REPORT CARD

Obama-Biden Administration

2009 – 2017

600 Campaign Promises
297 Kept / 303 Broken

JOHN E. BEAULIEU

REPORT CARD OBAMA-BIDEN ADMINISTRATION 2009 - 2017
"600 CAMPAIGN PROMISES 297 KEPT / 303 BROKEN"

Copyright © 2021 John E. Beaulieu.

All rights reserved. No part of this book may be used or reproduced by any means, graphic, electronic, or mechanical, including photocopying, recording, taping or by any information storage retrieval system without the written permission of the author except in the case of brief quotations embodied in critical articles and reviews.

iUniverse books may be ordered through booksellers or by contacting:

iUniverse
1663 Liberty Drive
Bloomington, IN 47403
www.iuniverse.com
844-349-9409

Because of the dynamic nature of the Internet, any web addresses or links contained in this book may have changed since publication and may no longer be valid. The views expressed in this work are solely those of the author and do not necessarily reflect the views of the publisher, and the publisher hereby disclaims any responsibility for them.

Any people depicted in stock imagery provided by Getty Images are models,
and such images are being used for illustrative purposes only.
Certain stock imagery © Getty Images.

ISBN: 978-1-6632-2902-1 (sc)
978-1-6632-2903-8 (e)

Library of Congress Control Number: 2021919150

Print information available on the last page.

iUniverse rev. date: 10/22/2021

Contents

1. **REPORT CARD OVERVIEW** 1
2. **DEPARTMENT OF AGRICULTURE** 3
   Agribusiness 3
   Conservation Security 6
   Forest Service 7
   Land Use 9
   Renewable Energy 9
   Research 10
3. **DEPARTMENT OF COMMERCE** 11
   Manufacturing 11
   National Oceanic and Atmospheric Administration (NOAA) 11
   Other Programs 13
   Patent & Trademark Office 15
4. **DEPARTMENT OF DEFENSE** 17
   Acquisition Reform 17
   Afghanistan 20
   Armed Forces - General 22
   Corps of Engineers 27
   Defense Spending 27
   Iraq 33
   Pakistan 35
   Reserves 36
   Russia 37
5. **DEPARTMENT OF EDUCATION** 41
   College Education 41
   Community College 43
   General Education 44
   Gulf Area Schools 54
   Research 55
   Student Aid 56
   Teaching 57
6. **DEPARTMENT OF ENERGY** 61
   Conservation 61
   Electrical Grid 62
   Energy Consumption 63

CONTENTS

    Energy - General 73
    Energy-Efficient Appliances 76
    Natural Resources 76
    Nuclear Waste 79
    Windfall Profits 79

7. DEPARTMENT OF HEALTH & HUMAN SERVICES 81
    Abortion 81
    Autism 81
    Cancer/Cancer Research 82
    Children 84
    Head Start 86
    Health Care System Overhaul 87
    Health Insurance 92
    Medicaid 95
    Medical Infrastructure 95
    Medicare 96
    Pharmaceuticals 99
    Pregnancy 100
    Research 101

8. DEPARTMENT OF HOMELAND SECURITY 103
    Border Security 103
    Coast Guard 104
    Cyber Security 105
    Federal Emergency Management Agency (FEMA) 111
    Guantanamo Bay Detention Facility 113
    Homeland Security General 115
    Immigration 122
    PATRIOT Act 127
    Terrorism 129

9. DEPARTMENT OF HOUSING & URBAN DEVELOPMENT 135
    Affordable Housing 135
    Community Development 138
    Foreclosures 139

10. DEPARTMENT OF THE INTERIOR 143
    Fish & Wildlife Service 143

CONTENTS

Habitat 145
National Parks.. 146
Natural Resources 147
U.S. Geological Survey (USGS)... 149
Wildland Fire Management 150

11. DEPARTMENT OF JUSTICE 151
Abortion 151
Anti-Trust Law 151
Civil Rights... 152
Crime 155
Crime – Katrina Related 162
Drug Enforcement Agency (DEA).. 162
Domestic Violence 162
Gay Rights 164
Torture/Rendition 164

12. DEPARTMENT OF LABOR.. 167
Corporate Bankruptcy 167
Employment... 168
Innovation 177
Retirement 178
Unemployment 180
Unions 180

13. DEPARTMENT OF STATE... 183
Africa 183
China 186
Consular Affairs 190
Europe 191
Export Controls 194
Foreign Affairs/Diplomacy 195
Foreign Aid 198
Foreign Policy 202
Latin America/Caribbean... 207
Middle East 210
U.S. Agency for International Development (USAID).. 217

CONTENTS

14. DEPARTMENT OF TRANSPORTATION 221
    Air Service 221
    Infrastructure 221
    Mass Transportation 222
    Public/Commuter Transportation 223
    Rail Service 224

15. DEPARTMENT OF THE TREASURY 227
    Corporate Taxes 227
    Individual Taxes 231
    International Programs 240
    Regulatory Reform 242
    Special Funds 245

16. DEPARTMENT OF VETERANS AFFAIRS 249
    General 249
    Health Care 250
    Homelessness 252
    Jobs 254
    Veterans' Benefits 255

17. APPOINTMENTS 259
    American Indian Advisor 259
    Autism Coordinator 259
    Cabinet Republican 259
    Chief Financial Officer 259
    Chief Performance Officer 260
    Chief Technology Officer 260
    Director, Federal Emergency Management Agency (FEMA) 261
    Federal Rebuilding Coordinator 261
    Federal Coordinating Officer 261
    General 262
    National Cyber Advisor 262
    Nuclear Security Advisor 263
    Privacy/Civil Liberties Board 263
    Science/Technology Advisor 264
    Special Envoy - Americas 264
    Urban Policy Director 265

CONTENTS

    Violence Against Women Advisor 265

18. TRANSPARENCY/ETHICS 267

    Ethics 267

    Transparency 269

19. INDEPENDENT ORGANIZATIONS 277

    Commodity Futures Trading Commission (CFTC) 277

    Corporation for National and Community Service (CNCS) 277

    Environmental Protection Agency (EPA) 281

    Federal Aviation Administration (FAA) 287

    Federal Communications Commission (FCC) 289

    Federal Trade Commission (FTC) 295

    National Archives and Records Administration (NARA) 296

    National Aeronautics and Space Administration (NASA) 296

    National Aeronautics and Space Council (NASC) 301

    National Infrastructure Bank 301

    National Endowment for the Arts (NEA) 302

    Office of Management and Budget (OMB) 303

    Overseas Private Investment Corporation (OPIC) 303

    Office of Personnel Management (OPM) 304

    Small Business Administration (SBA) 305

    Social Security Administration (SSA) 307

    U.S. Trade Representative 308

20. MISCELLANEOUS PROMISES 311

    Al Gore 311

    Bipartisanship 311

    Campaign Financing 313

    College Football 313

21. UNITED NATIONS 315

    Convention Participation 315

    Nuclear Non-Proliferation 317

    Appendix A – President Obama's Monthly Approval Rate (2009-2016) 323

    Appendix B – DOW-Jones Industrial Average by Month (2009-2016) 325

    Appendix C – U.S. National Monthly Unemployment Rate (2009-2016) 327

    Index 329

    About the Author 337

Preface

1. This campaign promise project was initiated when then-Senator Barack Hussein Obama II announced his candidacy for the presidency of the United States of America on February 10, 2007. Senator Obama picked Senator Joseph Robinette Biden Jr. to be his running mate on August 22, 2008. Singularly and together, they made innumerable promises to the American voter, regardless of his/her political affiliation. This project limited the number of Obama-Biden promises researched to 600, a manageable number.

2. This Report Card is a valuable tool for students majoring in political science, high school students studying government, and regular folks interested in learning how promises made to earn their votes were either fulfilled or broken. Thus, this research project reflects how a 'man or woman on the street' views Obama-Biden Administration performance based on the information publicly available to the American taxpayer.

3. This site is non-partisan, unbiased and objective. Personal views or political affiliation did not affect the results of this Report Card. It is an aid to remaining abreast of the Obama-Biden Administration's performance, tied to the specific wording of promises made. A further benefit of this research is that it serves as a handy tool to compare the Obama-Biden political playbook of years past in such critical areas as immigration to that of the current Biden-Harris Administration.

4. Like the report card children bring home through high school in which the completion of assignments factors heavily in final subject grades, each campaign promise made by President Obama and Vice President Biden is treated as an "assignment" under a general subject category filed under "Departments" or "Other/Miscellaneous." General subject categories have several sub-categories. The numerical results of all the sub-category "assignments" feed into the Grade Point Average (GPA) for the general category. For example, in the first section (Agriculture), go to the last page of that section. At the far right under the "Grade" column, you will see the GPA for promises related to Agriculture, in that case 0.5 out of a possible 1.0 (or 50% out of a possible 100%). The final GPA is converted to a letter/alpha score that is reflected on page 1 of this book. The average of all category/subject grades is reflected in the "Overall Grade" (C), top right of page 1 of this book.

5. It should be noted that this Report Card is based on a Pass/Fail system. Promises made, in some cases, could not be fulfilled totally for pragmatic, political or other reasons. In such cases, compromises were needed for partial promise fulfillment. If a promise made was not totally fulfilled, no grade points were awarded.

6. The following color codes were assigned to different letter/alpha grades simply for visual effect:
a. GPA of 0.87 to 1.00 = Blue (for grades of A and A-)
b. GPA of 0.66 to 0.86 = Green (for grades of B+, B and B-)
c. GPA of 0.35 to 0.65 = Yellow (for grades of C+, C and C-)
d. GPA of 0.14 to 0.34 = Orange (for grades of D+, D and D-)
e. GPA of 0.00 to 0.13 = Red (for grades of F+ and F)

7. Here's how the GPA numerical averages were converted to home page letter/alpha grades:
a. 0.94 to 1.00 = A.......... 0.87 to 0.93 = A-
b. 0.80 to 0.86 = B+........ 0.73 to 0.79 = B.......... 0.66 to 0.72 = B-
c. 0.59 to 0.65 = C+.........0.42 to 0.58 = C.......... 0.35 to 0.41 = C-
d. 0.28 to 0.34 = D+........ 0.21 to 0.27 = D.......... 0.14 to 0.20 = D-
e. 0.07 to 0.13 = F+.........0.00 to 0.06 = F

8. For this project the average of all 20 GPAs was 47%, which translates to a yellow "C" button.

9. Links to source documents come and go whereby a reliable web site available today may not be accessible anywhere tomorrow. This was problematic especially for promises accessible in their original form

from one source only and that source no longer hosts the document in question. In such cases, the original title and date of the document has been retained on the off chance that it will resurface somewhere in open-source documents in the future. In some cases, well-known sites such as "Politifact" were the only sources wherein the exact wording of promises could be confirmed as having been present in otherwise deleted source documents. Citing such sources was the extent of the influence those sources had on the conclusions attained during research of a particular promise.

10. By being reelected in 2012, President Obama got four more years to deliver on promises he did not fulfill during his first 2009-2012 term in office. To ensure continuity, this site remained focused on promises made that led to his first election, considering that promises made for his second election were largely duplications of those made during the campaign for the first election.

11. Please note that Congressional sessions last two years from the 3rd of January of the year following a Congressional election. For clarity, however, this project reflects a Congressional session as ending on the last day of the second calendar year of the session, knowing that Congress rarely works on New Years Day and on January 2 of any year. For example, the 114th Congress began on January 3, 2015 and ended on January 3, 2017. In this project, however, the expiration date of bills introduced during the 114th Congress but not signed into law is reflected as "end of CY2016" or words to that effect.

12. Some readers/researchers may be interested to learn how the American voter perceived President Obama's effectiveness while in office for two terms. His monthly approval rating as averaged by Real Clear Politics is reflected in Appendix A. Appendix B is a monthly market summary of how the DOW Jones Industrial Average performed while President Obama served as leader of the United States. Lastly, some may be interested to have an appreciation for how unemployment fared under President Obama's leadership. A monthly portrayal of the nation's unemployment percentages as reported by the Department of Labor's Bureau of Labor Statistics is included as Appendix C.

13. The original web site for this research project, the address of which is reflected on the front page of each chapter (Obama44reportcard.com), no longer exists, as the on-line version of this book became available coincident with its soft cover publication.

Enjoy!

The Author,
John E. Beaulieu

REPORT CARD
OBAMA44REPORTCARD.COM
Objective....Fact-Based....Unbiased

↑ Approval Rate ↑
↑ DOW ↑
↓ Unemployment ↓

Obama-Biden Administration 2009-2017

OVERALL GRADE: C

600 Campaign Promises
297 Kept / 303 Broken

Departments

Department	Grade
Agriculture	C
Commerce	B
Defense	C
Education	C+
Energy	C
Health & Human Services	B-
Homeland Security	C

Departments

Department	Grade
Housing & Urban Development	C
Interior	C
Justice	C
Labor	D
State	C
Transportation	B-
Treasury	C-

Departments

Department	Grade
Veterans Affairs	A-

Other/Miscellaneous

Appointments	C
Transparency/Ethics	D
Independent Organizations	C
Miscellaneous Promises	D+
United Nations	C-

Chapter 1 - Department of Agriculture

Campaign Promises

Departments -> Agriculture

ITEM	AGRICULTURE	
	AGRIBUSINESS	**GRADE**
AG-1	**The Promise:** "Will implement a $250,000 payment limitation so that we help family farmers, not large corporate agribusiness." **When/Where:** Obama-Biden Plan to Support Rural Communities. **Source:** https://www.supermarketguru.com/articles/wondering-what-president-obama-will-eat/ **Status:** When adopting the nation's FY2010 budget resolutions in 03/09, both the House and Senate rejected a proposal to cap subsidies to individual farmers at $250,000. Another proposal to phase out subsidies to farmers with gross annual retail sales of $500,000 or more was also rejected. In his FY2011 budget proposal, President Obama stated: "The Budget proposes to limit farm subsidy payments to wealthy farmers by reducing the cap on direct payments by 25 percent and reducing the Adjusted Gross Income (AGI) payment eligibility limits for farm and non-farm income by $250,000 over three years." The USDA's FY2011 budget reflected in the Department of Defense and Full-Year Continuing Appropriations Act, 2011 (H.R. 1473) did not specifically address the above proposal. The President's FY2012 budget proposal did not address any aspect of this promise except to state: "The Administration proposes that farm policy target payments to only those who really need them...by reducing payments to wealthy farmers." On 03/21/12, Senator Charles Grassley (R-IA) introduced the "Rural America Preservation Act" (S. 2217). This bill would have capped direct payments at $50,000, counter-cyclical payments at $75,000 and marketing loan gains (including forfeitures), loan deficiency payments and commodity certificates at $125,000 annually (for a total of $250,000). The bill would have also closed loopholes that some farmers use to evade statutory limits. This bill did not progress beyond initial committee review and expired with the 112th Congress. In President Obama's FY2013 budget request, he stated that his proposal "includes $32 billion in savings over 10 years by eliminating direct farm payments, providing disaster assistance, reducing subsidies to crop insurance companies..." The Farm Bill passed in 2008 covered a 5-year period until the end of CY2012. To replace it, the "Agriculture Reform, Food, and Jobs Act of 2012" (S. 3240) was introduced by Senator Debbie Ann Stabenow (D-MI) on 05/24/12. This bill proposed to repeal (1) direct payments, (2) counter-cyclical payments, and (3) the average crop revenue election program. However, the bill states in part: "in the case of any producer... that has an average adjusted gross income in excess of $750,000...the total amount of premium subsidy...shall be 15 percentage points less than the premium subsidy provided in accordance with this subsection that would otherwise be available for the applicable policy, plan of insurance, and coverage level selected by the producer." Thus, it is conceivable that	0.00

Chapter 1 - Department of Agriculture

payments to multi-millionaire farmers could exceed $250,000.

The above bill passed the Senate on 06/21/12 but lack of House action on it led to its expiration with the 112th Congress at the end of CY2012. Instead, the 2008 Farm Bill was extended to 09/30/13 under the "American Taxpayer Relief Act of 2012" signed into law by President Obama on 01/02/13. The $250,000 payment limitation was not addressed in that bill.

A new 5-year Farm Bill, dubbed the "Agricultural Act of 2014" (H.R. 2642), was signed into law by President Obama on 02/07/14. The basic tenet of this promise (a $250,000 payment limitation) was not addressed in this bill.

This promise was not fulfilled.

AG-2	**The Promise:** "...will increase funding for the National Organic Certification Cost-Share Program to help farmers afford the costs of compliance with national organic certification standards..." **When/Where:** Obama-Biden Plan: "Promoting a Healthy Environment," dated 10/08/08. **Source:** http://energy.gov/sites/prod/files/edg/media/Obama_Cap_and_Trade_0512.pdf **Status:** The National Organic Certification Cost Share Program (NOCCSP) was funded at the $22M level under the 2008 Farm Bill. This was mandatory funding to be spent starting in FY2008 until expended or the end of FY2012, whichever occurred first. Replacing the 2008 Farm Bill, the "Agricultural Act of 2014" (H.R. 2642), was signed into law by President Obama on 02/07/14. Section 10004(c) states in part that the Secretary of Agriculture shall fund the NOCCSP in the amount of "... $11,500,000 for each of fiscal years 2014 through 2018...", an increase of $37.5M over the previous Farm Bill. This promise was fulfilled.	1.00
AG-3	**The Promise:** "... will reform the U.S. Department of Agriculture (USDA) Risk Management Agency's crop insurance rates so that they do not penalize organic farmers." **When/Where:** Obama-Biden Plan: "Promoting a Healthy Environment," dated 10/08/08. **Source:** http://energy.gov/sites/prod/files/edg/media/Obama_Cap_and_Trade_0512.pdf **Status:** Under the Federal Crop Insurance Act (7 U.S.C. 1501-1524), the USDA's Risk Management Agency (RMA) administers the federal crop insurance on behalf of the Federal Crop Insurance Corporation (FCIC). In CY2000, the Agricultural Risk Protection Act (ARPA) recognized organic farming as a good farming practice, allowing the inclusion of organic production for coverage under all crop insurance policies in effect at that time. Citing insufficient experience with losses to organic agriculture because conventional mitigating practices to control insects, weeds, etc. would not be employed and based on data available to the RMA, organic loss ratios exceeded conventional farming losses. The RMA therefore determined that an additional insurance rate load of 5%, applied as a 5% surcharge, was appropriate for organic farming practices. The Farm Bill of 2008 mandated a review of this surcharge practice. The RMA issued a contract in 02/09 for a thorough study to "review actuarial appropriateness of RMA's organic rates and organic pricing arrangements" and "the Corporation shall eliminate or reduce the premium surcharge that the Corporation charges for coverage for organic crops, as determined in accordance with the results." The playing field for organic crop producers was finally leveled in 05/13 when the USDA announced the removal of the 5% surcharge for all organic crops starting in the CY2014 crop insurance cycle. This promise was fulfilled.	1.00

Chapter 1 - Department of Agriculture

AG-4

The Promise: "will also provide tax incentives to make it easier for new farmers to afford their first farm."
When/Where: Obama and Biden's Plan for America: "Blueprint for Change," dated 10/09/08.
Source: https://www.documentcloud.org/documents/550007-barack-obama-2008-blueprint-for-change.html
Status: Mandated under the Food, Conservation and Energy Act of 2008, which was vetoed by President Bush but which became law (Public Law 110-234) under a Senate Override on 05/22/08, the Office of Advocacy and Outreach at the Department of Agriculture (USDA) opened in mid December 2009 with an initial staffing budget of $3M. Its mission is to improve access to USDA programs of small farms and ranches, beginning and/or socially disadvantaged farmers and ranchers.

The opening of the USDA Office of Advocacy and Outreach did nothing to deliver on President Obama's campaign promise to provide federal tax incentives to new farmers.

This promise is not to be confused with state-level tax incentives provided to new farmers by some states (i.e. Wisconsin, Nebraska, Iowa) or to landowners who rent portions of their properties to new farmers.

The new 5-year Farm Bill, the "Agricultural Act of 2014" (H.R. 2642), was signed into law by President Obama on 02/07/14. It did not address any new tax incentives for starting farmers.

This promise was not fulfilled.

0.00

AG-5

The Promise: "...will create a rural revitalization program to attract and retain young people to rural America."
When/Where: Obama and Biden's Plan for America: "Blueprint for Change," dated 10/09/08.
Source: https://www.documentcloud.org/documents/550007-barack-obama-2008-blueprint-for-change.html
Status: The Rural Revitalization Act of 2009 (S. 323) was introduced by Senator Kent Conrad (D-ND) on 01/26/09 and was referred to the Senate Subcommittee on Finance. No further action taken on this bill by the 111th Congress and it expired at the end of CY2010.

Other than rudimentary rural development technologies minimally funded at the $12M per annum level under the Agriculture Act of 2014 (Farm Bill) signed into law by President Obama on 02/07/14, no specific, nation-wide "Rural Revitalization Program" was created during President Obama's two terms in office in support of rural development, rural housing services, rural business/cooperative services and rural utilities services.

While several multi-agency initiatives such as the "Jobs and Innovation Accelerator Challenge" were introduced during President Obama's tenure, these were limited in regional scope and served relatively few participants.

This promise was not fulfilled.

0.00

AG-6

The Promise: "...will strengthen anti-monopoly laws and strengthen producer protections to ensure independent farmers have fair access to markets, control over their production decisions, and fair prices for their goods."
When/Where: Obama and Biden's Plan for America: "Blueprint for Change," dated 10/09/08.
Source: https://www.documentcloud.org/documents/550007-barack-obama-2008-blueprint-for-change.html
Status: An anti-monopoly law prevents a company from being the sole supplier of specific goods or services, thereby preventing it from charging any price it desires.

Aside from the USDA's rule published in 12/09 to level the competitive playing field for the poultry

0.00

industry, there has been no other known initiative to "strengthen" existing anti-monopoly laws such as the Packers and Stockyard Act of 1921 or other producer protections.

This promise was not fulfilled.

	CONSERVATION SECURITY	GRADE
AG-7	**The Promise:** "...will fight to increase funding for the Conservation Security Program and the major set-aside programs such as the Conservation Reserve Program..." **When/Where:** Obama-Biden Plan: "Supporting the Rights and Traditions of Sportsmen" dated 08/06/08. **Source:** https://www.kentuckyhunting.net/threads/obama-sportsmen-issues.61174/ **Status:** The 2008 Farm Bill replaced the Conservation Security Program with a new Conservation Stewardship Program (CSP). The new program encourages participants to undertake new conservation activities in addition to maintaining and managing existing conservation activities. Also, the new program operates under an annual acreage limitation rather than a funding cap. The CSP is administered for the Department of Agriculture (USDA) by the Natural Resources Conservation Service (NRCS). The Conservation Reserve Program (CRP) is administered by the USDA Farm Service Agency (FSA). Here's how funding fared for the CSP and the CRP under President Obama: Conservation Stewardship Program (including Technical Assistance) from funding level of $9M in FY2009: FY2010.... $0.390B FY2011.... $0.601B FY2012.... $0.812B FY2013.... $0.975B FY2014.... $1.195B FY2015.... $1.383B FY2016.... $1.464B FY2017.... $1.383B Conservation Reserve Program (including Technical Assistance) from funding level of $1.919M in FY2009: FY2010.... $1.911B FY2011.... $1.939B FY2012.... $1.969B FY2013.... $1.993B FY2014.... $1.800B FY2015.... $1.821B FY2016.... $1.868B FY2017.... $1.994B This promise was fulfilled.	1.00
AG-8	**The Promise:** "...extending the swamp buster provisions of the Farm Bill..." **When/Where:** Obama-Biden Plan: "Supporting the Rights and Traditions of Sportsmen" dated 08/06/08. **Source:** https://www.kentuckyhunting.net/threads/obama-sportsmen-issues.61174/ **Status:** Swamp buster provisions originated under the Food Security Act of 1985 and essentially prevented landowners from using dredged or drained wetlands for agricultural purposes if these landowners expected to receive USDA benefits. Under the Farm Bill of 1996, swamp buster provisions were refined to permit the use of converted and abandoned wetlands as farmland.	0.00

Chapter 1 - Department of Agriculture

There was no retention of swamp buster provisions in the "Agriculture, Food, and Jobs Act of 2012" (S. 3240) that passed the Senate on 06/21/12 to replace the Farm Bill of 2008, nor is there any record that President Obama sought to extend those provisions, which expired on 10/01/12. This bill expired with the 112th Congress at the end of CY2012. Instead, the 2008 Farm Bill was extended to 09/30/13 under the "American Taxpayer Relief Act of 2012" signed into law by President Obama on 01/02/13. There is no mention of a swamp buster provision extension in this bill.

The new 5-year Farm Bill, dubbed the "Agricultural Act of 2014" (H.R. 2642), was signed into law by President Obama on 02/07/14. It contained nothing related to the extension of swamp buster provisions.

This promise was not fulfilled.

FOREST SERVICE | GRADE

AG-9

The Promise: "Will place a high priority on implementing cooperative projects to remove brush, small trees and other overgrown vegetation that serve as fuel for wildfires."
When/Where: Obama-Biden Plan: "Committed to Wildfire Management and Community Protection" dated 10/18/08.
Source: https://www.politifact.com/truth-o-meter/promises/obameter/promise/278/remove-more-brush-small-trees-and-vegetation-that/
Status: Source is cited for confirmation of exact promise wording only, as it existed before original "When/Where" campaign document was deleted from archival websites.

The "Tax Relief and Health Care Act of 2006" (H.R. 6111) signed into law by President Bush on 12/20/06 codified the requirement for the implementation of a comprehensive, cost effective, multi-jurisdictional hazardous fuels reduction and fire prevention plans for the Lake Tahoe Basin, Carson Range, Carson City and Spring Mountain areas of Nevada.

Further-reaching legislation such as the "Catastrophic Wildfire Prevention Act of 2012" introduced by Senator Mike Lee (R-UT) on 07/19/12 and its House counterpart bill (H.R. 5744) introduced by Congressman Paul Gosar (R-AZ) on 05/15/12 would have permitted the Secretaries of Agriculture and Interior to extend wildfire prevention projects and to streamline projects to reduce the potential for wildfires. Neither of these bills progressed beyond initial committee reviews and expired with the 112th Congress at the end of CY2012.

Congressman Gosar reintroduced this legislation under H.R. 1345 on 03/21/13. It expired with the 113th Congress at the end of CY2014. Senator Lee did the same under S. 2286 on 11/17/15. His bill expired with the 114th Congress at the end of CY2016.

Nonetheless, the economic stimulus American Recovery and Reinvestment Act of 2009, signed into law on 02/17/09 by President Obama, provided an additional $500M to the USDA and an additional $15M to the Department of the Interior for "Wildland Fire Management."

This promise was fulfilled.

Grade: 1.00

AG-10

The Promise: "Will use controlled burns and prescribed natural fire to reduce such fuels in close coordination with those communities that are most at risk"
When/Where: Obama-Biden Plan: "Committed to Wildfire Management and Community Protection" dated 10/18/08.
Source: https://www.politifact.com/truth-o-meter/promises/obameter/promise/279/more-controlled-burns-to-reduce-wildfires/
Status: Source is cited for confirmation of exact promise wording only, as it existed before original "When/Where" campaign document was deleted from archival websites.

Controlled burns and prescribed natural fires have been applied by communities since at least the

Grade: 1.00

Chapter 1 - Department of Agriculture

1930's according to the National Interagency Fire Center (NIFC). However, it is acknowledged that they sometimes haven't been applied in the areas most needed to prevent loss of individual properties.

On 03/10/09, Congressman Nick Rahall (D-WV) introduced the "Federal Land Assistance, Management and Enhancement Act" (H.R. 1404), referred to as the "FLAME Act of 2009," to "authorize supplemental funding for catastrophic emergency wildland fire suppression and...to develop a cohesive wildland fire management strategy."

On 10/29/09, the House and the Senate passed the "Interior, Environment, and Related Agencies Appropriations Act of 2010," which included Title V, the FLAME Act of 2009. President Obama signed this bill into law on 10/30/09. Annual appropriations since 2009 have continued to fund Forest Service, Department of Interior and other organizations responsible to implement provisions of the FLAME Act of 2009.

Based on NIFC-furnished statistics, the following represents the trend in number of prescribed fires by all participating organizations and affected acreage during President Obama's terms in office:

Year	# of Burns	# of Acres
2009	12,429	2,531,113
2010	16,882	2,423,862
2011	8,672	2,112,811
2012	16,626	1,971,834
2013	18,764	2,000,040
2014	17,044	2,389,798
2015	37,263	2,958,260
2016	83,005	4,015,511

This promise was fulfilled.

AG-11

The Promise: "...will fight to protect roadless areas on Forest Service lands from all new road construction."
When/Where: Obama-Biden Plan: "Supporting the Rights and Traditions of Sportsmen" dated 08/06/08.
Source: https://www.kentuckyhunting.net/threads/obama-sportsmen-issues.61174/
Status: Early in his administration, President Obama delegated authority to the Department of Agriculture (USDA) to approve applications to build roads and proceed with logging operations in land areas under the purview of the Forest Service.

The authorization was soon thereafter granted by Agriculture Secretary Tom Vilsack for the logging exploitation of a 381 acre tract of Alaska's Tongass National Forest, which necessitated the building of seven (7) miles of roads in this otherwise roadless area.

The promise to "fight to protect roadless areas" was not fulfilled.

0.00

AG-12

The Promise: "...will develop domestic incentives that reward forest owners, farmers, and ranchers when they plant trees, restore grasslands, or undertake farming practices that capture carbon dioxide from the atmosphere."
When/Where: Obama/Biden Plan: "Promoting a Healthy Environment" dated 10/08/08.
Source: https://www.energy.gov/sites/prod/files/edg/media/Obama_Cap_and_Trade_0512.pdf
Status: Instructions to all federal agencies to improve the environment and reduce greenhouse gas emissions were articulated in President Obama's 10/05/09 Executive Order 13514, replaced by Executive Order 13693 dated 03/19/15. However, these executive orders did not address any new domestic incentives for the capture of carbon dioxide applicable to individual forest owners, farmers and ranchers.

0.00

Chapter 1 - Department of Agriculture

The Air Quality Initiative portion of the Environmental Quality Incentive Program (EQIP) addressed in the 2014 Farm Bill, dubbed the "Agricultural Act of 2014" (H.R. 2642) and signed into law by President Obama on 02/07/14, provided assistance to farmers, ranchers etc. to (1) establish cover crops, (2) plant windbreak trees, (3) implement nutrient management practices, and (4) apply other conservation measures to reduce airborne particulate matter and greenhouse gases. None of these provisions were new when compared to previous farm bills.

This promise was not fulfilled.

LAND USE	GRADE

AG-13 — **The Promise:** "Will support the Open Fields Incentives legislation that provides incentives to farmers and ranchers who voluntarily open their land to hunting, fishing and other wildlife-related activities."
When/Where: Obama-Biden Plan: "Supporting the Rights and Traditions of Sportsmen" dated 08/06/08.
Source: https://www.kentuckyhunting.net/threads/obama-sportsmen-issues.61174/
Status: The Open Fields Initiative was introduced in 2005 by Senator Kent Conrad (D-ND). It found its way into the Farm Bill of 2008, with funding projected at $50M in financial support for voluntary, state-run access programs that provide incentives to private landowners to allow public access to their land for hunting and fishing purposes.

This program was in effect and grant money was available from the Department of Agriculture to fund state efforts to develop incentive-based programs that expanded public access to private lands for hunting, fishing, and other recreational purposes. While funding in the amount of $16.67M per year over the three years was reflected in President Obama's FY2010 budget proposal, the "Voluntary Public Access and Habitat Incentive Program" (VPA-HIP) under which the Open Fields Incentives fell was completely defunded by Congress in the final FY2012 budget.

There were no provision for Open Field Incentives in the Farm Bill of 2008 replacement legislation, the "Agricultural Act of 2014" (H.R. 2642) signed into law by President Obama on 02/07/14.

This promise was not fulfilled.

Grade: 0.00

RENEWABLE ENERGY	GRADE

AG-14 — **The Promise:** "... Will encourage the use of methane digesters that are being used to produce power from animal waste."
When/Where: Obama-Biden Plan: "Promoting a Healthy Environment," dated 10/08/08.
Source: https://www.energy.gov/sites/prod/files/edg/media/Obama_Cap_and_Trade_0512.pdf
Status: On 12/15/09 while at a climate conference in Copenhagen, Agriculture Secretary Vilsack announced an agreement with U.S. dairy producers to accelerate adoption of innovative manure-to-energy projects on American dairy farms. This would lead to a reduction of dairy farm greenhouse gas (GHG) emissions by 25% by 2020 while also extracting electricity from the raw manure using anaerobic digesters.

The USDA reports that it has several programs that support the installation of anaerobic digesters and other technologies that reduce GHG emissions from manure management practices. They include:
(1) Environmental Quality Incentives Program (EQIP), which includes conservation practice standards for both anaerobic digesters, solid separators, and roofs and covers with methane flaring;
(2) Rural Energy for America Program (REAP), which supports anaerobic digesters through grants and loans; and
(3) Research, education, and extension programs to explore the development and implementation of technologies and practices that reduce methane emissions from animal manure.

Under EQIP and REAP, the USDA has initiated Livestock Partnerships that explore mechanisms to prioritize anaerobic digesters and the appropriate associated electrical generation technology, covers

Grade: 1.00

9

Chapter 1 - Department of Agriculture

with flares, solid separators, and other manure management technologies that reduce GHG emissions.

This promise was fulfilled.

AG-15	**The Promise:** "...will expand USDA projects that focus on energy efficiency and conservation." **When/Where:** Obama-Biden Plan: "Promoting a Healthy Environment," dated 10/08/08. **Source:** https://www.energy.gov/sites/prod/files/edg/media/Obama_Cap_and_Trade_0512.pdf **Status:** Section 6407 of the 2014 Farm Bill, the "Agricultural Act of 2014" (H.R. 2642), signed into law by President Obama on 02/07/14, was new. Entitled the "Rural Energy Savings Program," this section did not exist under the 2008 Farm Bill. The purpose of this section is "to help rural families and small businesses achieve cost savings by providing loans to qualified consumers to implement durable cost- effective energy efficiency measures." This section of the 2014 Farm Bill provided funding to complete energy audits, provide renewable energy development assistance, make energy efficiency improvements and install renewable energy systems. The USDA also has programs that help convert older heating sources to cleaner technologies, produce advanced biofuels, install solar panels, build biorefineries, and other energy efficiency/conservation initiatives. The amount of $75M was authorized to be appropriated annually (FY2014 through FY2018) to carry out the provisions of Section 6407 of the 2014 Farm Bill. This promise was fulfilled.	1.00

RESEARCH	GRADE

AG-16	**The Promise:** "...will increase research and educational funding for land-grant colleges." **When/Where:** Obama and Biden's Plan for America: "Blueprint for Change," dated 10/09/08. **Source:** https://www.documentcloud.org/documents/550007-barack-obama-2008-blueprint-for-change.html **Status:** Under the Morrill Acts of 1862 and 1890, each eligible state received 30,000 acres of federal land for each member of congress the state had as of the 1860 census. Proceeds from the sale of this land were to be used for the establishment and funding of public colleges and a few state-supported contract colleges that fulfill the public land-grant critera. Approximately 100 colleges and universities across the USA and its territories (including Native American Tribal Colleges) are currently classified as land-grant colleges/universities. Under President Obama, funding for 1890 institution research, including 1890 facility improvements, managed by USDA's National Institute of Food and Agriculture (NIFA) grew from $104M in FY2009 as follows: FY2010 - $111M FY2011 - $113M FY2012 - $113M FY2013 - $106M FY2014 - $116M FY2015 - $116M FY2016 - $139M FY2017 - $139M Notwithstanding the funding reduction reflected for FY2013, this promise was fulfilled.	1.00

	AGRICULTURE GPA	0.50

Campaign Promises

Departments -> Commerce

ITEM	COMMERCE	
	MANUFACTURING	**GRADE**
CO-1	**The Promise:** "...will double funding for the Manufacturing Extension Partnership (MEP) so its training centers can continue to bolster the competitiveness of U.S. manufacturers." **When/Where:** Plan for America: "Blueprint for Change," dated 10/09/08 **Source:** https://www.documentcloud.org/ Obama and Biden's documents/550007-barack-obama-2008-blueprint-for-change.html **Status:** The Manufacturing Extension Partnership (MEP), known as the "Hollings MEP," operates out of the National Institute for Standards and Technology (NIST), working with state partnerships to provide business planning services and technical advice to small businesses. This is not to be confused with the Advanced Manufacturing Partnership (AMP) introduced by President Obama on 06/24/11 to bring industry, universities and the federal government together to invest in emerging technologies. FY2009 funding for the Hollings MEP program when President Obama was first elected was $111.8M. This was the amount to "double." Here's how the Hollings MEP was funded during President Obama's two terms in office: FY2010 - $125.2M FY2011 - $129.3M FY2012 - $130.9M FY2013 - $118.2M FY2014 - $122.6M FY2015 - $144.6M FY2016 - $140.9M FY2017 - $143.7M This promise was not fulfilled.	0.00
	NOAA	**GRADE**
CO-2	**The Promise:** "...the Obama administration will lean forward to deploy a global climate change research and monitoring system..." **When/Where:** Obama-Biden Plan: "A Robust and Balanced Program of Space Exploration and Scientific Discovery" dated 08/15/08. **Source:** http://www.nasa.gov/pdf/382369main_48%20-%2020090803.2.Space_Fact_Sheet_FINAL.pdf **Status:** Throughout his two terms in office, President Obama considered climate change as among his highest national and international priorities. An example of his commitment to this subject is reflected in his 06/13 "Climate Action Plan." The USA has had climate monitoring systems deployed for decades. The National Oceanic and Atmospheric Administration (NOAA), which falls under the Department of Commerce, manages the	1.00

Chapter 2 - Department of Commerce

National Environmental Satellite, Data, and Information Service (NESDIS). NESDIS acquires and manages the nation's operational environmental satellites, operates the NOAA National Data Centers, provides data and information services including earth system monitoring, performs official assessments of the environment, and conducts related research.

New generations of satellites under the purview of NOAA's NESDIS are being developed to succeed current polar orbiting and geosynchronous satellites:

(1) To replace aging weather satellites and to join an international network of satellites that share data among 191 countries, the Geostationary Operational Environmental Satellite - R Series (GOES-R) is the next generation of geosynchronous environmental satellites. It will provide atmospheric and surface measurements of the earth's Western Hemisphere for weather forecasting, severe storm tracking, space weather monitoring and meteorological research. GOES-R was launched from Cape Canaveral on 11/19/16, was renamed GOES-16 upon reaching orbit, and became fully operational on 12/18/17.

(2) Joint Polar Satellite System (JPSS) satellites will carry a suite of sensors designed to collect meteorological, oceanographic, climatological, and solar-geophysical observations of the earth's land, oceans, atmosphere, and near-earth space. The launch of JPSS-1 took place on 11/18/17.

President Obama's efforts to "lean forward" have been reflected in his annual multi-agency climate change related budget requests.

This promise was fulfilled.

CO-3

The Promise: "Will strengthen baseline climate observations and climate data records to ensure that there are long-term and accurate climate records."
When/Where: Obama-Biden Plan: "A Robust and Balanced Program of Space Exploration and Scientific Discovery" dated 08/15/08
Source: http://www.nasa.gov/pdf/382369main_48%20-%2020090803.2.Space_Fact_Sheet_FINAL.pdf
Status: The National Oceanic and Atmospheric Administration (NOAA) received $230M from the Stimulus Package of 2009 to supplement its $5.2B budget. $170M of the $230M supplement was intended to be used to improve climate observations and research.

The enacted budget for the NOAA in FY2010 was $4.9B, of which $1.3B was for the development and acquisition of weather satellites and climate sensors (an increase of $284.1M over FY2009) and $600M was for the construction and maintenance of NOAA research facilities and satellites.

President Obama's FY2011 budget submission for the NOAA was $6.1B, of which $2B was intended for the National Environmental Satellite, Data and Information Service (NESDIS) polar orbiting and geo-stationary weather satellite systems, satellite-borne measurement of climate variables and other space-based observations. In reality, the total FY2011 budget appropriation for the NOAA was annualized under Continuing Resolution procedures at the $4.8B level. Joint Polar-Orbiting Satellite System (JPSS) and other satellite projects took a funding hit.

For FY2012, the President's budget proposed NOAA funding at the $5.6B level but Congress appropriated $4.9B. Nonetheless, the appropriated funds were sufficient to allocate $1.88B for NOAA's NESDIS program.

For FY2013, the President requested $5.06B, $2.04B of which would be for the NESDIS program, which includes $1.848B for climate monitoring systems acquisition.

This promise was fulfilled.

1.00

Chapter 2 - Department of Commerce

	OTHER PROGRAMS	GRADE
CO-4	**The Promise:** "...will invest $250 million per year to increase the number and size of incubators in disadvantaged communities throughout the country." **When/Where:** Plan for America: "Blueprint for Change," dated 10/09/08 **Source:** https://www.documentcloud.org/ Obama and Biden's documents/550007-barack-obama-2008-blueprint-for-change.html **Status:** Business incubators help entrepreneurial companies survive and grow during the start-up period. There are currently over 1,250 business incubator programs in the United States. Business incubators are funded in large part under the Public Works (PW) and Economic Adjustment Assistance (EAA) portions of the Department of Commerce's Economic Development Assistance Program (EDAP). Appropriations for the above two organizations during most of President Obama's two terms in office were as follows: FY.............PW..............EAA 2010........$133.2M.....$38.6M 2011........$163.3M.....$43.6M 2012........$111.6M.....$50.0M 2013..........$77.2M.....$48.0M 2014..........$96.0M.....$42.0M 2015..........$99.0M.....$35.0M The totality of funds appropriated to PW and EAA in each of the years reflected above came nowhere close to the promised $250.0M per annum. And business incubators received only a fraction of the amounts reflected above. This promise was not fulfilled.	0.00
CO-5	**The Promise:** "Institute a common standard for securing such data across industries and protect the rights of individuals in the information age." **When/Where:** Obama-Biden Plan: "Protecting Our Information Networks," 11/16/08. **Source:** http://webarchive.loc.gov/all/20090429184932/http://change.gov/agenda/homeland_security_agenda/ **Status:** This promise refers to personal data. The development of a national "identity ecosystem" and standards was still in the works as of end-CY2016. The first meeting of the Identity Ecosystem Steering Group (IDESG) took place in 08/12, nearly a year and a half after the National Strategy for Trusted Identities in Cyberspace (NSTIC) was unveiled. In 10/15, more than three years later, the IDESG delivered version 1 of the Identity Ecosystem Framework (IDEF), which is now a final public document. As of end-CY2016, there were already numerous federal privacy-related laws that regulated the collection/use of personal data. Some applied to specific categories of information, such as financial or health information, or electronic communications. Others applied to activities that use personal information, such as telemarketing and commercial e-mail. Further, there were broad consumer protection laws that are not privacy laws as such, but have been used to prohibit unfair/deceptive practices involving the disclosure of personal information. But there was no common standard applicable across all industries. This promise was not fulfilled.	0.00

Chapter 2 - Department of Commerce

CO-6	**The Promise:** "...will create a federal program to support 'innovation clusters' -- regional centers of innovation and next-generation industries. This innovation clusters program will provide $200 million in planning and matching grants for regional business, government and university leaders to collaborate on leveraging a region's existing assets -- from transportation infrastructure to universities -- to enhance long-term regional growth." **When/Where:** Obama-Biden Plan: "Supporting Urban Prosperity" dated 09/11/08. **Source:** https://assets.documentcloud.org/documents/550008/barack-obama-2008-supporting-urban-prosperity.pdf **Status:** The America COMPETES Reauthorization Act of 2010 (H.R. 5116) was introduced by Congressman Barton Gordon (D-TN) on 04/22/10 and signed into law by President Obama on 01/04/11 (P.L. 111-358). Section 27 of this act directs the Secretary of Commerce to "establish a regional innovation program to encourage and support the development of regional innovation strategies, including regional innovation clusters and science and research parks." In advance of the above, here are examples of what was being done during President Obama's first term in support of this promise: - Led by the Department of Energy (DOE), seven organizations (Departments of Energy, Commerce, Education and Labor, the Manufacturing Extension Partnership, the Small Business Administration, and the National Science Foundation) issued a joint 5-year $129.7M funding opportunity on 02/12/10 to promote an Energy Regional Innovation Cluster (E-RIC) to improve the design of energy-efficient buildings. - $30M was provided in FY2010 to Nebraska, Iowa and Missouri for worker training in "green" jobs as an attempt to motivate the region's innovative cluster initiative. - The FY2011 budget submissions from the following organizations include line items for regional innovation ecosystems/clusters in the reflected amounts: Economic Development Administration (EDA) ($100M), Departments of Agriculture ($136.4M) and Labor ($108M), and the National Science Foundation ($12M). The FY2011 budget proposals made it through the appropriation/enactment process, satisfying Obama's promised funding level of $200M. Support of Regional Innovation Clusters program has been sustained for FY2012 through FY2016. This promise was fulfilled.	1.00
CO-7	**The Promise:** "Partner with industry and our citizens to secure personal data stored on government and private systems." **When/Where:** Obama-Biden Plan: "Protecting Our Information Networks," 11/16/08. **Source:** http://webarchive.loc.gov/all/20090429184932/http://change.gov/agenda/homeland_security_agenda/ **Status:** Identity theft is defined as the unauthorized use or attempted misuse of an existing credit card or other existing account, the misuse of personal information to open a new account or for another fraudulent purpose, or a combination of these types of misuse. The following represents the trends in identity theft since President Obama's first term in office: Year...Number of Victims...Estimated Cost CY2009..........11.1M......................$54B CY2010..........10.2M......................$23B CY2011..........11.6M......................$18B CY2012..........12.6M......................$21B CY2013..........13.1M......................$19B CY2014..........12.7M......................$16B	1.00

Chapter 2 - Department of Commerce

CY2015.........13.1M......................$15B
CY2016.........15.4M......................$16B

On 04/14/11, DOC unveiled its National Strategy for Trusted Identities in Cyberspace (NSTIC) that includes a national cyber-identity system -- an optional single, secure password and identity for all of a consumer's digital transactions. This system could be accessed via smart card, cell phone, or other website access method.

This promise was fulfilled.

	PATENT & TRADEMARK OFFICE	GRADE
CO-8	**The Promise:** "...update and reform our copyright and patent systems to promote civic discourse, innovation and investment while ensuring that intellectual property owners are fairly treated." **When/Where:** Obama-Biden Plan: "Connecting and Empowering All Americans Through Technology and Innovation" dated 11/13/07. **Source:** http://www.wired.com/images_blogs/threatlevel/2009/04/obamatechplan.pdf **Status:** Senator Patrick Leahy (D-VT) was joined by Congressman Lamar Smith (R-TX) on 03/30/11 to introduce the "Leahy-Smith America Invents Act" (H.R. 1249). This bill, which focused predominantly on patent reform, was signed into law by President Obama on 09/16/11. As a follow-on to the passage of the above bill, Congressman Tom Reed II (R-NY) introduced the Trade Facilitation and Trade Enforcement Act of 2015 (H.R. 644) on 02/02/15. This bill addressed, but was not limited to, the copyright and intellectual property protection aspects of this promise. President Obama signed this act into law on 02/24/16. This promise was fulfilled.	1.00
CO-9	**The Promise:** "...will improve "predictability and clarity in our patent system" helping to "foster an environment that encourages innovation." **When/Where:** Obama-Biden Plan: "Connecting and Empowering All Americans Through Technology and Innovation" dated 11/13/07. **Source:** http://www.wired.com/images_blogs/threatlevel/2009/04/obamatechplan.pdf **Status:** Senator Patrick Leahy (D-VT) was joined by Congressman Lamar Smith (R-TX) on 03/30/11 to introduce the "Leahy-Smith America Invents Act" (H.R. 1249). This bill made it through both houses of Congress and was signed into law by President Obama on 09/16/11. Section 3 of this new law improves the patent system from a "first to invent" to a "first inventor to file" system. When combined with the other provisions of this new law, the promise to improve "predictability and clarity in our patent system" was fulfilled. The only aspect of "predictability" that is compromised is the backlog of patent applications and time it takes for the Patent & Trademark Office (PTO) to process those applications. As of 04/16, the PTO had a backlog of 550,000 applications, taking 16 to 26 months to process. Nonetheless, this promise was fulfilled.	1.00
CO-10	**The Promise:** "...giving the Patent and Trademark Office (PTO) the resources to improve patent quality and opening up the patent process to citizen review will reduce the uncertainty and wasteful litigation that is currently a significant drag on innovation..." **When/Where:** Obama-Biden Plan: "Connecting and Empowering All Americans Through Technology and Innovation" dated 11/13/07. **Source:** http://www.wired.com/images_blogs/threatlevel/2009/04/obamatechplan.pdf **Status:** Senator Patrick Leahy (D-VT) was joined by Congressman Lamar Smith (R-TX) on 03/30/11 to introduce the "Leahy-Smith America Invents Act" (H.R. 1249). This bill made it through both houses of Congress and was signed into law by President Obama on 09/16/11.	1.00

Chapter 2 - Department of Commerce

	Section 11 of this new law sets the fees for the different aspects of patent application, examination, processing and appeal and states that "All fees...shall be credited to the United States Patent and Trademark Office Appropriation Account" and "shall remain available until expended...". Section 22 of the new law goes further by establishing a Patent and Trademark Fee Reserve Fund where funds exceeding the amount appropriated to the Patent and Trademark Office (PTO) on an annual basis are deposited for later use by the PTO. Throughout this new law are contained guidelines for public review. This promise was fulfilled.	
CO-11	**The Promise:** "...will ensure that our patent laws protect legitimate rights while not stifling innovation and collaboration."" **When/Where:** Obama-Biden Plan: "Connecting and Empowering All Americans Through Technology and Innovation" dated 11/13/07. **Source:** http://www.wired.com/images_blogs/threatlevel/2009/04/obamatechplan.pdf **Status:** Senator Patrick Leahy (D-VT) was joined by Congressman Lamar Smith (R-TX) on 03/30/11 to introduce the "Leahy-Smith America Invents Act" (H.R. 1249). This bill made it through both houses of Congress, was signed into law by President Obama on 09/16/11, and is a significant step forward to protect the interests of patent filers while promoting innovation and collaboration. This promise was fulfilled.	1.00
	COMMERCE GPA	**0.73**

Chapter 3 - Department of Defense

Campaign Promises
Departments -> Defense

ITEM	DEFENSE	
	ACQUISITION REFORM	**GRADE**
DE-1	**The Promise:** "Require the Pentagon to develop a strategy for figuring out when contracting makes sense and when it doesn't, rather than continually handing off governmental jobs to well-connected companies." **When/Where:** Obama Campaign Document "A 21st Century Military for America" dated 11/26/07. **Source:** https://www.scribd.com/document/6245756/Barack-Obama-on-Defense-Issues-A-21st-Century-Military-for-America **Status:** Obama signed an executive order on 03/04/09, calling for an examination of federal contracts. The Government Accountability Office (GAO) issued its report #11-192 in 01/11 entitled "Further Action Needed to Better Implement Requirements for Conducting Inventory of Service Contract Activities." The above GAO report indicated that as of FY2009, the Pentagon, its agencies and military departments employed 766.6K full time contractor employees at an estimated cost of $140.4B, an amount that went up to an estimated $200B in FY2010. On 11/22/11, the Pentagon issued its plan for near- and long-term documenting of the number of full-time contractor employees it and its agencies and military departments employ as mandated by the Department of Defense and Full Year Continuing Appropriations Act of 2011 (Public Law 112-10). As of end-CY2016, more than 26% or 268K of the 1.014M personnel working in the Pentagon's back-office bureaucracy (i.e. acquisition, supply & logistics, property management, human resources, etc.) were contractor personnel. This promise was for the Pentagon to develop a "strategy." That was done. This promise was fulfilled.	1.00
DE-2	**The Promise:** "Each major defense program will be reevaluated in light of current needs, gaps in the field, and likely future threat scenarios in the post 9/11 world" **When/Where:** Obama Campaign Document "A 21st Century Military for America" dated 11/26/07. **Source:** https://www.scribd.com/document/6245756/Barack-Obama-on-Defense-Issues-A-21st-Century-Military-for-America **Status:** With the key word being "reevaluated", OMB document "Terminations, Reductions, and Savings" released 05/06/09 supported promise fulfillment. But these efforts did not address the over-arching intent of this promise. The Quadrennial Defense Review (QDR) was mandated by Congress to look forward 20 years in the areas of threat assessment, military strategy, force structure, and long-term defense budget plans.	1.00

Chapter 3 - Department of Defense

The first QDR presented by the Obama Administration to Congress on 02/01/10 along with the President's FY2011 budget proposal failed to meet many of the statutory requirements (i.e. did not address risks associated with current funding and capability shortfalls) and failed to provide a 20-year roadmap. Four years later, faced with the realities of sequestration, the 2014 QDR reported that the Department of Defense had "capped and cancelled billions of dollars in programs that were inefficient and under-performing. As a result of a 2011 Secretary of Defense-led efficiency review, the Department realized five-year savings of $150 billion. In 2012, the Department identified another $60 billion in planned reductions over five years, with an additional $35 billion in 2013."

The promised reevaluation resulted in cancellation of the F-35 Joint Strike Fighter alternative F-136 engine programs as well as the F-22 Raptor Program after the 187th unit was delivered in 05/12. These are two significant examples.

This promise was fulfilled.

DE-3

The Promise: "Establish transparency standards for military contractors...create the reporting requirements, accounting, and accountability needed for good governance and actual money savings with contracting."
When/Where: Obama Campaign Document "A 21st Century Military for America" dated 11/26/07.
Source: https://www.scribd.com/document/6245756/Barack-Obama-on-Defense-Issues-A-21st-Century-Military-for-America
Status: The "Weapon Systems Acquisition Reform Act of 2009" was signed into law by President Obama on 05/22/09. This act reformed the way the Department of Defense (DoD) contracts for and purchases major weapon systems to mitigate waste and cost overruns in defense contracts, but fell short of establishing transparency standards for military contractors.

On 04/07/10, the DoD issued its "Open Government Plan." This plan, updated periodically through Version 4.0 dated 09/15/16, created a new "Defense Collaborative Service" to replace the "Defense Connect Online" program. The objective of this service is "to have all Departmental collaboration tools, capabilities and activities evolve to be based on common published enterprise standards; interoperable across the variety of internet protocol based communication environments."

On 09/14/10, Defense Secretary Gates issued stringent acquisition reform objectives by announcing 20 changes in defense purchasing procedures. Among these changes, the DoD is to provide preferential treatment to contractors with good cost-control records and requires more competitive bidding for service contracts.

Another positive step toward promise fulfillment was the 04/22/11 memo issued by the Under Secretary of Defense (Acquisition, Technology and Logistics) that implemented "Will-Cost and Should Cost" management designed to drive productivity improvements into acquisition programs during contract negotiations and throughout program execution and sustainment. Savings are to be identified through any of three methods: bottoms-up estimates, identification of cost reductions from "will-cost" estimates, and use of competitive contracting and contract negotiations to identify "should-cost" savings.

Further progress was made in the contractor cost control area such as the publication of Defense Federal Acquisition Regulations Supplement (DFARS) Notice 20111220 on 12/20/11 that updated guidelines for monitoring "the policies, procedures, and practices used by contractors to control direct and indirect costs related to Government business."

On 05/09/14, President Obama signed Public Law 113-101, the "Digital Accountability and Transparency Act (DATA Act) of 2014" (S. 994), introduced by Senator Mark Warner (D-VA). The DoD must comply with the transparency standards and reporting requirements of this law.

This promise was fulfilled.

1.00

Chapter 3 - Department of Defense

DE-4	**The Promise:** "...will...Enact a program of market incentives and sanctions for Pentagon contractors...to reward companies that perform well and come in under budget, while punishing firms that fail to perform as originally hired." **When/Where:** Obama Campaign Document "A 21st Century Military for America" dated 11/26/07. **Source:** https://www.scribd.com/document/6245756/Barack-Obama-on-Defense-Issues-A-21st-Century-Military-for-America **Status:** The Weapon Systems Acquisition Reform Act of 2009 (Public Law 111-23) was signed by President Obama on 05/22/09. This bill did not specifically address incentives for or sanctions against defense contractors. The Commission on Wartime Contracting estimated in 09/11 that over $60B in government contract spending was wasted or lost since CY2002 in Afghanistan and Iraq, approximately 20% of the $206B of U.S. taxpayer money spent in those war efforts at that time. An additional 9% was lost due to fraud, according to the Commission. On the reward side, the Pentagon's Principal Deputy Undersecretary for Acquisition, Technology and Logistics, Mr. Frank Kendall, introduced a new "Superior Supplier Incentive Program" on 07/18/11. Under this program, DoD contracting officers will be empowered to set contract terms that recognize businesses that demonstrate superior performance in delivering quality products and services to the warfighter. In addition, companies that demonstrate aggressive subcontract management, cost containment, and on-time delivery practices will be recognized. Recognition will be in the form of favorable progress payments, special award fee pools, and other advantages. On 03/02/12, the DOD published DFAR Rule 2012-D017 "Debarment as Ground for Termination for Default" as one of the means to address the punishment of firms that fail to perform as originally contracted. This promise was fulfilled.	1.00
DE-5	**The Promise:** "...will...Restore the government's ability to manage contracts, by rebuilding our contract officer corps." **When/Where:** Obama Campaign Document "A 21st Century Military for America" dated 11/26/07. **Source:** https://www.scribd.com/document/6245756/Barack-Obama-on-Defense-Issues-A-21st-Century-Military-for-America **Status:** Since CY2006, when the DoD "contract officer corps" had a total of 27,748 personnel, declines in manpower (to 26,838 in CY2007 and 25,680 in CY2008) exacerbated the DoD's ability to manage its ballooning contracting requirements. On 04/06/09, the Secretary of Defense announced plans to grow the entire acquisition workforce by 20,000 personnel by FY2015 -- 10,000 new federal employees and 10,000 contractor positions converted to federal positions. Of the 10,000 new federal positions, 5,600 were projected to be additions to the Defense Contracting career field. As of 06/10, 3,400 new contracting officers had been hired and 1,400 contractor positions had been converted to federal positions. Together, this exceeded by 1,300 the FY2010 goal of 3,500 for new hires and conversions. Success of this program will be hindered as experienced contracting officer retirements will likely peak around CY2018. By then, in-coming contracting officer interns will not likely have gained the experience needed to make a meaningful dent in contracting workloads. Nonetheless, there has been a steady increase in the number of contracting officers since the FY2007-FY2008 downward trend reflected above. In CY2009, the contracting segment of the Defense Acquisition Workforce consisted of 23,752 civilian and 3,903 military personnel for a total of 27,655 contracting personnel. In FY2010, the total was 29,792 and in FY2011 the number had risen to 30,327.	1.00

	By end-CY2016, the DOD's contracting officer corps was on a restoration path. This promise was fulfilled.		
DE-6	**The Promise:** "As part of it overall defense reforms, Obama administration will prioritize fixing the naval acquisitions system." **When/Where:** Obama Campaign Document "A 21st Century Military for America" dated 11/26/07. **Source:** https://www.scribd.com/document/6245756/Barack-Obama-on-Defense-Issues-A-21st-Century-Military-for-America **Status:** Navy Secretary Ray Mabus outlined the Navy's acquisition reform approach on 05/05/10 at the Navy League's Sea-Air-Space symposium just outside of Washington, D.C. The five principles of the Navy's acquisition reform effort were (1) clearly identify requirements, (2) raise the bar on contract performance, (3) rebuild the acquisition workforce, (4) support the industrial base, and (5) make every single dollar count. He gave the examples of the P-8 Poseidon maritime patrol aircraft, the SSN-774 Virginia-class submarine, and the T-AKE-1 Lewis and Clark class dry cargo ships as programs that are meeting benchmarks such as getting increased benefits from learning curves and, with time, reducing unit costs. He vowed that he would not hesitate to cancel Navy programs that do not meet his baseline goals of 'on time and on budget'. Secretary Mabus also stated that Navy acquisition professionals will be "going through every contract line by line to make sure the terms of those contracts make sense for what they are meant to do, and are fair to the contractor and the government." The U.S. Navy is implementing its plan to clean up its acquisiton processes in conjunction with the over-arching "Weapon Systems Acquisition Reform Act of 2009" that was signed into law by President Obama on 05/22/09. To that end, the U.S. Navy published its "Acquisition and Capabilities Guidebook" (SECNAV M-5000.2) on 05/09/12 for operation of the Defense Acquisition System and the Joint Capabilities Integration and Development System. This promise was fulfilled.	1.00
	AFGHANISTAN		**GRADE**
DE-7	**The Promise:** "As Obama removes our combat brigades from Iraq, he will send at least two additional brigades to Afghanistan, where the Taliban is resurgent." **When/Where:** Obama Campaign Document "A 21st Century Military for America" dated 11/26/07. **Source:** https://www.scribd.com/document/6245756/Barack-Obama-on-Defense-Issues-A-21st-Century-Military-for-America **Status:** As a result of an executive order signed by President Obama on 02/19/09, the 2nd Marine Expeditionary Brigade assumed its position in Afghanistan on 05/29/09. On 06/20/09, the Army 5th Stryker Brigade departed Fort Lewis, WA for duty in Afghanistan. This promise was fulfilled.	1.00
DE-8	**The Promise:** "Obama will strengthen the training and equipping of the Afghan army and police and increase Afghan participation in U.S. and NATO missions, so that there is more of an Afghan face on security." **When/Where:** Obama-Biden Plan: "The War We Need to Win" dated 07/31/07. **Source:** http://www.mattluedke.com/wp-content/uploads/2016/09/CounterterrorismFactSheet.pdf **Status:** Authorized 195,000 personnel, the Afghan National Army (ANA) reportedly had 170,000 personnel which included 6,600 members of the Afghan Air Force (AAF) as of 08/16. The Afghan National Police (ANP) has an authorized strength of 157,000, against which approximately 153,000 are assigned. Generally, progress is inhibited by reports that under the Afghanistan's corrupt and unreliable governments, officers regularly steal the salaries of enlisted men who do not have direct-deposit	1.00

Chapter 3 - Department of Defense

bank accounts; soldiers sell their coalition-provided clothing and equipment at the local bazaars -- where they can be purchased by the Taliban; and a 25% attrition rate due to desertion is common, with about 20% of the remaining force spaced out on hashish, heroin and other drugs. As a point of reference, "Transparency International" has ranked Afghanistan as the world's third most corrupt country -- after Somalia and Burma.

While superb U.S. military leadership and funding have been made available (cumulative funding for U.S. efforts in Afghanistan was over $700B at the end of FY2016), there's simply not much to show for it. There is apparently no Afghan political will for it to work and clan-based loyalties will likely prevail when coalition forces withdraw from Afghanistan after CY2017, much as they have for thousands of years.

It is relatively safe to conclude that neither the ANA nor ANP will be putting an "Afghan face on security" any time soon. According to Lieutenant General John Nicholson before the Senate Armed Services Committee on 01/28/16, the Afghan security forces there are not yet ready to stand on their own after more than a decade of trying to train the ANA and ALP at a cost of more than $70B.

The creation of a new local defense force, the Afghan Local Police (ALP) or "community police" under the Interior Ministry was announced on 07/14/10. This was followed on 07/20/10 by an announcement by President Karzai that Afghanistan would be able to ensure its own security by end-CY2014. That didn't happen. Instead, the Taliban's offensive in mid-CY2016 has shown the insurgents to be bolder and better organized, holding more territory in CY2016 than at any time since CY2001. The primary reason for this setback: weak leadership, lack of professionalism, complacency and corruption throughout the ANDSF, whose members simply aren't crazy about fighting for their pro-American government.

Efforts to strengthen the training and equipping of the Afghan army and police did take place during the Obama Administration, despite the fact that the results as of end-CY2016 were lamentable.

This promise was fulfilled.

DE-9	**The Promise:** "NATO currently has 39,000 troops in Afghanistan...some countries contributing forces are imposing restrictions on where their troops can operate, tying the hands of commanders on the ground...Obama will work with European allies to end these burdensome restrictions and strengthen NATO as a fighting force." **When/Where:** Obama-Biden Plan: "The War We Need to Win" dated 07/31/07. **Source:** http://www.mattluedke.com/wp-content/uploads/2016/09/CounterterrorismFactSheet.pdf **Status:** As of 12/31/16, the International Security Assistance Force (ISAF) operating in Afghanistan had approximately 13,332 troops from 39 countries (including 26 of 28 NATO countries - Canada and France are not participating), approximately 6,941 of whom were from the USA. Fatalities in Afghanistan during President Obama's first and second tours in office were as follows: - CY2009: 521 ISAF, 317 of whom were U.S. - CY2010: 711 ISAF, 499 of whom were U.S. - CY2011: 566 ISAF, 418 of whom were U.S. - CY2012: 402 ISAF, 310 of whom were U.S. - CY2013: 161 ISAF, 127 of whom were U.S. - CY2014: 75 ISAF, 55 of whom were U.S. - CY2015: 27 ISAF, 22 of whom were U.S. - CY2016: 16 ISAF, 14 of whom were U.S. During Operation Enduring Freedom (OEF), the number of coalition deaths reported as of end-CY2016 stood at 3,486 (2,351 of whom were U.S.), and 20,092 U.S. troops were reported as wounded in action. The issue was that during OEF, over half of the participating countries continued to impose "national	0.00

caveats". These caveats dictated what national forces could/could not do in Afghanistan. Some allied troops lacked the equipment necessary to operate in an integrated fashion with other allies; some nations did not allow their troops to be deployed where needed by the ISAF Commander; and some allies did not permit their soldiers to participate in combat operations unless in self-defense.

President Obama continued to be ineffective in influencing the removal of operational restrictions imposed by over half of the OEF participating nations in Afghanistan. This situation was not resolved as coalition engagements in Afghanistan transitioned to withdrawal of forces at the request of the Afghan Government.

This promise was not fulfilled.

	ARMED FORCES - GENERAL	GRADE
DE-10	**The Promise:** "Barack Obama supports plans to increase the size of the Army by 65,000 troops and the Marines by 27,000 troops." **When/Where:** Obama Campaign Document "A 21st Century Military for America" dated 11/26/07. **Source:** https://www.scribd.com/document/6245756/Barack-Obama-on-Defense-Issues-A-21st-Century-Military-for-America **Status:** Under the John Warner National Defense Authorization Act for FY2007 (Public Law 109-364) in effect when this promise was made, the authorized strength of the U.S. Army was 512,400. An increase by 65,000 would bring the authorized strength to 577,400. In FY2007 when this promise was made, the Marine Corps (USMC) authorized strength was 180,000. Adding 27,000 would bring the Marine Corps end strength to 207,000. Based on annual reporting by the Defense Manpower Data Center (DMDC), here's how the end-strength flutuated during President Obama's two terms in office: ..FY................ARMY................USMC 2010.............566,045.............202,441 2011.............565,463.............201,157 2012.............550,064.............198,193 2013.............532,043.............195,848 2014.............508,210.............187,417 2015.............491,365.............183,417 2016*...........474,472.............183,370 *As of 06/30/16 During President Obama's tenure in office, at no time was the U.S. Army and USMC end-strength at the level promised during his first presidential campaign, even during temporary increases to support Overseas Contingency Operations. In fact, under President Obama, the U.S. Army strength for FY2016 is the lowest since World War II. This promise was not fulfilled.	0.00
DE-11	**The Promise:** "I will work for a full repeal of Don't Ask/Don't Tell." **When/Where:** Statement to the Human Rights Campaign (HRC) dated 11/29/07. **Source:** http://www.dailykos.com/story/2011/6/27/988893/- **Status:** "Don't Ask, Don't Tell" (DADT) was codified under Public Law 103-160 signed by President Clinton on 11/30/93. This law permitted gay service members to serve as long as they hid their sexual orientation and the armed services could not prove that they engaged in homosexual conduct. The act also specified that service members who disclosed that they were homosexual or engaged in homosexual conduct should be discharged except when a service member's conduct was "for the purpose of avoiding or terminating military service" or when it "would not be in the best interest of the armed forces." Approximately 13,650 gay personnel were kicked out of the military under DADT.	1.00

Chapter 3 - Department of Defense

Repeal of the DADT law required Congressional action. On 05/24/10, a compromise was reached between the White House and Capitol Hill allowing votes on amendments that would repeal the 1993 law, but deferred its effectivity until the Pentagon concluded an implementation study by 12/01/10.

The Pentagon's study findings, revealed on 11/30/10, indicated that repealing the DADT law would present only a low risk to the armed forces' ability to fulfill their missions. 70% of service members polled during the Pentagon study opined that repeal of the DADT law would have little, if any, effect on their individual units. The principal recommendations of the study:
- Gays would not be restricted from any career fields such as combat arms or service in submarines;
- Prohibition against separate berthing or shower facilities for gays;
- Service members discharged under "Don's Ask, Don't Tell" could seek to re-enlist or re-commission.

President Obama signed the "Don't Ask, Don't Tell Repeal Act of 2010 (H.R.2965/S.4023) into law on 12/22/10. The law was not enforceable while procedural steps were in place within the Department of Defense to ensure that the repeal would be consistent with military standards for military "readiness, effectiveness, unit cohesion, recruiting and retention."

The Pentagon's certification was presented to President Obama on 07/22/11, who in turn signed a certification ending DADT. The repeal became effective on 09/20/11.

This promise was fulfilled.

DE-12

The Promise: "Existing U.S. programs of military to military exchanges, joint training, education, and human rights programs must be reoriented from their current Cold War standards to reflect new strategic priorities and ethical standards."
When/Where: Obama Campaign Document "A 21st Century Military for America" dated 11/26/07.
Source: https://www.scribd.com/document/6245756/Barack-Obama-on-Defense-Issues-A-21st-Century-Military-for-America
Status: During CY2009, President Obama effectively engaged with his Russian counterpart with a view to enhancing our respective bilateral/military-to-military relationship.

In CY2011, U.S. and Russian military forces successfully cooperated in bilateral anti-terrorism engagements such as Exercise Vigilant Eagle and Exercise Crimson Rider, as well as a Russian visit to the Pentagon's Joint Improvised Explosive Devise Defeat Organization (JIEDDO) in Northern Virginia.

On 04/18/12, senior U.S. and Russian military officials signed a "Military Cooperation Work Plan." This Work Plan included 110 events such as joint exercises, senior leadership exchange visits, subject matter expert exchanges, and port visits by respective navies.

Joint training and education exercises with Russia focused on the interoperability of U.S. and Russian forces and equipment to address respective national priorities. For example, a 05/12 joint exercise was conducted in Colorado between U.S. and Russian forces in parachuting, operation planning, reconnaissance, assault operations, and helicopter evacuations.

U.S. and Russian military organizations also established a working relationship in 05/12 to ensure improved energy, security and equipment interoperability, as well as a fuel-only Acquisition and Cross-Servicing Agreement.

In March CY2014, the short-lived U.S.-Russian military engagements, including military exercises, meetings and port visits, were halted due to Russian adventurism in Ukraine and annexation of Crimea. This brought the U.S.-Russian military relationship back to Cold War levels.

This promise was initially on the path toward fulfillment during President Obama's first term in office,

0.00

Chapter 3 - Department of Defense

but fell apart during his second. It was nearly impossible for the U.S. and Russia to coordinate their air operations over Syria against the Al Qaeda-linked Jabhat al-Nusra, which was primarily fighting forces loyal to Syrian President Bashar Al-Assad, as of end-CY2016.

The USA wanted to remove Al-Assad. Russia worked to protect him.

This promise was not fulfilled.

DE-13	**The Promise:** "Invest in foreign language training, cultural awareness, and human intelligence and other needed counterinsurgency and stabilization skillsets." **When/Where:** Obama Campaign Document "A 21st Century Military for America" dated 11/26/07. **Source:** https://www.scribd.com/document/6245756/Barack-Obama-on-Defense-Issues-A-21st-Century-Military-for-America **Status:** Section 529 of the Defense Budget signed into law by President Obama on 10/28/09 authorized the Secretary of Defense to "establish language training centers at accredited universities, senior military colleges, or other similar institutions of higher education for purposes of accelerating the development of foundational expertise in critical and strategic languages and regional area studies." The "cultural awareness" aspect of this promise is usually satisfied via intense regional area studies, provided for under Section 529. For Marines deploying to Iraq (until end-CY2011) and Afghanistan (until end-CY2014), the Center for Advanced Operational Culture Learning (CAOCL) at Camp Pendleton, CA developed training modules that incorporated language and cultural training. The U.S. Army's pre-commissioning programs at West Point include the Center for Language, Culture, and Regional Studies -- all cadets must learn a foreign language. Further, the Reserve Officer Training Corps (ROTC) has language programs at 12 universities designed to increase cadet skills in languages considered strategic to future DoD initiatives. The Army Training and Doctrine Command (TRADOC) and Defense Language Institute's Foreign Language Center (DLIFLC) are other avenues where linguistic and cultural awareness training were developed and/or provided. As to investments in "human intelligence and other needed counterinsurgency and stabilization skillsets", such investments were dealt a serious blow on 08/09/10 when the Secretary of Defense announced the cost-cutting elimination of the U.S. Joint Forces Command (USJFC). This command had as its mission, other than managing forces and coordinating deployments, the following responsibilities that were tied directly to this promise: (1) to train and provide forces from all services to commanders around the world to work together as a joint team; (2) to ensure the equipment each team brings to an operation is compatible; and (3) to provide teams with unique skills that can deploy at a moment's notice to assist an operation. This SecDef budget reduction proposal received significant pushback from Virginia's state and congressional elected officials, in a "not in my backyard" reaction, but President Obama sealed the fate of USJFC on 01/10/11 when he signed the order for its closure. As to "cultural awareness," training programs appear to be sound but a few troops on the ground appear oblivious to putting that training to practical use. The culturally insensitive burning of Korans (also referred to as "Qur'an") in Afghanistan in 02/12 was deemed reprehensible by the entire Muslim population and most of the rest of the world. This stupid action incited anti-U.S. manifestations, caused the killing of at least six U.S. soldiers, and further soured already-fragile bilateral Afghan-U.S. relations. Nonetheless, considering the balance between the positive and negative developments articulated	1.00

Chapter 3 - Department of Defense

above, President Obama continued to push for the promised investments.

This promise was fulfilled.

DE-14

The Promise: "Create a specialized military advisers corps, which will enable us to better build up local allies' capacities to take on mutual threats."
When/Where: Obama Campaign Document "A 21st Century Military for America" dated 11/26/07.
Source: https://www.scribd.com/document/6245756/Barack-Obama-on-Defense-Issues-A-21st-Century-Military-for-America
Status: By end-CY2016, the U.S. Army had announced definitive plans to develop/create at least one "train, advise, assist" brigade that would advise indigenous forces in Iraq and Afghanistan and elsewhere as needed. Formal activation of the U.S. Army's 1st Security Force Assistance Brigade was anticipated to occur in CY2018.

This promise was fulfilled.

1.00

DE-15

The Promise: "Create a Military Families Advisory Board: Consisting of experts and family representatives from each service, it would help identify and develop actionable policies to ease the burden on spouses and families."
When/Where: Obama Campaign Document "A 21st Century Military for America" dated 11/26/07.
Source: https://www.scribd.com/document/6245756/Barack-Obama-on-Defense-Issues-A-21st-Century-Military-for-America
Status: The promised board should not be confused with "Operation Military Family," created in CY2007 and run by a defense industry contractor.

The "Board" was actually created under the 2008 Defense Authorization Act signed into law by President George W. Bush on 01/28/08 and is known as the Military Family Readiness Council (MFRC). Thus, credit cannot be given to President Obama for creating the MFRC because it already existed under another name when he came into office.

The MFRC is chaired by the UnderSecretary of Defense for Personnel and Readiness and consists of (1) one representative of the Army, Navy, Air Force and Marine Corps, (2) three individuals representing military family organizations, and (3) senior enlisted advisors of the Army, Navy, Air Force and Marine Corps or the spouse of a senior enlisted member of these armed services. Meetings are open to the public on a space available basis. The MRFC must submit an annual report to the Secretary of Defense by 1 February.

Another advisory board referred to as "Joining Forces" announced on 04/12/11 failed to meet the specific criteria reflected in this promise.

This promise was not fulfilled.

0.00

DE-16

The Promise: "Restore the Deployment Policies Under Which the Reserve and Guard Enlisted...An Obama administration will...End the "Stop-Loss" program of forcing troops to stay in service beyond their expected commitments."
When/Where: Obama Campaign Document "A 21st Century Military for America" dated 11/26/07.
Source: https://www.scribd.com/document/6245756/Barack-Obama-on-Defense-Issues-A-21st-Century-Military-for-America
Status: On 03/18/09, Secretary of Defense Gates announced that the U.S. Army would phase out its "Stop-Loss" program, which forced soldiers to stay on active duty with the Army past their service obligations. The new policy prohibited the Army Reserve from mobilizing units under the "Stop-Loss" policy effective 08/09, with the Army National Guard following suit in 09/09 and the active U.S. Army in 01/10.

On 06/15/11, Defense Secretary Gates testified to the Senate Appropriations Defense Subcommittee that the Bush Administration's initiatives to increase manpower levels in the Army and Marine Corps

0.00

Chapter 3 - Department of Defense

to reduce troop deployment times and increase their at-home time had succeeded. He announced that stop-loss deployments had been terminated. Promise fulfillment appeared to be on track.

Not so. On 10/16/14, President Obama signed Executive Order 13680 authorizing the secretaries of defense and homeland security to recall Reserve and Individual Ready Reserve members to active duty in support of Operation United Assistance, a mission to fight the spread of the Ebola virus in West Africa. This move allowed the Army to continue reducing the active force by its goal of 80,000 soldiers while at the same time permitting the involuntary recall of former service members to active duty beyond their original enlistment and Reserve Component service commitments.

Further, in 10/15, in the aftermath of manpower reductions (discharging 19,000 airmen from its ranks in CY2014), the U.S. Air Force formalized its "stop-loss" program.

This promise was not fulfilled.

DE-17	**The Promise:** "Build up our special operations forces, civil affairs, information operations, engineers, foreign area officers, and other units and capabilities that remain in chronic short supply" **When/Where:** Obama Campaign Document "A 21st Century Military for America" dated 11/26/07. **Source:** https://www.scribd.com/document/6245756/Barack-Obama-on-Defense-Issues-A-21st-Century-Military-for-America **Status:** Special Forces: While actual manpower numbers are tightly controlled, we do know that when President Obama was first elected, the U.S. Army operated 7 groups consisting of 3 battions apiece. At an average strengh of 800 personnel per battalion, the Army Special Forces strengh was estimated to be about 16,800. In FY2011, the Department of Defense authorized the US Army Special Operations Command (SOCOM) to increase the authorized U.S. Army Special Forces strength by one third. To accomplish this, each of the 7 Special Forces groups would be augmented by one battalion by end-CY2012 for an estimated total Special Forces strength of 23,000. According to the 2016 SOCOM Fact Book, Special Forces personnel strength has risen to about 27,000. While the exact numbers may be off target, the promise was to "build up" the Special Forces, and this was accomplished. Foreign Area Officers (FAO): As of CY2010, there were 1,940 FAOs in active operational capacities, with about 25% of this number in training. Of that number, 1,236 were Army officers, 285 in the Marine Corps, 224 in the Navy, and about 195 in the Air Force. The services planned to add at least 1,239 to the rolls by FY2016. In late-11/16, the Obama Administration announced the creation of a new "Counter-External Operations Task Force," known within the Pentagon as "Ex-Ops," operating under the Joint Special Operation Command (JSOC) which is subordinate to SOCOM. Its mission: in collaboration with the Central Intelligence Agency (CIA), pursue terrorist networks and individuals plotting attacks against the USA and its allies. This promise was fulfilled.	1.00
DE-18	**The Promise:** "Establish regularity in deployments...so that active duty and reserves know what they must expect, rather than the current trend of changing the deployment schedules after they have left home, which harms the morale of troops and their families." **When/Where:** Obama Campaign Document "A 21st Century Military for America" dated 11/26/07. **Source:** https://www.scribd.com/document/6245756/Barack-Obama-on-Defense-Issues-A-21st-Century-Military-for-America **Status:** On 06/02/10, the Chairman of the Joint Chiefs of Staff (CJCS), Admiral Michael Mullen, announced at Fort Bragg, NC that between 06/11 and 06/12, active and reserve Army units would stay in the United States for two years before deploying again for 12 months. On 08/05/11, the U.S. Army announced that except for headquarters units, aviation specialties and military police, troop	0.00

deployments would be curtailed from 12 to 9 months starting in CY2012.

Six months after Admiral Mullen's 06/11 announcement, in early 12/11, the 4th Brigade Combat Team, 1st Armored Division from Fort Bliss, Texas returned from Iraq in time to spend Christmas with families. A few days later on 12/21/11, however, this unit was advised that it would be re-deployed to Afghanistan 7 months later in 05/12. The brigade stayed in Afghanistan until 06/13, playing havoc with family relations and morale.

The above is but one example where this promise, despite best intentions and supportive policy changes, was not fulfilled.

CORPS OF ENGINEERS	GRADE

DE-19

The Promise: "...will ensure that New Orleans has a levee and pumping system to protect the city against a 100-year storm by 2011, with the ultimate goal of protecting the entire city from a Category 5 storm."

When/Where: Obama-Biden Plan: "Rebuilding the Gulf Coast and Preventing Future Catastrophes", dated 09/11/08.

Source: https://www.documentcloud.org/documents/550006-barack-obama-2008-rebuilding-the-gulf-coast-and.html

Status: In the aftermath of Hurricane Katrina, rated as a Category 3 on the Saffir-Simpson Hurricane Scale with sustained winds of 100 to 140 miles per hour and classified as a 400-year storm with a 0.25% chance of occurring in any year, the U.S. Army Corps of Engineers repaired levees and temporarily repaired pumping systems in the New Orleans area and beyond.

The main concern for New Orleans residents was that although the pre-Katrina levee/pumping system was restored and strengthened, that restoration was limited to fast-moving, moderate Category 3 hurricane protection standards.

In 06/10, the Corps of Engineers delivered its 8,000 page Louisiana Coastal Protection and Restoration Study to Congress. In the study, the Corps estimated that it would cost between $70B and $136B to protect Louisiana's coastline at the Category 5 hurricane level. A Category 5 system around New Orleans would require 30-foot levees whereas some of the rebuilt levees and flood walls are 10.5 feet high, capable of withstanding a slow-moving Category 2 hurricane or a fast-moving Category 3 hurricane. Experts in these matters agree that the storm surge from a Category 5 hurricane would be greater than a 100-year storm.

By end-CY2016, the Corps of Engineers was on track to complete permanent canal closures and pump stations at the end of three New Orleans outfall canals by mid-CY2018. This effort was plagued by cost overruns and schedule delays. Despite these improvements, New Orleans was not protected from a Category 5 storm.

This promise was not fulfilled.

0.00

DEFENSE SPENDING	GRADE

DE-20

The Promise: "End the abuse of supplemental budgets ..."

When/Where: Obama Campaign Document "A 21st Century Military for America" dated 11/26/07.

Source: https://www.scribd.com/document/6245756/Barack-Obama-on-Defense-Issues-A-21st-Century-Military-for-America

Status: Six months after taking office, President Obama sought to add pork to the FY2010 war funding bill, $83.4B of which was earmarked for the wars in Iraq and Afghanistan. Items unrelated to the war effort he sought to add were $4B to combat the H1N1 virus, $5B to buttress the International Monetary Fund (IMF), the "cash for clunkers" program to jump-start lagging auto sales, $3.1B for aircraft (C-17's and C-130's) the Pentagon did not want, and others.

The $61.4B FY2011 supplementary war funding bill signed into law by President Obama on 07/29/10

0.00

contained non-war related items such as $24B to keep teachers, firefighters and police officers employed, $13B for Vietnam Veteran Agent Orange survivors, $5.7B for PELL grants, $2.8B for aid to Haiti, $275M for the Gulf Coast oil spill, and funding such special interest requirements as improving port facilities in Guam ($50M).

The above examples are provided as illustration that U.S. taxpayer monies for supplemental "war" purposes are not always used for those purposes.

This promise was not fulfilled.

DE-21	**The Promise:** "We need greater investment in advanced technology ranging from the revolutionary, like unmanned aerial vehicles and electronic warfare capabilities, to systems like the C-17 cargo and KC-X air refueling aircraft..." **When/Where:** Obama Campaign Document "A 21st Century Military for America" dated 11/26/07. **Source:** https://www.scribd.com/document/6245756/Barack-Obama-on-Defense-Issues-A-21st-Century-Military-for-America	0.00

Status: The FY2010 defense budget appropriated $88.5M for C-17 Multi-Year Procurement, $424M for C-17 Advance Procurement, a Senate plus-up for 10 additional C-17's valued at $2.5B, $120M for C-17 Modifications, and $161M for C-17 Research & Development Management. The 279th and final C-17 was completed at Boeing's Long Beach, California plant and flown on 11/29/15.

The Boeing KC-46 Pegasus was selected by the United States Air Force (USAF) in 02/11 as the winner in the KC-X tanker competition to replace older KC-135 Stratotankers. The first 18 combat-ready aircraft are scheduled to be delivered to the USAF by 08/17.

In FY2010, the MQ-1 Predator Unmanned Aerial Vehicle (UAV) procurement was funded at $754M for 24 each against a budget request of $955M for 36 each; the acquisition of five each MQ-4 UAVs for $802M was consistent with the President's budget proposal; the RQ-7 Shadow was fully funded at $666M for 11 each, as was the MQ-8 Fire Scout at $77M for 5 each.

Different electronic warfare systems also received funding consistent with the President's budget proposal such as the Lightweight Counter-Mortar Radar at $90M, the AN/SLQ-32 at $34M, electronic warfare technology at $88M, electronic warfare development at $248M, Joint Counter-Radio Controlled IED Electronic Warfare (JCREW), Space and Electronic Warfare Architecture Development at $42M.

In 09/10, the Defense Advanced Research Projects Agency (DARPA) awarded an $89M contract to Boeing/Qinetiq for their "Solar Eagle" concept capable of keeping 1,000 pounds of payload aloft for five years with 5kw of power. Boeing planned to prove an initial 30-day "Solar Eagle" airworthiness capability by CY2014, but the program was cancelled in CY2012.

While the above examples indicated that the promise to invest in these technologies was on track to be fulfilled, the deficit-cutting plan included in the overarching debt ceiling agreement reached and signed into law on 08/02/11 caused the Pentagon to cut an initial $325B from its FY2012 budget. These cuts affected sustained investments in advanced science and technology throughout the armed forces.

As an example, here's the DoD Science & Technology (S&T) funding profile, with the FY2009 amount of $13.4B as a baseline, during President Obama's tenure in office:

FY2010 - $13.7B
FY2011 - $11.8B
FY2012 - $12.2B
FY2013 - $11.9B
FY2014 - $12.0B

Chapter 3 - Department of Defense

FY2015 - $12.2B
FY2016 - $13.0B
FY2017 - $13.4B

As the above portrays, DoD funding for S&T during President Obama's two terms in office, in part attributed to sequestration, was rather anemic.

This promise was not fulfilled.

DE-22

The Promise: "Work to bring pay more in line with that of the private sector, as measured by the employment cost index (ECI)."
When/Where: Obama Campaign Document "A 21st Century Military for America" dated 11/26/07.
Source: https://www.scribd.com/document/6245756/Barack-Obama-on-Defense-Issues-A-21st-Century-Military-for-America
Status: Current law (Section 1009(c) of U.S.C. Title 37) states that military pay raises shall increase at the percentage of the Employment Cost Index (ECI) for the base quarter of the year before the preceding year, keyed to wages and salaries for private industry workers.

The automatic adjustment is tied to the increase in the ECI from the 3rd Quarter of the third preceding year to the 3rd Quarter of the second preceding year. For example, in the 12-month period between the quarter which ended in 09/10 and the quarter which ended in 09/11, the ECI increased by 1.7%. Hence the pay raise for CY2013, as calculated by the statutory formula, was 1.7%.

The following depicts the relationship between military pay raises and the prevailing ECI during President Obama's two terms in office:

YEAR	MILITARY PAY RAISE %	ECI
2010	3.4	2.9
2011	1.4	1.4
2012	1.6	1.6
2013	1.7	1.7
2014	1.0	1.8
2015	1.0	1.8
2016	1.3	2.3
2017	1.6	2.5

Fulfilling this promise looked promising during President Obama's first term but fell apart during his second.

This promise was not fulfilled.

0.00

DE-23

The Promise: "Fully Equip Our Troops for the Missions They Face...We must prioritize getting vitally needed equipment to our Soldiers and Marines before lives are lost."
When/Where: Obama Campaign Document "A 21st Century Military for America" dated 11/26/07.
Source: https://www.scribd.com/document/6245756/Barack-Obama-on-Defense-Issues-A-21st-Century-Military-for-America
Status: When President Obama assumed office in CY2009, a critical gap existed between reconciling the Defense Logistics Agency's (DLA's) spare parts inventory and field requirements. The Department of Defense (DoD) needed to do a better job in forecasting what the Armed Forces actually needed and more accurately calculate how long it took to produce these items and deliver them to the end user -- the war fighter.

For example, the U.S. Army in CY2007 confirmed a CY2003 requirement that the Soldier-Wearable Acoustic Targeting System (SWATS) was safe for soldiers to use. SWATS are rugged and lightweight (450 g) provide direction and distance in a fraction of a second and 360 degree coverage. Visual indication is shown on a shoulder display. The system is available in vehicle (VMS) and fixed-site

1.00

Chapter 3 - Department of Defense

(FSS) versions. As of end-CY2011, more than 18,000 units had been delivered to the warfighter.

The Mine-Resistent, Ambush-Protected (MRAP) vehicle started in CY2007 during the Bush Administration has saved thousands of lives. MRAP vehicles have a V-shaped hull that deflects the force of bombs and roadside Improvised Explosive Devices (IEDs) that blow up beneath them, in contrast with Humvee vehicles that have flat bottoms. According to a Congressional Research Service (CRS) report dated 01/18/11, Congress appropriated over $40B for the MRAP vehicle through FY2010. The President's FY2011 request for $3.4B for the MRAP Vehicle Fund was authorized in the National Defense Authorization Act of 2011 (Public Law 111-383). After delivering about 20,000 MRAP vehicles for efforts in Iraq and Afghanistan, the Pentagon focused on the development of a more agile Joint Light Tactical Vehicle (JLTV), the delivery of which would occur in CY2018 after a six-year delay.

The Pentagon's new "fast lane" system, initiated by former Defense Secretary Gates, also appeared promising to get needed equipment to the troops fast. A new "Boomerang" system to detect the origin of sniper gunshots was fast-tracked to outposts in Afghanistan in CY2011. Over 200K pairs of "Ballistic Underwear" were also expedited to Afghanistan in CY2011 to help minimize wounds received from bombs detonated by foot patrols.

Despite improvements in the delivery of protective equipment, lives continued to be lost and troops continued to be wounded. As of 12/31/16, the tally was:

3,481 Killed in Action (KIA), 929 deaths due to non-hostile actions, plus 13 DoD Civilian KIA for a total of 4,423 in Iraq during Operation Iraqi Freedom as well as 31,958 Wounded in Action (WIA);

38 KIA plus 35 deaths due to non-hostile actions for a total of 73 during Iraqi Operation New Dawn as well as 295 WIA;

1,833 KIA and 383 deaths due to non-hostile actions for a total of 2,216 under Afghanistan Operation Enduring Freedom (OEF). In addition, there were 131 campaign-related deaths at other locations as well as four (4) DoD civilians deaths, all totaling 2,351 KIA. OEF also resulted in 20,092 WIA;

Eight (8) KIA plus 23 deaths due to non-hostile actions and 21 WIA under Operation Inherent Resolve against ISIS/ISIL;

44 U.S. KIA and 16 deaths under non-hostile circumstances, plus 360 WIA reported to date under Afghan Operation Freedom's Sentinel.

In certain areas, progress was made to protect our troops by the Obama Administration. For FY2012 alone, $2.8B was provided for measures to counter Improvised Explosive Device (IED) activities in Iraq and Afghanistan; $3.2B was provided for MRAP vehicles; $453M was provided for upgrading M-1 Abrama tanks; and $1.5B was provided for the National Guard and Reserves to meet urgent equipment needs.

This promise was fulfilled.

DE-24	**The Promise:** "...support increased R&D for naval forces." **When/Where:** Obama Campaign Document "A 21st Century Military for America" dated 11/26/07. **Source:** https://www.scribd.com/document/6245756/Barack-Obama-on-Defense-Issues-A-21st-Century-Military-for-America **Status:** The U.S. Navy's (USN's) Research and Development (R&D) budget for FY2009 was set at $19.3B. This was the amount to be increased. Here's a profile of President Obama's requests for USN Research, Development, Test and Evalustion during his two terms in office: FY2010.......$19.9B FY2011.......$17.7B	0.00

Chapter 3 - Department of Defense

FY2012.......$17.6B
FY2013.......$16.8B
FY2014.......$15.9B
FY2015.......$16.2B
FY2016.......$17.8B
FY2017.......$17.3B

On 02/04/12, the Chief of Naval Operations (CNO), Admiral Jonathan Greenert, announced that the Future Years Defense Program (FYDP) provided for a battle force of 285 ships in FY2017. A new Force Structure Assessment (FSA) completed later in CY2012 increased the battle force projection to a goal of 306 ships, adjusted to 308 in CY2014. That level would be constituted by 11 aircraft carriers, 12 ballistic-missile submarines, 48 attack submarines, 88 large surface combatants, 52 small surface combatants, 34 amphibious warfare ships, 29 combat logistics force ships and 34 support vessels. As of mid-CY2016, excluding approximately 200 ready-reserve and mothballed/reserve ships that could be activated in case of a national or international crisis, the USN had a battle force of 282 ships.

The trend of President Obama's requests for USN RDT&E funding, with the exception of a small increase in FY2010, indicates that he requested less each year during the FY2011-FY2017 timeframe than the amount funded in FY2009.

This promise was not fulfilled.

DE-25

The Promise: "...will support sea basing ships capable of support humanitarian missions as well as combat mission."
When/Where: Obama Campaign Document "A 21st Century Military for America" dated 11/26/07.
Source: https://www.scribd.com/document/6245756/Barack-Obama-on-Defense-Issues-A-21st-Century-Military-for-America
Status: The Amphibious Assault Ship (Multi-Purpose) designated "LHD" is an example of the type of ship referred to in this promise. The LHD serves as the lead ship of a U.S. Navy (USN) Amphibious Readiness Group (ARG), embarks, transports, deploys, commands and fully supports all elements of a Marine Expeditionary Unit (MEU) of 2,000 Marines, inserting forces on shore via helicopters, landing craft and amphibious vehicles for humanitarian and other conventional purposes.

To support combat operations as well as non-combatant evacuations and humanitarian missions, LHD's have hospital facilities including 6 fully equipped operating rooms and other hospital facilities capable of treating up to 600 patients.

The Navy's 30-year plan released in 02/10 recognized the value of multi-purpose amphibious ships and planned to maintain an adaptable amphibious landing force of approximately 33 ships in the near term (2011-2020) with 11 of the 33 being LHA/D amphibious assault ships. As of mid-CY2016, the USN operated seven (7) LHA and eight (8) LHD ships, four (4) over the CY2010 plan.

1.00

Further, during President Obama's tenure in office, the USN planned to introduce the following ships to the fleet over the coming years, each with humanitarian assistance/disaster relief capabilities:
- 23 Joint High Speed Vessels (JHSV). This ship was renamed Expeditionary Fast Transport (EPF) in 09/15. As of mid-CY2016, six (6) had been delivered and two (2) were under construction
- up to 4 Mobile Landing Platform (MLP)/Afloat Forward Staging Base (AFSB) ships. These ships were renamed Expeditionary Transfer Dock (ESD) and Expeditionary Mobile Base (ESB) respectively in 09/15. Both have humanitarian aid/disaster relief capabilities. As of mid-CY2016, two (2) ESD and one (1) ESB ships had been delivered to the USN. One of each variant is under construction for an increased total of five (5).

This promise was fulfilled.

Chapter 3 - Department of Defense

DE-26	**The Promise:** "...will modernize the many capable ships that we now have and tilt the investment balance towards more capable, smaller combatants, while maintaining the Navy's ability to command the seas." **When/Where:** Obama Campaign Document "A 21st Century Military for America" dated 11/26/07. **Source:** https://www.scribd.com/document/6245756/Barack-Obama-on-Defense-Issues-A-21st-Century-Military-for-America **Status:** 1. Modernization: Under its Phased Modernization Plan (PMP) introduced in 03/14, the U.S. Navy (USN) would have placed 11 cruisers and three dock-landing ships into a reduced operating status primarily for modernization purposes. Under the plan, the cruisers were to be minimally manned for 5 to 12 years. In CY2015, Congress came up with a new modernization plan. Under this plan, the USN would pull 2 cruisers out of service each year with the modernization period not to exceed 4 years, and no more than 6 cruisers to be out of service at any point in time. This came to be referred to as the "2/4/6 Plan." Two years later for FY2017, President Obama's administration proposed to revert back to the USN's PMP and 'drydock' all 11 cruisers and one amphibious ship at the same time. Here's the profile for President Obama's annual budget requests for ship modernization: FY2010..........$343M (Down from $374M in FY2009) FY2011..........$414M FY2012..........$358M FY2013..........$348M FY2014..........$369M FY2015..........$294M FY2016..........$000M FY2017..........$000M 2. Investment in Smaller Combatants: In CY2001, the Littoral Combat Ship (LCS) Program was established, calling for 52 units to be produced. In CY2014, the Pentagon decided that the final 20 ships in the program were to be built as a variant of the original LCS design and were to be referred to as "Frigates." In 12/15, in view of budget limitations imposed by the deficit-cutting plan signed into law on 08/02/11 that caused the Pentagon to cut an estimated $350B to $450B through FY2023, the Obama Administration directed the USN to reduce the LCS/Frigate program to a total of 40 ships. Back on 02/04/12, the Chief of Naval Operation had announced that instead of a 301-ship Navy anticipated for FY2017, that number was adjusted downward to 285. Despite budget cuts, this number was later adjusted during CY2012 to 306, and further adjusted in CY2014 to 308. As of end-CY2016, not counting approximately 200 ready-reserve and mothballed ships that could be activated in case of a national or international crisis, the USN had 282 deployable battle force ships. This promise was not fulfilled.	0.00
DE-27	**The Promise:** "...humanitarian activities that build friends and allies at the regional and ground level...are presently not included in long-term planning and... actually take away funds from a unit's regular operational budget...The Obama administration will expand such programs, regularizing them into the annual budget so that our efforts to aid allies...are sustainable, rather than ad-hoc." **When/Where:** Obama Campaign Document "A 21st Century Military for America" dated 11/26/07. **Source:** https://www.scribd.com/document/6245756/Barack-Obama-on-Defense-Issues-A-21st-Century-Military-for-America	0.00

Chapter 3 - Department of Defense

Status: The Department of Defense (DoD) Overseas Humanitarian, Disaster and Civic Aid (OHDACA) program, which funds DoD's Humanitarian Assistance Program, the Humanitarian Mine Action Program, and the Foreign Disaster Relief and Emergency Response Program, has been in existence since the 10/06/94 issuance of DoD Directive 2205.2 ("Humanitarian and Civic Assistance (HCA) Provided in Conjunction with Military Operations"). This directive states that "Expenses incurred as a direct result of providing HCA (other than De Minimis HCA) to a foreign country shall be paid out of funds specifically appropriated for such purposes."

Thus, the mechanisms were in place long before the Obama Administration came into power for DoD's inclusion of humanitarian activities in its annual budget submissions.

This promise was not fulfilled because it didn't need to be.

DE-28

The Promise: "... creating a system of oversight for war funds as stringent as in the regular budget."
When/Where: Obama Campaign Document "A 21st Century Military for America" dated 11/26/07.
Source: https://www.scribd.com/document/6245756/Barack-Obama-on-Defense-Issues-A-21st-Century-Military-for-America
Status: To protect U.S. taxpayer funds committed for nonmilitary development and humanitarian assistance in Afghanistan from fraud, waste and abuse, the Office of the Special Inspector General for Afghanistan Reconstruction (SIGAR) was opened under the Bush Administration in CY2008, not under President Obama.

As of 04/15/16, the SIGAR had 288 open investigations:
- 105 Procurement/Contract Fraud
- 61 Public Corruption/Bribery
- 30 Theft of Property and Services
- 69 Miscellaneous Criminal Activity

In its 07/30/16 quarterly report to Congress, SIGAR reported that since its inception in 2008, "...SIGAR investigations had resulted in a cumulative total of 141 criminal charges, 103 convictions, and 91 sentencings. Criminal fines, restitutions, forfeitures, civil settlement recoveries, and U.S. government cost savings total $951 million."

SIGAR's oversight mission is supplemented by independent investigation and audit efforts by the Government Accountability Office (GAO) and the USAID Office of the Inspector General.

The oversight system instituted by President Obama's predecessor continued with stellar results during President Obama's two terms in office. But President Obama cannot be credited with "creating" that system.

This promise was not fulfilled.

Grade: 0.00

IRAQ | GRADE

DE-29

The Promise: "redeploy combat brigades from Iraq at a pace of 1 to 2 brigades a month that would remove them in 16 months."
When/Where: Plan for America: "Blueprint for Change," dated 10/09/08
Source: https://www.documentcloud.org/ Obama and Biden's documents/550007-barack-obama-2008-blueprint-for-change.html
Status: The oft-repeated campaign, vote-getting promise to "end the war" and pull all combat troops out of Iraq "within 16 months" of his inauguration sounded good at the time. However, reality set in and President Obama essentially kept the same timeline established by President Bush for withdrawal from Iraq. He formally ended U.S. military combat involvement in Iraq on 12/15/11, 35 months after his inauguration.

Meanwhile, more U.S. servicemen and women lost their lives or were wounded since "Operation

Grade: 0.00

New Dawn" started on 09/01/10. Since that date, 38 U.S. soldiers were killed in Iraq as a result of hostile actions, 35 died as a result of non-hostile actions, and 295 were wounded in action as of 12/31/16.

The above are the official numbers. We do know, for example, that there were more U.S. troops (specifically, members of a 200-strong Marine Expeditionary Unit) killed or wounded in early CY2016 near Makmour, Iraq. These losses were 'off the books' because those Marines were on a so-called "temporary" assignment to Iraq.

This promise was not fulfilled.

DE-30

The Promise: "...on my first day in office, I would give the military a new mission: ending this war."
When/Where: Obama campaign article printed in The New York Times entitled "My Plan for Iraq" dated 07/14/08.
Source: http://www.nytimes.com/2008/07/14/opinion/14obama.html
Status: Immediately after his inauguration on 01/21/09, President Obama met with diplomatic and military leaders responsible for the U.S. presence in Iraq. During that meeting, Obama directed immediate planning for a "responsible military drawdown" from Iraq.

On 10/21/11, President Obama announced that he and Prime Minister Al-Maliki agreed that all U.S. Forces in Iraq would be pulled out before the end of CY2011.

However, promise fulfillment was short-lived with the advent of successful Islamic State of Iraq and Syria (ISIS) incursions into Iraq resulting in the takeover of population centers such as Mosul and Ramadi.

In early CY2016, for example, the Administration sent 200 Marines from the Marine Expeditionary Unit with four artillery units to prop up the Iraqi 15th Division near Makmour. The Marines were attacked by ISIS elements occupying Mosul and at least one Marine death and several wounded resulted. This was not publicly reported at the time by the Administration.

By 09/28/16, U.S. troop strength in Iraq had crept up to about 4,565 from a low of 170 security personnel in 06/14. On that date, the Administration announced that an additional 615 soldiers would be sent to Iraq, bringing the total of combat-ready troops to 5,180. Uncounted were approximately 1,500 troops in Iraq for purely security reasons, bringing the in-country presence to 6,680 before end-CY2016. According to media reports, nobody believed that the 5,180 combat troops were in Iraq purely in an "advisory and training" capacity. Combat was believed to be inevitable as Iraqi forces tried to liberate Mosul from ISIS occupation -- with U.S. military assistance.

This promise was not fulfilled.

0.00

DE-31

The Promise: "I would not hold our military, our resources and our foreign policy hostage to a misguided desire to maintain permanent bases in Iraq."
When/Where: Obama Op-Ed Contribution to The New York Times, dated 07/14/08.
Source: http://www.nytimes.com/2008/07/14/opinion/14obama.html
Status: The National Defense Authorization Act for 2010 signed into law by President Obama on 10/28/09 specifies that "No funds ... may be obligated or expended ... for the permanent stationing of United States Armed Forces in Iraq." Under the terms of a 2008 Status of Forces Agreement (SOFA), all U.S. troops had to be out of Iraq by the end of CY2011.

On 10/21/11, President Obama announced that he and Prime Minister Al-Maliki agreed that all U.S. Forces in Iraq would be pulled out before the end of CY2011. This announcement was validated during Prime Minister Al-Maliki's visit to Washington on 12/12/11 and the last U.S. combat troops formally departed Iraq on 12/18/11.

1.00

Chapter 3 - Department of Defense

In the face of the takeover by ISIS of key cities such as Mosul and Ramadi, President Obama announced in 06/15 that the Pentagon was sending an additional 450 "advisors/trainers." By 08/16, U.S. troop strength in Iraq had crept up to about 4,650. Yet no "permanent" U.S. bases were re-opened. Instead, U.S. troops operated out of a few temporary "fire bases."

To maintain a rapid reaction force in case conditions in Iraq deteriorated, President Obama kept several brigades in neighboring Kuwait (i.e. 3rd Armored Brigade, 1st Armored Division; 2nd Brigade Combat Team, 1st Infantry Division; 17th Sustainment Brigade, 1st Sustainment Command) as well as some 10,000 troops in Qatar.

This promise was fulfilled.

	PAKISTAN	GRADE
DE-32	**The Promise:** "Obama would condition U.S. military aid to Pakistan on their making progress to close down the training camps, evict foreign fighters, and prevent the Taliban from using Pakistan as a base to strike inside of Afghanistan." **When/Where:** Obama-Biden Plan: "The War We Need to Win" dated 07/31/07. **Source:** http://www.mattluedke.com/wp-content/uploads/2016/09/CounterterrorismFactSheet.pdf **Status:** Historically, Pakistan considers that anything on its side of the Durand Line (the poorly marked 1,600 mile Afghanistan-Pakistan border established in 1893) is its sovereign territory and therefore its own business.	0.00

For FY2010, Pakistan gained approximately $2.5B in direct U.S. military aid: $288M in Foreign Military Financing, $5M for International Military Education and Training, $700M under the Pakistan Counterinsurgency Capability Fund, and $1.5B under the Coalition Support Fund as part of a $4.3B aid package.

Despite all this funding, U.S. Predator drone attacks and the use of other intelligence assets had to be increased in western Pakistan as early as CY2010. This reflected Obama Administration frustrations over Pakistan's failure to dislodge Haqqani Network, Taliban and Al-Qaeda operatives from North Waziristan -- using that area as a base from which to launch attacks against coalition troops in Afghanistan, an effort that continued unabated through CY2016.

For FY2011, an increase in funding for the Pakistan Counterinsurgency Capability Fund (from $700M to $1.2B) was requested by President Obama. Congress agreed to limit this amount to $800M in the Department of Defense and Full-Year Continuing Appropriations Act of 2011 (H.R. 1473).

For FY2012, President Obama proposed $1.6B for Pakistani police and military assistance. Congress froze $700M of this assistance while it sought proof that Pakistan was taking action against militants who used Improvised Explosive Devices (IEDs) against U.S. force operating in Afghanistan. Congress again temporarily blocked funds for Pakistan in early-CY2012 because Pakistan would not let supplies reach NATO forces in Afghanistan via shorter, less costly routes through Pakistan after Pakistani troops were killed during a U.S. drone attack on insurgent training sites in Pakistan.

All this time, the Haqqani Network, declared to be a terrorist group by the Obama Administration on 09/07/12, continued to operate with impunity in North Waziristan. Nonetheless, the Obama Administration's FY2013 budget proposal requested $2.2B in foreign operations funds for Pakistan, including $800M for the Pakistan Counterinsurgency Capability Fund (PCCF), a 6% increase over the FY2012 enacted level.

In 08/16, the Pentagon withheld $300M in military aid to Pakistan. According to a spokesman, "the funds could not be released to the government of Pakistan at this time because the secretary has not yet certified that Pakistan has taken sufficient action against the Haqqani Network." But this was only

$300M out of a $1B military aid package.

It was widely reported at the time that some of Pakistan's security services had been assisting the 60K-strong Taliban against NATO forces in Afghanistan since Operation Enduring Freedom started in late CY2001. At the same time, the 4K to 6K-strong Haqqani Network and terrorist training camps continued to operate in North Waziristan. Despite these documented facts, the Obama Administration continued to provide military aid to the Pakistani Government, with slight perturbations, through end-CY2016.

This promise was not fulfilled.

	RESERVES	GRADE
DE-33	**The Promise:** "Obama's plan will be to reverse the trend of "cross-leveling," the cannibalizing of soldiers and machines from units back home for missions abroad." **When/Where:** Obama Campaign Document "A 21st Century Military for America" dated 11/26/07. **Source:** https://www.scribd.com/document/6245756/Barack-Obama-on-Defense-Issues-A-21st-Century-Military-for-America **Status:** The purpose of cross-leveling of personnel and equipment is to improve an individual unit's readiness. Cross-leveling of one state's equipment to fulfill another state's shortage is the most common type of cross-leveling action. Distribution of personnel and non-excess equipment between states is done for mobilizations or other high priority events based on the Pentagon's requirements. There was no 'plus-up' in President Obama's FY2010-FY2017 budget proposals to mitigate the "cross-leveling" of troops and equipment situation. Nonetheless, when this promise was a serious issue during President Obama's first term in office (and less so during his second), nothing substantive was accomplished toward promise fulfillment. This promise was not fulfilled.	0.00
DE-34	**The Promise:** "Obama cosponsored legislation to elevate the Chief of the National Guard to the rank of four-star general and make the chief a member of the Joint Chiefs of Staff, the top military advisory panel to the president. As president, Obama will sign this legislation into law." **When/Where:** Obama Campaign Document "A 21st Century Military for America" dated 11/26/07. **Source:** https://www.scribd.com/document/6245756/Barack-Obama-on-Defense-Issues-A-21st-Century-Military-for-America **Status:** On 05/19/11, Senators Patrick Leahy (D-VT)Lindsey Graham (R-SC) introduced the "National Guard Empowerment and State-National Defense Integration Act of 2011 (S. 1025) with 50 senators as co-sponsors and supported by 65 senators for inclusion in the defense authorization for FY2012. This proposed bill included a provision to give the National Guard's senior officer, the Chief of the National Guard Bureau (CNGB), a seat at the Joint Chiefs of Staff (JCS) table. As submitted by Congress to the President for signature, Section 512 of the NDAA for FY2012 (H.R. 1540) granted membership of the CNGB on the Joint Staff. President Obama signed H.R. 1540 into law on 12/31/11. This promise was fulfilled.	1.00
DE-35	**The Promise:** "Restore the deployment policies under which the reserve and guard enlisted...An Obama administration will...limit lengthy deployments to one year for every six years...restore the 24-month limit on cumulative deployment time." **When/Where:** Obama Campaign Document "A 21st Century Military for America" dated 11/26/07. **Source:** https://www.scribd.com/document/6245756/Barack-Obama-on-Defense-Issues-A-21st-Century-Military-for-America **Status:** Prior to 01/07, Guard/Reserve members' cumulative time in active duty to support war efforts in Iraq or Afghanistan could not exceed 24 months. In 01/07, Secretary of Defense Gates announced	0.00

Chapter 3 - Department of Defense

that this cumulative limit was lifted. Since 01/09, any single mobilization cannot exceed 12 months. The 24-month limitation was not restored during subsequent years.

Under the CY2011 Army Force Generation (ARFORGEN) model, the objective was for active component (AC) units to have a deploy-to-dwell ratio of 1:2 meaning one year deployed to two years at home station. The U.S. Army Reserve (USAR) and Army National Guard (ARNG), referred to as Reserve Components (RC), were both reorganized to fill the role of an operational reserve, with an expected activation-to-dwell ratio of 1:5.

In reality the percentage of RC personnel who exceeded Activation-to-Dwell Ratios as of end-CY2016 was as follows:
Ratio:........1:5........1:4........1:3........1:2
USAR:.... 18.4%...16.4%...15.1%...6.0%
ARNG:... 17.7%...15.4%...13.9%...5.9%

Under a new CY2014 program known as "Associated Units," 14 ARNG and two USAR units were to be paired with AC units so they could train together and deploy together. Consequently, if an AC unit had a deploy-to-dwell ratio of 1:2, the reserve components would also be subjected to the same deploy-to-dwell ratio of 1:2.

This promise was not fulfilled.

RUSSIA	GRADE

DE-36

The Promise: "As a first step, I will seek Russia's agreement to extend essential monitoring and verification provisions of the {Strategic Arms Reduction Treaty} START I before it expires in December 2009."
When/Where: Candidate Obama response to "Arms Control Today" questionnaire dated 09/10/08.
Source: https://www.armscontrol.org/2008election
Status: On 04/01/09, Obama met with his Russian counterpart, Dmitry Medvedev, in Europe where the two established the groundwork for this promise to be kept by the deadline of 12/05/09. They met again at a summit in Moscow in 07/09 where they issued a "Joint Understanding" proposing a legally binding agreement to replace the START Treaty.

The expiration date of 12/05/09 passed without an agreement. On 03/26/10, Presidents Obama and Medvedev agreed on a new treaty that called for both sides to reduce their nuclear weapons stockpiles by 30%, allowing each to retain 1,550 warheads, down from the ceiling at that time of 2,200, as well as limiting deployed and non-deployed missile launchers to 800 (half of the authorized amount under the previous treaty). The agreement would also re-establish a weak system for monitoring and verification that had ended in 12/09.

0.00

The new treaty was signed on 04/08/10 in Prague. It was ratified by the U.S. Senate in a 71-26 vote on 12/22/10, was ratified by the Russian Government and was signed into law by President Medvedev on 01/28/11, signed into law by President Obama on 02/02/11, and implemented with an exchange of ratification documents by Secretary of State Clinton and Foreign Minister Lavrov in Munich on 02/05/11. Shortly thereafter on 02/07/11, both Deputy Foreign Minister Ryabkov and Deputy Defense Minister Antonov acknowledged that Russia reserved the right to withdraw from the "New START" treaty if the U.S. significantly boosted its missile shield in Europe to the detriment of Russia's missiles and nuclear deterrent forces.

While ratification of "New START" was a significant political and foreign policy victory (despite its apparent weaknesses), President Obama was specific about fulfilling this promise "before it expires in December 2009." This did not happen.

This promise was not fulfilled.

DE-37	**The Promise:** "....will also immediately stand down all nuclear forces to be reduced under the Moscow Treaty and urge Russia to do the same." **When/Where:** Candidate Obama response to "Arms Control Today" questionnaire dated 09/10/08. **Source:** https://www.armscontrol.org/2008election **Status:** When this promise was made in CY2008, the USA was very close to reaching the upper limit of 1,700-2,200 warheads set by the Strategic Offensive Reduction Treaty (SORT), also known as the Moscow Treaty. The target of 2,200 was reached shortly after President Obama was sworn in for his first term in office. Soon after President Obama's inauguration, his Administration entered into new rounds of negotiations with Russian counterparts, to include Obama-Medvedev talks, with the objective of signing a new treaty to replace the "START-1" Treaty signed in 07/91 and set to expire in 12/09. The "New START" Treaty was signed on 04/08/10 in Prague. It was ratified by the U.S. Senate on 12/22/10 and by the Russian Duma on 01/28/11 with an effective date of 02/05/11, marking the end of the Moscow Treaty. The "New START" Treaty further reduced the deployed warhead limit by both countries to 1,550 and the deployed delivery vehicle limit to 700 by 02/05/18. This promise was fulfilled.	1.00
DE-38	**The Promise:** "...will work with Russia to find common ground and bring significantly more weapons off hair-trigger alert." **When/Where:** Obama Campaign Document "A 21st Century Military for America" dated 11/26/07. **Source:** https://www.scribd.com/document/6245756/Barack-Obama-on-Defense-Issues-A-21st-Century-Military-for-America **Status:** "Hair-trigger" status is also referred to as "high alert," "ready alert," "day-to-day alert," "launch-on-warning status," or "prompt-launch status." Approximately 3,000 nuclear warheads maintained by Russia and the USA in silos, in submarines and elsewhere, remained on hair-trigger alert status through end-CY2016. Activities such as President Obama's Nuclear Posture Review (NPR) of 04/06/10, the various non-proliferation meetings, and signature of the "New START" treaty on 04/08/10 in Prague (ratified by the U.S. Senate on 12/22/10 and by the Russian Government on 01/28/11) did nothing to eliminate the "hair-trigger alert" status adopted by both sides. This determination was validated by the statement in the CY2010 NPR that "the current alert posture of U.S. strategic forces - with heavy bombers on full-time alert, nearly all ICBMs on alert, and a significant number of SSBNs at sea at any given time - should be maintained..." The above is contradicted by Department of State briefing slides (2015 U.S. National Report to the Nuclear NonProliferation Treaty Review Conference) which state in part that "...U.S. nuclear forces are not on hair-trigger alert..." Given the strained relations that prevailed with Russia since President Vladimir Putin was re-elected on 05/07/12, and given the provisions of the CY2010 NPR cited above, it was inconceivable that the USA was not in a position to react immediately if subjected to a nuclear threat by Russia. This promise was not fulfilled.	0.00
DE-39	**The Promise:** "...will seek deep, verifiable reductions in all U.S. and Russian nuclear weapons - whether deployed or non-deployed, whether strategic or non-strategic..." **When/Where:** Obama Campaign Document "A 21st Century Military for America" dated 11/26/07. **Source:** https://www.scribd.com/document/6245756/Barack-Obama-on-Defense-Issues-A-21st-Century-Military-for-America **Status:** When the original START I Treaty expired on 12/05/09 under President Obama's watch, the	1.00

Chapter 3 - Department of Defense

U.S. lost its ability to "boots on the ground" verify Russia's nuclear capabilities of approximately 2,500 nuclear missiles. Also on 12/05/09 and as a further detriment to U.S. national security, Russia stopped its notifications to the State Department Nuclear Risk Reduction Center on inspections, movement, ground-based and airborne nuclear capabilities, and destruction of launchers.

The "New START" Treaty was concluded between the USA and Russia on 04/08/10 in Prague. It was ratified by the U.S. Senate on 12/22/10 and the Russian Government on 01/28/11. It provides for extensive exchanges of data on the numbers, locations and technical features of nuclear weapon systems and facilities -- including the telemetry on up to 5 ICBM and SLBM launches per year. Under the Treaty, both parties have to share information on treaty-limited items and Russia will have to provide the USA with notifications on the movements and production of their long-range missiles and launchers.

New in this treaty was that for the first time, both parties would record and share unique identifiers on all Inter-Continental Balistic Missiles (ICBMs), Submarine-Launched Balistic Missiles (SLBMs), and heavy bombers covered under the treaty - not just mobile missiles as in the previous treaty. These unique identifiers (serial numbers) would enable both sides to track both deployed and non-deployed missiles, minimizing the potential for violating the provisions of the "New START" treaty, which called for a bilateral reduction of nuclear warheads to 1,550.

Further verifications would be assured through 18 annual on-site, short-notice inspection of Russian operating bases, storage facilities, test ranges, and conversion and elimination facilities.

However, Russia announced on 06/16/15 that it was adding 40 new ICBMs to its arsenal, missiles that it reported would be able to overcome "the most technically sophisticated missile defense systems." In the aftermath of Russia's annexation of the Crimean Peninsula in 03/14, this was tangible evidence that Russia would not sit back as NATO shored up its defenses.

Nonetheless, President Obama's promise to "seek deep, verifiable reductions in all U.S. and Russian nuclear weapons" was fulfilled.

DE-40 | **The Promise:** "...will set a goal to expand the U.S.-Russian ban on intermediate-range missiles so that the agreement is global." | **0.00**

When/Where: Obama and Biden's Plan for America: "Blueprint for Change," dated 10/09/08.
Source: https://www.documentcloud.org/documents/550007-barack-obama-2008-blueprint-for-change.html
Status: Intermediate-Range Ballistic Missiles (IRBM) are those that can travel 1,865 to 3,420 miles (3,000 to 5,500 kilometers). In CY1987, the USA and Russia signed an Intermediate-Range Nuclear Forces (INF) Treaty that called for the elimination of all nuclear and conventional ground-launched ballistic and cruise missiles held by both countries that have a range of 500 to 5,500 km. IRBMs fall within these ranges.

Germany, Hungary, Poland, Slovakia and the Czech Republic destroyed their IRBMs in the 1990's, followed by Bulgaria in CY2002. By end-CY2016, Russia and the USA had been joined in the INF Treaty by Belarus, Kazakhstan, and Ukraine.

On 07/28/14, President Obama informed Russian President Vladimir Putin that Russia had violated the INF Treaty. The US said Russia tested a new ground-launched cruise missile, possibly the Novator 9M729 (NATO nomenclature SSC-8). The first launch of this missile occurred on 09/02/15.

In 05/16, the USA started Aegis launch operations at Deveselu, Romania, while building another land-based Aegis launch facility near Redzikowo, Poland for CY2018 activation. Russia objected to this development, stating that the activation of such European missile defense shields violated the INF Treaty, despite U.S. assurances that the shields in Romania and Poland were to defend Europe from an unpredictable foe such as Iran. Russia countered by legitimately arguing that the MK-41

Vertical Launch System utilized by the Aegis missile system could easily be retrofitted to fire cruise missiles against Russia.

On the other hand, Russia was also suspected of having developed and flight-tested the R-500 (aka Iskander-K), a Ground-Launched Cruise Missile (GLCM) with a range estimated at between 500-3,000 km. That range was well within the Prohibited Range prescribed by the INF and the R-500 was therefore in violation of the INF. In its "2016 Report on Adherence to and Compliance With Arms Control, Nonproliferation, and Disarmament Agreements and Commitments" dated 04/11/16, the Department of State acknowledged that "Russia was in violation of its obligations under the INF Treaty not to possess, produce, or flight-test a ground-launched cruise missile (GLCM) with a range capability of 500 km to 5,500 km, or to possess or produce launchers of such missiles."

A global ban on INF missiles would have potentially removed missiles held by countries unfriendly to the USA such as Iran and North Korea. At the same time, however, it would have eliminated IRBMs from allies that need them for self-preservation such as Israel.

China (DF-4/CSS-3), India (Agni-III and K-4), Iran (BM-25/Musudan), Pakistan (Ghauri-3), Israel, and North Korea (Taepo Dong-2) still possessed IRBMs as of end-CY2016.

There was no expansion of the INF Treaty during President Obama's two terms in office. Rather, starting during the Bush Administration and lasting throughout the 8-year Obama Administration, Russia resumed production, testing and launching of intermediate-range conventional and nuclear missiles in contravention of the CY1987 INF Treaty.

This promise was not fulfilled.

DEFENSE GPA | **0.45**

Chapter 4 - Department of Education

Campaign Promises
Departments -> Education

ITEM	EDUCATION	GRADE
	COLLEGE EDUCATION	
ED-1	**The Promise:** "...will make college affordable for all Americans by creating a new American Opportunity Tax Credit." **When/Where:** Obama's Plan for America: "The Blueprint for Change" dated 07/29/08 **Source:** https://www.documentcloud.org/documents/550007-barack-obama-2008-blueprint-for-change.html **Status:** The American Recovery and Reinvestment Act (ARRA) of 2009, signed into law 02/17/09, approved the new American Opportunity Tax Credit for two years up to $2,500 (it was $1,800 prior to the stimulus bill). Passage of the ARRA trumped the American Opportunity Tax Credit Act of 2009 (H.R. 106) introduced on 01/05/09 by Congressman Chaka Fattah (D-PA), a bill that expired without action at the end of the 111th Congress. That bill would have increased the refundable tax credit for higher education expenses to $4,000. The American Opportunity Tax Credit was further extended for CY2011 and CY2012 on 12/17/10 when President Obama signed the Tax Relief, Unemployment Insurance Reauthorization, and Job Creation Act of 2010 (H.R. 4853). On 01/02/13, President Obama signed the "American Taxpayer Relief Act of 2012" (H.R. 8) into law. This bill extended the American Opportunity Tax Credit by five years through the end of CY2017. The Bipartisan Budget Act of 2015 (H.R. 1314) was then signed into law by President Obama on 11/02/15, making the American Opportunity Tax Credit permanent. This promise was fulfilled.	1.00
ED-2	**The Promise:** "...will create a national "Make College a Reality" initiative that has a bold goal to increase students taking AP or college-level classes nationwide 50 percent by 2016..." **When/Where:** Obama and Biden's Plan for America: "Blueprint for Change," dated 10/09/08. **Source:** https://www.documentcloud.org/documents/550007-barack-obama-2008-blueprint-for-change.html **Status:** When variants of this promise were made during the CY2007-08 school year, 1,580,821 students out of a total high school enrollment of 14.9M students had taken Advanced Placement (AP) courses and exams. During the CY2014-15 school year, 2,483,452 out of a total high school enrollment of 15.0M students (less than a 1% increase) took AP courses/exams according to The College Board, exceeding the 50% goal. This promise is not to be confused with the President's "2020 North Star Initiative" or First Lady Michelle Obama's "Reach Higher Initiative" to promote college attendance and completion as well as other initiatives to ensure college affordability. Rather, this promise was specifically to create a national "Make College a Reality" initiative applicable to high school students. While the goal to increase AP/college-level class participation by 50% was reached on its own	0.00

steam, the promised initiative/program did not come to fruition during President Obama's two terms in office.

This promise was not fulfilled.

ED-3

The Promise: "Some states have developed an Early Assessment Program that enables 11th graders and their families to ascertain if they are on track to be college ready by the time they graduate...will provide $25 million annually in matching funds for states to develop Early Assessment Programs."
When/Where: Obama-Biden Plan: "Making College Affordable for Everyone" dated 09/11/08.
Source: https://static.newamerica.org/attachments/7618-a-call-to-arms/College%20Affordability%20Fact%20Sheet.d9439c717ab24e9cbd5d2cef2db86cba.pdf
Status: There is no evidence that the Obama Administration requested matching funds for state-level "Early Assessment Programs" (EAP), during President Obama's two terms in office. Some states such as California already had excellent EAP's in place prior to President Obama's first term.

This promise was not fulfilled.

0.00

ED-4

The Promise: "...will support university programs that partner NASA, DOT, DOD and NOAA with academia to provide hands-on training experiences at the college level."
When/Where: Obama-Biden Plan: "Advancing the Frontiers of Space Exploration" dated 08/15/08.
Source: http://www.nasa.gov/pdf/382369main_48%20-%2020090803.2.Space_Fact_Sheet_FINAL.pdf
Status: The guiding principles that govern interactions between the Federal Government and universities that perform research are outlined by Executive Order 13185 signed by President Bill Clinton on 12/28/00. This was not an Obama Administration initiative.

(1) NASA has strategic partnerships with numerous universities such as the Universities of Arizona, Michigan, Southern California, California Santa Cruz, UCLA, MIT, Dartmouth College, Carnegie Mellon, Princeton, and others.

(2) The Department of Transportation (DOT) has a healthy research partnership with Ohio State University and with Cornell University to increase public involvement in the rulemaking process driven by a proposed rule to ban texting for truck and bus drivers and to reduce other risks posed by distracted driving. As a result, the DOT announced a new rule in 01/10 against texting and driving.

(3) The National Oceanic and Atmospheric Agency (NOAA) has established partnerships with the University of Mississippi for the Sea Grant Law Center, with the University of Southern California and Texas A&M for ports and harbors research, the University of Connecticut for geospatial research, the University of Rhode Island to foster a global capacity for sustainable resource use, and others.

(4) The Department of Defense, not only through its Defense Acquisition University, has significant partnerships with academia such as funding a unique corrosion engineering degree program at the University of Akron, Ohio State, and the Universities of Virginia, Hawaii and Southern Mississippi. Partnering with the DoD, the University of Michigan combats the stigma associated with seeking care for psychological health, traumatic brain injury among veterans and athletes. External/university research efforts and partnerships can also be funded by the Air Force Office of Sponsored Research (AFOSR), Office of Naval Research (ONR), Army Research Office (ARO), Defense Advance Research Projects Agency (DARPA), Army Corps of Engineers, National Security Agency (NSA), and others.

Funding for these partnership programs was routinely included in President Obama's budget proposals.

This promise was fulfilled.

1.00

Chapter 4 - Department of Education

	COMMUNITY COLLEGE	GRADE
ED-5	**The Promise:** "...provide grants for students seeking college level credit at community colleges if their school does not provide those resources." **When/Where:** Obama and Biden's Plan for America: "Blueprint for Change," dated 10/09/08. **Source:** https://www.documentcloud.org/documents/550007-barack-obama-2008-blueprint-for-change.html **Status:** This promise focused on high school students with the aptitude to pursue college level classes at their neighborhood community colleges but lacked the resources to do so. The "Student Aid and Fiscal Responsibility Act of 2009" (H.R. 3221) was introduced by Congressman George Miller (D-CA) on 07/15/09. It passed by the House on 09/17/09 but did not get through the Senate. This bill was developed to amend the College Access Challenge Grant Program which provides grants to state agencies designated by the governor of that state, not to individual student applicants. The bill intended to give grant priority to programs that: (1) served underrepresented students, dislocated workers, or veterans; (2) are offered by institutes that do not predominantly award bachelor's degrees (i.e. community colleges); (3) increase degree or certificate completion in the fields of science, technology, engineering, and mathematics; (4) enhance the financial literacy of students who are potentially eligible for assistance under the Act; or (5) encourage constructive partnerships between Institutions of Higher Education (IHEs) with high degree completion rates and those without such rates. On 03/18/10, the text of the "Student Aid and Fiscal Responsibility Act of 2009" (H.R. 3221) was included as a rider to the Health Care and Education Reconciliation Act of 2010 (H.R. 4872), signed into law on 03/30/10 by President Obama as an amendment to the Patient Protection and Affordable Care Act. This promise was fulfilled.	1.00
ED-6	**The Promise:** "...will make community college tuition completely free for most students." **When/Where:** Obama and Biden's Plan for America: "Blueprint for Change," dated 10/09/08. **Source:** https://www.documentcloud.org/documents/550007-barack-obama-2008-blueprint-for-change.html **Status:** During his 01/20/15 State of the Union Address to Congress, President Obama repeated his campaign promise to make two years of community college free. The proposed program would create a federal-state partnership with federal government funding covering 75% of community college tuition and states paying 25%. Responding to President Obama's national-level proposal, Congressman Robert Scott (D-VA) introduced the "America's College Promise Act of 2015" (H.R. 2962) on 07/08/15, as did Senator Tammy Baldwin (D-WI) on the same date (S. 1716). These bills would have authorized the Department of Education (DOE) to award grants to waive tuition and fees at community colleges on a national scale. These Acts expired when the 114th Congress closed at the end of CY2016. By end-CY2016 and in the absence of the promised national program, at least 14 states and the cities of San Francisco and Chicago had developed or passed legislation to enact their own tuition-free community college programs, based on varying eligibility criteria (i.e. family income, student high school GPA, etc.). This promise was not fulfilled.	0.00
ED-7	**The Promise:** "...will create a Community College Partnership Program to strengthen community colleges by providing grants to (a) conduct more thorough analysis of the types of skills and technical education that are in high demand from students and local industry; (b) implement new associate of	1.00

arts degree programs that cater to emerging industry and technical career demands; and (c) reward those institutions that graduate more students and also increase their numbers of transfer students to four-year institutions... the grants will support programs that facilitate transfers from two-year institutions to four-year institutions."

When/Where: Obama-Biden Plan: "Making College Affordable for Everyone" dated 09/11/08.
Source: https://static.newamerica.org/attachments/7618-a-call-to-arms/College%20Affordability%20Fact%20Sheet.d9439c717ab24e9cbd5d2cef2db86cba.pdf
Status: Prior to this promise, certain colleges/universities and some states had created their own community college partnership programs, such as Dickinson College of Carlisle, PA and Excelsior College of Albany, NY.

Starting in FY2011, the Departments of Education and Labor were both funded at the $500M level for community college/employer partnerships under the Trade Adjustment Assistance Community College and Career Training initiative. This initiative was signed into law by President Obama on 03/30/10 under the Health Care and Education Reconciliation Act (H.R. 4872), Section 1501. Funding was capped at $2B over a four-year period, essentially creating a Community College Partnership Program.

Beyond the above funding, President Obama's FY2013 budget proposal stated that he was asking for $8B for the Departments of Labor and Education to support "State and community college partnerships with businesses to build the skills of American workers." The creation of this "Community College to Career" fund was announced by President Obama at Northern Virginia Community College in Annandale, VA on 02/13/12. Its intent was to train 2M workers for high-demand industries.

In his FY2017 budget submission to Congress, President Obama proposed the establishment of a $2.5B "Community College Partnership Tax Credit" that would provide businesses with a new tax credit for hiring graduates from community and technical colleges as an incentive to encourage employer engagement and investment in these education and training pathways. The proposal would provide $500M in tax credit authority for each of the five years, FY2017 through FY2021. The tax credit authority would be allocated annually to states on a per capita basis and would be available to qualifying employers that hire qualifying community college graduates.

This promise was fulfilled.

GENERAL EDUCATION	GRADE

| ED-8 | **The Promise:** "Will use the bully pulpit and the example he will set in the White House to promote the importance of arts and arts education in America."
When/Where: Obama-Biden Plan: "Champions for Arts and Culture", dated 09/11/08.
Source: http://muzartworld.org/president-barack-obama-and-joe-biden-champions-for-arts-and-culture/
Status: Since taking office in 01/09, President Obama set the example by hosting numerous musical performances and workshops at the White House, covering classical music/ballet, jazz, Latin and country music. He added $100M in new funding for the arts including $50M under the American Recovery and Reinvestment Act of 2009 to preserve arts jobs. In addition to approximately $25M appropriated to the Department of Education for "Arts in Education" programs, both the national arts and humanities endowments received $167.5M in FY2010, their largest allocations in 16 years.

In terms of arts in education, President Obama's Education Secretary Arne Duncan addressed a letter in 08/09 to "School and Education Community Leaders", to bring to their "attention the importance of the arts as a core academic subject and part of a complete education for all students." The letter then reports on the results of a 2008 National Assessment of Educational Progress (NAEP) survey whereby only 57% of 8th graders attended schools where music instruction was offered "at least three or four times a week", and only 47% attended schools where visual arts were | 1.00 |

Chapter 4 - Department of Education

offered that often.

Finally, the letter announced the launching of another survey "to assess the condition of arts education in grade K-12." All of these actions and plans fed into promise fulfillment, as the promise was simply to "promote" arts and arts education.

This promise was fulfilled.

ED-9	**The Promise:** "Will double funding for the main federal support for afterschool programs, the 21st Century Learning Centers program, to serve one million more children." **When/Where:** Plan for America: "Blueprint for Change," dated 10/09/08 **Source:** https://www.documentcloud.org/ Obama and Biden's documents/550007-barack-obama-2008-blueprint-for-change.html **Status:** The level of funding for 21st Century Community Learning Centers (21st CCLC) established for FY2009, the last Bush Administration budget year, was $1.13B. This was the amount to "double." Here's how appropriated funds for the 21st CCLC looked like during most of President Obama's two terms in office: FY2010...$1.160B FY2011...$1.154B FY2012...$1.128B FY2013...$1.069B FY2014...$1.126B FY2015...$1.151B FY2016...$1.166B FY2017...$1.167B Doubling the FY2009 level of funding would have required $2.26B per annum. This goal was not met. Further, the 21st CCLC served 1.5M students in FY2009 and 1.8M students by end-FY2017. Therefore the goal to serve "one million more children" was also not met. This promise was not fulfilled.	0.00
ED-10	**The Promise:** "...will develop K-12 education activities to translate the successes of our civil space programs, particularly our nation's scientific discoveries, our technology developments, and space exploration activities, into instructional programs for our children." **When/Where:** Obama-Biden Plan: "Advancing the Frontiers of Space Exploration" dated 08/15/08. **Source:** http://www.nasa.gov/pdf/382369main_48%20-%2020090803.2.Space_Fact_Sheet_FINAL.pdf **Status:** In President Obama's FY2011 budget proposal for NASA, a section entitled "Inspires More Young People to Engage in Science, Technology, Engineering, and Mathematics" specifies that "The Budget supports NASA programs that are designed to meet the goals of the President's 'Educate to Innovate' campaign in Science, Technology, Engineering and Mathematics education." NASA's "Summer of Innovation," for example, works with thousands of middle school teachers and students to engage students in stimulating, evidence-based math and science-based education programs. Another example is the continuation of the NASA-led Digital Learning Network (DLN), an Internet or video conferencing medium through which over 600K students and teachers (K-through-College) have access to engineers, scientists and mathematicians at 10 NASA centers. Through DLN, educators can guide their students over 50 space-related modules addressing subject matters ranging from asteroids to robotics. NASA's FY2011 budget for Science, Technology, Engineering and Mathematics (STEM) education purposes was $75M. This budget line item increased to $80M for FY2012, but leveled off at about	1.00

$67M annually from FY2013 onward through FY2017.

This promise was fulfilled.

ED-11	**The Promise:** "...will require all schools of education to be accredited." **When/Where:** Obama and Biden's Plan for America: "Blueprint for Change," dated 10/09/08. **Source:** https://www.documentcloud.org/documents/550007-barack-obama-2008-blueprint-for-change.html **Status:** According to the Department of Education, the goal of accreditation "is to ensure that education provided by institutions of higher education meets acceptable levels of quality." Accrediting agencies, of which there are seven (7), develop evaluation criteria and conduct peer evaluations to assess whether or not those criteria are met. Institutions and/or programs that meet an agency's criteria are then "accredited" by that agency. The Secretary of Education is required by law to publish a list of nationally recognized accrediting agencies. In the United States, a school does not necessarily have to be accredited to operate, but the quality of education it provides is usually considered dubious. The Council for Higher Education Accreditation (CHEA) also maintains a database of accredited and nonaccredited institutions and programs. Their listing is considered more up-to-date than DOE's listing. The States of Michigan and Oregon also maintain their own listings of degree/diploma mills. Michigan's list has some 600 entries of bogus institutes. As of CY2016, the top 10 states harboring fake universities, unaccredited institutions of higher education, and unrecognized accrediting agencies were as follows: California (134) Hawaii (94) Washington (87) Florida (57) Texas (53) New York (44) Louisiana (39) Illinois (29) Nevada (29) Arizona (28) As of the end of President Obama's second term in office, CHEA's listing of nonaccredited schools was extensive. This promise was not fulfilled.	0.00
ED-12	**The Promise:** "...will establish a Presidential Early Learning Council to encourage necessary dialogue among programs at the federal and state levels, and within the private and nonprofit sectors to collect and disseminate the most valid and up-to-date research on early learning, and to highlight best practices and model programs at the state and local level." **When/Where:** Obama-Biden Plan: "Lifetime Success Through Education," dated 10/16/08. **Source:** http://doclibrary.com/MSC56/DOC/ObamaEducationPlan12084315.pdf **Status:** The cited plan stipulates that the creation of an Early Learning Council would be funded as part of a $10B effort along with Early Learning Challenge Grants, increasing Head Start funding, and other "zero to five" child education initiatives. In 08/10, Secretary of Education Arne Duncan and Secretary of Health and Human Services Kathleen Sebelius announced the creation of the Early Learning Interagency Policy Board designed, according to Department of Education documentation, "to improve the quality of early learning programs and outcomes for young children; increase the coordination of research, technical	1.00

assistance and data systems; and advance the effectiveness of the early learning workforce among the major federally funded early learning programs across the two departments."

This was not exactly the promised "Presidential Early Learning Council," but the Early Learning Interagency Policy Board's mission comes close to the articulated purpose of the proposed "Council."

This promise was fulfilled.

ED-13	**The Promise:** "...will launch a Children's First Agenda that provides care, learning and support to families with children from birth up to five years old." **When/Where:** Obama and Biden's Plan for America: "Blueprint for Change," dated 10/09/08. **Source:** https://www.documentcloud.org/documents/550007-barack-obama-2008-blueprint-for-change.html **Status:** President Obama supported initiatives to improve education for children in the 0-to-5 age bracket, and his annual budget requests throughout his two terms in office reflect that support. However, this promise was specifically to "launch a Children's First Agenda," sometimes referred to as the "Kids First Agenda". This didn't happen. This promise was not fulfilled.	0.00
ED-14	**The Promise:** "Fully funding IDEA [Individuals with Disabilities Education Act] will provide students with disabilities the public education they have a right to, and school districts will be able to provide services without cutting into their general education budgets. In addition to fully funding IDEA, ...will ensure effective implementation and enforcement of the Act." **When/Where:** Obama-Biden Plan: "Empower Americans with Disabilities," dated 09/06/08. **Source:** http://www.thearc.org/document.doc?id=3073 **Status:** When Congress enacted the Education of the Handicapped Act (EHA) of 1975, which later evolved to become the Individuals with Disabilities Education Act (IDEA) of 1990, it determined that the cost of educating children with disabilities was roughly twice as expensive as educating children without disabilities. Thus, Congress at that time agreed that the federal government would pay a percentage of the "excess" costs being experienced by states, utilizing the national Average Per-Pupil Expenditure (APPE) as the metric and 40% as the limit of the government's payment of "excess" costs. For FY2009, the annual appropriation for IDEA ($12.580B/16.8% of excess) was buttressed by the infusion of additional capital from the American Recovery and Reinvestment Act (ARRA) of 2009 ($12.2B) for a total of $24.7B representing 33.4% of excess costs. For FY2010, the appropriation for IDEA amounted to $12.32B or 16.9% of excess costs. For FY2011, the appropriated amount was $11.48B representing 16.1% of excess costs. For FY2012, the appropriated amount was $12.66B representing 17.2% of excess costs. An "IDEA Full Funding Act" was introduced by both houses of Congress during every Congress while President Obama was in office since CY2009. When the 114th Congress expired at the end of 12/16, S.130 and H.R. 551, Senate and House bills bearing the "IDEA Full Funding Act" title, also expired. This promise was not fulfilled.	0.00
ED-15	**The Promise:** "...will double funding for the Federal Charter School Program to support the creation of more successful charter schools..." **When/Where:** Obama and Biden's Plan for America: "Blueprint for Change," dated 10/09/08. **Source:** https://www.documentcloud.org/documents/550007-barack-obama-2008-blueprint-for-change.html **Status:** The U.S. Government funds three related programs: the Public Charter Schools Program	0.00

Chapter 4 - Department of Education

(CSP), the State Facilities Incentive Grants Program, and the Credit Enhancement for Charter School Facilities Program. Candidate Obama perhaps meant all three programs in this promise.

Excluding funding for Voluntary Public School Choice and Magnet Schools Assistance, the charter school grant programs were appropriated $216M for FY2009. This was the amount to "double."

The Federal Charter School Program followed the trend depicted below, being rolled into a subset of the "Expanding Educational Options Authority":

FY2010....$256.0M
FY2011....$255.5M
FY2012....$255.5M
FY2013....$254.8M
FY2014....$248.2M
FY2015....$253.2M
FY2016....$333.2M
FY2017....$253.0M

At no time was the FY2009 amount for the Charter School Program ($216M) doubled to $432M during President Obama's two terms in office.

This promise was not fulfilled.

ED-16

The Promise: "...will address the dropout crisis by passing his legislation to provide funding to school districts to invest in intervention strategies in middle school - strategies such as personal academic plans, teaching teams, parent involvement, mentoring, intensive reading and math instruction, and extended learning time."

When/Where: Obama and Biden's Plan for America: "Blueprint for Change," dated 10/09/08.

Source: https://www.documentcloud.org/documents/550007-barack-obama-2008-blueprint-for-change.html

Status: According to a National Center for Education Statistics study for the CY2007-08 school year, it was estimated that the national high school graduation rate was 63.5% for Hispanics, 61.5% for African Americans, 81% for White Americans, and 64.2% for Native Americans. The Average Freshman Graduation Rate was reported as 74.9% of the student population, leaving the dropout rate at about 25%. 2,000 of the nation's worst-performing schools reportedly accounted for 75% of the minority-student dropout rate.

The "Race to the Top" program, funded at a level of $4.35B under the American Recovery and Reinvestment Act of 2009, contained a provision for turning around the lowest achieving schools and, by extension, would improve the dropout rate at a few, select schools.

To mitigate the school dropout situation, the Graduation for All Act was introduced by Congressman George Miller (D-CA) on 11/19/09 to support high-need middle and high schools in order to improve students' academic achievement, graduation rates, post-secondary readiness, and preparation for citizenry. This bill expired without action at the end of the 111th Congress.

On 08/02/11, Senator Lisa Murkowski (D-MD) introduced the "Early Intervention for Graduation Success Authorization Act of 2011" (S. 1495). This bill was reintroduced as S.1109 by Senator Murkowski on 06/06/13. No action was taken on these bills during the 112th and 113th Congresses.

On 02/09/12, Congressman John Kline (R-MN) introduced the "Student Success Act" (H.R. 3989). This bill also expired with the 112th Congress. Congressman Kline again introduced this bill to the 113th Congress, it passed the House, but died with that Congress. He reintroduced it to the 114th Congress where it passed the House on 07/08/15 but was not voted upon by the Senate. Had the Senate passed this bill, President Obama announced his intention to veto it.

1.00

Chapter 4 - Department of Education

On 04/30/15, Senator Lamar Alexander (R-TN) introduced the "Every Student Succeeds Act" (S.1177) to address the basic tenets of this promise and which contains many of the provisions of the "Student Success Act" cited above. President Obama signed this legislation into law on 12/10/15.

The trend in high school graduation rates during President Obama's two terms in office was as follows, reflecting a steady reduction in the national high school dropout rate:

SY2009-10....75.0%
SY2010-11....79.0%
SY2011-12....80.0%
SY2012-13....81.4%
SY2013-14....82.3%
SY2014-15....83.2%
SY2015-16....84.1%

This promise was fulfilled.

ED-17	**The Promise:** "...will also prioritize supporting states that help the most successful charter schools to expand to serve more students." **When/Where:** Obama and Biden's Plan for America: "Blueprint for Change," dated 10/09/08. **Source:** https://www.documentcloud.org/documents/550007-barack-obama-2008-blueprint-for-change.html **Status:** The FY2009 appropriation for charter school programs was $216M. Under President Obama, annual appropriations were as reflected below: FY2010....$256.0M FY2011....$255.5M FY2012....$255.0M FY2013....$241.5M FY2014....$248.2M FY2015....$253.2M FY2016....$333.0M FY2017....$332.5M On 04/30/15, Senator Lamar Alexander (R-TN) introduced the "Every Student Succeeds Act" (S.1177). Section 4303 of this bill is entitled "Grants to Support High-Quality Charter Schools" and responds to the basic thrust of this promise. President Obama signed this legislation into law on 12/10/15. This promise was fulfilled.	1.00
ED-18	**The Promise:** "...will help Limited English Proficient students get ahead by holding schools accountable for making sure these students complete school." **When/Where:** Obama and Biden's Plan for America: "Blueprint for Change," dated 10/09/08. **Source:** https://www.documentcloud.org/documents/550007-barack-obama-2008-blueprint-for-change.html **Status:** On 12/10/15, President Obama signed the "Every Student Succeeds Act (ESSA)" (S.1177) to essentially replace the "No Child Left Behind Act" signed into law by President George W. Bush on 01/08/02. ESSA changes references to "Limited English Proficient" students to "English Learners." Title III of this law, entitled "Language Instruction for English Learners and Immigrant Students," states that one of its principal purposes is "to assist all English learners, including immigrant children and youth, to achieve at high levels in academic subjects so that all English Learners can meet the same challenging State academic standards that all children are expected to meet..." Title III also	1.00

Chapter 4 - Department of Education

articulates the accountability standards that must be met by schools with English Learner programs.

This promise was fulfilled.

ED-19	**The Promise:** "Reform No Child Left Behind [NCLB]: ...will also improve NCLB's accountability system so that we are supporting schools that need improvement, rather than punishing them." **When/Where:** Obama and Biden's Plan for America: "Blueprint for Change," dated 10/09/08. **Source:** https://www.documentcloud.org/documents/550007-barack-obama-2008-blueprint-for-change.html **Status:** On 12/10/15, President Obama signed the "Every Student Succeeds Act (ESSA)" (S.1177) to replace the "No Child Left Behind (NCLB) Act" signed into law by President George W. Bush on 01/08/02. This new law fixes NCLB practices at the national level to allow more flexibility and equality in the accountability area, additional investments in teachers and principals, and more attention to high-risk schools and students. This promise was fulfilled.	1.00
ED-20	**The Promise:** "Reform No Child Left Behind [NCLB]: ...will improve the assessments used to track student progress to measure readiness for college and the workplace..." **When/Where:** Obama and Biden's Plan for America: "Blueprint for Change," dated 10/09/08. **Source:** https://www.documentcloud.org/documents/550007-barack-obama-2008-blueprint-for-change.html **Status:** While the Department of Education (DOE) sets general policy on assessments, the application of assessment standards varies from state to state. The DOE approves or disapproves individual state assessment systems under Title I of the Elementary and Secondary Education Act (ESEA) as amended by the Improving America's Schools Act (IASA) of 1994. On 12/10/15, President Obama signed the "Every Student Succeeds Act (ESSA)" (S.1177) to replace the "No Child Left Behind Act" signed into law by President George W. Bush on 01/08/02. Title I, Section 112 of this law states in part: "Each State plan shall demonstrate that the State educational agency, in consultation with local educational agencies, has implemented a set of high-quality student academic assessments in mathematics, reading or language arts, and science." As a point of reference, the "College Board" report for the Class of 2017 indicated that students made significant progress during President Obama's tenure in improving basic skill sets requisite to succeed in college and in the workplace. It published its Graduating Class of 2017 national Scholastic Aptitude Test mean scores as 533 for reading and writing, up from 501 when President Obama assumed the Office of the Presidency in CY2009; 527 for mathematics, up from 515 in CY2009. This promise was fulfilled.	1.00
ED-21	**The Promise:** "Reform No Child Left Behind [NCLB]: Obama and Biden will reform NCLB, which starts by funding the law." **When/Where:** Obama and Biden's Plan for America: "Blueprint for Change," dated 10/09/08. **Source:** https://www.documentcloud.org/documents/550007-barack-obama-2008-blueprint-for-change.html **Status:** The Obama Administration dropped the moniker "No Child Left Behind" (NCLB) for the program by that name started under President Bush in CY2002. Under the structure of this program, grants to Local Educational Agencies (LEAs) were funded at $25.0B in FY2009 plus $14.0B received under American Recovery and Reinvestment Act (ARRA) of 2009 economic stimulus funding for a total of $39.0B, coming close to the authorized amount for the entire NCLB program of $39.4B.	1.00

The gap between authorized and actual funding increased in FY2010 with appropriations amounting to $25.1B leaving unfunded requirements of $14.3B. For FY2011, funding was $29.2B leaving an unfunded gap of $10.2B.

Title I of the NCLB Act ("Improving Basic Programs Operated by State and LEAs") was the cornerstone of the NCLB, codified as the Elementary & Secondary Education Act (ESEA). This Title was funded during subsequent years against the authorized per annum level of $25.0B as follows:
FY2012....$14.5B
FY2013....$13.7B
FY2014....$14.3B
FY2015....$14.4B
FY2016....$15.4B

On 12/10/15, President Obama signed the "Every Student Succeeds Act (ESSA)" (S.1177) to replace/reform the "No Child Left Behind Act." This new law came into effect starting in FY2017. For FY2017, President Obama requested $16.0B but Congress appropriated $15.4B for Title IA against the authorized level of $16.5B

The "funding the law" aspect of this promise was fulfilled, albeit at less than authorized amounts. Further, the Obama Administration did reform the NCLB as promised by replacing it with the ESSA.

This promise was fulfilled.

ED-22 **The Promise:** "...will make math and science education a national priority, and provide our schools with the tools to educate 21st-Century learners." **0.00**
When/Where: Obama and Biden's Plan: "Lifetime Success Through Education," dated 10/16/08.
Source: http://doclibrary.com/MSC56/DOC/ObamaEducationPlan12084315.pdf
Status: On 11/23/09, President Obama launched the Science, Technology, Engineering and Math (STEM) related "Educate to Innovate" campaign to move American students from the middle to the top of international pack in science and math achievements over the next decade.

In CY2010 alone, the STEM program had attracted over $700M in donations and in-kind support from Corporate America, philanthropies, service organizations, and private individuals to inspire young people to pursue careers in math and science.

However, the second half of this promise was to provide schools with the tools they need to achieve the 21st Century goal of making American students tops in the world in the areas of math and science.

MATHEMATICS: the National Assessment of Educational Progress (NAEP) test administered in CY2017 revealed that only 40% of Grade 4 (up from 39% in CY2009), 34% of Grade 8 (unchanged from CY2009) and 25% of Grade 12 students (down from 26% in CY2009) were performing at or above the "Proficient" level in mathematics.

SCIENCE: The most recent figures available for testing at or above the "Proficient" level in science was 38% for Grade 4 in CY2015 (up from 34% in CY2009), 34% for Grade 8 in CY2015 up from 32% in CY2009), and 22% for Grade 12 in CY2015 compared to 21% in CY2009.

Among 65 industrialized countries assessed triennially by the Organization for Economic Cooperation and Development (OECD) Program for International Student Assessment (PISA) in CY2009, the USA ranked 31st in math and 24th in science. By the time the CY2015 assessment was conducted, the results published by PISA in 12/16, were worse. The USA had gone down to 40th place in math among the 72 member countries participating in the assessment, and down one place to 25th in science proficiency.

Chapter 4 - Department of Education

With some exceptions, U.S. student performance in math and science was worse by end-CY2016 than it was when President Obama assumed the Presidency in CY2009, despite STEM and other tools he initiated.

This promise was not fulfilled.

ED-23   **The Promise:** "Science assessments need to do more than test facts and concepts...states like Connecticut, Maine, New Hampshire, and Vermont, use an assessment that calls for students to design and conduct investigations, analyze and present data, write up and defend results...will work with governors and educators to ensure that state assessments measure these skills."
When/Where: Obama-Biden Plan for Lifetime Success Through Education, dated 10/16/08.
Source: http://doclibrary.com/MSC56/DOC/ObamaEducationPlan12084315.pdf
Status: The perfect opportunity to address this promise was in President Obama's "Blueprint for Reform - The Reauthorization of the Elementary and Secondary Education Act," presented to Congress on 03/15/10.

In Page 8 of the "Blueprint for Reform," under the heading of "Rigorous College-and Career-Ready Standards," the following statement is made: "States will continue to implement statewide science standards and aligned assessments in specific gradespans, and may include such assessment -- as well as statewide assessments in other subjects, such as history -- in their accountability system."

Further to the above, President Obama signed the "Every Student Succeeds Act (ESSA)" (S.1177) into law on 12/10/15 to replace the "No Child Left Behind Act." Section 1201(a)(2)(G) of ESSA specifically calls on states to refine "...science assessments required under section 1111(b)(2) in order to integrate engineering design skills and practices into such assessments."

This promise was fulfilled.

Score: 1.00

ED-24   **The Promise:** "...we'll fight to make sure we are once again first in the world when it comes to high school graduation rates."
When/Where: Candidate Obama Campaign Speech on Education, dated 10/15/08.
Source: http://www.youtube.com/watch?v=_vEg-deTXkc#t=2m33s
Status: In CY2009, the USA ranked 21st out of 26 Organization for Economic Cooperation and Development (OECD) developed countries in terms of high school graduation rates. Studies also indicated that the United States ranked 7th among the G-8 countries with regard to high school graduation rates.

With a national graduation rate hovering around 75% when President Obama started his first year in office in CY2009, it climbed to 83.2% by the end of the CY2014-15 school year. There remain problem areas, however. The graduation rate for the District of Columbia for school year CY2014-15 was only 69%.

Attaining President Obama's promised "first in the world" status was an unrealistic goal, given that CY2015 high school graduation rates in countries like Slovenia (96%), Japan (95%), Finland (95%) and others with a higher completion rate than the USA are not expected to experience significant reductions in their graduation rate.

This promise was not fulfilled.

Score: 0.00

ED-25   **The Promise:** "...will create 20 Promise Neighborhoods in cities that have high levels of poverty and crime and low levels of student academic achievement...Cities and private entities will be required to pay 50 percent of the program costs."
When/Where: Obama-Biden Plan: "Supporting Urban Prosperity", dated 09/11/08.
Source: https://assets.documentcloud.org/documents/550008/barack-obama-2008-supporting-urban-prosperity.pdf

Score: 1.00

Chapter 4 - Department of Education

Status: Promise Neighborhoods are intended to model the Harlem Children's Zone and seek to engage all resident children and their parents in an achievement program based on tangible goals, including college for every participating student, strong physical and mental health outcomes for children as well as retention of meaningful employment and parenting schools for parents.

The Congressional budget appropriation for the Department of Education for FY2010 included $10M under the Fund for the Improvement of Education (FIE) Programs of National Significance line item for the creation of Promise Neighborhoods.

On 09/21/10, Education Secretary Arne Duncan announced that on a competitive basis, 21 nonprofit organizations and higher education institutions (out of over 300 applicants from 48 states and the District of Columbia) would receive Promise Neighborhood grants of up to $500K. Recipients of these grants (cities/private entities) had to provide 50% of their respective program costs.

The funding profile for subsequent years was as follows:
FY2011...................$29.9M for new awards (20 Promise Neighborhoods)
FY2012...................$59.9M for new awards (17 Promise Neighborhoods) plus $25.9M for program continuation awards
FY2013-FY2015....$56.7M each year for program continuation awards only
FY2016..................$37.0M for program continuation awards only

This promise was fulfilled.

ED-26

The Promise: "...will support nontraditional approaches, such as student design competitions and internet-based collaborations to engage students and develop the next generation of scientists and engineers."
When/Where: Obama-Biden Plan: "Advancing the Frontiers of Space Exploration" dated 08/15/08.
Source: http://www.nasa.gov/pdf/382369main_48%20-%2020090803.2.Space_Fact_Sheet_FINAL.pdf
Status: Numerous competitions exist to permit the design of fresh solutions to next generation technological challenges. The NASA-sponsored Lunabotics Mining Competition held in 05/10 and involving 22 schools is but one example. Another example is the CY2010-CY2011 "green aviation" competition for students and teams to submit ideas and designs for vehicle/propulsion concepts that could lower noise, emissions and fuel consumption goals by CY2020.

There was also no shortage of online collaboration mediums such as "The Globe Program" to allow students to participate in world-wide data gathering on the global environment, NASA's "Cube Quest Challenges" project to connect K-12 students to NASA experts, and the "Internet Science and Technology Fair (ISTF)" to permit collaboration between students/teachers and scientists/engineers.

Further, President Obama's "Educate to Innovate" initiative resulted in over $1B in public-private partnership financial and in-kind support for STEM programs, showcased annually in the White House Science Fair. President Obama's "support" for these programs appeared to be solid despite uncertain fiscal resources during his presidency.

This promise was fulfilled.

1.00

ED-27

The Promise: "...will increase resources for the U.S. Department of Education's Arts Education Model Development and Dissemination Grants, which develop public/private partnerships between schools and arts organizations..."
When/Where: Obama-Biden Plan: "Champions for Arts and Culture", dated 09/11/08.
Source: http://muzartworld.org/president-barack-obama-and-joe-biden-champions-for-arts-and-culture/
Status: In FY2009, the Arts in Education Model Development and Dissemination (AEMDD) Program was funded at the $4.2M level. Under President Obama, the appropriation for FY2010 increased to

1.00

$14.0M followed by $14.2M for FY2011. In FY2011, the Obama Administration did not seek separate funding for the "Arts in Education" program. Instead, "Arts in Education" became a subset of a new program entitled "Effective Teaching and Learning for a Well-Rounded Education."

The final appropriation for "Arts in Education" in FY2012 was $24.9M, but declined slightly to $23.6M in FY2013. Efforts to "increase resources" continued in subsequent years as follows:

FY2014....$25.0M
FY2015....$25.0M
FY2016....$27.0M
FY2017....$26.9M

This promise was fulfilled.

ED-28 — **The Promise:** "...will engage the foundation and corporate community to increase support for public/private partnerships...[between schools and arts organizations]"
When/Where: Obama-Biden Plan: "Champions for Arts and Culture", dated 09/11/08.
Source: http://muzartworld.org/president-barack-obama-and-joe-biden-champions-for-arts-and-culture/
Status: Since FY2011 and for the remainder of President Obama's tenure in office, the Department of Education's "Arts in Education" program has been funded with the stipulation that funds were to be allocated to "a number of arts education activities through grants to Local Educational Agencies (LEAs), State educational agencies (SEAs), nonprofit organizations, institutions of higher education, organizations with expertise in the arts, and partnerships of these entities.

Such partnerships included the National Endowment for the Arts' relationship with select, arts-deprived schools through its "Our Town Grantee Program."

This promise was fulfilled.

Grade: 1.00

GULF AREA SCHOOLS — GRADE

ED-29 — **The Promise:** "Will help communities in the Gulf make necessary school infrastructure investments so all kids from all backgrounds have safe and supportive environments to learn."
When/Where: Obama-Biden Plan: "Rebuilding the Gulf Coast and Preventing Future Catastrophes" dated 09/11/08.
Source: https://assets.documentcloud.org/documents/550006/barack-obama-2008-rebuilding-the-gulf-coast-and.pdf
Status: When Hurricane Katrina hit the Gulf Coast in 08/05, it caused significant damage to 110 of New Orleans' 126 public schools among the 261 schools damaged/destroyed throughout Louisiana.

Soon after he was sworn in for his first term in office, President Obama's "American Recovery and Reinvestment Act (ARRA) of 2009" allocated $1.4B in education funds for Louisiana and $1.1B for Mississippi, the hardest hit states. In addition, as of CY2015, the two states had respectively received $3.37B and $334M for education infrastructure improvements from the Federal Emergency Management Agency (FEMA).

Of the $3.37B allocated to Louisiana, New Orleans received $1.8B in FEMA grants to rebuild and/or repair over 80 destroyed or damaged schools.

On top of ARRA funding, President Obama's FY2010 budget proposal included an additional $30M to improve both school infrastructures and programs in the Gulf Region. Additionally, FEMA was improving some schools in the region under a separate $650M allocation.

As of the start of the CY2015-16 school year, FEMA reported that 33 school projects had been completed, 31 were under construction, four were in the procurement phase, 16 were in the design

Grade: 1.00

phase and four had yet to begin, for a total of 88 schools.

As of CY2016, post-Katrina federal funding for Hurricane Katrina recovery totaled approximately $120.5B, $45.5B of which went toward infrastructure improvements/rebuilding projects, including schools.

The campaign promise was to "help" Gulf communities recover from the damage caused to the education infrastructure by Hurricane Katrina in CY2005.

This promise was fulfilled.

	RESEARCH	GRADE
ED-30	**The Promise:** "...will provide new research grants to the most outstanding early-career researchers in the country." **When/Where:** Obama-Biden Plan: Invest in University-Based Research, undated. **Source:** http://webarchive.loc.gov/all/20090429185018/http://change.gov/agenda/technology_agenda/ **Status:** The Early Career Research Program is administered by the Department of Energy's Office of Science in support of Department of Education's (DOE's) Office of Science Opportunities. Approximately $85M in American Recovery and Reinvestment Act of 2009 funding was awarded in early CY2010 to support at least 50 early-career researchers for five years at U.S. academic institutions and laboratories. Budget limits for this initiative were set to at least $150K for universities for five years and $500K per year for five years for DOE's national laboratories. This promise was fulfilled.	1.00
ED-31	**The Promise:** "...will...task his Secretary of Education with researching: the barriers that keep students with disabilities from seeking and completing higher education; the barriers that prevent students from making a direct transition to work; the extent to which students with disabilities are able to access loans and grants; reasons college students with disabilities drop out at a higher rate; and best practices from schools that have effectively recruited and graduated students with disabilities that can be implemented more widely." **When/Where:** Obama-Biden Plan: "Empower Americans with Disabilities", dated 09/06/08. **Source:** http://www.thearc.org/document.doc?id=3073 **Status:** Operating under the Department of Education's Office of Special Education and Rehabilitative Services (OSERS), the National Institute on Disability and Rehabilitation Research (NIDRR) has existed to conduct the research intended under this promise. The basic tenets of this promise are reflected in NIDRR's "Long-Range Plan for Fiscal Years 2010 Through 2014" dated 01/22/09. In CY2012, under contract to the Department of Education, the Mathematica Center for Studying Disability Policy started a 5-year research project entitled "National Longitudinal Transition Study (NLTS)" to gather information on students with and without disabilities. In CY2015, as a result of the "Workforce Innovation and Opportunity Act" (H.R. 803) signed into law by President Obama on 07/22/14, NIDRR became part of the Administration for Community Living (ACL) within the Department of Health and Human Services (HHS), and changed its name to "National Institute on Disability, Independent Living, and Rehabilitation Research (NIDILRR)." NIDILRR's updated mission was to generate new knowledge and promote its effective use to improve the abilities of people with disabilities to perform activities of their choice in the community, and also to expand society's capacity to provide full opportunities and accommodations for its citizens with disabilities. This research continues. This promise was fulfilled.	1.00

Chapter 4 - Department of Education

	STUDENT AID	GRADE
ED-32	**The Promise:** "Will ... ensure that the maximum Pell Grant award is increased for low-income students...will ensure that the award keeps pace with the rising cost of college inflation." **When/Where:** Obama-Biden Plan to Make College Affordable for Everyone, dated 09/11/08. **Source:** https://static.newamerica.org/attachments/7618-a-call-to-arms/College%20Affordability%20Fact%20Sheet.d9439c717ab24e9cbd5d2cef2db86cba.pdf **Status:** The American Recovery and Reinvestment Act of 2009, signed into law by President Obama on 02/27/09, raised the maximum Pell Grant limit to $5,350. The FY2010 Department of Education budget included sufficient funds ($17.4B) to raise the maximum Pell Grant to $5,550 for the 2010-2011 award year and thereafter. The President's FY2011 budget proposed "to make that increase permanent and put them on a path to grow faster than inflation every year" and to make Pell Grant funding mandatory. The Health Care and Education Reconciliation Act of 2010, signed into law by President Obama on 03/30/10, stipulated that for future years, awards will be "increased by a percentage equal to the annual adjustment percentage." The term "annual adjustment percentage" was defined in the Act as being "equal to the estimated percentage change in the Consumer Price Index." This promise was fulfilled.	1.00
ED-33	**The Promise:** "....eliminate wasteful subsidies to private student lenders....and invest the savings in additional student aid." **When/Where:** Obama-Biden Plan to Make College Affordable for Everyone, dated 09/11/08. **Source:** https://static.newamerica.org/attachments/7618-a-call-to-arms/College%20Affordability%20Fact%20Sheet.d9439c717ab24e9cbd5d2cef2db86cba.pdf **Status:** The President's FY2010 Budget proposal of 02/26/09 asked Congress not to reduce, but to eliminate lender subsidies under the Federal Family Education Loan (FFEL) program and originate all student lending through Government-run Direct Loans as of 07/01/2010. Under the Health Care and Education Reconciliation Act signed into law by President Obama on 03/30/10, subsidies to private lenders were eliminated. This promise was fulfilled.	1.00
ED-34	**The Promise:** "...will simplify the financial aid process by eliminating the FAFSA and its complicated calculations altogether... The aid process will be streamlined by enabling families to apply simply by checking a box on their tax form..." **When/Where:** Obama-Biden Plan to Make College Affordable for Everyone, dated 09/11/08. **Source:** https://static.newamerica.org/attachments/7618-a-call-to-arms/College%20Affordability%20Fact%20Sheet.d9439c717ab24e9cbd5d2cef2db86cba.pdf **Status:** On 06/24/09, Education Secretary announced plans to simplify the process for the Free Application for Federal Student Aid (FAFSA), but not eliminate it as promised in the Obama-Biden plan cited above. As of end-CY2016, the FAFSA program was alive and well. It remained the primary form that the federal government, states and colleges used to award grants, scholarships, work study and student loans. Grants and scholarships were free, but students had to earn the work study dollars and pay back the loans. FAFSA's web site offers a simplified 3-step process for filling out requisite forms. To assist in this process, the site offers an IRS Data Retrieval Tool to access tax return information to be used on FAFSA application documents. As of Tax Year 2016, there was no provision for simply "checking a box" on tax forms. This promise was not fulfilled.	0.00

Chapter 4 - Department of Education

	TEACHING	**GRADE**
ED-35	**The Promise:** "Will recruit math and science degree graduates to the teaching profession and will support efforts to help these teachers learn from professionals in the field. They will also work to ensure that all children have access to a strong science curriculum at all grade levels" **When/Where:** Obama-Biden Plan for Lifetime Success Through Education, dated 10/16/08. **Source:** http://doclibrary.com/MSC56/DOC/ObamaEducationPlan12084315.pdf **Status:** The American Recovery and Reinvestment Act of 2009 provided $4.3B targeted for the State Incentive Grant Fund, popularly referred to as the "Race to the Top" fund, and $2.5B for the National Science Foundation (NSF). The Department of Education's (DOE's) "Transition to Training" program was designed to recruit and retain highly qualified mid-career professionals to teach at high-need schools. This program was funded at the $43.7M level in FY2009 and FY2010, but funding started to decrease in FY2011 with a $41.1M appropriation. For FY2012, Congress appropriated $26.0M for this program. In his budget proposal for FY2013, President Obama requested $1B for the creation of a Science, Technology, Engineering and Math (STEM) Master Teacher Corps. This Corps would be comprised of some of the nation's best educators in STEM subjects beginning with 50 exceptional STEM teachers at 50 sites, particularly in high-need and rural schools. President Obama signed the "Every Student Succeeds Act (ESSA)" (S.1177) into law on 12/10/15 to replace the "No Child Left Behind Act." Title II of this Act, entitled "Preparing, Training, and Recruiting High-Quality Teachers, Principals, or Other School Leaders," focuses on "...developing and providing professional development and other comprehensive systems of support for teachers, principals, or other school leaders to promote high-quality instruction and instructional leadership in science, technology, engineering, and mathematics subjects, including computer science." The STEM Master Teacher Corps was codified under Part A of Title II of the ESSA. Part A is authorized to be funded at the $2.295B level each fiscal year from FY2017 through FY2020. This promise was fulfilled.	1.00
ED-36	**The Promise:** "...will create new Teacher Service Scholarships that will cover four years of undergraduate or two years of graduate teacher education, including high-quality alternative programs for mid-career recruits in exchange for teaching for at least four years in a high-need field or location." **When/Where:** Obama and Biden's Plan for America: "Blueprint for Change," dated 10/09/08. **Source:** https://www.documentcloud.org/documents/550007-barack-obama-2008-blueprint-for-change.html **Status:** Students aspiring to pursue a teaching profession have hundreds of sources, both public and private, from which to seek scholarships. Throughout President Obama's two terms in office, there was no known initiative to create a "new Teacher Service Scholarships" program at the national level. This promise was not fulfilled.	0.00
ED-37	**The Promise:** "...create a voluntary national performance assessment so we can be sure that every new educator is trained and ready to walk into the classroom and start teaching effectively." **When/Where:** Obama and Biden's Plan for America: "Blueprint for Change," dated 10/09/08. **Source:** https://www.documentcloud.org/documents/550007-barack-obama-2008-blueprint-for-change.html **Status:** In CY1987, the National Board for Professional Teaching Standards (NBPTS) was created to define and recognize accomplished teaching. National Board Standards are created by teachers, for teachers, as is National Board Certification, which is a voluntary process to certify teachers against	0.00

those standards.

The standards define what accomplished teachers should know and be able to do in 25 certificate areas. They represent 16 different subject areas, four developmental levels, and are applicable to most teachers in U.S. public schools.

As of end-CY2016, more than 112,000 teachers in all 50 states and the District of Columbia had achieved National Board Certification. At that time, the National Board was revising the certification process to incorporate the latest research on best practices in teaching and to remove a few existing barriers so that more teachers could have the opportunity to achieve voluntary certification.

There was no evidence that the creation of a new "voluntary national performance assessment" was being pursued during President Obama's two terms in office.

This promise was not fulfilled.

ED-38	**The Promise:** "...will expand mentoring programs that pair experienced teachers with new recruits. They will also provide incentives to give teachers paid common planning time so they can collaborate to share best practices." **When/Where:** Obama and Biden's Plan for America: "Blueprint for Change," dated 10/09/08. **Source:** https://www.documentcloud.org/documents/550007-barack-obama-2008-blueprint-for-change.html **Status:** On 02/17/09, less than one month after being sworn in for his first term, President Obama signed into law the "American Recovery and Reinvestment Act of 2009 (ARRA)." The ARRA provided $4.35B for the "Race to the Top Fund," a competitive grant program designed to reward States for creating the conditions for education innovation and reform; achieving significant improvement in student outcomes; ensuring student preparation for success in college and careers; and implementing ambitious plans in four core education reform areas. One of the four core education reform areas was "...recruiting, developing, rewarding, and retaining effective teachers and principals." One of the measures to accomplish this goal included "observation-based assessments of teacher performance or evidence of leadership roles (which may include mentoring or leading professional learning communities) that increase the effectiveness of other teachers in the school..." The Department of Education's (DOE) FY2010 appropriation included $2.9B for state grants for improving teacher quality. This program helped states carry out activities that included support during initial teaching phases such as mentoring programs. The Teacher Incentive Fund (TIF) was designed to support the use of performance-based compensation. The TIF was funded at $97M for FY2009 under President Bush, supplemented by $200M under the ARRA initiated by President Obama. Funding was further increased to $400M under President Obama's first budget year, FY2010. In light of prevailing fiscal constraints, funding for the TIF new awards and continuation awards experienced general reductions during subsequent years as follows: FY2011....$399.2M FY2012....$299.4M FY2013....$283.7M FY2014....$288.7M FY2015....$230.0M FY2016....$225.4M FY2017....$201.4M This promise was fulfilled.	1.00

Chapter 4 - Department of Education

ED-39

The Promise: "...will promote new and innovative ways to increase teacher pay"
When/Where: Obama and Biden's Plan for America: "Blueprint for Change," dated 10/09/08.
Source: https://www.documentcloud.org/documents/550007-barack-obama-2008-blueprint-for-change.html
Status: According to National Education Association (NEA) reports, the average teacher salary for the 2009-10 School Year (SY) when President Obama assumed the presidency was about $55.2K with the highest average in New York State ($71.6K) and the lowest in South Dakota ($38.8K). For SY2014-15, the U.S. average public school teacher salary went up to $57.4K. New York again had the highest average ($77.6K), and South Dakota remained with the lowest average ($40.9K).

The NEA estimated that over the decade from SY2004-05 to SY2014-15, in constant dollars (an adjusted value to compare dollar values from one period to another), average salaries for teachers decreased 1.6%.

Under President Obama's education reform blueprint, merit pay would be replaced by a "pay-for-performance" plan, the premise of which was to reward teachers for evaluations, test scores and other new criteria. The President's blueprint stated: "Grantees may use funds to reform compensation systems to provide differentiated compensation and career advancement opportunities to educators who are effective in increasing student academic achievement...". The blueprint further stated: "Rewards may include financial rewards...to share best practices and replicate successful strategies to assist low-performing schools and districts."

To help the blueprint become reality, President Obama proposed $5B in teacher incentives as part of his FY2013 $69.8B Department of Education budget proposal. This initiative was not accepted by Congress. Nonetheless, using grants available to them such as the Teacher and Leader Innovation Fund, some states have robust "pay-for-performance" programs.

President Obama's promise was to "promote" ways to increase teacher pay, and he did.

This promise was fulfilled.

1.00

ED-40

The Promise: "...will also create Teacher Residency Programs that will supply 30,000 exceptionally well-prepared recruits to high-need schools."
When/Where: Obama and Biden's Plan for America: "Blueprint for Change," dated 10/09/08.
Source: https://www.documentcloud.org/documents/550007-barack-obama-2008-blueprint-for-change.html
Status: Teacher Residency Programs existed in cities such as Boston, Baltimore, Denver, Philadelphia, Memphis, San Francisco, and many more long before President Obama arrived on the national political scene.

At the national level, funding for these programs was assured under the Department of Education's budget line item entitled "Teacher Quality Partnership" (TQP). This program aimed to improve the quality of teachers in high-need schools and early childhood education programs by creating model teacher preparation programs and teaching residency programs.

FY2009 funding for TQP was $43M, supplemented by $100M under the American Recovery and Reinvestment Act (ARRA) of 2009. TQP funding for FY2014 and FY2015 was $40.5M respectively and $42.5M for FY2016.

The bottom line is that this was an empty promise which could not be fulfilled because Teacher Residency Programs already existed when President Obama assumed the Presidency in CY2009.

This promise was not fulfilled.

0.00

EDUCATION GPA **0.65**

Campaign Promises
Departments -> Energy

ITEM	ENERGY	
	CONSERVATION	**GRADE**
EN-1	**The Promise:** "Will call on businesses, government and the American people to meet the goal of reducing our demand for electricity 15 percent by the end of the next decade." **When/Where:** Obama-Biden Plan: "New Energy for America" dated 09/06/08. **Source:** http://energy.gov/sites/prod/files/edg/media/Obama_New_Energy_0804.pdf **Status:** U.S. Energy Information Administration (EIA) data in its "Annual Energy Outlook" report for CY2012 indicated that the demand for electricity in the USA would grow by 22% from 3.877B kilowatthours in CY2010 to 4.716B kilowatthours by CY2035. The same report indicated that residential electricity demand would grow 18% and commercial demand would grow by 28% over the same timeframe. Electricity demand in the transportation sector will reportedly triple from 7B kilowatthours in CY2010 to 22B kilowatthours by CY2035. While President Obama did call on the nation to double its production of renewable electricity by CY2020 and double its energy efficiency by CY2030 in his 02/12/13 State of the Union address, he did not specifically call on America to reduce its electricity demand by 15% at any time during his two terms in office. A later EIA report indicates that as of the end of CY2016 and based on long-term trends and "the growing demand for chargeable electronic devices of every description," the nation's demand for electricity is expected to increase by 5% per year through CY2050. This promise was not fulfilled.	0.00
EN-2	**The Promise:** "...will require governors and local leaders in our metropolitan areas to make energy conservation a required part of their planning for the expenditure of federal transportation funds." **When/Where:** Barack Obama's "Plan to Make America a Global Energy Leader" dated 10/18/07 **Source:** https://grist.org/article/obama-energy-fact-sheet/ **Status:** The American Recovery and Reinvestment Act (ARRA) of 2009 funded the Energy Efficiency and Conservation Block Grant (EECBG) Program which, in part, was designed to develop, promote, implement and manage energy efficiency and conservation projects down to the state, county and city level to improve energy efficiency in the transportation sector. Initially funded at $3.2B under the ARRA, the EECBG had $1.8B for cities and counties, $767M for states, $54M for Indian Tribes, and $454M for competitive grants. Title 23, Highways, of the Code of Federal Regulations (23 CFR) Section 450.316 (Metropolitan Transportation Planning Process) has long mandated "consistency of metropolitan transportation planning with applicable federal, state, and local energy conservation programs, goals, and objectives." President Obama championed energy conservation throughout his two terms in office. To that end, the Federal Highway Administration (FHWA) and the Federal Transit Administration (FTA) published	1.00

a Final Rule on 05/27/16 (81 FR 34049) requiring governors and local leaders to make energy conservation an integral part of their transportation plans under the aegis of the "Moving Ahead for Progress in the 21st Century (MAP-21) Act" signed into law by President Obama on 06/07/12 and the "Fixing America's Surface Transportation (FAST) Act" signed into law by President Obama on 12/04/15. The Final Rule states in part that states and metropolitan/non-metropolitan areas must adopt measures to "...protect and enhance the environment, promote energy conservation..."

With regard to funding being contingent upon performance, the Final Rule cited above further states: "U.S.C. Title 23 U.S.C. 104(f) and 49 U.S.C. 5305(g) authorize funds to support transportation planning at metropolitan and statewide levels. As a condition to receive this funding, requirements are established for metropolitan and statewide transportation planning under 23 U.S.C. 134 and 135 and 49 U.S.C. 5303 and 5304." These sections call for development of transportation plans and Transportation Improvement Programs (TIPs) in all States and metropolitan areas. The information collection activities to prepare federally required plans and programs, and the planning studies proposed for funding in Unified Planning Work Programs (UPWPs) and State Planning and Research (SP&R) work programs, are necessary to monitor and evaluate current and projected usage and performance of transportation systems nationwide, statewide, and in each urbanized area.

This promise was fulfilled.

	ELECTRICAL GRID	GRADE
EN-3	**The Promise:** "Will establish a Grid Modernization Commission to facilitate adoption of Smart Grid practices across the nation's electricity grid to the point of general adoption and ongoing market support in the U.S. electric sector." **When/Where:** Obama-Biden Plan: "New Energy for America" dated 09/06/08. **Source:** http://energy.gov/sites/prod/files/edg/media/Obama_New_Energy_0804.pdf **Status:** The Energy Independence and Security Act of 2007, signed into law by President Bush on 12/19/07, created a Smart Grid Advisory Committee and a Smart Grid Task Force. The need for another organization, this one called the "Grid Modernization Commission," based on a promise made by then-Candidate Obama nine months after the above act was signed into law, was questionable. Nonetheless, in late-CY2014 the Department of Energy (DOE) created a "Grid Modernization Laboratory Consortium," a partnership between DOE headquarters and national laboratories to bring together leading experts and resources to collaborate on the goal of modernizing the USA's electricity grid. Not exactly a "commission," but close enough to satisfy promise fulfillment. This promise was fulfilled.	1.00
EN-4	**The Promise:** "...will pursue a major investment in our national utility grid using smart metering, distributed storage and other advanced technologies to accommodate 21st century energy requirements..." **When/Where:** Obama-Biden Plan: "New Energy for America" dated 09/06/08. **Source:** http://energy.gov/sites/prod/files/edg/media/Obama_New_Energy_0804.pdf **Status:** The American Recovery and Reinvestment Act (ARRA) of 2009 included $11B for smart grid technologies, transmission system expansion and upgrades, and other investments to modernize and enhance the electric transmission infrastructure to improve energy efficiency and reliability. Of that amount, $4.5B was for grid modernization. This promise was fulfilled.	1.00
EN-5	**The Promise:** "...will instruct the Secretary of Energy to: (1) establish a Smart Grid Investment Matching Grant Program to provide reimbursement of one-fourth of qualifying Smart Grid investments..." **When/Where:** Obama-Biden Plan: "New Energy for America" dated 09/06/08. **Source:** http://energy.gov/sites/prod/files/edg/media/Obama_New_Energy_0804.pdf	1.00

Status: On 04/16/09, Vice President Biden announced that nearly $4B under the American Recovery and Reinvestment Act of 2009 would be distributed in the form of Department of Energy's (DOE's) Smart Grid Investment Grant Program ($3.375B) and $615M for smart grid storage, monitoring and technology initiative demonstration projects.

Also on 04/16/09, the DOE released a Notice of Intent (NOI) for the Smart Grid Investment Grant Program and a Funding Opportunity Announcement for a smart grid regional demonstration initiative.

The program for federal matching funds for smart grid investment costs was codified in 42 USC, Chapter 152, Section 17386 which became law on 01/03/12. This law states "The Secretary shall establish a Smart Grid Investment Matching Grant Program to provide grants of up to one-half (50 percent) of qualifying Smart Grid investments." This went beyond Candidate Obama's 25% promise.

This promise was fulfilled.

ENERGY CONSUMPTION	GRADE

EN-6

The Promise: "Half of all cars purchased by the federal government will be plug-in hybrids or all-electric by 2012."
When/Where: Obama-Biden Plan: "New Energy for America" dated 09/06/08.
Source: http://energy.gov/sites/prod/files/edg/media/Obama_New_Energy_0804.pdf
Status: E.O. 13423, signed by President George W. Bush on 01/24/07, required federal agencies to use plug-in hybrid electric vehicles (PHEVs) when commercially available at a cost reasonably comparable to non-PHEVs. This E.O. was superceded by E.O. 13693, issued by President Obama on 03/19/15.

0.00

The American Recovery and Reinvestment Act (ARRA) of 2009 signed into law on 02/17/09 included $300 million to buy more high efficiency motor vehicles for the federal fleet, including hybrids, hybrid plug-ins and all-electric cars.

Executive Order 13514 dated 10/05/09 established policy for federal fleet vehicles to reduce the use of fossil fuels by using low greenhouse gas emitting vehicles including alternative fuel vehicles (i.e. electric fueled vehicles, hybrid electric vehicles, plug-in hybrid vehicles, etc.).

Based on the most recent data available from the General Services Administration (GSA) Federal Fleet Report as of end-FY2012, the federal government (civilian agencies, military and Postal Service) operated just over 650K vehicles worldwide. Of these, 234K were acquired by the Federal Government during the timeframe CY2009-CY2012. The total acquisition breakout by fuel type was as follows during this timeframe:
Gasoline - 94,774
Diesel - 17,683
Gasoline Hybrid - 13,853
Diesel Hybrid - 117
Gasoline Low Greenhouse Gas (LGHG) - 1,346
Diesel LGHG - 24
Gasoline Plug-In Hybrid - 150
Compressed Natural Gas (CNG) - 327
E-85 (85 percent ethanol, 15 percent gasoline) - 103,638
Electric - 2,091
Hydrogen - 9
Liquid Petroleum Gas (LPG) - 51

Total: 234,063

Total Plug-In Hybrid and Electric: 2,241 or less than 1%

Total Inventory of Passenger Vehicles ("cars") as of end-FY2012: 115,451.

Assuming that most Plug-In Hybrid and Electric vehicles acquired during the CY2009-CY2012 timeframe were Passenger Vehicles, the percentage remains less than 1% for the timeframe established by President Obama.

This promise was not fulfilled.

EN-7	**The Promise:** "...will implement legislation that phases out traditional incandescent light bulbs by 2014. This measure alone will save American consumers $6 billion per year on monthly electricity bills..." **When/Where:** Barack Obama's "Plan to Make America a Global Energy Leader" dated 10/18/07 **Source:** https://grist.org/article/obama-energy-fact-sheet/ **Status:** The Energy Independence and Security Act of 2007 contained legislation to make incandescent light bulbs more efficient by setting maximum wattage requirements for all general service incandescent light bulbs producing 310-2600 lumens of light. Exempt were several classes of specialty lights, including appliance lamps, rough service bulbs, 3-way, colored lamps, stage lighting, plant lights, candelabra lights under 60 watts, outdoor post lights less than 100 watts, nightlights and shatter resistant bulbs. This law effectively banned the manufacturing or importing of most incandescent bulbs. The major U.S. producer of standard incandescent light bulbs, General Electric, shut its last production facility in Winchester, VA in 09/10. The leading replacement light bulbs, compact fluorescents (CFLs), are mainly produced in China. President Obama announced new "standards" for incandescent light bulbs on 06/29/09. In response to these new standards, Sylvania and other light bulb manufacturers introduced new incandescent light bulbs that met the standards. The Republican-led House failed to obtain a two-thirds majority vote on 07/12/11 to overturn the above standards. The standards went into effect in CY2012 with the phase-out of 100-watt traditional incandescent light bulbs. The production of 75-watt traditional incandescent light bulbs ceased in CY2013, followed by 40- and 60-watt traditional incandescent light bulbs in CY2014. This promise has been fulfilled.	1.00
EN-8	**The Promise:** "Will create a competitive grant program to award those states and localities that take the first steps in implementing new building codes that prioritize energy efficiency, and provide a federal match for those states with leading-edge public benefits funds that support energy efficiency retrofits of existing buildings." **When/Where:** Obama-Biden Plan: To Combat Climate Change and Create a Green Economy" dated 02/07/08. **Source:** https://www.politifact.com/truth-o-meter/promises/obameter/promise/498/provide-grants-to-encourage-energy-efficient-build/ **Status:** Source is cited for confirmation of exact promise wording only, as it existed before original "When/Where" campaign document was deleted from archival websites. The American Recovery and Reinvestment Act (ARRA) of 2009 signed into law by President Obama on 02/17/09 provided $3.2B in initial grants to fund the Energy Efficiency and Conservation Block Grant (EECBG) Program administered by the Department of Energy's Office of Weatherization and Intergovernmental Programs (WIP). Of that amount, $454M was allocated to competitive grants for building energy audit and retrofits, as well as building code development, implementation and	0.00

inspections.

The first grants were awarded to 9 cities and 10 counties on 07/24/09.

However, this competitive grant program was first authorized under the Energy Independence and Security Act of 2007, signed into law by President Bush on 12/19/07. There was no need for President Obama to "create" this competitive grant program.

This promise was not fulfilled.

EN-9	**The Promise:** "Will make a national commitment to weatherize at least 1 million low-income homes each year for the next decade, which can reduce energy usage across the economy and help moderate energy prices for all" **When/Where:** Obama-Biden Plan: "New Energy for America" dated 09/06/08. **Source:** https://www.energy.gov/sites/prod/files/edg/media/Obama_New_Energy_0804.pdf **Status:** The American Recovery and Reinvestment Act (ARRA) of 2009 signed into law by President Obama on 02/17/09 included $5B to expand the Weatherization Assistance Program (WAP). Of that amount, $4.746B was earmarked for low-income home weatherization, $90M for Sustainable Energy Resources for Consumers (SERC) Grants, and $29M for WAP training centers. Under ARRA funding, the Department of Energy (DOE) reported that more than 806K homes had been weatherized over the period CY2010-CY2012. In recent years, the WAP targets for the number of low-income homes to be weatherized was as follows: FY2014: 24,600. This target was exceeded. 38,000 homes were weatherized. FY2015: 30,000 homes FY2016: 33,000 homes FY2017: 35,000 homes Restated, this promise was to weatherize 1M low-income homes "each year for the next decade." This promise was not fulfilled.	0.00
EN-10	**The Promise:** "...we will get one million 150 mile-per-gallon plug-in hybrids on our roads within six years..." **When/Where:** Obama Campaign Speech, Lansing, MI, dated 08/04/08, as reported in the New York Times with credit to CQ Transcriptions, Inc. **Source:** http://www.nytimes.com/2008/08/04/us/politics/04text-obama.html?pagewanted=all **Status:** None of the statistics studied supported the concept that PHEVs would be capable of attaining 150 Miles Per Gallon (MPG) by CY2015, six years after President Obama first assumed the presidency. In CY2016, for example, some of the more popular PHEVs were rated as follows by the U.S. Environmental Protection Agency (EPA): -2016 Chevy Volt: 106 MPGe (combined electric/gas) and 42 MPG (gas only) -2016 Cadillac ELR Sport: 80 MPGe/30 MPG -2016 Ford C-Max Energi: 88 MPGe/38 MPG -2016 Ford Fusion Energi: 88 MPGe/38 MPG -2016 Toyota Prius: 95 MPGe/50 MPG While the above are PHEV vehicles, they should not be confused with the all-electric vehicles such as the Chevrolet Bolt, which had an EPA-certified range of 238 miles when it became available in late-CY2016. According to the EPA, the difference between Miles Per Gallon equivalent (MPGe) and MPG is that MPGe takes into consideration the efficiency of a car when it is running on both gas and battery	0.00

power, and is intended to give an overall efficiency rating.

During the period CY2009-CY2015, approximately 2.6M PHEVs were sold in the USA, none of which had a 150 mile-per-gallon capability.

This promise was not fulfilled.

EN-11	**The Promise:** "Will 'flip' incentives to utility companies by: requiring states to conduct proceedings to implement incentive changes; and offering them targeted technical assistance. These measures will benefit utilities for improving energy efficiency, rather than just from supporting higher energy consumption." **When/Where:** Obama-Biden Plan: "New Energy for America" dated 09/06/08. **Source:** http://energy.gov/sites/prod/files/edg/media/Obama_New_Energy_0804.pdf **Status:** The American Recovery and Reinvestment Act of 2009 included $3.1 billion for DOE's State Energy Program (SEP). Allocation of this funding depended on whether or not states adopted utility rate "decoupling" and new building codes. Although only half of the states and the District of Columbia had electricity and/or gas decoupling mechanisms in place as of end-CY2010, all 50 states, the District of Columbia and 5 territories benefited from these funds. With regard to compliance with new building codes, the American Society of Heating, Refrigerating and Air Conditioning Engineers (ASHRAE) publishes its recommended standards (Standard 90.1) every three years. The Department of Energy (DOE) has one year to decide whether the new standards are more energy efficient than the previous codes. If so, states are required under the Energy Policy Act of 1992 to certify to the DOE that their building energy codes meet the new standards. The most recent ASHRAE Standard 90.1 for CY2016 was approved by the DOE, after lengthy analysis, in 03/18. The DOE determined that Standard 90.1-2016 would achieve greater energy efficiency in buildings subject to the code and estimated that the following savings would accrue based on ASHRAE Standard 90.1-2016: 8.2% energy cost savings; 7.9% source energy savings; and 6.7% site energy savings. This promise was fulfilled.	1.00
EN-12	**The Promise:** "...will increase fuel economy standards 4 percent per year..." **When/Where:** Obama-Biden Plan for America: "Blueprint for Change" dated 10/09/08. **Source:** https://www.documentcloud.org/documents/550007-barack-obama-2008-blueprint-for-change.html **Status:** On 03/27/09, the Obama administration announced the first increase in fuel economy standards for cars in more than 25 years. The move increased fuel economy standards for light vehicles in CY2011 to 27.3 miles per gallon (mpg), or 8% over the CY2010 model year requirement. On 04/01/10, Transportation Secretary Ray Lahood announced new rules, co-signed with the Environmental Protection Agency (EPA), setting fuel efficiency standards for model years 2012-2016. The goal was to achieve the equivalent of 35.5 mpg for cars and trucks by CY2016, an increase of nearly 6% per year. On 11/16/11, the Department of Transportation and the EPA announced new standards for light vehicles for the CY2017-2025 timeframe equivalent to 54.5 mpg, an increase of nearly 5% per year. This promise was fulfilled.	1.00
EN-13	**The Promise:** "Within one year of becoming President, the entire White House fleet will be converted to plug-ins as security permits."	0.00

Chapter 5 - Department of Energy

When/Where: Obama-Biden Plan: "New Energy for America" dated 09/06/08.
Source: http://energy.gov/sites/prod/files/edg/media/Obama_New_Energy_0804.pdf
Status: Secret Service requirements for vehicle security for the President and members of his Cabinet prevail and no "plug-in" limosine hybrids are likely to ever make it into that part of the White House fleet.

The American Recovery and Reinvestment of 2009 provided $285M for the purchase of about 17,600 commercially available, fuel efficient vehicles for the government fleet. Of that number, 2,500 would be hybrids (but not necessarily "plug-ins"). Non-sensitive White House vehicles would be included in this number.

But the President's campaign promise was to convert the "entire" White House fleet to plug-ins, not hybrids vehicles, "within one year" of taking office. This didn't happen.

This promise was not fulfilled.

EN-14

The Promise: "...a proposal that alone removes 50 million cars' worth of pollution from the road and reduces our oil consumption 2.5 million barrels a day by 2020."
When/Where: Campaign Speech, Portsmouth, NH, 10/08/07.
Source: https://grist.org/article/obamas-speech/
Status: Enacted by Congress in CY1975, the purpose of the Corporate Average Fuel Economy (CAFE) Program is to reduce energy consumption by increasing the fuel economy of cars and light trucks.

On 05/21/10, President Obama released a memorandum with the subject "Improving Energy Security, American Competitiveness and Job Creation, and Environmental Protection through a Transformation of our Nation's Fleet of Cars and Trucks." This memorandum set the stage for the establishment of updated CAFE standards for fuel emissions.

The Department of Transportation (DOT) and the Environmental Protection Agency (EPA) immediately established the standards for cars and light trucks for CY2011-2016, raising average fuel efficiency by CY2016 to the equivalent of 35.5 Miles Per Gallon (MPG). On 08/28/12, the Obama Administration went further, setting standards to increase fuel economy to the equivalent of 54.5 MPG for cars and light-duty trucks by CY2025.

According to the National Highway Traffic Safety Administration (NHTSA), these new standards could improve fuel economy, reduce greenhouse gas emissions, save consumers more than $1.7T at the gas pump, and reduce vehicular oil consumption by 12B barrels. This means U.S. reliance on foreign oil for its vehicles could be significantly reduced and oil consumption could be further reduced by more than 2.4M barrels per day by CY2030.

According to a report issued by the Union of Concerned Scientists, for every gallon of gasoline saved as a result of these standards, 24 pounds of global warming emissions could be avoided (5 pounds for drilling, refining, and distributing gasoline and 19 pounds while burning gasoline during vehicle operation). The CY2017-CY2025 standards, when combined with the first round of standards (CY2011-CY2016), could reduce global warming emissions by 470 million metric tons. Based on this determination, coupled with an EPA estimate that the average amount of carbon dioxide emitted per passenger vehicle is 4.75 metric tons per vehicle, per year, it is conceivable that nearly 50M vehicles' worth of pollution (carbon dioxide, nitrogen oxide, etc.) could be removed from the U.S. air by CY2020.

This promise was fulfilled.

1.00

EN-15

The Promise: "...will establish a National Low Carbon Fuel Standard (LCFS) to speed the introduction of low-carbon non-petroleum fuels..."

0.00

When/Where: Obama's "Plan to Make America a Global Energy Leader," dated 10/18/07
Source: https://grist.org/article/obama-energy-fact-sheet/
Status: As of end-CY2016, no "National Low Carbon Fuel Standard" (LCFS) had been established.

Despite the absence of a national LCFS but recognizing the need for low/no carbon fuel solutions, U.S. industry took the initiative to introduce vehicles powered by fuels other than diesel and gasoline. Examples are biofuels, advanced diesel, natural gas, hydrogen (for fuel cells), and electricity (for plug-in and plug-in hybrid vehicles).

In 12/11, as a result of a lawsuit by oil industry and out-of-state farm groups, the U.S. District Court for the Eastern Division of California ruled that some aspects of California's LCFS were unconstitutional. A CY2013 decision by the 9th U.S. Circuit Court of Appeals upheld California's LCFS. In 06/14, the U.S. Supreme Court declined to hear this case, letting stand the 9th Circuit Court's decision, indirectly validating California's LCFS as a possible model for the establishment of a national LCFS.

An opportunity also presented itself for promise fulfillment under the "Moving Ahead for Progress in the 21st Century Act" (MAP-21) (S. 1813) signed into law by President Obama on 04/06/12. LCFS was not addressed in that bill.

In CY2014, a study conducted by Charles River Associates (CRA) revealed that a nationwide LCFS would increase average U.S. gasoline and diesel prices by as much as 80% within five years and up to 170% within 10 years, suggesting that the average national price for gasoline would be about $5 per gallon by CY2020 and about $7.50 a gallon by CY2025. Further, the study indicated that a national LCFS would cause a net loss of up to 4.5M jobs.

This promise was not fulfilled.

EN-16

The Promise: "...putting in place policies like conservation, development of alternative fuels and investments in new technologies to reduce our dependence on foreign oil..."
When/Where: Obama's "Plan to Make America a Global Energy Leader," dated 10/18/07
Source: https://grist.org/article/obama-energy-fact-sheet/
Status: The American Recovery and Reinvestment Act of 2009 included more than $80B for the generation of renewable energy sources, expanding manufacturing capacity for clean energy solutions, advancing vehicle and fuel technologies, and building a smarter electric grid.

According to U.S. Energy Information Administration (EIA) data, oil and other petroleum products imported by the USA from all sources when President Obama assumed the presidency in CY2009 and during ensuing years was as follows:
CY2009....4.267B barrels or 11.7M barrels per day (b/d)
CY2010... 4.304B barrels or 11.8M b/d
CY2011....4.174B barrels or 11.4M b/d
CY2012....3.878B barrels or 10.6M b/d
CY2013....3.598B barrels or 9.8M b/d
CY2014....3.372B barrels or 9.2M b/d
CY2015....3.431B barrels or 9.4M b/d
CY2016....2.865B barrels or 7.9M b/d

Imports of oil from all sources decreased by 3.8M b/d between CY2009 and CY2016.

This promise was fulfilled.

1.00

EN-17

The Promise: "...will work to ensure that these clean alternative fuels are developed and incorporated into our national supply as soon as possible...will require at least 60 billion gallons of advanced biofuels by 2030..."

1.00

Chapter 5 - Department of Energy

When/Where: Obama-Biden Plan: "New Energy for America" dated 09/06/08.
Source: http://energy.gov/sites/prod/files/edg/media/Obama_New_Energy_0804.pdf
Status: According to the Global Renewable Fuels Alliance (GRFA), the USA had the capability to produce 12B gallons of corn-based ethanol in CY2010.

On 08/01/10, a technology center in Denver, WY announced that it is producing up to 400 gallons of synthetic jet fuel daily, a first step in reducing the airline industry's consumption of an estimated 23B gallons of jet fuel each year, producing about 2% of the world's carbon emissions according to the International Air Transport Association (IATA). The prospects for attaining this goal was further improved on 07/01/11 when the American Society for Testing and Materials (ASTM) International, an organization that sets standards for airlines, approved the mixing of organic waste and non-food plants with aircraft fuel.

In CY2012, four commercial cellulosic or advanced biorefineries were created which, when they became operational in CY2014, had a combined capacity to produce over 80M gallons of advanced biofuels per year. These are the four facilities:
1. DuPont-Nevada Site Cellulosic Ethanol Facility at Nevada, Iowa. Capacity: 30M gallons per year.
2. Abengoa-Bioenergy Hugoton Cellulosic Ethanol Facility at Hugoton, Kansas. Capacity: 25M gallons per year plus 21 Megawatts of renewable electricity.
3. POET-DSM Project Liberty at Emmetsburg, Iowa. Capacity: 25M gallons per year.
4. Quad County Corn Adding Cellulosic Ethanol, or ACE at Galva, Iowa. Capacity: 3.75M gallons per year.

The military has also been making great strides in the adaptation of its resources to utilize biofuels. The USAF C-17 Globemaster has been certified for flight operations using hydro-processed blended biofuels. The Lockheed-Martin F-22 Raptor fighter aircraft successfully flight tested a biofuel camelina/JP-8 jet fuel blend in 03/11. The U.S. Navy's F/A-18 Hornets and helicopters are among its airborne assets flying with mixtures of biofuels and jet fuel. The Navy's "Great Green Fleet" became a reality in 01/16 when the aircraft carrier John C. Stennis left on a Far East deployment accompanied by five biofuel-powered ships. Those ships (three destroyers, one cruiser and one fast combat support ship) were powered by a biofuel blend made from tallow (rendered beef fat). These innovations by the military come at a higher cost, however:
USAF: $59/gallon for alcohol-to-jet fuel;
USN: $26/gallon for biofuels.

This promise was fulfilled.

EN-18	**The Promise:** "...will strategically invest $150 billion over 10 years to accelerate the commercialization of plug-in hybrids, promote development of commercial scale renewable energy, encourage energy efficiency, invest in low emissions coal plants, advance the next generation of biofuels and fuel infrastructure, and begin transition to a new digital electricity grid." **When/Where:** Obama-Biden Plan: "New Energy for America" dated 09/06/08. **Source:** http://energy.gov/sites/prod/files/edg/media/Obama_New_Energy_0804.pdf **Status:** The principal government entity to carry out this promise is Office of Energy Efficiency and Renewable Energy (EERE) within the Department of Energy. During President Obama's two terms in office, the EERE was funded as follows: FY2010....$2.216B FY2011....$1.772B FY2012....$1.781B FY2013....$1.692B FY2014....$1.825B FY2015....$1.914B FY2016....$2.069B FY2017....$2.073B	0.00

Chapter 5 - Department of Energy

The above totals $15.342B, with two years to go to reach the 10 year mark. Even if a combination of other agencies/organizations have received similar levels of funding, it was inconceivable that the promised $150B investment would be a reality by CY2019.

This promise was not fulfilled.

EN-19

The Promise: "...will make the federal government a leader in the green building market, achieving a 40 percent increase in efficiency in all new federal buildings within five years and ensuring that all new federal buildings are zero-emissions by 2025."
When/Where: Obama-Biden Plan: "New Energy for America" dated 09/06/08.
Source: http://energy.gov/sites/prod/files/edg/media/Obama_New_Energy_0804.pdf
Status: The American Recovery and Reinvestment Act of 2009 of 02/17/09 includes at least $4.5 billion to turn federal buildings into "high-performance green buildings". As of 03/30/11, $5.8B had been invested in energy efficiency projects for federal buildings.

Supporting the stated goal, the General Services Administration (GSA) appointed Ms. Eleni Reed to the newly created position of "Chief Greening Officer" on 06/09/10. In this role, Ms. Reed's mandate was to oversee the "greening" of 1,500 federally owned and 8,100 federally leased buildings.

However, Executive Order 13514 issued by President Obama on 10/05/09 lowered federal building energy efficiency expectations. It mandated that at least 15% (not 40%) of existing federal buildings and leases met "Energy Efficiency Guiding Principles" by CY2015 (not CY2014 - within five years of President Obama's first term inauguration) and that all new federal buildings met 100% conformance goals by CY2030 (not CY2025).

This promise was not fulfilled.

0.00

EN-20

The Promise: "I showed up at this event in a government vehicle that does not have a flexible-fuel tank. When I'm President, I will make sure that every vehicle purchased by the federal government does."
When/Where: Obama Campaign Speech to Detroit Economic Club, Detroit, MI, dated 05/07/07.
Source: https://en.wikisource.org/wiki/Remarks_of_Senator_Barack_Obama_to_the_Detroit_Economic_Club
Status: Flexible-Fuel Vehicles (FFV) are capable of operating on E85 (a blend of 85% ethanol and 15% gasoline). The main advantage of employing E85 is that it reduces demand on petroleum, but ethanol contains less energy than gasoline and by some accounts provides 25-30% fewer miles per gallon.

The Energy Policy Act of 2005 (EPACT) signed into law by President Bush on 08/08/05 mandated the use of light duty FFVs in "covered" federal fleets (fleets operating in a Metropolitan Statistical Area (MSA) with 20 or more vehicles, which are capable of being centrally fueled, barring exceptions). Under this law, 75% of all covered light duty vehicle acquisitions had to be FFVs (law enforcement, emergency vehicles and vehicles located outside the 125+ MSAs covered by EPACT were exempt). It also mandated 100% use of alternative fuel in FFVs.

Executive Order (EO) 13423, "Strengthening Federal Environment, Energy and Transportation Management," was signed by President Bush on 01/24/07. It required federal agencies to exercise leadership in petroleum reduction through improvements in fleet efficiency and the use of alternative fuel vehicles and alternative fuels. This EO was revoked by President Obama on 03/19/15 and replaced by EO 13963 entitled "Planning for Federal Sustainability in the Next Decade."

EO 13963 steps back from the basic tenet of this promise. It stated that by 12/31/20, use of alternative fuel vehicles, including E-85 compatible vehicles, zero emission and plug-in hybrid vehicles, and compressed natural gas powered vehicles must "account for 20 percent of all new

0.00

agency passenger vehicle acquisitions and by December 31, 2025, zero emission vehicles or plug-in hybrid vehicles account for 50 percent of all new agency passenger vehicles."

The words "every vehicle" in this promise were interpreted to mean 100% of non-exempt vehicles.

This promise was not fulfilled.

EN-21

The Promise: "...will work with Congress and auto companies to ensure that all new vehicles have FFV [Flexible Fuel Vehicle] capability -- the capability by the end of his first term in office."
When/Where: Obama-Biden Plan: "New Energy for America" dated 09/06/08
Source: http://energy.gov/sites/prod/files/edg/media/Obama_New_Energy_0804.pdf
Status: Although all major U.S. auto manufacturers have aggressive FFV programs in place, it was unrealistic to think that "all new vehicles" manufactured by the end of CY2012 (the end of President Obama's first term in office) would have some type of FFV capability.

The Open Fuel Standard Act of 2011 (H.R. 1687 and S. 1603), introduced by Congressman John Shimkus and Senator Maria Cantwell on 5/3/11 and 9/22/11 respectively promoted the adoption of non-petroleum based fuels (ethanol, methanol, natural gas, hydrogen, biodiesel, plug-in electric, fuel cell) by the following goals: 50% of automobiles manufactured in Model Year (MY) 2014, 80% in MY2016 and 95% by MY2017. Both bills expired with the 112th Congress at the end of CY2012.

This bill was reintroduced by Congressman Eliot Engel (D-NY) as H.R. 2493 on 06/25/13, modified as being applicable to:
- not less than 30% of qualified vehicles manufactured beginning in MY2016 (not 50% by MY2014); and
- not less than 50% of qualified vehicles beginning in MY2017 and each subsequent year (not 80% in MY2016).

In this proposed bill, the term "qualified vehicle" meant a covered vehicle that has been warranted by its manufacturer (1) to operate on natural gas, hydrogen, or biodiesel; is a flexible fuel vehicle; (2) is a plug-in electric drive vehicle; (3) is propelled solely by a fuel cell that produces power without the use of petroleum or a petroleum-based fuel; or (4) is propelled solely by something other than an internal combustion engine and produces power without the use of petroleum or a petroleum-based fuel. This bill expired with the 113th Congress at the end of CY2014,

This promise was not fulfilled.

0.00

EN-22

The Promise: "...will invest in cost-effective retrofits to achieve a 25 percent increase in efficiency of existing federal buildings within 5 years."
When/Where: Obama-Biden Plan: "New Energy for America" dated 09/06/08.
Source: http://energy.gov/sites/prod/files/edg/media/Obama_New_Energy_0804.pdf
Status: While Promise Number EN-19 appears closely related, it pertains to 40% of "new" federal buildings. This promise pertains to 25% of "existing" federal buildings.

Executive Order 13514 issued by President Obama on 10/05/09 lowered federal building energy efficiency expectations. It mandated that at least 15% (not 25%) of "existing" federal buildings and leases meet "Energy Efficiency Guiding Principles" by CY2015, not CY2014, which would have been within five years of President Obama's first term inauguration.

This promise was not fulfilled.

0.00

EN-23

The Promise: "...will put forward the resources necessary to achieve a 15 percent reduction in federal energy consumption by 2015."
When/Where: Obama-Biden Plan: "New Energy for America" dated 09/06/08.
Source: http://energy.gov/sites/prod/files/edg/media/Obama_New_Energy_0804.pdf
Status: The American Recovery and Reinvestment Act (ARRA) of 2009 provided $4.5B for the

1.00

Chapter 5 - Department of Energy

greening of federal buildings as well as $300M for the acquisition of federal motor vehicles with higher fuel economy, including: hybrid vehicles; electric vehicles; and commercially-available, plug-in hybrid vehicles.

On 10/05/09, President Obama signed Executive Order 13514 that set energy consumption reduction goals for federal agencies. However, the Energy Independence and Security Act of 2007, signed into law by President Bush on 12/19/07, had already mandated a federal building energy reduction goal of 30% by CY2015.

The ARRA funding reflected above and follow-on annual appropriations provided the "resources necessary" to satisfy the basic tenets of this promise.

This promise was fulfilled.

EN-24

The Promise: "...will use a portion of the revenue generated from the cap-and-trade permit auction to make investments that will reduce our dependence on foreign oil and accelerate deployment of low-carbon technologies. The investments will focus on three critical areas: 1) Basic Research; 2)Technology Demonstration and 3) Aggressive Commercial Deployment and Clean Market Creation."
When/Where: Obama-Biden Plan: "New Energy for America" dated 09/06/08.
Source: http://energy.gov/sites/prod/files/edg/media/Obama_New_Energy_0804.pdf
Status: The American Clean Energy and Security Act of 2009 (ACES) (H.R. 2454) was introduced by Congressmen Henry Waxman (D-CA) and Edward Markey (D-MA) on 05/15/09 and was thus also known as the "Waxman-Markey Bill." This legislation would have regulated and taxed carbon emissions of power plants and private companies. It narrowly passed the House by a vote of 219 to 212 on 06/26/09. It never reached the Senate floor for discussion or a vote due to Republican opposition based in part on their belief that the "Cap-and-Trade" portion of the ACES amounted to a massive energy tax (a 15% increase according to Department of Treasury estimates). This bill died when the 111th Congress expired at the end of CY2010.

Undaunted, President Obama stated on 11/03/10, after his Democratic party lost control of the Senate, that "cap-and-trade was just one way of skinning the cat; it was not the only way." At his direction, the Environmental Protection Agency (EPA) produced a 1,560-page Clean Power Plan (CPP) regulation which was publicly implemented by President Obama on 08/03/15.

A group of 29 states, along with utility and energy companies, immediately challenged the CPP, elevating their opposition through the judicial system to the Supreme Court.

On 02/09/16 the Supreme Court stayed implementation of the CPP pending judicial review, which meant that until the Supreme Court announced a final ruling, the CPP had no legal effect. While the stay is in effect, the EPA cannot impose CPP requirements on any state that does not voluntarily recognize those requirements. By end-CY2016, the Supreme Court had not issued its final ruling on this topic.

This promise was not fulfilled.

0.00

EN-25

The Promise: "...will establish a 10 percent federal Renewable Portfolio Standard (RPS) to require that 10 percent of electricity consumed in the U.S. is derived from clean, sustainable energy sources...by 2012."
When/Where: Obama-Biden Plan: "New Energy for America" dated 09/06/08
Source: http://energy.gov/sites/prod/files/edg/media/Obama_New_Energy_0804.pdf
Status: The goal of the Renewable Portfolio Standard (RPS) was to stimulate market and technology development so that renewable energy would be competitive with conventional forms of electric power.

0.00

Chapter 5 - Department of Energy

The American Clean Energy and Security Act of 2009 (ACES) (H.R. 2454) was introduced by Congressmen Henry Waxman (D-CA) and Edward Markey (D-MA) on 05/15/09. It narrowly passed the House on 06/26/09. But in the absence of any Senate action, this bill died when the 111th Congress expired at the end of CY2010.

ACES would have established a federal RPS, requiring that 6% of electric power come from renewable resources by CY2012, and 20% by 2020.

As of end-CY2016, 38 states had established state-level RPS or goals. The establishment of a 10% RPS by CY2012 at the national/federal level did not happen.

This promise was not fulfilled.

ENERGY - GENERAL	GRADE

EN-26

The Promise: "I will report to the American people every year on the State of our Energy Future..."
When/Where: Campaign Speech, Portsmouth, NH, dated 10/08/07.
Source: https://2008election.procon.org/sourcefiles/Obama20071008.pdf
Status: To one extent or another, President Obama addressed the nation's energy status during his annual "State of the Union" reports to Congress. But this promise was to deliver an annual "State of our Energy Future" report to the American people.

CY2010: President Obama had until 01/20/10 (one year after his first term inauguration) to initially honor this promise. He didn't do so.

CY2011: On 03/30/11, he delivered a speech at Georgetown University entitled "A Secure Energy Future." This non-national speech was delivered in conjunction with the Department of Energy's release of its "Blueprint for a Secure Energy Future."

CY2012: On 02/23/12, he delivered a major address at the University of Miami focused on energy.

CY2013: A national address, entitled "Taking Control of Our Energy Future," was delivered by the President in his weekly address to the nation on 03/03/13.

CY2014: On 05/09/14, President Obama delivered remarks on "American Energy" at a Walmart in Mountain View, CA.

CY2015: On 08/25/15, President Obama was a principal speaker at the National Clean Energy Summit held in Las Vegas, NV.

CY2016: President Obama delivered a weekly address on 02/06/16 entitled "Doubling Our Clean Energy Funding to Address the Challenge of Climate Change" as well as the weekly address of 08/13/16 entitled "Providing a Better, Cleaner, Safer Future for Our Children."

This promise was not fulfilled.

Grade: 0.00

EN-27

The Promise: "...will swap oil from the Strategic Petroleum Reserve...to help bring down prices at the pump."
When/Where: Obama and Biden's Plan for America: "Blueprint for Change," dated 10/09/08.
Source: https://assets.documentcloud.org/documents/550007/barack-obama-2008-blueprint-for-change.pdf
Status: When this promise was made in 10/08, gasoline cost an average of $3.80 per gallon, having peaked in 07/08 at around $4.10 per gallon. The ensuing months to President Obama's inauguration saw national average prices per gallon of regular gasoline decline to around $1.90 per gallon.

By 05/09/11, the national average cost of regular gasoline had climbed to $3.97 per gallon. In

Grade: 1.00

Chapter 5 - Department of Energy

response on 06/23/11, the Obama Administration released 30M barrels of oil from the Strategic Petroleum Reserve to help Americans during their CY2011 summer vacation travels.

As of 12/31/16, the national average cost of one gallon of regular gasoline was $2.33. In the Contiguous United States (CONUS), California had the highest average cost per gallon at $2.75 whereas South Carolina enjoyed the lowest at $2.08 for regular gasoline. Gasoline prices are usually higher in Hawaii and Alaska when compared to the CONUS average with $3.00 and $2.64 respectively per gallon of regular gasoline on the same date. Source: www.gasbuddy.com.

This promise was fulfilled.

EN-28	**The Promise:** "...will launch a Clean Technologies Venture Capital Fund that will provide $10 billion a year for five years to get the most promising clean energy technologies off the ground." **When/Where:** Campaign Speech, Portsmouth, NH, dated 10/08/07. **Source:** https://2008election.procon.org/sourcefiles/Obama20071008.pdf **Status:** The promised "Clean Technologies Venture Capital Fund" had not been created as of end-CY2016. In fact, the Brookings Institute has since reported that venture capital funding for clean technologies, which includes sectors like solar, energy storage and smart grid, dropped by 30% between 2011 and 2016. Loan guarantees for clean technologies initiatives were included in the American Recovery and Reinvestment Act (ARRA) of 2009, but did not satisfy the exact specifications stated in this promise. This promise was not fulfilled.	0.00
EN-29	**The Promise:** "...will invest federal resources, including tax incentives, cash prizes and government contracts into developing the most promising technologies with the goal of getting the first two billion gallons of cellulosic ethanol into the system by 2013." **When/Where:** Obama-Biden Plan: "Make America a Global Energy Leader," dated 10/07/07. **Source:** https://grist.org/article/obama-energy-fact-sheet/ **Status:** Cellulosic ethanol is made from corn stalks, wood chips and other biomass such as grass clippings, and not food such as corn. The Renewable Fuels Reinvestment Act of 2010 (H.R. 4940), introduced by Congressman Earl Pomeroy (D-ND) on 03/25/10, would have extended the $1.01 per gallon tax credit for cellulosic ethanol producers beyond 12/31/10. This bill was referred to the Subcommittee on Trade and no further action was taken when the 111th Congress expired at the end of CY2010. No similar bill was introduced during the 112th, 113th or 114th Congress. Cellulosic ethanol production didn't begin in earnest until CY2012. Financing was the biggest impediment to progress in building the needed cellulosic ethanol production plants on an industrial/national scale. Banks considered financing the first of these plants too risky. By end-CY2016, POET Biorefining LLC, the nation's premier producer of cellulosic ethanol, had ethanol productions sites at Hanlontown, Iowa; Hudson, South Dakota; and Caro, Michigan. The combined production capability of these three facilities was 171M gallons per year (MGPY). This promise was not fulfilled.	0.00
EN-30	**The Promise:** "...will provide $4 billion retooling tax credits and loan guarantees for domestic auto plants and parts manufacturers, so that the new fuel-efficient cars can be built in the U.S. by American workers rather than overseas." **When/Where:** Obama-Biden Plan: "New Energy for America" dated 09/06/08. **Source:** http://energy.gov/sites/prod/files/edg/media/Obama_New_Energy_0804.pdf **Status:** During CY2009 and CY2010, retooling tax credits were provided to the auto industry at the city and state levels.	1.00

As to loans for retooling, the Department of Energy (DOE) has been effective in providing loans to the auto industry such as the $1.4B loan to Nissan in 01/10 to retool a Smyrna, TN plant where it will build its electric LEAF sedan and batteries for that vehicle. Six months prior, Nissan had won a conditional $1.6B loan guarantee under the DOE's Advanced Technology Vehicles Manufacturing (ATVM) program. On 08/29/12, Forbes Magazine reported additional success stories:

Ford: used a $5.9B loan from the DOE to convert two truck plants to small-car production and to develop more fuel-efficient vehicles like the Ford Focus EV and C-Max Energi plug-in hybrid.

Nissan: received a $1.4B loan from the DOE to build a battery plant and modify an existing car factory in Tennessee to produce the electric Nissan Leaf instead of producing that vehicle in Japan.

Tesla: used a $465M DOE loan to build a battery plant and retool part of a former Toyota-GM factory to build the Model S, its second electric car.

Vehicle Production Group: used a $50M DOE loan to add a compressed natural gas version of its MV-1 handicapped accessible van.

Johnson Controls: used a $300M DOE grant to build an advanced-battery cell plant in Michigan to relocate work to the USA from Europe.

Dow Kokam: a joint venture between Dow Chemical, a Korean battery maker and a French engineering company used a $161M DOE grant to build an advanced-battery factory in Michigan.

This promise was fulfilled.

EN-31	**The Promise:** "...will...invest $150 billion over ten years to deploy clean technologies..." **When/Where:** Obama-Biden Plan for America entitled: "Blueprint for Change" dated 10/09/08. **Source:** https://assets.documentcloud.org/documents/550007/barack-obama-2008-blueprint-for-change.pdf **Status:** The American Recovery and Reinvestment Act (ARRA) of 2009 included over $90B for energy efficiency and renewable energy.	1.00

The breakout of this $90B of ARRA funding was roughly $29B for energy efficiency, $21B for renewable generation, $18B for traditional and high speed rail, $10B for grid modernization, $6B for advanced batteries, advanced vehicles and fuels technologies, $3B for carbon capture and sequestration technologies, $3B for green innovation and job training, and $2B for clean energy equipment manufacturing tax credits.

President Obama's FY2012 budget request included but was not limited to:
- $5.4B for the Office of Science, including $2.0B for basic energy sciences to discover new ways to produce, store, and use energy.
- $457M for a program to reduce the cost of solar power and other solar energy research and development (R&D);
- $550M for the Defense Advanced Research Projects Agency (DARPA) to support the development of new energy technologies;
- $102M investment in geothermal energy;
- $341M for biofuels and biomass R&D;
- $95M for wind energy research;
- $853M for nuclear energy to include research into the development of modular nuclear reactors; and
- $453M for a fossil energy R&D portfolio focused on carbon capture and storage technologies.
The total of the above is roughly $8.3B.

Chapter 5 - Department of Energy

When looking at the $90B of funding across all federal entities provided under the ARRA in CY2009, followed by an average of about $8B per year for the period FY2010-FY2017 under the Obama Administration, it is anticipated that the goal of investing $150B for clean energy technologies over 10 years (through FY2020), across all federal entities, will be attained.

This promise was fulfilled.

ENERGY-EFFICIENT APPLICANCES	GRADE

EN-32 **The Promise:** "...will provide more resources to his Department of Energy so it implements regular updates for efficiency standards."
When/Where: Obama-Biden Plan: "New Energy for America" dated 09/06/08.
Source: http://energy.gov/sites/prod/files/edg/media/Obama_New_Energy_0804.pdf
Status: Under the Energy Policy and Conservation Act of 1975 (EPCA), the Department of Energy (DOE) is required to establish by certain dates energy efficiency standards for a broad class of residential and commercial products.

These products are appliances and other equipment used in consumers' homes and in commercial establishments. National appliance, equipment and lighting standards were first enacted by Congress in 1988. In the Energy Policy Act of 2005 (EPACT), the Congress directed the DOE to develop a plan to issue expeditiously efficiency standards for those products with respect to which the DOE had not yet met the deadlines specified in the EPCA. New standards were added under the Energy Policy Acts of 1992 and 2005 and the Energy Independence and Security Act of 2007.

During CY2009, the DOE did a bit of catching up. It completed several appliance standards rules: codified the standards prescribed by the Energy Independence and Security Act of 2007, established standards for fluorescent and incandescent lamps, beverage vending machine, ranges and ovens, and some commercial equipment contained in the American Society of Heating, Refrigerating and Air Conditioning Engineers Standard (ASHRAE) 90.1, commercial clothes washers, small electric motors, residential water heaters, direct heating equipment, and gas pool heaters.

Between funding increases provided by the American Recovery and Reinvestment Act of 2009 and other annual plus-ups ($35M in FY2010 and FY2011, an amount President Obama requested be doubled in FY2012), the DOE has benefited from "more resources" to update efficiency standards as promised.

As of CY2016, the DOE's Appliance and Equipment Standards Program continues to experience backlogs. However, these are mostly attributed to snail-paced action by the White House Office of Management & Budget (OMB), which must analyze and clear rules/regulations before they are published in the Federal Register.

This promise was fulfilled.

Grade: 1.00

NATURAL RESOURCES	GRADE

EN-33 **The Promise:** "Obama will federal double [sic] science and research funding for clean energy projects including those that make use of our biomass, solar and wind resources."
When/Where: Obama-Biden Plan: Make America a Global Energy Leader, dated 10/07/07.
Source: https://grist.org/article/obama-energy-fact-sheet/
Status: The Department of Energy's Office of Energy Efficiency and Renewable Energy (EERE) appropriation for FY2009 was $2.157B. This appropriation was supplemented by an additional $16B under the American Recovery and Reinvestment Act (ARRA) of 2009. This more than "doubled" the FY2009 budget for clean energy initiatives managed by the EERE.

This promise was fulfilled.

Grade: 1.00

EN-34 **The Promise:** "...will enter into public private partnerships to develop five 'first-of-a-kind' commercial scale coal-fired plants with clean carbon capture and sequestration technology."

Grade: 1.00

Chapter 5 - Department of Energy

When/Where: Obama and Biden's Plan for America: "Blueprint for Change," dated 10/09/08.
Source: https://assets.documentcloud.org/documents/550007/barack-obama-2008-blueprint-for-change.pdf
Status: The "FutureGen" project, a public-private partnership to develop coal gasification, carbon capture, and sequestration technologies was cancelled by the Bush Administration. The Obama Administration revived this initiative under what was referred to as the "Clean Coal Power Initiative (CCPI) Round Three." A FutureGen 2.0 project at Meredosia, Ill was killed by the Department of Energy (DOE) on 02/03/15 under DOE's belief that it was not economically feasible to retrofit existing coal plants with carbon capture technology.

Under President Obama, the DOE started support of the Petra Nova Project near Houston, Texas. By end-CY2016, the DOE had provided $190M under the original CCPI, which included funding from the American Recovery and Reinvestment Act (ARRA) of 2009, and an additional $23M in 02/16 under the FY2016 Consolidated Appropriations Act, which included the "Furthering Carbon Capture, Utilization, Technology, Underground Storage, and Reduced Emissions (FUTURE) Act" (S.1535) that extended tax credits for Carbon Capture, Utilization, and Storage (CCUS) projects. This plant, one of two worldwide (the other is in Canada), became fully operational by the end of President Obama's second term in office in 01/17. Petra Nova can reportedly capture over 90% of the carbon dioxide released from the equivalent of a 240 megawatt coal unit, which translates into 5K tons of carbon dioxide per day or over 1M tons per year.

The Texas Clean Energy Project (TCEP) is an Integrated Gasification Combined Cycle (IGCC) facility near Odessa, TX that proposed to incorporate CCUS technology in a first-of-its-kind commercial clean coal power plant. This project was expected to be operational in CY2018 as the first US-based power plant to combine both IGCC and capture 90% of its emissions. By end-CY2016, TCEP was filing for bankruptcy and their clean coal power plant project was ultimately cancelled.

The promise to "enter into public private partnerships to develop five..." was honored and exeeded by four for a total of nine. Nonetheless, including TCEP above, eight of the nine CCUS start-ups/initiatives either failed or were terminated during President Obama's two terms in office or shortly thereafter.

This promise was fulfilled.

EN-35	**The Promise:** "Prioritize the Construction of the Alaska Natural Gas Pipeline...will work with the Canadian government, state of Alaska, oil and gas producers, and other stakeholders to facilitate construction of the pipeline."	0.00

When/Where: Obama and Biden's Plan for America: "Blueprint for Change," dated 10/09/08.
Source: https://www.documentcloud.org/documents/550007-barack-obama-2008-blueprint-for-change.html
Status: In CY1967, significant natural gas reserves (30T cubic feet) were discovered in Prudhoe Bay and Point Thompson, Alaska. When then-Candidate Obama campaigned for election to the presidency, building a 1,700 mile, 48-inch pipeline capable of carrying natural gas from Alaska's North Slope to Calgary, Alberta had been in planning stages since CY1973.

From Alberta, the original plan was for the pipeline to be extended an additional 1,500 miles to the Chicago area with producers in North Dakota and Montana authorized to tap into it to support local consumption requirements. An alternative routing under consideration at the time would have the natural gas flow to Valdez, Alaska from where it could be transported to markets in the western USA, Mexico, Hawaii and Asia.

In CY2010, President Obama appointed Larry Persily as his Federal Coordinator for Alaska Gas Line Projects, a key figure in bilateral talks with Canada. In late CY2011, the Alaska Gas Pipeline announced the cancellation of its Natural Gas Pipeline development efforts as originally planned (to

Alberta and potentially to the lower 48 states) due to market changes and lack of popular support in Canada.

A few years later, Mr. Persily announced that his office had not been funded by Congress for FY2015. The efforts of the Federal Coordinator for Alaska Gas Line Projects ceased.

This promise was not fulfilled.

EN-36

The Promise: "Oil companies have access to 68 million acres of land, over 40 million offshore, which they are not drilling on. Drilling in open areas could significantly increase domestic oil and gas production. Barack Obama and Joe Biden will require oil companies to diligently develop these leases or turn them over so that another company can develop them."
When/Where: Obama-Biden Plan: "New Energy for America" dated 09/06/08.
Source: http://energy.gov/sites/prod/files/edg/media/Obama_New_Energy_0804.pdf
Status: On 03/31/10, reversing a 20-year ban, President Obama announced the opening of specific areas along the Atlantic seaboard from the northern tip of Delaware down to central Florida, a new section of the Gulf of Mexico and the Cook Inlet in Alaska.

On 10/18/15, the Department of the Interior announced it was calling off two auctions for oil and gas drilling rights in the Arctic off Alaska and denied requests for lease extensions by Shell and Statoil. The two canceled auctions were for the Chukchi and Beaufort seas, potentially scheduled for CY2016 and the first half of CY 2017, respectively.

Requests for "lease suspensions" from Shell and Statoil that would have allowed them to keep their leases beyond their primary 10-year terms set to expire in CY2017 for the Beaufort Sea and in CY2020 for the Chukchi Sea were denied. According to Interior Secretary Jewell, "among other things, the companies did not demonstrate a reasonable schedule of work for exploration and development under the leases."

On 11/18/16, the Obama Administration banned offshore drilling/exploration in the Arctic (specifically Chukchi and Beaufort seas), with the exception of Cook Inlet, until CY2022. The ban also applies to plans for companies to drill for natural gas and oil off the Atlantic coast of four eastern seaboard states. Citing the Outer-Continental Shelf Lands Act of 1953, President Obama solidified this ban on 12/20/16. Retained were 10 potential leases in the Gulf of Mexico plus Cook Inlet near Anchorage, Alaska.

This promise was fulfilled.

1.00

EN-37

The Promise: "...will establish a 25 percent federal Renewable Portfolio Standard (RPS) to require that 25 percent of electricity consumed in the U.S. is derived from clean, sustainable energy sources, like solar, wind and geothermal by 2025."
When/Where: Obama-Biden Plan: "Promoting a Healthy Environment," dated 10/08/08.
Source: https://www.energy.gov/sites/prod/files/edg/media/Obama_Cap_and_Trade_0512.pdf
Status: See Promise EN-25. The goal of RPS is to stimulate market and technology development so that renewable energy will be competitive with conventional forms of electric power.

The American Clean Energy and Security Act of 2009 (ACES) (H.R. 2454) was introduced by Congressmen Henry Waxman (D-CA) and Edward Markey (D-MA) on 05/15/09. It narrowly passed the House on 06/26/09. But in the absence of any Senate action, this bill died when the 111th Congress expired at the end of CY2010. ACES would have established a federal RPS, requiring that 6% of electric power come from renewable resources by CY2012, and 20% by CY2020. CY2025 was not mentioned as a goal year in this bill.

Only Nevada, Illinois, Delaware, New Hampshire and Oregon have established targets exactly consistent with President Obama's promise of 25% by CY2025. Several have exceeded the

0.00

President's goal: Alaska (50% by CY2025), California (33% by CY2020), Colorado (30% by CY2020), Maryland (25% by CY2020), Michigan (35% by CY2025), Minnesota (26.5% by CY2025), Maine (40% by CY2017), Hawaii (30% by CY2020), Vermont (55% by CY2017) and U.S. Virgin Islands (30% by CY2025).

Legislation to support this promise such as S.433 (A bill to amend the Public Utility Regulatory Policies Act of 1978 to establish a renewable electricity standard, and for other purposes) failed to get through the 111th Congress. Senator Tom Udall (D-NM) tried again by reintroducing the bill as S.741 during the 112th Congress. Under these proposed bills, 25% of electricity consumption would have to be from clean, renewable sources by CY2025. S.741 died when the 112th Congress expired at the end of CY2013.

As of end-CY2016, there is no law establishing the 25% RPS national objective by CY2025.

This promise was not fulfilled.

NUCLEAR WASTE	GRADE

EN-38 — **The Promise:** "...will make safeguarding nuclear material both abroad and in the U.S. a top anti-terrorism priority. In terms of waste storage...do not believe that Yucca Mountain is a suitable site...will lead federal efforts to look for safe, long-term disposal solutions based on objective, scientific analysis...will develop requirements to ensure that the waste stored at current reactor sites is contained using the most advanced dry-cask storage technology available."
When/Where: Obama-Biden Plan: "New Energy for America" dated 09/06/08.
Source: http://energy.gov/sites/prod/files/edg/media/Obama_New_Energy_0804.pdf
Status: As of end-CY2016, the national inventory of commercial spent nuclear fuel amounted to nearly 70K metric tons stored at 75 site-specific and general license sites in 34 states.

GLOBAL SAFEGUARDING: Under President Obama's leadership, the first international Nuclear Security Summit (NSS) to prevent nuclear terrorism worldwide was held in Washington, D.C., on 04/12-13/10. The second summit was held at Seoul, South Korea on 03/26-27/12; the third at The Hague, Netherlands, on 03/24-25/14; and the fourth in Washington, D.C. on 03/31-04/01/16.

YUCCA MOUNTAIN: President Obama's FY2010 budget submission included $197M to shutter the Yucca Mountain, NV nuclear waste storage program while the Administration devised "a new strategy toward nuclear waste disposal." The U.S. Government had already invested nearly $12B for the development of the Yucca Mountain waste disposal site. As of end-CY2016, the Yucca Mountain site had been abandoned since 04/11 and nothing existed but a boarded up, five-mile exploratory tunnel developed at a cost of $8B by the Department of Energy (DOE).

DRY-CASK STORAGE: Dry-cask storage is meant to be an interim storage solution. Dry casks are designed to hold nuclear waste for a few decades while permanent geological storage capabilities are developed. To that end and at an estimated cost of $19B, the Waste Isolation Pilot Plant (WIPP) near Carlsbad, New Mexico, in operation since CY1999, is now the nation's first deep geological repository for nuclear waste.

This promise was fulfilled.

Grade: 1.00

WINDFALL PROFITS	GRADE

EN-39 — **The Promise:** "I'll make oil companies like Exxon pay a tax on their windfall profits, and we'll use the money to help families pay for their skyrocketing energy costs and other bills."
When/Where: Obama Campaign Speech on the Economy, Raleigh, NC, 06/09/08.
Source: https://2008election.procon.org/sourcefiles/Obama20080609.pdf
Status: This promise was made in 06/08 when U.S. crude oil prices reached $151.72 per barrel. On 12/31/16, that price had fallen to $53.72 per barrel.

Grade: 0.00

Chapter 5 - Department of Energy

On 05/10/11, Senate Democrats announced a plan to eliminate tax breaks for the nation's five biggest oil companies. The "Close Big Oil Tax Loopholes Act" (S 258 and S. 940) introduced by Senator Robert Menendez (D-NJ) on 02/02/11 and 05/10/11 respectively failed to progress beyond preliminary committee review.

Another opportunity to accomplish the elimination of tax breaks for the oil industry also presented itself when a supercommittee was appointed in 08/11 to trim $1.2T from the national budget, an initiative that failed to materialize by the mandated 11/23/11 deadline.

Initiatives to close big oil tax loopholes were also included in the "Clean Energy Jobs Act of 2012" (H.R. 4108) introduced by Congresswoman Shelley Berkley (D-NV) on 02/29/12. This and other related bills expired with the 112th Congress.

On 08/04/15, Senator Menendez reintroduced the "Close Big Oil Tax Loopholes Act" (S. 1907) during the 114th Congress. That bill would have repealed tax subsidies for the "Big 5" oil companies and raise $22B in savings towards deficit reduction over 10 years. This bill expired with the 114th Congress at the end of CY2016.

It should be noted the top 25 oil and gas companies on the Forbes Global 2000 reaped $2.6 trillion in sales during the 04/15-04/16 measurement period and pocketed $81 billion in profit during that 12-month period.

This promise was not fulfilled.

ENERGY GPA | **0.49**

Campaign Promises

Departments -> Health & Human Services

ITEM	HEALTH & HUMAN SERVICES	
	ABORTION	**GRADE**
HE-1	**The Promise:** "...reproductive care is ... basic care, so it is at the center and at the heart of the plan that I propose...we're going to set up a public plan that all ... women can access if they don't have health insurance...including reproductive services..." **When/Where:** Candidate Obama speech before the Planned Parenthood Action Fund, dated 07/17/07. **Source:** http://lauraetch.googlepages.com/barackobamabeforeplannedparenthoodaction **Status:** The Patient Protection and Affordable Care Act (ACA) (H.R. 3590) (Public Law 111-148) was signed into law by President Obama on 03/23/10. Section 1303, as amended by Section 10104, states in part that qualified health plans may elect whether or not to cover abortions and further includes "conscience language" that prohibits qualified health plans from discriminating against any health care provider because of unwillingness to provide, pay for, provide coverage of, or refer for abortions. Congressman Bart Stupak (D-MI) was co-sponsor of an amendment that would have prohibited the use of federal funds "to pay for any abortion or to cover any part of the costs of any health plan that includes coverage of abortion." This language did not make it into the final version of the ACA which Congressman Stupak voted for anyway. Consequently, the ACA provided $317M for the Family Planning Program to serve 5.2M women and prevent 1M unintended pregnancies during FY2010 alone. Other funds in the ACA (about $11B) could be used to support abortions. This promise was fulfilled.	1.00
	AUTISM	**GRADE**
HE-2	**The Promise:** "...will fully fund the Combating Autism Act, which provides nearly $1 billion in autism-related funding over 5 years." **When/Where:** Obama-Biden Plan: "Supporting Americans with Autism Spectrum Disorders (ASD)" dated 10/30/08. **Source:** https://assets.documentcloud.org/documents/1556436/obamaautismspectrumdisorders.pdf **Status:** FY2010 budget appropriation for the Department of Health and Human Services (HHS) included $48M to the Health Resources and Services Administration (HRSA)/Autism and Other Developmental Disorders (a $6M increase over FY2009), $141M to the National Institutes of Health (NIH) and $22M for the Centers for Disease Control (CDC), all for activities associated with autism spectrum disorders (ASD), for a total of $211M against the authorized amount of $210M stipulated in "Combating Autism Act of 2006" (S. 843) (Public Law 109-416). On top of the foregoing, ASD research benefited from an additional $123.9M from tha American Recovery and Reinvestment Act (ARRA) of 2009. For FY2011, President Obama's budget proposal included $222M across HHS activities for research, detection, treatment etc. related to improving the lives of individuals and families affected by ASD. The authorized amount for FY2011 was $231M as stipulated in the "Combating Autism Act of 2006."	1.00

On 09/30/11, President Obama signed into law the "Combating Autism Reauthorization Act (CARA) of 2011" (H.R. 2005) which authorized $924M in continued federal funding for FY2011-FY2014 ($231M per year) for autism research, treatment and services (source: "autismvotes.org"). This was followed by President Obama's signature of the FY2012 budget bill on 12/23/11 which authorized $230M for FY2012 CARA requirements.

The "Combating Autism Reauthorization Act of 2014," also known as the "Autism Collaboration, Accountability, Research, Education, and Support Act of 2014" (or "Autism CARES Act of 2014") (H.R. 4631) amended the Public Health Service Act to reauthorize research, surveillance, and education activities related to autism conducted by the Department of Health and Human Services (HHS). This bill was signed into law by President Obama on 08/08/14 and authorized $1.3B in funding for FY2015-2019 ($260M per year), an increase of $29M per year over the CARA of FY2011 authorization.

This promise was fulfilled.

HE-3	**The Promise:** "...will mandate insurance coverage of autism treatment and will also continue to work with parents, physicians, providers, researchers, and schools to create opportunities and effective solutions for people with ASD." **When/Where:** Obama-Biden Plan: "Supporting Americans with Autism Spectrum Disorders (ASD)" dated 10/30/08. **Source:** https://assets.documentcloud.org/documents/1556436/obamaautismspectrumdisorders.pdf **Status:** Although the Patient Protection and Affordable Care Act (ACA) of 2010 does not mention autism or Autism Spectrum Disorder (ASD) by name, insurance is mandated across the board for "behavioral health treatment", "developmental delays or disabilities", and other category descriptors under which ASD normally falls, to include the prohibition of pre-existing condition exclusions or discrimination based on health status (Section 2704). In addition, funds are set aside in the Act for "mental and behavioral health education and training grants," "early identification and referral for children at risk for developmental or behavioral problems," screening activities for "mental health/behavioral health disorders," etc. In 11/12, the Department of HHS advised states that if they did not have autism insurance reform laws in effect by 12/13, they could not have autism coverage for CY2014 and CY2015. As of end-CY2016, 46 states and the District of Columbia (DC) had autism insurance coverage. The promise was to "mandate" that all states have insurance coverage for autism. This promise was not fulfilled.	0.00
	CANCER/CANCER RESEARCH	**GRADE**
HE-4	**The Promise:** "Will double federal funding for cancer research within 5 years." **When/Where:** Obama-Biden Plan to Combat Cancer, 09/06/08. **Source:** http://www.testicularcancersocietyblog.org/wp-content/uploads/2010/11/Obama-Cancer-Statement.pdf **Status:** While several federal entities were involved in cancer research other than the National Institutes of Health (NIH) such as the Food & Drug Administration (FDA), the Centers for Disease Control (CDC), the Veterans Administration (VA) and others, the principal recipient of federal funding for cancer research during the five-year period articulated in this promise was the NIH's National Cancer Institute (NCI). For FY2009, the NIC was appropriated $4.964B for cancer research by Congress. This was the amount to "double."	0.00

Chapter 6 - Department of Health & Human Services

For subsequent years during the five-year period addressed in this promise, the NIC was appropriated the following amounts:
FY2010....$5.103B
FY2011....$5.103B
FY2012....$5.081B
FY2013....$5.072B
FY2014....$4.923B

This promise was not fulfilled.

HE-5

The Promise: "...will immediately direct his Secretary of Health and Human Services...to comprehensively examine the various cancer-related efforts of federal agencies, and provide recommendations to eliminate barriers to effective coordination across federal agencies and between the federal government and other stakeholders."
When/Where: The Obama-Biden Plan to Combat Cancer, dated 09/06/08.
Source: http://www.testicularcancersocietyblog.org/wp-content/uploads/2010/11/Obama-Cancer-Statement.pdf
Status: On 12/14/10, President Obama's Cancer Panel published a memorandum documenting its recommendation that the President should create a task force led by the Secretary of Health and Human Services (HHS), in collaboration with agency officials, academic researchers, and patient advocates to comprehensively examine the various cancer-related efforts of federal agencies and the silos that exist among and between them.

On 01/28/16, President Obama signed a memorandum establishing a "Cancer Moonshot Task Force," to be headed by Vice President Biden, bringing together federal agencies that have a direct or indirect role in cancer research. Federal organizations represented in this task force included: National Aeronautics and Space Administration (NASA); Department of Health and Human Services (HHS); Food and Drug Administration (FDA); Department of Defense(DOD); National Endowment for the Arts (NEA); National Institutes of Health (NIH); National Science Foundation (NSF); White House Office of Management and Budget (OMB); Centers for Disease Control and Prevention (CDC); White House Office of Science and Technology Policy (OSTP); National Cancer Institute (NCI); Environmental Protection Agency (EPA); Department of Veterans Affairs (VA); Department of Energy (DOE); White House Domestic Policy Council; Department of Commerce (DOC); Centers for Medicare & Medicaid Services (CMS); Department of Agriculture (DOA); and the White House National Economic Council.

The "Cancer Moonshot Task Force" was tasked to ensure that the Federal Government made the most of its cancer-related investments, research and data, computing capabilities, targeted incentives, private-sector efforts, and patient-engagement initiatives.

This promise was fulfilled.

1.00

HE-6

The Promise: "Will provide the CDC $50 million in new funding to determine the most effective approaches that assist not only navigation of cancer patients through diagnosis and treatment processes, but also provide easy-to-understand information on the necessary follow-up steps to ensure continued lifelong health."
When/Where: The Obama-Biden Plan to Combat Cancer, dated 09/06/08.
Source: http://www.testicularcancersocietyblog.org/wp-content/uploads/2010/11/Obama-Cancer-Statement.pdf
Status: The Centers for Disease Control (CDC) FY2009 budget for cancer prevention and control was $340M.

During subsequent years, cancer prevention and control was funded as follows:
FY2010....$370M (+$30M)
FY2011....$325M (-$45M)

0.00

Chapter 6 - Department of Health & Human Services

FY2012....$371M (+$46M)
FY2013....$337M (-$34M)
FY2014....$350M (+$13M)
FY2015....$352M (+$2M)
FY2016....$356M (+$4M)
FY2017....$355M (-$1M)

Over President Obama's two terms in office, no "new funding" amounting to $50M was provided to the CDC for cancer prevention and control. Despite the ups and downs experienced in funding over those years, the CDC received a net gain of $15M over the FY2009 start point of $340M, as of President Obama's last budget in FY2017.

This promise was not fulfilled.

HE-7

The Promise: "...will seek to increase participation in clinical trials to 10 percent of adult cancer patients by requiring coverage of patient clinical trial costs..."
When/Where: Obama-Biden Plan to Combat Cancer, 09/06/08.
Source: http://www.testicularcancersocietyblog.org/wp-content/uploads/2010/11/Obama-Cancer-Statement.pdf
Status: The Patient Protection and Affordable Care Act (ACA) signed into law by President Obama on 03/23/10 includes regulations regarding insurance coverage of clinical trials. Specifically, the ACA states that health plans or insurers cannot:
- Keep patients from joining a clinical trial.
- Limit or deny coverage of routine costs to patients who join an approved clinical trial.
- Increase costs because a patient joins a clinical trial.

As to participation in clinical trials, according to a Lancet Oncology Journal study published in 02/06, two of the main barriers to patient participation in clinical trials were (1) concern that joining a trial might reduce the patient's quality of life and (2) that the patient might receive a placebo instead of real medication to combat the cancer the patient is experiencing. The National Cancer Institute estimated in 07/09 that less than 5% of adults diagnosed with cancer each year would participate in clinical trials.

A CY2016 report issued by the American Society of Clinical Oncology (ASCO) stated the following: "...assembling and analyzing data from millions of electronic health records...will allow us to learn from every individual treated for cancer - not just the fewer than 5% of patients who currently participate in clinical trials."

This promise was not fulfilled.

0.00

CHILDREN	GRADE

HE-8

The Promise: "Will provide affordable high-quality child care to working families."
When/Where: President-Elect Barack Obama's Plans to Fight Poverty, 11/08
Source: https://www.childrensdefense.org/wp-content/uploads/2018/08/president-elect-obama-plan-cdf-priorities-americas-child.pdf
Status: The American Recovery and Reinvestment Act of 2009 pumped an additional $2B into the Child Care and Development Block Grant (CCDBG) coffers to supplement the $2.127B appropriated for the CCDBG during the regular FY2009 budget process. With these funds, most states were able to sustain their child care assistance programs.

The Child Care and Development Block Grant Act of 2014 (S. 1086) was signed into law by President Obama on 11/19/2014. This law authorized the following levels of funding for child care and development:
FY2015....$2.360B
FY2016....$2.478B

1.00

Chapter 6 - Department of Health & Human Services

	FY2017....$2.540B FY2018....$2.603B FY2019....$2.669B FY2020....$2.749B This promise was fulfilled.	
HE-9	**The Promise:** "...will work with schools to create more healthful environments for children, including assistance with contract policy development for local vendors, grant support for school-based health screening programs and clinical services, increased financial support for physical education, and educational programs for students." **When/Where:** Obama-Biden Plan: "To Lower Health Care Costs and Ensure Affordable, Accessible Health Coverage For All," dated 10/03/08. **Source:** http://courses.ischool.berkeley.edu/i202/f08/lectures/Obama_Healthcare-1.pdf **Status:** Fulfillment of this promise got off to a very slow start, with only $100K enacted to promote a "healthful environment" for children in FY2010. President Obama's FY2011 budget submission did a bit of catching up by proposing $6.3M to create healthier school environments for all children. In light of Obama Administration objectives to reduce obesity in children, the first/critical step was the reauthorization of the Child Nutrition Act of 1966, which was extended to 09/30/10 under the Agriculture Appropriations Bill of 2009. Senator Blanche Lincoln (D-AR) introduced the "Healthy, Hunger-Free Kids Act of 2010" (S. 3307) on 05/05/10. This bill passed the Senate on 08/05/10 and the House on 12/02/10. President Obama signed S. 3307 into law on 12/13/10. S.3307 supported every aspect of this promise including vendor contracting policy, clinical services, child physical activity and education programs. This legislation remained in effect through FY2015. This promise was fulfilled.	1.00
HE-10	**The Promise:** "Part of Obama's early childhood intervention plan will be directed at coordinating fragmented community programs to help provide parents with information about screening for disabilities as infants and again as two-year olds." **When/Where:** Obama-Biden Plan: "Empower Americans with Disabilities," dated 09/06/08. **Source:** http://www.thearc.org/document.doc?id=3073 **Status:** Section 2951 of the Patient Protection and Affordable Health Care Act (ACA) of 2010 stipulated in part that the purpose of the Maternal, Infant, and Early Childhood Home Visiting Programs amendment to Title V of the Social Security Act (42 U.S.C. 701 et seq.) was to "improve coordination of services for at risk communities." The Act further specified that within 6 months of its enactment, each State would conduct a statewide needs assessment. This research had to address community-wide strategic planning and assessments conducted under the Head Start Act, as well as an "inventory of unmet needs and community-based and prevention-focused programs." Under the ACA, this effort was authorized funding at the following levels: FY2010....$100M FY2011....$250M FY2012....$350M FY2013....$400M FY2014....$450M. This was a significant step toward "coordinating fragmented community programs" that should have led to the dissemination of information to parents about having their children screened for disabilities. This promise was fulfilled.	1.00
HE-11	**The Promise:** "...will expand the highly-successful Nurse-Family Partnership to all 570,000 low-	1.00

income, first-time mothers each year. The Nurse-Family Partnership provides home visits by trained registered nurses to low-income expectant mothers and their families."
When/Where: Plan for America: "Blueprint for Change," dated 10/09/08
Source: https://www.documentcloud.org/ Obama and Biden's documents/550007-barack-obama-2008-blueprint-for-change.html
Status: Section 2951 of the Patient Protection and Affordable Care Act, signed into law by President Obama on 03/23/10, provided "grants to eligible entities to enable the entities to deliver services under early childhood home visitation programs." $1.5B was authorized by Congress for this purpose.

This promise was fulfilled.

	HEAD START	GRADE
HE-12	**The Promise:** "...Quadruple the number of eligible children for Early Head Start..." **When/Where:** Obama-Biden Plan: "Lifetime Success Through Education," dated 10/16/08. **Source:** http://doclibrary.com/MSC56/DOC/ObamaEducationPlan12084315.pdf **Status:** In CY2009, 66K children were enrolled in the Early Head Start (EHS) program. By end-CY2016, according to a 10/23/18 Congressional Research Service report, 168K children under the age of four were enrolled in EHS. 264K enrollments were needed to "quadruple" the CY2009 number of enrollments. This promise was not fulfilled.	0.00
HE-13	**The Promise:** "...will invest $10 billion per year in early intervention educational and developmental programs for children between zero and five. Their plan will help expand Early Head Start..." **When/Where:** Obama-Biden Plan: "Empower Americans with Disabilities," dated 09/06/08. **Source:** http://www.thearc.org/document.doc?id=3073 **Status:** More than $1.1 billion earmarked for the Early Head Start (EHS) program under the American Recovery and Reinvestment Act (ARRA) of 2009 helped increase participation in the EHS program from 66K in FY2009 to 168K in FY2017. For FY2015 and FY2016, for example, a combination of Head Start (including Early Head Start) and Child Care and Development Block Grants totaled $10.958B and $11.646B respectively. This promise was fulfilled.	1.00
HE-14	**The Promise:** "The Obama-Biden comprehensive "Zero to Five" plan will provide critical support to young children and their parents...will create Early Learning Challenge Grants to promote state "zero to five" efforts and help states move toward voluntary, universal pre-school." **When/Where:** Obama and Biden's Plan for America: "Blueprint for Change," dated 10/09/08. **Source:** https://www.documentcloud.org/documents/550007-barack-obama-2008-blueprint-for-change.html **Status:** The proposed Early Learning Challenge Fund was administered as a collaborative effort between the Departments of Education (DOE) and Health & Human Services (HHS). This fund challenged Governors to develop new model systems that (1) drove results-oriented, standards reform across programs, (2) funded and implemented pathways to improve existing early learning programs, and (3) ensured that more children enter kindergarten ready. On 5/25/11, the Secretaries of DOE and HHS announced that the Obama Administration would use $500M from the "Race to the Top" Program to fund an initial round of grants to states under what became the Race to the Top-Early Learning Challenge (RTT-ELC) Program. The period of effectivity for this program was 48 months from its inception and funding for it ceased after FY2013. This promise was fulfilled.	1.00

Chapter 6 - Department of Health & Human Services

	HEALTH CARE SYSTEM OVERHAUL	GRADE
HE-15	**The Promise:** "Invest $10 billion a year over the next five years to move the U.S. health care system to broad adoption of standards-based electronic health information systems, including electronic health records." **When/Where:** Obama-Biden Plan: "To Lower Health Care Costs and Ensure Affordable, Accessible Health Coverage For All," dated 10/03/08. **Source:** http://mendocinohre.org/rhic/200812/HealthCareFullPlan.pdf **Status:** The Health Information Technology for Economic and Clinical Health (HITECH) Act of 2009 was enacted under Title XIII of the American Recovery and Reinvestment Act of 2009 (Pub.L. 111-5). Under the HITECH Act, the United States Department of Health and Human Services (HHS) reportedly spent $25.9B to promote and expand the adoption of health information technology. The budget authorization for the Office of the National Coordinator for Health Information Technology (ONC) was about $60M for FY2014. Given that the cumulative total of this promise amounted to $50B ($10B per year for five years), the stated goal was not achieved by FY2014. This promise was not fulfilled.	0.00
HE-16	**The Promise:** "...implementing and funding evidence-based interventions, such as patient navigator programs" **When/Where:** Obama-Biden Plan: "To Lower Health Care Costs and Ensure Affordable, Accessible Health Coverage For All," dated 10/03/08. **Source:** http://mendocinohre.org/rhic/200812/HealthCareFullPlan.pdf **Status:** The American Recovery and Reinvestment Act of 2009 included $650 million "to carry out evidence-based clinical and community-based prevention and wellness strategies." Implementation of the Patient Navigator Program is further codified in the Patient Protection and Affordable Care Act (ACA) of 2010 (Section 3510), signed into law by President Obama on 03/30/10. Under the ACA, the Patient Navigator Program was funded in the amount of "$3,500,000 for fiscal year 2010, and such sums as may be necessary for each of fiscal years 2011 through 2015." This promise was fulfilled.	1.00
HE-17	**The Promise:** "... will increase funding to expand community based preventive interventions to help Americans make better choices to improve their health." **When/Where:** Obama-Biden Plan: "To Lower Health Care Costs and Ensure Affordable, Accessible Health Coverage For All," dated 10/03/08. **Source:** http://mendocinohre.org/rhic/200812/HealthCareFullPlan.pdf **Status:** Announced by Mrs. Obama on 06/29/09, $851M was authorized under the American Recovery and Reinvestment Act (ARRA) of 2009, signed into law by President Obama 02/17/09, to expand community based preventive interventions. This promise was fulfilled.	1.00
HE-18	**The Promise:** "...the government must invest in ...modernizing our physical structures, particularly our public health laboratories." **When/Where:** Obama-Biden Plan: "To Lower Health Care Costs and Ensure Affordable, Accessible Health Coverage For All," dated 10/03/08. **Source:** http://courses.ischool.berkeley.edu/i202/f08/lectures/Obama_Healthcare-1.pdf **Status:** The American Recovery and Reinvestment Act (ARRA) of 2009 (Economic Stimulus Bill) provided $1B "to construct, renovate or repair existing non-Federal research facilities." This promise was fulfilled.	1.00
HE-19	**The Promise:** "Establish a National Health Insurance Exchange with a range of private insurance	0.00

options as well as a new public plan based on benefits available to members of Congress..."
When/Where: Obama-Biden Plan on Health Care
Source: http://webarchive.loc.gov/all/20090429185902/http://change.gov/agenda/health_care_agenda/
Status: This promise refers to the establishment of a "public option." The Patient Protection and Affordable Care Act (Public Law 111-148) signed into law by President Obama on 03/23/10, did not include a "public option."

This promise was not fulfilled.

HE-20

The Promise: "Large employers that do not offer meaningful coverage or make a meaningful contribution to the cost of quality health coverage for their employees will be required to contribute a percentage of payroll toward the costs of the national plan. Small businesses will be exempt from this requirement."
When/Where: Obama-Biden Plan on Health Care
Source: http://webarchive.loc.gov/all/20090429185902/http://change.gov/agenda/health_care_agenda/
Status: Section 1304 of the Patient Protection and Affordable Care Act (ACA) (Public Law 111-148), signed into law by President Obama on 03/23/10, defines "large employer" as one that "employed an average of at least 101 employees on business days during the preceding calendar year and employs at least 1 employee on the first day of the plan year."

Section 1513 of the ACA stated: "Large Employers Not Offering Health Coverage....then there is hereby imposed on the employer an assessable payment equal to the product of the applicable payment amount and the number of individuals employed by the employer as full-time employees...".

The ACA also considered that businesses with 50 to 100 employees were considered small employers.

Effective in CY2015, the penalty for small businesses not covering their workers was $2K per employee (minus the first 30 full-time employees) if an employer did not offer coverage. For employers who provided coverage but that coverage did not provide minimum value or was not affordable, the fee was the lesser of $3K per full-time employee receiving a subsidy, or $2K per full-time employee (minus the first 30).

Small businesses were not required to contribute a percentage of their payroll toward the costs of the national plan as a penalty for not offering "meaningful" coverage.

This promise was fulfilled.

1.00

HE-21

The Promise: "...will also phase in requirements for full implementation of health IT and commit the necessary federal resources to make it happen."
When/Where: Obama-Biden Plan: "To Lower Health Care Costs and Ensure Affordable, Accessible Health Coverage For All," dated 10/03/08.
Source: http://mendocinohre.org/rhic/200812/HealthCareFullPlan.pdf
Status: Under the American Recovery and Reinvestment Act (ARRA) of 2009, $250M was made available to 17 "beacon communities" for clinicians, hospitals and consumers to work together to implement "health IT."

In addition to funds made available to the Office of the National Coordinator for Health Information Technology, nearly $29M was provided on an annual basis to the Agency for Health Care Research and Quality (AHRQ) to advanced the use of "health IT" and to the Office of Civil Rights to strengthen and enforce "health IT" privacy rules.

President Obama's FY2011 budget proposal included $110M for continuing efforts to "strengthen

1.00

Chapter 6 - Department of Health & Human Services

health IT policy, coordination and research activities."

This promise was fulfilled.

HE-22

The Promise: "Require that plans that participate in the new public plan, Medicare or the Federal Employee Health Benefits Program (FEHBP) utilize disease management programs to improve efficiency and lower costs."
When/Where: Obama-Biden Plan to Lower Health Care Costs and Ensure Affordable, Accessible Health Coverage For All, dated 10/03/08.
Source: http://mendocinohre.org/rhic/200812/HealthCareFullPlan.pdf
Status: To keep the background of this promise in perspective, in CY2004, a Congressional Budget Office (CBO) study revealed that there was "insufficient evidence to conclude that disease management programs can generally reduce overall health spending."

Further, the Centers for Medicare & Medicaid Services (CMS) awarded grants in CY2005 to see whether disease management programs would cut Medicare costs and improve quality of care. CMS shut this program down in CY2008 because three of the eight grantees dropped out of the study citing cost overruns. The remaining five could not substantiate cost reductions in terms of fewer hospitalizations or emergency room visits by the approximately 150,000 Medicare recipients studied.

A CY2009 CBO report further stated that there was "no conclusive evidence that [disease management] reduces overall costs and only limited evidence that it can improve quality care for some conditions."

However, the FEHBP, in which approximately 250 local and national plans participate to serve about 8M enrollees, has had a robust disease management program targeted to care for members with chronic or life-threatening diseases in the areas of asthma, diabetes, cardiovascular disease, and cancer.

Multiple sections of the Patient Protection and Affordable Care Act (ACA) (Public Law 111-148), signed into law by President Obama on 03/23/10, address "disease management" initiatives and incentives either directly or under the umbrella of a Patient-Centered Medical Homes (PCMH) program. However, nowhere in the ACA does it specifically levy a requirement that plans utilize disease management programs to improve efficiency and lower costs, except that the participation in such programs would be directly tied to a health care provider's reimbursement structure starting in CY2012.

The Health Care and Education Act of 2010 (H.R. 4872) signed into law by President Obama on 03/30/10 makes no mention of disease management program participation.

This promise was not fulfilled.

0.00

HE-23

The Promise: "...will require hospitals and providers to collect and publicly report measures of health care costs and quality, including data on preventable medical errors, nurse staffing ratios, hospital-acquired infections, and disparities in care and costs."
When/Where: Obama-Biden Plan: "To Lower Health Care Costs and Ensure Affordable, Accessible Health Coverage For All," dated 10/03/08.
Source: http://mendocinohre.org/rhic/200812/HealthCareFullPlan.pdf
Status: The Patient Protection and Affordable Care Act (ACA) of 2010 signed into law by President Obama on 03/30/10, contains provisions for the reporting of medical errors. On nurse staffing ratios, however, reporting requirements are limited to nurse staffing levels for "skilled nursing facilities and nursing facilities" (Sections 6103 and 6112).

Reporting on hospital-acquired infections is mandated by Section 10303 of the ACA.

1.00

Reporting requirements for disparities in health care provision and related costs are also addressed extensively in the ACA, notably in Sections 4201 and 4302.

This promise was fulfilled.

HE-24

The Promise: "...will also challenge the medical system to eliminate inequities in health care by requiring hospitals and health plans to collect, analyze and report health care quality for disparity populations and holding them accountable for any differences found..."
When/Where: Obama-Biden Plan: "To Lower Health Care Costs and Ensure Affordable, Accessible Health Coverage For All," dated 10/03/08.
Source: http://mendocinohre.org/rhic/200812/HealthCareFullPlan.pdf
Status: The Patient Protection and Affordable Care Act (ACA) of 2009, signed into law by President Obama on 03/30/10, includes "programs that address, identify, and ameliorate health care disparities among principal at-risk subpopulations." Specifically:

- Section 4201 of the ACA (Community Transformation Grants) makes funds available for entities for "prioritizing strategies to reduce racial and ethnic disparities, including social, economic, and geographic determinants of health."
- Section 4302 of the ACA (Understanding Health Disparities Data Collection and Analysis) mandates that by 03/30/12, "any federally conducted or supported health care or public health program, activity or survey...collects and reports...any other demographic data as deemed appropriate by the Secretary [of Health and Human Services] regarding health disparities."

Lacking in the ACA of 2009 was the requirement for hospitals and health care plans to report on the quality of health care provided to disparity populations.

In the interim, the "HHS Action Plan to Reduce Racial and Ethnic Health Disparities" of 04/11 acknowledged HHS' limited ability "to identify disparities and effectively monitor efforts to reduce them by a lack of specificity, uniformity, and quality in data collection and reporting procedures" and outlined the steps HHS would take to address this situation, to include steps it would take to ensure accountability. Also in 04/11, the Obama Administration released its "National Stakeholder Strategy for Achieving Health Equity" which further reflected a reporting and accountability commitment.

The "Health Equity and Accountability Act (HEAA)" (H.R. 5475) to codify reporting requirements excluded from the ACA of 2009, introduced by Congresswoman Robin Kelly (D-IL) on 06/14/16, was not enacted.

Nonetheless, this promise was fulfilled.

1.00

HE-25

The Promise: "Reimburse employer health plans for a portion of the catastrophic costs they incur above a threshold if they guarantee such savings are used to reduce the cost of workers' premiums."
When/Where: Obama-Biden Plan: "To Lower Health Care Costs and Ensure Affordable, Accessible Health Coverage For All," dated 10/03/08.
Source: http://mendocinohre.org/rhic/200812/HealthCareFullPlan.pdf
Status: Section 1102 of the Patient Protection and Affordable Care Act (ACA) (Public Law 111-148), signed into law by President Obama on 03/23/10, states that "...the Secretary [of Health and Human Services] shall reimburse such plan for 80 percent of that portion of the costs attributable to such claim that...shall not be less than $15,000 nor greater than $90,000..." and "shall be used to lower costs of the plan....Such payments shall not be used as general revenues for an entity...".

The reimbursements under the ACA did not directly relate to "catastrophic costs they [employer health plans] incur above a threshold." By some accounts, such costs typically exceeded $90,000.

This promise was not fulfilled.

0.00

HE-26 | **The Promise:** "...will expand funding, including loan repayment, adequate reimbursement, grants for | 1.00

Chapter 6 - Department of Health & Human Services

training curricula, and infrastructure support to improve working conditions to ensure a strong workforce that will champion prevention and public health activities."

When/Where: Obama-Biden Plan to Lower Health Care Costs and Ensure Affordable, Accessible Health Coverage For All, dated 10/03/08.

Source: http://courses.ischool.berkeley.edu/i202/f08/lectures/Obama_Healthcare-1.pdf

Status: The American Recovery and Reinvestment Act (ARRA) of 2009 provided $1.5B to the Department of Health and Human Services (HHS) for "grants for construction, renovation and equipment...for health centers" and $300M for the National Health Service Corps (NHSC) "to address professions shortages...to provide scholarships, loan repayment, and grants to training programs...". Of this amount, $240M was for the recruitment of clinicians to serve in health professional shortage areas and the balance is for field operations.

The Patient Protection and Affordable Care Act (ACA) of 2010 goes even further. The levels of funding authorized for the NHSC under the ACA were as follows: FY2010-$320M, FY2011-$414M, FY2012-$535M, FY2013-$691M, FY2014-$893M, and FY2015-$1.1B. For FY2016 and each fiscal year thereafter, the amount appropriated was to be the preceding year's authorization plus adjustments. Starting from a workforce baseline of 3.6K NHSC health care providers in CY2008, the number nearly tripled to about 10.5K by end-CY2016.

This promise was fulfilled.

HE-27

The Promise: "...will build on America's unparalleled talent and advantage in science, technology, and engineering, and the powerful insights into biological systems that are emerging, to create new drugs, vaccines, and diagnostic tests and to manufacture these vital products much more quickly and efficiently than is now possible."

When/Where: Obama-Biden Plan on Homeland Security

Source: http://webarchive.loc.gov/all/20090429184932/http://change.gov/agenda/homeland_security_agenda/

Status: Under the American Recovery and Reinvestment Act (ARRA) of 2009, $100B was dedicated to developing science and technology capabilities and, by extension, provided funding for about 12K research projects with $750M going toward advanced heart, lung and blood disease research.

This promise was fulfilled.

1.00

HE-28

The Promise: "...will attract more doctors to rural areas."

When/Where: Obama and Biden's Plan for America: "Blueprint for Change," dated 10/09/08.

Source: https://www.documentcloud.org/documents/550007-barack-obama-2008-blueprint-for-change.html

Status: Section 5606, Subpart II of the Patient Protection and Affordable Health Care Act of 2010 included $4M in grants per year from FY2010 through FY2013 to attract medical students to complete their residencies in rural/underserved communities or at "local residency training programs that support and train physicians to practice in underserved rural communities."

This promise was fulfilled.

1.00

HE-29

The Promise: "...will also work to ensure that environmental health issues in the wake of man-made or terrorist disasters are promptly addressed by federal, state and local officials."

When/Where: Obama-Biden Plan: Promoting a Healthy Environment" dated 10/08/08.

Source: https://www.energy.gov/sites/prod/files/edg/media/Obama_Cap_and_Trade_0512.pdf

Status: Section 10323 of the Patient Protection and Affordable Care Act (ACA) of 2010 addresses environmental health conditions related to "asbestosis, pleural thickening, or pleural plaques...mesothelioma...and any other medical condition which the Secretary determines is caused by exposure to a hazardous substance or pollutant or contaminant at a Superfund site..." No mention was made of environmental health issues as a result of man-made or terrorist disasters.

However, in partnership with the Federal Emergency Management Agency (FEMA) the Centers for

1.00

Disease Control (CDC) developed an on-line Environmental Health Training in Emergency Response (EHTER) course in CY2012 to address the role of environmental health responders in preparing for, responding to, and recovering from natural and/or man-made emergencies and disasters. EHTER training covers issues and challenges in the areas of disaster management, responder safety and health, safe water, food safety, wastewater, building assessments, vectors and pests, solid waste and debris, shelters, and radiation. EHTER instructs participants on how to identify problems, hazards, and risks; plan for team response; select appropriate equipment and instrumentation; perform required tasks using environmental health response protocols; and report and participate in follow-up activities. Most of the course involves hands-on operation practice and response to simulated events. The on-line nature of EHTER training renders it available to federal, state and local environmental health responders.

This promise was fulfilled.

	HEALTH INSURANCE	GRADE
HE-30	**The Promise:** "Create a "National Health Insurance Exchange to help Americans and businesses purchase private health insurance." **When/Where:** Obama-Biden Plan to Lower Health Care Costs and Ensure Affordable, Accessible Health Coverage For All, dated 10/03/08. **Source:** http://courses.ischool.berkeley.edu/i202/f08/lectures/Obama_Healthcare-1.pdf **Status:** On 07/14/09, the House tabled its version of America's Affordable Health Choices Act (AAHCA) of 2009. Title III, Section 301 of the bill presented by the House proposed to create a National Insurance Exchange under a Health Choices Administration, with a Commissioner to run it. Section 1311 of the Senate version of the health care reform bill stated in part "Each State shall, not later than January 1, 2014, establish an American Health Benefit Exchange." The final language included in the Patient Protection and Affordable Care Act (Public Law 111-148), signed into law by President Obama on 03/23/10, supported the Senate version of the Health Care Reform effort in that the exchange was to be established at the State level, not the National level. This promise was not fulfilled.	0.00
HE-31	**The Promise:** "Require insurance companies to cover pre-existing conditions...at fair and stable premiums." **When/Where:** Obama-Biden Plan to Lower Health Care Costs and Ensure Affordable, Accessible Health Coverage For All, dated 10/03/08. **Source:** http://courses.ischool.berkeley.edu/i202/f08/lectures/Obama_Healthcare-1.pdf **Status:** Section 2704 of the Patient Protection and Affordable Care Act (Public Law 111-148) signed into law by President Obama on 03/23/10, is entitled "Prohibition of Preexisting Condition Exclusions or Other Discrimination Based on Health Status." This promise was fulfilled.	1.00
HE-32	**The Promise:** "If you don't have insurance, or don't like your insurance, you'll be able to choose from the same type of quality private plans as every federal employee...All of these plans will cover essential medical services including prevention, maternity, disease management and mental health care. No one will be turned away because of a pre-existing condition. If you change jobs, this insurance will go with you. And if you can't afford this insurance, you'll receive a tax credit to help pay for it." **When/Where:** Obama Campaign Speech, Newport News, VA dated 10/04/08. **Source:** https://2008election.procon.org/sourcefiles/Obama20081004.pdf **Status:** Section 1312 of the Patient Protection and Affordable Case Act (ACA) of 2010, signed into law on 03/30/10, stipulates that "the only health plans that the Federal Government may make available to Members of Congress and congressional staff...shall be health plans that are created under this Act...or offered through an Exchange established under this Act...".	1.00

Promised medical services are included in the ACA such as prevention (Title IV), maternity (Section 10213), and disease management and mental health care (both under Section 1302).

On 11/14/11, the Supreme Court agreed to hear the legal challenges to the ACA filed by 26 states and the National Federation of Independent Business. On 06/28/12, the Supreme Court upheld the ACA as constitutional. The majority ruled that the "individual mandate" for most U.S. citizens to obtain insurance or pay a penalty was authorized by Congressional power to levy taxes. The Supreme Court again upheld the ACA on 06/25/15.

Health plan tax credits for low-income individuals are addressed in Section 1331(e) of the ACA. As of end-CY2016, tax credits payable to insurers under the ACA were based on income and available to American taxpayers making between 100% and 400% of the Federal Poverty Level (between $11,770-$47,080 for an individual and between $24,250-$97,000 for a family of four).

This promise was fulfilled.

HE-33

The Promise: "...will expand the number of options for young adults to get coverage by allowing young people up to age 25 to continue coverage through their parents' plans."
When/Where: Obama-Biden Plan to Lower Health Care Costs and Ensure Affordable, Accessible Health Coverage For All, dated 10/03/08.
Source: http://courses.ischool.berkeley.edu/i202/f08/lectures/Obama_Healthcare-1.pdf
Status: Under the Patient Protection and Affordable Care Act (Public Law 111-148) signed into law by President Obama on 03/23/10, children will be able to get health insurance coverage under their parents' insurance plans as long as they do not have the possibility of acquiring coverage through their own employers and have not yet turned 26 -- one year longer than originally proposed by then-candidate Obama.

This promise was fulfilled.

1.00

HE-34

The Promise: "I will sign a universal health care bill into law by the end of my first term as president that will cover every American and cut the cost of a typical family's premium by up to $2,500 a year."
When/Where: Obama Campaign Speech, Hartford, CT, dated 06/23/07.
Source: http://www.presidency.ucsb.edu/ws/index.php?pid=76986
Status: President Obama signed the Patient Protection and Affordable Care Act (ACA) of 2010 on 03/23/10. This promise did not address the cost of premiums after tax credits, etc., simply the cost of premiums.

In CY2009, when President Obama became President, premiums for a "typical" family where the principal earner worked for a small business (3 to 199 employees) was about $12,696. This rose to $17,546 by CY2016 under the ACA. Premiums for workers in large companies (200 or more employees) rose from $13,704 in CY2009 to $18,142 in CY2016.

On 10/03/16, former President Bill Clinton provided his views on ACA, also referred to as "Obamacare:" "So you've got this crazy system where all of a sudden 25 million more people have health care and then the people who are out there busting it, sometimes 60 hours a week, wind up with their premiums doubled and their coverage cut in half. It's the craziest thing in the world."

As more insurance providers withdrew from ACA exchange participation such as Aetna, Humana and UnitedHealth Group, premium costs were expected to skyrocket by CY2017 with the national average increasing by about 25%. Such increases were expected to vary by state but in Phoenix, AZ alone, individual benchmark insurance premiums in the ACA marketplace were expected to increase by an estimated 145%. In Birmingham, AL, the increase was estimated to be 71% by CY2017.

One of the root problems of this evolving situation was that the number of older, sicker enrollees

0.00

outpaced the number of younger, healthier people signing up for health insurance, preferring to pay an annual fine over more expensive coverage. Another issue was that instead of the 20M insurance purchasers estimated by the Office of Management and Budget (OMB) by end-CY2016 to make ACA work, only between 11M and 13.8M people had signed up for coverage.

This promise was not fulfilled.

HE-35

The Promise: "Health plans will be required to disclose the percentage of premiums that actually goes to paying for patient care as opposed to administrative costs."
When/Where: Obama-Biden Plan: "To Lower Health Care Costs and Ensure Affordable, Accessible Health Coverage For All," dated 10/03/08.
Source: http://mendocinohre.org/rhic/200812/HealthCareFullPlan.pdf
Status: Section 2718 of the Patient Protection and Affordable Case Act of 2010, signed into law by President Obama on 03/30/10, stipulates that "A health insurance issuer offering group or individual health insurance coverage shall, with respect to each plan year, submit to the Secretary a report concerning the percentage of total premium revenue that such coverage expends (1) on reimbursement for clinical services provided to enrollees under such coverage; (2) for activities that improve health care quality; and (3) on all other non-claims costs, including an explanation of the nature of such costs, and excluding State taxes and licensing or regulatory fees."

This promise was fulfilled.

1.00

HE-36

The Promise: "In markets where the insurance business is not competitive, their plan will force insurers to pay out a reasonable share of their premiums for patient care instead of keeping exorbitant amounts for profits and administration."
When/Where: Obama-Biden Plan: "To Lower Health Care Costs and Ensure Affordable, Accessible Health Coverage For All," dated 10/03/08.
Source: http://courses.ischool.berkeley.edu/i202/f08/lectures/Obama_Healthcare-1.pdf
Status: Section 2718 of the Patient Protection and Affordable Care Act of 2010, entitled "Bringing Down the Cost of Health Care Coverage," states in part: "a State shall seek to ensure adequate participation by health insurance issuers, competition in the health insurance market in the State, and value for consumers so that premiums are used for clinical services and quality improvements."

Section 2718 also requires insurance providers to rebate part of the premiums it received if 85% of those premiums were not spent on doctor or hospital bills or activities to improve health care quality. For CY2011, for example, the UnitedHealthcare insurance company met only 84% of the established expenditure criteria and had to issue rebates equivalent to 1% of its earned premium dollars to employers or group policyholders by 08/01/12.

This promise was fulfilled.

1.00

HE-37

The Promise: "Under the plan, if you like your current health insurance, nothing changes..."
When/Where: Obama-Biden Plan to Lower Health Care Costs and Ensure Affordable, Accessible Health Coverage For All, dated 10/03/08.
Source: http://courses.ischool.berkeley.edu/i202/f08/lectures/Obama_Healthcare-1.pdf
Status: Commencing in CY2011, $132B in federal subsidies to support Medicare Advantage (MA) plans started to be phased out. With the gradual elimination of these subsidies, coverage for expenditures such as for dental care, hearing aids and eyeglasses were reduced or eliminated. Costs of premiums for these services increased as seniors tried to find similar coverage elsewhere.

So for seniors who liked their health insurance coverage under MA through CY2010, their plan started to change in CY2011. In testimony before Congress on 01/26/11, Medicare Actuary Richard Foster supported this view by stating that he expected 7M MA participants to be forced to purchase supplementary health insurance over time because of the Government's curtailment of support to the MA plans they liked and selected prior to CY2010.

0.00

Between 2.6M (an Urban Institute number) and 4.7M (as reported by the Associated Press) health insurance policies were cancelled between CY2010 and CY2014 regardless of whether a policyholder was happy with his/her plan. In most cases, the cancelled plans did not meet the coverage standards mandated by the ACA. Insurers that did not leave the individual health insurance market altogether offered their policyholders alternative plans, often plans the policyholders did not like.

Since the implementation of the Patient Protection and Affordable Care Act (ACA) on 10/01/13, not only have insurance premium rates continued to rise, but millions of health insurance policies that policyholders liked have been cancelled.

It should be noted that there was no guarantee in the ACA that policyholders would get to keep their health insurance policies just because they liked those policies.

This promise was not fulfilled.

MEDICAID	GRADE
HE-38 **The Promise:** "Expand eligibility for the Medicaid and SCHIP [State Children's Health Insurance Fund] programs and ensure that these programs continue to serve their critical safety net function." **When/Where:** Obama-Biden Plan to Lower Health Care Costs and Ensure Affordable, Accessible Health Coverage For All, dated 10/03/08. **Source:** http://courses.ischool.berkeley.edu/i202/f08/lectures/Obama_Healthcare-1.pdf **Status:** The Children's Health Insurance Program Reauthorization Act of 2009 (H.R. 2) expanded the State Children's Health Insurance Program (SCHIP) over the period CY2009-CY2014. President Obama signed this Act into law on 02/04/09. The SCHIP was further reinforced under the Medicare and Medicaid Extenders Act of 2010 (H.R. 4994) signed by President Obama on 12/15/10. The Medicaid eligibility expansion part of this promise was kept by inclusion of $87B for this purpose in the American Recovery and Reinvestment Act (ARRA) of 2009 of 02/17/09. Under the Patient Protection and Affordable Care Act (ACA) (Public Law 111-148) signed into law by President Obama on 03/23/10, Medicaid was further expanded starting in CY2014 for individuals "who are under 65 years of age, not pregnant, not entitled to, or enrolled for, benefits under Part A of Title XVIII, or enrolled for benefits under Part B of Title XVIII....and whose income...does not exceed 133 percent of the poverty line...". In CY2011, however, additional Medicaid assistance provided by the government to states ran out. Consequently, more than half of the states reduced payments to health providers, 23 lowered spending on prescription drugs, and 20 restricted coverage of other services. Nonetheless, expanding eligibility for Medicaid became a reality when the ACA Act was fully implemented starting in CY2014. This promise was fulfilled.	1.00

MEDICAL INFRASTRUCTURE	GRADE
HE-39 **The Promise:** "...will rebuild broken facilities and provide incentives, such as loan forgiveness, to lure medical professionals back to the region." **When/Where:** Obama-Biden Plan: "Rebuilding the Gulf Coast and Preventing Future Catastrophes", dated 09/11/08. **Source:** https://assets.documentcloud.org/documents/550006/barack-obama-2008-rebuilding-the-gulf-coast-and.pdf **Status:** On 08/29/05 when Hurricane Katrina hit New Orleans, the city's health care infrastructure was devastated with its inpatient bed capacity reduced from 4,080 in the parishes of Orleans, Jefferson, Plaquemine and St. Bernard to 664.	1.00

Chapter 6 - Department of Health & Human Services

During President Obama's tenure in office, work continued to improve the availability of medical facilities in New Orleans. Examples: (1) New Orleans East Hospital, 80 beds, opened 08/14; (2) University Medical Center, 446 beds, opened 08/15; (3) VA Hospital Complex, 200 beds, opened 11/16.

The number of ambulatory care clinics in the New Orleans area was reduced from 90 to about 19 by Hurricane Katrina. As of CY2016, there were about 195 fully functional care centers and clinics in/around New Orleans.

In the aftermath of Hurricane Katrina, an estimated 4,500 physicians were dislocated, approximately 35% of them being primary care doctors. The Department of Health and Human Services (HHS) stepped in with a $100M Primary Care and Stabilization Grant (PCASG) to support neighborhood primary and behavioral health care system, administered by the Louisiana Public Health Institute (LPHI).

The College Cost Reduction Act, signed into law by President Obama in 07/09, allowed students to pay off loans backed by federal guarantees at rates tied to their income, and have those loans forgiven after 10 years of public service in all levels of government and 501(c)3 or nonprofit organizations. This program served as a means to provide loan forgiveness for some physicians to return to New Orleans.

This promise was fulfilled.

HE-40

The Promise: "...will fight to establish a major medical complex in downtown New Orleans that will serve the entire community."
When/Where: Obama-Biden Plan: "Rebuilding the Gulf Coast and Preventing Future Catastrophes", dated 09/11/08.
Source: https://assets.documentcloud.org/documents/550006/barack-obama-2008-rebuilding-the-gulf-coast-and.pdf
Status: Ground was broken on 04/18/11 for a new $1.2B University Medical Center (UMC) to be built in New Orleans. The facility opened for business on 08/01/15.

Strategically located to permit the sharing of facilities and services with the future New Orleans VA Medical Center (opened in 11/16 with 200 beds), the new UMC occupies 37 acres in the Biosciences District and acts as a Level 1 trauma center to provide critical care for the area's most severely injured patients. The bed count for this new facility is 446. To avoid a repeat of the destruction caused by Hurricane Katrina, the UMC was constructed more than 20 feet above sea level and can withstand a Category 3 hurricane.

This promise was fulfilled.

Grade: **1.00**

MEDICARE — GRADE

HE-41

The Promise: "...eliminate the excessive subsidies to Medicare Advantage plans and pay them the same amount it would cost to treat the same patients under regular Medicare."
When/Where: Obama-Biden Plan: "To Lower Health Care Costs and Ensure Affordable, Accessible Health Coverage For All," dated 10/03/08.
Source: http://mendocinohre.org/rhic/200812/HealthCareFullPlan.pdf
Status: The Department of Health and Human Services budget for 2010 provided $311M for greater program integrity oversight for the Medicare program, including Medicare Advantage (Part C) against fraud, waste and abuse. According to a Government Accountability Office (GAO) analyses, Part C cost the American taxpayer $48B in fraudulent Medicare claims in CY2010 alone.

Section 3308 of the Patient Protection and Affordable Case Act of 2010, signed into law by President Obama on 03/30/10 and entitled "Reducing Part D Premium Subsidy for High-Income Beneficiaries,"

Grade: **1.00**

supported promise fulfillment.

Further, under the Health Care and Education Reconciliation Act of 2010 also signed into law by President Obama on 03/30/10 to amend the ACA, government subsidies to Medicare Advantage, the private-health plan alternative to traditional Medicare, were cut back steeply. Prior to this Act, the government paid the private plans an average of 14% more than traditional Medicare. This law, besides reducing payments overall, shifted the funding -- some high-cost areas would be paid 5% less than traditional Medicare, while some lower cost areas would be paid up to 15% more.

This promise was fulfilled.

HE-42

The Promise: "...close the 'doughnut hole' in the Medicare Part D Prescription Drug Program that limits benefits for seniors with more than $2,250 but less than $5,100 in annual drug costs."
When/Where: Obama-Biden Plan: "Helping America's Seniors" dated 10/26/07.
Source: https://www.politifact.com/truth-o-meter/promises/obameter/promise/48/close-the-donut-hole-in-medicare-prescription-dr/
Status: Source is cited for confirmation of exact promise wording only, as it existed before original "When/Where" campaign document was deleted from archival websites.

The CY2010 numbers were actually more than $2,800 but less than $4,550. In application, after a $310 deductible, drug costs were reimbursed at 75% when they were less than $2,800 annually, and Medicare covered 95% of the cost of drugs once their accumulated cost rose above $4.550 annually. Between these two numbers ($1,750 - called the "donut hole" or gap), there was no reimbursement.

Under the Patient Protection and Affordable Care Act (ACA) (Public Law 111-148) signed into law by President Obama on 03/23/10, any Medicare Part D beneficiary who crossed into the donut hole in CY2010 received a $250 check to help defray their prescription drug costs.

1.00

By CY2016, the coverage gap (donut hole) began once a beneficiary's Medicare Part D plan's initial coverage limit ($3,310) and ended when the beneficiary spent a total of $4,850, a gap of $1,540. Enrollees received a 55% discount on the total cost of their brand-name drugs purchased while in the donut hole. The 50% discount paid by the brand-name drug manufacturer applied to getting out of the donut hole, however the additional 5% paid by Medicare Part D plan did not count toward an enrollee's True Out-of-Pocket (TrOOP) expenses. Enrollees also paid a maximum of 58% co-pay on generic drugs purchased while in the coverage gap (a 42% discount).

Dependent upon the coverage plan selected, Part D premiums range from $10 to $100 per month. The maximum deductible for Part D in CY2016 was $360.

While President Obama didn't close the doughnut hole during his two terms in office, he is credited with laying the groundwork in the ACA for its elimination by CY2020.

This promise was fulfilled.

HE-43

The Promise: "...will ensure seniors are provided with information about the best prescription drug plans for them every year....will require companies to send Medicare Part D beneficiaries a complete list of the drugs the individual used the past year as well as the pertinent fees paid the previous year. Companies will also be required to provide seniors with online versions of this information, so that they can use it at a third-party comparison shopping site, similar to Priceline.com."
When/Where: Obama-Biden Plan: "Helping America's Seniors" dated 10/26/07.
Source: https://www.politifact.com/truth-o-meter/promises/obameter/promise/49/provide-easy-to-understand-comparisons-of-the-medi/
Status: Source is cited for confirmation of exact promise wording only, as it existed before original "When/Where" campaign document was deleted from archival websites.

1.00

Chapter 6 - Department of Health & Human Services

The Patient Protection and Affordable Care Act (H.R. 3590) signed into law on 03/23/10 includes Section 3021 entitled "Health Information Technology Enrollment Standards and Protocols" that provides a "...capability for individuals to apply, recertify and manage their eligibility information online, including at home, at points of service, and other community-based locations." This is the closest reference toward a simplified, automated process for individual health care subscibers.

The Center for Medicare and Medicaid Services (CMS) provides access to information related to prescribed drugs and medications to beneficiaries through its MyMedicare.gov website. The CMS publication "Medicare and You" further states that "Each month that you fill a prescription, your drug plan mails you an "Explanation of Benefits" (EOB) notice." Some plans give the beneficiary the option of accessing the EOB online. The EOB is a summary of the services and items a beneficiary has received and how much he or she may owe for them. It tells the beneficiary how much the provider billed, the approved amount the plan has paid, and how much the beneficiary has to pay to the provider.

Also, the CMS Medicare Prescription Drug Benefit Manual, Chapter 14, Section 50.2 states in part that "Beginning in 2010...Part D sponsors are required to notify each beneficiary of his/her other prescription drug coverage information reflected in the Coordination of Benefits (COB) file from CMS, and request that the beneficiary review the information and report back only updates (that is, corrections to existing information and new coverage information) to the sponsor."

This promise was fulfilled.

HE-44	**The Promise:** "Allow Medicare to negotiate for cheaper drug prices...repeal the ban on direct negotiation with drug companies..." **When/Where:** Obama-Biden Plan: "To Lower Health Care Costs and Ensure Affordable, Accessible Health Coverage For All," dated 10/03/08. **Source:** http://mendocinohre.org/rhic/200812/HealthCareFullPlan.pdf **Status:** Widely reported backroom deals between President Obama and the Pharmaceutical Research and Manufacturers of America (PhRMA) on 08/04/09 resulted in an agreement for the brand name drug manufacturers to pay new fees and, with effect in CY2011, provide a 50% discount on Medicare Part D prescriptions. The Patient Protection and Affordable Care Act of 2009 made numerous references to "negotiated" drug prices, but fell short of specifying the negotiating parties when it came to Medicare Part D. Despite 92% of the American people favoring the federal government's ability to negotiate drug prices for Medicare Part D beneficiaries, the Secretary of the Department of Health and Human Services (HHS) is explicitly prohibited, under current law, from negotiating directly with drug manufacturers on behalf of these enrollees. A majority of members of Congress (96% of Democrats, 92% of Republicans, and 92% of Independents) support such negotiations. On 01/06/15, Senator Amy Klobuchar (D-MN) introduced the "Medicare Prescription Drug Price Negotiation Act of 2015" (S. 31). On 09/15/15, Congressman Elijah Cummings introduced the "Prescription Drug Affordability Act of 2015" (H.R. 3513). Either of these bills would have enabled HHS to negotiate cheaper drugs with pharmaceutical companies. Neither of these bills were given a chance of being signed into law before the 114th Congress expired at the end of CY2016. This promise was not fulfilled.	0.00
HE-45	**The Promise:** "Amend the Medicare 'homebound' rule, which requires severely disabled recipients to stay in their homes to retain benefits, so that they have the freedom to leave their homes without fear of having their home-health benefits taken away." **When/Where:** Obama-Biden Plan: "Empower Americans with Disabilities," dated 09/06/08. **Source:** http://www.thearc.org/document.doc?id=3073	1.00

Status: Section 30.1.1 of the Centers for Medicare and Medicaid Services (CMS) Medicare Benefit Policy Manual (Revision 208 effective 01/01/15) defines the homebound policy as "Any absence of an individual from the home attributable to the need to receive health care treatment, including regular absences for the purpose of participating in therapeutic, psychosocial, or medical treatment in an adult day-care program that is licensed or certified by a State, or accredited to furnish adult day-care services in a State, shall not disqualify an individual from being considered to be confined to his home. Any other absence of an individual from the home shall not so disqualify an individual if the absence is of an infrequent or of relatively short duration. For purposes of the preceding sentence, any absence for the purpose of attending a religious service shall be deemed to be an absence of infrequent or short duration. It is expected that in most instances, absences from the home that occur will be for the purpose of receiving health care treatment. However, occasional absences from the home for nonmedical purposes, e.g., an occasional trip to the barber, a walk around the block or a drive, attendance at a family reunion, funeral, graduation, or other infrequent or unique event would not necessitate a finding that the patient is not homebound if the absences are undertaken on an infrequent basis or are of relatively short duration and do not indicate that the patient has the capacity to obtain the health care provided outside rather than in the home."

Thus a Medicare beneficiary may leave his/her home on an "infrequent or short duration" basis without fear of having their home-health benefits taken away.

This promise was fulfilled.

	PHARMACEUTICALS	GRADE
HE-46	**The Promise:** "Prevent drug companies from blocking generic drugs from consumers...will work to ensure that market power does not lead to higher prices for consumers.." **When/Where:** Obama-Biden Plan: "To Lower Health Care Costs and Ensure Affordable, Accessible Health Coverage For All," dated 10/03/08. **Source:** http://mendocinohre.org/rhic/200812/HealthCareFullPlan.pdf **Status:** For decades, some brand-name drug manufacturers have resorted to "product switching" or "product hopping" tactics designed to delay or prevent entirely the entry of generic drugs into the market, thereby protecting their market shares. Reportedly, brand name drug manufacturers have benefited from price fixing deals (reverse payment agreements to protect patent holders) with generic drug manufacturers to delay the entry of generic drugs on the market, as authorized under the Drug Price Competition and Patent Term Restoration Act of 1984. The Patient Protection and Affordable Care Act (ACA) of 2009 included a provision mandating that the Secretary of Health and Human Services shall "facilitate generic substitution when a generic covered outpatient drug is available at a lower price" but fell far short of preventing brand name drug manufacturers from blocking generic drug manufacturers. In fact, the Section 7002 of the ACA protects the brand name drug manufacturers by stipulating that applications for generic (biosimilar) drugs "may not be made effective by the Secretary until the date that is 12 years after the date on which the reference product was first licensed...". President Obama's FY2010 budget proposal included language "prohibiting anticompetitive agreements and collusion between brand name and generic drug manufacturers intended to keep generic drugs off the market" and prohibiting drug manufacturers from "reformulating existing products into new products." Several bills to codify the objective of this promise were introduced in Congress since CY2009. On 09/22/15, Senator Amy Klobuchar (D-MN) introduced a new iteration of the "Preserve Access to Affordable Generics Act" (S.2019) which had as its purpose: "(1) to enhance competition in the pharmaceutical market by stopping anticompetitive agreements between brand name and generic	0.00

drug manufacturers that limit, delay, or otherwise prevent competition from generic drugs; and (2) to support the purpose and intent of antitrust law by prohibiting anticompetitive practices in the pharmaceutical industry that harm consumers." This bill was not enacted before the 114th Congress expired at the end of CY2016.

This promise was not fulfilled.

HE-47

The Promise: "... will allow Americans to buy their medicines from other developed countries if the drugs are safe and prices are lower outside the U.S."
When/Where: Obama-Biden Plan: "To Lower Health Care Costs and Ensure Affordable, Accessible Health Coverage For All," dated 10/03/08.
Source: http://mendocinohre.org/rhic/200812/HealthCareFullPlan.pdf
Status: In return for pledges by the pharmaceutical companies to put up $80B over 10 years in pledged drug cost reductions, it appeared that the White House had assented to move away from permitting the importation of cheaper drugs from developed countries such as Canada.

On 12/20/09, however, the White House reaffirmed President Obama's commitment to allow the re-importation of drugs initially produced in the U.S., exported, then imported back into the country at a lower cost than the same drug costs in the U.S.

Neither the Patient Protection and Affordable Care Act of 2010 nor the Health Care and Education Reconciliation Act of 2010 mentioned any authorization to reimport drugs from such developed countries as Canada.

Back on 10/28/00, provisions of the "Medicine Equity and Drug Safety Act" (MEDSA) and the "Prescription Drug Import Fairness Act" were signed into law by President Bill Clinton as incorporated into the "Agriculture, Rural Development, Food and Drug Administration, and Related Agencies Appropriations Act of 2001" (H.R. 4461) as Sections 745 and 746 respectively. This law permitted the importation of safe and cost effective pharmaceuticals into the USA from high-income countries such as Australia, Canada, Israel, Japan, New Zealand, Switzerland, South Africa and the European Union so long as the Secretary of Health and Human Services (HHS) certified that there was no additional risk to the purchaser and that the importation would result in "significant" savings to purchasers.

As of end-CY2016, the cited provisions of the above law had not been implemented by any Secretaries of HHS of the Obama Administrations or preceding administrations.

This promise was not fulfilled.

0.00

PREGNANCY	GRADE

HE-48

The Promise: "...will work to reduce unintended pregnancy by guaranteeing equity in contraceptive coverage, providing sex education and offering rape victims accurate information about emergency contraception."
When/Where: Obama and Biden's Plan for America: "Blueprint for Change," dated 10/09/08.
Source: https://www.documentcloud.org/documents/550007-barack-obama-2008-blueprint-for-change.html
Status: The "Safe Motherhood/Infant Health" line item in the FY2010 appropriation for the Department of Health and Human Services (HHS) includes $15.8M to provide "medically accurate and age appropriate" information on contraception to youth. This was an increase of $5M over FY2009 funding.

The Patient Protection and Affordable Care Act of 2010 authorized an additional $10M for grants "to implement innovative youth pregnancy prevention strategies and target services to high-risk, vulnerable, and culturally under-represented youth populations...".

1.00

In 10/10, the Obama Administration announced a $110M campaign to support a range of unintended pregancy prevention initiatives to include sex education and the benefits of contraception, as well as focusing on encouraging teens to delay sex.

This promise was fulfilled.

RESEARCH	GRADE

HE-49

The Promise: "As President, I will lift the current administration's ban on federal funding of research on embryonic stem cell lines created after August 9, 2001 through executive order."
When/Where: Science Debate 2008, Obama Response to Top Science Questions, 08/30/08.
Source: https://abcnews.go.com/Health/Politics/story?id=6224566&page=1
Status: Embryonic Stem Cells (ESC) are cells that can morph into any cell of the body. Potentially, they could someday cure such ailments as spinal cord injuries, quadriplegia, diabetes, and Parkinson's Disease.

President Obama signed Executive Order 13505 on 03/09/09 entitled "Removing Barriers to Responsible Scientific Research Involving Human Stem Cells". This Executive Order revoked the Presidential Statement of 08/09/01 limiting federal funding for embryonic stem cell research as well as its supplementing Executive Order 13435 dated 06/20/07.

According to Executive Order 13505, the Secretary of Health and Human Services (HHS), through the Director of National Institutes of Health (NIH), "may support and conduct responsible, scientifically worthy human stem cell research, including human embryonic stem cell research, to the extent permitted by law."

The U.S. District Court of Washington, D.C. ruled on 08/23/10 that federal funding could not be used for Embryonic Stem Cell (ESC) research under the Dickey-Wicker Amendment (P.L. 104-99) of CY1996 until that law was changed by Congress. On 07/27/11, the same court ruled (in Sherley v. Sebelius) in favor of federally funded embryonic stem cell research because such research was not "research in which a human...embryos are destroyed." The ruling further stated that the "policy question is not answered by any congressional law, and it has fallen on three presidential administrations to provide an answer. For all three such administrations, Democratic and Republican, the answer has been to permit federal funding. They have differed only as to the path forward."

The NIH authorized the first 13 lines of cells on 12/02/09. By end-CY2016, nearly 400 lines were eligible for NIH-funded research as listed in the NIH Human Embryonic Stem Cell Registry.

This promise was fulfilled.

1.00

HE-50

The Promise: "I will ensure that all research on stem cells is conducted ethically and with rigorous oversight."
When/Where: Science Debate 2008, Obama Response to Top Science Questions, 08/30/08.
Source: https://abcnews.go.com/Health/Politics/story?id=6224566&page=1
Status: Executive Order 13505 lifting restrictions on stem cell research that was signed on 03/09/09 by President Obama also directed the Secretary of Health and Human Services to issue new guidelines for the research within 120 days (by mid-07/09). According to President Obama's Executive Order, these guidelines were to include "provisions establishing appropriate safeguards," and should be updated "periodically..."

On 04/23/09, the National Institutes of Health (NIH) published draft stem cell guidelines for public comment. By 05/26/09, nearly 50,000 comments on the draft guidelines had been received and NIH published them on its web site. The final guidelines were published with an effective date of 07/07/09.

This promise was fulfilled.

1.00

Chapter 6 - Department of Health & Human Services

HE-51	**The Promise:** "...will establish an independent institute to guide reviews and research on comparative effectiveness, so that Americans and their doctors will have accurate and objective information to make the best decisions for their health and well-being." **When/Where:** Obama-Biden Plan to Lower Health Care Costs and Ensure Affordable, Accessible Health Coverage For All, dated 10/03/08. **Source:** http://courses.ischool.berkeley.edu/i202/f08/lectures/Obama_Healthcare-1.pdf **Status:** The American Recovery and Reinvestment Act of 2009 signed into law by President Obama on 02/17/09 started promise fulfillment by investing $700M for "comparative effectiveness research". Under the Patient Protection and Affordable Care Act (Public Law 111-148) signed into law by President Obama on 03/23/10, a new Patient-Centered Outcomes Research Institute was created to fund comparisons of medical treatments. This promise was fulfilled.	1.00
HE-52	**The Promise:** "...making steady increases that double NIH's [National Institutes of Health] budget over ten years..." **When/Where:** Obama-Biden Plan for Science and Innovation, dated 09/25/08. **Source:** http://www.faseb.org/portals/2/pdfs/opa/2008/ObamaFactSheetScience.pdf **Status:** The NIH budget in FY2009 was enacted at $30.5B. This was the amount to "double" by FY2019. The FY2009 authorization was supplemented by $10.4B under the American Recovery and Reinvestment Act (ARRA) of 2009 for a total of $40.9B. The following represents NIH budget authorizations during subsequent years: FY2010....$31.2B FY2011....$30.9B FY2012....$30.8B FY2013....$29.1B FY2014....$30.1B FY2015....$29.3B FY2016....$31.3B FY2017....$33.1B As reflected above, the promised "steady increases" that could have led to doubling the NIH budget in 10 years did not happen during President Obama's two terms in office. This promise was not fulfilled.	0.00
	HEALTH & HUMAN SERVICES GPA	**0.69**

Campaign Promises

Departments -> Homeland Security

ITEM	HOMELAND SECURITY	
	BORDER SECURITY	**GRADE**
HS-1	**The Promise:** "Support the virtual and physical infrastructure and manpower necessary to secure our borders and keep our nation safe." **When/Where:** Obama-Biden Plan for Homeland Security dated 11/16/08. **Source:** http://webarchive.loc.gov/all/20090429184932/http://change.gov/agenda/homeland_security_agenda/ **Status:** According to the Department of Homeland Security (DHS), the USA was home to approximately 12M illegal immigrants as of CY2016. In CY2009, 132K of 392K illegal aliens apprehended were classified as "criminal aliens" by the Immigration and Customs Enforcement (ICE) agency and deported. In CY2016, 135K criminal aliens were apprehended and deported. The American Recovery and Reinvestment Act (ARRA) of 2009 provided $280M for technology improvements along the southern border, $420M for construction of Customs & Border Protection (CBP) facilities, and $1B for airport explosives detection systems. The Total Budget Authority (TBA) for the Department of Homeland Security (DHS) for FY2010 was $56.0B, a $3.3B increase over the FY2009 authorization (excluding $2.8B from the ARRA) and included $368M to support 20,000 CBP agents protecting 7,479 miles of U.S. borders with Mexico and Canada, as well as the coastal waters around Florida and Puerto Rico. Under President Obama, the TBA for DHS had risen to $68.3B for FY2017. Six (6) unarmed "Predator B" Unmanned Aerial Systems (UAS) provided border surveillance in the Southwest as of CY2016 with another three (3) operating along the border with Canada between Minnesota and the State of Washington. These are supplemented by eight (8) aerostats that form the Tethered Aerostat Radar System (TARS) to provide surveillance of the U.S./Mexico border, south Florida and Puerto Rico, as well as some 16,800 vehicles, 245 aircraft, 295 watercraft, and 300 camera towers. On 05/25/10, President Obama ordered the deployment of 1,200 National Guard troops to the border under "Operation Phalanx." This broke down to 524 for Arizona, 250 for Texas, 224 for California, 72 for New Mexico, and 130 for Command and Control and other support functions. A Government Accountability Office (GAO) report at that time, indicated that only 44% of the Southwest border (about 860 miles) was under the CBP's operational control. On 08/11/10, the Senate approved $600M for an additional 1,000 border agents, 250 CBP agents, and 250 ICE agents. President Obama signed this bill on 08/13/10, bringing the number of agents along the border with Mexico to 18,200. FY2009 enacted authorizations were $11.30B plus $680M under the ARRA for the CBP and $6.03B plus $20M under the ARRA for ICE. The operational budget numbers under President Obama were as follows:	1.00

Year.............CBP..............ICE
FY2010....$11.84B........$5.82B
FY2011....$11.24B........$5.80B
FY2012....$11.78B........$5.98B
FY2013....$11.66B........$5.62B
FY2014....$12.39B........$5.94B
FY2015....$12.77B........$6.18B
FY2016....$13.26B........$6.17B
FY2017....$14.33B........$6.70B

For Border Security Fencing, Infrastructure and Technology:
FY2009....$745.0M
FY2010....$800.0M
FY2011....$573.0M
FY2012....$385.1M
FY2013....$307.4M
FY2014....$351.5M
FY2015....$420.3M
FY2016....$447.5M
FY2017....$533.0M

By end-CY2016, nearly 700 of the 1,969 mile border with Mexico had been fenced off. Recorded apprehensions accounted for about 80% of 500K suspected illegal crossings.

Manpower to enforce the nation's border security did not fare well under President Obama. CBP Agent staffing in CY2009 was 20,119 (17,408 for the Southwest Border, 1,887 for the Northern Border, and 223 for Coastal Border sectors). By end-CY2016, despite manpower increases in CY2010-CY2012, the total number of agents had dropped to 19,828 (17,026 Southwest, 2,059 Northern, and 211 for Coastal sectors). Total ICE personnel strength went up from about 12,500 in CY2009 to about 19,300 in CY2015.

As of end-CY2016, President Obama had delivered on his promise to "support" border security initiatives in terms of personnel, infrastructure and technology.

This promise was fulfilled.

COAST GUARD	GRADE

| HS-2 | **The Promise:** "...will increase investment in riverine craft and small coastal patrol craft, and ensure the maximum interoperability between the Navy and the Coast Guard."
 When/Where: Obama Campaign Document "A 21st Century Military for America" dated 11/26/07.
 Source: https://www.scribd.com/document/6245756/Barack-Obama-on-Defense-Issues-A-21st-Century-Military-for-America
 Status: Although classified as one of the nation's armed forces, the homeland security aspect of the U.S. Coast Guard's (USCG) mission dictates that this promise be included under the Department of Homeland Security (DHS).

 As of CY2009, 56% of the the USCG's mission performance was dedicated to Homeland Security, including 11% for illegal drug interdiction, 11% for the interdiction of illegal immigrants, and 8% for defense readiness. Non-Homeland Security missions included 14% for aids-to-navigation services, 13% for "living marine resources," 8% for search and rescue services, and 7% for marine safety services.

 For years, U.S. Navy (USN) and USCG interoperability has been assured through joint exercises and operations as mandated by a Joint Navy/Coast Guard Policy Statement signed by the Chief of Naval | 1.00 |

Operations and the Commandant of the Coast Guard, on 03/03/06. The objective of that statement was to implement the National Strategy for Maritime Security (NSMS). In 08/15, the USN Chief of Naval Operations and the USCG Commandant refined the implementation of the NSMS by signing the National Fleet Plan which articulates the joint interoperability objectives related to: integrated logistics; training; maritime security cooperation; command, control and communications systems; sensors; weapon systems; engineering systems; platforms; and intelligence and information integration.

The investment in riverine and small patrol craft falls under the purview of the USCG. In his FY2010 DHS budget submission, President Obama included $103M for 30 boats to replace the USCG's aging 41-foot utility boats and other non-standard boats.

The FY2011 budget submission included $45M for the design of a new Offshore Patrol Cutter to replace an aging fleet of cutters and patrol boats. The FY2012 request included $358M to construct six more Fast Response Cutters and $130M to acquire two more Maritime Patrol Aircraft. The FY2013 budget request included $658M to construct the 6th USCG National Security Cutter and $8M for the USCG to initiate acquisition of a new polar icebreaker to replace aging vessels.

This promise to increase investments in USCG assets to improve interoperability with the USN was fulfilled.

	CYBER SECURITY	GRADE
HS-3	**The Promise:** "....will ensure that his administration develops a Cyber Security Strategy that ensures that we have the ability to identify our attackers and a plan for how to respond that will be measured but effective." **When/Where:** Fact Sheet: Obama's New Plan to Confront 21st Century Threats, 07/16/08 **Source:** https://www.presidency.ucsb.edu/documents/press-release-fact-sheet-obamas-new-plan-confront-21st-century-threats **Status:** On 02/09/09, Obama ordered a 60-day intra-agency review to determine the USG's reactive posture toward cyber warfare. The resulting report was released on 05/29/09 by President Obama and is entitled "Cyberspace Policy Review - Assuring a Trusted and Resilient Information and Communications Infrastructure."	1.00

One of the near-term goals articulated in the above document was: "Prepare for the President's approval an updated national strategy to secure the information and communications infrastructure."

On 05/16/11, the White House presented a set of cybersecurity policy proposals. According to President Obama, the initiative represented "not only a vision for the future of cyberspace but an agenda for realizing it." His "International Strategy for Cyberspace" reinforced the Administration's focus on cybersecurity and counter-censorship.

In 07/11, the Department of Defense (DoD) released its "Strategy for Operating in Cyberspace," making it clear that the Pentagon reserved the right to respond to foreign attacks on its cyber networks with military force. This provision was retained in the Pentagon's release of its "Cyberspace Policy Report" in mid-11/11. Further to that report, DoD released its specific five-point strategy to secure its cybersecurity initiatives on 04/17/15. That strategy was summarized as: (1) Build and maintain ready forces and capabilities to conduct cyberspace operations; (2) Defend the DoD information network, secure DoD data, and mitigate risks to DoD missions; (3) Be prepared to defend the U.S. homeland and U.S. vital interests from disruptive or destructive cyberattacks of significant consequence; (4) Build and maintain viable cyber options and plan to use those options to control conflict escalation and to shape the conflict environment at all stages; and (5) Build and maintain robust international alliances and partnerships to deter shared threats and increase international security and stability.

After nearly a decade of partisan haggling, the "Cybersecurity Act of 2015" was signed into law on 12/18/15 as Division N of the FY2016 omnibus spending bill, the "Consolidated Appropriations Act of

Chapter 7 - Department of Homeland Security

2016" (H.R. 2019). Less than a month later on 01/08/16, Congressman Amash Justin (R-MI) introduced H.R. 4350 entitled "To Repeal the Cybersecurity Act of 2015" which would delete Division N in its entirety. The premise for the repeal is that the "Cybersecurity Act of 2015" won't prevent cyber attacks, threatens personal privacy, and is considered by some to be illegitimate. This legislation expired with the 114th Congress at the end of CY2016.

Meanwhile, the Office of Personnel Management (OPM) revealed in 06/15 that over 21M personnel records had been hacked since 03/14. The fingerprints of 5.6M personnel were compromised in the process. In 02/16, the contact information of 20K FBI and 9K DHS personnel was made public by a hacker. Also in 02/16, the Internal Revenue Service (IRS) was hacked. Approximately 700K social security numbers were stolen, increasing identity theft risks for the owners of those social security numbers.

Nonetheless, a national Cyber Security Strategy was developed under President Obama.

This promise was fulfilled.

HS-4	**The Promise:** "Barack Obama will also initiate a grant and training program to provide federal, state, and local law enforcement agencies the tools they need to detect and prosecute cyber crime." **When/Where:** Fact Sheet: Obama's New Plan to Confront 21st Century Threats, 07/16/08 **Source:** https://www.presidency.ucsb.edu/documents/press-release-fact-sheet-obamas-new-plan-confront-21st-century-threats **Status:** The Comprehensive National Cybersecurity Initiative (CNCI) under which the proposed grant/training programs would be funded, was actually started in January 2008 during the President Bush administration, so the Obama Administration cannot lay claim to initiating these programs. A review of the Department of Homeland Security Grant Program (HSGP), established in CY2003, reveals that funds from each of the HSGP State, Local, Tribal and Territorial (SLTT) grant components (i.e. State Homeland Security Program, Urban Areas Security Initiative, Metropolitan Medical Response System and Citizen Corps Program) can be used for SLTT cybersecurity programs. Under President Obama, the Law Enforcement Cyber Center (LECC) was created on 05/18/15. The LECC enters into strategic partnerships with organizations that provide training, technical assistance, and other resources to law enforcement agencies and criminal justice practitioners to prevent, investigate, prosecute, and respond to cyber threats and cyber crimes. Organizations participating in the LECC on-line training mission include but are not limited to: - FBI Cyber Shield Alliance - Virtual Academy Cyber Certification Program; - National White Collar Crime Center (NW3C); - Secret Service - National Computer Forensics Institute (NCFI); - Department of Homeland Security The Federal Virtual Training Environment (FedVTE); - Defense Cyber Crime Center (DC3); - Department of Justice, Computer Crime and Intellectual Property Section (CCIPS); - National Computer Forensics Institute (NCFI); - National Criminal Justice Training Center (NCJTC); and - Regional Computer Forensics Laboratory (RCFL). This promise was fulfilled.	1.00
HS-5	**The Promise:** "The federal government must partner with industry and our citizens to secure personal data stored on government and private systems. An Obama administration will institute a common standard for securing such data across industries." **When/Where:** Fact Sheet: Obama's New Plan to Confront 21st Century Threats, 07/16/08 **Source:** https://www.presidency.ucsb.edu/documents/press-release-fact-sheet-obamas-new-plan-confront-21st-century-threats **Status:** Throughout the Obama Administration, multiple bills were introduced in Congress that could	0.00

have potentially addressed this promise. None of those bills passed both houses of Congress.

A small sampling of such bills:
- Data Accountability and Trust Act (H.R. 2221)
- PASS ID Act (S. 1261) "to amend Title II of the Homeland Security Act of 2002 to protect the security, confidentiality, and integrity of personally identifiable information."
- Cybersecurity Act of 2009 (S. 773)
- Cybersecurity and Internet Freedom Act of 2011 (S. 413)
- Cybersecurity Act of 2012 (S. 2105)
- A new version of the "Cybersecurity Act of 2012" (S. 3414)
- Cybersecurity Enhancement Act of 2012 (H.R. 2096) to "advance cybersecurity research, development, and technical standards."

In 01/15, President Obama released draft language to Congress for the establishment of a national data security standard. His proposal was incorporated in the Senate's "Data Security and Breach Notification Act of 2015" (S. 177) and in the House's bill by the same title (H.R.1770). Neither of these bills were signed into law before the 114th Congress expired at the end of CY2016.

The "Cybersecurity Act of 2015" (S. 754) signed into law on 12/18/15 by President Obama as Division N of the Consolidated Appropriations Act of 2016 (H.R. 2029), did not include provisions for the institution of a common standard for the protection of personal data "across industries."

Despite the efforts made by the Obama Administration to address cybersecurity matters and protect personal data, no legislation was signed into law to codify the promised "common standard."

This promise was not fulfilled.

| HS-6 | **The Promise:** "California and other states have laws requiring a company that may have disclosed a resident's personal information without authorization to inform the victim of the disclosure. Barack Obama believes that all Americans deserve the same right to know and will push for comparable federal legislation."
When/Where: Fact Sheet: Obama's New Plan to Confront 21st Century Threats, 07/16/08
Source: https://www.presidency.ucsb.edu/documents/press-release-fact-sheet-obamas-new-plan-confront-21st-century-threats
Status: The National Strategy for Trusted Identities in Cyberspace (NSTIC) was created in early-CY2011 under President Obama to improve the privacy, security and convenience of sensitive online transactions through collaborative efforts with the private sector, advocacy groups, government agencies, and other organizations.

The NSTIC was based on an online environment where individuals and organizations could trust each other because they mutually identify and authenticate their digital identities.

The "Identity Ecosystem," a less formal term for the NSTIC initiative will, when designed, developed and implemented, allow consumers to gain greater privacy and security protection from the innumerable companies that collect data on their web-surfing activities. Use of the future "Identity Ecosystem" will be voluntary.

But the thrust of this promise was to have laws in place at the national level that would require companies to notify consumers when their personal data has been disclosed to a third party. In the absence of national-level legislation and in view of the urgency associated with identity theft notifications, as of end-CY2016, residents of 47 states (less Alabama, New Mexico and South Dakota), the District of Columbia, Puerto Rico and the Virgin Islands can expect to be contacted by a business or bank should their personal data get lost or stolen.

Bills that, if combined, could have fulfilled this promise were routinely introduced during President | 0.00 |

Chapter 7 - Department of Homeland Security

Obama's two terms in office. The most recent bills include:
* Data Breach Notification and Punishing Cyber Criminals Act of 2015 (S. 1027), introduced by Senator Mark Kirk (R-IL) on 04/21/15, to require notification of information security breaches and to enhance penalties for cyber criminals.
* Data Security and Breach Notification Act of 2015 (S. 177), introduced by Senator Bill Nelson (D-FL) on 01/13/15, to protect consumers by requiring reasonable security policies and procedures to protect data containing personal information, and to provide for nationwide notice in the event of a breach of security.
* Data Security and Breach Notification Act of 2015 (H.R. 1770), introduced by Congresswoman Marshaw Blackburn (R-TN) on 04/14/15, to require certain entities who collect and maintain personal information of individuals to secure such information and to provide notice to such individuals in the case of a breach of security involving such information.
* Personal Data Notification and Protection Act of 2015 (H.R. 1704), introduced by Congressman James Langevin (D-RI) on 03/26/15, to establish a national data breach notification standard.

None of the above bills were given a chance of being signed into law before the 114th Congress expired at the end of CY2016, according to Congressional activity monitoring web site govtrack.us.

This promise was not fulfilled.

HS-7

The Promise: "...will work with industry to develop the systems necessary to protect our nation's trade secrets and our research and development."
When/Where: Obama-Biden Plan: Prevent Corporate Cyber-Espionage, undated.
Source:
https://webarchive.loc.gov/all/20090429184932/http://change.gov/agenda/homeland_security_agenda/
Status: On 02/20/13, the U.S. Attorney General Eric Holder, Acting Secretary of Commerce Rebecca Blank and Victoria Espinel, White House Intellectual Property Enforcement Coordinator at the White House, released a document entitled "Administration Strategy on Mitigating the Theft of U.S. Trade Secrets." Part of this strategy is to "promote voluntary best practices by private industry to protect trade secrets."

With support from a broad industry coalition of manufacturers such as the Boeing Company and General Electric, as well as organizations such as the Software & Information Industry Association (SIIA) and the U.S. Chamber of Commerce, President Obama signed the "Defend Trade Secrets Act of 2016" (S.1890) into law on 05/11/16.

This law provides federal jurisdiction over the theft of trade secrets. This means that U.S. companies and inventors whose trade secrets and intellectual property are proven to have been stolen by any means can seek monetary compensation for those losses in federal court.

Thus, a strategy is in place to address this promise, and some legislation is being enacted for that strategy to become a reality.

This promise was fulfilled.

1.00

HS-8

The Promise: "...will support an initiative to develop next-generation secure computers and networking for national security applications."
When/Where: Obama-Biden Plan: Initiate a Safe Computing R&D Effort and Harden our Nation's Cyber Infrastructure, undated.
Source:
https://webarchive.loc.gov/all/20090429184932/http://change.gov/agenda/homeland_security_agenda/
Status: One day after he was sworn into his first term, President Obama released his strategy for cyber security. One of the goals of that strategy was to "develop next-generation secure computers and networking for national security applications," words identical to his promise of 10/17/08.

1.00

Chapter 7 - Department of Homeland Security

The term "national security application," by default, lent itself to the handling of classified information. This aspect gained prominence and heightened attention after the release of thousands of classified documents to the web site "Wikileaks" in CY2010.

The National Intelligence Programs (NIP), exclusive of military intelligence, were funded as follows under President Obama:
FY2010....$53.1B
FY2011....$54.6B
FY2012....$53.9B
FY2013....$49.0B (Reduced from $52.6B under Sequestration)
FY2014....$50.5B
FY2015....$50.3B
FY2016....$53.0B
FY2017....$54.6B

While there is no other disclosure of currently classified NIP budget information because such disclosures could harm national security, one part of NIP's responsibilities is to "maintain the security of federal cyber networks." Further, the NIP budget supports the protection of the critical networks that facilitate Intelligence Community information sharing and operational requirements and accelerates various information protection and access-control mechanisms.

Under the NIP funding umbrella, the National Security Agency (NSA) manages a High Assurance Platform (HAP) Program, a multi-year program dedicated to develop a next generation secure computing systems to further improve protection for national security data, applications and networks. NSA conducts this effort in collaboration with industry, academia, and other government organizations.

Through President Obama's sustained funding requests for NIP and, by extension, NSA's HAP initiative, this promise was fulfilled.

HS-9

The Promise: "...will shut down the mechanisms used to transmit criminal profits by shutting down untraceable Internet payment schemes."
When/Where: Obama-Biden Plan: Develop a Cyber Crime Strategy to Minimize the Opportunities for Criminal Profit, undated.
Source:
https://webarchive.loc.gov/all/20090429184932/http://change.gov/agenda/homeland_security_agenda/
Status: On 02/09/09, President Obama ordered a 60-day review of the highly classified Comprehensive National Cyber Initiative (CNCI) established by the Bush Administration in 01/08. One of the objectives of the review reportedly included "shutting down untraceable Internet payment schemes."

In CY2011, the highly reputed cybersecurity firm "RSA" reported alarming trends in the effectiveness of such financial cybercrime trojans as "Zeus," "Spyeye," "Ice IX" and others. Their report also indicated that cybercriminals were successfully finding new ways to monetize non-financial data such as utility bills, medical records, gaming accounts and other sources.

As of end-CY2016, the following untraceable Internet payment schemes proliferated, any of which could be used to mask the transmission of criminal profits:
- DASH: A Bitcoin-based electronic currency focused on privacy. Anonymity is an option.
- CloakCoin: Every CloakCoin participant becomes part of a network, which increases anonymity
- ShadowCash: Decentralised cryptocurrency with the option of making anonymous payments.
- LEOCoin: This is a decentralized peer-to-peer payment system. The public ledger is encrypted. There have reportedly been substantiated scam accusations against the developers of this currency.
- AnonCoin: Anonymous cryptocurrency also anonymizes computer IPs when one connects to a client.
- Monero: An open source untraceable currency that uses peer-to-peer transactions and a distributed

0.00

Chapter 7 - Department of Homeland Security

public ledger, receipts and money transfers remain private by default. Ring signatures add a degree of ambiguity to make it harder to link a transaction to an individual computer.
- BitcoinDark: Employing a unique approach to currency anonymity, BitcoinDark uses what they call "Teleport" to clone and exchange currency denominations.

The promise was not fulfilled.

HS-10

The Promise: "...will work with the private sector to establish tough new standards for cyber security and physical resilience."
When/Where: Obama-Biden Plan: Protect the IT Infrastructure That Keeps America's Economy Safe, undated.
Source:
https://webarchive.loc.gov/all/20090429184932/http://change.gov/agenda/homeland_security_agenda/
Status: On 02/12/13, President Obama signed Presidential Policy Directive 21 (PPD-21) entitled "Critical Infrastructure Security and Resilience." At the same time, he issued Executive Order 13636, entitled "Improving Critical Infrastructure Cybersecurity."

PPD-21 introduced three strategic imperatives designed to "drive the Federal approach to strengthen critical infrastructure security and resilience: (1) Refine and clarify functional relationships across the Federal Government to advance the national unity of effort to strengthen critical infrastructure security and resilience; (2) Enable effective information exchange by identifying baseline data and systems requirements for the Federal Government; and (3) Implement an integration and analysis function to inform planning and operations decisions regarding critical infrastructure." PPD-21 led to the release of The National Infrastructure Protection Plan (NIPP 2013) on 12/20/13, entitled "Partnering for Critical Infrastructure Security and Resilience." This Plan outlined how government and private sector participants in the critical infrastructure community are to cooperate to manage risks and achieve security and resilience outcomes and meets the requirements of PPD-21.

NIPP 2013 represented an evolution from concepts introduced in the initial version of the NIPP released in CY2006 by the Bush Administration and updated in CY2009 by the Obama Administration. It was developed through a collaborative process involving stakeholders from all 16 critical infrastructure sectors, all 50 states, and from all levels of government and industry. It provides a clear call to action to leverage partnerships, innovate for risk management, and focus on outcomes by providing the foundation for an integrated and collaborative approach to achieve the vision of a "nation in which physical and cyber critical infrastructure remain secure and resilient, with vulnerabilities reduced, consequences minimized, threats identified and disrupted, and response and recovery hastened."

As to standards, NIPP 2013 included the following direction to the Department of National Security: "Develop interoperability standards to enable more efficient information exchange through defined data standards and requirements, to include: (1) a foundation for an information-sharing environment that has common data requirements and information flow and exchange across entities; and (2) sector-specific critical reporting criteria to allow for improved information flow and reporting to produce more complete and timely situational awareness for security and resilience."

The above requirements were codified in Section 208 of Division N (Cybersecurity Act of 2015) of the Consolidated Appropriations Act of 2016 (H.R. 2029), which states in part that the Secretary of Homeland Security shall, among other responsibilities: "provide information to the appropriate congressional committees on the feasibility of producing a risk-informed plan to address the risk of multiple simultaneous cyber incidents affecting critical infrastructure, including cyber incidents that may have a cascading effect on other critical infrastructure" and "...a report on cybersecurity vulnerabilities for the 10 United States ports that the Secretary determines are at greatest risk of a cybersecurity incident and provide recommendations to mitigate such vulnerabilities."

This promise was fulfilled.

1.00

Chapter 7 - Department of Homeland Security

HS-11	**The Promise:** "...will strengthen privacy protections for the digital age and will harness the power of technology to hold government and business accountable for violations of personal privacy." **When/Where:** Obama-Biden Plan: "Connecting and Empowering All Americans Through Technology and Innovation" dated 11/13/07. **Source:** https://www.wired.com/images_blogs/threatlevel/2009/04/obamatechplan.pdf **Status:** The National Strategy for Trusted Identities in Cyberspace (NSTIC) was created in early-CY2011 under President Obama to improve the privacy, security and convenience of sensitive online transactions through collaborative efforts with the private sector, advocacy groups, government agencies, and other organizations. The "Identity Ecosystem," a less formal term for the NSTIC initiative will, when fully implemented, allow consumers to gain greater privacy and security protection from the innumerable companies that collect data on their web surfing activities. Within the Identity Ecosystem Steering Group's Identity Ecosystem Framework (IDEF), the strategy states that "...to truly enhance privacy in the conduct of online transactions, the Fair Information Practice Principles (FIPPs) must be universally adopted and applied in the Identity Ecosystem. The FIPPs are the widely accepted framework of defining principles to be used in the evaluation and consideration of systems, processes, or programs that affect individual privacy." The strategy further states that "...organizations should be accountable for complying with these principles, providing training to all employees and contractors who use personally identifiable information (PII), and auditing the actual use of PII to demonstrate compliance with these principles and all applicable privacy protection requirements." As of end-CY2016, the National Institute of Standards and Technology (NIST) continued to award grants to eligible applicants to pilot online identity solutions that embrace the IDEF...a work in progress but not yet institutionalized. This promise was not fulfilled.	0.00

	FEMA	GRADE
HS-12	**The Promise:** "...will ensure resources reach the communities that need it..." **When/Where:** Obama-Biden Plan: "Rebuilding the Gulf Coast and Preventing Future Catastrophes", dated 09/11/08. **Source:** https://assets.documentcloud.org/documents/550006/barack-obama-2008-rebuilding-the-gulf-coast-and.pdf **Status:** Since Hurricane Katrina in 08/05, which killed more than 1,800 people, uprooted over 1M Gulf Coast residents, and left 80% of New Orleans submerged, the $143B government reconstruction effort has fixed 220 miles of levees and floodwalls, rebuilt hundreds of public facilities, reconstructed miles of roads and bridges, and provided money to tens of thousands of residents to help them get on with their lives. The white, middle-class, insured population has benefited from the government's $8.6B "Roads Home" program to get back into their homes and resume their lives. For the black, low-income, uninsured segment of the New Orleans population, the story is different. Black storm victims, largely renters without insurance or homeowners without insurance, did not qualify for grants to repair storm damage. Those whose homes suffered wind damage but did not have wind insurance were also denied assistance. The result is that only about 80% of the New Orleans city population has returned, leaving many traditional black neighborhoods looking as they did immediately after Hurricane Katrina. For example, as of end-CY2016, many of those neighborhoods, like the Lower Ninth Ward, are blighted by block after block of damaged homes abandoned by their owners. With few exceptions, resources did not reach those who needed them the most -- the Gulf Coast	0.00

Chapter 7 - Department of Homeland Security

black, uninsured, low-income community. As quoted in an article by Ben Casselman on web site "fivethirtyeight.com" on 08/24/15, Beverly Wright, a Dillard University sociologist, stated that "the black middle class has been completely ignored and overlooked in this whole recovery, period. We've just been left to languish."

New Orleans' black middle class was further decimated after Hurricane Katrina by the decision to fire over 4,000 teachers as part of a post-storm "school reform" effort that converted most of the city's public schools to charter schools. This school reform came at the expense of poor and disadvantaged children, who were either "counseled out" of the educational system or simply disappeared when their families moved elsewhere. During President Obama's two terms in office, resources were not provided to mitigate this negative evolution.

This promise was not fulfilled.

HS-13	**The Promise:** "...will streamline the application process so that communities feel that FEMA is a partner in reconstruction, not an opponent." **When/Where:** Obama-Biden Plan: "Rebuilding the Gulf Coast and Preventing Future Catastrophes", dated 09/11/08. **Source:** https://assets.documentcloud.org/documents/550006/barack-obama-2008-rebuilding-the-gulf-coast-and.pdf **Status:** In 07/10, severe storms devastated large segments of Milwaukee, Waukesha and Grant counties in Wisconsin. On 08/11/10, President Obama signed a major disaster area declaration for those parts of Wisconsin struck by tornados and flooding. In Milwaukee County where flood damage was estimated at $50M, 95% of homes have basements where furnaces, washers and dryers are located. It is the flooding of these basements, many of which are used as living quarters, that rendered homes uninhabitable. FEMA immediately rejected requests for individual, family and business disaster relief assistance. FEMA's position was that assistance priority was granted to residential first floors and above. To Wisconsin residents, regardless of any improvements made to the application process, FEMA was an opponent. The benefits of a streamlined application process were considered questionable at best, if one whose property was devastated could not apply for those benefits. In 10/12, Hurricane Sandy caused severe property destruction along the eastern seaboard of the USA, especially in the states of New York and New Jersey. Years later, on 04/28/16, several former FEMA insurance claim reviewers submitted affidavits and one came forward to publicly state that claims reviewers were instructed by FEMA to deny or underpay claims exceeding pre-set dollar ranges when deciding the level of compensation for Superstorm Sandy victims, regardless of data contained in damage reports. Reportedly, those dollar ranges were set by a software program. If a reviewer recommended that FEMA pay more on a claim than the programmed threshold predicted by the software, FEMA systematically disapproved the recommendation and ordered the reviewers to change their estimates. Again, FEMA came across as the opponent. This scenario led Congressman Tom MacArthur (R-NJ) to call for a congressional hearing on the matter as well as the resignation of FEMA Administrator Craig Fugate. This promise was not fulfilled.	0.00
HS-14	**The Promise:** "...will further improve coordination between all levels of government, create better evacuation plan guidelines, ensure prompt federal assistance to emergency zones, and increase medical surge capacity." **When/Where:** Obama-Biden Plan: "Supporting Urban Prosperity", dated 09/11/08. **Source:** https://assets.documentcloud.org/documents/550008/barack-obama-2008-supporting-urban-prosperity.pdf **Status:** The National Incident Management System (NIMS) exists under Department of Homeland Security (DHS) management so that (according to a FEMA website) "departments and agencies at all	1.00

Chapter 7 - Department of Homeland Security

levels of government, nongovernmental organizations, and the private sector can work together to prevent, protect against, respond to, recover from, and mitigate the effects of incidents, regardless of cause, size, location, or complexity..."

President Obama issued Presidential Policy Directive #8 (PPD-8) entitled "National Preparedness" on 03/30/11. This PPD required the DHS to submit to him a "National Preparedness Goal" by 10/01/11. This goal document, coordinated with other federal departments/agencies and based on inputs from state, local, tribal and territorial governments, private and nonprofit partners and the general public was released on 10/07/11.

PPD-8 also required the submission to the President of a description of a new "National Preparedness System" by 12/01/11. In 11/11, DHS unveiled the framework for the new system and on 05/07/12 released its first "National Preparedness Report" tied to the five principal mission areas outlined in the National Preparedness Goal: prevention, protection, mitigation, response and recovery.

This promise was fulfilled.

GUANTANAMO BAY DETENTION FACILITY	GRADE

HS-15 **The Promise:** "As president, Barack Obama will close the detention facility at Guantanamo."
When/Where: Obama-Biden Plan: "The War We Need to Win," dated 07/31/07
Source: http://www.mattluedke.com/wp-content/uploads/2016/09/CounterterrorismFactSheet.pdf
Status: In an attempt to deliver on this promise, Obama signed an Executive Order on 01/22/09 ordering that the Guantanamo facility be closed within a year. A few months later on 05/19/09, Senate Democrats rejected Obama's request for $80 million in funding for this promised closure. The main sticking point: absence of a detailed plan on where to send the detainees. In the words of Senate Leader Harry Reid (D-NV): "We will never allow terrorists to be released in the United States."

Despite the Senate leader's position at the time, the House voted on 10/15/09 to allow select foreign terrorism suspects from the Guantanamo Bay prison into the United States to face trial. Likewise, the Senate voted 79 to 19 on 10/20/09 in favor of transferring terrorist suspects to the United States for trial.

On 11/17/09, the Senate voted in favor of using defense spending bill funds to build or modify prisons in the United States to hold detainees from Guantanamo Bay. An underused facility in Thomson, Illinois was being considered to house about 100 of the Guantanamo detainees.

President Obama acknowledged on 11/18/09 that while progress was being made on this promise, he would not be able to keep it by 01/22/10.

The FY2011 Defense Authorization Bill imposed restrictions on U.S. action on Guantanamo detainees, including provisions that made it difficult for the Obama Administration to resettle or repatriate detainees abroad.

Further, President Obama formally capitulated on this promise on 03/07/11 by issuing a written statement to the effect that military commission trials would resume at Guantanamo, ending the ban he imposed the day he was inaugurated for his first term in office.

As of end-CY2016, 41 individuals remained incarcerated at the Guantanamo Detention Facility. Since it opened in 01/02, a total of 779 individuals have been incarcerated at Guantanamo Bay as of end-CY2016.

This promise was not fulfilled.

0.00

HS-16 **The Promise:** "Obama strongly supports bipartisan efforts to restore habeas rights. He firmly believes that those who pose a danger to this country should be swiftly tried and brought to justice, but those

0.00

Chapter 7 - Department of Homeland Security

who do not should have sufficient due process to ensure that we are not wrongfully denying them their liberty."
When/Where: Obama-Biden Plan: "The War We Need to Win," dated 07/31/07
Source: http://www.mattluedke.com/wp-content/uploads/2016/09/CounterterrorismFactSheet.pdf
Status: Habeas Corpus is a writ (court order) which directs law enforcement officials who have custody of a prisoner to appear in court with that prisoner to help a judge determine whether the prisoner is lawfully in prison or jail. It is a protection against illegal confinement when due process has been denied as could be the case with some Guantanamo detainees.

Under U.S. Supreme Court case Boumediene v. Bush of CY2008, it was established that Guantanamo detainees have a right to habeas corpus and are able to bring their petitions to U.S courts. It was also ruled that Guantanamo detainees are entitled to the legal protections of the U.S. Constitution and that the Combatant Status Review Tribunal at Guantanamo would be inadequate.

Of the 41 prisoners held at Guantanamo as of endCY2016, 21 had lost their habeas corpus petitions challenging their detention.

Under the Obama Administration, 32 detainees were held for indefinite detention without charge or trial. President Obama's toleration of the continued imprisonment without charges of these 32 individuals, some of whom were reportedly not involved in military operations, runs counter to his promise to reverse the wrongful imprisonments he repeatedly blamed on the Bush Administration during his first campaign for the presidency.

This promise was not fulfilled.

HS-17 — **The Promise:** "...will reject the Military Commissions Act, which allowed the U.S. to circumvent Geneva Conventions in the handling of detainees."
When/Where: Obama-Biden Plan: "The War We Need to Win," dated 07/31/07.
Source: http://www.mattluedke.com/wp-content/uploads/2016/09/CounterterrorismFactSheet.pdf
Status: Military commissions are courts established by military commanders to try persons accused of crimes allegedly committed during war. These commissions may also try persons accused of committing ordinary crimes during periods of martial law or military occupation, when regular civil courts are either nonexistent or unable to function. The first military commissions were established by a military order issued by President Bush on 11/13/01.

0.00

On President Obama's first Inauguration Day, 01/21/09, federal prosecutors were directed to file a motion seeking to suspend legal proceedings against detainees at Guantanamo. One day later, he signed Executive Order (EO) 13492 entitled "Closure Of Guantanamo Detention Facilities." That EO stated in part "...that all proceedings of such military commissions to which charges have been referred but in which no judgment has been rendered, and all proceedings pending in the United States Court of Military Commission Review, are halted."

Undeterred by the above EO, the House passed a bill (HR 2647) on 10/09/09 that created the Military Commissions Act (MCA) of 2009. That bill, an integral part of the National Defense Authorization Act of 2010 (S. 1391) (P.L. 111-84) was signed into law by President Obama on 10/28/09. It limited the use of hearsay or coerced evidence, provided greater access to witnesses and evidence, but still denied Guantanamo detainees due process required by the U.S. Constitution and Geneva Conventions. While that law was an improvement over the MCA of 2006 (H.R. 6166), it contained no outright rejection of the provisions of that Act. In fact, Section 948b(f) under Chapter 47A specifically states that "no alien unprivileged enemy belligerent subject to trial by military commission under this chapter may invoke the Geneva Conventions as a basis for a private right of action." The term "unprivileged enemy belligerent" was defined in the Act as an individual who "(A) has engaged in hostilities against the United States or its coalition partners; (B) has purposefully and materially supported hostilities against the United States or its coalition partners; or (C) is a member of Al Qaeda." A "privileged belligerent," on the other hand, is defined as an individual belonging to one of

Chapter 7 - Department of Homeland Security

the eight categories of prisoners listed in Article 4 of the Geneva Convention Relative to the Treatment of Prisoners of War.

On President Obama's watch, seven (7) prisoners at Guantanamo were tried and convicted by military commissions between CY2009 and CY2014. As of end-CY2016, three (3) of the convicted prisoners remained at Guantanamo and the trial of seven (7) additional prisoners by military commissions was ongoing. Among those: Khalid Sheikh Mohammed who allegedly masterminded the 9/11/01 attacks on the USA and four of his co-conspirators, as well as Abd Al-Rahim Al-Nashiri who allegedly organized the attack on the USS Cole in CY2000.

This promise was not fulfilled.

HS-18

The Promise: "He will develop a fair and thorough process based on the Uniform Code of Military Justice to distinguish between those prisoners who should be prosecuted for their crimes, those who can't be prosecuted but who can be held in a manner consistent with the laws of war, and those who should be released or transferred to their home countries."
When/Where: Obama-Biden Plan: "The War We Need To Win" dated 07/31/07.
Source: http://www.mattluedke.com/wp-content/uploads/2016/09/CounterterrorismFactSheet.pdf
Status: On 05/22/09, President Obama addressed the nation and discussed a plan dividing Guantanamo prisoners into five categories:
1. Those who have violated American criminal laws are to be tried in U.S. federal courts.
2. Those who violated laws of war are to be tried under the Military Commission system.
3. Those who have been released by the courts.
4. Those who can be transferred safely to another country.
5. Those who cannot be prosecuted but pose a clear danger to the American people and who may be held indefinitely.

Except for #1 above, there are no provisions of the U.S. Uniform Code of Military Justice that are directly applicable to items #2 thru #5.

The Military Commissions Act of 2009, an integral part of the National Defense Authorization Act of 2010 signed into law by President Obama on 10/28/09, still denied Guantanamo detainees the due process required by the U.S. Constitution and Geneva Conventions. As of end-CY2016, it was still considered substandard, offering only a second class system of justice for 41 detainees remaining at Guantanamo.

This promise was not fulfilled.

Grade: 0.00

HOMELAND SECURITY GENERAL — GRADE

HS-19

The Promise: "...the President and Congress should direct our precious homeland security dollars according to risk, not as a form of general revenue sharing."
When/Where: Obama-Biden Plan: "The War We Need to Win," dated 07/31/07.
Source: http://www.mattluedke.com/wp-content/uploads/2016/09/CounterterrorismFactSheet.pdf
Status: There is specific mention of "risk" in the President's FY2010 Homeland Security budget proposal such as the following entry: "Risk-based exercise assistance grants will assist state, local and tribal partners in offsetting costs of critical homeland security activities...".

In the FY2011 budget proposal for Homeland Security: "...funding of $1.1 billion for the Urban Area Security Initiative will direct resources to the metropolitan vicinities with the highest threats based on a risk management methodology."

From the FY2012 Homeland Security budget proposal: "...the Budget proposes the elimination of six stove-piped and duplicative stand-alone grant programs, consolidating them into broader State or local grants that are awarded based on risk."

Grade: 1.00

Chapter 7 - Department of Homeland Security

Examples in the FY2016 DHS budget state in part: (1) "The Budget enables TSA to maintain its steadfast focus on maturing into a high-performing counterterrorism organization that applies intelligence-driven, risk-based security (RBS) principles across all operations." (2) Federal Insurance and Mitigation Administration (FIMA) strengthens communities' resilience to disasters through risk analysis, risk reduction, and risk insurance.

There are numerous other references substantiating the view that taxpayer dollars were being appropriated and spent largely based on the implementation of risk management practices by DHS.

This promise was fulfilled.

HS-20 | **The Promise:** "...will develop a meaningful critical infrastructure protection plan across the nation..." | 1.00
When/Where: Obama-Biden Plan: "The War We Need to Win," dated 07/31/07.
Source: http://www.mattluedke.com/wp-content/uploads/2016/09/CounterterrorismFactSheet.pdf
Status: The CY2009 National Infrastructure Protection Plan (NIPP) superceded the CY2006 version and met the requirements set forth in Homeland Security Presidential Directive 7 (HSPD-7) entitled "Critical Infrastructure Identification, Prioritization and Protection".

On 02/12/13, President Obama signed Presidential Policy Directive 21 (PPD-21) entitled "Critical Infrastructure Security and Resilience." At the same time, he issued Executive Order 13636, entitled "Improving Critical Infrastructure Cybersecurity."

PPD-21 articulated the following strategic imperative designed to "drive the Federal approach to strengthen critical infrastructure security and resilience:...Refine and clarify functional relationships across the Federal Government to advance the national unity of effort to strengthen critical infrastructure security and resilience."

PPD-21 led to the release of an updated National Infrastructure Protection Plan (NIPP 2013) on 12/20/13, entitled "Partnering for Critical Infrastructure Security and Resilience." This Plan outlined how government and private sector participants in the critical infrastructure community are to cooperate to manage risks and achieve security and resilience outcomes.

NIPP 2013 provides the overarching approach for integrating the nation's many Critical Infrastructure and Key Resources (CIKR) protection initiatives into a single national effort.

This promise was fulfilled.

HS-21 | **The Promise:** "...will work with the private sector to ensure that all real targets are prepared for disasters both natural and man-made." | 1.00
When/Where: Obama-Biden Plan: "The War We Need to Win," dated 07/31/07.
Source: http://www.mattluedke.com/wp-content/uploads/2016/09/CounterterrorismFactSheet.pdf
Status: This promise was made in reference to the ineffectiveness of the National Asset Database (NADB) which contained information on over 77,000 individual assets ranging from dams, hazardous materials sites and nuclear power plants to local festivals and sporting goods stores. According to a 07/16/07 Congressional Research Service report to Congress, the database was reportedly being used inappropriately as the basis upon which federal resources, including infrastructure protection grants, were being allocated.

Efforts to revamp the NADB and morph it into a new "Infrastructure Information Collection Program-IICP" were addressed in the updated National Infrastructure Protection Plan (NIPP 2009), released to the public on 06/28/10. The IICP would have a repository that contained quantitative, asset-specific risk data for the assets within the 17 critical infrastructure and key resources (CIKR) sectors.

NIPP 2009 addressed a "common plan and unifying structure for the government and private sector to prevent, deter, neutralize, or mitigate deliberate attempts to destroy, incapacitate, or exploit critical

Chapter 7 - Department of Homeland Security

infrastructure and key resources." These are words from the original Bush Administration NIPP of CY2006. What was new in the Obama Administration update to NIPP 2006 was a focus on the preparedness of: chemical facilities; sports arenas and stadiums; "soft targets" such as retail and lodging facilities; critical manufacturing sector; attention to the resilience and preparedness of dams; levee security; and nuclear facilities.

On 02/12/13, President Obama signed Presidential Policy Directive 21 (PPD-21) entitled "Critical Infrastructure Security and Resilience." PPD-21 led to the release of The National Infrastructure Protection Plan (NIPP 2013) on 12/20/13, entitled "Partnering for Critical Infrastructure Security and Resilience." NIPP 2013 was developed, in part, through a collaborative process that included the active participation of private industry; public and private sector owners and operators; state, local, tribal, and territorial government agencies; non-governmental organizations; and other entities/government agencies.

NIPP 2013 made no mention of either the IICP or the CIKR sectors, but nonetheless updated the listing of facilities/targets to be protected from natural and man-made disasters. These include: chemical facilities; commercial facilities; communications; critical manufacturing; dams; defense industrial base; emergency services; energy sector; financial services; food and agriculture; government facilities; health care and public health; information technology; nuclear reactors, materials, and waste; transportation systems; and water and wastewater systems.

This promise was fulfilled.

HS-22

The Promise: "I'll give an annual 'State of the World' address to the American people in which I lay out our national security policy."
When/Where: Obama Campaign Speech entitled "A New Beginning," Chicago, IL, 10/02/07.
Source: http://www.presidency.ucsb.edu/ws/index.php?pid=77015
Status: By law, the President must deliver an annual "State of the Union" address to a joint session of Congress and to the American people. A "State of the World" address on national security policy is not mandated by law.

After two terms in office, President Obama failed to live up to this "annual" address promise.

This promise was not fulfilled.

0.00

HS-23

The Promise: "Obama is committed ... to increasing federal resources and logistic support to local emergency planning efforts."
When/Where: Obama-Biden Plan: "The War We Need to Win" dated 07/31/07.
Source: http://www.mattluedke.com/wp-content/uploads/2016/09/CounterterrorismFactSheet.pdf
Status: Under President Obama, the Homeland Security Grant Program (HSGP) annual allocations focused predominantly on three areas to prevent, protect against, mitigate, respond to, and recover from acts of terrorism and other threats:
(1) State Homeland Security Program (SHSP) to support the implementation of risk-driven, capabilities-based State Homeland Security Strategies to address capability targets. States are required to dedicate 25% of SHSP funds to law enforcement terrorism prevention activities.
(2) Urban Area Security Initiative (UASI) to enhance regional preparedness and capabilities in 29 high-threat, high-density areas. States and Urban Areas are required to dedicate 25% of UASI funds to law enforcement terrorism prevention activities.
(3) Operation Stonegarden (OPSG) to enhance cooperation and coordination among local, tribal, territorial, state and federal law enforcement agencies to jointly enhance security along the United States land and water borders.

Here's how the three grant programs fared while President Obama was in office. It should be noted that Operation Stonegarden was not funded until FY2010 and that the Citizen Corps Program (CCP) and Metropolitan Medical Response System (MMRS) were no longer funded as grant programs within

0.00

HSGP after FY2011. Starting with the last budget signed by President Bush (FY2009) as a comparative baseline (in $million):

Program......SHSP......UASI......OPSG......MMRS......CCP......Total
FY2009......$861.2....$798.6....-------........$39.8....$14.6......$1.714B
FY2010......$842.0....$832.5....$60.0........$39.4....$12.5......$1.786B
FY2011......$526.9....$662.6....$54.9........$34.9......$9.9......$1.289B
FY2012......$294.0....$490.4....$46.6................................$831.0M
FY2013......$354.6....$558.7....$55.0................................$968.3M
FY2014......$401.3....$587.0....$55.0................................$1.043B
FY2015......$402.0....$587.0....$55.0................................$1.044B
FY2016......$402.0....$580.0....$55.0................................$1.037B

Except for the short-lived and relatively minor uptick noted for FY2010, when viewed against the baseline established under his predecessor's presidency, a sustained increase in federal resources (i.e. funding) did not occur during President Obama's tenure.

This promise was not fulfilled.

HS-24

The Promise: "...will create a National Catastrophe Insurance Reserve that would be funded by private insurers contributing a portion of the premiums they collect from policyholders...With this program in place, disaster victims would no longer have to depend solely on taxpayerfunded federal disaster aid loans."

When/Where: Obama-Biden Plan: "Rebuilding the Gulf Coast and Preventing Future Catastrophes", dated 09/11/08.

Source: https://assets.documentcloud.org/documents/550006/barack-obama-2008-rebuilding-the-gulf-coast-and.pdf

Status: When President Obama assumed office in CY2009, insurers were not allowed the option of establishing tax-deferred, pre-event reserves to fund catastrophe losses. Generally Accepted Accounting Principles (GAAP) prohibited the use of catastrophe reserves for future events. U.S. companies were only permitted to set aside loss reserves for events that had already occurred. State regulators generally endorsed the idea of letting insurers set up catastrophe reserves, but accounting and tax provisions to make it worthwhile to insurers had not been enacted.

According to the National Association of Insurance Commissioners (NAIC), insurance companies should be allowed to set aside, on an objective formulaic basis, some portion of the premiums paid by the policyholders into a reserve for future catastrophic events. This ability would require a modification of the U.S. Tax Code to allow insurers to establish pre-event reserves on a tax-deferred basis.

Initiatives in this direction had been introduced during the George W. Bush Administration by Representatives Ginny Brown-Waite (R-FL) and Vern Buchanan (R-FL) on 01/04/07 under the Homeowners Insurance Protection Act of 2007 (H.R. 91). This was a comprehensive catastrophic insurance bill that would have established a federal reinsurance catastrophic fund as a federal backstop for future natural disasters. The bill called for all cost savings achieved through the legislation to be passed along to the consumer, and not kept as corporate profits.

Additionally, the Section 9 of H.R. 91 created Catastrophic Capital Reserve Funds; essentially tax deferred savings accounts that could be used by private insurance companies to help offset the costs of catastrophic events. Nothing happened with this bill.

During the Obama Administration, the CY2007 bill was again introduced by Congressman Dennis Ross (R-FL) on 01/14/13 as the Homeowners Insurance Protection Act of 2013 (H.R. 240). It contained the same Section 9 (Catastrophic Capital Reserve Funds) with the same provisions as H.R. 91 of seven years prior. This bill did not go far and died when the 113th Congress expired at the end of CY2014.

0.00

Chapter 7 - Department of Homeland Security

As of end-CY2016, there was no known "National Catastrophe Insurance Reserve."

This promise was not fulfilled.

HS-25

The Promise: "Even though recent attacks have happened on public transit in Madrid, Mumbai and London, the Bush administration has invested only a small fraction of the $6 billion that transportation officials have said is necessary to implement needed security improvements. Barack Obama believes that this critical hole in our homeland security network must be addressed."
When/Where: Obama-Biden Plan: "Strengthening America's Transportation Infrastructure" dated 02/08.
Source: https://transportist.org/2008/02/
Status: The Transit Security Grant Program (TSGP) was funded at the level of $348.6M in FY2009 under the President George W. Bush Administration. The trend during subsequent years under President Obama was as follows:

FY2010.........$288.0M
FY2011.........$200.0M
FY2012..........$87.5M
FY2013..........$83.7M
FY2014..........$90.0M
FY2015..........$87.0M
FY2016..........$87.0M
FY2017..........$88.0M
Sub-Total:...$1,011.2B

Other funds to ensure transit security and made available predominantly through grant programs administered by the Department of Homeland Security are as follows: Intercity Passenger Rail (IPR); Emergency Management Performance Grants (EMPG); Intercity Bus Security Grant Program (IBSGP); Port Security Grant Program (PSGP); Freight Rail Security Grant Program (FRSGP); Tribal Homeland Security Grant Program (THSGP); Nonprofit Security Grant Program (NSGP); and National Special Security Event (NSSE) Grant Program. Combined, the level of funding for these grant programs under President Obama was as follows (not all of the programs identified above were funded each year):

FY2010..........$647.9M
FY2011..........$596.3M
FY2012..........$453.0M
FY2013..........$455.2M
FY2014..........$483.1M
FY2015..........$483.1M
FY2016..........$483.1M
FY2017..........$602.1M
Sub-Total:....$4,203.8B

The combined total of the above two listings amounts to $5.215B, short of the $6B stated in this promise as the goal to be met to meet the nation's transit security needs.

This promise was not fulfilled.

0.00

HS-26

The Promise: "Protect our Energy Infrastructure...will prioritize security investments in our refineries and pipelines and power grids."
When/Where: Obama-Biden Plan: "The War We Need to Win" dated 07/31/07.
Source: http://www.mattluedke.com/wp-content/uploads/2016/09/CounterterrorismFactSheet.pdf
Status: ELECTRICITY GRID: The nation's electricity grid can be disrupted for prolonged periods by a number of man-caused events, like physical assaults, power surges, cyber warfare, or high-altitude electromagnetic pulse (EMP) caused by the detonation of a nuclear weapon outside the atmosphere above the United States. Such events could disable or destroy key parts of the power grid, prompting

1.00

the cascading collapse of every one of the other critical infrastructures that assure the availability of water, food, medicine, finance, transportation, telecommunications, etc.

President Obama recognized the need for additional funds to ensure power grid security. Page 24 of the American Recovery and Reinvestment Act (ARRA) of 2009 authorizes $4.5B "...to modernize the electric grid to include demand responsive equipment, enhance security..."

On 03/26/14, Congressman Henry Waxman (D-CA) introduced the "Grid Reliability and Infrastructure Defense (GRID) Act" (H.R. 4298). This bill sought to amend the Federal Power Act to protect the bulk-power system and electric infrastructure critical to the defense of the USA against cybersecurity, physical, and other threats and vulnerabilities. Electric utilities opposed the GRID Act. The National Rural Electric Cooperative Association (NRECA) said the bill would give the Federal Energy Regulatory Commission (FERC) too much power over utilities. This bill died when the 113th Congress expired at the end of CY2014.

Congresswoman Sheila Jackson Lee (D-TX) introduced the "Terrorism Prevention and Critical Infrastructure Protection Act of 2015" (H.R. 85) on 01/06/15. This bill would codify the objective of Presidential Policy Directive 21 (PPD-21) entitled "Critical Infrastructure Security and Resilience" signed by President Obama on 02/12/13. Enhanced electricity grid security measures are addressed in H.R. 85, which has not progressed beyond initial committee review as of 11/16. This bill expire with the 114th Congress at the end of CY2016.

PIPELINES: President Obama addressed the need to improve security of the nation's 2.6M miles of pipelines by proposing to support "a more robust, rigorous, and data-driven pipeline safety program to ensure the highest level of safety for America's pipeline system" in his FY2013 and FY2014 budget proposals.

Under the aegis of his FY2014 and FY2015 budget proposals, President Obama announced the creation of a "Pipeline Safety Reform (PSR) initiative" for a three-year program to increase pipeline inspection personnel, modernize pipeline data collection and analysis, and improve federal investigation of pipeline accidents.

On 06/22/16, President Obama signed the "Protecting our Infrastructure of Pipelines and Enhancing Safety (PIPES) Act of 2016 (S. 2276) to renew the federal government's pipeline safety program and give regulators new emergency authorities. This bill reauthorized the Pipeline and Hazardous Materials Safety Administration's (PHMSA) oil and gas pipeline programs through FY2019.

REFINERIES: On 12/19/2014, President Obama signed the "Intelligence Authorization Act for Fiscal Year 2015" (H.R. 4681). An integral part of that bill (Section 326) requires the Department of Homeland Security to conduct an intelligence assessment of the security of domestic oil refineries and related rail transportation, submitting to appropriate intelligence committees within 180 days from the Act's signature (1) the results of the assessment; and (2) any recommendations with respect to intelligence sharing or intelligence collection to improve the security of domestic oil refineries and related rail transportation infrastructure to protect the communities surrounding such refineries or such infrastructure from potential harm.

This promise was fulfilled.

HS-27	**The Promise:** "We have to put resources where our infrastructure is most vulnerable. That means tough and permanent standards for securing our chemical plants." **When/Where:** Obama Campaign Speech entitled "The War We Need to Win", Wilson Center, Washington, D.C., dated 08/01/07. **Source:** https://2008election.procon.org/sourcefiles/Obama20070801.pdf **Status:** On 12/18/14, President Obama signed into law the "Protecting and Securing Chemical Facilities from Terrorist Attacks Act of 2014" (the "CFATS Act of 2014"), which recodified and	1.00

reauthorized the CFATS program through CY2018 for the nation's 4,569 chemical facilities regulated by the Department of Homeland Security (DHS).

Initially authorized by Congress in CY2007, the program uses a dynamic multi-tiered risk assessment process and requires facilities identified as high-risk to meet and maintain performance-based security standards appropriate to the facilities and the risks they pose. DHS chemical security inspectors work in all 50 states to help ensure facilities have security measures in place to meet CFATS requirements.

DHS has a chemical plant ranking system from 1 through 4 where 1 is the highest risk and 4 is the lowest. The new bill established an "Expedited Approval Program," which could allow chemical facilities in Tiers 3 and 4 to move to an approved Site Security Plan (SSP) more quickly.

Based on current DHS documentation, "performance standards are particularly appropriate in a security context because they provide individual facilities the flexibility to address their unique security challenges. Using performance standards rather than prescriptive standards also helps to increase the overall security of the sector by varying the security practices used by different chemical facilities. Security measures that differ from facility to facility mean that each presents a new and unique problem for an adversary to solve."

The risk-based performance standards established by DHS and to be met by chemical facilities pertain to: (1) Restricted-Area Perimeter; (2) Secure Site Assets; (3) Screen and Control Access; (4) Deter, Detect, and Delay; (5) Shipping, Receipt, and Storage; (6) Theft and Diversion; (7) Sabotage; (8) Cyber; (9) Response (10) Monitoring; (11) Training; (12) Personnel Surety; (13) Elevated Threats; (14) Specific Threats, Vulnerabilities, or Risks; (15) Report of Significant Security Incidents; (16) Significant Security Incidents; (17) Officials and Organizations; and (18) Records.

This promise was fulfilled.

HS-28 | **The Promise:** "...will fight for greater information-sharing between national intelligence agents and local officials and provide local law enforcement agencies with the everyday tools they need to protect their transportation systems." | **1.00**

When/Where: Obama-Biden Plan: "Strengthening America's Transportation Infrastructure" dated 02/08.

Source: https://transportist.org/2008/02/

Status: On 08/18/10, President Obama issued Executive Order 13549 entitled "Classified National Security Information Program for State, Local, Tribal and Private Sector (SLTPS) Entities." This order established an SLTPS Policy Advisory Committee to "recommend changes to policies and procedures that are designed to remove undue impediments to the sharing of information..."

Prior to CY2010, National Counterterrorism Center (NCTC) analysts had to manually search for and integrate information from multiple DHS and Intelligence Community (IC) databases. In CY2012, the creation of a new Counterterrorism Data Layer (CTDL) automated this process in a single data collection environment.

In addition, DHS introduced a pilot intelligence information networking and collaboration tool called "Homeland Space" (HSpace) in 03/12 to support analysts in the Top Secret/Sensitive Compartmented Information environment.

On 02/10/15, the White House announced the formation of the Cyber Threat Intelligence Integration Center (CTIIC). Operating under the Office of the DNI, the CTIIC works like the NCTC to amalgamate threat information in a single place and disseminate it to those who need it, including law enforcement. The CTIIC is not an intelligence gathering institution. Rather, it serves to analyze, integrate and share intelligence information already collected. Much of this sharing is done through Fusion Centers found in each of the 50 states plus the District of Columbia, Guam, Puerto Rico and the U.S. Virgin Islands.

Chapter 7 - Department of Homeland Security

The above reflects improvement of intelligence information sharing, not only between federal agencies/departments, but also at the local law enforcement level to protect all aspects of American life, including the country's transportation systems.

This promise was fulfilled.

HS-29

The Promise: "...will work to ensure intellectual property is protected in foreign markets, and promote greater cooperation on international standards that allow our technologies to compete everywhere."
When/Where: Obama-Biden Plan: "Connecting and Empowering All Americans Through Technology and Innovation" dated 11/13/07.
Source: https://www.wired.com/images_blogs/threatlevel/2009/04/obamatechplan.pdf
Status: On 06/22/10, the Director of Homeland Security and Vice President Biden announced the Administration's Joint Strategic Plan for Intellectual Property (IPR) Enforcement, prepared by the Office of Management and Budget's Office of the U.S. Intellectual Property Enforcement Coordinator (IPEC). This is a multi-agency effort (Commerce, Agriculture, Health & Human Services, Homeland Security, Justice, State, and others) to enhance intellectual property protection by strengthening efforts to combat civil and criminal violations of trademark and copyright infringement.

The plan calls for the U.S. Immigration and Customs Enforcement (ICE) National Intellectual Property Rights Coordination Center (IPR Center) to serve as the focal point to bring the efforts of the following contributing organizations under one roof: the departments listed above, ICE, Customs and Border Protection (CBP), U.S. Food & Drug Administration (FDA), the FBI, the Naval Criminal Investigative Service (NCIS), the Defense Criminal Investigative Service (DCIS), the U.S. Army Criminal Investigation Command Major Procurement Fraud Unit, the GSA Office of Inspector General, the U.S. Patent & Trademark Office, and the Government of Mexico Tax and Revenue Service.

In the first half of CY2010 alone, the IPR Center's efforts reportedly resulted in 166 criminal arrests, 56 indictments, 34 convictions, and 1,078 seizures valued at more than $358M.

On 05/11/11, Senator Patrick Leahy (D-VT) and others introduced the Protect Intellectual Property Act (PIPA) (S. 968) to prevent online threats to economic creativity and theft of intellectual property. On the House side, Congressman Lamar Smith (R-TX) and others introduced the "Stop Online Piracy Act" (SOPA) (H.R. 3261) on 10/26/11 to combat the theft of copyrighted intellectual property. Both PIPA and SOPA received pushback from search engine advocates, as they were perceived as a form of censorship of internet content that could negatively affect social networks and other legitimate sites. Consequently both bills were shelved on 01/20/12 and expired with the 112th Congress at the end of CY2012.

On 10/01/11, the United States signed Anti-Counterfeiting Trade Agreements (ACTA) along with 22 European Union (EU) member states. This resulted in widespread protests across Europe. Chapter 2 of the ACTA spells out the conditions under which signatories agree to enforce intellectual property rights. The full European Parliament voted on the issue on 07/04/12 and declined consent to ACTA, essentially rejecting it. The reasoning for this rejection was that ACTA was intended, among other things, to cover infringements of copyright through internet use.

Once ACTA has been ratified by six signatories, its implementation will take effect. As of end-CY2016, it had only been ratified by Japan and was therefore not in force.

Regardless of the above contretemps related to ACTA, this promise was fulfilled.

1.00

IMMIGRATION	GRADE

HS-30

The Promise: "...we'll crack down on employers who hire undocumented immigrants..."
When/Where: Obama Campaign Speech at the Congressional Hispanic Caucus Institute Gala, Washington, D.C., dated 09/10/08.
Source: http://www.presidency.ucsb.edu/ws/index.php?pid=78613

0.00

Chapter 7 - Department of Homeland Security

Status: As of 07/09/09, as reported in the Washington Post, President Obama appeared to be abandoning a campaign promise to "crack down" on employers who hire illegal (undocumented) immigrants. The Department of Homeland Security (DHS), instead, would focus on federal contract employers who hired approximately 4M illegal immigrants, while the majority of such people (another 7-8M) did not work under federal contracts. Illegals working as household help, in the nation's "strawberry patches", etc. would be given a pass.

On 08/18/11, DHS Secretary Napolitano voiced support for the institution of what appeared to be, in the words of Arizona Governor Jan Brewer, a "backdoor amnesty" whereby the cases of approximately 300K illegal immigrants (except the most hardened criminals or those who posed a security risk) would be reviewed and reprieves from deportation granted for those who arrived in the USA as children, or who served in the U.S. military.

On 08/31/11, Labor Secretary Hilda Solis announced that illegal immigrants, once in the USA, have all the workplace rights enjoyed by U.S. citizens and legal immigrants -- notably the right to lodge complaints without fear of being fired or deported. This appeared to be in contravention of Department of Labor (DOL) policies that direct U.S. employers to first seek the certification of foreign nationals through the DOL. The employer then had to petition the U.S. Citizen and Immigration Services for work visas for those non-U.S. workers. Applicants had to establish that they were admissible to the U.S. under provisions of the Immigration and Nationality Act (INA). What Secretary Solis advocated, based on agreements reached with countries such as Mexico, is that it was OK for illegal immigrants to work in the USA. If they filed grievances against their employers with the DOL, they would receive full protections equal to those afforded to U.S. citizens.

On 06/15/12, Secretary Napolitano announced that as many as 800K illegal immigrants who were brought to the USA as children and who had never committed a crime would be issued work permits. By implementing these actions at the executive and not the legislative level, according to some members of Congress, the Obama Administration usurped Congress' authority by implementing its own amnesty program.

By implementing the above tactic effective 08/15/12, the Obama Administration created a significant incentive for foreigners to enter the USA illegally. In the longer term, their offspring would be granted an amnesty if they were brought to the USA before their 16th birthday, were younger than 31 years old on 06/15/12, had not been charged with any crimes, had graduated from a U.S. high school or equivalent, or had served in the U.S. armed forces. Upon payment of a $465 application fee, these offsprings of illegal immigrants would receive a two-year deferment from deportation proceedings. During that timeframe, eligible offspring could apply for work permits. Their parents, however, were permitted to continue working in the USA illegally as undocumented immigrants.

In CY2014, out of 554K employers participating in the U.S. Citizenship and Immigration Services (USCIS) E-Verify system to electronically verify the employment eligibility of newly hired employees, only 2,022 audits were initiated and only 172 employers were arrested by the U.S. Immigration and Customs Enforcement (ICE) Agency for criminal violations related to the knowing employment of aliens not authorized to work in the USA. This is reflective of 'business as usual' rather than a 'crack down'.

The official numerical pattern of illegal immigrants in the USA during President Obama's presidency was as follows:
CY2009 - 10.8M
CY2010 - 11.6M
CY2011 - 11.5M
CY2012 - 11.4M
CY2013 - 11.3M
CY2014 - 11.3M

CY2015 - 11.9M
CY2016 - 11.3M

At best, these numbers are "guesstimates," given that illegal aliens tend to hide or to deny their real status to government officials (i.e. USCIS, DHS, Census Bureau) or to the respected Pew Research Center. The actual number, according to some sources, is between 15M and 20M.

This promise was not fulfilled.

HS-31	**The Promise:** "...Support a system that allows undocumented immigrants who are in good standing to pay a fine, learn English, and go to the back of the line for the opportunity to become citizens." **When/Where:** Obama-Biden Plan on Immigration, dated 09/06/08. **Source:** https://webarchive.loc.gov/all/20090429184836/http://change.gov/agenda/immigration_agenda/ **Status:** President Obama did not address immigration reform in CY2009, preferring to focus on health care reform, financial regulations reform, cap-and-trade, and other priorities.	0.00

On 03/18/10, Senators Schumer (D-NY) and Graham (R-SC) released an outline of a bill that encouraged President Obama to proclaim that he would "do everything in my power" to get immigration reform legislation moving in Congress during CY2010.

On 12/18/10, the Development, Relief, and Education for Alien Minors (DREAM) Act (S.3992) was killed from further consideration by the 111th Congress when the Senate failed to attain the 60-vote majority needed for further advancement of the bill. This proposed act would have granted legal status to young people who entered the USA illegally as children and who agreed to either go to college or join the military -- if they do not have a criminal record and meet other eligibility critera.

Senator Richard Durbin (D-IL) reintroduced the DREAM Act (S. 952) on 05/11/11. On the House side, Congressman Howard Berman (D-CA) also reintroduced the DREAM Act (H.R. 1842) on the same date. Neither bill progressed beyond the initial committee phase as of end-CY2012 and prospects for any version of the DREAM Act becoming law during President Obama's terms in office died with the 112th Congress at the end of CY2012.

Undeterred, the Obama Administration issued a Deferred Action for Childhood Arrivals (DACA) policy memorandum, announced to the public by President Obama on 06/15/12. DACA grants deferred deportation to people under age 31 who came to the USA under age 16 before CY2007 and met other criteria. Upon paying a $465 application fee and producing supporting documents, qualified applicants were allowed to be in the USA legally for a period of two years, after which the DACA protection could be renewed for another $465. Some Republican lawmakers denounced DACA as an abuse of executive power.

On 11/20/14, the White House announced a new executive action expanding DACA to include undocumented immigrants who entered the country before CY2010 (vice CY2007), eliminate the requirement that applicants be younger than 31 years old, and lengthen the renewable deferral period from two to three years. That executive action also created a Deferred Action for Parents of Americans (DAPA) program to provide qualified individuals the opportunity to request temporary relief from deportation and obtain a work authorization for three years at a time. DAPA required individuals to register, submit biometric data, pass background checks, pay fees, and show that their child was born prior to 11/14.

An injunction against DACA and DAPA was issued by the U.S. District Court for the Southern District of Texas on 02/16/16. By a 4-4 split decision on 06/23/16, the U.S. Supreme Court effectively upheld the Texas court's decision and blocked President Obama's executive actions on DACA and DAPA. These legal decisions did not affect the original DACA of 06/12.

Chapter 7 - Department of Homeland Security

As of end-CY2016, more than 787K undocumented immigrants had benefited from DACA protection. Qualified illegals continued to request an initial grant of DACA or renew their quasi-legal status. DACA participants are not considered "citizens," nor has a clear path to citizenship been established for them nor, by some accounts, for the 11M and possibly up to 20M illegal immigrants in the USA.

This promise was not fulfilled.

HS-32

The Promise: "...will do more to promote economic development in Mexico to decrease illegal immigration."
When/Where: Obama-Biden Plan for America: "Blueprint for Change" dated 10/09/08.
Source: https://www.documentcloud.org/documents/550007-barack-obama-2008-blueprint-for-change.html
Status: Unemployment in Mexico reached a high of 5.93% in 05/09, and decreased to 4.1% by 09/16. Unemployment is not considered to be a principal factor driving illegal immigration. Rather, the average income for Mexicans in CY2015 was about $14,800 compared with an average income of $58,700 in the USA during the same year.

The Obama Administration sought only $3M for the State Department's Economic Support Fund (ESF) for Mexico in FY2010. Wiser heads in Congress prevailed and the authorized amount for FY2010 was boosted to $9M for grants in economic and social aid. For subsequent years, the ESF for Mexico was appropriated as follows:
FY2011 - $18.0M
FY2012 - $33.3M
FY2013 - $32.1M
FY2014 - $35.0M ($11.8M was designated for Global Climate Change (GCC) programs)
FY2015 - $33.6M ($12.5 million was designated for GCC programs)
FY2016 - $39.0M
FY2017 - $40.9M

Of course, the ESF is not the only source of assistance to Mexico. The above was recorded solely to illustrate that the amount of ESF accorded to Mexico on an annual basis is negligible. When viewed in the context of Mexico's high drug-trafficking crime rate, its poor human rights adherence record, its paltry wage structure and other national issues, it's no surprise that the "grass looks greener" across Mexico's northern border.

Sweetening the illegal immigration pot, Department of Labor Secretary Hilda Solis announced on 08/31/11 that illegal immigrants from countries like Mexico, once in the USA, have all the workplace rights enjoyed by U.S. citizens and legal immigrants. Consequently, Mexicans managing to sneak into the USA and finding a job enjoyed all the workplace rights afforded to U.S. citizens and legal immigrants under prevailing laws.

Further, DHS Secretary Napolitano announced on 06/15/12 that as many as 800K illegal immigrants who were brought to the USA as children and had never committed a crime would be issued work permits.

The foregoing decisions were interpreted by Mexicans and others transiting Mexico as incentives for entry by any means, legal or otherwise, into the USA.

This promise was not fulfilled.

0.00

HS-33

The Promise: "What I can guarantee is that we will have in the first year, an immigration bill that I strongly support."
When/Where: Candidate Obama interview with Jorge Ramos, dated 05/28/08,
Source: http://www.thedailybeast.com/articles/2010/06/28/univisions-jorge-ramos-obamas-immigration-promise.html

0.00

Chapter 7 - Department of Homeland Security

Status: Despite lots of pressure from southern border states, President Obama was ineffective in pushing for an immigration reform bill during his two terms in office.

Out of frustration, on 04/23/10, Arizona Governor Jan Brewer signed a state law banning illegal immigration to protect Arizona's citizens against trans-border drug related violence. Careful scrutiny of this law revealed that it mirrored federal immigration laws and, specifically, prohibited any form of racial profiling.

The legality of the Arizona bill was challenged by the Obama Administration. Its position was that immigration reform must be accomplished at the federal level. To that end, on 07/28/10 Judge Susan Bolton (a federal judge for the U.S. District Court of Arizona appointed in CY2000 by President Bill Clinton) blocked the most controversial sections of Arizona's immigration law from taking effect. On 04/11/11, the U.S. Court of Appeals for the 9th Circuit ruled that Judge Bolton acted lawfully when she blocked provisions of the Arizona law that would, among other things, have required police to check immigration status if they stopped someone while enforcing other laws. On 06/25/12, the Supreme Court ruled that this provision of the Arizona law was permissible under the Constitution but struck down three other provisions. Those provisions had made it a crime for immigrants to seek employment without work permits, made the non-carrying of immigration papers a crime by those who actually possess such documentation, and allowed law enforcement personnel to arrest anyone suspected of having committed a deportable offense.

Other states such as Utah, Georgia and Alabama introduced their own versions of laws designed to crack down on illegal immigration. These too were challenged by advocacy groups because they were considered unconstitutional and, in the case of Alabama, racist. Federal Judge Sharon Blackburn temporarily blocked enforcement of Alabama's immigration law (Act 2011-535) on 08/29/11 but on 09/28/11 ruled that key provisions of the law such as permitting the verification of student immigrant status would be upheld.

On 12/18/10, the Senate killed the Development, Relief, and Education for Alien Minors (DREAM) Act (S.3992/H.R. 1751) which would have been a critical first step toward immigration reform. Senator Richard Durbin (D-IL) reintroduced the DREAM Act (S. 952) on 05/11/11. Congressman Howard Berman (D-CA) also reintroduced a House version of the DREAM Act (H.R. 1842) on the same date. Neither bill progressed beyond the initial committee review phase and expired with the 112th Congress at the end of CY2012.

On 08/18/11, DHS Secretary Napolitano voiced support for the institution of what appeared to be, in the words of Governor Jan Brewer, a "backdoor amnesty" whereby the cases of approximately 300K illegal immigrants would be reviewed and reprieves from deportation granted for those who arrived in the USA as children or served in the U.S. military. The guidelines to be followed consisted of 19 factors, some of which were identical to the provisions of the defeated DREAM Act. By launching this initiative, the Obama Administration essentially usurped Congress' authority by implementing its own amnesty program without benefit of the promised immigration reform bill.

Two viable immigration reform bills were in play in the 112th Congress. Congressman Kenny Marchant (R-TX) introduced H.R. 2064 on 05/31/11 to amend the "Illegal Immigration Reform and Immigrant Responsibility Act of 1996" while Senator Robert Menendez (D-NJ) introduced the "Comprehensive Immigration Reform Act of 2011" (S. 1258). Both bills did not progress beyond initial committee reviews as of end-CY2012 and expired with the 112th Congress. Because the Administration decided to circumvent Congress by initiating what looks like an amnesty program for just about any illegal immigrant (except for convicted felons) without a supporting law in 08/11, Republicans in Congress denied consideration of any further immigration reform legislation during President Obama's two terms in office.

On 06/15/12, Secretary Napolitano announced that as many as 800K illegal immigrants who were

Chapter 7 - Department of Homeland Security

brought to the USA as children and have never committed a crime would be granted a two-year deportation deferral if they applied (at a cost of $465) for such reprieves under the Obama Administration's Deferred Action for Childhood Arrivals (DACA) initiative. See Promise HS-31 for details on DACA.

As of end-CY2016, the nation still awaited the promised immigration bill.

This promise was not fulfilled.

	PATRIOT ACT	GRADE
HS-34	**The Promise:** "Revise the PATRIOT Act...to avoid jeopardizing the rights and ideals of all Americans..." **When/Where:** Obama-Biden Plan: "The War We Need to Win" dated 07/31/07. **Source:** http://www.mattluedke.com/wp-content/uploads/2016/09/CounterterrorismFactSheet.pdf **Status:** Under Section 215 of the "Uniting and Strengthening America by Providing Appropriate Tools Required to Intercept and Obstruct Terrorism (USA PATRIOT) Act of 2001" (H.R. 3162) signed into law by President George W. Bush on 10/26/01 in reaction to the terrorist attack on the U.S. homeland on 09/11/01, the FBI could secretly conduct a physical search or wiretap of American citizens to obtain evidence of crime without proving probable cause as stipulated in the 4th Amendment of the U.S. Constitution. Another problem with Section 215 was that a Federal Bureau of Investigation (FBI) wiretapping order application could be approved "ex parte," meaning that the authorization could be granted in the absence of and without representation or notification of the party being investigated. The rationale for this provision was that involving the other party could potentially jeopardize the investigation. In 03/07, a Justice Department audit found that the FBI improperly and, in some cases, illegally used the PATRIOT Act to secretly obtain personal information about U.S. citizens. Stating "I think it is an important tool for us to continue dealing with an ongoing terrorist threat," President Obama signed a four-year extension of the PATRIOT Act into law on 05/26/11. Section 215 was left intact, thereby authorizing the continued conduct of roving wiretaps in pursuit of terrorists. On 06/02/15, President Obama not only revised but replaced many tenets of the PATRIOT Act by signing the "USA Freedom Act" (H.R. 2048) into law. This law amended Section 215, essentially prohibiting the National Security Agency (NSA) and the FBI from continuing the practice of collecting massive amounts of wiretapped telephone data (metadata). Instead, phone companies retain the data and the NSA and FBI can obtain information about targeted individuals from those phone companies if requested from a federal court by the Director of the FBI, a designee of the Director whose rank shall be no lower than Deputy Assistant Director at Bureau headquarters or a Special Agent in Charge of a Bureau field office. That official must certify that the absence of a prohibition of disclosure could result in (1) a danger to the national security of the United States; (2) interference with a criminal, counterterrorism, or counterintelligence investigation; (3) interference with diplomatic relations; or (4) danger to the life or physical safety of any person. This promise was fulfilled.	1.00
HS-35	**The Promise:** "As president, Obama would update the Foreign Intelligence Surveillance Act to provide greater oversight and accountability to the congressional intelligence committees to prevent future threats to the rule of law." **When/Where:** Obama-Biden Plan: "The War We Need to Win" dated 07/31/07. **Source:** http://www.mattluedke.com/wp-content/uploads/2016/09/CounterterrorismFactSheet.pdf **Status:** On 06/15/12, Congressman Lamar Smith (R-TX) introduced the "FISA Amendments Act Reauthorization Act of 2012" (H.R. 5949) to extend the FISA Amendments Act of 2008 for five years. President Obama signed this bill into law on 12/30/12. H.R. 5949 would have been a perfect opportunity to address any loopholes in the FISA that permit government entities to monitor the communications of American citizens without warrant or any other	1.00

Chapter 7 - Department of Homeland Security

lawful authorization. But these loopholes were not addressed in the above bill.

On 06/02/15, President Obama signed the "USA Freedom Act" (H.R. 2048) into law. Title IV of the USA Freedom Act (Foreign Intelligence Surveillance Court Reforms) directed the appointment of an "Amicus Curiae" (an impartial adviser to a court of law including the U.S. Supreme Court). An Amicus Curiae appointed under this Act serves to provide "...expertise in privacy and civil liberties, intelligence collection, communications technology, or any other area that may lend legal or technical expertise to a court..." By signing H.R. 2048 with its Title IV as written, President Obama improved accountability and oversight of FISA-related matters.

This promise was fulfilled.

HS-36	**The Promise:** "As president, Barack Obama would revisit the PATRIOT Act to ensure that there is real and robust oversight of tools like National Security Letters, sneak-and-peek searches, and the use of the material witness provision." **When/Where:** Obama-Biden Plan: "The War We Need to Win" dated 07/31/07. **Source:** http://www.mattluedke.com/wp-content/uploads/2016/09/CounterterrorismFactSheet.pdf **Status:** The three extensions to the Providing Appropriate Tools Required to Intercept and Obstruct Terrorism (PATRIOT) Act of 2001 signed by President Obama (02/27/10, 02/27/11, 05/26/11) kept it essentially intact. These periodic extensions were required to keep in check roving wiretaps, access to business records, and surveillance of non-American "lone wolf" suspects lacking confirmed ties to terrorist organizations.	0.00

National Security Letters (NSLs). These are administrative subpoenas used by the FBI, CIA, DIA and other intelligence agencies. They required no probable cause or judicial oversight and are used to request transactional records, phone numbers and e-mail addresses. Gag orders preventing the recipient of an NSL from disclosing the NSL's existence were ruled unconstitutional against 1st Amendment (free speech) rights in CY2008. The ruling also mandated semi-annual reporting to Congress on the use of NSLs.

Title V of the Uniting and Strengthening America by Fulfilling Rights and Ensuring Effective Discipline Over Monitoring (USA FREEDOM) Act (H.R. 2048) signed into law by President Obama on 06/02/15, reformed provisions of the PATRIOT Act pertaining to NSLs. Specifically, the reform extended the ban on bulk collection, except by way of application based on a "specific selection term" (specifically identifies a person, account, address, or personal device in a way that limits the scope of tangible things sought consistent with the purpose for seeking the tangible things) to various provisions in the U.S. Code that would otherwise permit the FBI to issue the bulk collection of NSLs. As of end-CY2016, many of the controversial NSL provisions from the PATRIOT Act remain in place and the FBI continues to issue thousands of NSLs every year.

"Sneak and Peak" search provisions in the USA PATRIOT Act allowed intelligence agencies to delay notification of the execution of search warrants to recipients of those warrants. These "sneak and peak" provisions were struck down on 09/26/07 after an Oregon circuit court found them to be in violation of the provisions of the 4th Amendment to the U.S. Constitution which prohibits unreasonable searches. However, when the PATRIOT Act was reauthorized in 02/11, the "sneak and peak" provisions were retained but notification of the execution of search warrants was changed to occur not more than 30 days after such execution. There was no specific oversight connected to this change.

Improved oversight of NSLs pre-dated President Obama's presidency. "Sneak and peak" oversight under the USA FREEDOM Act appears limited to the original provisions of that PATRIOT Act (Section 502 of Public Law 107-56) wherein the Attorney General must report activities under the Act to the Senate and House Select Committees on Intelligence and Judiciary Committees on a semiannual basis.

As of end-CY2016, there was no specific "material witness" provision in the USA FREEDOM Act,

Chapter 7 - Department of Homeland Security

therefore no "oversight" of such a provision is addressed therein.

No NSL or "sneak and peak" oversight improvements can be attributed directly to President Obama. "Material witness provisions" date back to the First Judiciary Act of 1789, as amended by the Bail Reform Act of 1984. Consequently "material witness provisions" were not included in the original PATRIOT Act and therefore did not require the related PATRIOT Act oversight improvements promised by President Obama.

This promise was not fulfilled.

	TERRORISM	GRADE
HS-37	**The Promise:** "I will address the problem in our prisons, where the most disaffected and disconnected Americans are being explicitly targeted for conversion by al Qaeda and its ideological allies." **When/Where:** Candidate Obama Speech at the Wilson Center, Washington, D.C., dated 08/01/07. **Source:** https://2008election.procon.org/sourcefiles/Obama20070801.pdf **Status:** Approximately 15% of the U.S. prison population is comprised of Muslim inmates. Prisons are known to be fertile grounds for converting Muslim and other inmates to a radicalized form of Islam. In recent years, radical Muslim chaplains are believed to have monopolized Islamic religious activities in U.S. state, federal, and city prisons and jails. When Muslim prisoners are released from incarceration, they are reportedly strongly encouraged to contact specific Islamic communities and mosques, where they can continue their Islamic jihad training. These training camps are known as "Muslims of the Americas" (MOA) compounds. A direct link between Al Qaeda and/or its ideological allies and U.S. federal or state prisons is known to exist, according to a former New York State Department of Correctional Services official testifying before a Congressional Homeland Security Committee hearing led by Representative Peter King (R-NY) on 06/15/11. That official testified that "individuals and groups that subscribe to radical Islamic ideology have made sustained efforts to target inmates for indoctrination." There have been many similar hearings in Congress. The trouble with these hearings is that little-to-nothing was done to resolve the issue...with one recent exception. On 12/17/15, Congressman Stephen Fincher (R-TN) introduced the "Prevent Terrorism from Entering our Prisons Act of 2015" (H.R. 4285) to require the screening of volunteers at federal prisons for terrorist links. This bill was given a 1% chance (by website govtrack.us) of being signed into law before the 114th Congress expires at the end of CY2016. After President Obama assumed the presidency in CY2009, the FBI was directed to remove all references to Islam or jihad from its training materials. Agents are even prohibited from vocalizing those terms. Further, the FBI's CY2013 "National Domestic Threat Assessment" made no mention of Islam in any form. As of end-CY2016, there was no evidence that the Obama Administration took any special steps to thwart the influence that Al Qaeda operatives and their ideological allies such as members of the Islamic State of Iraq and Syria (ISIS) were believed to have inside U.S. prisons. This promise was not fulfilled.	0.00
HS-38	**The Promise:** "Chemical plants are potential terrorist targets because they are often located near cities, are relatively easy to attack, and contain multi-ton quantities of hazardous chemicals...Obama will establish a clear set of federal regulations that all plants must follow, including improving barriers, containment, mitigation, and safety training..." **When/Where:** Obama-Biden Plan: "The War We Need to Win" dated 07/31/07. **Source:** http://www.mattluedke.com/wp-content/uploads/2016/09/CounterterrorismFactSheet.pdf **Status:** The Chemical Facility Anti-Terrorism Standards (CFATS), enforced by the Department of Homeland Security (DHS) came into effect on 06/08/07 with Appendix A for Chemicals of Interest	1.00

Chapter 7 - Department of Homeland Security

(COI) revisions that became effective on 11/20/07. The resulting Interim Final Rule (IFR) became codified under Title 6, Part 27 of the Code of Federal Regulations (CFR) and introduced a uniform process for assessing our nation's chemical facilities against Risk-Based Performance Standards.

To implement CFATS, DHS devised a Chemical Security Assessment Tool (CSAT) so that nearly 50K organizations that manufacture, use, store or distribute any COI can register in the system's on-line "Top Screen" process, except for organizations governed under the Maritime Transportation Security Act.

Upon reviewing "Top Screen" entries, organizations are ranked according to 4 tiers, with the highest being Tier 1 for companies possessing the highest risk. Upon receiving their initial tier notification, organizations complete a Security Vulnerability Assessment (SVA) so that DHS can conduct further assessments and assign a final tier classification.

Companies then prepare a Site Security Plan (SSP) documenting how they will satisfy the 18 standards identified in the IFR. Upon approval of the SSP by DHS, DHS issues an operating permit to the organization and thereafter conducts periodic site audits and inspections.

On 12/18/14, President Obama signed into law the "Protecting and Securing Chemical Facilities from Terrorist Attacks Act of 2014" (the "CFATS Act of 2014"), which recodified and reauthorized the CFATS program through CY2018 for the nation's 4,569 chemical facilities regulated by the Department of Homeland Security (DHS). Initially authorized by Congress in CY2007, the program uses a dynamic multi-tiered risk assessment process and requires facilities identified as high-risk to meet and maintain performance-based security standards appropriate to the facilities and the risks they pose. DHS chemical security inspectors work in all 50 states to help ensure facilities have security measures in place to meet CFATS requirements.

Further to the above, the DHS has routinely published updates to regulations contained in Title 6, Part 27 of the CFR, addressing the basic tenets of this promise.

This promise was fulfilled.

HS-39

The Promise: "...will expand the U.S. government's bioforensics program for tracking the source of any biological weapon so that the U.S. will be able to rapidly identify any adversary who uses a biological weapon and respond surely and swiftly."
When/Where: Fact Sheet: Obama's New Plan to Confront 21st Century Threats, 07/16/08
Source: https://www.presidency.ucsb.edu/documents/press-release-fact-sheet-obamas-new-plan-confront-21st-century-threats
Status: The nation's bioforensics capabilities were expanded by the opening of the Department of Homeland Security's Directorate for Science and Technology's $143M National Biodefense Analysis and Countermeasures Center (NBACC) at Fort Detrick, MD in 03/09. NBACC's mission is to provide the scientific basis for the characterization of biological threats and bioforensic analysis to support attribution of their planned or actual use. NBACC components include the National Bioforensic Analysis Center (NBFAC) and the National Biological Threat Characterization Center (NBTCC). Its core competencies include: Aerobiology; Biocontainment Operations; Bioforensics; Genomics and Bioinformatics; and broad capabilities in Bacteriology, Virology, and Toxinology Operations.

Although the contractor-operated NBACC was planned and funded long before President Obama entered presidential politics in 02/07, where President Obama comes into the picture is the extent to which he has supported the NBACC's 150 employees and their work. The financial crisis of CY2008 caused the NBACC's budget to be reduced from $32.9M in FY2009 to $30.0M in FY2010. For the following years, NBACC's budget authority was steadily increased as follows:
FY2011....$30.3M
FY2012....$30.8M
FY2013....$32.1M

1.00

FY2014....$33.4M
FY2015....$34.6M
FY2016....$35.8M

In 09/15, the Obama Administration provided additional NBACC funding in the form of a 10-year, $481M contract to Battelle National Laboratories.

As of end-CY2016, funding for a new $1.25B National Bio and Agro-Defense Facility (NBAF) has included federal, state and City of Manhattan, KS contributions. With the final federal commitment of $300M in FY2015 for a total of $938M in federal appropriations, NBAF laboratory facilities construction is well under way for completion in 12/20 and an anticipated Initial Operating Capability in 05/21. The NBAF will replace the antiquated Plum Island Animal Disease Center in New York State.

This promise was fulfilled.

HS-40

The Promise: "Fully implement the Lugar-Obama legislation to help our allies detect and stop the smuggling of weapons of mass destruction."
When/Where: Obama-Biden Plan: Secure Nuclear Weapons Materials in Four Years and End Nuclear Smuggling, undated.
Source:
https://webarchive.loc.gov/all/20090429184932/http://change.gov/agenda/homeland_security_agenda/
Status: The "Nuclear Non-Proliferation and Conventional Weapons Threat Reduction Act" was introduced by U.S. Senator Richard Lugar (R-IN) and then-Senator Barack Obama (D-IL) to expand U.S. cooperation to destroy conventional weapons stockpiles and to expand the State Department's ability to detect and interdict weapons and materials of mass destruction worldwide.

The basic provisions of the Lugar-Obama Initiative were incorporated in the "Department of State Authorities Act of 2006" (H.R. 6060) signed into law by President George W. Bush on 01/11/07.

The Lugar-Obama Initiative strengthened the ability of America's allies to detect and interdict illegal shipments of weapons and materials before these nuclear, chemical, biological and other weapons of mass destruction reached terrorists.

Since becoming President, Obama has gone several steps further than those mandated by the Lugar-Obama initiative of CY2007. For example, his FY2011 budget proposal for the Department of Energy's National Nuclear Security Administration (NNSA) for preventing proliferation was $2.7B, a 25.8% increase over FY2010. Highlights of this proposal were: (1) $590M for International Nuclear Materials Protection and Cooperation, including $265 for Second Line of Defense and Megaports programs; (2) $558.8 (up 67%) for the Global Threat Reduction Initiative to secure vulnerable nuclear and radiological materials; (3) $1B to work with Russia to permanently eliminate 68 metric tons of surplus weapons plutonium; (4) $351.5M (up 11%) for nonproliferation-related research and development; and (5) $155M to strengthen global nuclear safeguards and nuclear controls to verify arms control agreements.

It should be noted, however, that on 12/16/14, largely due to increased diplomatic hostilities between the USA and Russia fed by Russia's invasion and annexation of Crimea in 03/14, Russia informed the Obama Administration that they were cancelling previous agreements whereby they would accept U.S. assistance in protecting their stockpiles of about 700 metric tons of weapons-grade highly enriched uranium and 130 metric tons of military-grade plutonium from being stolen or sold on the black market.

Nonetheless, this promise was fulfilled.

1.00

HS-41

The Promise: "...if we have Osama bin Laden in our sights and the Pakistani government is unable or unwilling to take them out, then I think that we have to act, and we will take them out. We will kill bin

1.00

Laden."
When/Where: Second Presidential Debate, Nashville, TN, 10/02/08
Source: http://elections.nytimes.com/2008/president/debates/transcripts/second-presidential-debate.html
Status: Osama bin Laden was eliminated by U.S. Navy SEALS Team Six on 05/02/11.

This promise was fulfilled.

HS-42   **The Promise:** "We will crush al-Qaida. That has to be our biggest national security priority."   0.00
When/Where: Second Presidential Debate, Nashville, TN, 10/02/08
Source: http://elections.nytimes.com/2008/president/debates/transcripts/second-presidential-debate.html
Status: The elimination of the titular head of Al-Qaeda, Osama bin Laden, on 05/02/11 was not viewed as the crushing of Al-Queda as a terrorist organization.

When Al-Qaeda emerged as a radically ideological organization, it was known to have four main branches: Al-Qaeda Central (Pakistan), Al-Qaida Arabian Peninsula (AQAP), Al-Qaeda Maghreb (AQIM) in North Africa, and Al-Qaeda in the Land of Two Rivers - Iraq (AQIZ).

Egyptian Ayman al-Zawahiri, bin Laden's principal deputy and chief strategist was confirmed as bin Laden's successor on 06/16/11.

Jihadist terrorism is believed to extend far beyond Al-Qaeda. Countries like Indonesia and Saudi Arabia have done their best to neutralize jihadist franchise groups, but these groups simply relocate and re-affirm their intent to destroy the United States and its allies. Taking advantage of the turbulence created by pro-democracy movements in Yemen during most of CY2011 and CY2012, for example, AQAP seized significant amounts of land and power around Zinjibar and other areas of southern Yemen.

Neutralizing Al-Qaeda on a worldwide basis would go a long way toward ensuring the security of the United States and the rest of the world. But we have seen no progress on a global scale under Obama Administration leadership or influence to "crush" this organization. Rather, Al-Qaeda as an organization has survived Osama bin Laden's elimination, the elimination of AQAP's radical Yemeni-American cleric leader Anwar Al-Awlaki, and the elimination of Al-Qaeda's #2, Abu Yahya al-Libi.

In fact, more than three years into President Obama's first term in office, the State Department released its "Country Reports on Terrorism 2011" on 07/31/12 that reflected the growing strength of Al-Qaeda affiliates AQAP, AQIM and AQIZ and the expansion of Al-Qaeda resources in countries such as Syria -- largely due to increased funding assistance for training from Iran.

As of the start of President Obama's second term in office, the Al-Qaeda core group led by Ayman al-Zawahiri continued to operate in the Pakistani-Afghani theater.
- AQIM was operating in Algeria and Mali, bringing their threat closer to Europe. French forces tried to neutralize this threat with limited U.S. assistance.
- AQIZ was reportedly stronger than it was when U.S. troops disbanded from Iraq. They are reportedly effective in both Iraq and Syria.
- AQAP was still effective as a terrorist force.
- AQIS (Al-Qaeda in the Indian Sub-continent) - This was a new Al-Qaeda element, the formation of which was announced by leader Ayman Al-Zawahiri in CY2014. AQIS was believed to be headquartered in Pakistan with an operational responsibility that included Pakistan, India and the rest of southern Asia.

The closure of 22 U.S. Embassies/Consulates in the Middle East on 08/04/13 in reaction to a specific and credible Al-Qaeda threat was further proof that the Obama Administration was unable to "crush" that terrorist organization. In 01/14, two key cities in Iraq's Anbar Province (Fallujah and Ramadi), fell to Al-Qaeda militants.

In sum, as of end-CY2016, AQAP, AQIM, AQIZ, AQIS and Shabaab, formal branches of Al-Qaeda, had made their allegiance to Zawahiri evident. Jabhat Fath al Sham (formerly known as Al Nusrah) and other organizations continued to serve Al-Qaeda's agenda as well. Thus, Al-Qaeda elements were believed to be thriving in varying degrees in Iraq, Pakistan, Algeria, Yemen, Syria, Libya, Mali, Somalia and elsewhere.

As late as 11/16, New York, Texas and Virginia were declared to be possible targets for some type of terrorist attack prior to the 11/08/16 general elections, although no specific locations were identified by intelligence information sources. There was reportedly pressure on Al-Qaeda and its affiliates to regain relevance with their mission. As of end-CY2016, Al-Qaeda had not been crushed.

This promise was not fulfilled.

HOMELAND SECURITY GPA	**0.50**

Campaign Promises
Departments -> Housing & Urban Dev

ITEM	HOUSING & URBAN DEV	
	AFFORDABLE HOUSING	**GRADE**
HU-1	**The Promise:** "Will support efforts to create an Affordable Housing Trust Fund to develop affordable housing in mixed-income neighborhoods." **When/Where:** Obama-Biden Plan: "Supporting Urban Prosperity", dated 09/11/08. **Source:** https://assets.documentcloud.org/documents/550008/barack-obama-2008-supporting-urban-prosperity.pdf **Status:** The key words in this promise,"create an Affordable Housing Trust Fund" may have sounded great to low income earners and garnered votes for then-Candidate Obama. In reality, a National Housing Trust Fund (NHTF) was enacted in Public Law 110-289 on 07/30/08, a few months prior to the publication of the Obama-Biden plan sourced above. The President's Budget proposal for FY2010, and almost every year thereafter, included $1B "to capitalize and launch an Affordable Housing Trust Fund that will develop, rehabilitate, and preserve affordable housing targeted to very low income households." This was, in essence, the already-enacted NHTF. However, the FY2010 budget Final Conference Report (111-366) did not view funding the NHTF favorably. It was the only budget item in the Housing and Urban Development (HUD) budget requested by President Obama that received absolutely no funding. The reason for this was because the Federal National Mortgage Association (Fannie Mae) and the Federal Home Loan Mortgage Corporation (Freddie Mac) were both considered by Congress at the time to be failed Government-Sponsored Enterprises (GSEs) models. To remedy this situation and in response to the Dodd-Frank Wall Street Reform and Consumer Protection Act signed into law by President Obama on 07/21/10, HUD issued its report entitled "Reforming America's Housing Finance Market, A Report to Congress," on 02/11/11. In that report, HUD recommended better Government support for affordable housing by asking Congress to capitalize targeted access and affordability initiatives such as those mandated by Public Law 110-289. On 03/03/11, Senator Jack Reed (D-RI) introduced the "Preserving Homes and Communities Act" (S. 489). This was followed by the introduction by Congressman Elijah Cummings (D-MD) on 04/12/11 of a companion bill (H.R. 1477). These bills were designed to provide the $1B capitalization needed by the NHTF from profits accrued from the sale of warrants that the federal government received from banks that were bailed out under the Troubled Assets Recovery Program (TARP). Neither bill got past the introduction phase and both expired with the 112th Congress. Finally in FY2016, far from the annual request for $1B, the Housing Trust Fund was appropriated $182M and President Obama requested $136M for FY2017. These funds come from assessments from Fannie Mae and Freddie Mac. They will finance the development, rehabilitation and	0.00

Chapter 8 - Department of Housing & Urban Development

preservation of affordable housing for extremely low-income (ELI) residents, and will result in over 1,000 housing units produced over time.

The "Affordable Housing Trust Fund" did not require creation and the NHTF was not funded for most of President Obama's two terms in office.

This promise was not fulfilled.

HU-2	**The Promise:** "As President, Obama will work with the state to establish a goal for approving all Road Home applications within two months." **When/Where:** Obama-Biden Plan: "Rebuilding the Gulf Coast and Preventing Future Catastrophes", dated 09/11/08. **Source:** https://assets.documentcloud.org/documents/550006/barack-obama-2008-rebuilding-the-gulf-coast-and.pdf **Status:** The "Road Home" Program was funded at $10.4B to allow grants up to $150K per homeowner victim of Hurricanes Katrina and Rita. As of the end of CY2010, approximately 130,000 families (out of 230,000 applicants) had received affordable housing assistance valued at $8.9B from the state's housing recovery program administered by the Louisiana's Office of Community Development (OCD) via a contract with ICF International. However, according to the Louisiana Recovery Authority (LRA), by the end of 2009 approximately 3,500 homeowners were still working their applications through the system and more than 200 still had open appeals cases. The LRA ceased to exist on 06/30/10 and its functions were assumed by the Disaster Recovery Unit of Louisiana's OCD. The OCD reported that as of end-CY2010, only 66 applications were in the appeal process. More than $700M in Road Home funds remained unspent and about 3,000 files remained open as of early CY2011 -- some of these being more than a year old. This promise was not fulfilled.	0.00
HU-3	**The Promise:** "Will also work to increase the supply of rental property, which is particularly important in New Orleans where 57 percent of pre-Katrina residents were renters." **When/Where:** Obama-Biden Plan: "Rebuilding the Gulf Coast and Preventing Future Catastrophes", dated 09/11/08. **Source:** https://assets.documentcloud.org/documents/550006/barack-obama-2008-rebuilding-the-gulf-coast-and.pdf **Status:** Hurricane Katrina, according to the New Orleans Office of Community Development (OCD), destroyed 70% of housing stock including 51,000 rental units. According to the Greater New Orleans Community Data Center (GNOCDC), the CY2010 number of new federally subsidized rental units needed was 20,896. Against this requirement, only about one third (7,754) were subsidized, leaving 13,429 not subsidized. Projected subsidized rental unit requirements were provided by the GNOCDC as 23,034 in CY2012 and 26,837 by CY2015, escalating to 36,151 by CY2020. As of end-CY2012, the OCD reported that New Orleans still had 43,755 blighted homes and that an estimated $9.9B was needed to complete the city's reconstruction needs, including rental properties. Against this need, federal grants in FY2012 amounted to about $17M broken out as follows: - $10.830M from Community Development Block Grant (CDBG) - $1.590M from HOME Investment Partnerships Program (HOME) - $1.291 from Emergency Solutions Grant (ESG) Program - $3.584 from Housing Opportunities for Persons with AIDS (HOPWA) By end-CY2015, 35% of renters in the New Orleans-Metairie-Kenner statistical area devoted 50% or	0.00

Chapter 8 - Department of Housing & Urban Development

more of their income to rent and utilities. Only Miami was higher where 37.5% of renters shelled out 50% or more of their income to rent and utilities.

As of end-CY2016, New Orleans remained far behind in rebuilding its supply of apartment rentals following the total loss of at least 12,000 units after Hurricane Katrina. The metro area had added only about 3,100 units since CY2012.

This promise was not fulfilled.

HU-4	**The Promise:** "...will create a Homeowner Obligation Made Explicit (HOME) score, which will provide potential borrowers with a simplified, standardized borrower metric (similar to APR) for home mortgages. The HOME score will allow Americans to easily compare various mortgage products and understand the full cost of the loan." **When/Where:** Obama-Biden Plan: "Supporting Urban Prosperity", dated 09/11/08. **Source:** https://assets.documentcloud.org/documents/550008/barack-obama-2008-supporting-urban-prosperity.pdf **Status:** The Dodd-Frank Wall Street Reform and Consumer Protection Act signed into law by President Obama on 07/21/10 created a Consumer Financial Protection Bureau (CFPB). One of the CFPB's missions was to "prescribe rules to ensure that the features of any consumer financial product or service, both initially and over the term of the product or service, are fully, accurately, and effectively disclosed to consumers." In CY2015, the CFPB introduced the "CFPB Mortgage Tool" to help potential borrowers see the lowest interest rate available to them. Borrowers can use this tool to input their credit score, down payment, loan amount and zip code. The CFPB, using real data, will show the average and best interest rates available in the market in real time. In 09/15, the CFPB introduced its second tool to assist potential borrowers, a clear, three-page loan disclosure form written in simple language that any borrower can understand. The disclosure form simplifies the following: - The first part of the document reflects the loan amount, interest rate, monthly payment and any prepayment penalties or balloon payments as well as the total closing costs and cash required to close. - The second part breaks the costs into two sections. The first section details closing costs that "you cannot shop for" and closing costs that "you can shop for." For example, a borrower cannot shop for a better mortgage insurance deal, but can shop around for better deals on title insurance and property inspections. - The last section of the disclosure form is entitled "Comparisons," which simplifies the borrower's understanding of how much he/she will pay over a five-year period, including all expenses. When the borrower is shopping for mortgages, he/she can compare those five-year costs to see which lender is giving him/her the best deal when all costs are included. Although these CFPB initiatives do not ultimately provide the potential borrower with a "score," the intent of this promise has been fulfilled.	1.00
HU-5	**The Promise:** "...will also restore cuts to public housing operating subsidies, and ensure that all Department of Housing and Urban Development (HUD) programs are restored to their original purpose." **When/Where:** Obama-Biden Plan: "Supporting Urban Prosperity", dated 09/11/08. **Source:** https://assets.documentcloud.org/documents/550008/barack-obama-2008-supporting-urban-prosperity.pdf **Status:** President Obama's FY2010 budget request included $4.600B for the Public Housing Operating Fund (PHOF), which represented 100% of funding requirements for operating subsidies (since CY2002) as calculated by a formula devised through negotiated rule making. The amount appropriated by Congress for PHOF in FY2010 was actually $4.775B to mitigate prior year	1.00

	shortages. For subsequent years, funds requested for PHOF compared to the amount authorized by Congress were as follows: FY2011....Requested $4.829B / Received $4.626B FY2012....Requested $3.962B / Received $3.962B FY2013....Requested $4.524B / Received $4.262B FY2014....Requested $4.600B / Received $4.400B FY2015....Requested $4.600B / Received $4.400B FY2016....Requested $4.600B / Received $4.500B FY2017....Requested $4.569B / Received $4.400B Serious attempts were made by the Obama Administration, within budget constraints (i.e. sequestration), to reach the annual goal of $4.600B for the PHOF. This promise was fulfilled.	

	COMMUNITY DEVELOPMENT	GRADE
HU-6	**The Promise:** "...will work to provide states and local governments with the resources they need to address sprawl and create more livable communities." **When/Where:** Obama-Biden Plan: "Strengthening America's Transportation Infrastructure" dated 10/09/08. **Source:** https://transportist.org/2008/02/ **Status:** On 05/21/10, HUD Secretary Shaun Donovan correlated the alarming rate of home foreclosures with access to transportation, good schools and economic opportunity (i.e. jobs). Under President Obama, the federal government took steps to advance sustainability among buildings and communities under a $3.25B "Sustainable Communities Planning Grants" program administered by the Department of Housing and Urban Development (HUD) under the aegis of its Leadership in Energy and Environmental Design for Neighborhood Development (LEED-ND) initiative. The objective of the above grant program was to integrate green building into community development, help reduce sprawl, increase transportation choices, decrease automobile dependence, encourage healthy living, and protect endangered species. This is where a role for the Environmental Protection Agency (EPA) and Department of Transportation was defined in a partnership with HUD on 10/21/10. The President's "Sustainable Housing and Communities Initiative" became an integral part of the Community Development Block Grants (CDBG) Program, later renamed the "Community Development Fund" (CDF). Starting with FY2009, the $3.900B appropriated for the CDBG under President Bush was supplemented by $3.000B under the American Recovery and Reinvestment Act (ARRA) of 2009, signed into law on 02/17/09 by President Obama. During subsequent years, the CDBG/CDF was funded as follows: FY2010....$4.450B plus $100M for disaster relief FY2011....$3.501B FY2012....$3.408B FY2013....$3.308B plus $15.007B for disaster relief FY2014....$3.100B FY2015....$3.066B FY2016....$3.359B FY2017....$3.000B This promise was fulfilled.	1.00
HU-7	**The Promise:** "The Community Development Block Grant (CDBG) program is an important program that helps strengthen cities and towns throughout the nation by providing housing and creating jobs	1.00

Chapter 8 - Department of Housing & Urban Development

primarily for low- and moderate-income people and places...will restore funding for the CDBG program."
When/Where: Obama-Biden Plan: "Supporting Urban Prosperity", dated 09/11/08.
Source: https://assets.documentcloud.org/documents/550008/barack-obama-2008-supporting-urban-prosperity.pdf
Status: Under the Bush Administration, the Community Development Block Grant (CDBG) program faced an uncertain future. Some members of Congress had thoughts of holding sustained funding in abeyance and making future funding contingent upon mandated reforms and proof that the taxpayers dollars were reaping the intended results.

As part of the Community Planning and Development (CPD) Program, the CDBG Program is the largest community and economic development program in the U.S. Government, reaching an estimated 7,000 local governments annually. It assists urban, suburban and rural communities to improve housing and living conditions, expands economic opportunities for low and moderate income persons, helps to create jobs through the expansion and retention of businesses, and helps local governments tackle serious challenges facing their communities. Counties use the flexibility of CDBG funds to partner with private and non-profit sectors to develop and upgrade local housing, water and infrastructure projects and human services programs.

The annual appropriation for CDBG formula funding is split so that 70% is allocated among entitlement cities and counties and 30% among the states. See Promise HU-6 above for CDBG funding levels.

President Obama requested and received sustained funding and kept the CDBG program alive by proposing adequate levels of funding in light of severe budget constraints during his two terms in office.

This promise was fulfilled.

FORECLOSURES	GRADE
HU-8 **The Promise:** "I'll put a three-month moratorium on foreclosures so that we give homeowners the breathing room they need to get back on their feet." **When/Where:** Campaign Speech, Richmond, VA, 10/22/08. **Source:** http://www.presidency.ucsb.edu/ws/index.php?pid=84619 **Status:** While some states (i.e. California) voluntarily applied the proposed 90-day moratorium, Obama failed to make the promised moratorium a national commitment. In 09/10, tens of thousands of eviction applications were issued by "robosigners" without their accuracy being verified. Individual states (Texas, Connecticut, California, Colorado) moved quickly to institute their own foreclosure moratoriums, while the Bank of America announced on 10/07/10 that it would halt foreclosures nationwide due to reports of mortgage document mishandling. On 10/10/10, White House Senior Advisor David Axelrod announced that the Obama Administration did not favor a national moratorium on foreclosures, stating that foreclosures where documentation was neither inaccurate nor fraudulent should proceed. This promise was not fulfilled.	0.00
HU-9 **The Promise:** "...Chapter 13 law prohibits bankruptcy judges from modifying the original terms of home mortgages for ordinary families, regardless of whether the loan was predatory or unfair or is otherwise unaffordable...will repeal this provision so that ordinary families can also get relief that bankruptcy laws were intended to provide." **When/Where:** Obama-Biden Plan: "Supporting Urban Prosperity", dated 09/11/08. **Source:** https://assets.documentcloud.org/documents/550008/barack-obama-2008-supporting-urban-prosperity.pdf	0.00

Chapter 8 - Department of Housing & Urban Development

Status: Bankruptcy Law is contained in Title 11 of the United States Code. Congress passed the Bankruptcy Code under its constitutional grant of authority to "establish... uniform laws on the subject of bankruptcy throughout the United States." Its codification occurred with the enactment of the "Bankruptcy Law of 1800."

Chapter 13 of the Bankruptcy Law permits the discharge of some debts, as well as the repayment of others over a period of three to five years. It may also permit either a reduction in principal owed on secured debts or the elimination of these debts altogether. It can also be used to structure a repayment plan for debts that cannot be settled in bankruptcy.

On 05/20/09, President Obama signed the "Helping Families Save Their Homes Act of 2009" (S. 896). One of the original intents of this law was to allow bankruptcy judges to modify mortgages on primary residences. However, the Democrat-controlled Senate deleted this "cram down" provision from the above law.

On 12/11/09, the Democrat-controlled House voted against Amendment #534 to H.R. 4173 (188 for, 241 against) that would have permitted foreclosure-prone house owners to extend repayment periods, reduce excessive interest rates and fees, and adjust the principal balance of the mortgage to a home's fair market value as necessary to prevent foreclosure. It would further have permitted the Veterans Administration (VA) and Federal Housing Administration (FHA) and others to take steps to facilitate mortgage modifications.

On 02/01/12, President Obama called on Congress to support a new mortgage refinancing plan that would make it easier for homeowners whose mortgages are higher than their homes are worth to refinance their mortgages at lower interest rates. The Home Affordable Refinance Program (HARP 2.0) went into effect on 03/17/12 and permits homeowners to refinance their mortgages without paying down principal.

To improve upon HARP 2.0, which lacked sustainability, President Obama proposed HARP 3.0 on 01/24/12 which would have further expanded the mortgage refinancing process to homeowners whose mortgages were non-Fannie Mae or non-Freddie Mac and other eligibility criteria. The "Responsible Homeowners Refinancing Act of 2012" (S.3085) introduced by Senator Robert Menendez (D-NJ) on 05/10/12, could have codified provisions of HARP 3.0, but this bill died with the 112th Congress at the end of CY2012. This bill was reintroduced by Senator Menendez on 02/17/13 as the "Responsible Homeowner Refinancing Act of 2013" (S. 249). It died with the 113th Congress at the end of CY2014.

The expiration date for HARP 2.0 was 09/30/17. If HARP 3.0 had been signed into law by that date, the new program would have had no cutoff date and would not have limited borrowers to a single use. However, HARP 3.0 would have only serviced loans held by Fannie Mae and Freddie Mac. Underwater homeowners with non-Government-Sponsored Enterprise (GSE) held loans would still have lacked an alternative to refinance out of their high interest loans.

Chapter 13 of the "Bankruptcy Law of 1800" has not been repealed, nor has it been amended since 04/05.

This promise was not fulfilled.

| HU-10 | **The Promise:** "Obama will create a Foreclosure Prevention Fund to help people facing foreclosure stay in their homes and renegotiate with their lenders or sell their homes."
 When/Where: Obama-Biden Plan: Protecting Homeownership and Cracking Down on Mortgage Fraud, dated 01/13/08.
 Source: http://www.orthogonalthought.com/blog/wp-content/uploads/2008/06/mortgagefactsheet.pdf
 Status: Created under President George W. Bush on 10/03/08, the "Troubled Assets Relief Program" (TARP) could have served to fulfill this promise. TARP was originally authorized at the $700B level | 0.00 |

Chapter 8 - Department of Housing & Urban Development

but was reduced under President Obama to $475B by Congress under the Dodd-Frank Wall Street Reform and Consumer Protection Act of 07/21/10, against which $426.4B was disbursed. TARP funding expired on 10/01/10 reportedly because the fund failed to live up to expectations, one of which was to mitigate foreclosures in the wake of the CY2008 financial crisis.

During the Obama Administration, the nation continued to experience high foreclosure filings. A breakout of the number of filings by year follows, with improvements noted in CY2012 and subsequent years:
CY2009....3.4M
CY2010....3.8M
CY2011....3.9M
CY2012....2.3M
CY2013....1.3M
CY2014....1.1M
CY2015....1.1M
CY2016....0.9M

A "Foreclosure Prevention Fund" at the national level was not created under President Obama.

This promise was not fulfilled.

HU-11

The Promise: "...will make stabilizing our housing crisis a top priority..."
When/Where: Obama-Biden Plan: "Supporting Urban Prosperity," dated 09/11/08.
Source: https://assets.documentcloud.org/documents/550008/barack-obama-2008-supporting-urban-prosperity.pdf
Status: Housing prices peaked in early CY2006 and started to decline in late CY2006 and CY2007. It simply became more difficult for borrowers to refinance their loans. As adjustable-rate mortgages began to reset at higher interest rates (causing higher monthly payments), mortgage delinquencies soared, peaking by CY2012. Securities backed with mortgages, including subprime mortgages, lost most of their value. Global investors reduced purchases of mortgage-backed debt and other securities as part of a decline in the capacity of the private financial system to support lending. A tightening of credit around the world and slowing economic growth in the USA and Europe ensued. The credit crisis resulting from this bursting of the housing bubble was a major cause of the credit default swap bubble of the CY2008 recession.

From the outset, the Obama Administration accorded top priority to stabilize the housing market and provide security for homeowners. To achieve these goals, the Administration developed a broad approach implementing state and local housing agency initiatives, tax credits for homebuyers, neighborhood stabilization and community development programs, mortgage modifications and refinancing, housing counseling, continued Federal Housing Administration (FHA) engagement, support for Fannie Mae and Freddie Max and increased consumer protections. In addition, Federal Reserve and Department of Treasury mortgage-backed securities purchase programs helped to keep mortgage interest rates at record lows.

This promise was fulfilled.

1.00

HOUSING & URBAN DEV GPA	0.45

Campaign Promises

Departments -> Interior

ITEM	INTERIOR	GRADE
	FISH AND WILDLIFE SERVICE	
IN-1	**The Promise:** "Will provide state game and fish agencies with additional resources and encouragement to reach out to young men and women to educate them about hunting and fishing opportunities, hunter safety, and the basic principles of fish and wildlife management." **When/Where:** Obama-Biden Plan: "Supporting the Rights and Traditions of Sportsmen" dated 08/06/08. **Source:** https://www.kentuckyhunting.net/threads/obama-sportsmen-issues.61174/ **Status:** The Department of the Interior's (DOI) FY2010 budget proposal included $30M for the creation of a program entitled "Educating Young Hunters and Anglers." This proposed program was scrapped by Congress. While the DOI manages other youth-oriented programs such as the "Youth in the Great Outdoors" program and the "Youth Conservation Corps," none is specifically earmarked for youth hunting and fishing education or fish and wildlife management. This promise was not fulfilled.	0.00
IN-2	**The Promise:** "...devote billions of dollars annually to state game and fish agencies and federal land management agencies to help them ensure that fish and wildlife survive the impacts of climate change." **When/Where:** Obama-Biden Plan: "Supporting the Rights and Traditions of Sportsmen" dated 08/06/08. **Source:** https://www.kentuckyhunting.net/threads/obama-sportsmen-issues.61174/ **Status:** "Adaptation" is defined in the Department of Interior's (DOI's) 09/10 "Climate Change Strategic Plan" as "...planned, science-based management actions that we take to help reduce the impacts of climate change on fish, wildlife, and their habitats." In other words, DOI intended to help fish and wildlife "adapt" to climate change. Fulfillment of this "billions of dollars" promise was dependent upon passage of the American Clean Energy and Security (ACES) Act of 2009 (H.R. 2454) in CY2009. This Act (also known as the Waxman-Markey Bill or Cap-and-Trade Bill), was approved by the House but failed to pass the Senate. No other legislation containing the language found in the ACES Act of 2009, informally referred to as the "Cap & Trade Bill," was enacted during the remainder of President Obama's two terms in office. Multiple federal and state organizations run climate change programs. However none are known to have benefited from "billions of dollars" specifically aimed at helping fish and wildlife adapt to climate change. This promise was not fulfilled.	0.00
IN-3	**The Promise:** "...full funding for the North American Wetlands Conservation Act and fulfilling the goal	0.00

of "no net loss"..."

When/Where: Obama-Biden Plan: "Supporting the Rights and Traditions of Sportsmen" dated 08/06/08.

Source: https://www.kentuckyhunting.net/threads/obama-sportsmen-issues.61174/

Status: The North American Wetlands Conservation Act (NAWCA) of 1989 encourages "partnerships among public agencies and other interests to protect, enhance, restore, and manage wetland ecosystems and other habitats for migratory birds, fish and other wildlife..." Under the "No Net Loss Wetlands Policy," wetland loss is to be balanced with wetlands reclamation, mitigation, and restoration so that the total wetlands acreage in the USA does not decrease.

The latest available "Status and Trends of Wetlands in the Conterminous United States" provides data up to CY2009 only and shows that the goal of "no net loss," at that time, was not being achieved. Absent any current information as of end-CY2016, the focus is on the funding aspects of this promise.

In 2006, Congress reauthorized the NAWCA to extend its appropriation authorization up to $75M per year to 2012. This was the amount to be reached in the first few years of President Obama's first term to ensure the promised "full funding" was met.

Under President Obama, the North American Wetlands Conservation Fund received the following funding:

FY2010....$47.6M
FY2011....$37.5M
FY2012....$35.4M
FY2013....$33.6M
FY2014....$31.1M
FY2015....$34.1M
FY2016....$35.1M
FY2017....$35.0M

Additional program funding comes from fines, penalties, and forfeitures collected under the Migratory Bird Treaty Act of 1918; from federal fuel excise taxes on small gasoline engines; and from interest accrued on the fund established under the Federal Aid in Wildlife Restoration Act of 1937.

Efforts to reauthorize the NAWCA were unsuccessful. Notably, the North American Wetlands Conservation Extension Act of 2014 (S. 741), introduced on 04/16/13 by Senator David Vitter (R-LA), would have reauthorized the NAWCA in the amount of $55M per year during the period FY2014 through FY2019, down from the previously authorized $75M per year through FY2012. This bill expired at the end of the 113th Congress in 12/14.

The Sportsmen's Conservation and Outdoor Recreation Enhancement Act (H.R. 3173) was introduced by Congressman Timothy Walz (D-MN) on 07/23/15. A provision of this bill would have reauthorized the NAWCA for the period FY2016 to FY2020 in the amount not to exceed $50M per year. This bill expired with the 114th Congress at the end of CY2016.

As late as 11/03/15, President Obama acknowledged in a memorandum entitled "Mitigating Impacts on Natural Resources from Development and Encouraging Related Private Investment" that "no net loss" goals had not yet been met. In this memorandum, he directed that "Agencies' mitigation policies should establish a net benefit goal or, at a minimum, a no net loss goal for natural resources the agency manages that are important, scarce, or sensitive, or wherever doing so is consistent with agency mission and established natural resource objectives."

This promise was not fulfilled.

Chapter 9 - Department of the Interior

	HABITAT	GRADE
IN-4	**The Promise:** "...will support the use of tax incentives and other financial mechanisms to encourage private landowners to restore and protect habitat." **When/Where:** Obama-Biden Plan: "Supporting the Rights and Traditions of Sportsmen" dated 08/06/08. **Source:** https://www.kentuckyhunting.net/threads/obama-sportsmen-issues.61174/ **Status:** Tax incentives for restoring and protecting habitat, formally known as the "Enhanced Easement Incentive," were extended to 12/31/11 under the Tax Relief, Unemployment Insurance Reauthorization and Job Creation Act signed into law by President Obama on 12/17/10. Section 111, Division Q of the Consolidated Appropriations Act of 2016 (H.R. 2029) signed into law by President Obama on 12/18/15 made permanent the conservation easement tax incentive. Under this provision, non-farmer/rancher landowners who donate land for conservation easement purposes can deduct 50% of their annual income for 15 years. Qualifying farmer and rancher landowners can deduct 100% of their annual income for 15 years for the same purpose. This promise was fulfilled.	1.00
IN-5	**The Promise:** "...will direct the Departments of Agriculture and the Interior to place a special emphasis on restoration of habitat for important game species associated with specific regions of the United States..." **When/Where:** Obama-Biden Plan: "Supporting the Rights and Traditions of Sportsmen" dated 08/06/08. **Source:** https://www.kentuckyhunting.net/threads/obama-sportsmen-issues.61174/ **Status:** To fulfill this promise, the American Rovery and Reinvestment Act of 2009 authorized $165M for the U.S. Fish and Wildlife Service Resource Management account for "deferred maintenance, construction, and capital improvement projects on national wildlife refuges and national fish hatcheries and for high priority habitat restoration projects." Started in 01/08, The State Acres for Wildlife Enhancement (SAFE) program allows for individual states to offer special projects within the Conservation Reserve Program (CRP) to benefit threatened, endangered, and other high-priority species through habitat restoration. The SAFE program sets aside 500K acres under CRP for this purpose. President Obama's FY2010 budget submission included $119M, a $34M million increase over FY2009, for Forest Service funding through the Land and Water Conservation Fund to acquire easements to provide habitat for threatened or endangered wildlife and fish. In the FY2010 budget, another $230M was proposed for the National Oceanic and Atmospheric Administration (NOAA) for habitat restoration. For FY2011, President Obama's budget submission included $300M for ecosystem restoration efforts in the Great Lakes area, $17M for the Mississippi River Basin, $13M for the Chesapeake Bay, and other initiatives. This promise was fulfilled.	1.00
IN-6	**The Promise:** "...will make the restoration of America's Everglades a top environmental priority in their administration. They will honor the federal government's promise to be a 50-50 partner with Florida to complete the CERP and will provide the national leadership necessary to restore the natural flows of water to Everglades National Park, including the bridging of Tamiami Trail, and assure that the water flowing to the Everglades ecosystem and Park is fresh and clean." **When/Where:** Obama-Biden Plan: "Protecting Florida's Waterways" dated 10/16/08. **Source:** http://news.caloosahatchee.org/docs/Obama_On_Florida_Waters.pdf **Status:** Under the Comprehensive Everglades Restoration Plan (CERP) approved by Congress in	0.00

Chapter 9 - Department of the Interior

FY2000, the South Florida Water Management District (SFWMD) is responsible for 50% of the cost to implement the $10.9B, 30-year plan. The federal government, primarily the Department of the Interior (DOI) and the U.S. Army Corps of Engineers (USACE) is responsible for paying the other half.

During the period FY2010 through FY2017, the federal government (DOI and USACE) spent an additional $1.5B in support of design and construction of CERP projects. The funding breakdown is roughly as follows:
FY2010....$246.7M
FY2011....$201.6M
FY2012....$249.0M
FY2013....$162.3M
FY2014....$121.7M
FY2015....$135.9M
FY2016....$200.8M
FY2017....$195.5M

The Tamiami Trail, built in 1928, runs for 275 miles from Miami along the northern edge of Everglades National Park, through Big Cypress National Preserve, and ends in Tampa. This trail is considered to be environmentally damaging as it acts as a dam for Everglades waterflow as it cuts the "River of Grass" through its center. Most damaging is an 11-mile section of the trail that lays on top of the Northeast Shark River Slough, a deep waterway that is the primary source of water for Everglades National Park and Florida Bay. These areas are starved of freshwater while polluted water is diverted to fragile estuaries in the ocean.

As of end-CY2016, only one of five needed Tamiami Trail bridges was completed at a cost of $95M. On 04/22/16, work began on a second bridge, 2.6 miles in length, at a cost of $144M. This bridge could be completed by CY2020. Three additional bridges are needed at an estimated cost of $400M.

This promise was not fulfilled.

IN-7

The Promise: "...will increase incentives for farmers and private landowners to...protect wetlands, grasslands, and forests."
When/Where: Obama and Biden's Plan for America: "Blueprint for Change," dated 10/09/08.
Source: https://www.documentcloud.org/documents/550007-barack-obama-2008-blueprint-for-change.html
Status: Other than the pre-existing Landowner Incentive Program (LIP) as of mid-CY2012, no "additional incentives" are known to have been created by the Obama Administration specifically to encourage private landowner protection and restoration of wetlands, grasslands, forests and other wildlife habitat.

During the years preceding President Obama's two terms in office, and since CY1998, the LIP was funded in the amount of $136.5M, funds that were disbursed on a grant basis. The LIP received no new funding while President Obama was in office.

While Section 111, Division Q of the Consolidated Appropriations Act of 2016 (H.R. 2029) signed into law by President Obama on 12/18/15 made permanent the conservation easement tax incentive, this initiative is not considered to respond specifically to the intent of this promise.

This promise was not fulfilled.

Grade: 0.00

NATIONAL PARKS | GRADE

IN-8

The Promise: "Will repair the damage done to our national parks by inadequate funding and emphasize the protection and restoration of our National Forests."
When/Where: Obama-Biden Plan: "Promoting a Healthy Environment" dated 10/08/08.

Grade: 1.00

Source: https://www.energy.gov/sites/prod/files/edg/media/Obama_Cap_and_Trade_0512.pdf

Status: In this promise, the Bush Administration preceding President Obama was blamed for inadequately funding the National Park Service (NPS). The last appropriation under President Bush (FY2009) for the NPS was $2.532B.

On 10/30/09, President Obama signed into law a bill granting $2.7B to the Department of the Interior for the National Park Service, an increase of $198M over FY2009. The NPS received an additional $750M under the American Recovery and Reinvestment Act (ARRA) of 2009. This increase over previous year/administration funding was a step in the right direction, but still left the National Park Service short of about $9.2B to cover projected infrastructure maintenance/repair requirements, an amount estimated at the time to grow to over $12B by end-CY2016.

Here's how NPS funding fared under President Obama:
FY2010....$2.744B
FY2011....$2.611B
FY2012....$2.580B
FY2013....$2.775B
FY2014....$2.562B
FY2015....$2.616B
FY2016....$2.852B
FY2017....$2.932B
Total by end-CY2016: $21.672B

This promise was fulfilled.

NATURAL RESOURCES	GRADE
IN-9 — **The Promise:** "Will support federal policies to encourage voluntary water banks, wastewater treatment, and other market-based conservation measures to address the water shortage in western states." **When/Where:** Obama-Biden Plan: "Promoting a Healthy Environment" dated 10/08/08. **Source:** https://www.energy.gov/sites/prod/files/edg/media/Obama_Cap_and_Trade_0512.pdf **Status:** The American Recovery and Reinvestment Act (ARRA) signed into law on 02/17/09 included $1B for the Department of the Interior's Bureau of Reclamation for "Water and Related Resources". Not less than $126M of this amount was earmarked for water reclamation and reuse projects. On 09/25/09, for example, Secretary of the Interior Salazar announced the award of a $21.4M contract utilizing ARRA funds for a water conservation project in Sunnyside, WA. The Water Conservation Initiative Challenge Grants also funneled funds to the western states to optimize water conservation efforts. In CY2015 alone, the Obama Administration made $300M available to western states in new drought aid to provide relief for farmers, displaced workers and rural communities that ran out of drinking water. This promise was fulfilled.	1.00
IN-10 — **The Promise:** "Will support increased funding for the Land and Water Conservation Fund (LWCF), which supports land acquisition and maintenance of parks." **When/Where:** Obama-Biden Plan: "Promoting a Healthy Environment" dated 10/08/08. **Source:** https://www.energy.gov/sites/prod/files/edg/media/Obama_Cap_and_Trade_0512.pdf **Status:** The Land and Water Conservation Fund Act of 1965 mandates "congressional appropriations...to make the income of the Fund not less than $900,000,000 for each fiscal year until the Fund's expiration date, September 30, 2015." Only in FY1998 and FY2001 did the fund receive appropriations meeting that threshold.	1.00

Chapter 9 - Department of the Interior

On 09/08/09, Congressman Nick Rahall (D-WV) introduced the "Consolidated Land, Energy, and Aquatic Resources Act of 2009" (H.R. 3534) and would have required full funding of the LWCF for FY2011 and succeeding fiscal years. This bill passed the House on 07/30/10, but never passed the Senate. It expired at the end of CY2010 with the 111th Congress.

The "Land and Water Conservation and Funding Act of 2009" was introduced by Senator Jeff Bingaman (D-NM) on 11/06/09 as S-2747. The bill did not get beyond the Senate Committee on Energy and Natural Resources and it too expired when the 111th Congress adjourned at the end of CY2010. Senator Bingaman reintroduced this bill before the 112th Congress on 06/23/11 (S. 1265) but it did not gain any passage momentum and expired with the 112th Congress.

Shared between the Departments of Interior and Agriculture, the LWCF's budget for FY2010 to FY2014 was as follows:
FY2010....$450.4M
FY2011....$300.5M
FY2012....$322.3M
FY2013....$303.3M
FY2014....$306.0M

Starting in FY2015, President Obama requested the full/mandated amount of $900.0M. In light of fiscal constraint realities, Congress limited LWCF funding as follows:
FY2015....$306.1M (34% of requested amount)
FY2016....$450.0M (50% of requested amount)
FY2017....$400.0M (44% of requested amount)

The promise to "support increased funding" was fulfilled.

IN-11	**The Promise:** "...will lead efforts to acquire and conserve new parks and public lands, focusing on ecosystems such as the Great Plains and Eastern forests which do not yet have the protection they deserve." **When/Where:** Obama-Biden Plan: "Promoting a Healthy Environment" dated 10/08/08. **Source:** https://www.energy.gov/sites/prod/files/edg/media/Obama_Cap_and_Trade_0512.pdf **Status:** The President's budget proposal for FY2010 stated in part: "...there are many landscapes and ecosystems that do not have adequate protection. One way to protect these landscapes is to increase funding through the LWCF to acquire and conserve new parks and public lands...". In CY2010 alone, the Department of the Interior's (DOI's) Land and Water Conservation Fund (LWCF) stewardship protection was extended to 34,367 additional acres and 133 additional park sites. During his two terms in office, President Obama is credited with creating and/or enlarging 29 national parks or national monuments totaling, by some accounts, over 550M acres of land and water from Hawaii to Maine and points in between. This promise was fulfilled.	1.00
IN-12	**The Promise:** "...will advance legislation that works with landowners and follows in the tradition of the Wilderness Act, the Clean Water Act, and the Clean Air Act to focus federal attention and increased resources for this key environmental issue." **When/Where:** Obama-Biden Plan: Promoting a Healthy Environment" dated 10/08/08. **Source:** https://www.energy.gov/sites/prod/files/edg/media/Obama_Cap_and_Trade_0512.pdf **Status:** On 03/08/12, Agriculture Secretary Tom Vilsack and Secretary of the Interior Ken Salazar announced a new $33M partnership with farmers, ranchers and forest landowners to use innovative approaches to restore and protect habitats for wildlife.	0.00

Chapter 9 - Department of the Interior

The Department of Agriculture's Natural Resources Conservation Service (NRCS) and the Department of Interior's Fish and Wildlife Service jointly manage the new Working Lands for Wildlife (WLFW) program. This program provides technical and financial assistance for landowners who voluntarily choose to implement specific conservation practices for a particular species while continuing to manage the property as working lands. Those species include the bog turtle, golden-winged warbler, gopher tortoise, greater sage-grouse, lesser prairie-chicken, New England cottontail and southwestern willow flycatcher.

During President Obama's two terms in office, WLFW participants helped restore 6.7M acres of habitat for targeted species

Nonetheless, President Obama is not known to have advanced any new legislation that would further encourage private landowners to pursue conservation initiatives beyond those that already existed under such programs as the Conservation Reserve Program (CRP), the Wetland Reserve Program (WRP), the Wildlife Habitat Incentive Program, and others. No legislation was needed to create the WLFW.

This promise was not fulfilled.

IN-13

The Promise: "...will push for the passage of the Great Lakes Collaboration Implementation Act, which will move us past playing defense against environmental problems and toward a comprehensive restoration of the Great Lakes."
When/Where: Obama-Biden Plan: Promoting a Healthy Environment" dated 10/08/08.
Source: https://www.energy.gov/sites/prod/files/edg/media/Obama_Cap_and_Trade_0512.pdf
Status: The Great Lakes Collaboration Implementation Act (aka the National Invasive Species Council Act or National Invasive Species Act) was first introduced during the 109th Congress (S. 2545) in CY2006.

After repeated failures during the Bush Administration, it was reintroduced during the Obama Administration, notably during the 111th Congress in CY2009 (S. 237/H.R. 500) and repeatedly all the way through the 114th Congress (CY2015-CY2016) when it acquired a new name, the "Great Lakes Restoration Initiative Act of 2016" (S. 1024/H.R. 223). Also during the 114th Congress, related bills were introduced such as the "Great Lakes Water Protection Act" (H.R. 2809) and the "Great Lakes Ecological and Economic Protection Act" (S. 504), all of which failed to pass Congress and secure bill enactment.

This promise was not fulfilled.

0.00

USGS	GRADE

IN-14

The Promise: "Will continue support for the Landsat Data Continuity Mission, which allows study of the earth's land surfaces and provides valuable data for agricultural, educational, scientific, and government use."
When/Where: Obama-Biden Plan: "Advancing the Frontiers of Space Exploration" dated 08/15/08.
Source: http://www.nasa.gov/pdf/382369main_48%20-%2020090803.2.Space_Fact_Sheet_FINAL.pdf
Status: With the U.S. Geological Survey, NASA developed the Landsat Data Continuity Mission (LDCM) to replace aging Landsat satellites that were operating beyond their projected service periods. The Landsat-8 satellite was launched on 02/11/13 and was officially transferred to the USGS on 05/30/13.

For FY2010 and FY2011, the Landsat program was funded at the $59.6M level. For FY2012, the USGS Landsat operations budget of $99.8M included $48M for the establishment of National Land Imaging Program (NLIP), a permanent budgetary and managerial home for the Landsat program.

The promise to "support" the Landsat Program was fulfilled.

1.00

Chapter 9 - Department of the Interior

WILDLAND FIRE MANAGEMENT	GRADE

IN-15

The Promise: "Will aggressively pursue an effective fire prevention, mitigation and land and forest management plan that decreases the fire risks that many communities are now facing."

When/Where: Obama-Biden Plan: "Committed to Wildfire Management and Community Protection" dated 10/18/08.

Source: https://www.politifact.com/truth-o-meter/promises/obameter/promise/277/pursue-a-wildfire-management-plan/

Status: Source is cited for confirmation of exact promise wording only, as it existed before original "When/Where" campaign document was deleted from archival websites.

The American Recovery and Reinvestment Act (ARRA) of 2009, signed into law on 02/17/09 by President Obama, provided $500 million for "Wildland Fire Management" to the Forest Service under the Department of Agriculture (DOA). $250M of this amount was for "hazardous fuels reduction, forest health protection, rehabilitation and hazard mitigation activities on Federal lands" and $250M was for "State and private forestry activities including hazardous fuels reduction, forest health and ecosystem improvement activities on State and private lands using all the authorities available to the Forest Service."

There was also a provision for "Wildland Fire Management" funds in the ARRA for the Department of the Interior (DOI) in the amount of $15M.

DOI funding for Wildland Fire Management activities, including preparedness, suppression and hazardous fuels reduction was $855.9M (enacted) for FY2010. The same amount was to be authorized by Congress under the FY2011 Continuing Resolution, however actual funding was capped at $778.9M. Funding during the ensuing years of the Obama Presidency was as follows:
FY2012....$575.4M
FY2013....$794.7M
FY2014....$861.5M
FY2015....$896.8M
FY2016....$993.7M
FY2017....$1.007B

Further to the above DOI appropriations, the annual DOA Forest Service appropriations for Wildfire Management were as follows:
FY2010....$2.562B
FY2011....$2.097B
FY2012....$2.087B
FY2013....$2.579B
FY2014....$3.077B
FY2015....$2.636B
FY2016....$3.909B
FY2017....$3.175B

This promise was fulfilled.

Grade: 1.00

| INTERIOR GPA | 0.53 |

Chapter 10 - Department of Justice

Campaign Promises

Departments -> Justice

ITEM	JUSTICE	
	ABORTION	**GRADE**
JU-1	**The Promise:** "The first thing I'll do as President is sign the Freedom of Choice Act." **When/Where:** Obama Statement on 35th Anniversary of Roe v. Wade Decision, Chicago, IL, 01/22/08 **Source:** http://www.youtube.com/watch?v=pf0XIRZSTt8 **Status:** The 110th Congress Freedom of Choice Act (H.R. 1964/S. 1173) was aimed to provide women with the right to choose to bear a child, terminate a pregnancy prior to fetal viability, or to terminate a pregnancy at any time to protect their own lives. This bill got nowhere, nor was it reintroduced during the Obama Presidency. On 04/29/09, President Obama stated in a press conference that the Freedom of Choice Act was not his "highest legislative priority." This promise was not fulfilled.	0.00
	ANTI-TRUST LAW	**GRADE**
JU-2	**The Promise:** "Strengthen antitrust laws to prevent insurers from overcharging physicians for their malpractice insurance." **When/Where:** Obama-Biden Plan: "To Lower Health Care Costs and Ensure Affordable, Accessible Health Care for All," dated 10/03/08. **Source:** http://courses.ischool.berkeley.edu/i202/f08/lectures/Obama_Healthcare-1.pdf **Status:** On 09/17/09, Senator Patrick Leahy (D-VT) introduced the "Health Insurance Industry Antitrust Enforcement Act of 2009" (S. 1681). No action was taken on this bill prior to the 111th Congress' expiration at the end of CY2010. Also on 09/17/09, Congressman John Conyers Jr. (D-MI) introduced a House version of the "Health Insurance Industry Antitrust Enforcement Act of 2009" (H.R. 3596). This bill was intended to provide that medical malpractice insurance issuers would be subject to antitrust laws. Since no action was taken on this bill by the 111th Congress prior to its expiration, it was reintroduced by Congressman Conyers to the 112th Congress as H.R. 5838 on 05/18/12. This bill expired with the 112th Congress at the end of CY2012. It was reintroduced yet again by Congreeman Conyers on 01/03/13 as H.R. 99 and died again with the 113th Congress. In a final attempt during the Obama Presidency, Congressman Conyers reintroduced the "Health Insurance Industry Antitrust Enforcement Act" on 01/06/15 (H.R. 99). It died with the 114th Congress. Meanwhile the Secretary of Health and Human Services administered a $23M portfolio under the Patient Protection and Affordable Care Act of 2010 (H.R. 3590) for states to experiment with alternatives to medical malpractice lawsuits. The objective of this exercise was to minimize what was considered over-litigation that ultimately drove the high prices for malpractice insurance -- costs usually passed on to the health care recipient. As of end-CY2016, this promise was not fulfilled.	0.00
JU-3	**The Promise:** "...will reinvigorate antitrust enforcement, which is how we ensure that capitalism	0.00

works for consumers."
When/Where: Obama-Biden Plan: "Connecting and Empowering All Americans Through Technology and Innovation" dated 11/13/07.
Source: https://www.wired.com/images_blogs/threatlevel/2009/04/obamatechplan.pdf
Status: Antitrust enforcement is a joint responsibility of the Department of Justice (DOJ) Antitrust Division and the Federal Trade Commission (FTC). The authoritative Hart-Scott-Rodino (HSR) Annual Report was used at the macro level to assess whether the antitrust enforcement efforts of the DOJ and FTC were "reinvigorated" during the first seven years of the Obama Administration (numbers for FY2016 not available) when compared to the same period during the preceding Bush-43 Administration.

Number of Antitrust Enforcement Transactions Initiated/Number Pursued (Additional Information and/or Documentary Material Requested - "Second Requests")/Percentage of Total Investigated:
Bush 1st Year (FY2001) - 2,376 / 70 / 3.0%
Obama 1st Tear (FY2009) - 716 / 31 / 4.4%
Bush 2nd Year (FY2002) - 1,187 /49 / 4.2%
Obama 2nd Year (FY2010) - 1,166 /46 /4.0%
Bush 3rd Year (FY2003) - 1,014 / 35 / 3.5%
Obama 3rd Year (FY2011) - 1,450 / 55/ 3.8%
Bush 4th Year (FY2004) - 1,428 / 35 / 2.5%
Obama 4th Year (FY2012) - 1,429 / 49 / 3.4%
Bush 5th Year (FY2005) - 1,675 / 50 / 3.0%
Obama 5th Year (FY2013) - 1,326 / 47 / 3.6%
Bush 6th Year (FY2006) - 1,768/ 45 / 2.6%
Obama 6th Year (FY2014) - 1,663 / 51 / 3.1%
Bush 7th Year (FY2007) - 2,201 / 63 / 2.9%
Obama 7th Year (FY2015) - 1,801 /47 / 2.6%

Totals:
Under President Bush: 11,649 / 347 / 3.0%
Under President Obama: 9,551 / 326 / 3.4%

During the first seven years of the Obama Administration, the number of transactions processed as well as the number of "second requests" investigated by the DOJ and FTC (combined) were inferior to the first seven years of the Bush-43 Administration. The slight increase in percentage of antitrust investigations during the first seven years of the Obama Administration is unimpressive, given the lesser total number of transactions processed by DOJ/FTC during that period. Based on the above limited data, the envisioned antitrust enforcement re-invigoration did not occur during President Obama's Administration when compared to the Bush Administration.

This promise was not fulfilled.

	CIVIL RIGHTS	GRADE
JU-4	**The Promise:** "Obama will work to overturn the Supreme Court's recent ruling that curtails racial minorities' and women's ability to challenge pay discrimination." **When/Where:** Obama-Biden Plan for America: "Blueprint for Change" dated 10/09/08. **Source:** https://www.documentcloud.org/documents/550007-barack-obama-2008-blueprint-for-change.html **Status:** Obama signed the "Lily Ledbetter Fair Pay Act" on 01/29/09. This bill amends the Civil Rights Act of 1964 by stating that the 180-day statute of limitations for filing an equal pay lawsuit regarding pay discrimination resets with each new discriminatory paycheck. This promise was fulfilled.	1.00
JU-5	**The Promise:** "Will sign into law the Equal Remedies Act of 2007 "to do away with the caps on	1.00

Chapter 10 - Department of Justice

compensatory and punitive damages under Title VII that presently impede the ability of victims of racial and gender discrimination to fully recover for the wrongs they have suffered."
When/Where: Obama-Biden Plan: "Creating Equal Opportunity and Justice For All", dated 09/11/08.
Source: https://www.politifact.com/truth-o-meter/promises/obameter/promise/298/eliminate-caps-on-damages-for-discrimination-cases/
Status: Source is cited for confirmation of exact promise wording only, as it existed before original "When/Where" campaign document was deleted from archival websites.

The "Equal Remedies Act of 2007" (S. 1928) was introduced by Senator Edward Kennedy (D-MA) on 08/01/07 but was not enacted.

Under Title VII, compensatory and punitive damages that a jury can award to a plaintiff for discrimination are capped as follows: companies with 15-100 employees: $50K; 101-200: $100K; 201-500: $200K; and 500 or more: $300K. The proposed bill (S. 1928) would have removed the limits on the dollar amount of awardable damages, in cases of intentional employment discrimination, for pecuniary and non-pecuniary losses and punitive damages.

This promise could potentially have been fulfilled under the Civil Rights Act of 2008 (H.R. 5129) (into which the Equal Remedies Act of 2007 was initially rolled) which was introduced by Representative John Lewis (D-GA) on 01/23/08 to restore, reaffirm and reconcile legal rights and remedies under civil rights statutes. This bill expired with the 110th Congress and was not reintroduced during subsequent sessions of Congress.

But the basic thrust of this promise was fulfilled under the Lilly Ledbetter Fair Pay Act of 2009, signed into law by President Obama on 1/29/09. Section 3 of that act (Discrimination in compensation because of race, color, religion, sex, or national origin) states that "an unlawful employment practice occurs...when a discriminatory compensation decision or other practice is adopted, when an individual becomes subject to a discriminatory compensation decision or other practice, or when an individual is affected by application of a discriminatory compensation decision or other practice, including each time wages, benefits, or other compensation is paid, resulting in whole or in part from such a decision or other practice. No dollar caps were stipulated in this act.

This promise was fulfilled.

JU-6 | **The Promise:** "...will ban racial profiling by federal law enforcement agencies and provide federal incentives to state and local police departments to prohibit the practice."
When/Where: Plan for America: "Blueprint for Change," dated 10/09/08
Source: https://www.documentcloud.org/ Obama and Biden's documents/550007-barack-obama-2008-blueprint-for-change.html
Status: Versions of the "End Racial Profiling Act" (ERPA) have been in the works for over a decade. | 0.00

During President Obama's two terms in office, several bills were introduced to end racial profiling. Among those bills, none of which were passed by Congress and thus not enacted:
- End Racial Profiling Act of 2010 (H.R. 5748), 111th Congress
- End Racial Profiling Act of 2011 (S. 1670), 112th Congress
- Racial Profiling Prevention Act of 2012 (H.R. 4398), 112th Congress
- End Racial Profiling Act of 2013 (S. 1038), 113th Congress
- End Racial Profiling Act of 2015 (H.R. 1933), 114th Congress
- End Racial Profiling Act of 2015 (S. 1056), 114th Congress
- Racial Profiling Prevention Act (H.R. 2381), 114th Congress

This promise was not fulfilled.

JU-7 | **The Promise:** "...will encourage states to adopt a law...requiring videotaping of interrogations and confessions in capital cases to ensure that prosecutions are fair." | 0.00

Chapter 10 - Department of Justice

When/Where: Obama-Biden Plan: "Creating Equal Opportunity and Justice For All", dated 09/11/08.
Source: Source document was available online throughout the Obama Administration. It has since been deleted from all archival websites.
Status: As of CY2009, 10 states, the District of Columbia (DC), and over 500 U.S. jurisdictions had adopted the requirement through legislation/statute to videotape specified interrogations. As of end-2016, 21 states, DC, and about 1,000 jurisdictions had laws/rules in place to mandate the recording of specified interrogations/confessions.

There is no evidence that President Obama took any action during his two terms in office to encourage the remaining 29 states to follow suit by making the recording of interrogations/confessions a legal requirement at the state level.

This promise was not fulfilled.

JU-8

The Promise: "...will also require the Assistant Attorney General for Civil Rights to provide him with a report for its plan to diversify the Division's workforce in his first 100 days, particularly in the Criminal Section."
When/Where: Obama-Biden Plan: "Creating Equal Opportunity and Justice For All", dated 09/11/08.
Source: https://www.politifact.com/truth-o-meter/promises/obameter/promise/295/vigorously-pursue-hate-crimes-and-civil-rights-abu/
Status: Source is cited for confirmation of exact promise wording only, as it existed before original "When/Where" campaign document was deleted from archival websites.

The Civil Rights Division at the Department of Justice (DOJ) was founded in CY1957 to enforce anti-discrimination laws.

While reports from various sources, coupled with Congressional testimonies, indicate that the DOJ Civil Rights Division was active in diversifying its hiring and training practices during CY2009, the Assistant Attorney General for Civil Rights, Thomas Perez, is not known to have presented a report to President Obama, within 100 days of his first inauguration in CY2009, on his plan to diversify the Civil Rights Division and particularly its Criminal Section.

This promise was not fulfilled.

0.00

JU-9

The Promise: "...will ensure that the Criminal Section of the Civil Rights Division vigorously pursues cases involving hate crimes and civil rights abuses by local officials."
When/Where: Obama-Biden Plan: "Creating Equal Opportunity and Justice For All", dated 09/11/08.
Source: https://www.politifact.com/truth-o-meter/promises/obameter/promise/295/vigorously-pursue-hate-crimes-and-civil-rights-abu/
Status: Source is cited for confirmation of exact promise wording only, as it existed before original "When/Where" campaign document was deleted from archival websites.

The Matthew Shepard and James Byrd, Jr. Hate Crimes Prevention Act was signed into law by President Obama on 10/28/09 as Division E of the National Defense Authorization Act for Fiscal Year 2010 (H.R. 2647).

Given that the key words of this promise are "abuses by local officials," the above Act was the perfect vehicle through which President Obama could have addressed the responsibilities of the DOJ's Civil Rights Division Criminal Section. This did not occur...not even a mention.

As of end-CY2016, there was no evidence that President Obama specifically/personally weighed in to strengthen the Criminal Section's responsibilities regarding hate crimes and civil rights abuses at the local level.

This promise was not fulfilled.

0.00

JU-10	**The Promise:** "...will sign into law his legislation that establishes harsh penalties for those who have engaged in voter fraud and provides voters who have been misinformed with accurate and full information so they can vote." **When/Where:** Plan for America: "Blueprint for Change," dated 10/09/08 **Source:** https://www.documentcloud.org/ Obama and Biden's documents/550007-barack-obama-2008-blueprint-for-change.html **Status:** Then-Senator Obama introduced the "Deceptive Practices and Voter Intimidation Prevention Act of 2007" (S. 453) on 01/31/07. This bill never gained traction and died with the 110th Congress. Congressman John Conyers (D-MI) introduced similar legislation on 01/06/09 (H.R. 97) and it also failed to gain traction in Congress. This bill expired with the 111th Congress at the end of CY2010. On 12/14/11, Senator Charles Schumer (D-NY) introduced the "Deceptive Practices and Voter Intimidation Prevention Act of 2011" (S. 1994). This was followed by Congressman Rush Holt (D-NJ) introducing the "Deceptive Practices and Voter Intimidation Prevention Act of 2012" (H.R. 5815) on 05/17/12. Neither bill progressed beyond preliminary committee review and expired with the 112th Congress. Similar bills have not been introduced in subsequent sessions of Congress through end-CY2016 This promise was not fulfilled.	0.00
	CRIME	**GRADE**
JU-11	**The Promise:** "...will crack down on mortgage professionals found guilty of fraud by increasing enforcement and creating new criminal penalties." **When/Where:** Candidate Obama speech, Washington, D.C., 07/18/07, Topic: "Changing the Odds for Urban America." **Source:** http://www.presidency.ucsb.edu/ws/index.php?pid=77007 **Status:** On 05/20/09, President Obama signed into law the "Fraud Enforcement and Recovery Act." This new law changed the mortgage applications statute (18 U.S.C. Section 1014) to make it a crime to make a materially false statement or to willfully overvalue a property in order to influence any action by a mortgage lending business. On 02/01/12, President Obama announced new standards to protect mortgage borrowers in their dealings with mortgage professionals. This promise was fulfilled.	1.00
JU-12	**The Promise:** "Will fully fund the Community Oriented Policing Services (COPS) program to combat crime and help address police brutality and accountability issues in local communities." **When/Where:** Obama-Biden Plan: "Supporting Urban Prosperity" dated 09/11/08. **Source:** https://assets.documentcloud.org/documents/550008/barack-obama-2008-supporting-urban-prosperity.pdf **Status:** The American Recovery and Reinvestment Act (ARRA) of 2009 provided an over-and-above infusion of $1B to state, local and tribal governments for the hiring or rehiring of additional career law enforcement officers. This was expected to fund an estimated 5,500 local police officers and brought the total appropriation for COPS in FY2009 to $1.55B. The COPS program funding requirement for FY2010 was $798M. $792M was appropriated by Congress. For FY2011, the appropriation for the COPS program went down to $307M. It is noteworthy that in CY2011, the House voted to eliminate the COPS program entirely. In FY2012, COPS program funding was further decreased to the $198.5M level. With minor fluctuations, but still far below program requirements, here's how COPS program funding fared	0.00

during the remainder of President terms in office:

FY2013....$289M Required....$198M Enacted
FY2014....$439M Required....$214M Enacted
FY2015....$274M Required....$208M Enacted
FY2016....$303M Required....$212M Enacted
FY2017....$286M Required....$221.5 Enacted

Except for a significant uptick in COPS funding for FY2009, at no time did annual appropriations meet program requirements during President Obama's two tours in office.

This promise was not fulfilled.

JU-13

The Promise: "The (Bush) administration has consistently proposed to cut or eliminate funding for the Byrne Justice Assistance Grant (Byrne/JAG) program, which funds anti-drug and anti-gang task forces across the country...Since 2000, this program has been cut more than 83 percent...As president, Obama will restore funding."
When/Where: Obama-Biden Plan: "Renewing U.S. Leadership in the Americas", dated 06/06/08.
Source: https://www.politifact.com/truth-o-meter/promises/obameter/promise/224/restore-funding-for-the-byrne-justice-assistance-g/
Status: Source is cited for confirmation of exact promise wording only, as it existed before original "When/Where" campaign document was deleted from archival websites.

The Byrne/JAG Grant Program was created under the Omnibus Crime Control and Safe Streets Act of 1968 (P.L. 90-351 as amended through P.L. 114-324, enacted 12/16/16). Administered by the DOJ Bureau of Justice Assistance (BJA), its purpose is to improve the functioning of the criminal justice system through flexible, multi-purpose formula grants to states, local governments, and Indian tribes. The awards support a wide range of criminal justice and public safety initiatives, including (1) law enforcement, (2) courts, crime prosecution and indigent defense, (3) crime prevention and education, (4) corrections and community corrections, (5) drug treatment and enforcement, (6) justice system strategic planning, (7) technology for law enforcement and public safety, and (8) crime victim and witness services and programs. The cited law does not specifically call out "anti-drug and anti-gang" task force initiatives.

Under the 1968 law cited above, Congress is authorized to spend up to $1.095B per year for the Byrne/JAG Grant Program. However, annual funding has been less than 50% of the authorized amount since before the Bush Administration. Therefore the "restore funding" aspect of this promise was interpreted to apply to the Byrne/JAG Grant Program in its entirety. President Obama had to request and obtain the above-cited authorized funding level of $1.095B for Byrne/JAG for this promise to be fulfilled. Here are the annual appropriations for Byrne/JAG under President Obama:
FY2010....$511M
FY2011....$424M
FY2012....$352M
FY2013....$352M
FY2014....$376M
FY2015....$376M
FY2016....$376M
FY2017....$403M

Other than the "plus-up" authorized under the ARRA, we see a steady year-to-year decline in funding for the Byrne/JAG Grant Program (including anti-drug and anti-gang activities mitigation) during the timeframe FY2010-FY2013, with the remaining years funded at roughly one third of the authorized amount.

This promise was not fulfilled.

0.00

Chapter 10 - Department of Justice

JU-14	**The Promise:** "Barack Obama and Joe Biden believe the [sentencing] disparity between crack and powder-based cocaine is wrong, cannot be justified and should be eliminated....will work in a bipartisan way to eliminate these disparities." **When/Where:** Obama-Biden Plan: "Creating Equal Opportunity and Justice for All" dated 09/11/08. **Source:** Source document was available online throughout the Obama Administration. It has since been deleted from all archival websites. **Status:** Section 4713 of the National Defense Authorization Act for Fiscal Year 2010, signed into law by President Obama on 10/28/09, states in part: "Not later than 1 year after the date of enactment of this Act, the United States Sentencing Commission shall submit to the Committee on the Judiciary of the Senate and the Committee on the Judiciary of the House of Representatives a report on mandatory minimum sentencing provisions under Federal law. The report ... shall include...an assessment of the effect of mandatory minimum sentencing provisions under Federal law on the goal of eliminating unwarranted sentencing disparity and other goals of sentencing..." The Senate voted in favor of a bill on 03/17/10 to reduce the sentencing disparity between cocaine and crack offenses to a ratio of 18 to 1. This was far from the 1 to 1 ratio sought by the House, but the House approved a similar bill on 07/28/10, retaining the 18 to 1 ratio. President Obama signed the Fair Sentencing Act of 2010 into law on 08/03/10. This promise was fulfilled.	1.00
JU-15	**The Promise:** "...will immediately review (mandatory minimum) sentences to see where we can be smarter on crime and reduce the ineffective warehousing of nonviolent drug offenders." **When/Where:** Obama-Biden Plan: "Creating Equal Opportunity and Justice For All", dated 09/11/08. **Source:** https://www.politifact.com/truth-o-meter/promises/obameter/promise/300/reform-mandatory-minimum-sentences/ **Status:** Source is cited for confirmation of exact promise wording only, as it existed before original "When/Where" campaign document was deleted from archival websites. Section 4713 of the National Defense Authorization Act for Fiscal Year 2010, signed into law by President Obama on 10/28/09, states in part: "Not later than 1 year after the date of enactment of this Act, the United States Sentencing Commission shall submit to the Committee on the Judiciary of the Senate and the Committee on the Judiciary of the House of Representatives a report on mandatory minimum sentencing provisions under Federal law." On 11/22/16, President Obama commuted the sentences of 79 drug offenders, bringing the total number of similar commutations during his two terms in office to 1,032. Of these inmates serving life sentences prior to commutation: 342. This promise was fulfilled.	1.00
JU-16	**The Promise:** "...would repeal the Tiahrt Amendment and give police officers across the nation the tools they need to solve gun crimes and fight the illegal arms trade." **When/Where:** Obama-Biden Plan: "Supporting Urban Prosperity", dated 09/11/08. **Source:** https://assets.documentcloud.org/documents/550008/barack-obama-2008-supporting-urban-prosperity.pdf **Status:** While an FY2010 improvement to this amendment permits state and local law enforcement officials to have full access to gun trace databases to analyze gun trafficking patterns, President Obama's promise was to "repeal" this amendment, a repeal supported by the Brady Campaign and "Mayors Against Illegal Guns." Rather, President Obama's FY2011 budget proposal maintained language that required the destruction of most Brady Law background check records, banned the government from requiring gun dealers to fully account for firearms in their possession, and prohibited public access to information about guns used to commit crimes.	0.00

Chapter 10 - Department of Justice

Nonetheless, Congresswoman Barbara Lee (D-CA) introduced the "Tiahrt Restrictions Repeal Act" (H.R. 661) on 02/13/13 (113th Congress) and again before the 114th Congress (H.R. 1449) on 03/18/15. These bills expired without enactment action at the end of CY2014 and CY2016 respectively.

As of end-CY2016, despite renewed gun control efforts, the Tiahrt Amendment, which enjoys strong support from the National Rifle Association (NRA), had not been repealed.

This promise was not fulfilled.

JU-17	**The Promise:** "Establish the legal status of contractor personnel, making possible prosecution of any abuses committed by private military contractors." **When/Where:** Obama Campaign Document "A 21st Century Military for America" dated 11/26/07. **Source:** https://www.scribd.com/document/6245756/Barack-Obama-on-Defense-Issues-A-21st-Century-Military-for-America **Status:** The Military Extraterritorial Jurisdiction Enforcement Act (MEJA)/Expansion and Enforcement Act of 2007 was introduced by Representative David Price (D-NC) on 06/15/07. This legislation was initially passed by the House on 10/04/07, but didn't get any further in the Senate. It was felt at the time that DoD and other agency contractors serving in such areas as Iraq or Afghanistan could engage in criminal conduct with impunity because they operated outside of the jurisdiction of the United States criminal code. On 02/02/10, Congressman David Price (D-NC) and Senator Patrick Leahy (D-VT) introduced bills (H.R. 4567 and S. 2979 respectively) entitled "Civilian Extraterritorial Jurisdiction Act (CEJA) of 2010." No action beyond initial Committee reviews was taken on these bills during the 111th Congress and both expired at the end of CY2010. Congressman Price and Senator Leahy reintroduced their CEJA bills to the 112th Congress (H.R. 2136 and S. 1145) on 06/03/11 and 06/06/11 respectively. Both bills expired with the 112th Congress at the end of CY2012. Senator Leahy again reintroduced a CEJA to the 113th Congress (S. 2598) on 07/14/14 and to the 114th Congress (S. 1377) on 05/19/15. These bills expired without further enactment action at the end of CY2014 and CY2016 respectively. This promise was not fulfilled.	0.00
JU-18	**The Promise:** "...will direct his Attorney General and Homeland Security Secretary to meet with their Latin American and Caribbean counterparts in the first year of his presidency to produce a regional strategy to combat drug trafficking, domestic and transnational gang activity, and organized crime. A hemispheric pact..." **When/Where:** Obama-Biden Plan: "Renewing U.S. Leadership in the Americas" dated 06/06/08. **Source:** https://www.politifact.com/truth-o-meter/promises/obameter/promise/223/direct-attorney-general-and-homeland-security-secr/ **Status:** Source is cited for confirmation of exact promise wording only, as it existed before original "When/Where" campaign document was deleted from archival websites. In the first 100 days of the Obama Administration, the Departments of Justice (DOJ) and Homeland Security (DHS) launched new initiatives to combat Mexican drug cartels both in the USA and in Mexico in close coordination with their Mexican counterparts. Attorney General Eric Holder's first foreign trip was to Mexico in early 04/09, accompanied by DHS Secretary Janet Napolitano. During meetings with Mexican President Calderon and Mexican Attorney General Medina-Mora, the framework of a new regional strategy was discussed, but no further action is known to have taken place towards its production.	0.00

Chapter 10 - Department of Justice

The fifth Summit of the Americas held at Port of Spain, Trinidad and Tobago, on 04/17-19/09 provided a 'one-stop-shopping' opportunity for DOJ and DHS high level officials to meet with all their Latin American and Caribbean counterparts to agree on the framework for the promised "regional strategy." This didn't happen.

It should be noted that programs to thwart Latin America/Caribbean drug trafficking, gang activity and organized crime were in place long before President Obama assumed the presidency. When this promise was made, effective programs included but were not limited to the International Criminal Investigative Training Assistance Program (ICITAP), Colombia's Justice Sector Reform Program (JSRP), the Partnership for Growth Program, the "Merida Initiative" for Mexico and Central America, and others.

While DOJ/DHS focused exchanges based on specific regional/bilateral drug/criminal incidents with Mexico, Colombia and others throughout CY2009, there was no concentrated effort (beyond high level bilateral discussions) during President Obama's "first year" in office to develop a new USA/Latin America/Caribbean "hemispheric pact" to combat organized crime, drug trafficking or cross-border gang activity.

This promise was not fulfilled.

JU-19

The Promise: "...signing a law that would authorize federal magistrates to preside over drug courts and federal probation officers to oversee the offenders' compliance with drug treatment programs. They will ensure that our federal courts and probation offices have adequate resources to deal with this new program."
When/Where: Obama-Biden Plan: "Creating Equal Opportunity and Justice For All", dated 09/11/08.
Source: https://www.politifact.com/truth-o-meter/promises/obameter/promise/301/enhance-drug-courts/
Status: Source is cited for confirmation of exact promise wording only, as it existed before original "When/Where" campaign document was deleted from archival websites.

The Omnibus Crime Control and Safe Streets Act of 1994 authorized the Attorney General to make grants to state and local governments to establish drug courts. Attempts to federalize drug courts go back to at least CY2000 (106th Congress, S. 3191) but never passed either the Senate or the House.

In a 06/06 DOJ document entitled "Report to Congress on the Feasibility of Federal Drug Courts," the DOJ concluded that the establishment of such courts was not feasible. The rationale for this conclusion:
(1) There are already substantial programs that help federal offenders overcome their substance abuse problems during the pretrial, incarceration, and supervised release phases of their cases.
(2) The majority of drug offenders in the federal criminal system have committed serious drug trafficking offenses and are not amenable to, or eligible for, drug-court-type programs.
(3) The diversion of prosecutorial and financial resources necessary to create and maintain a federal drug court program would harm efforts to target drug traffickers and other serious offenders and reduce funds available to existing state drug court programs.

Nonetheless, when President Obama assumed the presidency in 01/09, among the nearly 3,000 drug courts in the nation at the time, 30 Federal reentry courts already existed. These Federal Drug Courts have programs for federal offenders with documented substance abuse problems who are on supervised release in the community and who volunteer to join the program.

The bottom line is that during President Obama's two terms in office, no new law was enacted to authorize federal magistrates to preside over drug courts. Some would argue that none was needed.

This promise was not fulfilled.

0.00

Chapter 10 - Department of Justice

JU-20	**The Promise:** "...will create a prison-to-work incentive program, modeled on the Welfare-to-Work Partnership, to create ties with employers, third-party agencies that provide training and support services to ex-offenders, and to improve ex-offender employment and job retention rates." **When/Where:** Obama-Biden Plan: "Creating Equal Opportunity and Justice For All", dated 09/11/08. **Source:** https://www.politifact.com/truth-o-meter/promises/obameter/promise/305/create-a-prison-to-work-incentive-program/ **Status:** Source is cited for confirmation of exact promise wording only, as it existed before original "When/Where" campaign document was deleted from archival websites. The "Federal Prison Work Incentive Act of 2009" (H.R. 1475) introduced by Congressman Danny Davis (D-IL) on 03/12/09, although not directly related, could have been used as a vehicle to address the provisions of this promise as regards the transition of an ex-offender from prison to mainstream society -- but wasn't. This bill died when the 111th Congress adjourned at the end of CY2010. The "Prisoner Incentive Act of 2011" (H.R. 2344) introduced by Congressman Robert Scott (D-VA) on 06/23/11 also could have been used as a vehicle to address a prison-to-work incentive program. It wasn't. To his credit, President Obama's FY2011 budget proposal provided $144M for prisoner re-entry programs, including $100M for the Office of Justice Programs to administer grant programs authorized by the "Second Chance Act of 2007," signed into law by President Bush on 04/09/08. However, no prison-to-work incentive program modeled on the Welfare-to-Work Partnership was created during President Obama's two terms in office. This promise was not fulfilled.	0.00
JU-21	**The Promise:** "...will give first-time, nonviolent drug offenders a chance to serve their sentence, where appropriate, in the type of drug-rehabilitation programs that have proven to work better than a prison term in changing bad behavior." **When/Where:** Candidate Obama Speech, Howard University Convocation, 09/28/07. **Source:** http://www.presidency.ucsb.edu/ws/index.php?pid=77014 **Status:** The Fair Sentencing Act of 2010 (S. 1789) was signed into law by President Obama on 08/03/10. This would have been a perfect opportunity to define revised sentencing procedures for first-time, nonviolent drug offenders. This did not happen. As of end-CY2016, the tail end of President Obama's two terms in office, minimum mandatory sentences and/or sentencing guidelines were in effect at both the Federal and State levels and most involved incarceration for varying periods of time for first-time, nonviolent drug offenders. This promise was not fulfilled.	0.00
JU-22	**The Promise:** "...will also repeal the mandatory minimum sentence for first time offenders convicted of simple possession of crack, as crack is the only drug that a non-violent first-time offender can receive a mandatory minimum sentence for possessing." **When/Where:** Obama-Biden Plan: "Creating Equal Opportunity and Justice For All", dated 09/11/08. **Source:** https://www.politifact.com/truth-o-meter/promises/obameter/promise/299/eliminate-disparity-in-sentencing-for-crack-and-co/ **Status:** Source is cited for confirmation of exact promise wording only, as it existed before original "When/Where" campaign document was deleted from archival websites. Prior to 08/10, a person convicted of possessing five grams of crack cocaine received a mandatory five year prison sentence. President Obama signed the Fair Sentencing Act of 2010 (S. 1789) into law on 08/03/10. This law	1.00

repealed the mandatory minimum sentence for simple possession of crack as required by Section 401(a) of the Controlled Substances Act (21 U.S.C. 844(a)).

This promise was fulfilled.

JU-23

The Promise: "...supports tough penalties, increased enforcement resources and forensic tools for law enforcement, and collaboration between law enforcement and the private sector to identify and prosecute people who abuse the Internet to try to exploit children."
When/Where: Obama-Biden Plan: "Connecting and Empowering All Americans Through Technology and Innovation" dated 11/13/07.
Source: https://www.wired.com/images_blogs/threatlevel/2009/04/obamatechplan.pdf
Status: The Child Online Protection Act (COPA) was enacted on 10/21/98, during the Clinton Administration. Its stated purpose was to restrict access by minors to any material defined as harmful to such minors on the Internet. The law, however, never took effect, as three separate rounds of litigation (including U.S. Supreme Court review without action) led to a permanent injunction against the law on 01/21/09, one day after President Obama's first inauguration.

Under Title 18, Part I, Chapter 110, Section 2251 of the U.S. Code, first violators of sexual exploitation of children are subject to not less than 15 years of imprisonment. Persons with a previous conviction of aggravated sexual abuse, sexual abuse, abusive sexual contact involving a minor, sex trafficking of children, or the production, possession, receipt, mailing, sale, distribution, shipment, or transportation of child pornography shall be fined and imprisoned for not less than 25 years. Persons with two or more prior convictions shall be fined and imprisoned for not less than 35 years.

To strengthen the above law, Senator Richard Blumenthal (D-CT) introduced the "Child Protection Act of 2012" (S. 3456) on 07/30/12 pertaining to child pornography and child exploitation offenses. This bill specifically addressed tougher penalties than those articulated in Title 18 above. In fact, it addressed the penalty for pornography (any visual depiction or imagery) involving prepubescent or minors younger than 12 years of age as being "fined...and imprisoned for not more than 20 years...," more than the requirement addressed in Title 18 for first-time offenders. S. 3456 was incorporated 100% into the House version of the "Child Protection Act of 2012" (H.R. 6063) introduced by Congressman Lamar Smith (R-TX) on 06/29/12 and signed into law by President Obama on 12/07/12. Referred to as Public Law (P.L.) 112-206, this law also incorporates relevant portions of the "Protecting Children From Internet Pornographers Act of 2011" (H.R. 1981 and S. 1308).

The Internet Crimes Against Children (ICAC) Task Force Program helps state and local law enforcement agencies develop an effective response to technology-facilitated child sexual exploitation and Internet crimes against children. The ICAC program is a national network of 61 coordinated task forces representing over 3,500 federal, state, and local law enforcement and prosecutorial agencies. These agencies are engaged in both proactive and reactive investigations, forensic investigations, and criminal prosecutions. With increased funding to help state and local agencies to develop effective responses to online child victimization, including responses to the online sharing of child sexual abuse images, the DOJ's Office of Juvenile Justice and Delinquency Prevention (OJJDP) has increased the capacity of thousands of communities across the country to combat Internet crimes against children.

During the 6-year period FY2003-FY2008, the ICAC Task Force was funded at an average of $13.9M per annum. Under President Obama and buttressed by a $50M plus-up under the "American Recovery and Reinvestment Act of 2009," the average funding of the ICAC Task Force over the 6-year period FY2009-FY2014 was $35.4M per annum, settling at the $27M per annum level starting in FY2014, more than twice the average per annum ICAC funding during the Bush Administration.

This promise was fulfilled.

1.00

Chapter 10 - Department of Justice

	CRIME - KATRINA RELATED	GRADE
JU-24	**The Promise:** "Will finish rebuilding the region's criminal justice system so that we do not have to rely on the National Guard to patrol city streets..Will establish a special "COPS for Katrina" program to allow communities impacted by the storm to hire and retain new officers and community prosecutors, develop community-based crime fighting strategies, and rebuild their lost infrastructure..." **When/Where:** Obama-Biden Plan: "Rebuilding the Gulf Coast and Preventing Future Catastrophes" dated 09/11/08. **Source:** https://assets.documentcloud.org/documents/550006/barack-obama-2008-rebuilding-the-gulf-coast-and.pdf **Status:** The American Recovery and Reinvestment Act of 2009 included nearly $160 million to fund Community Oriented Policing Services (COPS) for the region devastated by Hurricane Katrina. 173 regional law enforcement agencies benefited from these funds which facilitated the hiring of over 850 police officers, replacing National Guard personnel. This promise was fulfilled.	1.00

	DEA	GRADE
JU-25	**The Promise:** "Will strengthen Drug Enforcement Administration efforts to stop the reestablishment of drug gangs across the region." **When/Where:** Obama-Biden Plan: "Rebuilding the Gulf Coast and Preventing Future Catastrophes" dated 09/11/08. **Source:** https://assets.documentcloud.org/documents/550006/barack-obama-2008-rebuilding-the-gulf-coast-and.pdf **Status:** The Drug Enforcement Agency (DEA) was funded (less any supplement) in the amount of $1.544B in FY2009 to combat domestic, drug-related organized crime. Under the Obama Administration, this was increased by nearly half a billion dollars to $1.604B in FY2010, an amount maintained for FY2011 under Continuing Resolution funding. For FY2012, this line item was slightly decreased to $1.602M, the same amount enacted for FY2013. Subsequent year funding for Domestic Enforcement operations was as follows: FY2014....$1.592B FY2015....$1.587B FY2016....$1.610B FY2017....$1.631B The DEA's Domestic Enforcement resources were significantly "strengthened" in Gulf of Mexico littoral states to thwart the re-establishment of drug gangs in the post-Katrina era. This was despite the fact that critical resources in the fight against narco-trafficking across the Gulf region took a direct hit with the 9/30/12 decommissioning of the Navy's Airborne Early Warning (AEW) squadron (VAW-77) stationed at Belle Chase, LA. This squadron had been effective in supporting DEA's mission by detecting the movement by sea and air of illicit drugs destined for the Southeast USA from the Caribbean and Latin America. Nonetheless, this promise was fulfilled.	1.00

	DOMESTIC VIOLENCE	GRADE
JU-26	**The Promise:** "...will also issue a joint report on "best practices" across agencies and disseminate that information to the states." **When/Where:** Obama-Biden Plan: "Ending Violence Against Women and Children" dated 10/31/07. **Source:** https://www.politifact.com/truth-o-meter/promises/obameter/promise/120/issue-a-best-practices-report-for-states-on-redu/ **Status:** Source is cited for confirmation of exact promise wording only, as it existed before original "When/Where" campaign document was deleted from archival websites.	1.00

H.R.3401, entitled "Improving Assistance to Domestic and Sexual Violence Victims Act of 2009" was introduced on 07/30/09 by Representative Debbie Wasserman Shultz (D-FL). This proposed legislation was referred to the Subcommittee on Crime, Terrorism, and Homeland Security on 08/19/09 where it sat until it expired with the 111th Congress at the end of CY2010.

On the Senate side, S.327 with the same title was introduced by Senator Patrick Leahy (D-VT) on 01/26/09 and this initiative resulted in a Committee on the Judiciary Report No. 111-85 filed on 10/01/09. This bill also died with the 111th Congress at the end of CY2010.

On 04/27/12, Congresswoman Sandy Adams (R-FL) introduced the "Violence Against Women Reauthorization Act of 2012" (H.R. 4970) which specifically addressed the adoption of "best practices" to be shared with states. This bill passed the House on 05/16/12 but did not receive passage in the Senate before the 112th Congress expired at the end of CY2012.

On 01/22/13, Senator Leahy reintroduced his bill as the "Violence Against Women Reauthorization Act of 2013" (S. 47). This bill addressed best practices for "responding to domestic violence, dating violence, sexual assault, and stalking" and directs inter-agency reporting and information sharing with states. This bill was signed into law by President Obama on 03/07/13.

This promise was fulfilled.

JU-27

The Promise: "Senator Obama co-sponsored and helped reauthorize the Violence Against Women Act (VAWA). Reauthorized in January 2006, the bill provides funds to help communities, nonprofit organizations and police combat domestic violence, sexual assault and stalking. The legislation also establishes a sexual assault services program and provides education grants to prevent domestic violence. As president, Obama will fully fund and implement VAWA."
When/Where: Obama-Biden Plan: "Ending Violence Against Women and Children" dated 10/31/07.
Source: Source document was available online throughout the Obama Administration. It has since been deleted from all archival websites.
Status: The FY2010 Consolidated Appropriations Act signed into law by President Obama on 12/16/09 provided $444.5M to the Department of Justice's Office on Violence Against Women (OVW) for the VAWA program. In addition, the law provided $181.4M to the Department of Health and Human Services (HHS) for domestic violence programs. $415.5M was the enacted amount for OVW activities in FY2010.

For FY2011, President Obama's budget submission included $457M for VAWA (plus $192.3M for HHS domestic violence programs). Under Continuing Resolution procedures, $418.5M was appropriated for OVW for FY2011.

On 11/30/11, Senator Patrick Leahy (D-VT) introduced the "Violence Against Women Reauthorization Act of 2011" (S. 1925). This bill passed the Senate on 04/26/12, but did not pass the House as of end-CY2012 when the 112th Congress expired.

Nonetheless, for FY2012, the OVW was funded at the $412.5M level against the President's request for $431.7M, an amount President Obama requested again for FY2013.

On 01/22/13, Senator Leahy reintroduced his bill as the "Violence Against Women Reauthorization Act of 2013" (S. 47). This bill passed the Senate in a 78 to 22 vote on 02/12/13, authorizing $659M for VAWA related programs. This bill was signed into law by President Obama on 03/07/13.

This promise was fulfilled.

1.00

JU-28

The Promise: "...the Responsible Fatherhood and Healthy Families Act "to remove some of the government penalties on married families, crack down on men avoiding child support payments...will

0.00

sign this bill into law..."
When/Where: Obama-Biden Plan: "Supporting Urban Prosperity", dated 09/11/08.
Source: https://assets.documentcloud.org/documents/550008/barack-obama-2008-supporting-urban-prosperity.pdf
Status: After several unsuccessful attempts during previous sessions of Congress, Congressman Danny Davis (D-IL) reintroduced the "Julia Carson Responsible Fatherhood and Healthy Families Act of 2015" (H.R. 3005) on 07/09/15. No action was taken on this bill and it expired with the 114th Congress at the end of CY2016.

This promise was not fulfilled.

GAY RIGHTS	GRADE

JU-29
The Promise: "I will place the weight of my administration behind the enactment of the Matthew Shepard Act to outlaw hate crimes."
When/Where: Open Letter from Barack Obama to the LGBT Community dated 02/28/08.
Source: http://bilerico.lgbtqnation.com/2008/02/open_letter_from_barack_obama_to_the_lgb.php
Status: On 04/29/09, Obama verbally supported passage of the Local Law Enforcement Hate Crimes Prevention Act of 2009. The House voted in favor of this proposed law on 04/29/9, followed by the Senate on 10/22/09. The bill was attached to the Defense Budget for FY2010, which was signed into law by the President on 10/28/09.

This promise was fulfilled.

Grade: 1.00

JU-30
The Promise: "Will support "repeal the Defense of Marriage Act (DOMA) and enact legislation that would ensure that the 1,100+ federal legal rights and benefits currently provided on the basis of marital status are extended to same-sex couples in civil unions and other legally-recognized unions."
When/Where: Open Letter from Barack Obama to the LGBT Community dated 02/28/08.
Source: http://bilerico.lgbtqnation.com/2008/02/open_letter_from_barack_obama_to_the_lgb.php
Status: DOMA is a 1996 law signed by President Bill Clinton that barred the federal government from recognizing same-sex marriages.

The Supreme Court heard oral arguments in a case supporting the repeal of the DOMA on 03/27/13 and overturned a provision in the DOMA on 06/26/13 that limited the definition of marriage as a union between a man and a woman. This development permitted same-sex marriages to benefit from the same federal benefits afforded to opposite-sex marriages in states where same same-sex unions were legal.

The Supreme Court ruling did not repeal DOMA, as the outright repeal of any law is a legislative branch, not a judicial branch, responsibility.

On 06/26/15, the U.S. Supreme Court ruled that same-sex marriage is a constitutional right. By striking down Section 3 of DOMA, the Supreme Court therefore allowed gay and lesbian couples to marry in all 50 states.

This promise was fulfilled.

Grade: 1.00

TORTURE/RENDITION	GRADE

JU-31
The Promise: "...will eliminate the practice of extreme rendition, where we outsource our torture to other countries."
When/Where: Obama's Plan: The War We Need to Win" dated 07/31/07.
Source: http://www.mattluedke.com/wp-content/uploads/2016/09/CounterterrorismFactSheet.pdf
Status: Executive Order 13491 signed by President Obama on 01/22/09 directed the creation of a special task force to study this issue. Led by the Attorney General, the newly-formed Interrogation and Transfer Policy Task Force conducted a review of the Army Field Manual interrogation guidelines and looked at rendition and other policies for transferring individuals to third countries. The purpose of this review was to ensure that U.S. policies and practices complied with all obligations and were

Grade: 0.00

Chapter 10 - Department of Justice

sufficient to ensure that individuals did not face torture and cruel treatment if transferred.

The task force's recommendations were provided to the White House on 08/24/09 and found that Army Field Manual 2-22.3 provided appropriate guidance on interrogation for military interrogators and that no additional or different guidance was necessary for other agencies.

The task force also recommended that the interrogation of the most dangerous terrorists could be improved by forming a High-Value Detainee Interrogation Group (HIG) composed of experienced interrogators from across the Intelligence Community, the Department of Defense and law enforcement.

Under the new guidelines, the Department of State was directed to seek "assurances from the receiving country" that a transferred suspect would not be tortured. Further, the Inspector Generals of the Departments of State, Defense and Homeland Security were directed to submit annual reports on transfers they initiate. Finally, the report recommended that a monitoring mechanism be established to ensure that transferred individuals would not be tortured.

The task force's recommendations did not lead to the full cessation of extreme renditions. The only significant change is that the U.S. Government now relies on foreign governments to (1) grant access to transferred prisoners, and (2) assure the U.S. Government that such prisoners are not being tortured.

During the Obama Administration, there was no effective mechanism put in place to ensure that a receiving country is not employing torture as a means to obtain actionable intelligence information.

This promise was not fulfilled.

JU-32

The Promise: "Obama will end the use of torture without exception."
When/Where: Obama's Plan: "The War We Need To Win" dated 07/31/07.
Source: http://www.mattluedke.com/wp-content/uploads/2016/09/CounterterrorismFactSheet.pdf
Status: On 01/22/09, President Obama signed Executive Order (EO) 13491 entitled "Ensuring Lawful Interrogations."

EO 13491 states in part: "Effective immediately, an individual in the custody or under the effective control of an officer, employee, or other agent of the United States Government, or detained within a facility owned, operated, or controlled by a department or agency of the United States, in any armed conflict, shall not be subjected to any interrogation technique or approach, or any treatment related to interrogation, that is not authorized by and listed in Army Field Manual 2-22.3" which is entitled "Human Intelligence Collector Operations."

EO 13491 also established a Special Task Force to review interrogation and transfer policies.

This promise was fulfilled.

1.00

JUSTICE GPA | **0.44**

Chapter 11 Department of Labor

Campaign Promises

Departments -> Labor

ITEM	LABOR	GRADE
	CORPORATE BANKRUPTCY	
LA-1	**The Promise:** "Protect the jobs and benefits of workers and retirees when corporations file for bankruptcy by telling companies that they cannot issue bonuses for executives during bankruptcy while their workers watch their pensions disappear." **When/Where:** Obama-Biden Plan: Helping America's Seniors, dated 10/26/07. **Source:** https://webarchive.loc.gov/all/20090429185714/http://change.gov/agenda/seniors_and_social_security_agenda/ **Status:** This was a provision of the "Protecting Employees and Retirees in Business Bankruptcies Act of 2007" which President Obama co-wrote when he was in the Senate. It never became law. On 02/24/10, Senator Richard Durbin (D-IL) reintroduced the above bill (S. 3033). Likewise on the same date, Congressman John Conyers Jr. (D-MI) reintroduced a House version of this bill (H.R. 4677). Both bills expired without action when the 111th Congress expired at the end of CY2010. Undaunted, Senator Durbin reintroduced this bill during subsequent sessions of Congress: S. 3381 (112th), S. 2589 (113th) and S.1156 (114th). Congressman Conyers did the same: H.R. 6117 (112th), H.R. 100 (113th), and H.R. 97 (114th). All of these bills expired without enactment with their respective sessions of Congress. It's noteworthy that a 01/12 Wall Street Journal report revealed that chief executives at 21 companies involved in bankruptcy proceedings in CY2011 received bigger bonuses during bankruptcy proceedings than in years prior to the initiation of such proceedings. This promise was not fulfilled.	0.00
LA-2	**The Promise:** "...will protect pensions by...increasing the amount of unpaid wages and benefits workers can claim in court..." **When/Where:** Plan for America: "Blueprint for Change," dated 10/09/08 **Source:** https://www.documentcloud.org/ Obama and Biden's documents/550007-barack-obama-2008-blueprint-for-change.html **Status:** The "Protecting Employees and Retirees in Business Bankruptcies Act of 2007," initially co-sponsored by then-Senator Obama during the 110th Congress, would have protected workers' and retirees' wages and benefits when a company files for bankruptcy. On 02/24/10, Senator Richard Durbin (D-IL) reintroduced the above bill (S. 3033). Likewise on the same date, Congressman John Conyers Jr. (D-MI) reintroduced a House version of this bill (H.R. 4677). Both bills expired without action with the 111th Congress at the end of CY2010. Senator Durbin reintroduced this bill during subsequent sessions of Congress: S. 3381 (112th), S. 2589 (113th) and S.1156 (114th). Congressman Conyers did the same: H.R. 6117 (112th), H.R. 100 (113th), and H.R. 97 (114th). All of these bills expired without enactment with their respective sessions of Congress. This promise was not fulfilled.	0.00

Chapter 11 Department of Labor

	EMPLOYMENT	GRADE

LA-3 **The Promise:** "I will place the weight of my administration behind...a fully inclusive Employment Non-Discrimination Act [ENDA] to outlaw workplace discrimination on the basis of sexual orientation and gender identity."
When/Where: Candidate Obama letter to the Lesbian, Gay, Bisexual and Transsexual (LGBT) community dated 02/28/08.
Source: http://bilerico.lgbtqnation.com/2008/02/open_letter_from_barack_obama_to_the_lgb.php
Status: Both the Senate and the House introduced legislation in 08/09 and 06/09 respectively (S. 1584/H.R. 3017), toward fulfillment of President Obama's promise to get the dialogue toward ENDA passage reactivated. The 111th Congress expired at the end of CY2010 with no action taken on either of these legislative initiatives.

During the 112th Congress, the ENDA was reintroduced in the House (H.R. 1397) by Congressman Barney Frank (D-MA) on 04/06/11. Senator Jeff Merkley (D-OR) reintroduced a Senate version of this bill (S. 811) on 04/13/11. Both bills expired with the 112th Congress at the end of CY2012.

Senator Merkley again reintroduced this bill on 04/25/13 (S. 815). It was passed by the Senate on 11/7/13, but died in the House. It expired with the 113th Congress at the end of CY2015.

This promise was not fulfilled.

Grade: 0.00

LA-4 **The Promise:** "will...create 5 million 'green' jobs..."
When/Where: Obama-Biden Plan for America entitled: "Blueprint for Change" dated 10/09/08.
Source: https://www.documentcloud.org/documents/550007-barack-obama-2008-blueprint-for-change.html
Status: The Department of Labor (DOL) defines "green jobs" as (1) jobs in businesses that produce goods or provide services that benefit the environment or conserve natural resources; and (2) jobs in which workers' duties involve making their establishment's production processes more environmentally friendly or use fewer natural resources.

In early CY2012, President Obama stated during a campaign speech that 2.7M green jobs existed in clean energy industries, based on a 07/11 study conducted by the highly reputed Brookings Institution. That number was widely disputed at the time.

On 03/01/13, President Obama ordered into effect the sequestration measures mandated by the "Balanced Budget and Emergency Deficit Control Act." Required to cut $30M from its budget as a consequence of that order, the Bureau of Labor Statistics (BLS) eliminated all "measuring green jobs" products, in essence killing its initiatives for counting "green" jobs created or preserved.

According to the International Renewable Energy Agency (IRENA), as of end-CY2016 there were approximately 9.823B "green" jobs worldwide. Examining the fields of wind power, solar heating/cooling, solar photovoltaic, solid biomass, biogas, geothermal energy, hydropower (large and small), and liquid biofuels, the USA accounted for 806M or about 8.2% of the 9.823B "green" jobs worldwide. China and Brazil led the world with 3.955B and 1.058B "green" jobs respectively as of end-CY2016.

This promise was not fulfilled.

Grade: 0.00

LA-5 **The Promise:** "I will invest $150 billion over the next ten years in alternative sources of energy..."
When/Where: Obama Campaign Speech, Las Vegas, NV, dated 06/24/08.
Source: http://www.presidency.ucsb.edu/ws/index.php?pid=77554
Status: Under the American Recovery and Reinvestment Act (ARRA) of 2009 of 02/17/09, $39B was appropriated for renewable energy and energy efficiency activities. Additional funding proposed by President Obama during his first term in office for alternative/renewable sources of energy include but are not limited to the following:

For FY2010, President Obama's first budget proposal included:
- Department of Agriculture: $250M in renewable fuels loans and grants.
- Department of the Interior: $50M to promote renewable energy projects on Federal lands and waters.
Total funding proposed for FY2010 outside of ARRA funding: $300M

Grade: 0.00

Chapter 11 Department of Labor

For FY2011:
- Department of Energy: $500M in credit subsidy to support up to $5B in loan guarantees for innovative energy efficiency and renewable energy projects, $302M for solar energy, $220M for biofuels and biomass R&D,
- Department of the Interior: $65M to review and permit renewable energy projects on Federal lands.
- National Science Foundation: $766M for cross-agency sustainability research effort focused on renewable energy technologies.
Total funding proposed for FY2011: $1.551B

For FY2012:
- Department of Agriculture: $6.5B for renewable and clean energy.
- Department of Energy: $457M for solar energy; $341M for biofuels and biomass R&D, $102M for geothermal energy, $853M to support nuclear energy, $453M for fossil energy capture and storage R&D, $550M for the Advanced Research Projects Agency-Energy, and $200M in credit subsidies to support up to $2B in loan guarantees for innovative energy efficiency and renewable energy projects. Total: $2.956B.
- Department of the Interior: $73M to maintain capacity to review and permit new renewable energy projects on Federal lands.
- National Science Foundation: $998M for a cross-agency sustainability research effort focused on renewable energy technologies.
Total proposed by President Obama for FY2012: Just over $11B.

For FY2013:
- Department of Agriculture: $6.1B for renewable and clean energy.
- Department of Energy: $310M for the SunShot Initiative to make solar energy cost competitive nationwide without subsidies, $95M for wind energy, $65M for geothermal energy and enhanced geothermal systems, $770M for advanced small modular reactors R&D, and $350M for the Advanced Research Projects Agency-Energy. Total: $1.590B.
- Department of the Interior: $86M to maintain capacity to review and permit new renewable energy projects on federal lands.
- National Science Foundation: $203M for a cross-agency sustainability research effort focused on renewable energy technologies.
Total proposed for FY2013 for alternative/renewable energy initiatives: $7.979B

Including ARRA funding for alternative/renewable sources of energy, the above actual and proposed levels of funding during President Obama's first term in office amounted to $59.8B, leaving $90.2B to be funded for alternate energy sources during his second term for this promise to be fulfilled.

Although difficult to quantify, and in light of no new ARRA during his second term, it is prudent to assume that the $150B goal was not met during President Obama's two terms in office and will not be met during the first two years of President Trump's first term in office (for a total of 10 years).

This promise was not fulfilled.

LA-6	**The Promise:** "Will increase funding for federal workforce training programs and direct these programs to incorporate green technologies training, such as advanced manufacturing and weatherization training, into their efforts to help Americans find and retain stable, high-paying jobs..." **When/Where:** Obama-Biden Plan: "New Energy for America," dated 09/06/08. **Source:** http://energy.gov/sites/prod/files/edg/media/Obama_New_Energy_0804.pdf **Status:** Title VIII of the American Recovery and Reinvestment Act of 2009 signed into law by President Obama on 02/17/09 states that "$500,000,000 shall be for research, labor exchange and job training projects that prepare workers for careers in energy efficiency and renewable energy...". This promise was fulfilled.	1.00
LA-7	**The Promise:** "Will restore funding to these vital agencies (the EEOC and the U.S. Department of Labor's Office of Federal Contract Compliance Programs), reduce their charge backlog..." **When/Where:** Obama-Biden Plan: "Creating Equal Opportunity and Justice For All" dated 09/11/08. **Source:** https://www.politifact.com/truth-o-meter/promises/obameter/promise/297/restore-funding-to-the-eeoc-	1.00

and-the-us-departmen/
Status: Source is cited for confirmation of exact promise wording only, as it existed before original "When/Where" campaign document was deleted from archival websites.

The Equal Employment Opportunity Commission (EEOC) appropriated funding level for FY2009 was $343.9M, supplemented by $15M under the American Recovery and Reinvestment Act (ARRA) for a total of $358.9M against the Department of Labor's estimated funding requirement for EEOC operations of $357M.

For FY2010, the EEOC funding requirement increased to $367.3M, which was totally funded by Congress. FY2010 was the only year when EEOC's requirement was fully satisfied. For subsequent years, the President's request (EEOC's requirement) did not meet similar results as follows:
EEOC Requirement/Enactment by Congress
FY2011....$385.3M/$366.5M
FY2012....$385.5M/$360.0M
FY2013....$373.7M/$344.2M
FY2014....$372.9M/$364.0M
FY2015....$365.5M/$364.5M
FY2016....$373.1M/$364.5M

The backlog of requests for EEOC action at the beginning of FY2009 was 95,402, reduced to 85,768 at the beginning of FY2010.

In FY2016, the EEOC resolved 97,443 cases, 6.5% more than the 91,503 cases the agency received that year. Its backlog was down to 73,508 cases with an average of 9 months case processing time.

The Federal Contracting Compliance Program (FCCP) had a budget of $83.8M in FY2009, supplemented by $7.2M under the ARRA for a total of $91M. Under President Obama's first budget, this was increased to $105.3M in FY2010. Subsequent year funding was as follows:
FY2011....$105.0M
FY2012....$105.1M
FY2013....$ 99.5M
FY2014....$104.9M
FY2015....$106.4M
FY2016....$105.4M

As depicted above, there was increased funding for the EEOC and the FCCP, coupled with a reduction in EEOC's complaint processing backlog.

This promise was fulfilled.

LA-8 | **The Promise:** "Will establish a federal investment program to help manufacturing centers modernize and help Americans learn new skills to produce green products...the $1 billion per year investment will help spur sustainable economic growth in communities across the country." | 0.00
When/Where: Obama-Biden Plan: "Supporting Urban Prosperity", dated 09/11/08.
Source: https://assets.documentcloud.org/documents/550008/barack-obama-2008-supporting-urban-prosperity.pdf
Status: The $787B American Recovery and Reinvestment Act of 2009 (ARRA) included about $3.1 billion for state-level energy grant programs, focusing generally on green job creation and the adaptation of new energy efficient technologies.

Additional funding was made available to the Department of Energy (DOE) under the ARRA to help companies design and manufacture clean energy products. For example, DOE distributed $564M in 12/09 to support the development of advanced biofuel refineries in 15 states (facilities that make biofuel out of woodchips, grass and other organic waste products).

While the above are commendable initiatives (while acknowledging that some of the start-ups failed), this promise was to establish a specific "federal investment program." No such specific program was created.

Chapter 11 Department of Labor

This promise was not fulfilled.

LA-9

The Promise: "Obama will reinstate Executive Order No. 13173 which President Clinton issued just before he left office. Executive Order No. 13173 failed to achieve its mandate of hiring an additional 100,000 federal employees with disabilities within five years. Obama will issue this executive order early in his first term..."
When/Where: Obama-Biden Plan: "Empower Americans with Disabilities" dated 09/06/08.
Source: http://www.thearc.org/document.doc?id=3073
Status: This promise actually referred to Executive Order 13163 ("Increasing the Opportunity for Individuals with Disabilities to be Employed in the Federal Government") signed by President Clinton on 07/26/00.

On 07/26/10, President Obama signed Executive Order 13548, "Increasing Federal Employment of Individuals with Disabilities." This Executive Order mandated the hiring of an additional 100,000 persons with disabilities during the timeframe FY2011-FY2015 and called on each federal agency to "designate a senior-level agency official to be accountable for enhancing employment opportunities for individuals with disabilities and individuals with targeted disabilities within their agency, consistent with law, and for meeting the goals of this order." Responsibility for keeping the President apprised of Executive Order 13548 compliance was vested in the Director of the Office of Personnel Management (OPM) in consultation with the Office of Management and Budget (OMB).

On 10/27/16, the OPM announced that From FY2011 to FY2015, the Federal Government hired 109,575 part-time and full-time career employees with disabilities, exceeding the Obama Administration's goal to hire 100,000 people with disabilities.

This promise was fulfilled.

1.00

LA-10

The Promise: "As president, Barack Obama will announce the creation of a National Commission on People with Disabilities, Employment, and Social Security which will include presidential appointees, congressional appointees and the Commissioner of the Social Security Administration and the Secretaries of Labor and Health & Human Services as ex officio members."
When/Where: Obama-Biden Plan: "Empower Americans with Disabilities" dated 09/06/08.
Source: http://www.thearc.org/document.doc?id=3073
Status: One of the responsibilities of this commission was to have been "examining and proposing solutions to work disincentives in the Social Security Disability Insurance (SSDI), Supplementary Security Income (SSI), Medicare, and Medicaid programs".

In other words, the commission would have to find the means whereby recipients of the stated benefits would still be motivated to find work.

The promised commission was not formed during President Obama's two terms in office.

This promise was not fulfilled.

0.00

LA-11

The Promise: "...would further raise the minimum wage to $9.50 an hour by 2011, index it to inflation and increase the Earned Income Tax Credit to make sure that full-time workers can earn a living wage that allows them to raise their families and pay for basic needs such as food, transportation, and housing..."
When/Where: Obama-Biden Plan: "Supporting Urban Prosperity" dated 09/11/08.
Source: https://assets.documentcloud.org/documents/550008/barack-obama-2008-supporting-urban-prosperity.pdf
Status: The last minimum wage legislation to be passed was the "Fair Minimum Wage Act of 2007" which was signed into law on 05/25/07 during the Bush Administration under the "U.S. Troop Readiness, Veterans' Care, Katrina Recovery, and Iraq Accountability Appropriations Act of 2007".

Under the above law, the federal minimum wage could be raised in three increments of 70 cents each: from $5.15 to $5.85 on 07/24/07; to $6.55 on 07/24/08; and to $7.25 on 07/24/09.

It is noteworthy that an amendment to the Fair Minimum Wage Act of 2007 was signed into law by President Obama on 09/30/10 (Public Law 111-244) to deny the North Mariana Islands and American Samoa an increase

0.00

in their minimum wages.

As of end-CY2016, 29 states and the District of Columbia (DC) had set their their minimum wage levels above the national level of $7.25, with DC being the highest at $11.50 per hour.

Meanwhile, median household incomes, adjusted for inflation, increased only slightly from $55,478 when President Obama was inaugurated in CY2009 to $55,775 as of end-CY2015 according to the latest available Census Bureau survey data.

The national minimum wage of $7.25 per hour was unchanged during President Obama's two terms in office.

This promise was not fulfilled.

LA-12 **The Promise:** "...will work to ban the permanent replacement of striking workers, so workers can stand up for themselves without worrying about losing their livelihoods."
When/Where: Obama and Biden's Plan for America: "Blueprint for Change," dated 10/09/08.
Source: https://www.documentcloud.org/documents/550007-barack-obama-2008-blueprint-for-change.html
Status: Nothing was done to address this promise during President Obama's first term in office. In fact, this promise was repeated during President Obama's bid for a second term in office, by the end of which this promise had been forgotten.

This promise was not fulfilled.

0.00

LA-13 **The Promise:** "...will create a program to inform businesses about the benefits of flexible work schedules; help businesses create flexible work opportunities; and increase federal incentives for telecommuting."
When/Where: Obama and Biden's Plan for America: "Blueprint for Change," dated 10/09/08.
Source: https://www.documentcloud.org/documents/550007-barack-obama-2008-blueprint-for-change.html
Status: The federal government has a telecommuting program in place referred to as the "Flexiplace" program. Individual agencies have their own approaches for managing this program such as the Department of Agriculture's Telework Management System (TMS).

To refine and enforce policies under which federal employee can participate in telecommuting initiatives, President Obama signed into law the "Telework Enhancement Act of 2010" on 12/09/10. This was followed by a Presidential Memorandum on 06/23/14 entitled "Enhancing Workplace Flexibilities and Work-Life Program," again geared toward federal employees.

On the business side, however, the Department of Labor (DOL) advised that "Alternative work arrangements such as flexible work schedules are a matter of agreement between the employer and employee (or the employee's representative)."

While much progress was been made on federal employee telework initiatives, there is no evidence that the Obama Administration took any steps to "create a program" to encourage businesses to follow suit.

This promise was not fulfilled.

0.00

LA-14 **The Promise:** "...will initiate a 50-state strategy to encourage all of the states to adopt paid-leave systems (as part of the Family and Medical Leave Act). ...will provide a $1.5 billion fund to assist states with start-up costs and to help states offset the costs for employees and employers..."
When/Where: Obama-Biden Plan: "Empower Americans with Disabilities" dated 09/06/08.
Source: http://www.thearc.org/document.doc?id=3073
Status: President Obama's FY2011 budget proposal included $50M to establish a State Paid Leave Fund within the Department of Labor (DOL) "that will provide competitive grants to help States that choose to launch paid-leave programs to cover their start-up costs." The proposed budget also requested "almost $2M for the DOL to explore ways to improve the collection of data related to intersection of work and family responsibilities."

For FY2012, the President's request included "...a $23 million State Paid Leave Fund within the Department of Labor that will provide competitive grants to help States cover their start-up costs that choose to launch paid-leave programs."

0.00

Chapter 11 Department of Labor

For FY2013, the President's request is "$5 million State Paid Leave Fund within the Department of Labor that will provide technical assistance and support to States that want to establish paid-leave programs."

The above and subsequent funding proposals were not adopted by Congress in its final annual budgets. No $1.5B fund was established to help states with a paid leave system.

This promise was not fulfilled.

LA-15	**The Promise:** "...will require that employers provide seven paid sick days per year - which may be taken on an hourly basis - so that Americans with disabilities can take the time off they need without fear of losing their jobs or a paycheck." **When/Where:** Obama-Biden Plan: "Empower Americans with Disabilities" dated 09/06/08. **Source:** http://www.thearc.org/document.doc?id=3073 **Status:** Leave authorized under the Family and Medical Leave Act is unpaid leave, although the statute allows for the substitution of paid leave. The "Healthy Families Act" (H.R. 2460) introduced by Congresswoman Rosa DeLauro (D-CT) on 05/18/09 would have required "employers to permit employees to earn up to 56 hours of paid sick time including paid time for family care...". No further action was taken on this bill and it died with the 111th Congress at the end of CY2010. Congresswoman DeLauro reintroduced the "Healthy Families Act" (H.R. 1876) to the 112th Congress on 05/12/11. Senator Thomas Harkin (D-IA) introduced a Senate version of this bill on the same date (S. 984). Both bills died with the 112th Congress. The 56-hour paid sick leave provision is also included in the "Rebuild America Act" (S. 2252) introduced by Senator Harkin on 03/29/12. Legislation by the same name (H.R. 5727) was introduced by Congresswoman DeLauro on 05/10/12. Neither bill progressed beyond preliminary committee review and both expired with the 112th Congress. On 09/07/15, President Obama signed Executive Order 13706 (Establishing Paid Sick Leave for Federal Contractors). Other than federal contractors, 36% of U.S. businesses did not offer employees paid sick leave as of end-CY2016. This promise was not fulfilled.	0.00
LA-16	**The Promise:** "...will guarantee that millions more workers have access to FMLA [Family and Medical Leave Act] leave by reducing the threshold for which employers are covered from companies with 50 or more employees to those with 25 or more." **When/Where:** Obama-Biden Plan: "Empower Americans with Disabilities" dated 09/06/08. **Source:** http://www.thearc.org/document.doc?id=3073 **Status:** An amendment to the Family and Medical Leave Act was included in the National Defense Authorization Act of 2010, signed into law by President Obama on 10/28/09. However, this amendment addressed only the obligations of employers to provide leave for the families of military members by extending 12 weeks of job-protected leave to "covered active duty" personnel instead of limiting this coverage to military personnel serving in support of "contingency operations." Congresswoman Rosa Delauro (D-CT) introduced a new Healthy Families Act (H.R. 1876) on 05/12/11. This bill would have lowered the threshold for current employers to those who employ "15 or more employees for each working day during each of 20 or more calendar workweeks in the current or preceding calendar year." The same language could be found in a similar bill introduced by Senator Tom Harkin (D-IA) on the same date (S.984). Both bills expired with the 112th Congress at the end of CY2012. The 15 employee provision is also included in the "Rebuild America Act" (S. 2252) introduced by Senator Harkin on 03/29/12. Legislation by the same name (H.R. 5727) was introduced by Congresswoman DeLauro on 05/10/12. Both bills also expired with the 112th Congress.	0.00

Chapter 11 Department of Labor

As of end-CY2016, the threshold remained applicable to private sector employers who employ 50+ employees for at least 20 workweeks.

This promise was not fulfilled.

LA-17 **The Promise:** "...the Disabled Access Tax Credit, a Tax Deduction for Architectural and Transportation Barrier Removal, and the Work Opportunity Tax Credit...very few employers actually take advantage of these credits...will launch an aggressive effort to educate employers about these tax benefits so that more employers use them to hire greater numbers of employees with disabilities."
When/Where: Obama-Biden Plan: "Empower Americans with Disabilities" dated 09/06/08.
Source: http://www.thearc.org/document.doc?id=3073
Status: The Work Opportunity Tax Credit alone provides up to $9,600 in tax credit incentives to employers hiring individuals with disabilities.

The Department of Labor's Office of Disability Employment Policy (ODEP) created robust web sites such as https://www.dol.gov/odep/topics/FinancialEducationAssetDevelopment.htm that explain in great detail all the tax credits that could accrue to employers hiring certified disabled persons.

After President Obama came into office in 01/09, the number of disabled persons certified to permit the granting of tax credits to employers rose from 719K in FY2009 to about 1.3M by FY2014.

This increase is attributed in part to the Department of Labor's creation of a "Guide to Hiring Incentives" that describes tax benefits that can accrue to employers hiring disabled persons (accessible through www.disability.gov), as well as other ODEP information sharing initiatives such as the Employer Assistance and Resource Network on Disability Inclusion (EARN), Job Accommodation Network (JAN), Leadership for Emplyment and Economic Advancement for Individuals with Disabilities (LEAD), National Collaborative on Workforce and Disability for Youth (NCWD/Youth), and Partnership on Employment and Accessible Technology (PEAT).

This promise was fulfilled.

1.00

LA-18 **The Promise:** "...will direct his Secretary of Labor, the Labor Department's Office of Disability Employment Policy, and its Job Accommodation Network to bring together employers, employer associations, human resources professionals, disability advocates, service providers, and the labor movement to identify, promote, and disseminate best practices in accommodating workers with disabilities."
When/Where: Obama-Biden Plan: "Empower Americans with Disabilities" dated 09/06/08.
Source: http://www.thearc.org/document.doc?id=3073
Status: Established in CY1983 and managed by Labor's Office of Disability Employment Policy (ODEP), the Job Accommodation Network (JAN) originally focused on helping individuals with sensory disabilities (hearing, vision, touch, or speech impairments). With the arrival of automated capabilities in the 1990's, JAN's services expanded to include motor/mobility, sensory and cognitive/neurological teams. JAN inquiries have risen to about 50K annually and its website is visited by more than 8M customers annually as of end-CY2016.

JAN supports private employers by providing customized webcasts. These webcasts are accomplished either through partnerships or collaborations with public and corporate entities ranging from the Equal Employment Opportunity Commission (EEOC), to Gettinghired.com, to the National Multiple Sclerosis Society, to ODEP's "America's Heroes at Work" program for veterans and others.

34 years after ODEP instituted JAN, its mission remains the same as cited in recent appropriation language: "to provide leadership, develop policy and initiatives, and award grants furthering the objective of eliminating barriers to the training and employment of people with disabilities." For this, ODEP's budget under the Omnibus Appropriations Act of 2010 was $39.1M, an amount decreased to about $38.2M by end-FY2016. Not surprisingly, the DOL's CY2016 Annual Report on Disability Statistics and Demographics indicated that the employment of disabled people between the ages of 18 and 64 fell from 39.1% in CY2008 to 34.9% in CY2015.

What may be a contributing factor to the above statistics is that there is no public record indicating that President Obama specifically tasked his Secretary of Labor and ODEP to take action to bring interested entities together to fulfill the intent of this promise other than programs already existing prior to his presidency.

0.00

Chapter 11 Department of Labor

It is acknowledged, however, that President Obama signed Executive Order (E.O.) 13548 on 07/26/10. This E.O. pertained to "Increasing Federal Employment of Individuals with Disabilities," and not to the non-federal employers etc. for which this promise was also intended.

This promise was not fulfilled.

LA-19 **The Promise:** "...affirmative action under the Rehabilitation Act is largely ineffective. Barack Obama will direct his Secretary of Labor to make changes to the regulations implementing Section 503 so that they more closely resemble those implementing Executive Order No. 11246."
When/Where: Obama-Biden Plan: "Empower Americans with Disabilities" dated 09/06/08.
Source: http://www.thearc.org/document.doc?id=3073
Status: Executive Order 11246 was signed on 09/24/65, in the days of President Lyndon Johnson and was at the origin of the term "Equal Opportunity Employment."

Section 503 of the Rehabilitation Act of 1973 prohibits discrimination and requires employers with federal contracts or subcontracts that exceed $10K to take affirmative action to hire, train, and promote qualified individuals with disabilities and is enforceable by the Department of Labor's (DOL)Employment Standards Administration's Office of Federal Contract Compliance Programs (OFCCP).

On 09/24/13, the OFCCP published a Final Rule that makes changes to the regulations implementing Section 503 of the Rehabilitation Act of 1973.

This promise was fulfilled.

1.00

LA-20 **The Promise:** "...will also expand the purposes for which leave can be taken under the Family Medical Leave Act to include reasons related to domestic violence or sexual assault."
When/Where: Obama-Biden Plan: "Ending Violence Against Women and Children" dated 10/31/07.
Source: https://www.politifact.com/truth-o-meter/promises/obameter/promise/122/expand-the-family-medical-leave-act-to-include-lea/
Status: Source is cited for confirmation of exact promise wording only, as it existed before original "When/Where" campaign document was deleted from archival websites.

The "Healthy Families Act" (H.R. 2460) introduced by Congresswoman Rosa DeLauro (D-CT) on 05/18/09 stated that "Paid sick time earned...may be used by an employee for...an absence resulting from domestic violence, sexual assault..." No further action was taken on this bill and it died with the 111th Congress at the end of CY2010.

Congresswoman DeLauro reintroduced the "Healthy Families Act" (H.R. 1876) to the 112th Congress on 05/12/11. This bill expired with the 112th Congress at the end of CY2012. Senator Thomas Harkin (D-IA) introduced a Senate version of this bill on the same date (S. 984). This bill also expired with the 112th Congress.

The domestic violence and sexual assault provision was also included in the "Rebuild America Act" (S. 2252) introduced by Senator Harkin on 03/29/12. Legislation by the same name (H.R. 5727) was introduced by Congresswoman DeLauro on 05/10/12. Neither bill progressed beyond preliminary committee reviews and expired with the 112th Congress at the end of CY2012.

An opportunity to fulfill this promise presented itself in the "Violence Against Women Reauthorization Act of 2013" (S.47) signed into law by President Obama on 03/07/13. The Obama Administration passed on this opportunity.

Another opportunity to address this promise was the "Family and Medical Leave Enhancement Act of 2016" (H.R, 5518) introduced by Congresswoman Carolyn Maloney on 6/16/16. This bill expired with the 114th Congress at the end of CY2016.

This promise was not fulfilled.

0.00

Chapter 11 Department of Labor

LA-21	**The Promise:** "...reauthorize the Workforce Investment Act (WIA) and ensure that it strengthens federal investments needed for success in the 21st Century." **When/Where:** Obama-Biden Plan: "Supporting Urban Prosperity" dated 09/11/08. **Source:** https://assets.documentcloud.org/documents/550008/barack-obama-2008-supporting-urban-prosperity.pdf **Status:** The Workforce Investment Act of 1998 was reauthorized under and replaced by the "Workforce Innovation and Opportunity Act" (H.R. 803), signed into law by President Obama on 07/22/14. This promise was fulfilled.	1.00
LA-22	**The Promise:** "...will fight job discrimination for aging employees by strengthening the Age Discrimination in Employment Act and empowering the Equal Employment Opportunity Commission to prevent all forms of discrimination." **When/Where:** Obama and Biden's Plan for America: "Blueprint for Change," dated 10/09/08. **Source:** https://www.documentcloud.org/documents/550007-barack-obama-2008-blueprint-for-change.html **Status:** Since President Obama's inauguration in 01/09, the Age Discrimination in Employment Act of 1967 has been weakened, not strengthened. The Lilly Ledbetter Fair Pay Act of 2009 (S. 181/H.R. 11) signed into law by President Obama on 01/29/09 addressed discrimination in "compensation" because of age, but did not address discrimination in hiring because of age, nor did it address the empowerment of the Equal Employment Opportunity Commission (EEOC) to prevent all forms of discrimination. The Supreme Court, on 06/18/09, weakened the Age Discrimination in Employment Act by making it harder for plaintiffs to demonstrate age discrimination. The burden of proof now rests with the plaintiff and not the employer. To undo the above ruling, Senator Thomas Harkin (D-IA) introduced the "Protecting Older Workers Against Discrimination Act" (S. 2189) on 03/13/12. This bill expired with the 112th Congress at the end of CY2012. Congressman Robert Scott (D-VA) introduced the "Protecting Older Workers Against Discrimination Act" (H.R. 5574) on 06/24/16. This bill expired with the 114th Congress at the end of CY2016. This promise was not fulfilled.	0.00
LA-23	**The Promise:** "...will invest $1 billion over five years in transitional jobs and career pathways programs that implement proven methods of helping low-income Americans succeed in the workforce." **When/Where:** Obama-Biden Plan: "Supporting Urban Prosperity", dated 09/11/08. **Source:** https://assets.documentcloud.org/documents/550008/barack-obama-2008-supporting-urban-prosperity.pdf **Status:** The American Recovery and Reinvestment Act (ARRA) of 2009 signed into law by President Obama on 02/17/09 included a $5B Temporary Assistance for Needy Families (TANF) Emergency Fund. Of this amount, $1.3B was earmarked to create new subsidized employment programs or expand existing ones. The remaining $3.7B was used to cover costs associated with providing basic assistance and short-term benefits such as assistance to low-income families/individuals to avoid eviction and potential homelessness. Except for FY2009, the Career Pathways Innovation Fund (CPIF) has not been a line item in the Department of Labor's (DOL's) annual budget. That year, CPIF was funded in the amount of $125M. There is no specific Transitional Jobs (TJ) Program under the DOL. Rather, TJ funding requirements are satisfied in the form of grants and other funding vehicles administered by the DOL, such as the "Trade Adjustment Assistance Community College and Career Training Grant Program" which was funded at the $500M level for FY2011 and FY2012 under the Health Care and Education Reconciliation Act of 2010 (P.L. 111-152) and the Workforce Innovation Fund. The Department of Education and other organizations also have programs that support TJ objectives. Nonetheless, the ARRA appropriation for subsidized employment programs alone exceeded the promised $1B investment to help low-income families succeed in the American workforce.	1.00

Chapter 11 Department of Labor

This promise was fulfilled.

LA-24 **The Promise:** "...will fight to ensure more Katrina-related recovery or reconstruction activities can be done by local residents...will work to improve job training in the area as well."
When/Where: Obama-Biden Plan: "Rebuilding the Gulf Coast and Preventing Future Catastrophes", dated 09/11/08.
Source: https://www.documentcloud.org/documents/550006-barack-obama-2008-rebuilding-the-gulf-coast-and.html
Status: It is likely that the $300M allocated to Katrina-related reconstruction initiatives under the American Recovery and Reinvestment Act (ARRA) of 2009 resulted in job creation for local residents. However, there is no specific evidence that President Obama personally fought to send reconstruction business to local companies in areas devastated by Hurricane Katrina over and above initiatives started during the President George W. Bush Administration.

Other than regular job training programs managed by the Department of Labor to the benefit of all 50 states and U.S. territories, there is no evidence that unique job training initiatives were introduced in the areas affected by Hurricane Katrina during President Obama's two terms in office.

This promise was not fulfilled.

0.00

LA-25 **The Promise:** "...will work with YouthBuild to grow from 8,000 slots today to 50,000 slots over the next eight years in order to meet the demand from young people and communities for this valuable program."
When/Where: Obama-Biden Plan: "Helping All Americans Serve Their Country" dated 09/11/08.
Source: http://i2.cdn.turner.com/cnn/2008/images/07/02/national.service.fact.sheet.final.pdf
Status: YouthBuild programs give at-risk youth ages 16-24 the opportunity to earn their GED or high school diploma, learn to be community leaders, and prepare for college and other post-secondary training opportunities.

YouthBuild used to be under the Department of Housing and Urban Development (HUD), but has since transitioned to the Department of Labor for its funding. The program received $50M under the American Recovery and Reinvestment Act of 2009 and as of end-CY2016 has a capacity of less than 5,500 student slots annually.

Addressing participation, taking FY2014 as an example, the DOL's authorized grant program for YouthBuild amounted to $77.5M to serve approximately 5,210 participants with about 75 programs. [NB: YouthBuild USA, Inc. annual report indicates that there were 10,000 participating students in CY2014.] Jumping to FY2017, the DOL's budget authorization for YouthBuild was $84.5M to support 5,200 slots (about 10% of the promised 50,000 slots) and 82 programs.

This promise was not fulfilled.

0.00

INNOVATION	GRADE

LA-26 **The Promise:** "...will support doubling federal funding for basic research over ten years...This will foster home-grown innovation, help ensure the competitiveness of US technology-based businesses, and ensure that 21st century jobs can and will grow in America."
When/Where: Obama-Biden Plan: "Connecting and Empowering All Americans Through Technology and Innovation" dated 11/13/07.
Source: https://www.wired.com/images_blogs/threatlevel/2009/04/obamatechplan.pdf
Status: The authorized funding level for federal research and development (R&D) in FY2009 was $147.0B. This was the amount to be doubled under this promise, excluding $18.4B for federal R&D authorized under the American Recovery and Reinvestment Act (ARRA) of 2009.

According to Congressional Research Service (CRS) reports issued annually to address the status of federal R&D funding across all agencies and based largely on President Obama's annual requests, authorized funding was as follows:

FY2010....$147.1B

0.00

FY2011....$142.7B
FY2012....$140.9B
FY2013....$130.3B
FY2014....$136.3B
FY2015....$138.2B
FY2016....$146.1B
FY2017....$125.2B

Instead of "doubling" funding for federal R&D during President Obama's two terms in office, notwithstanding the ARRA plus-up reflected above, annual appropriations were actually less than the FY2009 authorized amount to be doubled ($147.0) each year except for FY2010.

This promise was not fulfilled.

RETIREMENT	GRADE

LA-27 **The Promise:** "...will automatically enroll workers in a workplace pension plan."
When/Where: Obama and Biden's Plan for America: "Blueprint for Change," dated 10/09/08.
Source: https://www.documentcloud.org/documents/550007-barack-obama-2008-blueprint-for-change.html
Status: The thrust of this promise wasn't anything new or innovative. The Pension Protection Act of 2006 encouraged automatic 401(k) enrollment. While bigger businesses offer 401(k) participation, it isn't really common for smaller businesses to offer this savings/investment capability.

President Obama addressed this promise in his FY2010 budget proposal (Table S-6). Under this proposal, employees would be automatically enrolled in workplace pension plans and would be allowed to opt out if they chose.

On 07/07/09, the Treasury Department issued final regulations on two automatic enrollment alternatives: (1) the Qualified Automatic Contribution Arrangement (QACA) and (2) the Eligible Automatic Contribution Arrangement (EACA). Under the QACA, escalating salary deferrals coupled with an employer contribution that vests after two years are authorized. Under the EACA, salary deferrals with or without employer contributions are authorized and distribution of automatic deferrals is permitted within 90 days after the first such deferral if an employee opts out of the program within that time frame.

The Departments of Labor (DOL) and Treasury announced in 02/10 that they were seeking to bring employer-sponsored 401(k) and Individual Retirement Accounts (IRAs) under structures created and administered by the U.S. Government, dubbed Guaranteed Retirement Accounts (GRAs). Republicans expressed strong opposition to federalize private sector 401(k) and IRAs and public comments were largely negative, expressing distrust over the government's ability to manage retirement accounts.

President Obama devoted an entire paragraph in his FY2011 budget proposal on this topic, wherein it states: "The Administration will streamline the process for 401(k) plans to adopt automatic enrollment." In reality, by 05/15, DOL Bureau of Labor Statistics data indicates that only 51% of the U.S. workforce was participating in a direct contribution (DC) plan such as 401(K) or IRA.

In 11/15, the Department of Treasury launched a new savings bond program called "MyRA" to encourage employees without a workplace 401(K) or IRA plan to build a safe, no-cost savings account with a reasonable, no-risk return on investment. By end-CY2016, only 20,000 people had signed up for the "MyRA" program, leaving an estimated 55M employees without a mandated, automatic 401(K) or IRA participation program.

This promise was not fulfilled.

0.00

LA-28 **The Promise:** "Create a retirement savings tax credit for low incomes."
When/Where: Interview with Tax Policy Center of Urban and Brookings Institutions dated 08/15/08.
Source: https://www.politifact.com/truth-o-meter/promises/obameter/promise/23/create-a-retirement-savings-tax-credit-for-low-inc/
Status: Source is cited for confirmation of exact promise wording only, as it existed before original "When/Where" campaign document was deleted from archival websites.

0.00

Conceptually, this tax credit has been in effect since its inception in 2001. For the 2009 tax year, singles with incomes up to $26,500, married couples with incomes up to $53,000, and heads of household with incomes up to $39,750 could claim the Retirement Savings Contributions Credit, commonly known as the "Savers Credit".

If eligible contributions are made to a qualified IRA, 401(k) or other qualified retirement plans, credits can be granted up to $1,000 (singles) or up to $2,000 (married filing jointly).

Nonetheless, President Obama's FY2010 budget proposal included modification of the existing Savers Credit to provide a 50% match on the first $1,000 of retirement savings for couples that earned less than $65,000 ($32,500 for singles). This amount was raised to $85,000 for couples in President Obama's FY2011 budget proposal. This credit would have been fully refundable.

However, Congress did not support the above initiatives. With the passage of time, the retirement savings tax credit for low incomes was dropped from President Obama's agenda.

This promise was not fulfilled.

LA-29 **The Promise:** "... employers who do not currently offer a retirement plan will be required to enroll their employees in a direct-deposit [automatic] IRA account..."
When/Where: Obama and Biden's Plan for America: "Blueprint for Change," dated 10/09/08.
Source: https://www.documentcloud.org/documents/550007-barack-obama-2008-blueprint-for-change.html
Status: This promise was reflected in President Obama's FY2010 Budget Plan (Table S-6). Employers who did not offer a retirement plan would be required to enroll their employees in a direct-deposit IRA account that is compatible with existing direct-deposit payroll systems.

President Obama went further in his FY2011 budget proposal. In a section entitled "Establishing Automatic Workplace Pensions," he stated: "...employers who do not currently offer a retirement plan will be required to enroll their employees in a direct-deposit IRA account that is compatible with existing direct-deposit payroll systems. Employees may opt-out if they choose. The smallest firms would be exempt." This proposal got nowhere.

On 08/05/10, Senator Jeff Bingaman (D-NM) introduced the "Automatic IRA Act of 2010" (S. 3760). This bill expired without action at the end of the 111th Congress. Senator Bingaman tried again on 09/14/11 by introducing the "Automatic IRA Act of 2011" (S. 1557). Likewise, Congressman Richard Neal (D-MA) introduced the "Automatic IRA Act of 2012" (H.R. 4049) on 02/16/12. Both of these bills expired without action at the end of the 112th Congress. Senator Sheldon Whitehouse (D-RI) introduced the "Automatic IRA Act of 2015" (S.245) on 01/22/15. This bill expired without action at the end of the 114th Congress at end-CY2016.

This promise was not fulfilled.

0.00

LA-30 **The Promise:** "...will ensure that all employees who have company pensions receive detailed annual disclosures about their pension fund's investments. This will provide retirees important resources to make their pension fund more secure."
When/Where: Plan for America: "Blueprint for Change," dated 10/09/08
Source: https://www.documentcloud.org/ Obama and Biden's documents/550007-barack-obama-2008-blueprint-for-change.html
Status: The Department of Labor Employee Benefits Security Administration (EBSA) issued final regulations relating to service provider disclosures under the Employee Retirement Income Security Act (ERISA) on 02/02/12. Under these new rules, "initial annual disclosure of 'plan-level' and 'investment-level' information...must be furnished no later than August 30, 2012...The first quarterly statement must then be furnished no later than November 14, 2012." Disclosures must be provided quarterly thereafter.

In 09/14, the Department of Labor published a "Reporting and Disclosure Guide for Employee Benefit Plans." Section 3 of this guide, entitled "Additional Disclosure Requirements for Pension Plans" specifies, among its 22 reporting requirements, the following:

- Periodic Pension Benefit Statement: Quarterly benefit statements for an employee or beneficiary account plan

1.00

must provide the value of each investment to which assets in the account have been allocated.
- Qualified Default Investment Alternative Notice: 30 days advance notice to participants and beneficiaries describing the circumstances under which contributions or other assets will be invested on their behalf in a qualified default investment alternative with the option to opt-out of such investments.
- Participant Plan and Investment Fee Disclosures: General information about the pension plan and potential administrative and individual costs, as well as a "comparative chart" of key information about plan investment options, must be furnished annually. On at least a quarterly basis, participants must receive a statement of the dollar amount of administrative and individual (investment) fees that were charged to their accounts.

The objective of the above is to provide greater transparency to help employees plan for retirement and actively manage their retirement savings prior to and after retirement.

This promise was fulfilled.

UNEMPLOYMENT	GRADE

LA-31 **The Promise:** "...extend unemployment insurance for an additional 13 weeks..."
When/Where: Obama-Biden Plan to Revitalize the Economy, dated 11/07/08.
Source: https://webarchive.loc.gov/all/20090429185145/http://change.gov/agenda/economy_agenda/
Status: The economic stimulus bill (American Recovery and Reinvestment Act of 2009) signed into law on 02/17/09 extended unemployment insurance benefits eligibility criteria.

On 04/15/10, President Obama signed another bill further extending unemployment benefits for those whose 26 weeks of state-paid benefits had expired and would last for up to 99 weeks. Valued at $18B, this bill was in effect until 06/02/10.

On 07/22/10, another bill was signed into law, this one valued at $34B, extending the eligibility dates for benefits extensions to 11/28/10.

Under the Tax Relief, Unemployment Insurance Reauthorization, and Job Creation Act of 2010 (H.R. 4853) signed into law by President Obama on 12/17/10, an additional 13 months (not weeks as promised) extension of unemployment benefits was authorized for eligible unemployed persons.

This promise was fulfilled.

Grade: 1.00

LA-32 **The Promise:** "...temporarily suspend taxes on unemployment insurance benefits..."
When/Where: Obama-Biden Plan to Revitalize the Economy, dated 11/07/08.
Source: https://webarchive.loc.gov/all/20090429185145/http://change.gov/agenda/economy_agenda/
Status: While the economic stimulus bill (American Recovery and Reinvestment Act of 2009) signed into law on 02/17/09 extended unemployment insurance, tax relief was extended only to the first $2,400 of unemployment benefits received in 2009 ($4,800 if both spouses were unemployed). The interpretation of this promise is that all unemployment insurance would be temporarily tax exempt.

For the CY2010 tax year, the exemption from taxes for the first $2,400 of unemployment benefits expired under the "Tax Relief, Unemployment Insurance Reauthorization, and Job Creation Act of 2010" (H.R. 4853). Since CY2010, all unemployment benefits have been taxable at the federal level, although some states do not tax these benefits. Recipients of such benefits must file IRS Form 1099-G.

This promise was not fulfilled.

Grade: 0.00

UNIONS	GRADE

LA-33 **The Promise:** "I will fight for...I intend to sign the Employee Free Choice Act when it lands on my desk in the White House."
When/Where: Campaign Speech "Alliance for American Manufacturing," Pittsburg, PA, dated 04/14/08.
Source: http://www.presidency.ucsb.edu/ws/index.php?pid=76997
Status: The purpose of the Employee Free Choice Act is to "establish an efficient system to enable employees to form, join, or assist labor organizations, to provide for mandatory injunctions for unfair labor practices during the organizing effort..."

Grade: 0.00

Chapter 11 Department of Labor

Introduced in both houses of Congress on 03/10/09 (H-1409 and S-560) by Congressman George Miller (D-CA) and Senator Edward Kennedy (D-MA) respectively as the "Employee Free Choice Act of 2009", the requisite Congressional votes to make these bills happen were lagging throughout the 111th Congress. Additionally, constituent employers were generally against them. Given that previous supporters on both sides of the aisles withdrew their support for these bills, they died with the adjournment of the 111th Congress at the end of CY2010.

The promised Act is not to be confused with the "Employer Free Choice Act" (H.R. 2854) introduced on 09/07/11 for the purpose of repealing a rule on the notification of employee rights under the National Labor Relations Act.

The "Employee Free Choice Act of 2016" (H.R. 5000) was reintroduced by Congressman Alan Grayson on 04/20/16. This bill expired with the 114th Congress at the end of CY2016.

This promise was not fulfilled.

LA-34 **The Promise:** "...I support collective bargaining rights for all workers...I will review decisions by the Bush Administration that have denied these rights to federal employees and seek to restore them."
When/Where: Candidate Obama letter to President, American Federation of Federal Employees, dated 10/20/08.
Source: https://www.politifact.com/truth-o-meter/promises/obameter/promise/499/restore-collective-bargaining-rights-to-federal-em/
Status: As of end-CY2011, 37% of public sector workers and 6.9% of private sector workers were represented by a union according to the Department of Labor's Bureau of Labor Statistics.

0.00

President Bush's Executive Order (E.O.) 13480 entitled "Exclusions from the Federal Labor-management Relations Program" of 11/26/08 eliminated the collective bargaining rights of numerous organizations belonging to the Departments of Energy, Homeland Security, Justice, Transportation and Treasury on the basis that those organizations "have as a primary function intelligence, counterintelligence, investigative, or national security work."

On 10/28/09, President Obama signed into law the National Defense Authorization Act for FY2010 (Public Law 111-84). This law repealed the statutory authority for the National Security Personnel System (NSPS) created under the Bush Administration and required the Department of Defense (DoD) to transition approximately 226K civilian employees from NSPS back to the appropriate statutory non-NSPS pay and personnel system by 01/01/12. NSPS would have imposed significant restrictions on regular civil servants' collective bargaining rights. With the return of the old pay and personnel system (i.e. General Schedule - GS), collective bargaining rights were returned as well.

The Transporation Security Agency (TSA) is another organization where 40K employees (mainly airport screeners) did not have collective bargaining rights. In 04/11, under the aegis of the Federal Labor Relations Authority (FLRA), employees were invited to vote for union representation by either the National Treasury Employees Union (NTEU) or the American Federation of Government Employees (AFGE). Since less than 50% of eligible employees voted, a runoff election was called by the FLRA. The NTEU won this runoff election as announced by the FLRA on 06/23/11.

The situation is much different for 1,500 Bureau of Alcohol, Tobacco and Firearms (ATF) employees, however. No known action has been taken by the Obama Administration to reinstate their collective bargaining rights, which could have been accomplished easily by President Obama issuing an executive order of his own.

President Obama will also be remembered as the President who turned his back on Wisconsin public employees who sought to restore their collective bargaining rights in FY2011 but failed. He promised them during his presidential election campaign that he'd have their backs but was a "no-show."

As of CY2015, the percentage of wage and salary workers who were members of unions was as follows according to the website FedSmith.com:
Private Sector - 6.7%

Federal Government - 27.3%
State Government - 30.2%
Local Government - 41.3%

This promise was not fulfilled.

LA-35 **The Promise:** "And if American workers are being denied their right to organize when I'm in the White House, I will put on a comfortable pair of shoes and I will walk on that picket line with you as President of the United States."
When/Where: Campaign Speech entitled "A Change We Can Believe In," Spartanburg, SC, dated 11/03/07.
Source: http://www.presidency.ucsb.edu/ws/index.php?pid=77018
Status: In this promise, then-candidate Obama promised to support the protection of union collective bargaining rights.

An for opportunity President Obama to deliver on this promise presented itself in early CY2011 when the Governor of Wisconsin cut collective bargaining rights of most public employees in his efforts to reduce the state's budget deficit. Governor Scott Walker (R-WI) signed this decision into law on 03/11/11. On 09/14/12, Dane County Circuit Judge Juan Colas ruled that this law violated both the U.S. Constitution and state equal protection laws, thereby declaring it null and void. This decision was appealed.

Other than statements in support of unions in general, President Obama did not "put on a comfortable pair of shoes and...walk on the picket line" in Madison as promised. This situation led to a recall election on 06/05/12. Republican Governor Walker won (the first governor to win a recall election in history) and the Wisconsin democrats lost. On 08/04/14, the Wisconsin Supreme Court ruled that Governor Walker's initiative did not violate constitutional protections limiting the right of workers to collectively bargain through unions.

This promise was not fulfilled.

0.00

LABOR GPA	**0.26**

Chapter 12 - Department of State

REPORT CARD
OBAMA44REPORTCARD.COM
Objective....Fact-Based....Unbiased

Campaign Promises
Departments -> State

ITEM	STATE	GRADE
	AFRICA	
ST-1	**The Promise:** "As president, Obama will take immediate steps to end the genocide in Darfur..." **When/Where:** Obama and Biden's Plan for America: "Blueprint for Change," dated 10/09/08 **Source:** https://www.documentcloud.org/ Obama and Biden's documents/550007-barack-obama-2008-blueprint-for-change.html **Status:** Early in his presidency, President Obama named Major General (Ret.) J. Scott Gration as his special envoy to Sudan on 03/18/09. On 06/17/09 Gration told reporters in Washington that the Government of Sudan was no longer engaged in a campaign of mass murder in Darfur. Months later on 10/19/09, however, President Obama referred to the situation in Darfur as "genocide," acknowledging that "hundreds of thousands of people" had been killed in Darfur and "millions more displaced." As the South completed its 01/11 referendum on self-determination and independence from the North/Khartoum government and moved ahead to become the world's newest country (South Sudan) on 07/09/11, the Obama Administration appeared to focus only on the North-South secession challenge over the continuing lack of a cease fire in the Western Sudanese region of Darfur. President Obama appointed Princeton Lyman as Special Envoy to South Sudan and Sudan on 03/31/11 to replace Gration. The "Doha Document for Peace in Darfur (DDPD)," was signed in 07/11 between the Government of Sudan and the Darfuri rebel groups to end their conflict that was the root cause of the genocide. Insignificant progress was made after the document was signed to resolve the Darfur situation because of lack of implementation and enforcement. In fact, mass murders in Darfur are known to have continued through the end of President Obama's two terms in office, although on a lesser scale than in previous years. For example, in 09/16, the Sudanese government reportedly launched chemical weapon attacks on civilian populations in Darfur, killing at least 250 people, mostly children. By end-CY2016, about 600K people were known to have been killed in Darfur and nearly 3M displaced. This promise was not fulfilled.	0.00
ST-2	**The Promise:** "...will hold the government in Khartoum accountable for abiding by its commitments under the Comprehensive Peace Accord that ended the 30 year conflict between the north and south." **When/Where:** Plan for America: "Blueprint for Change," dated 10/09/08 **Source:** https://www.documentcloud.org/documents/550007-barack-obama-2008-blueprint-for-change.html **Status:** The Comprehensive Peace Agreement (CPA) signed on 01/09/05 by the southern Sudan People's Liberation Movement (SPLM), based in Juba (south), and the ruling National Congress Party (NCP) in Khartoum (north). Among its provisions: withdrawal of northern troops from the south,	0.00

Chapter 12 - Department of State

national elections, a census, the sharing of southern oil revenues with the north, power-sharing, and it set a timetable for a referendum on independence for southern Sudan. The CPA expired on 07/07/11, the date South Sudan became an independent nation.

Through the years, U.S.-Sudan relations have been strained. After a six-year closure, the U.S. Embassy in Khartoum reopened in CY2002 with a Charge d'Affaires as the senior U.S. diplomat, not an Ambassador, a situation that exists to the present day. Compounding this situation, the International Criminal Court (ICC) in The Hague issued two warrants for the arrest of the President of Sudan, Omar Hassan Ahmad Al Bashir for war crimes and crimes against humanity as well as for being a criminally responsible suspect and an indirect co-perpetrator. As of end-CY2016, President Bashir remained at large, traveling with impunity to countries that do not recognize the jurisdiction of the ICC with regard to its warrants against Bashir.

Despite the best efforts of special envoys and others, the CPA is believed to have failed in its overarching goals of reconciliation between the north and south and national unity. The following CPA objectives also failed by the time it expired in 07/11:
- Setting aside 30% of the Sudanese civil service for southerners;
- Introduction of legislation to reform land ownership;
- Settlement of boundary disputes along the oil-rich Abyei region;
- Demobilization of soldiers and termination of support for proxy militias;
- Investment in chronically impoverished rural areas for roads, schools, hospitals and other infrastructure;
- Involvement of international community with regard to CPA implementation.

Faced with the above failures, there was no accountability by the Khartoum Government led by fugitive President Bashir who, it seems, simply disregarded President Obama's overtures as well as the terms of the CPA.

This promise was not fulfilled.

ST-3	**The Promise:** "...In order to increase the incomes of subsistence producers, decrease the pressure on shrinking arable lands, and minimize the vulnerability of commodity exports to global price shocks, an Obama administration will launch the AVTA Initiative..." **When/Where:** Obama-Biden Plan: "Strengthening Our Common Security by Investing in Our Common Humanity," dated 09/11/08. **Source:** https://www.cgdev.org/sites/default/files/archive/doc/blog/obama_strengthen_security.pdf **Status:** The intent of the Add Value to Agriculture (AVTA) Initiative promise was to spur research and innovation aimed at bringing about a Green Revolution in Africa by partnering with land grant institutions, private philanthropies and business to support agricultural processing through increased investment in research and development for improved seeds, irrigation methods, and affordable and safe fertilizers. The initiative would also address food security issues in order to alleviate high food costs. Under President Obama, according to public domain Congressional Research Service Report R41072, appropriations for all international food aid programs was as follow: FY2009....$2.642B (Last Bush era appropriation) FY2010....$2.561B FY2011....$2.324B FY2012....$2.431B FY2013....$2.275B FY2014....$2.671B FY2015....$2.816B FY2016....$2.071B FY2017....$1.801B	0.00

Chapter 12 - Department of State

Although President Obama continued previous Administration programs to alleviate global hunger, programs that have existed since the Eisenhower Administration (1954), he very specifically promised to establish AVTA. As of the end of his second term in office, he had not established a specific AVTA Initiative.

This promise was not fulfilled.

ST-4	**The Promise:** "...will launch the Global Energy and Environment Initiative to ensure African countries have access to low carbon energy technology and can profitably participate in the new global carbon market so as to ensure solid economic development even while the world dramatically reduces its greenhouse gas emissions." **When/Where:** Plan for America: "Blueprint for Change," dated 10/09/08 **Source:** https://www.documentcloud.org/ Obama and Biden's documents/550007-barack-obama-2008-blueprint-for-change.html **Status:** As of end-CY2016 the Obama Administration had not launched an Africa-focused Global Energy and Environment Initiative (GEEI). Educational institutions such as Johns Hopkins University and the Massachusetts Institute of Technology (MIT) have their own energy and environment programs that could have served as launching pads for the promised program. However, President Obama promised that his Administration would launch a GEEI specifically focused on the sharing of energy technology in support of economic development with certain African countries. Also problematic in this promise is Obama's statement that the world is reducing its greenhouse gas emissions. While this is true for many countries, more than half of the estimated 7B tons of coal burned annually is burned in China alone. To meet its increasing demands during the Obama Administration and contributing to sustained greenhouse gas emissions, China stepped up its annual importation of more than 150M tons of coal from Wyoming, Montana and Australia. This promise was not fulfilled.	0.00
ST-5	**The Promise:** "...will also strengthen the African Growth and Opportunity Act to ensure that African producers can access the U.S. market and will encourage more American companies to invest on the continent." **When/Where:** Plan for America: "Blueprint for Change," dated 10/09/08 **Source:** https://www.documentcloud.org/ Obama and Biden's documents/550007-barack-obama-2008-blueprint-for-change.html **Status:** The African Growth and Opportunity Act (AGOA) was signed into law (P.L. 106-200) by President Clinton on 05/18/00. To strengthen this Act, "AGOA II" and "AGOA III" were signed by President Bush in CY2002 and CY2004 respectively. On 12/20/06, President Bush also signed the Africa Investment Incentive Act further amending portions of the AGOA and is known as "AGOA IV." President Obama signed into law an amendment to the AGOA on 08/10/12 (H.R. 5986). This amendment extended through FY2015 the duty-free treatment of the products of beneficiary sub-Saharan African countries. With its original 15-year period of validity expiring in CY2015, the AGOA was extended by President Obama on 06/29/15 for an additional 10 years through CY2025 under the Trade Preferences Extension Act of 2015 (S. 1267). Amendments and additional clauses pertinent to the AGOA and included in this law served to strengthen it. This promise was fulfilled.	1.00

Chapter 12 - Department of State

	CHINA	GRADE
ST-6	**The Promise:** "...will use all diplomatic means at his disposal to achieve change in China's manipulation of the value of its currency, a practice that contributes to massive global imbalances and provides Chinese companies with an unfair competitive advantage." **When/Where:** Obama-Biden Plan: "Protecting U.S. Interests and Advancing American Values in our Relationship with China" dated 09/11/08. **Source:** http://www.scribd.com/doc/6245761/Barack-Obama-Joe-Biden-Protecting-US-Interests-Advancing-American-Values-in-our-Relationship-with-China **Status:** At the start of the Obama Administration, American manufacturers considered the Chinese yuan (also called the "renminbi") to be undervalued by about 40%, contributing to the USA's massive trade deficit with China and the loss of millions of American jobs. On 07/08/10, the Obama Administration announced that it would not make an issue of China's apparent currency manipulation to gain an unfair trade imbalance. Chinese Premier Wen Jiabao stated on 09/22/10 that the exchange rate of the yuan was not the "main cause" of the bilateral trade imbalance (which was valued at about $350B) by end-CY2016 and that the U.S. trade deficit with China was not intentional. President Obama tried to get leading economic powers to follow his plan to end global trade imbalances during the 11/10 G-20 Summit in Korea. He was soundly rebuffed. President Obama's sour reaction was to refer to the yuan issue as an "irritant." No progress was made during President Hu's 01/11 visit to the USA to change China's manipulation of its currency. It must be recognized, however, that the yaun's value against the U.S. dollar was 6.84 at the start of the Obama Administration and 6.94 yuan to the dollar at the end of CY2016. This is viewed in the context of the yuan's record low value of 1.53 in 01/81 and a record high of 8.73 on 01/94. During the 11/12-13/11 Asia-Pacific Economic Cooperation (APEC) conference in Hawaii, President Obama used strong language to press China to reform the U.S. belief that China's currency was being kept artificially low, thereby keeping American businesses at a disadvantage and driving up China's trade surpluses. As in the past, China pushed back against this pressure with Chinese President Hu Jintau telling President Obama that "China's foreign exchange policy is a responsible one," and that China will "continue reforming its exchange rate mechanism." Translation: the Chinese would not reform the perceived manipulation of their currency. On 12/28/11, the Obama Administration decided not to designate China as a currency manipulator, thereby avoiding a potential trade war rooted in low export prices against high import costs. Since then, research indicates that China has endeavored to raise the value of the yuan whenever it fell rather than further lowering that value. This promise was not fulfilled.	0.00
ST-7	**The Promise:** "...will insist that our imports from China and other countries be safe." **When/Where:** Obama-Biden Plan: "Protecting U.S. Interests and Advancing American Values in our Relationship with China" dated 09/11/08. **Source:** http://www.scribd.com/doc/6245761/Barack-Obama-Joe-Biden-Protecting-US-Interests-Advancing-American-Values-in-our-Relationship-with-China **Status:** During the first term of the Obama Administration, concerns prevailed over the safety of Chinese products. These concerns ranged from much-publicized corrosive effects of Chinese-manufactured drywall with hydrogen sulfide content (affecting more than 20K homes), to lead content in children's toys, to defective tires. A Memorandum of Understanding (MOU) was signed between the U.S. Consumer Product Safety	0.00

Chapter 12 - Department of State

Commission (CPSC) and China's General Administration of Quality Supervision, Inspection and Quarantine (AQSIQ) back in CY2004. Its provisions were generally ignored by China largely due to the absence of cooperation and reciprocal inspections.

The CPSC signed another MOU in 04/10, but this one was with the U.S. Customs and Border Protection (CBP) organization, following an increase in civil penalties from $8K to $100K for each violation of the Consumer Product Safety Improvements Act of 2008 and from $1.8M to $15M for repeated violations. This 04/10 MOU mandated the allocation of increased CBP resources to inspect and prevent noncompliant products from entering the USA. The new rules apply to all imports -- not only those from China.

China objected to the 04/10 MOU between the CPSC and CBP, and cited it as an example of American protectionism, further exacerbating an already strained bilateral trade relationship. With other pressing issues at hand such as economic relations, China's military buildup, North Korea's nuclear capabilities buildup and its provocative actions in the region, this import concern was not brought up during Chinese President Hu Jintao's visit to the USA in 01/11.

During President Obama's tenure in office, China continued to put our military men and women at risk by delivering counterfeit parts for such critical military warfighting systems as the F-15 fighter, Maverick missile, V-22 Osprey tilt-rotor aircraft and some of the U.S. Navy's submarines. While the extent of parts counterfeiting cannot be quantified exactly, the Government Accountability Office (GAO) has acknowledged that it is taking place.

The Obama Administration fell far short of ensuring that militarily significant parts obtained from China met the standards necessary to ensure the safety of military personnel.

This promise was not fulfilled.

ST-8

The Promise: "From Tibet to cracking down on democracy and religious freedom activists, China has failed to live up to international standards of human rights. Barack Obama and Joe Biden...will press them to respect human rights."
When/Where: Obama-Biden Plan: "Protecting U.S. Interests and Advancing American Values in our Relationship with China" dated 09/11/08.
Source: http://www.scribd.com/doc/6245761/Barack-Obama-Joe-Biden-Protecting-US-Interests-Advancing-American-Values-in-our-Relationship-with-China
Status: The Communist Chinese government acknowledges that its form of government is a "socialist democracy" under which public debate on certain issues is permitted, so long as the Communist Party's leadership is not challenged. However, that Party continued to disregard basic human rights, including religious freedom, during President Obama's two terms in office.

Secretary of State Clinton, during her first trip to China on 02/09, appeared to push human rights concerns to a low priority by stating that human rights issues "can't interfere with the global economic crisis, the global climate change crisis, and the security crisis."

Meanwhile, those who spoke out against the Communist Party continued to be persecuted, critical internet postings were viewed as subversive, web sites were and continue to be routinely shut down, and their authors hunted down and jailed.

The U.S.-China "Human Rights Dialogue," a forum that permits direct engagement with China on U.S. concerns over specific human rights issues, resumed in mid-CY2010. One of the issues discussed was the continued incarceration of Dr. Xue Feng, a U.S. citizen, serving an 8-year sentence and $30,000 fine for allegedly revealing state secrets when he published information about China's oil fields in CY2007 -- in other words, for espionage. In 04/15, after serving nearly the full 8 years in a Chinese prison, Dr. Xue was released and immediately deported to the USA.

0.00

Chapter 12 - Department of State

By hosting Chinese President Hu Jintau on 01/19/11, President Obama became the first U.S. President to host a head of state whose country continued to imprison a Nobel Peace Prize laureate, democracy advocate and writer Liu Xiaobo (who has since died of liver cancer) who was serving an 11-year prison term for "suspicion of inciting subversion of state power." During the visit, President Hu first tried to deflect a direct question regarding China's poor human rights record. When pressed to answer the question, President Hu simply stated that "a lot still needs to be done in China in terms of human rights." It's interesting that this comment was censored from the press briefing version aired in China.

In a joint statement released on 01/19/11, the U.S. and China addressed their differences on human rights in a "spirit of equality and mutual respect." Translation: no progress. Shortly thereafter on 04/02/11, one of China's best-known and sometimes provocative contemporary artists, Ai Weiwei, was arrested. He was released nearly three months later, after considerable international pressure, but only after signing a confession of having "committed crimes against the state."

Hundreds of Chinese activists and intellectuals were detained or simply disappeared in China's efforts to thwart the possibility of a popular uprising such as the "Arab Spring" uprisings in Egypt, Tunisia, Bahrain, Syria, Libya and other Middle East countries during the first half of CY2011.

The 19th U.S.-China "Human Rights Dialogue" took place in mid-08/15. The State Department acknowledged in its briefing to Congress following this conference that "...we discussed the Chinese Government's crackdown on lawyers, which has resulted in over 250 attorneys, activists, and their family members being detained, questioned, interrogated, or held incommunicado...many are still in custody, many reportedly have been denied access to defense counsel. Some have been forced to make televised confessions...that run contrary to China's own criminal procedure law."

Another example: the State Department's Bureau of Democracy, Human Rights and Labor painted an extremely bleak human rights picture for Tibet in its "2016 Country Reports on Human Rights Practices," released in 03/17. The abuses portrayed therein are no different and in some cases worse than during the pre-Obama era.

The bottom line: the Obama Administration failed to improve China's human rights record, with the latter maintaining the status quo ante.

This promise was not fulfilled.

ST-9	**The Promise:** "...will press China to end its support for regimes in Sudan, Burma, Iran and Zimbabwe." **When/Where:** Obama-Biden Plan: "Protecting U.S. Interests and Advancing American Values in our Relationship with China" dated 09/11/08. **Source:** http://www.scribd.com/doc/6245761/Barack-Obama-Joe-Biden-Protecting-US-Interests-Advancing-American-Values-in-our-Relationship-with-China **Status:** Iran: While China provided support for U.S.-led United Nations watered-down sanctions against Iran's nuclear energy program in 06/10, China remained Iran's largest oil customer. However, China was extremely vocal about its opposition to U.S. unilateral sanctions against Iran. As Japanese and Western investments dried up in Iran, China increased its own investments, thereby maintaining its support of Iran's regime. In CY2014, trade between China and Iran was estimated to be $52B, as China depends on Iran for nearly 15% of its oil requirement. In 01/16 during a visit to Iran by President Xi Jinping, the two countries agreed to increase bilateral trade to $600B over the ensuing decade. Iran's Supreme Leader Ayatollah Ali Khamenei praised China for standing by Iran during its many years of economic isolation imposed by United Nations, U.S. and European Union sanctions due to Iran's nuclear proliferation activities. Burma (now Myanmar): In 03/10, China defended the Burmese regime's controversial election laws at the UN Security Council by taking the position that any transition to democracy is an internal affair.	0.00

A year later the first democratically elected President of Myanmar (Thein Sein) visited China during which China reaffirmed its "respect for Myanmar's independence, sovereignty and territorial integrity." Nonetheless, as of end-CY2016, Myanmar continued to be concerned about Chinese influence due to China's size, power, and proximity, as well as the way China's economic development projects have been carried out without due consideration for the well-being of Myanmar's population and ecology.

Zimbabwe: Through end-CY2016, China continued to be Zimbabwe's largest investor (by some accounts providing 74% of Zimbabwe's foreign direct investment), while exploiting the country's natural resources to develop its own economy. This was greatly facilitated by Zimbabwe's "Look East Policy" established in CY2000 by President Mugabe. On 09/11/11, Mugabe stated: "The imperialist countries of Britan, Europe and the U.S. have continued to undermine our country...we are grateful to the stance China has always taken in defending our sovereignty." As of end-CY2016, China remained as a key supplier of military hardware to Zimbabwe. Recent major sales included a radar system, jet trainers and fighters, military vehicles and AK-47 assault rifles and ammunition.

Sudan: China imports about 80% of Sudan's oil, and continues to deliver weapons, ammunition, tanks, helicopters, fighter aircraft etc. to the Sudanese regime in Khartoum. During the 01/11 visit of Chinese President Hu Jintao to the USA, China agreed to fully support Sudan's Comprehensive Peace Agreement (CPA). For China, this ensured uninterrupted acquisition of oil from the oil-rich South after the South became an independent country in 07/11, while continuing to arm the Khartoum regime. At the same time, China continued to favor the Khartoum regime of President Omar Al-Bashir by adopting a "look the other way" non-interference policy in Darfur where, according to UN reports, more than 300K people were killed and nearly 3M people were displaced. During President Hu's 01/11 visit to the USA, he only acknowledged that progress should be made in the political process to resolve the Darfur issue. Meanwhile, China agreed on 07/08/13 to finance the construction of a new $700M Khartoum International Airport.

With the exception of Myanmar where new-found democracy came about outside of Chinese influence and where Chinese support of a repressive regime was no longer an issue, Chinese support of the regimes in Iran, Zimbabwe and Sudan as of end-CY2016 was either at the same level or at a higher level than when President Obama assumed the presidency in CY2009.

This promise was not fulfilled.

ST-10	**The Promise:** "...will vigorously enforce our trade laws and trade agreements to ensure that American companies have a fair opportunity to compete..." **When/Where:** Obama-Biden Plan: "Protecting U.S. Interests and Advancing American Values in our Relationship with China" dated 09/11/08. **Source:** http://www.scribd.com/doc/6245761/Barack-Obama-Joe-Biden-Protecting-US-Interests-Advancing-American-Values-in-our-Relationship-with-China **Status:** From the start of his Administration, President Obama made enforcement of U.S. trade rights a top priority. To that end, between CY2009 and CY2016, the U.S. filed 25 trade enforcement actions with the World Trade Organization (WTO). The U.S. won every one of its challenges that were decided by the WTO by end-CY2016, including seven against China alone. Export figures confirm that these enforcement victories are worth billions of dollars for American farmers and ranchers; manufacturers of high-tech steel, aircraft and automobiles; solar energy manufacturers; cutting edge service providers, and many others. Among the successes, the Obama Administration, through its U.S. Trade Representative (USTR), the Department of Commerce, Customs and Border Patrol, and Immigration and Customs Enforcement (ICE) took positive action against China on the following: - Discriminatory aircraft tax exemptions; - Excessive government support to the Chinese agricultural sector;	1.00

Chapter 12 - Department of State

- Raw materials (rare earth) quotas/restrictions;
- Unlevel playing field affective seven export sectors such as agriculture, textiles, and medical products;
- Excessive duties on American poultry, high-tech steel, American automobiles and SUVs; and
- Enforcement of anti-dumping/countervailing duty orders pertaining to non-oriented electrical steel, corrosion-resistant steel, cold-rolled steel, and cut-to-length plate.

Further, President Obama was proactive in discussing trade imbalance issues with President Xi Jinping whenever they met. This led to President Xi's commitments to address these issues.

This promise was fulfilled.

ST-11

The Promise: "will vigorously...counteract piracy of intellectual property."
When/Where: Obama-Biden Plan: "Protecting U.S. Interests and Advancing American Values in our Relationship with China" dated 09/11/08.
Source: http://www.scribd.com/doc/6245761/Barack-Obama-Joe-Biden-Protecting-US-Interests-Advancing-American-Values-in-our-Relationship-with-China
Status: U.S. manufacturers have validated their claims that China routinely counterfeits U.S. goods, offering these goods on the U.S. and world markets at cut-rate prices, thereby furthering China's goals to hold the USA at a competitive export disadvantage and feeding the estimated $346B+ trade imbalance as of end-CY2016.

The U.S. position on mitigating cyber crimes and theft of Intellectual Property (IP) during the Obama Administration was weak at best. In fact, an early CY2017 report published on behalf of The Commission on the Theft of American Intellectual Property by The National Bureau of Asian Research states that "The commissioners were discouraged by the Obama administration's inaction on IP theft and cyber-espionage...Although the president took steps to bring his emergency economic powers to bear on cyber-enabled IP theft, the Obama Administration failed to bring any cases against the perpetrators of cyber crime or IP theft" during his two terms in office.

This promise was not fulfilled.

Grade: 0.00

CONSULAR AFFAIRS | GRADE

ST-12

The Promise: "...will streamline the visa process to return America to its rightful place as the world's top destination for artists and art students."
When/Where: Obama-Biden Plan: "Champions for Arts and Culture", dated 09/11/08.
Source: http://muzartworld.org/president-barack-obama-and-joe-biden-champions-for-arts-and-culture/
Status: Since 09/11/01, artists and art organizations faced considerable red tape and bureaucratic delays when applying for O-1A (individuals with an extraordinary ability in the sciences, education, business, or athletics), O-1B (individuals with an extraordinary ability in the arts or extraordinary achievement in motion picture or television industry) or O-2 (an individual who will accompany an O-1 visa applicant who has critical skills and experience with the O-1 visa applicant that cannot be readily performed by a U.S. worker and which are essential to the successful performance of the O-1 visa applicant), and P-1B (Member of Internationally Recognized Entertainment Group) non-immigrant visas to enter the USA to perform.

As of end-CY2016, artists filing State's I-129 Form (Petition for Nonimmigrant Worker) had to allow 5.5 months for their applications to be processed. Dependent upon individual applicant circumstances, the processing time could be longer or shorter.

The processing times typically required since the terrorist attacks of 09/11/01 are as follows:
- O-1A, O-1B and O-2: 60 to 90 days
- P-1B: 2 to 5 months
The above processing times could be longer or shorter, depending upon applicant circumstances

Grade: 1.00

Chapter 12 - Department of State

and application completeness. To mitigate this issue, the Homeland Security U.S. Citizenship and Immigration Service (USCIS) announced on 07/23/10 that artist/art student visa applications filed by "creative organizations" could be adjudicated within 15 calendar days upon payment of a premium processing fee (currently $1,225.00).

As of end-CY2016, the USCIS web site reflected 60-90 days as the norm for processing "O" (Extraordinary Ability) visas and 3-6 months for "P" (Athletes, Artists and Entertainers) visas. These processing times can be reduced to 15 days upon payment of a hefty ($1,000+) surcharge.

This promise was fulfilled.

ST-13

The Promise: "...will stop shuttering consulates and start opening them in the tough and hopeless corners of the world - particularly in Africa."
When/Where: Obama-Biden Plan for America: "Blueprint for Change" dated 10/09/08.
Source: https://www.documentcloud.org/documents/550007-barack-obama-2008-blueprint-for-change.html
Status: Since President Obama came into office in 01/09, the following are examples of consulates that have either been opened, reopened or were planned under the State Department's Bureau of Overseas Buildings Operations (OBO):

Afghanistan: Herat, Kandahar and Jalalabad
China: Guangzhou
India: Hyderabad
Iraq: Basra and Erbil
Kazakhstan: Almaty (Upgrade from Embassy Branch Office to Consulate)
Egypt: Alexandria
Mexico: Monterrey and Tijuana
Equatorial Guinea: Malabo
Morocco: Casablanca
Saudi Arabia: Dhahran

With the exception of Afghanistan, where security concerns caused the cancellation of plans to open a Consulate in Mazar-e-Sharif in CY2012, and Iraq where security is sometimes tenuous, none of the other sites are considered "tough and hopeless," -- not even the two African sites.

On the "shuttering" side, the State Department closed the U.S. Embassy and consular activities in Syria on 02/06/12 as the regime of President Bashar al-Assad intensified its efforts to crush internal dissidence.

This promise was not fulfilled.

Grade: 0.00

EUROPE	GRADE

ST-14 — **1.00**

The Promise: "...will insist that the rights of the Serb community in Kosovo and the security of Serbian religious sites be vigilantly protected and will work to encourage Serbia to seek its future in a stable and prosperous West."
When/Where: Obama-Biden Plan: "A Stronger Partnership with Europe for a Safer America" dated 10/14/08.
Source: http://www.scribd.com/doc/6245758/Barack-Obama-Joe-Biden-A-Stronger-Partnership-with-Europe-for-a-Safer-America
Status: According to UN Security Council Resolution 1244, Serbia has the right to place up to 1,000 personnel at the most important religious and historical sites in Kosovo. The Kosovan Minister of the Interior, Bajram Regjepi, rejected this engagement of Serbian personnel.

The NATO-led Kosovo Force (KFOR) announced in 08/10 that it would hand over the responsibility for protection of most Serbian monasteries and churches in Kosovo and Metohija to the largely

Chapter 12 - Department of State

ethnic-Albanian Kosovo police. The announcement was immediately condemned by the Serbian Orthodox Church. As of end-CY2016, KFOR was still protecting major Serbian Orthodox Church sites and a few monasteries such as the 14th Century Serbian Orthodox Visoki Decani Monastery near Decani, Kosovo.

U.S. silence on the control of security of Serbian religious/historical sites by the mostly ethnic-Albanian Kosovo police, despite the provisions of UN Resolution 1244, is a situation that served to inhibit the prospects for true peace and security in that region for the foreseeable future.

Following a visit to Serbia by Vice President Biden in 05/09, the U.S. committed to provide Serbia with an annual $50M aid package to support reforms needed for Serbia's integration in the European Union (EU) and other global institutions. In this area, there was support forthcoming from the USA for Serbia as it seeks a "future in a stable and prosperous West."

The U.S. foreign aid package to Serbia, across all agencies (which saw a high of $99M in CY2001), was provided as follows during the Obama Administration:
FY2010 - $43M
FY2011 - $61M
FY2012 - $32M
FY2013 - $35M
FY2014 - $36M
FY2015 - $28M
FY2016 - $33M

The need to maintain a KFOR security presence in Serbia and the provision of aid below the promised $50M per year during most of President Obama's two terms in office are indicative of the slow progress Serbia is making toward achieving true peace and security. As of end-CY2016, Serbia remained as a candidate for membership in the European Union, a process started in CY1998.

This promise was fulfilled.

ST-15

The Promise: "...will show U.S. leadership in seeking to negotiate a political settlement on Cyprus...believes strongly that Cyprus should remain a single, sovereign country in which each of the two communities on the island is able to exercise substantial political authority within a bi-zonal, bi-communal federation."

When/Where: Obama-Biden Plan: "A Stronger Partnership with Europe for a Safer America" dated 10/14/08.

Source: http://www.scribd.com/doc/6245758/Barack-Obama-Joe-Biden-A-Stronger-Partnership-with-Europe-for-a-Safer-America

Status: The so-called Cypriot issue or conflict is an ongoing dispute between Greek Cypriots and Turkish Cypriots since the CY1974 Turkish military invasion and occupation of the northern third of Cyprus. Historically, relations between the USA and Cyprus have been considered good-to-excellent and the USA routinely uses Cypriot military bases, ports and airports such as the Port of Limassol and the Larnaca International Airport to support its activities in the Middle East.

As of end-CY2010, the Obama Administration, according to the U.S. Embassy Nicosia web site, still viewed the status quo on Cyprus as unacceptable, but preferred that United Nations inter-communal negotiations lead the way to achieve a fair and permanent settlement between the Greek Cypriot and Turkish Cypriot communities.

In FY2005, the USA provided approximately $36M in foreign aid to Cyprus (across all agencies) to reduce tensions and promote peace and cooperation between the two communities, and creating conditions conducive to resolution of the long-standing Cyprus conflict by reuniting the island.

A few years later under President Obama, foreign aid to Cyprus took a big hit as depicted below:

0.00

FY2010 - $15.0M
FY2011 - $9.0M
FY2012 - $1.2M
FY2013 - $4.8M
FY2014 - $880K
FY2015 - $420K
FY2016 - $303K

The Obama Administration did not show any "U.S. leadership" needed to resolve the Cypriot issue. Rather, Turkey was recognized by the Obama Administration as a key ally in the Middle East, an ally that continually moved toward closer relationships with Iran, Russia and others not considered allies of the USA, to the detriment of any resolution of the Cyprus partition situation.

Frustration on the lack of U.S. leadership for a political settlement on Cyprus was articulated by the President of the "Justice of Cyprus" International Coordinating Committe, Philip Christopher, on 06/04/12 in Washington, D.C. when he stated: "We are very disappointed with the administration. It has basically maintained the status quo...they have offered the same rhetoric." That status quo was maintained through end-CY2016.

This promise was not fulfilled.

ST-16

The Promise: "They [Obama and Biden] recognize that the historic political achievements of 2007 must be followed by economic development that benefits all of the people of Northern Ireland...will work closely with the Irish Taoiseach, the British Prime Minister, and the Northern Ireland Executive to continue on this path of peace and prosperity."
When/Where: Obama-Biden Plan: "A Stronger Partnership with Europe for a Safer America" dated 10/14/08.
Source: http://www.scribd.com/doc/6245758/Barack-Obama-Joe-Biden-A-Stronger-Partnership-with-Europe-for-a-Safer-America
Status: The first step in fulfilling this promise was the appointment of the U.S. Special Economic Envoy to Northern Ireland, businessman Declan Kelly, in 09/09. This position had remained vacant during the preceding Bush Administration. Mr. Kelly resigned in 05/11 and was replaced by former Senator Gary Hart in 10/14. Mr. Hart served as Special Economic Envoy to Northern Ireland until the end of the Obama Administration in 01/17.

The Special Envoy's mission was to work with the Northern Ireland Government and private sectors in fostering new opportunities for trade and investment. Relations between the Obama Administration and the Taoiseach (Irish head of government/prime minister) and President have been cooperative.

The Obama Administration has also been supportive of the International Fund for Ireland (IFI), established in CY1986 with the USA, Canada, New Zealand, Australia and the European Union as contributors. This fund provides grants and loans to businesses to improve their economy, redress inequalities of employment opportunity, and improve cross-border business and community ties.

The U.S. contribution to the IFI in FY2010 was $17M, up from $15M in FY2009. For FY2011, $18M was appropriated under the Continuing Appropriations Act (H.R. 3081) but this funding was eliminated under Public Law 112-6 on 03/18/11. Instead, the IFI received $2.5M from the FY2011 Economic Support Fund in the form of a grant. Subsequent year funding for the IFI was as follows:
FY2012 - $5M
FY2013 - $0
FY2014 - $2.1M
FY2015 - $1.25M
FY2016 - $750K

This promise was fulfilled.

1.00

Chapter 12 - Department of State

EXPORT CONTROLS	GRADE
ST-17 **The Promise:** "...will direct a review of the International Traffic in Arms Regulations (ITAR) to reevaluate restrictions imposed on American companies, with a special focus on space hardware that is currently restricted from commercial export." **When/Where:** Obama-Biden Plan: "Advancing the Frontiers of Space Exploration" dated 08/15/08. **Source:** http://www.nasa.gov/pdf/382369main_48%20-%2020090803.2.Space_Fact_Sheet_FINAL.pdf **Status:** Since CY1999, the International Traffic in Arms Regulations (ITAR) have imposed severe export controls not only on the USA's defense/weapons systems, but on communications satellites and virtually all spacecraft and space hardware, software and related materials. These restrictions came about after two U.S. satellite manufacturers were found to have aided China missile development efforts by advising the Chinese on the causes of U.S. missile launch failure. These restrictions were viewed by some as a declaration of economic and technological war by the U.S. Government against U.S. businesses and national interests. On 08/14/09, President Obama announced his decision to undertake a comprehensive review of U.S. export controls, referred to as the Export Control Reform (ECR) Initiative. This Initiative was to be accomplished in three phases: Phases 1 and 2 - reconcile various definitions, regulations, and policies for export controls Phase 3 - create a single export control list, a single licensing agency, a single enforcement coordination agency, and a unified information technology system. In response to this challenge, the Department of Defense, in cooperation with the Departments of State, Commerce, Homeland Security, the Director of National Intelligence and National Security Agency devised a blueprint for implementing the President's direction with the understanding that some of the above changes could be implemented via Executive Order, while others would require Congressional notification/action. On 03/11/11, the Department of State Directorate of Defense Trade Controls published a new proposed rule that establishes conditions under which an ITAR license would not be required for the export of a defense article incorporated into an end-item that is subject to export controls under the Department of Commerce's Export Administration Regulations (EAR). On 07/12/11, the Department of Commerce Bureau of Industry and Security (BIS) published a proposed rule for the transfer of items on the U.S. Munitions List (USML) that the President determines no longer warrant control under the Arms Export Control Act (AECA) to the Commerce Control List (CCL) once Congressional notification requirements are met. In 04/12, the Department of Defense issued its report recommending that some U.S.-built satellites and components be transferred from the USML to the CCL. On 05/22/12, Senator Michael Bennett (D-CO) introduced the "Safeguarding United States Leadership and Security Act of 2012" (S. 3211) which would give the President the authority to transfer certain satellites and their components from the USML to the less restrictive CCL. While this bill did not advance through Congress, its provisions were included in the House version of the FY2013 National Defense Authorization Act. On 11/10/14, some satellites, spacecraft, and components were moved from the USML (ITAR control) to CCL (EAR control): - Communications satellites that do not contain classified components or capability; - Remote sensing satellites with performance parameters below certain thresholds; and	**1.00**

- Systems, subsystems parts, and components associated with these satellites and with performance parameters below a certain threshold.

This promise was fulfilled.

ST-18	**The Promise:** "...will also direct revisions to the licensing process to ensure that American suppliers are competitive in the international aerospace markets, without jeopardizing American national security." **When/Where:** Obama-Biden Plan: "Advancing the Frontiers of Space Exploration" dated 08/15/08. **Source:** http://www.nasa.gov/pdf/382369main_48%20-%2020090803.2.Space_Fact_Sheet_FINAL.pdf **Status:** As of end-CY2016, the processing time for export licenses was about 45 days, and about 95% of applications were approved. Viewed against 21st Century technological advances, 45 days is an eternity for U.S. companies trying to satisfy their international customers. In 08/09, President Obama directed a top-to-bottom review of the nation's export control system. A major component of this review involved licensing procedures. In 04/10, an Interagency Task Force reported its findings and concluded that a single licensing agency should be formed (State, Commerce and Defense currently have licensing responsibilities that often do not complement one another) and that licencing reform should ensue in three phases: Phase 1: Implement regulatory-based improvements to streamline licensing processes and standardize policy and processes to increase efficiencies. Phase 2: Complete transition to mirrored control list system and fully implement licensing harmonization to allow export authorizations within each control tier to achieve a significant license requirement reduction which is compatible with national security equities. Phase 3: Implement a single licensing agency. Also in 04/10, Defense Secretary Gates announced a "4 Singles" approach to export licensing reform. The basic tenets of the "4 Singles" initiative: (1) a more predictable, efficient and transparent technology control regime that will create a single control list, (2) a single primary enforcement coordination agency, (3) a single information technology system, and (4) a single licensing agency. Years later, the Obama Administration and Congress were still working to develop and codify the "4 Singles," whereas a simple amendment to Executive Order 11958, Administration of Arms Export Controls, could have accomplished this objective. By creating a single licensing agency as proposed by Secretary Gates, conflicting State, Defense and Commerce regulations could be eliminated and the licensing process simplified. As of end-CY2016, the arms export licensing process had not been significantly improved. This promise was not fulfilled.	0.00
	FOREIGN AFFAIRS/DIPLOMACY	**GRADE**
ST-19	**The Promise:** "Increase the size of the foreign service." **When/Where:** Obama-Biden Plan "Strengthening Our Common Security by Investing in Our Common Humanity," dated 09/11/08. **Source:** https://www.cgdev.org/sites/default/files/archive/doc/blog/obama_strengthen_security.pdf	1.00

Chapter 12 - Department of State

Status: In CY2009, the State Department launched a four-year plan known as "Diplomacy 3.0" to increase its foreign service officer strength by 25% by end-FY2018. Fiscal realities suggested that this goal might not be met until FY2023. According to General Accountability Office (GAO) Report 12-721 entitled "Foreign Service Workforce Gaps" dated 06/14/12, the State Department faced "experience gaps in 28 percent of overseas Foreign Service positions...14 percent are vacant...14 percent are filled through upstretch assignments" (where the incumbent has not attained the grade of the position he or she fills).

The same GAO report indicated that the State Department had failed to develop a strategic plan to exercise the authority it had to address Foreign Service mid-level personnel gaps, relying instead on its practice of employing Foreign Service retirees on a When Actually Employed (WAE) basis and converting a few of its 10,569 (a CY2011 figure) Civil Service personnel to Foreign Service positions.

Mid-level personnel gaps were expected to continue for the foreseeable future due to fiscal realities coupled with personnel attrition attributed to the graying of the employees, the mandatory retirement age for Foreign Service personnel (65), and the built-in Reduction in Force (RIF) in the Foreign Service with its "up or out" system.

According to the State Department Bureau of Human Resources, and in spite of the above GAO report, during President Obama's two terms in office, and with the exception of slight dips in CY2013 and CY2015, the Foreign Service grew as follows to support 275 posts abroad as of end-CY2016:
CY2009 - 7,070 Officers/5,189 Specialists = 12,268
CY2010 - 7,458 Officers/5,401 Specialists = 12,859
CY2011 - 7,775 Officers/5,657 Specialists = 13,432
CY2012 - 7,940 Officers/5,736 Specialists = 13,676
CY2013 - 7,915 Officers/5,752 Specialists = 13,667
CY2014 - 8,042 Officers/5,759 Specialists = 13,801
CY2015 - 8,026 Officers/5,734 Specialists = 13,760
CY2016 - 8,106 Officers/5,740 Specialists = 13,846

Without specifying numerical goals, President Obama promised to increase the size of the foreign service and has done so.

This promise was fulfilled.

ST-20 | **The Promise:** "Unfortunately, our resources for cultural diplomacy are at their lowest level in a decade. Barack Obama and Joe Biden will work to reverse this trend and improve and expand public-private partnerships to expand cultural and arts exchanges throughout the world." | 1.00

When/Where: Obama-Biden Plan: "Champions for Arts and Culture" dated 09/11/08.
Source: http://muzartworld.org/president-barack-obama-and-joe-biden-champions-for-arts-and-culture/
Status: Funding for State's Educational and Cultural Exchange (ECE) program for FY2008 was $501M and $538M for FY2009.

The Consolidated Appropriations Act of 2010, signed into law by President Obama on 12/16/09, provided $635M to the Department of State for an increase of $97M over the FY2009 appropriation, to "fund educational, cultural and professional exchange programs worldwide to foster mutual understanding between the United States and more than 160 other nations."

For FY2011, the State Department requested $635M to sustain ECE programs but received $599M. For FY2012, State's requirement was $637.1M but received $598.8M. Subsequent FY appropriations for ECE were as follows:
FY2013....$574M
FY2014....$567M
FY2015....$594M

FY2016....$590M
FY2017....$634M

From the very beginning of his Administration, President Obama fulfilled this promise to improve/expand ECE activities based on increased funding when weighed against the FY2008/FY2009 funding levels.

This promise was fulfilled.

ST-21	**The Promise:** "...will pursue direct diplomacy with all nations, friend and foe. He will do the careful preparation necessary, but will signal that America is ready to come to the table, and that he is willing to lead." **When/Where:** Obama-Biden Plan for America: "Blueprint for Change" dated 10/09/08. **Source:** https://www.documentcloud.org/documents/550007-barack-obama-2008-blueprint-for-change.html **Status:** While relations with most of America's friends were maintained during the Obama Administration, some cooled (i.e. United Kingdom, France, Germany), while others became severely strained (i.e. Russia, Israel, Afghanistan).	0.00

China continued to deeply distrust the USA over its continued relationship with and support of Taiwan. On the other hand, Taiwan's continuing need for 66 new F-16C/D fighter aircraft and upgrades for its aging fleet of F-16/A/B aircraft were repeatedly blocked during the first three years of the Obama Administration, gaining traction only in 04/12 when the Administration reversed its position and declared that it would give "serious consideration" to an F-16C/D sale. To that end, the House approved the "National Defense Authorization Act for Fiscal Year 2013" (H.R. 4310) which included Section 1240 that reads: "The President shall carry out the sale of no fewer than 66 F-16C/D multirole fighter aircraft to Taiwan." This potential sale was rejected by China and was one of the root causes for continued strained relationships between the USA and China.

China also saw the USA as encircling Chinese assertive expansion efforts in Southeast Asia by establishing new transpacific relationships with Vietnam, Cambodia, Indonesia and others that were viewed as running against China's free trade objectives with Association of Southeastern Asian Nation (ASEAN) member countries.

There was no known demarche or meaningful pursuit of improved, highest level diplomatic relations between the Obama Administration and countries the USA considers its foes (i.e. Venezuela, Iran, Syria, North Korea).

The collapse of climate negotiations in Copenhagen was considered a serious defeat for the Obama Administration. His brokering of a separate deal with the Chinese left his European allies stymied by what was referred to in European media as President Obama's "pomposity and arrogance."

President Obama's failure to show up at the 20th anniversary of the fall of the Berlin Wall in 11/09 further infuriated his British, French and German counterparts. These relationships slowly mended during President Obama's visit to London in 05/11 and his hosting of German Chancellor Merkel in the first state visit he accorded to a European leader, 2 1/2 years into his first term in office.

In 11/10, he failed again to deal effectively with China on the issue of the latter's currency manipulation.

In 05/12, the new Russian President Vladimir Putin elected not to attend the Group of Eight (G8) Summit at Camp David, Maryland for the first time since Russia became the 8th member of this forum in CY1997. Russia sent its Prime Minister instead, a move that was interpreted by international observers as a sign of the high level of tension that existed between the U.S. and Russian presidencies. This strained bilateral relationship got worse as a result of the mid-09/12 closure of

Chapter 12 - Department of State

USAID activities in Russia because of funding provided by USAID to "Golos," a group that reported on widespread fraud during recent parliamentary and presidential elections that, in part, returned Putin to presidential power.

In 08/12, President Obama declared that the use of chemical weapons by Syrian President Bashar al-Assad would cross a "red line for us" and might trigger a U.S. military response. On 08/21/13, Bashar fired rockets loaded with outlawed toxins against his people near Damascus, killing nearly 1,500 civilians, including at least 426 children. Obama did nothing.

In 09/12, President Obama decided not to meet with any foreign leaders during the annual United Nations General Assembly, further straining relationships with traditional allies, especially Israel. Instead, his priority was to hit the campaign trail to secure a second term in office.

In 08/13, President Obama cancelled a planned summit with Russia's President Putin, indicating that Obama's "reset" of bilateral relations announced during his first term had failed.

In 02/14, Russian President Vladimir Putin invaded and seized Crimea. Obama did nothing.

These are a few examples where President Obama's lack of diplomatic leadership skills were perceived negatively and as a sign a weakness by the international community. For the remainder of his second term through end-CY2016, the USA was generally viewed internationally as militarily strong, but strategically, diplomatically and geo-politically impotent, feckless, untrustworthy, and lacking integrity.

This promise was not fulfilled.

	FOREIGN AID	GRADE
ST-22	**The Promise:** "Double U.S. spending on foreign aid to $50 Billion a year by 2012" **When/Where:** Obama's Plan: "The War We Need To Win" dated 07/31/07. **Source:** http://www.mattluedke.com/wp-content/uploads/2016/09/CounterterrorismFactSheet.pdf **Status:** For FY2009, the last Bush Presidency budget cycle, foreign assistance amounted to about $53.9B for all entities involved in foreign assistance/aid (i.e. DOD, Overseas Contingency Operations etc.), not counting supplementals such as the American Recovery and Reinvestment Act (ARRA) signed into law by President Obama in 02/09 and other agency-specific supplementary funding per year. The $50B goal of U.S. spending on foreign aid had already been met prior to President Obama assuming office. Subsequent funding under the Obama Administration was as follows FY2010....$55.4B FY2011....$55.2B FY2012....$55.2B FY2013....$49.5B FY2014....$45.8B FY2015....$52.0B FY2016....$51.3B FY2017....$48.9B Foreign Aid spending by the U.S. was not doubled during President Obama's two terms in office and in some years was less than enacted during his predecessor's last year in office. This promise was not fulfilled.	0.00
ST-23	**The Promise:** "Barack Obama will double the Peace Corps to 16,000 by its 50th anniversary in 2011..." **When/Where:** Plan for America: "Blueprint for Change," dated 10/09/08	0.00

Chapter 12 - Department of State

Source: https://www.documentcloud.org/ Obama and Biden's documents/550007-barack-obama-2008-blueprint-for-change.html

Status: In FY2009, total Peace Corps strength was 7,671 volunteers serving in 65 countries.

By end-CY2016, the Peace Corps had 7,376 personnel serving in 65 countries.

The promise was not fulfilled.

ST-24

The Promise: "Use part of increased U.S. assistance to establish a $2 billion Global Education Fund to offer an alternative to extremist schools."

When/Where: Obama's Plan: "The War We Need To Win" dated 07/31/07.

Source: http://www.mattluedke.com/wp-content/uploads/2016/09/CounterterrorismFactSheet.pdf

Status: A Global Education Fund (GEF) has existed since CY1998. It originally focused on providing books and literacy tools to orphanages and learning centers in Latin America. By CY2007, it had expanded to 22 countries. Since 2007, GEF has focused on removing obstacles to education in three high-need countries: Kenya, India and Guatemala.

The purpose of President Obama's GEF would have been to finance schools that would counter the message of radical Islamist madrasas (schools for teaching Islamic theology and religious law) in Afghanistan, Pakistan and elsewhere. The State Department budget for FY2010 included $1B for this effort, $19M above the President's request and $300M above FY2009, to increase access to quality education and provide alternatives to madrasas.

In Pakistan alone by end-CY2016, an estimated 1.9M Pakistani children attended madrasas, which have also proliferated in India, Afghanistan and other Middle East countries.

The logical entity to manage a GEF would have been the State Department's Office of Global Educational Programs. This didn't happen and a formal "Global Education Fund" was not established at the $2B level.

This promise was not fulfilled.

0.00

ST-25

The Promise: "...more than four million Iraqis are refugees or are displaced inside their own country. Obama and Biden will form an international working group to address this crisis. They will provide at least $2 billion to expand services to Iraqi refugees in neighboring countries, and ensure that Iraqis inside their own country can find sanctuary."

When/Where: Plan for America: "Blueprint for Change," dated 10/09/08

Source: https://www.documentcloud.org/ Obama and Biden's documents/550007-barack-obama-2008-blueprint-for-change.html

Status: The Department of State budget for FY2010 included $1.68B for Migration and Refugee Assistance (MRA), which was $197M above the President's request and $6.8M above the FY09 level. For FY2011, State's budget for MRA was $1.647B, an amount reduced to $1.600B in FY2012. The Emergency MRA (EMRA) account was funded at $27.2M in FY2012, down from $49.9M in FY2011.

On top of the above, International Organizations & Conferences (CIO) were funded at the $1.69B level, which was $100 million below the President's FY2010 request but $92.6M above the FY2009 enacted level. For FY2011, CIO funding was enacted at the reduced level of $1.311B but increased to $1.440B in FY2012.

The CIO account provides funds to 47 international organizations, including the United Nations, for which the U.S. is treaty-obligated. There is no evidence that a specific obligation of $2B was made by the Obama Administration to help resolve the unique Iraqi refugee issue, one which could perhaps best be addressed through the United Nations High Commission on Refugees (UNHCR).

0.00

Chapter 12 - Department of State

One must keep in mind that MRA, EMRA and CIO funds are appropriated to address global issues, not solely Iraqi issues.

By end-CY2016, following prior year funding trends, the State Department's Bureau of Population, Refugees, and Migration was funded at the $2.8B level. Of this amount, $1.35B was earmarked for Near East countries, Iraq being just one of approximately 20 countries that constitute the Near East.

The formation of an "international working group" didn't happen. Neither did the dedication of $2B annually for Iraqi refugees.

This promise was not fulfilled.

ST-26	**The Promise:** "...invest at least $50 billion by 2013 for the global fight against HIV/AIDS, including our fair share of the Global Fund." **When/Where:** Plan for America: "Blueprint for Change," dated 10/09/08 **Source:** https://www.documentcloud.org/ Obama and Biden's documents/550007-barack-obama-2008-blueprint-for-change.html **Status:** The Global Fund is a partnership between governments, civil society, the private sector, and affected communities to prevent and treat not only HIV/AIDS, but also malaria and tuberculosis. On 10/05/10, U.S. Global AIDS Coordinator Eric Goosby announced that the USA pledged $4B to the Global Fund -- for the multiyear period of FY2011-FY2013. Against this pledge, the Obama Administration committed $1.05B in FY2011, $1.3B in FY2012, and $1.56B in FY2013. The goal of $4B for the Global Fund by FY2013 was not met. The FY10 appropriation for the Department of State to combat worldwide HIV/AIDS was enacted at $5.5B (including $350M for USAID HIV/AIDS programs). For FY2011 and FY2012, the President's request and resultant appropriations for USAID HIV/AIDS programs was flat and unchanged at $350M. The President requested that this line item be reduced to $330M for FY2013. The total FY2011 Global/International request for HIV/AIDS under the President's Emergency Plan for AIDS (PEPFAR) was $6.7B. The enacted amount was $5.5B. For FY2012, PEPFAR funding was enacted at the $4.6B level and President Obama's request for FY2013 proposes to increase this amount to $7.6B, an amount that was reduced to $3.86B in light of sequestration related budget constraints. During President Obama's first term in office, the promise of fully funding the Global Fund pledge ($4B) and meeting the $50B goal for HIV/AIDS mitigation was not met, given that the cumulative funding for the FY2010-FY2013 timeframe came in at less than $20B to combat HIV/AIDS. This promise was not fulfilled.	0.00
ST-27	**The Promise:** "The Civilian Assistance Corps [CAC]...would provide each federal agency a pool of volunteer experts willing to deploy in crises. They would be pre-trained and screened for deployment to supplement departments' expeditionary teams...would ensure that true experts carry out tasks such as restoring electricity or creating banking systems, rather than the current practice of expecting already over-burdened soldiers to assume these roles...will set a goal of creating a national CAC of 25,000 personnel." **When/Where:** Obama Campaign Document "A 21st Century Military for America" dated 11/26/07. **Source:** https://www.scribd.com/document/6245756/Barack-Obama-on-Defense-Issues-A-21st-Century-Military-for-America **Status:** Based on a Congressional Research Service report entitled "Peacekeeping/Stabilization and	0.00

Chapter 12 - Department of State

Conflict Transitions: Background and Congressional Action on the Civilian Response/Reserve Corps and Other Civilian Stabilization and Reconstruction Capabilities" dated 01/12/12, Congress approved $50M for the creation of a Civilian Response Corps (CRC) under the President Bush era Supplemental Appropriations Act of 2008.

The Obama Administration further refined the organization of the CRC into three components as follows:
- Active Component (CRC-A) of 250 personnel
- Standby Component (CRC-S) of 2,000 personnel
- Reserve Component (CRC-R) of 2,000 personnel.

The CRC-R most closely resembled the Civilian Assistance Corps (CAC) then-Candidate Obama promised to establish. The intent of the CRC-R, to be manned by 2,000 volunteers from the public and private sectors, was to deploy experts within 60 days to areas of conflict or disaster.

Following receipt of an initial authorization of $50M from Congress for a CRC in FY2008, State requested CRC funding in the amount of $323M for FY2010 under the Civilian Stabilization Initiative (CSI). Congress turned down this request because neither the CRC-A nor CRC-S programs were considered to have been effectively established. President Obama did not seek funding for CRC-R in either FY2011 or FY2012.

As of end-CY2016, the envisioned 25,000-strong Civilian Assistance Corps (CAC), now referred to as CRC-R, had not been realized.

This promise was not fulfilled.

ST-28

The Promise: "...will...develop the capacity of our civilian aid workers to work alongside the military."
When/Where: Obama-Biden Plan for America: "Blueprint for Change" dated 10/09/08.
Source: https://www.documentcloud.org/documents/550007-barack-obama-2008-blueprint-for-change.html
Status: In theory, USAID's Office of Military Affairs Planning Division has a well-articulated mission to coordinate USAID civilian-military relationships with the Pentagon, the State Department and other organizations. USAID's participation in the development of the next iteration of the "Guidance for the Employment of the Force," a strategic planning document used by Combatant Commanders (COCOMs), its participation in COCOM regional/theater campaign planning, and its participation in DoD's Quadrennial Defense Review (QDR) are all, on the surface, indicative that there exists good collaboration between USAID and the military.

In its first Quadrennial Diplomacy and Development Review (QDDR) of CY2010, the State Department acknowledged the need for closer civilian/military working relationships as one of the pillars of an effective national security strategy. Several of State's strategic goals directly supported, on paper, this objective. The QDDR of CY2015 did not mention any civilian/military working relationship.

As of end-CY2016, the DoD remained as the country's most significant instrument in dealing with the world's most pressing needs. At the same time, the civilian-led foreign aid system during the Obama Administration was considered by some to be politically weak, largely dysfunctional, generally unable to deliver aid consistent with State's longer-term strategic vision/goals, and lacked international partner confidence.

To fully deliver on this promise, the Foreign Assistance Act of 1961 needed to be rewritten. This particular legislative reform was not on President Obama's or Congress' agenda throughout the Obama Administration.

This promise was not fulfilled.

0.00

Chapter 12 - Department of State

FOREIGN POLICY		GRADE
ST-29	**The Promise:** "Obama will personally lead diplomacy efforts beginning with a speech at a major Islamic forum in the first 100 days of his administration." **When/Where:** Obama's Plan: "The War We Need to Win" dated 07/31/07. **Source:** http://www.mattluedke.com/wp-content/uploads/2016/09/CounterterrorismFactSheet.pdf **Status:** President Obama found his "major Islamic forum" when he addressed the Turkish Parliament on 04/06/09. According to the CIA World Factbook, Turkey is nominally 99.8% Muslim and Obama's speech was reportedly monitored by a majority of the worldwide Muslim and Arab community as broadcast by the Al Jazzera and Al Arabiya news networks. This promise was fulfilled.	1.00
ST-30	**The Promise:** "We'll establish a program for the Department of Energy and our laboratories to share technology with countries across the region." **When/Where:** Obama-Biden Plan: "Renewing U.S. Leadership in the Americas", dated 06/06/08. **Source:** https://www.politifact.com/truth-o-meter/promises/obameter/promise/494/share-enviromental-technology-with-other-countries/ **Status:** Source is cited for confirmation of exact promise wording only, as it existed before original "When/Where" campaign document was deleted from archival websites. During the 2009 Summit of the Americas at Port of Spain, Trinidad and Tobago on 04/17-19/09, President Obama announced the creation of the "Energy and Climate Partnership of the Americas". On 04/19/09, President Obama and his Mexican counterpart (President Calderon) established the US-Mexico Bilateral Framework on Clean Energy and Climate Change, a key tenet of which is "...expanding our extensive bilateral collaboration on clean energy technologies to facilitate renewable power generation...". This promise was fulfilled.	1.00
ST-31	**The Promise:** "Barack Obama and Joe Biden...will significantly increase funding for the National Endowment for Democracy (NED) and other nongovernmental organizations to support these civic activists." **When/Where:** Obama-Biden Plan: "Strengthening Our Common Security by Investing in Our Common Humanity", dated 09/11/08. **Source:** https://www.cgdev.org/sites/default/files/archive/doc/blog/obama_strengthen_security.pdf **Status:** NED funding is usually under an appropriation provided by Congress to the Department of State largely for the U.S. Agency for International Development (USAID). The FY2008 budget allocation for the NED was $99.190M, but this amount was funded under the Democracy Fund, not under the conventional State/USAID route. The enacted NED budget for FY2009 was $115M. Under President Obama, the NED enacted budget for FY2010 was $118M, the same amount appropriated under Continuing Resolution procedures for FY2011. For FY2012, President Obama requested that the NED's funding be reduced to $104M but the budget enacted by Congress remained at $118M. For FY2013, President Obama again requested a reduction to $104M. Despite this early trend of trying to reduce NED funding, the Obama Administration regrouped and by FY2015, NED funding was increased to $148M and in FY2016 to $185M. It's interesting to note that in CY2015, NED became the first Non-Government Organization (NGO) to be banned in Russia under a law against "undesirable" international nongovernmental organisations. This promise was fulfilled.	1.00
ST-32	**The Promise:** "Restore U.S. leadership on space issues by seeking code of conduct for space-faring	0.00

nations, including a worldwide ban on weapons to interfere with satellites and a ban on testing anti-satellite weapons."
When/Where: Obama Campaign Document "A 21st Century Military for America" dated 11/26/07.
Source: https://www.scribd.com/document/6245756/Barack-Obama-on-Defense-Issues-A-21st-Century-Military-for-America
Status: On 06/28/10, the Obama Administration released its "National Space Policy of the United States of America." This new policy failed to address the main thrust of this promise, as it does not include any statement supporting the notion that the Obama Administration is seeking "a worldwide ban on weapons to interfere with satellites and a ban on testing anti-satellite weapons."

On 09/27/10, The European Union (EU) presented an updated version of its "Draft Code of Conduct for Outer Space Activities" to potential signatories for preventing harmful interference with space objects and refraining from intentional damage to satellites.

In 01/12, the State Department announced the Obama Administration's position that instead of signing the EU's proposed Code of Conduct, the USA would work with the EU and other nations to develop an "International Code of Conduct for Outer Space Activities." Yet on 02/17/12, Secretary Clinton endorsed the EU Code on behalf of the United States (joining Canada, Australia, Japan and India) while recognizing that the code was not legally binding and had no enforcement mechanisms.

As of end-CY2016, a finalized EU Code of Conduct was not yet in place. There are a total of nine countries with launch capabilities and more than 50 countries that have assets in space (space-faring nations) that would have to endorse the Code before it would be considered effective. If/when this happens, it will be impossible to monitor and enforce the Code's provisions.

It is clear that the EU, not the USA, exercised leadership in the drafting and finalization of the Code of Conduct for Outer Space Activities. Secondly, the USA has not been effective in introducing a worldwide ban on anti-satellite weapons.

As recently as 05/16, Russia tested its Nudol anti-satellite (ASAT) capability, joining China and the USA in their own development and testing of ASAT capabilities.

This promise was not fulfilled.

ST-33	**The Promise:** "He will open "America Houses" in cities across the Arab world...America Houses would offer state-of-the-art English-language training programs, discussions, and a wide selection of current periodicals, newspapers, and literature. They would offer free Internet access and moderated programs that promote direct exchange with Americans through the use of modern information technology." **When/Where:** Obama-Biden Plan: "The War We Need To Win" dated 07/31/07. **Source:** http://www.mattluedke.com/wp-content/uploads/2016/09/CounterterrorismFactSheet.pdf **Status:** On 12/02/10, an "America House" was opened at the Pacific Place Mall in Jakarta, Indonesia, a non-Arab country in which the majority is of the Muslim faith. Opened with corporate support provided by Microsoft, Google, Cisco and others, this high-tech outreach center (known as "@america") was the first American cultural center of its kind in the world. This promise was to open America Houses "in cities across the Arab world". Other than Indonesia, not considered an "Arab" country, another America House was established at the U.S. Consulate in East Jerusalem in CY2010. This promise was not fulfilled.	0.00
ST-34	**The Promise:** "Obama also would launch a new "America's Voice Corps" to rapidly recruit and train fluent speakers of local languages (Arabic, Bahasa Melayu, Bahasa, Farsi, Urdu, and Turkish) with public diplomacy skills, who can ensure our voice is heard in the mass media and in our efforts on	0.00

Chapter 12 - Department of State

the ground."
When/Where: Obama-Biden Plan: "The War We Need To Win" dated 07/31/07.
Source: http://www.mattluedke.com/wp-content/uploads/2016/09/CounterterrorismFactSheet.pdf
Status: There has been no known initiative to provide any funds, either in President Obama's FY2010 thru FY2016 Department of State budget proposals, for the creation of the promised "America's Voice Corps."

This promise has not been fulfilled.

ST-35

The Promise: "They will work to double the IAEA budget in the next four years (increasing the U.S. annual share to about $225 million)."
When/Where: Obama -Biden Plan: "Confronting 21st Century Threats" dated 09/23/08.
Source: https://www.presidency.ucsb.edu/documents/press-release-fact-sheet-obamas-new-plan-confront-21st-century-threats
Status: The International Atomic Energy Agency (IAEA) total budget for CY2009 was 350M Euros ($503M at the exchange rate prevailing on 12/31/09), meaning that to double its budget in four years required a commitment by the 151 member states to fund the IAEA by approximately $1B by CY2013. By end-CY2013, IAEA's total budget was 409M Euros ($560M at the 12/31/13 exchange rate).

The USA contributes to the IAEA via four separate appropriations:
(1) Direct Contributions to the IAEA's Regular Budget
(2) Voluntary Contributions to IAEA
(3) $10M per year for IAEA's Peaceful Use Initiative
(4) An average of $18M per year for IAEA contributions within the budgets of the Department of Energy, the Nuclear Regulatory Commission, and the Department of Agriculture.

The State Department's FY2009 budget for the U.S. portion of the International Atomic Energy Agency (IAEA)'s budget was about $200M, an amount maintained for FY2010. Ensuing year contributions were as follows:
FY2011 - $213M
FY2012 - $219M
FY2013 - $224M

First, the IAEA's budget did not "double" during the four years of President Obama's first term in office. Second, the funding goal of $225M reflected in this promise was not met. Still, the U.S. FY2013 contribution represented about 40% of IAEA's total budget. The only conceivable way IAEA's budget could have been doubled during the period CY2009-CY2013 would have been for President Obama to encourage the other 159 IAEA member nations to increase their contributions.

By end-CY2016, IAEA's total budget was 500.6M Euros ($526M at the exchange rate of 12/31/16). In dollars, this was only slightly above the original CY2009 total budget.

This promise was not fulfilled.

0.00

ST-36

The Promise: "...will lead a multilateral effort to address the issue of "odious debt" by investigating ways in which "loan sanctions" might be employed to create disincentives for private creditors to lend money to repressive, authoritarian regimes."
When/Where: Obama-Biden Plan: "Strengthening Our Common Security by Investing in Our Common Humanity", dated 09/11/08.
Source: https://www.cgdev.org/sites/default/files/archive/doc/blog/obama_strengthen_security.pdf
Status: "Odious debt" is debt incurred by a repressive government for spending that is not for the benefit of its people or debt incurred to finance the repression of those people. Repressive regimes exist in Africa, South America, Middle East and elsewhere. This promise was intended to be an an international initiative, led by the United States, with global application.

0.00

Chapter 12 - Department of State

As of end-CY2016, no significant political progress had been made on this promise since President Obama raised the odious debt issue during his initial election campaign in CY2008. While unilateral loan sanctions were imposed on a selective basis (such as on North Korea, Central African Republic, Yemen, Syria, Iran), this was not the "multilateral" intent of this promise.

This promise was not fulfilled.

ST-37

The Promise: "...will take the lead at the G-8, working with and leveraging the engagement of the private sector and private philanthropy, to launch Health Infrastructure 2020 - a global effort to work with developing countries to invest in the full range of infrastructure needed to improve and protect both American and global health."
When/Where: Obama-Biden Plan: "Strengthening Our Common Security by Investing in Our Common Humanity", dated 09/11/08.
Source: https://www.cgdev.org/sites/default/files/archive/doc/blog/obama_strengthen_security.pdf
Status: The 35th G-8 Summit held in Italy in 2009 did not include the establishment of a "Health Infrastructure 2020" as an agenda item. Neither was this topic addressed at the following summits:
- 36th G-8 Summit (dubbed the "Muskoka Summit") held at Huntsville, Ontario on 06/25-26/10,
- 37th G-8 Summit at Deauville, France on 05/26-27/11,
- 38th G-8 Summit at Camp David, Maryland on 05/18-19/12,
- 39th G-8 Summit at Lough Erne, Northern Ireland on 06/17-18/13,
- 40th G-7 summit at Brussels, Belgium on 06/04-05/14 (Russia was disinvited from the G-8 Summit due to its invasion and annexation of Crimea. The summit became a G7),
- 41st G-7 summit at Schloss Elmau, Germany on 06/07-08/15, and the
- 42nd G-7 summit at Kashiko Island, Japan on 05/26-27/16 where some international health issues were discussed but not the Health Infrastructure 2020.

This promise was not fulfilled.

0.00

ST-38

The Promise: "...will extend opportunities for older individuals such as teachers, engineers, and doctors to serve overseas. This effort will include a Global Energy Corps to help reduce greenhouse gas emissions overseas and promote low-carbon and affordable energy solutions in developing nations..."
When/Where: Obama-Biden Plan: "Helping All Americans Serve Their Country" dated 09/11/08.
Source: http://i2.cdn.turner.com/cnn/2008/images/07/02/national.service.fact.sheet.final.pdf
Status: This promise, had it been fulfilled, would have been an extension of U.S. foreign policy much like the Peace Corps run by the State Department.

The creation of a "Global Energy Corps" did not materialize during President Obama's two terms in office.

This promise was not fulfilled.

0.00

ST-39

The Promise: "...will establish a Shared Security Partnership Program to invest $5 billion over three years to improve cooperation between U.S. and foreign intelligence and law enforcement agencies. This program will include information sharing, funding for training, operations, border security, anti-corruption programs, technology, and the targeting of terrorist financing."
When/Where: Obama-Biden Plan: "The War We Need to Win" dated 07/31/07.
Source: http://www.mattluedke.com/wp-content/uploads/2016/09/CounterterrorismFactSheet.pdf
Status: On 05/08/09, the State Department presented its FY2010 budget proposal. In it, State requested $90M to launch the "Shared Security Partnership" (SSP) to help address the "wide array of threats posed by terrorist organizations by building on previous law enforcement and counter-terrorist efforts to create a regional and global information-sharing and coordination infrastructure."

The Congressional authorization for FY2010 SSP activities included:
- $21.2M for Central America/Caribbean cross-cutting initiative to coordinate regional and global law

0.00

205

enforcement and anti-terrorist efforts;
- $49.4M for border security, nonproliferation of weapons of mass destruction, anti-corruption and anti-terrorism efforts;
- $9.4M for cross-cutting initiatives in Africa to coordinate regional and global law enforcement and anti-terrorist efforts;
- $3.3M for the Trans-Sahara SSP.
- $10M for SSP air and maritime equipment, training, and command, control, and communications (C3) equipment for the Caribbean;

The "National Security Strategy" presented by President Obama on 05/27/10 addressed the fact that the U.S. was "strengthening our partnership with foreign intelligence services and sustaining strong ties with our close allies." To that end, the SSP program was funded to the level of at least $93.3M in FY2010, as outlined above.

Since the FY2010 budget, there has been no specific mention of the SSP program in subsequent presidential and State Department budget submissions except as a mention as a subset of the International Law Enforcement Academy (ILEA) budget line item. Even if SSP program funding was sustained at $90M-$1B for FY2010-FY2012, it is evident that the investment of "$5 billion over three years" in the SSP program did not occur.

This promise was not fulfilled.

ST-40	**The Promise:** "...will work for the release of jailed scholars, activists, and opposition party leaders such as Ayman Nour in Egypt." **When/Where:** Obama-Biden Plan: "Strengthening Our Common Security by Investing in Our Common Humanity", dated 09/11/08. **Source:** https://www.cgdev.org/sites/default/files/archive/doc/blog/obama_strengthen_security.pdf **Status:**- Egyptian Aymasn Nour was released from imprisonment for alleged electoral fraud on 02/18/09 reportedly on "medical grounds," but whose release within a month of President Obama's inauguration was viewed as an attempt by President Mubarak to repair relations with the USA that had been strained during the Bush Administration because of Nour's incarceration. - Nobel Peace Prize laureat Myanmarian Aung San Suu Kyi, a pro-democracy opposition leader and Nobel Peace Prize winner in Myanmar, was released from house arrest on 11/13/10 by the oppressive military's proxy political party that was replaced by a nominally civilian government in 03/11. On 04/01/12, she was elected to the lower house of the Myanmar parliament. - Under pressure caused by President Obama's 05/22/16 visit to the Socialist Republic of Vietnam, Vietnamese Father Thaddeus Nguyen Van Ly, a human rights campaigner, was released from jail on 05/19/16. - Russian oil tycoon Mikhail Khodorkovsky and his associate Platon Lebedev received an initial sentence of nine years in 05/05 for fraud, plus another three years on 12/30/10 for embezzlement and money laundering. U.S. Senate Resolution #65 on 02/16/11 stated in part that the conviction of the above individuals "constitutes a politically motivated case of selective arrest and prosecution that flagrantly undermines the rule of law and independence of the judicial system of Russia." Primarily due to the Khodorkovsky and Lebedev imprisonments, President Obama decided not to send any high level Administration delegation to the Sochi Winter Olympic games. This snub led President Vladimir Putin to pardon Khodorkovsky, releasing him from jail on 12/20/13 while Lebedev was released by the Russian Supreme Court on 01/23/14. - Chinese Nobel Peace Prize laureate, democracy advocate and writer Liu Xiaobo was sentenced to 11 years in jail and 2 years deprivation of political rights on 12/25/09. The charge: "inciting subversion of state power." This was his fourth prison term. President Obama called for Liu Xiaobo's release on 10/08/10 and again on 12/10/10 when Liu Xiaobo was honored in absentia in Oslo as	1.00

Chapter 12 - Department of State

Nobel Peace Prize winner. As a Nobel Peace Prize winner himself (2009), it would have been inappropriate for President Obama not to recognize his fellow laureate in this manner. There were no formal demarches to the Chinese Government on this matter since then and Liu Xiaobo remained incarcerated for the remainder of President Obama's tenure in office.

- Iranian Pastor Youcef Nadarkhani was originally sentenced to be executed for refusing to renounce his Christian faith in accordance with Sharia law. The American Center for Law and Justice (ACLJ) received assistance from the State Department in its efforts to secure Pastor Nadarkhani's release with a plea from Secretary Clinton on 12/10/11 that called for his "immediate and unconditional" release. He was released from custody by the Iranian Government on 09/08/12 as a face-saving measure.

The above are but very few, high-visibility examples where the Obama Administration attempted to influence the release of jailed scholars, activists, and opposition party leaders.

This promise was fulfilled.

ST-41

The Promise: "...will increase support for the building blocks of durable democracies -- strong legislatures, independent judiciaries, free press, vibrant civil society, honest police forces, religious freedom, and the rule of law."
When/Where: Plan for America: "Blueprint for Change," dated 10/09/08
Source: https://www.documentcloud.org/ Obama and Biden's documents/550007-barack-obama-2008-blueprint-for-change.html
Status: This promise was headed toward non-fulfillment when the Obama Administration failed to support the popular uprising in Iran in CY2009, an excellent opportunity to influence the Iranian people's deep desire for democracy. On this matter, the Obama Administration hit the "mute button."

In early 08/10, future leaders from 46 African countries gathered in Washington, D.C. as guests of the U.S. Government to participate in conferences with American businesses and nongovernmental organizations. The conference themes included youth empowerment, good governance, and economic opportunity. When President Obama addressed this group on 08/04/10, he stressed his belief that good governance is at the center of economic development on the African continent and that there needed to be a "clear sense of the rule of law" for growth and opportunity to flourish. This was a key lesson for Africa's future leaders, a lesson that was heard throughout the world.

Grade: 1.00

In 02/11, the people of Egypt demanded the cessation of the 30-year Mubarak autocratic government. The Obama Administration's supportive reaction was commendable. Mubarak quit. In comments made during a press brief on 02/15/11, President Obama stated that governments in the Middle East "can't maintain power through coercion" and that "you have a young, vibrant generation in the Middle East that is looking for greater opportunity...you've got to get out ahead of change - you can't be behind the curve."

This campaign promise was to "increase support" for fledgling democracies. The above serve as examples where President Obama voiced that support early in his Administration.

Tangible assistance (i.e. funds) to support this promise was also provided to fledgling democracies such as Iraq, Aghanistan, Myanmar, Egypt, Tunisia and others during the Obama Administration on condition that they respect the building blocks for attaining durable democracies.

This promise was fulfilled.

LATIN AMERICA/CARIBBEAN	GRADE

ST-42 — **The Promise:** "...as president, Obama will grant Cuban Americans unrestricted rights to visit family and send remittances to the island."
When/Where: Obama-Biden Plan: "Renewing U.S. Leadership in the Americas", dated 06/06/08.

Grade: 1.00

Chapter 12 - Department of State

Source: https://www.politifact.com/truth-o-meter/promises/obameter/promise/222/grant-americans-unrestricted-rights-to-visit-famil/

Status: Source is cited for confirmation of exact promise wording only, as it existed before original "When/Where" campaign document was deleted from archival websites.

On 04/13/09, President Obama issued an executive order eliminating limits on travel and raising remittance levels by Cuban Americans to relatives in Cuba.

On 01/14/11, President Obama ordered his Administration to find ways to ease travel to Cuba by non-Cuban Americans (primarily academics, students, religious groups, and journalists). Money transfers to Cuba would be permitted to non-government persons in an amount not exceeding $2,000 per year.

This promise was fulfilled.

ST-43

The Promise: "...will rebuild diplomatic links throughout the hemisphere through aggressive, principled, and sustained diplomacy in the Americas from Day One. He will bolster U.S. interests in the region by pursuing policies that advance democracy, opportunity, and security and will treat our hemispheric partners and neighbors with dignity and respect."

When/Where: Plan for America: "Blueprint for Change," dated 10/09/08

Source: https://www.documentcloud.org/ Obama and Biden's documents/550007-barack-obama-2008-blueprint-for-change.html

Status: Barely 4 months in office in 04/09, President Obama attended the 5th Summit of the Americas in Trinidad & Tobago along with 33 other democratically elected Heads of State and Government of the Western Hemisphere. President Obama used this meeting to start engaging in new relationships with countries of the Americas to work together on common challenges: the economic crisis, our common energy and climate future, and public safety.

During the meeting, President Obama committed to continue working with Western Hemisphere counterparts for the reduction of poverty, social inclusion, and democratic governance.

The resumption of diplomatic relations with Cuba announced by President Obama on 12/17/14 was significant, followed by the opening of Cuban and U.S. embassies in mid-CY2015.

This promise was fulfilled.

1.00

ST-44

The Promise: "...will bring together the countries of the region in a new Energy Partnership for the Americas to forge a path toward sustainable growth and clean energy."

When/Where: Plan for America: "Blueprint for Change," dated 10/09/08

Source: https://www.documentcloud.org/ Obama and Biden's documents/550007-barack-obama-2008-blueprint-for-change.html

Status: During the 04/09 Summit of the Americas in Port of Spain, Trinidad & Tobago, President Obama invited all governments of the Western Hemisphere to join in an Energy and Climate Partnership of the Americas (ECPA).

He suggested that the ECPA focus on energy efficiency, renewable energy, cleaner and more efficient use of fossil fuels, energy poverty, and infrastructure. This focus was developed at the 06/09 Americas Energy and Climate Symposium in Lima, Peru.

During his first trilateral North American Leaders meeting held at Guadalajara, Mexico on 08/10/09, President Obama led the establishment of a partnership with the President of Mexico and the Prime Minister of Canada on future emissions trading systems and building a smart grid across the region for more efficient and reliable electricity inter-connections. The partnership established between these three countries was a step in the right direction toward promise fulfillment.

1.00

Chapter 12 - Department of State

In 04/10, Energy Secretary Chu invited Western Hemisphere energy ministers to the "Energy and Climate Ministerial of the Americas". During this meeting, State Secretary Clinton proposed that ECPA's mandate be expanded to include initiatives regarding sustainable forests and land use, as well as climate change adaptation.

To jump-start the ECPA's efforts, the Administration named three top scientists to serve as ECPA fellows, to serve as consultants, advisors or educators for any of the member countries: Dr. Daniel Kammen, a professor of energy at the University of California-Berkeley; Dr. Ruth Defries, a professor of sustainable development at Columbia University; and Dr. Gerry Galloway, an engineering professor at the University of Maryland.

This promise was fulfilled.

ST-45

The Promise: "...will substantially increase our aid to the Americas..."
When/Where: Obama-Biden Plan: "To Secure America and Restore our Standing," undated.
Source: Source document was available online throughout the Obama Administration. It has since been deleted from all archival websites.
Status: Foreign aid extended to Latin America and the Caribbean during the Obama Administration included funding for:
- Development Assistance (DA)
- Global Health Programs (GHP)
- Food for Peace (P.L. 480)
- Economic Support Fund (ESF)
- Migration and Refugee Assistance (MRA)
- International Narcotics Control and Law Enforcement (INCLE) provided through the Central America Regional Security Initiative (CARSI)
- Nonproliferation, Anti-terrorism, De-mining, and Related programs (NADR)
- Foreign Military Financing (FMF), and
- International Military Education and Training (IMET)

Foreign aid provided by fiscal year for the Americas was:
FY2010 - $3.30B
FY2011 - $1.85B
FY2012 - $1.82B
FY2013 - $1.68B
FY2014 - $1.47B
FY2015 - $1.58B
FY2016 - $1.73B

The reduction in funding from FY2011 onward was attributed by the Administration to the effects of the CY2008 financial crisis.

This promise was not fulfilled.

0.00

ST-46

The Promise: "...we need to target all sources of insecurity through a new hemispheric security initiative. This initiative will foster cooperation within the region to combat gangs, trafficking and violent criminal activity."
When/Where: Plan for America: "Blueprint for Change," dated 10/09/08
Source: https://www.documentcloud.org/ Obama and Biden's documents/550007-barack-obama-2008-blueprint-for-change.html
Status: On 05/27/10, the Caribbean Basin Security Initiative (CBSI) was launched during the first "U.S.-Caribbean Security Dialogue" in Washington, D.C. The CBSI supplements three other related initiatives: the Merida Initiative, the Central American Regional Security Initiative, and the Colombian Security Development Initiative.

1.00

Chapter 12 - Department of State

By covering the different regions of Latin America and the Caribbean through these initiatives, the Obama Administration attempted to "mitigate any balloon effect" - criminal spillover resulting from successful reductions in drug trafficking and transnational crime elsewhere in the region."

There were three objectives stipulated in the CBSI: (1) substantially reduce illicit trafficking, (2) increase public safety and security, and (3) promote social justice.

To accomplish the above objectives, the FY2010 Foreign Operations Appropriations Bill allocated $37M for CBSI. President Obama requested $79M for CBSI in his FY2011 budget proposal, $62M of which would be used for police and military assistance, and $17M for economic and social assistance.

This promise was fulfilled.

	MIDDLE EAST	GRADE
ST-47	**The Promise:** "I strongly support passage of the Armenian Genocide Resolution (H.Res.106 and S.Res.106), and as President I will recognize the Armenian Genocide." **When/Where:** Senator Obama Campaign Statement of 01/19/08. **Source:** http://www.armenian-genocide.org/Affirmation.413/current_category.4/affirmation_detail.html **Status:** President Obama's statement on 04/24/09, a day of memorial for the Armenian Genocide, failed to mention the key word that interested parties wanted to hear: "genocide". On 03/05/10, the House Foreign Affairs Committee voted 23-22 on a resolution officially recognizing the Armenian Genocide. This action prompted the Turkish Government to recall its Ambassador to the U.S. home for "consultations." The Turkish Foreign Ministry issued a statement stating: "Secretary Clinton emphasized that the U.S. administration opposes both the decision accepted by the committee and the decision reaching the general assembly." The White House went further by opposing House Resolution 306 which called for Turkey to return christian churches that were confiscated during the Armenian Genocide. During his two terms in office, President Obama never publicly uttered the words "Armenian Genocide." This promise was not fulfilled.	0.00
ST-48	**The Promise:** "...will launch an aggressive diplomatic effort to reach a comprehensive compact on the stability of Iraq and the region. This effort will include all of Iraq's neighbors -- including Iran and Syria." **When/Where:** Plan for America: "Blueprint for Change," dated 10/09/08 **Source:** https://www.documentcloud.org/ Obama and Biden's documents/550007-barack-obama-2008-blueprint-for-change.html **Status:** The appointment of former Senator George Mitchell as Special Envoy for Middle East Peace on 01/22/09 was a critical first step in honoring this promise. Senator Mitchell resigned from this post on 05/13/11 out of frustration that no progress was being made with any of the principal Middle East players in the desired peace process. Senator Mitchell was replaced by his deputy, Ambassador David Hale, who himself was replaced in 6/14 by Ambassador Martin Indyk who stayed on the job only one year. The promised "comprehensive compact" remained elusive since regional security could not be attained unless meaningful dialogue was initiated with the likes of Iran, Syria, Pakistan, the Palestinians and others.	0.00

Chapter 12 - Department of State

When the USA pulled its remaining troops out of a marginally stable Iraq at the end of CY2011 as announced by President Obama on 10/21/11 (and requested by the Iraqi Government), the Obama Administration needed to engage with Iran and other unfriendly Middle East nations at the senior diplomatic level. This was in part to ensure that Iran did not dominate Iraq and the Persian Gulf region after the USA's departure. Lack of immediate engagement with Iran paved the way for Iran to instigate increased subversive activities against remaining U.S. assets and resources in Iraq and the Iraqian Government itself. This was a U.S. diplomatic "faux pas."

As of end-CY2016, there was no "comprehensive compact" for Iraqi and regional stability,

This promise was not fulfilled.

ST-49

The Promise: "...will lead a diplomatic effort to bring together Turkish and Iraqi Kurdish leaders and negotiate a comprehensive agreement that deals with the PKK threat, guarantees Turkey's territorial integrity, and facilitates badly needed Turkish investment in and trade with the Kurds of northern Iraq."
When/Where: Obama-Biden Plan: "A Stronger Partnership with Europe for a Safer America", dated 10/14/08.
Source: http://www.scribd.com/doc/6245758/Barack-Obama-Joe-Biden-A-Stronger-Partnership-with-Europe-for-a-Safer-America
Status: During his first overseas trip in 04/09, President Obama made stops in Ankara and Istanbul, Turkey. His message was to pledge support for Turkey's efforts to thwart the terrorism tactics of the Kurdistan Workers Party (in Kurdish: Partiya Karkeren Kurdistan or "PKK").

Although much more work was required to build a real cooperative relationship between Turkey and Iraq (including the Kurds), Turkey had to look within its own borders to ensure that the Kurds there received equitable attention in the fields of education, health care, economic opportunities and assistance, etc.

While the Turkish Government met resistance as it tried to resolve problems with the Kurds, it announced its determination to do so. The first step agreed to by the Obama Administration was the disarmament of the PKK under Turkish-US-Iraqi supervision, where the weapons would be handed over to U.S. Forces in northern Iraq.

The next step was to clear all the northern Iraq PKK camps and return those camp areas to control by the regional northern Iraqi administration. Meanwhile, Turkey opened a consulate in the northern Iraqi city of Erbil, based upon an agreement reached between Turkish Foreign Minister Davutoglu and the leader of the northern Iraqi regional government, Massoud Barzani.

The above was a clear indication that the two sides were talking. President Obama did not promise success. He promised to "lead a diplomatic effort" to give success a chance, which he did.

This promise was fulfilled.

1.00

ST-50

The Promise: "...will support its efforts to join the European Union."
When/Where: Obama-Biden Plan: "A Stronger Partnership with Europe for a Safer America", dated 10/14/08.
Source: http://www.scribd.com/doc/6245758/Barack-Obama-Joe-Biden-A-Stronger-Partnership-with-Europe-for-a-Safer-America
Status: This campaign promise was in reference to Turkey.

Turkey was officially recognized as a candidate for full membership in the European Union (EU) on 12/12/99 at the Helsinki Summit of the European Council.

In a speech before the Turkish Parliament in 04/09, President Obama stated: "The United States

1.00

strongly supports Turkey's bid to become a member of the European Union...Centuries of shared history, culture, and commerce bring you together...And Turkish membership would broaden and strengthen Europe's foundation once more."

Although President Obama voiced his support for Turkey in its bid to become a member of the European Union, those words did not lead to membership as of end-CY2016.

This promise was fulfilled.

ST-51	**The Promise:** "Obama also will increase aid to Pakistan for development and secular education to counter extremists." **When/Where:** Obama-Biden Plan: "The War We Need to Win" dated 07/31/07. **Source:** http://www.mattluedke.com/wp-content/uploads/2016/09/CounterterrorismFactSheet.pdf **Status:** In Pakistan, a country of 180M people, youth literacy was a little over 60%, while adult literacy rate was closer to 50% by end-CY2016. Of the 21.6M school-age (5 to 9) children in Pakistan, 6.2M or 29% (2.6M boys and 3.6M girls) were out of school. Only 32% of Pakistani children get a secondary education. One way in which U.S. education assistance was being used during the Obama Administration was to offer stipends to poor Pakistani families to offset the cost of education with the objective of reducing militancy resulting from education received from madrasas. Total funding by the U.S. taxpayer for assistance to Pakistan in FY2010 was $4.289B, up from $2.925B in FY2009. Of this amount, only $180M was specifically earmarked for education reform. Amid calls from various sectors to cut off all foreign aid to Pakistan for many well-founded reasons (i.e. allegedly harboring/hiding Osama bin Laden, blocking supplies from reaching U.S. troops in Afghanistan), Congress immediately decreased total funding for Pakistan in FY2011 (to $2.369B) and FY2012 (to $2.102B). By FY2014, foreign aid to Pakistan totaled $1.162B, only $53M of which went toward education reform under the Economic Support Fund. Undaunted by dwindling financial resources but buttressed by the first "over-and-above" Kerry-Lugar "Enhanced Partnership with Pakistan Act of 2009" ($1.5B authorized annually for five years starting in CY2010), the U.S. Agency for International Development (USAID) managed to accomplish the following in Pakistan by end-CY2016: - built or repaired over 1,400 schools across Pakistan, - trained over 35,900 teachers and school administrators, - provided over 18,000 scholarships for talented students to attend tertiary education in Pakistan, and - reached more than 1,349,000 primary-level learners through reading programs. As of end-CY2016, the promise to "increase" development and education funding to combat extremist influences in Pakistan was not fulfilled. USAID accomplishments aside, Pakistani madrasas continued to proliferate during the Obama Administration. This promise was not fulfilled.	0.00
ST-52	**The Promise:** "Provide at least $2 billion to expand services to Iraqi refugees in neighboring countries." **When/Where:** "Blueprint for Change: Obama and Biden's Plan for America" dated 10/09/08. **Source:** https://www.documentcloud.org/documents/550007-barack-obama-2008-blueprint-for-change.html **Status:** By United Nations High Commission for Refugees (UNHCR) estimates, approximately 4.5M Iraqis (one sixth of Iraq's population) were displaced as of end-CY2016. Nearly 4M were internally displaced, and most of the rest were living in countries in the region such as Lebanon, Jordan, Turkey, Iran, Syria and Egypt.	1.00

Chapter 12 - Department of State

According to State Department estimates, the Obama Administration provided over $2.5B of humanitarian assistance for displaced Iraqis in Iraq and in neighboring countries during President Obama's two terms in office, this allocation being on top of other foreign aid given to Iraq during the same period (CY2009-CY2016).

This promise was fulfilled.

ST-53	**The Promise:** "...will implement a Memorandum of Understanding that provides $30 billion in assistance to Israel over the next decade - investments to Israel's security that will not be tied to any other nation." **When/Where:** Candidate Obama Speech to the American-Israel Public Affairs Committee (AIPAC), Washington, D.C., dated 06/04/08. **Source:** http://www.presidency.ucsb.edu/ws/index.php?pid=77433 **Status:** The Memorandum of Understanding (MOU) in question was actually signed on 08/16/07 and provided for a $30B hand-out to Israel over the timeframe 10/08-10/18, an increase of $6B over the $24B provided in the previous decade. The Obama Administration lived up to the terms of the MOU and provided funding to Israel in the following amounts: FY2010 - $2.803B FY2011 - $3.029B FY2012 - $3.098B FY2013 - $3.118B FY2014 - $3.118B FY2015 - $3.118B FY2016 - $3.110B FY2017 - $3.107B On 09/14/16, the USA and Israel signed a new 10-year MOU covering the period FY2019-FY2028. Under the terms of the new MOU, the USA pledged to provide Israel $38 billion in military aid ($33B for Foreign Military Financing grants plus $5B for missile defense. This promise was fulfilled.	**1.00**
ST-54	**The Promise:** "...would work with key European allies to persuade the European Union as a whole to end its practice of extending large-scale credit guarantees to Iran." **When/Where:** Obama-Biden Plan: "A Stronger Partnership with Europe for a Safer America" dated 10/14/08. **Source:** http://www.scribd.com/doc/6245758/Barack-Obama-Joe-Biden-A-Stronger-Partnership-with-Europe-for-a-Safer-America **Status:** On 07/26/10, European Union (EU) Foreign Policy Chief Catherine Ashton announced that all 27 EU countries were united in imposing sanctions on Iran in an effort to encourage the Iranian regime to halt uranium enrichment as proof that it is not seeking a nuclear weapons capability. These sanctions would reportedly go beyond United Nations Security Council Resolution 1929 of 06/09/10, and deepen Iran's international isolation. EU sanctions (referred to as "restrictive measures") are documented in EU Council Regulation 961/2010 dated 10/25/10. Chapter IV (Freezing of Funds and Economic Resources), Article 25 states: "It shall be prohibited: (a) to sell or purchase public or public-guaranteed bonds issued after 26 July 2010, directly or indirectly, to or from any of the following: (i) Iran or its Government, and its public bodies, corporations and agencies; (ii) a credit or financial institution domiciled in Iran, including the Central Bank of Iran, or any credit or financial institution referred to in Article 23(2); (iii) a natural person or a	**1.00**

legal person, entity or body acting on behalf or at the direction of a legal person, entity or body referred to in (i) or (ii); (iv) a legal person, entity or body owned or controlled by a person, entity or body referred to in (i), (ii) or (iii);

(b) to provide brokering services with regard to public or public-guaranteed bonds issued after 26 July 2010 to a person, entity or body referred to in point (a);

(c) to assist a person, entity or body referred to in point (a) in order to issue public or public-guaranteed bonds, by providing brokering services, advertising or any other service with regard to such bonds."

In summary, the announced EU sanctions include a ban on investing or selling equipment to Iran's oil and natural gas industries, restrictions on export-credit guarantees and insurance, and closer monitoring of banks doing business with Iran.

The extent of U.S. influence in the EU's actions is unclear.

Nonetheless, this promise was fulfilled.

ST-55

The Promise: "...would conduct direct talks with Iran..."
When/Where: Obama-Biden Plan: "A Stronger Partnership with Europe for a Safer America" dated 10/14/08.
Source: http://www.scribd.com/doc/6245758/Barack-Obama-Joe-Biden-A-Stronger-Partnership-with-Europe-for-a-Safer-America
Status: On 08/02/10, Iranian President Mahmoud Ahmadinejad stated that he was ready to meet/debate with President Obama when the two were attending a General Assembly meeting at the United Nations in 09/10.

The Obama Administration rebuffed this call for a meeting on 08/03/10. In the words of White House Press Secretary Robert Gibbs: "We have always said that we'd be willing to sit down and discuss Iran's illicit nuclear program, if Iran is serious about doing that. To date, that seriousness has not been there."

Three years later, President Obama spoke directly via telephone with President Hassan Rouhani on 09/27/13, just before President Rouhani left New York where he had been attending the 68th session of the United Nations General Assembly.

White House officials described the 15 minute conversation, initiated by President Rouhani, as cordial. During the same timeframe, Secretary of State John Kerry held a rare meeting with his Iranian counterpart, Mohammad Javad Zarif.

This promise was fulfilled.

1.00

ST-56

The Promise: "...supports tough, direct presidential diplomacy with Iran without preconditions...would offer the Iranian regime a choice. If Iran abandons its nuclear program and support for terrorism, we will offer incentives like membership in the World Trade Organization, economic investments, and a move toward normal diplomatic relations. If Iran continues its troubling behavior, we will step up our economic pressure and political isolation."
When/Where: Obama-Biden Plan on Iran, undated.
Source: https://webarchive.loc.gov/all/20090429185412/http://change.gov/agenda/foreign_policy_agenda/
Status: As a direct result of President Obama's "carrot and stick" approach in dealing with the Islamic Republic of Iran, a nuclear deal framework agreement was reached on 04/02/15 between Iran and the P5+1 Group (permanent members of the United Nations Security Council - the USA, United Kingdom, Russia, France and China plus Germany) and the European Union. The resultant

1.00

Chapter 12 - Department of State

agreement was the Joint Comprehensive Plan of Action (JCPOA).

Under the terms of the JCPOA, sanctions relief would affect the economy of Iran in four ways:
- release of Iran's frozen funds abroad, estimated at $29B, representing approximately one third of Iran's foreign held reserves,
- the removal of sanctions against exports of Iranian oil,
- allow foreign firms to invest in Iran's oil and gas, automobiles, hotels and other sectors, and
- allow Iran to trade with the rest of the world and use global banking systems.

On 01/16/16, the International Atomic Energy Agency (IAEA) announced that Iran had adequately dismantled its nuclear weapons program. The United Nations immediately lifted all sanctions against Iran, allowing Iran to immediately have access to more than $100B in assets frozen around the world and resume selling oil on international markets.

Iran's accession to the World Trade Organization (WTO) will take years, as there will likely be efforts by Iran's foes (i.e. Saudi Arabia, Israel and others) to thwart membership, much as the establishment of full diplomatic relations between the USA and Iran will not be forthcoming in the foreseeable future.

Strong-arming Iran early in the Obama Administration produced cautiously positive results.

This promise was fulfilled.

ST-57 | **The Promise:** "... strongly supports the U.S.-Israel relationship. He believes that our first and incontrovertible commitment in the Middle East must be to the security of Israel, America's strongest ally in the Middle East. Obama believes that we should deepen and strengthen the friendship and cooperation between the United States and Israel." | **0.00**

When/Where: Plan for America: "Blueprint for Change," dated 10/09/08
Source: https://www.documentcloud.org/ Obama and Biden's documents/550007-barack-obama-2008-blueprint-for-change.html
Status: During the first three years of the Obama Administration, it in fact distanced itself from Israel because of the latter's building of Jewish settlements in East Jerusalem. The relationship between the U.S. and Israel was considered by some as being at the lowest point in over 35 years.

The bilateral relationship between the U.S. and Israel reached a new low on 05/19/11 when President Obama called for the establishment of a Palestinian state based on pre-1967 Six-Day War borders behind which more than 350K Jews reside. In the words of Republican presidential contender Mitt Romney, Obama threw Israel "under the bus" when he stated this position. Prime Minister Netanyau immediately described Obama's call for a Palestinian state based on pre-1967 borders as "indefensible." Prime Minister Netanyahu was seen as placating his constituency and preserving his weak coalition government by disagreeing with any plan to exchange land for peace.

President Obama offered clarifications during a speech to the American-Israel Public Affairs Committee (AIPAC) on 05/22/11, stating that his 1967 border statement of 05/19/11 had been misrepresented.

While no one questioned President Obama's commitment to the Israeli-Palestinian peace process, Israeli perceptions of the U.S. President were exactly the opposite, because President Obama unwittingly created tension between the U.S. and Israel at the highest levels.

But this strained relationship has not affected continued financial support to Israel promised under the President Carter-era Camp David accords with Egypt -- assistance that President Obama supports.

Nonetheless, tensions between the USA and Israel festered during the remainder of President

Obama's tenure in office.

This promise was not fulfilled.

ST-58	**The Promise:** "...Israel should not be pressured into a ceasefire that did not deal with the threat of Hezbollah missiles. He believes strongly in Israel's right to protect its citizens" **When/Where:** Plan for America: "Blueprint for Change," dated 10/09/08 **Source:** https://www.documentcloud.org/ Obama and Biden's documents/550007-barack-obama-2008-blueprint-for-change.html **Status:** In 05/10, Israeli Intelligence Minister Dan Meridor estimated that Hezbollah had 42K missiles "aimed at Israel." He claimed that they could reach anywhere in Israel. The missiles possessed by Hamas in Gaza and Hezbollah in Lebanon originated in North Korea and reached these organizations via Iran and Syria. As one of many examples, with U.S. support, Israel's "Iron Dome" short range missile defense system successfully shot down a Grad rocket fired against Israel from the Gaza strip on 04/07/11. To President Obama's credit, peace talks between Israel and Palestine resumed on 09/02/10 in Washington, D.C. At that time, the State Department anticipated that those talks would continue toward a final resolution by 09/11 -- although either side could break off the talks for myriad reasons. By end-CY2011, talks between the Israelis and Palestinians stalled. This failure was largely attributed to the terrorist group Hamas' unity agreement with the Palestinian political party "Fatah." The Hamas charter called then as it does now for the eradication of Israel. A potential peace agreement between Israel and Palestine, orchestrated by U.S. Special Envoy George Mitchell and other third parties such as Jordan and Egypt, also failed. This draft agreement addressed the disposition of the Hezbollah missile/rocket threats, including Hezbollah's receipt of approximately 10 SCUD-D from Syria. Special Envoy Mitchell announced on 05/13/11 that he was quitting his job, a sign of frustration that neither a ceasefire nor peace agreement would become reality in the foreseeable future. His successors were equally unable to influence peace in the region. The new Lebanese cabinet announced by Prime Minister Najib Mikati on 06/13/11 gave Hezbollah 16 of 30 seats, making it the dominant political and military force in Lebanon. In practical terms, peace with Israel was seen by many as less likely than when President Obama assumed the presidency. On the plus side, however, the Obama Administration was supportive of Israel's "Iron Dome," "David's Sling," and "Arrow Defense" capabilities, while approving the sale of 19 F-35 stealth fighter jets with an option for 75 more to replace aging F-16 fighter aircraft. Further, the Administration has routinely authorized the conduct of large-scale U.S. military exercises with the Israeli armed forces, and has conducted joint intelligence operations with the Mossad. Despite strained relationships at the senior level between the USA and Israel, the Obama Administration has maintained support of Israel's efforts to protect its citizens. This promise was fulfilled.	1.00
ST-59	**The Promise:** "...continuing U.S. cooperation with Israel in the development of missile defense systems." **When/Where:** Plan for America: "Blueprint for Change," dated 10/09/08 **Source:** https://www.documentcloud.org/ Obama and Biden's documents/550007-barack-obama-2008-blueprint-for-change.html **Status:** From FY2007 to the start of the Obama Administration, more than $750M had been appropriated for Israel's Arrow and David's Sling anti-missile systems.	1.00

Chapter 12 - Department of State

The Department of Defense and Full-Year Continuing Appropriations Act, 2011 (H.R. 1473) signed into law on 04/14/11 included $205M for the procurement of the Iron Dome defense system to counter short-range rocket threats, $84.7M for the Short Range Ballistic Missile Defense (SRBMD) program including cruise missile defense research and development under the SRBMD program, $58.9M for an upper tier component to the Israeli Missile Defense Architecture, and $66.4M for the Arrow System Improvement Program including development of a long range, ground and airborne detection suite.

"Iron Dome" was first activated in 04/11 and is credited with shooting down 80% of an estimated 300 rockets launched against Israel in 03/12 alone. At these initial stages, however, "Iron Dome" was not expected to be fully capable of protecting all Israeli cities from all rockets/guided missiles that Hamas was acquiring from Syria, Iran and other sources. Attainment of this goal was exacerbated by U.S. fiscal constraints causing the reduction of the FY2011 appropriation of $205M for "Iron Dome" in FY2011 to $0.0M in FY2012.

In summary, here are some of the principal Israeli missile defense systems which took place with active U.S. cooperation during the the Obama Administration:

- "Iron Dome" for missile threats less than 70 kilometers from Israel;
- "David's Sling" for cruise and ballistic missiles launched less than 300 kilometers from Israel;
- Upgrades to the U.S.-provided Patriot missile interceptor system; and
- "Arrow-2" and "Arrow-3" interceptors against Iran's Shabab class ballistic missiles.

The above signified continued U.S. cooperation with Israel in the development of missile defense systems.

This promise was fulfilled.

	USAID	GRADE
ST-60	**The Promise:** "will introduce a new Rapid Response Fund - a seed fund that will provide a shot of adrenaline to young democracies and post-conflict societies, through foreign aid, debt relief, technical assistance and investment packages that show the people of newly hopeful countries that democracy and peace deliver, and the United States stands by them." **When/Where:** Obama-Biden Plan: "Strengthening Our Common Security by Investing in Our Common Humanity", dated 09/11/08. **Source:** https://www.cgdev.org/sites/default/files/archive/doc/blog/obama_strengthen_security.pdf **Status:** The proposed "Rapid Response Fund" evolved to become the "Complex Crises Fund" (CCF), which is a mechanism appropriated by Congress that provided much-needed flexible money to USAID "to prevent and respond to emerging or unforeseen crises, filling a critical gap when stove-piped assistance funds cannot be reprogrammed." This funding mechanism quickly became one of the most highly demanded tools in the U.S. foreign policy toolkit, and was used to help mitigate violence in 19 countries, including Tunisia, Kenya, Mali and Sri Lanka. In the Central African Republic, for example, CCF funding has been used to help improve access to timely and accurate information, and lay the framework for a peaceful political transition by working to prevent further atrocities and rebuilding social cohesion through community peace-building. Managed by USAID, funding for CCF during the Obama Administration was as follows: FY2010 - $50M FY2011 - $40M FY2012 - $40M FY2013 - $38M	1.00

FY2014 - $20M
FY2015 - $20M
FY2016 - $10M

The future of the CCF, given fast-dwindling funds, is questionable. The promise did not have a dollar amount attached to it, so credit is given for the creation and funding of this initiative by the Obama Administration.

This promise was fulfilled.

ST-61

The Promise: "...will mobilize our civilian agencies to address a new set of global challenges and boost the stature of the government's long-term development mission to attract the most talented professionals."
When/Where: Obama-Biden Plan: "Strengthening Our Common Security by Investing in Our Common Humanity", dated 09/11/08.
Source: https://www.cgdev.org/sites/default/files/archive/doc/blog/obama_strengthen_security.pdf
Status: On 12/15/10, Secretary of State Clinton unveiled the first Quadrennial Diplomacy and Development Review (QDDR) following President Obama's release of a National Security Strategy (NSS) released on 05/27/10, after the Presidential Study Directive on Global Development (PSD-7) was leaked to the public earlier in 05/10.

As of CY2010, there were no less than 12 departments, 25 agencies, and 60 government offices involved in U.S. foreign assistance programs. The greatest hindrance to progress on this promise appeared to be the age-old turf conflict between the State Department and USAID. The State Department recruits for policy and communications skills, while USAID recruits more for sector and management expertise. Another fly in the ointment is that the Administrator of USAID continued to report to the Secretary of State.

The QDDR called for the State Department and USAID to change the way they did business by mandating reform in four areas:
- adapt to a 21st Century diplomatic landscape,
- elevate and modernize development,
- strengthen the civilian capacity to prevent and respond to crises and conflicts, and
- work smarter to develop results for the American taxpayer.

Reacting to President Obama's challenge in this promise, one of the key goals articulated in State's QDDR was to "focus and deepen our investments and empower our development professionals to deliver in areas that build on our core strengths."

This promise was fulfilled.

1.00

ST-62

The Promise: "...will coordinate and consolidate PEPFAR [President's Emergency Plan for AIDS Relief], Millennium Challenge Corporation, Middle East Partnership Initiative and many foreign assistance programs currently housed in more than 20 executive agencies into a restructured, empowered and streamlined USAID."
When/Where: Obama-Biden Plan: "Strengthening Our Common Security by Investing in Our Common Humanity", dated 09/11/08.
Source: https://www.cgdev.org/sites/default/files/archive/doc/blog/obama_strengthen_security.pdf
Status: Launched by President Bush in FY2003, the President's Emergency Plan for AIDS Relief (PEPFAR) was reauthorized in the amount of $48B in FY2009 for a period of five years through FY2013. In addition to funds to fight HIV/AIDS, it also includes funding for tuberculosis and malaria.

In 03/14, USAID partnered with the Millennium Challenge Corporation (MCC) to help other countries take the reins and empower themselves to confront development challenges like HIV/AIDS.

0.00

Chapter 12 - Department of State

Since its creation in CY2004, the MCC remained an independent foreign aid agency of the U.S. Government. Similarly, the Middle East Partnership Initiative (MEPI) has existed since CY2002 as a separate State Department program that supports reform efforts in the Middle East and North Africa (MENA).

However, there was no sign of any initiative by the Obama Administration to consolidate PEPFAR, MCC, and the Middle East Partnership Initiative (MEPI) under the U.S. Agency for International Development (USAID).

Rather, a 09/29/10 statement by Ambassador Eric Goosby, U.S. Global AIDS Coordinator, before the House Committee on Foreign Affairs confirmed that "the Center for Disease Control (CDC), the Department of Health and Human Services (HHS), Department of Defense (DOD), Department of Commerce (DoC), Department of Labor (DoL), Peace Corps, the Institute of Medicine (IOM), Millennium Challenge Corporation, Middle East Partnership Initiative and other government organisms continue to share PEPFAR implementation with USAID under President Obama's Global Health Initiative (GHI)."

This promise to consolidate PEPFAR activities with those of the MCC and MEPI under a "streamlined USAID" did not materialize during the Obama Administration.

This promise was not fulfilled.

STATE GPA | **0.45**

Campaign Promises
Departments -> Transportation

ITEM	TRANSPORTATION	
	AIR SERVICE	**GRADE**
TR-1	**The Promise:** "Will support the continuation of the Small Community Air Service Development Program that helps small and mid-sized communities attract new air service..." **When/Where:** Obama-Biden Plan: "Strengthening America's Transportation Infrastructure" dated 10/09/08. **Source:** https://evansparks.wordpress.com/2008/09/08/aviation08-the-obama-aviation-plan/ **Status:** President Obama's FY10 Budget proposal of 02/26/09 did not specifically include money for the Small Community Air Service Development Program (SCASDP), but did increase Essential Air Service funding for air service in small communities. Compared to previous years, funding for the SCASDP generally remained level in the first year of the Obama Administration ($6.0M in FY2010) with a $1M plus-up from other DOT organizations. For FY2011, Senate Report 111-230 recommended $6.0M for the SCASDP, "equal to the fiscal year 2010 enacted level." Obama Administration support for SCASDP started to increase in FY2012 with 33 communities in the United States plus Puerto Rico receiving $13.9M from the Department of Transportation's SCASDP grant program, this based on a 08/15/12 announcement by DOT Secretary Ray LaHood. This promise was fulfilled.	1.00
	INFRASTRUCTURE	**GRADE**
TR-2	**The Promise:** "...will enter into a new partnership with state and local civic, political, and business leaders to enact a truly national infrastructure policy that recognizes that we must upgrade our infrastructure to meet the demands of a growing population, a changing economy, and our short and long-term energy challenges." **When/Where:** Obama-Biden Plan: "Strengthening America's Transportation Infrastructure" dated 10/09/08. **Source:** https://www.politifact.com/truth-o-meter/promises/obameter/promise/477/upgrade-nations-infrastructure-through-new-partne/ **Status:** Source is cited for confirmation of exact promise wording only, as it existed before original "When/Where" campaign document was deleted from archival websites. On 12/04/15, President Obama signed the "Fixing America's Surface Transportation (FAST) Act. That Act, a $305B infrastructure improvement initiative, established many features of the promised partnership between federal, state and local entities. The Secretary of Transportation was directed under FAST to reinforce those partnerships by encouraging state and local agencies to take full advantage of engineering industry capabilities to strengthen project performance, improve domestic competitiveness, and create jobs.	1.00

Chapter 13 - Department of Transportation

	FAST also included a plan for partnering with the private sector or public agencies, including multimodal and multijurisdictional entities, research institutions, organizations representing transportation and technology leaders, and other transportation stakeholders. This promise was fulfilled.	
TR-3	**The Promise:** "...to mandate states and Metropolitan Planning Organizations create policies to incentivize greater bicycle and pedestrian usage of roads and sidewalks." **When/Where:** Obama-Biden Plan: "Strengthening America's Transportation Infrastructure" dated 10/09/08. **Source:** https://transportist.org/2008/02/ **Status:** On 03/11/10, the Department of Transportation (DOT) issued a "Policy Statement on Bicycle and Pedestrian Accommodation Regulations and Recommendations." The main thrust of this policy statement was to "incorporate safe and convenient walking and bicycling facilities into transportation projects." Further, the policy statement directs transportation agencies to "plan, fund, and implement improvements to their walking and bicycling networks, including linkages to transit." This promise was fulfilled.	1.00
TR-4	**The Promise:** "...will re-evaluate the transportation funding process to ensure that smart growth considerations are taken into account." **When/Where:** Obama-Biden Plan: "Build More Livable and Sustainable Communities" dated 10/09/08. **Source:** https://webarchive.loc.gov/all/20090429184744/http://change.gov/agenda/urbanpolicy_agenda/ **Status:** The Departments of Housing and Urban Development (HUD) and Transportation (DOT) and the Environmental Protection Agency (EPA) formed a partnership to provide American communities more transportation options and lower transportation costs. This partnership was embodied in the "Partnership for Sustainable Communities" announced by President Obama on 10/21/10, and included the integration of "smart growth" initiatives into the Transportation Investment Generating Economic Recovery (TIGER) grant program that was created under the American Recovery and Reinvestment Act (ARRA) of CY2009. This promise was fulfilled.	1.00
	MASS TRANSPORTATION	**GRADE**
TR-5	**The Promise:** "Will re-commit federal resources to public mass transportation projects across the country." **When/Where:** Obama-Biden Plan: "Strengthening America's Transportation Infrastructure" dated 10/09/08. **Source:** https://www.politifact.com/truth-o-meter/promises/obameter/promise/483/invest-in-public-transportation/ **Status:** Source is cited for confirmation of exact promise wording only, as it existed before original "When/Where" campaign document was deleted from archival websites. The American Recovery and Reinvestment Act of 2009, signed into law 02/17/09, provided $8.4 billion for improvements to the nation's public transportation systems, to include "buses, subways, light rail, commuter rail, streetcars, monorail, passenger ferry boats, inclined railways and people movers." In addition, Transportation Investment Generating Economic Recovery (TIGER) grants valued at about $500M annually were made available to economically depressed communities striving to	1.00

develop multi-mode transportation projects.

This promise was fulfilled.

PUBLIC/COMMUTER TRANSPORTATION	GRADE

TR-6

The Promise: "...will reform the tax code to make benefits for driving and public transit or ridesharing equal."
When/Where: Obama-Biden Plan: "Strengthening America's Transportation Infrastructure" dated 10/09/08.
Source: https://www.politifact.com/truth-o-meter/promises/obameter/promise/484/equalize-tax-breaks-for-driving-and-public-transit/
Status: Source is cited for confirmation of exact promise wording only, as it existed before original "When/Where" campaign document was deleted from archival websites.

Section 1151 of the American Recovery and Reinvestment Act (ARRA) of 2009 is entitled "Increased exclusion amount for commuter transit benefits and transit passes."

For CY2009 the maximum monthly pre-tax contribution for mass transit was $120.00, and $230.00 for parking. However the $120.00 transit expense was increased to $230.00 by the Treasury Department under the ARRA, signed into law by President Obama on 02/17/09. This brought parity between those who drove their own vehicles to a public parking lot and then commuted to work, and those who relied totally on public transit assets. However, this incentive was temporary and expired at the end of CY2011.

Starting in CY2012, employers were authorized to provide employees up to $125 per month in tax-free transit and vanpool benefits and qualified parking benefits went up to $240 per month. These rates went up to $130 and $250 per month respectively in CY2014.

As a result of a tax deal concluded in Congress on 12/16/15, the playing field leveled out to $255 per month for both drivers and transit riders. The tax break for those who use their bicycles to work is $20 per month.

This promise was fulfilled.

1.00

TR-7

The Promise: "...will double the federal Jobs Access and Reverse Commute (JARC) program to ensure that additional federal public transportation dollars flow to the highest-need communities..."
When/Where: Obama-Biden Plan: "Strengthening America's Transportation Infrastructure" dated 10/09/08.
Source: https://transportist.org/2008/02/
Status: The FY2009 apportionment for the JARC program by the Federal Transit Administration (FTA) was $183.1M. The FTA's apportionment in FY2010 for the JARC program was $68M. The promised doubling of funds for this grant program did not occur in President Obama's first years in office.

President Obama's FY2011 budget proposal included $166.6M for the JARC program, still a long way from doubling the baseline FY2009 apportionment of $183.1M. Of this requested amount, Congress apportioned only $69.7M for JARC in FY2011.

For FY2012, the JARC program was apportioned $95M of the Federal Transit Administration's budget.

On 10/1/13, the JARC Program was repealed by Congress under the Moving Ahead for Progress in the 21st Century Act (MAP-21).

This promise was not fulfilled.

0.00

Chapter 13 - Department of Transportation

TR-8	**The Promise:** "...will help the New Orleans area develop regional transit partnerships so that public transit can be integrated across parish lines, providing seamless transportation options, including a possible light rail line to connect New Orleans and Baton Rouge through the petrochemical corridor in between." **When/Where:** Obama-Biden Plan: "Rebuilding the Gulf Coast and Preventing Future Catastrophes", dated 09/11/08. **Source:** https://www.documentcloud.org/documents/2270775-katrinafactsheetfinal.html **Status:** Louisiana House Bill 1410, passed by the House on 05/18/10 and the Senate on 06/17/10 allows two or more Louisiana cities or parishes to establish rail compacts as a way to help launch intrastate railway or rapid transit systems. This bill was signed into law by Governor Bobby Jindal on 06/30/10 with no known assistance from the Obama Administration. Previously, Governor Jindal declined to apply for $300M in stimulus money to start a New Orleans-Baton Rouge light rail project, because annual operating costs of $18M could not be supported by the state. For a few years after Hurricane Katrina in CY2004, "LA Swift," funded to the tune of $2.3M annually by the Department of Transportation, operated as a commuter bus service between New Orleans and Baton Rouge. In CY2013, the federal government asked Louisiana to provide $750K annually as its share of the costs for operating LA Swift. Louisiana's Governor Jindal declined and the commuter bus service ended. At a cost of $60M, $45M of which were federal funds, New Orleans started operating the less-than-a-mile-long Loyola Avenue streetcar which did little to improve inner-city transit. Some called it the streetcar "from nowhere to nowhere." The New Orleans inner transit system and its ability to interconnect with other parishes was worse by end-CY2016 than it was before Hurricane Katrina While a passenger rail system linking New Orleans to Baton Rouge and other points is still being planned by Governor Jindal's successor since 01/16, Governor John Bel Edwards, no specific/formal transit partnership between the Government of the State of Louisiana and the federal government is known to have been formed during the Obama Administration other than grants provided under the "Partnership for Sustainable Communities" and similar programs. This promise was not fulfilled.	0.00
	RAIL SERVICE	**GRADE**
TR-9	**The Promise:** "Will "support development of high-speed rail networks across the country"." **When/Where:** Obama-Biden Plan: "Strengthening America's Transportation Infrastructure" dated 10/09/08. **Source:** https://transportist.org/2008/02/ **Status:** The Federal Railroad Administration (FRA) defines "high speed" as the ability for a train to travel 90 mph or faster. The American Recovery and Reinvestment Act of 2009, signed into law 02/17/09, provided an initial $8 billion, to be spent over two years, and an addition $1 billion per year over the next five years toward the accomplishment of this campaign promise. During his 01/10 State of the Union address, President Obama stated that "There's no reason Europe or China should have the fastest train." The FY2010 transporation budget appropriation passed on 07/17/09 saw a surprising increase for high-speed rail from the planned $1B to $4B, despite Senate attempts to peel back $3B and transfer	1.00

Chapter 13 - Department of Transportation

that amount to the Highway Trust Fund.

For FY2012, President Obama's budget proposal included $53B over six years for "high-speed rail and other passenger rail programs as part of an integrated national strategy."

President Obama showcased high-speed rail in Tampa on 01/28/10, launching the building of a high-speed rail link between Tampa and Orlando. However, the Governor of Florida (as well as those of Ohio and Wisconsin) adopted the position that Florida would not accept federal funding for any high-speed rail projects.

The $33B California high speed rail project between Sacramento and San Diego is not on track. By end-CY2016, only 160 of the originally planned 703 miles was under construction between Merced and Bakersfield, California. These points are 131 miles from San Francisco and 113 miles from Los Angeles respectively, requiring eventual users to either drive or use rental cars to get to the embarkation point or from the debarkation point to destination.

By end-CY2016, the Texas Central Railway, to be built from Houston to Dallas with speeds up to 205 mph, was expected to be constructed between CY2020 and CY2026.

The above are just examples. There are also plans for higher-speed rail and high-speed rail in the Midwest, New England, Pennsylvania, the Pacific Northwest, Colorado, New Mexico and the Southwestern United States and other locations.

This promise was fulfilled.

TR-10	**The Promise:** "...will continue to fight for Amtrak funding and reform so that individuals, families and businesses throughout the country have safe and reliable transportation options." **When/Where:** Obama-Biden Plan: "Strengthening America's Transportation Infrastructure" dated 10/09/08. **Source:** https://transportist.org/2008/02/ **Status:** The Passenger Rail Investment and Improvement Act (PRIIA) of 2008 authorized Amtrak through FY2013, later reauthorized through FY2020 under the FAST Act (H.R. 22). The original PRIIA authorized the appropriation of about $3B in operating funds and $5.3B in capital funding not including debt service. The American Recovery and Reinvestment Act (ARRA) of 2009 provided an additional $1.3B to supplement Amtrak's capital program through 02/11 as part of a $9.5B investment in passenger trains. Under the PRIIA funding plan, Amtrak's total funding was to go up incrementally from $1.8B in FY2010 to $1.9B in FY2011, $2.1B in FY2012 and $2.2B in FY2013. In reality, the following represents actual federal outlays for AMTRAK's operating and operating and capital expenses for the period FY2010 to FY2016: FY2010 - $1.565B FY2011 - $1.483B FY2012 - $1.418B FY2013 - $1.334B FY2014 - $1.390B FY2015 - $1.390B FY2016 - $1.450B FY2017 - $1.500B Federal funds for AMTRAK steadily declined from President Obama's first budget submission for FY2010.	0.00

The PRIIA also required Amtrak to address "reform initiatives" in each of its five-year plans, to be submitted by the first day of the fiscal year or 60 days after the enactment of an appropriations Act, whichever is later.

Clearly, Amtrak funding under the Obama Administration did not keep pace with requirements and was considerably less than the funding levels authorized under the PRIIA.

This promise was not fulfilled.

TRANSPORTATION GPA	0.70

Chapter 14 - Department of the Treasury

Campaign Promises

Departments -> Treasury

ITEM	TREASURY	
	CORPORATE TAXES	**GRADE**
TY-1	**The Promise:** "Eliminating special tax breaks for oil and gas companies: including repealing special expensing rules, foreign tax credit benefits, and manufacturing deductions for oil and gas firms." **When/Where:** Barak Obama's "Comprehensive Tax Plan" dated 08/20/08. **Source:** http://plancksconstant.org/blog1/pdfs/Factsheet_Tax_Plan_FINAL.pdf **Status:** As of end-CY2016, oil and gas companies continued to benefit from the following tax breaks: - domestic manufacturing deduction for oil and gas production; - deductions for the depletion of oil and gas deposits; - deductions for tertiary injectants; - deductions for the depletion of oil shale deposits; - marginal wells tax credit; - deductions for the costs of oil shale exploration and development; - amortization of geological and geophysical expenditures; - deductions for the costs of drilling wells; and - exception to passive loss limitation for working interests in oil and natural gas properties. By some accounts, repealing the above tax breaks would have potentially saved the U.S. taxpayer $40B over a period of 10 years. This promise was not fulfilled.	0.00
TY-2	**The Promise:** "Will eliminate all capital gains taxes on investments in small and start-up firms." **When/Where:** Barak Obama's "Comprehensive Tax Plan" dated 08/20/08. **Source:** http://plancksconstant.org/blog1/pdfs/Factsheet_Tax_Plan_FINAL.pdf **Status:** Under the American Recovery and Reinvestment Act of 2009, signed into law 02/17/09, investors in small businesses were able to exclude 75% of their gain from capital gains taxes -- not 100% ("all capital gains taxes") as promised. The Small Business Jobs and Credit Act of 2010 (H.R. 5297), signed into law by President Obama on 09/27/10, exempted 100% of the taxes on capital gains for angel and venture capital investors on small business investments if held for five years. This was a short term solution to spur investment in small businesses immediately and applied only for stocks bought prior to the end of CY2010. By end-CY2011, the exclusion rates returned to 50% for C-Corporations with less than $50M in assets and 60% for select businesses in empowerment zones. By end-CY2016, the exclusion rate remained at 50% of capital gains for small businesses. This exclusion on the small business capital gains tax was limited to $10M or 10 times the cost basis of shares. The maximum capital gains tax rate on long-term capital gains profits remained at 15%. This promise was not fulfilled.	0.00

Chapter 14 - Department of the Treasury

TY-3	**The Promise:** "Raise the small business investment expensing limit to $250,000 through the end of 2009." **When/Where:** Obama-Biden Plan: Raise the small business investment expensing limit to $250,000 through the end of 2009, undated. **Source:** https://webarchive.loc.gov/all/20090429185145/http://change.gov/agenda/economy_agenda/ **Status:** Section 179 of the American Recovery and Reinvestment Act of 2009 (ARRA) stipulated that small businesses could elect to expense up to $250,000 of the cost of qualifying property. The $250,000 amount provided under the new law was to be reduced if the cost of all section 179 property placed in service by the taxpayer during the tax year exceeded $800,000. These provisions were repeated in Section 201 of the Hiring Incentives to Restore Employment Act (H.R. 2847) signed into law by President Obama on 03/18/10 and remained in effect until 12/31/10. This promise was fulfilled.	1.00
TY-4	**The Promise:** "During 2009 and 2010, existing businesses will receive a $3,000 refundable tax credit for each additional full-time employee hired." **When/Where:** Obama-Biden Plan: A New American Jobs Tax Credit, undated. **Source:** https://webarchive.loc.gov/all/20090429185145/http://change.gov/agenda/economy_agenda/ **Status:** Initial estimates were that this promise would have cost $40-50B over the two-year CY2009-CY2010 period. This promise was excluded from American Recovery and Reinvestment Act of 2009, signed into law 02/17/09. The promise was also excluded from the President's FY2010 budget proposal. Unemployment realities in CY2009 (rising to 10% by 10/31/09) forced reconsideration, as President Obama proposed raising the tax credit level for each newly hired person to $5,000 during his State of the Union address of 01/27/10. At that time, he said that the $5,000 per-worker tax credit he proposed would be available to businesses of any size, and would be retroactive to the start of 2010. On 03/18/10, President Obama signed the Hiring Incentives to Restore Employment (HIRE) Act (H.R. 2847) into law. Section 101 of this bill provided a tax exemption for non-federal or state employers for qualified employees hired between 02/03/10 and 12/31/10 who had not been employed for more than 40 hours during the 60-day period prior to employment. The non-refundable tax credit was limited to the lesser of $1,000 or 6.2% of wages paid during the 52-week period following employment. The estimated cost of this initiative stood at $30-100B, reportedly to be funded from left-over Troubled Asset Relief Program (TARP) funds. Thus, the tax credit that ultimately came into effect in CY2010 did not apply to CY2009 as promised, was not refundable, and was limited to $1,000, not $3,000. This promise was not fulfilled.	0.00
TY-5	**The Promise:** "Will extend the federal Production Tax Credit (PTC) for 5 years to encourage the production of renewable energy." **When/Where:** Obama-Biden Plan: "New Energy for America", dated 09/06/08. **Source:** http://energy.gov/sites/prod/files/edg/media/Obama_New_Energy_0804.pdf **Status:** The American Recovery and Reinvestment Act of 2009, signed into law 02/17/09, extended the PTC for 3 years to CY2012, not 5 years as promised. On 08/02/12, the Senate Finance Committee added an additional one-year extension of the $12B PTC as part of a larger tax credit extension bill.	1.00

Chapter 14 - Department of the Treasury

On 01/01/13, President Obama signed the "American Taxpayer Relief Act of 2012" (H.R. 8), extending the PTC for facilities producing energy from renewable resources by one additional year to 01/01/14. The federal PTC was in fact extended for a total of five years during President Obama's first term in office.

This promise was fulfilled.

TY-6

The Promise: "Require publicly traded financial partnerships to pay the corporate income tax."
When/Where: Tax Policy Center Urban Institute and Brookings Institute document dated 08/15/08
Source: https://www.taxpolicycenter.org/sites/default/files/alfresco/publication-pdfs/411749-An-Updated-Analysis-of-the-Presidential-Candidates-Tax-Plans-Updated-September--.PDF
Status: Participants in Publicly Traded Partnerships (PTP) are taxed on the money distributed by the partnership. Unlike a corporation, a PTP itself does not pay taxes on its income. Income is only taxed once when it is distributed to general and limited partners.

This is why businesses organized as PTPs are known not to pay one penny in federal corporate income tax. Rather, they rely on "pass-throughs," meaning that they pass profits to investors. It is these investors who pay taxes through their individual tax returns on dividends received.

As of end-CY2016, a PTP could still avoid paying corporate taxes if 90% or more of the PTP's gross income consisted of qualifying income. Examples of qualifying income:
- interest;
- dividends;
- royalties;
- real property rents;
- gain from the sale/disposition of real estate;
- income and gains from the exploration, development, mining, or production, processing, refining, transportation, or marketing of any mineral or natural resource, industrial source carbon dioxide, or the transportation or storage of specified renewable fuels;
- income and gains from commodities, if buying and selling of commodities is the PTP's principal activity; and
- any income that would be qualifying income for a regulated investment company (RIC) or a real estate investment trust (REIT).

This promise was not fulfilled.

0.00

TY-7

The Promise: "...will also create a new Small Business Health Tax Credit to provide small businesses with a refundable tax credit of up to 50 percent on premiums paid by small businesses on behalf of their employees."
When/Where: Obama-Biden Plan: "To Lower Health Care Costs and Ensure Affordable, Accessible Health Coverage for All" dated 10/03/08.
Source: http://courses.ischool.berkeley.edu/i202/f08/lectures/Obama_Healthcare-1.pdf
Status: The definition of a "small business" in the USA is one having fewer than 500 employees for manufacturing businesses, has less than $7.5M in annual receipts for most non-manufacturing businesses, and meets regulatory requirements established by the Small Business Administration (SBA) under 13 CFR Part 121.

Under the Patient Protection and Affordable Care Act (Public Law 111-148) signed into law by President Obama on 03/23/10, small businesses with no more than 25 employees received a non-refundable tax credit of 35% of contributions made toward the health care premiums of their employees during the period CY2010-2013. That percentage increased to 50% starting in CY2014.

The tax credit did not apply to all businesses classified as "small business" by the SBA and it was not refundable.

0.00

This promise was not fulfilled.

TY-8	**The Promise:** "Will target tax incentives to lure businesses to the hardest hit areas of the Gulf Coast including downtown New Orleans and St. Bernard Parish." **When/Where:** Obama-Biden Plan: "Rebuilding the Gulf Coast and Preventing Future Catastrophes", dated 09/11/08. **Source:** https://assets.documentcloud.org/documents/550006/barack-obama-2008-rebuilding-the-gulf-coast-and.pdf **Status:** The Gulf Opportunity Zone (GO Zone) Act of 2005 was signed into law on 12/22/05 by President Bush. It provided tax relief for recovery efforts in the states of Louisiana, Mississippi and Alabama, devastated by Hurricane Katrina, for a period of five years. It also provided incentives and tax relief to states affected by Hurricanes Rita and Wilma, similar to the assistance provided under the Katrina Emergency Tax Relief Act (Public Law 109-73) signed into law by President Bush on 09/23/05. Since these CY2005 initiatives, there have been no new tax incentives or credits introduced by the Obama Administration to lure businesses to the Gulf, New Orleans, and/or Saint Bernard Parish other than the one-year extension of the above bonds under the Tax Relief, Unemployment Insurance Authorization and Job Creation Act of 2010. The New Orleans and Saint Bernard Parish areas have benefitted from the "New Market Tax Credit" (NMTC) since its inception in CY2000. For FY2011, Louisiana was the beneficiary of $295M in NMTC, all of which, except for $53M for Baton Rouge, went to New Orleans. In addition, Louisiana has continued to benefit from pre-CY2009 federal-level Rehabilitation Tax Credits, GO Zone Bonus Depreciation, and GO Zone Bonds programs as well as other state-level tax incentives/credits. Other than the incentives (and their extension) that existed when President Obama assumed office, incentives that he extended by two years by signing the Tax Relief, Unemployment Insurance Authorization and Job Creation Act of 2010 on 12/17/10, he is not credited with having "targeted" any new tax incentives to lure new businesses to the GO Zone. This promise was not fulfilled.	0.00
TY-9	**The Promise:** "Make permanent...renewable energy production tax credit." **When/Where:** Interview with Tax Policy Center of Urban and Brookings Institutions dated 08/15/08. **Source:** https://www.taxpolicycenter.org/sites/default/files/alfresco/publication-pdfs/411749-An-Updated-Analysis-of-the-Presidential-Candidates-Tax-Plans-Updated-September--.PDF **Status:** The American Recovery and Reinvestment Act of 2009 provided a 3-year extension of the Renewable Energy Production Tax Credit (PTC) through 12/31/12. President Obama's FY2010 budget proposal included $75B to make this tax credit permanent. Congress didn't go along. On 01/01/13, President Obama signed the "American Taxpayer Relief Act of 2012" (H.R. 8), extending the PTC for facilities producing energy from renewable resources by one additional year to 01/01/14 (not permanent). As of end-CY2016, the PTC was extended as part of the Consolidated Appropriations Act of 2016 (P.L. 114-113). This legislation extended the PTC for two years, through CY2016, for all eligible technologies. The PTC for wind was also extended an additional three years, through CY2019, but at reduced credit rates for wind facilities beginning construction in CY2017 thru CY2019.	0.00

Chapter 14 - Department of the Treasury

	The renewable energy PTC did not become permanent during President Obama's two terms in office. This promise was not fulfilled.	
TY-10	**The Promise:** "...provide a 20 percent tax credit on up to $50,000 of investment in small owner-operated businesses." **When/Where:** Obama-Biden Plan for Small Businesses, dated 09/11/08. **Source:** https://www.politifact.com/truth-o-meter/promises/obameter/promise/25/establish-a-small-business-initiative-for-rural-am/ **Status:** Source is cited for confirmation of exact promise wording only, as it existed before original "When/Where" campaign document was deleted from archival websites. Considerable assistance was provided to small businesses under the American Recovery and Reinvestment Act of 2009. However, this Act did not provide a 20% tax credit on up to $50,000 of owner-operator investments. An opportunity to deliver on this promise presented itself when President Obama signed the Small Business Jobs Act of 2010 (H.R. 5297) on 09/27/10. The Democrat-controlled Congress and President Obama did not seize this opportunity. Another opportunity to support fulfillment of this promise presented itself by the introduction by Congressman Ron Kind (D-WI) on 07/31/14 of the Rural Microbusiness Investment Credit Act of 2014 (H.R. 5346). This proposed Act would have provided a tax credit of $10,000 (20% of $50,000) for rural microbusinesses. This Act did not advance through the House and expired with the 113th Congress. This promise was not fulfilled.	0.00
TY-11	**The Promise:** "Make permanent R&D credit and renewable energy production tax credit" **When/Where:** Interview with Tax Policy Center of Urban and Brookings Institutions dated 08/15/08. **Source:** https://www.taxpolicycenter.org/sites/default/files/alfresco/publication-pdfs/411749-An-Updated-Analysis-of-the-Presidential-Candidates-Tax-Plans-Updated-September--.PDF **Status:** The Research and Development (R&D) tax credit was permanently extended by Congress retroactively as of 01/01/15 when President Obama signed the "Protecting Americans from Tax Hikes (PATH) Act of 2015" on 12/18/16. This bill was incorporated as Division Q of the Consolidated Appropriations Act of 2016 (H.R. 2029). This promise was fulfilled.	1.00
	INDIVIDUAL TAXES	**GRADE**
TY-12	**The Promise:** "Will eliminate all income taxation of seniors making less than $50,000 per year. This will eliminate taxes for 7 million seniors -- saving them an average of $1,400 a year-- and will also mean that 27 million seniors will not need to file an income tax return at all." **When/Where:** Barak Obama's "Comprehensive Tax Plan" dated 08/20/08. **Source:** http://plancksconstant.org/blog1/pdfs/Factsheet_Tax_Plan_FINAL.pdf **Status:** This promise was not addressed in the American Recovery and Reinvestment Act of 2009, signed into law 02/17/09. Nor was it addressed in the Tax Relief, Unemployment Insurance Reauthorization, and Job Creation Act of 2010, signed into law by President Obama on 12/17/10. As of end-CY2016, depending upon individual circumstances and income, seniors qualifying for the 10% or 15% tax brackets (less than $50,000) continued to pay taxes at those rates. This promise was not fulfilled.	0.00
TY-13	**The Promise:** "Extend aspects of the Bush tax cuts such as child credit expansions and changes to marriage bonuses and penalties."	1.00

When/Where: Interview with Tax Policy Center of Urban and Brookings Institutions dated 08/15/08.
Source: https://www.taxpolicycenter.org/sites/default/files/alfresco/publication-pdfs/411749-An-Updated-Analysis-of-the-Presidential-Candidates-Tax-Plans-Updated-September--.PDF
Status: The American Recovery and Reinvestment Act of 2009, signed into law 02/17/09, increased existing credits for children by reducing the minimum earned income used to calculate the tax credit from $12,550 to $3,000 and was applicable for tax years 2009 and 2010. President Obama's FY2010 and FY2011 budget submissions proposed to make the child tax credit permanent starting in CY2013.

The law that eases the "marriage penalty" (forcing married couples with two incomes to pay more tax than two single people living together) would have sunset on 12/31/10, affecting 36M couples.

The Tax Relief, Unemployment Reauthorization, and Job Creation Act of 2010 (H.R. 4853) signed into law by President Obama on 12/17/10, extended and expanded the child tax credit and eased the marriage penalty through CY2012.

This promise was fulfilled.

TY-14

The Promise: "Freeze the 2009 estate tax law, which exempts the first $3.5 million and has a top rate of 45 percent."
When/Where: Interview with Tax Policy Center of Urban and Brookings Institutions dated 08/15/08.
Source: https://www.taxpolicycenter.org/sites/default/files/alfresco/publication-pdfs/411749-An-Updated-Analysis-of-the-Presidential-Candidates-Tax-Plans-Updated-September--.PDF
Status: Estate taxes with the rate of 45% for anything above $3.5 million (individuals) and $7 million (couples) were left to expire at the end of CY2009, despite President Obama's promise to maintain the CY2009 exemption and maximum rate levels beyond CY2009.

For 2010, the total gift and Estate Tax exemptions were unlimited and estate taxes were expected to revert back, in CY2011, to where they were in the pre-Bush era: exemption only on the first $1 million and anything above that would be taxed at 55%.

Under the The Tax Relief, Unemployment Reauthorization, and Job Creation Act of 2010 (H.R. 4853) signed into law by President Obama on 12/17/10, the first $5M per person ($10M for married couples) of an estate was exempt from taxes and a rate of 35% was assessed against any estate amount exceeding $5M for individuals and $10M for married couples.

By signing the "American Taxpayer Relief Act of 2012" (H.R. 8) on 01/01/13, President Obama again changed the estate tax law. Under that law, the maximum tax rate for estates over $1M was $345,800 plus 40% of anything over that amount.

By end-CY2016, the estate and gift tax exemption for CY2017 had risen to $5.490M per individual ($10.980M per couple) up from $5.450M ($10.900M per couple) in CY2016. Any amount exceeding these amounts was taxed at 40%.

Bottom line: Estate taxes were not frozen at the CY2009 level.

This promise was not fulfilled.

0.00

TY-15

The Promise: "Extend the Bush tax cuts for those making less than $250,000 (couples) or $200,000 (single)."
When/Where: Interview with Tax Policy Center of Urban and Brookings Institutions dated 08/15/08.
Source: https://www.taxpolicycenter.org/sites/default/files/alfresco/publication-pdfs/411749-An-Updated-Analysis-of-the-Presidential-Candidates-Tax-Plans-Updated-September--.PDF
Status: This promise was addressed in President Obama's FY10 budget submission, particularly in Tables S-2, S-5 and S-6. Again in his FY2011 budget submission, President Obama proposed to

1.00

Chapter 14 - Department of the Treasury

allow Bush tax cuts for "families earning more than $250,000" to expire at the end of CY2010.

If action had not been taken by Congress by the end of CY2010 on the Bush-era tax cuts, everyone's taxes (income, dividends and capital gains) would have gone up, even for individuals earning less than $200,000 or households earning less than $250,000.

Under the Tax Relief, Unemployment Reauthorization, and Job Creation Act of 2010 (H.R. 4853) signed into law by President Obama on 12/17/10, Bush-era tax cuts for families earning less than $250K and individuals earning less than $200K were extended for tax years 2011 and 2012.

On 07/09/12, President Obama called for a one-year extension through end-CY2013 of the Bush-era tax cuts for families earning less than $250,000, arguing that 98% of all U.S. taxpayers earn less than $250,000.

By signing the "American Taxpayer Relief Act of 2012" (H.R. 8) on 01/01/13, President Obama made permanent Bush-era tax cuts for taxpayers earning less than $400,000 (individuals) and $450,000 (couples).

This promise was fulfilled.

TY-16

The Promise: "Repeal the Bush tax cuts for those making more than $250,000 (couples) or $200,000 (single)."
When/Where: Interview with Tax Policy Center of Urban and Brookings Institutions dated 08/15/08.
Source: https://www.taxpolicycenter.org/sites/default/files/alfresco/publication-pdfs/411749-An-Updated-Analysis-of-the-Presidential-Candidates-Tax-Plans-Updated-September--.PDF
Status: Bush tax cuts on the "wealthy" were set to expire in FY2011. President Obama's FY2010 Budget Request presented to Congress on 02/26/09 (Table S-6) proposed to raise those in a 33% bracket to 36% and those in a 35% bracket to 39.6%. The FY2011 budget submission (Table S-8) had a similar line item.

The Tax Relief, Unemployment Reauthorization, and Job Creation Act of 2010 (H.R. 4853) signed into law by President Obama on 12/17/10 extended Bush-era tax cuts for everyone, including those earning more than $200K (individuals) and over $250K (couples).

On 10/04/11, President Obama's own party (Senate Democrats) canned his proposal to raise taxes on families making over $250K, instead proposing to raise the threshold to $1M. Further, Senate Democrats wanted to impose a 5% surtax on the tax liability of millionaires, a move that by some accounts could have potentially raised $445B over 10 years. This proposal did not gain any bipartisan traction.

On 01/01/13, President Obama signed the "American Taxpayer Relief Act of 2012" (H.R. 8) into law. This law did not repeal Bush-era tax cuts for those making more than $250,000 (couples) or $200,000 (single). Rather it raised the bar to $450,000 for couples and $400,000 for individuals.

This promise was not fulfilled.

0.00

TY-17

The Promise: "Phaseout personal exemptions and itemized deductions for those making more than $250,000 (couples) or $200,000 (single), with thresholds indexed for inflation."
When/Where: Interview with Tax Policy Center of Urban and Brookings Institutions dated 08/15/08.
Source: https://www.taxpolicycenter.org/sites/default/files/alfresco/publication-pdfs/411749-An-Updated-Analysis-of-the-Presidential-Candidates-Tax-Plans-Updated-September--.PDF
Status: The Tax Relief, Unemployment Reauthorization, and Job Creation Act of 2010 (H.R. 4853) signed into law by President Obama on 12/17/10, extended Bush-era tax rates, including exemptions and deductions, for individuals earning more than $200K or couples earning more than $250K through end-CY2012.

1.00

Chapter 14 - Department of the Treasury

The "American Taxpayer Relief Act of 2012" signed into law by President Obama on 01/01/13 increased the overall limitation on itemized deductions from $250,000 for couples to $300,000 and from $200,000 for individuals to $250,000. It re-instituted phase-out limitations for itemized deductions at 3% of adjusted gross income for amounts above these thresholds, and 2% for each $2,500 above the thresholds.

As of end-CY2016, the threshold Adjusted Gross Income (AGI) amounts were $259,400 for single filers, $285,350 for individuals filing as heads of households, $311,300 for married couples filing jointly and $155,650 for married individuals filing separately. The phaseout factors were as follows:

- Personal Exemption: The allowable exemption amounts were reduced by 2% for each $2,500 or part of $2,500 ($1,250 for a married taxpayer filing separately) that the taxpayer's AGI exceeded the threshold amount for the taxpayer's filing status.

- Itemized Deductions: The total amount of itemized deductions was reduced by 3% of the amount by which the taxpayer's AGI exceeded the threshold amount, with the reduction not to exceed 80% of the allowable itemized deductions.

This promise was fulfilled.

TY-18

The Promise: "...codifying the economic substance doctrine (requiring that transactions qualifying for tax benefits have economic justification beyond those benefits)..."
When/Where: Interview with Tax Policy Center of Urban and Brookings Institutions dated 08/15/08.
Source: https://www.taxpolicycenter.org/sites/default/files/alfresco/publication-pdfs/411749-An-Updated-Analysis-of-the-Presidential-Candidates-Tax-Plans-Updated-September--.PDF
Status: President Obama's FY2010 budget submission included a line item in Table S-6 entitled "Codify Economic Substance Doctrine".

According to Treasury Department documentation, the law prior to CY2010 contained an accuracy-related penalty that applied to an underpayment of tax attributable to a substantial understatement of income tax. The penalty equaled 20 percent of the tax underpayment. The penalty rate increased to 30 percent if the taxpayer had not disclosed the transaction as required by law.

The proposed change to the Economic Substance Doctrine would clarify that a transaction satisfies the economic substance doctrine only if it changed in a 'meaningful way' the taxpayer's economic position, and the taxpayer had a substantial purpose (other than a federal tax purpose) for entering into the transaction.

The codification of these changes took place under Section 1409 of the Health Care and Education Reconciliation Act of 2010, signed into law by President Obama on 03/30/10.

This promise was fulfilled.

1.00

TY-19

The Promise: "Increase capital gains and dividends taxes from 15 to 20 percent for those making more than $250,000 (couples) or $200,000 (single)."
When/Where: Interview with Tax Policy Center of Urban and Brookings Institutions dated 08/15/08.
Source: https://www.taxpolicycenter.org/sites/default/files/alfresco/publication-pdfs/411749-An-Updated-Analysis-of-the-Presidential-Candidates-Tax-Plans-Updated-September--.PDF
Status: Under President Obama's FY2010 budget proposal (Table S-6), upper income tax payers, those earning above the $200,000 (individuals) and $250,000 (couples) thresholds, would have paid a 20% rate on capital gains and dividends. This did not happen.

By signing the Tax Relief, Unemployment Reauthorization, and Job Creation Act of 2010 (H.R. 4853) into law on 12/17/10, President Obama extended the 15% capital gains and dividend tax rates until

0.00

Chapter 14 - Department of the Treasury

the end of CY2012 for high income earners.

Under the "American Taxpayer Relief Act of 2012" (H.R. 8) signed into law by President Obama on 01/01/13, the capital gains and dividend income taxes for single filers with taxable income exceeding $400,000 ($450,000 for married filers) increased from 15 to 20 percent.

Because the income thresholds subject to increased capital gains and dividend taxes from 15 to 20% were increased from $200K (single)/$250K (couple) to $400K (single)/$450K (couple), the basic tenets of this promise were not satisfied.

As of end-CY2016, a married couple in the highest tax bracket of 39.6% and earning more than $470,701 paid 20% for long term capital gains. Between $250K and $470K, the original rate of 15% was maintained.

This promise was not fulfilled.

TY-20

The Promise: "I can make a firm pledge. Under my plan, no family making less than $250,000 a year will see any form of tax increase. Not your income tax, not your payroll tax, not your capital gains taxes, not any of your taxes."
When/Where: Obama Campaign Speech "On Taxes", Dover, NH 09/12/08.
Source: http://www.presidency.ucsb.edu/ws/index.php?pid=78612
Status: During President Obama's two terms in office, the tax rate for families earning $250K or less remained stable with the highest bracket of 33% for single filers, married couples filing jointly and heads of households.

The picture is different for married people filing separately. In CY2010, these filers were taxed at the 35% rate for any amount above $186,825. The American Taxpayer Relief Act of 2012 (Public Law 112-240), signed into law by President Obama on 01/02/13, permanently extended tax cuts in effect at that time, but added a top marginal tax rate of 39.6% for those with higher incomes.

For married people filing separately, the CY2013 tax rate went up from $35% to 39.6% for earnings exceeding 225 (less than $250K). By end-CY2016, the tax rate for married people filing separately was 39.6% for earnings exceeding $233,476 (still less than $250K).

This promise was not fulfilled.

0.00

TY-21

The Promise: "Expand the earned income tax credit for workers without children and taxpayers with more than three children. Equalize thresholds for married filers and head of household filers."
When/Where: Interview with Tax Policy Center of Urban and Brookings Institutions dated 08/15/08.
Source: https://www.taxpolicycenter.org/sites/default/files/alfresco/publication-pdfs/411749-An-Updated-Analysis-of-the-Presidential-Candidates-Tax-Plans-Updated-September--.PDF
Status: For CY2012, single filers (head of household) with three or more children and married couples with three or more children could each receive a maximum Earned Income Tax Credit (EITC) of $5,891 if income was less than $45,060 and $50,270 respectively.

For CY2013, childless workers earning less than $14,340 ($19,680 for childless married couples) could receive an EITC of $487, a $12 increase over CY2012. Head of household and married tax payers filing jointly with three or more qualifying children and earning less than $46,227 and $51,567 respectively could receive an EITC of $6,044.

This promise was fulfilled.

1.00

TY-22

The Promise: "Enact a Making Work Pay tax credit that would equal 6.2 percent of up to $8,100 of earnings (yielding a maximum credit of approximately $500), indexed for inflation."
When/Where: Interview with Tax Policy Center of Urban and Brookings Institutions dated 08/15/08.
Source: https://www.taxpolicycenter.org/sites/default/files/alfresco/publication-pdfs/411749-An-

1.00

Updated-Analysis-of-the-Presidential-Candidates-Tax-Plans-Updated-September--.PDF
Status: A "Making Work Pay" maximum tax credit of $400 for working individuals (and $800 for working married couples) was funded in the amount of $116.2 billion by Congress under the American Recovery and Reinvestment Act of 2009, signed into law 02/17/09.

For single filers in CY2010, this credit started phasing out at $75,000 of Adjusted Gross Income (AGI) and terminated at $95,000. Phase-out for joint filers started at $150,000 and ended at $190,000 of AGI.

Instead of the "Making Work Pay" tax credit which expired at the end of CY2010, all American workers received a 2% Social Security withholding break on their payroll taxes in CY2011 and CY2012, a reduction from 6.2% to 4.2% on wages up to $106,800. This tax break expired on 12/31/12 and payroll taxes reverted to the 6.2% level.

When this promise was made, then-Candidate Obama did not specify how long the "Making Work Pay" tax credit would remain in effect.

This promise was fulfilled.

TY-23

The Promise: "The child and dependent care credit is a nonrefundable tax credit available to individuals paying for child care needed so they can either work or look for work. Senator Obama's tax plan would make the credit refundable and increase the maximum rate from 35 to 50 percent."
When/Where: Interview with Tax Policy Center of Urban and Brookings Institutions dated 08/15/08.
Source: https://www.taxpolicycenter.org/sites/default/files/alfresco/publication-pdfs/411749-An-Updated-Analysis-of-the-Presidential-Candidates-Tax-Plans-Updated-September--.PDF
Status: Since its inception in CY1976, the Child and Dependent Case Tax Credit (CDCTC) has been a non-refundable tax credit designed to help defray the expenses of providing care for children under 13 years of age or disabled dependents as long as a parent or care-giver was working or looking for work.

Under the Economic Growth and Tax Relief Reconciliation Act (EGTRRA) of 2001, the CDCTC's top credit rate was set at 35%, boosted the maximum childcare expenses eligible for the credit to $3,000, $6,000 if a family had two or more children, and increased the threshold above which the credit rate declined from $10,000 to $15,000.

By end-CY2016, the CDCTC was still calculated by multiplying the amount of qualifying expenses (a maximum of $3,000 if the taxpayer had one qualifying individual, and up to $6,000 if the taxpayer had two or more qualifying individuals) by the appropriate credit rate. The credit rate depended on the taxpayer's Adjusted Gross Income (AGI), with a maximum credit rate still at 35% declining, as AGI increased, to 20% for taxpayers with an AGI above $43,000. Even though the credit formula (due to the higher credit rate) was more generous toward lower-income taxpayers, many lower-income taxpayers received little or no credit since the credit remained nonrefundable.

This promise was not fulfilled.

0.00

TY-24

The Promise: "Tax carried interest as ordinary income."
When/Where: Campaign Interview with Tax Policy Center of Urban and Brookings Institutions dated 08/15/08.
Source: https://www.taxpolicycenter.org/sites/default/files/alfresco/publication-pdfs/411749-An-Updated-Analysis-of-the-Presidential-Candidates-Tax-Plans-Updated-September--.PDF
Status: Carried interest is generally earned by those who manage partnership-structured funds, such as venture capital, private equity, hedge, real estate and infrastructure. Most carried interest is treated for tax purposes as a capital gain or a dividend (i.e. at a much lower rate than ordinary income tax rates).

0.00

Chapter 14 - Department of the Treasury

President Obama's FY10 budget submission (Table S-6) proposed to tax carried interest as ordinary income instead of at the lower capital gains rate. His FY2011 budget submission included similar language. This would have meant that carried interest would be taxed, at the time, at 35% (increased in CY2013 to 39.6%) instead of the capital gains rate of 15%, a 157% tax hike. Congress did not concur with this proposal, viewing it as a tax hike.

As of end-CY2016, no legislation had been passed to address this issue. Carried interest was not taxed as ordinary income during the Obama Administration.

This promise was not fulfilled.

TY-25 — **The Promise:** "Extend and index the temporary fix to the Alternative Minimum Tax that was passed in 2007."
When/Where: Campaign Interview with Tax Policy Center dated 09/12/08.
Source: https://www.politifact.com/truth-o-meter/promises/obameter/promise/40/extend-and-index-the-2007-alternative-minimum-tax-/
Status: Source is cited for confirmation of exact promise wording only, as it existed before original "When/Where" campaign document was deleted from archival websites.

Without annual "patches" to raise the Alternative Minimum Tax (AMT) income exemption consistent with inflation, the AMT exemption amounts would return to CY2000 levels -- $45,000 for joint filers and $33,750 for singles. This would result in the imposition of an AMT on a large percentage of the tax-paying population the AMT program was never intended to tax.

A feature of the AMT for qualified taxpayers is that it eliminates standard tax brackets.

An AMT patch was included in the American Recovery and Reinvestment Act (ARRA) of 2009. In late 12/10, the CY2010 levels were set at $74,450 for joint filers and $48,450 for singles through CY2011.

On 01/01/13, President Obama signed the "American Taxpayer Relief Act of 2012" (H.R. 8). This bill provided a permanent patch to the AMT at the $78,750 level for joint filers and $50,600 for single filers, to be indexed for inflation.

By end-CY2016, the AMT rate was 26% if income was $186,300 or less ($93,150 or less if married filing separately) and an AMT of 28% if income was more than $186,300.

This promise was fulfilled.

(1.00)

TY-26 — **The Promise:** "...calling for legislation that would allow withdrawals of 15% up to $10,000 from retirement accounts without penalty (although subject to the normal taxes). This would apply to withdrawals in 2008 (including retroactively) and 2009."
When/Where: Obama-Biden Plan: Penalty-free hardship withdrawals from IRAs and 401(k)s in 2008 and 2009, undated.
Source: https://webarchive.loc.gov/all/20090429185145/http://change.gov/agenda/economy_agenda/
Status: Penalty-free withdrawals from Individual Retirement Accounts (IRAs) and 401(k) accounts are permissible prior to the age of 59 1/2 for one or more of the following: (1) education purposes, (2) first-time home buyers (up to $10,000), (3) unreimbursed medical expenses less than or equal to or less than the expenses minus 7.9% of one's adjusted gross income, (4) if one is a military reservist called to active duty for at least 180 days, (5) health insurance premiums if unemployed for 12 weeks, (6) qualified as disabled by an insurance company or the Social Security Administration, and (7) victim of a natural disaster.

This promise was to apply to withdrawals in CY2008 and CY2009. That didn't happen.

(0.00)

As of end-CY2016, no legislation had been signed into law by President Obama that would allow withdrawals of 15% up to $10,000 from retirement accounts without penalty.

This promise was not fulfilled.

TY-27	**The Promise:** "...closing loopholes in the corporate tax deductibility of CEO pay." **When/Where:** Interview with Tax Policy Center of Urban and Brookings Institutions dated 08/15/08. **Source:** https://www.taxpolicycenter.org/sites/default/files/alfresco/publication-pdfs/411749-An-Updated-Analysis-of-the-Presidential-Candidates-Tax-Plans-Updated-September--.PDF **Status:** One of several loopholes affecting Chief Executive Officer (CEO) pay is that businesses can deduct CEO pay as a business expense up to $1M. Beyond that amount, CEO's can be paid with stock options or other performance-based pay that can be exempted from taxation. Despite numerous opportunities to address this promise during his two terms in office, President Obama elected not to challenge non-salary compensation for CEOs. This promise was not fulfilled.	0.00
TY-28	**The Promise:** "...will ensure that the IRS uses the information it already gets from banks and employers to give taxpayers the option of pre-filled tax forms to verify, sign and return." **When/Where:** Plan for America: "Blueprint for Change," dated 10/09/08 **Source:** https://www.documentcloud.org/ Obama and Biden's documents/550007-barack-obama-2008-blueprint-for-change.html **Status:** Representative Jim Cooper (TN-D) introduced the "Simple Return Act of 2010" (H.R. 5050) on 04/15/10 that would allow the Internal Revenue Service (IRS) to automatically fill out basic tax return (i.e. W-2, 1099) information for every American citizen, based on information it receives from employers and financial institutions. This bill expired with the 111th Congress but was reintroduced to the 112th Congress (H.R. 1069) on 03/14/11. No action beyond initial committee referral was taken on this bill by the 112th Congress and it expired at the end of CY2012. Under the above bill, use of the IRS-generated data and forms would have been optional. Approximately 40M Americans would have potentially benefited from this initiative. This promise was not fulfilled.	0.00
TY-29	**The Promise:** "Create a refundable tax credit equal to 10 percent of mortgage interest for nonitemizers, up to a maximum credit of $800" **When/Where:** Interview with Tax Policy Center of Urban and Brookings Institutions dated 08/15/08. **Source:** https://www.taxpolicycenter.org/sites/default/files/alfresco/publication-pdfs/411749-An-Updated-Analysis-of-the-Presidential-Candidates-Tax-Plans-Updated-September--.PDF **Status:** As of end-CY2016, tax reductions for payment of home mortage interest still required itemization on annual individual tax filings. This promise was not fulfilled.	0.00
TY-30	**The Promise:** "Obama believes that one strong option is increasing the maximum amount of earnings covered by Social Security by lifting the payroll tax cap on earnings above $250,000." **When/Where:** Obama-Biden Plan: "Helping America's Seniors" dated 08/13/08. **Source:** https://www.politifact.com/truth-o-meter/promises/obameter/promise/44/lift-the-payroll-tax-cap-on-earnings-above-25000/ **Status:** Source is cited for confirmation of exact promise wording only, as it existed before original "When/Where" campaign document was deleted from archival websites. The wage base for Social Security taxes for CY2009 was $106,800, unchanged for CY2010 and CY2011. By end-CY2016, the wage base had increased to $118,500, unchanged from CY2015.	0.00

Chapter 14 - Department of the Treasury

Senator Bernard Sanders (I-VT) introduced the "Keeping Our Social Security Promises Act" (S. 1558) on 09/14/11 to apply payroll taxes "to remuneration in excess of $250,000," as does the "Act for the 99%" (H.R. 3638) introduced by Congressman Raul Grijalva (D-AZ) on 12/13/11. Both bills expired with the 112th Congress at the end of CY2012.

During President Obama's two terms in office, there was no lifting of payroll tax caps on earnings above $250,000, which would have left a "doughnut hole" for those earning between $118,500 and $250,000.

This promise was not fulfilled.

TY-31

The Promise: "Through the Exchange, any American will have the opportunity to enroll in the new public plan or an approved private plan, and income-based sliding scale tax credits will be provided for people and families who need it."
When/Where: Obama-Biden Plan: "To Lower Health Care Costs and Ensure Affordable, Accessible Health Coverage for All" dated 10/03/08.
Source: http://courses.ischool.berkeley.edu/i202/f08/lectures/Obama_Healthcare-1.pdf
Status: The Patient Protection and Affordable Care Act (ACA) (Public Law 111-148) signed into law by President Obama on 03/23/10, addressed sliding scale tax credits for individuals and families whose earnings were between 133% and 400% of the poverty level.

For CY2012, the poverty level was defined as $11,170 for an individual and $27,010 for a family of five in the contiguous States and D.C. These rates were $13,970 and $12,860 for an individual in Alaska and Hawaii respectively, and $33,770 and $31,060 for a family of five in Alaska and Hawaii respectively.

This promise was fulfilled.

1.00

TY-32

The Promise: "...will support the Artist-Museum Partnership Act, introduced by Sen. Patrick Leahy, D-Vt. The Act amends the Internal Revenue Code to allow artists to deduct the fair market value of their work, rather than just the costs of the materials, when they make charitable contributions"
When/Where: Obama-Biden Plan: "Champions for Arts and Culture", dated 09/11/08.
Source: http://muzartworld.org/president-barack-obama-and-joe-biden-champions-for-arts-and-culture/
Status: Under current law, artists who donate self-created works are only able to deduct the cost of supplies such as canvas, pen, paper and ink, not their true value. Prior to CY1969, artists were able to take a deduction equivalent to the fair market value of a work, but Congress changed the law with respect to artists in the Tax Reform Act of 1969.

To address this situation, Senator Patrick Leahy (D-VT) introduced the Artist-Museum Partnership Act (S-548) on 02/12/07 during the 110th Congress. This bill did not get beyond the Senate Committee on Finance and died at the end of CY2008 with the 110th Congress.

Congressman John Lewis (D-GA) introduced a similar bill (H.R. 1126) to the 111th Congress on 02/23/09. His version of this bill was referred to the House Committee on Ways and Means the same date and no further action was taken toward its passage by the time the 111th Congress expired at the end of CY2010.

Congressman Lewis introduced a new bill, the Artist-Museum Partnership Act of 2011 (H.R. 1190) on 03/17/11. On the Senate side, Senator Charles Schumer (D-NY) introduced the "Art and Collectibles Capital Gains Tax Treatment Parity Act" (S. 930) on 05/10/11. Both of these bills proposed to provide a tax deduction equal to fair market value for charitable contributions of literary, musical, artistic, or scholarly compositions created by the donor. Neither bill progressed beyond preliminary committees to which they were submitted before they expired with the 112th Congress at the end of CY2012.

0.00

TY-33

The Promise: "...we'll give consumers a $7,000 tax credit to buy these vehicles."
When/Where: Obama Campaign Speech, Lansing, MI, dated 08/04/08, as reported in the New York Times with credit to CQ Transcriptions, Inc.
Source: http://www.nytimes.com/2008/08/04/us/politics/04text-obama.html?pagewanted=all
Status: This promise pertains to then-Candidate Obama's promise to "...get one million 150 mile-per-gallon plug-in hybrids on our roads within six years..." (Promise EN-10 refers).

The American Recovery and Reinvestment Act of 2009 of 02/17/09 provided tax credits of up to $7,500 for those who purchased Plug-in Hybrid Electric Vehicles (PHEV). This tax credit expired after a PHEV manufacturer sold 200,000 qualified vehicles. As of end-CY2016, no plug-in hybrid vehicles met the 150 mpg criteria.

This promise was fulfilled.

Grade: 1.00

INTERNATIONAL PROGRAMS — GRADE

TY-34

The Promise: "...creating an international tax haven watch list of countries that do not share information returns with the United States (and potentially enacting sanctions against those countries)..."
When/Where: Interview with Tax Policy Center of Urban and Brookings Institutions dated 08/15/08.
Source: https://www.taxpolicycenter.org/sites/default/files/alfresco/publication-pdfs/411749-An-Updated-Analysis-of-the-Presidential-Candidates-Tax-Plans-Updated-September--.PDF
Status: The G-20 meeting of 04/03/09 led the United Nations Organization for Economic Cooperation and Development (OECD) to publish its most recent report on countries that agreed to exchange tax information. This initiative was not new -- the OECD tax haven monitoring initiative has existed since the G20 Finance Ministers meeting held in Berlin in CY2004.

The OECD report included a listing of countries that exchange such information, countries that agreed to exchange tax information but had not yet implemented the process, and countries that had not committed to share tax information such as Malaysia, Philippines, Costa Rica and Uruguay.

What is still missing is a U.S. international tax haven watch list, which would come under the purview of the Department of the Treasury and the Securities and Exchange Commission. Reference to such a list is made in the country-by-country reporting requirements contained in the "Stop Tax Haven Abuse Act" (S. 1346) introduced by Senator Carl Levin (D-MI) on 07/12/11, and H.R. 2669 by the same name introduced by Congressman Lloyd Doggett (D-TX) on 07/27/11. No action was taken on either of these bills and they expired with the 112th Congress at the end of CY2012, as did the reintroduction of this act during the 113th and 114th congresses -- they also failed.

Further, no action was taken on the "Cut Unjustified Tax Loopholes Act" (S. 2075) introduced by Senator Levin on 02/07/12 which also had country-by-country tax haven listing requirements. It too died with the 112th Congress. A subsequent introduction of the same act during the 113th Congress also failed.

This promise was not fulfilled.

Grade: 0.00

TY-35

The Promise: "...want to see 100 percent debt cancellation for the world's heavily-indebted poor countries. They are committed to living up to the promise to fully fund debt cancellation for Heavily-Indebted Poor Countries (HIPC)."
When/Where: Obama-Biden Plan: "Strengthening Our Common Security by Investing in Our Common Humanity", dated 09/11/08.
Source: https://www.cgdev.org/doc/blog/obama_strengthen_security.pdf
Status: 100% debt cancellation for HIPC-eligible countries is a multi-decade untaking involving not

Grade: 0.00

Chapter 14 - Department of the Treasury

less than 25 donor countries plus the European Union and several multilateral donor organizations.

At the 07/05 G-8 Summit in Gleneagles, Scotland (pre-dating this promise), G-8 leaders pledged to cancel the debts of the world's most indebted countries, many of them located in Africa. Following this declaration, the Board of Governors of both the International Monetary Fund (IMF) and World Bank endorsed the principles of the 100% debt cancellation deal, formally called the Multilateral Debt Relief Initiative (MDRI), in 09/05. The MDRI provides 100% debt cancellation on eligible multilateral debts to countries that have completed the Highly Indebted Poor Country (HIPC) Initiative process.

There are two major milestones that must be reached before an HIPC country's debt can be cancelled:

--Decision Point: when a country is considered to be eligible for HIPC initiative assistance by (1) having a track record of macroeconomic stability, (2) having prepared an Interim Poverty Reduction Strategy Paper (PRSP), and (3) having cleared any outstanding arrears. As of end-CY2010, Chad, Comoros, Cote d'Ivoire, and Guinea had reached the Decision Point and were between that point and the Completion Point.

-- Completion Point: a country can receive full reduction in debt available under the HIPC initiative and the Multilateral Debt Relief Initiative (MDRI) by (1) maintaining macroeconomic stability under an International Monetary Fund (IMF) Poverty Reduction and Growth Facility (PGRF) supported program, (2) carrying out key structural and social reforms as agreed upon at the Decision Point, and (3) implementing the provisions of their PRSP satisfactorily for one year.

In FY2010, the estimated amount of eligible country debt was approximately $75B. The U.S. appropriated amount for the HIPC Trust Fund was $56M, far below the $90.63M Administration request. An amount of $20M was diverted to allow developing countries to redirect funds from debt payments to forest conservation programs under the Tropical Forest Conservation Act (TFCA).

For FY2011, the Treasury Department requested $1.235B for the second of three installments of $1.235B plus $50M to clear a portion of U.S. pledge arrears for a total of $1.285B payable to the IDA, representing 20.12% of pledges made to the MDRI by the donor community. Only $1.235B was appropriated by Congress under State Department funding.

Also for FY2011, the estimated amount of eligible country debt was approximately $72B. The Administration's budget proposal for the HIPC Trust Fund was $50M (with another $20M going toward forest conservation under the TFCA). Treasury Department documentation indicates that this $50M in FY2011 was "to be used to make a substantial contribution towards meeting the $75.4M in pledges to the HIPC Trust Fund that have not yet been fulfilled," thereby acknowledging that the U.S. was in arrears in honoring its HIPC Trust Fund pledges.

For the African Development Fund (AfDF) in FY2011, the Treasury Department requested $155.9M to cover the third of three installments. Congress appropriated only $110M under State Department funding.

On 12/16/09, Congresswoman Maxine Waters (D-CA) reintroduced H.R. 2634 (110th Congress) as the "Jubilee Act for Responsible Lending and Expanded Debt Cancellation of 2009" (H.R. 4405) for "expanded cancellation of debts owed to the United States and the international financial institutions by low-income countries." This bill did not progress beyond initial committee review and expired with the 111th Congress at the end of CY2010. It was not renewed during the 112th and subsequent congresses.

As of end-CY2016, 36 of 39 eligible countries had reached the Completion Point and received debt relief under both the HIPC Initiative and MDRI. MDRI contributions are made through the

International Development Association (IDA) and the AfDF). Three countries remained potentially eligible for debt relief as of end-CY2016: Eritrea, Somalia and Sudan.

In view of the extreme national debt and budget deficit the U.S. experienced since CY2008 and later years, full funding of the HIPC Trust Fund did not occur during President Obama's two terms in office.

This promise was not fulfilled.

	REGULATORY REFORM	GRADE
TY-36	**The Promise:** "...a critical step in restoring fiscal discipline is enforcing pay-as-you-go (PAYGO) budgeting rules which require new spending commitments or tax changes to be paid for by cuts to other programs or new revenue." **When/Where:** Obama-Biden Plan for America "Blueprint for Change" dated 10/09/08. **Source:** https://www.documentcloud.org/documents/550007-barack-obama-2008-blueprint-for-change.html **Status:** Without fanfare, President Obama signed the Statutory Pay-As-You-Go Act of 2010 into law on 02/12/10. The basic premise of PAYGO was that any new spending or tax relief was to be offset through reductions in spending elsewhere or increase in other taxes in order to hold the national deficit at bay. The law also raised the government's debt ceiling from $12.4T to $14.3T. Since signing the PAYGO bill, new spending measures such as the American Protection and Affordable Care Act of 2010 signed into law on 03/23/10 (and its counterpart Health Care and Education Reconciliation Act of 2010, signed into law by President Obama on 03/30/10) were not offset by "reductions in spending elsewhere". Under the Tax Relief, Unemployment Reauthorization, and Job Creation Act of 2010 (H.R. 4853) signed into law by President Obama on 12/17/10, there are no PAYGO provisions for tax cut extensions for those earning more than $250K ($200K for single tax filers). So, the typical American taxpayer considered that PAYGO, as codified by President Obama in CY2010, was ineffective as a means to balance new government spending with comparable cuts elsewhere. Another method to arrive at the stated goal would have been via a balanced budget amendment to the U.S. Constitution, a move advocated by the majority of Congressional Republicans. On 11/25/11, the Republican-led House failed to obtain the 290 votes needed for a balanced budget amendment, obtaining only 261 such votes. This initiative expired with the 112th Congress at the end of CY2012. The Congress was largely ineffective in its application of PAYGO law provisions when they passed spending bills for the remainder of President Obama's two terms in office. This promise was not fulfilled.	0.00
TY-37	**The Promise:** "I'll put in place the common-sense regulations and rules of the road...rules that will keep our market free, fair, and honest; rules that will restore accountability and responsibility in our corporate boardrooms." **When/Where:** Campaign Speech, Saint Louis, MO, 10/18/08. **Source:** http://www.presidency.ucsb.edu/ws/index.php?pid=84570 **Status:** Department of Treasury document "Financial Regulatory Reform: A New Foundation" was released on 06/17/09. That document provided the framework for future legislation to (1) promote robust supervision and regulation of financial firms; (2) establish comprehensive supervision of financial markets; (3) protect consumers and investors from financial abuse; (4) provide the government with the tools it needs to manage financial crises; and (5) raise international regulatory standards and improve international cooperation.	1.00

Chapter 14 - Department of the Treasury

President Obama signed the Dodd-Frank Wall Street Reform and Consumer Protection Act (H.R. 4173) into law on 07/21/10. This law reshaped oversight of the U.S. financial industry, included the creation of a new consumer protection agency, set new limits on banks using capital for trading and investing in hedge funds, and gave the government power to close down troubled financial firms.

Under H.R. 4173, the Consumer Financial Protection Bureau (CFPB) was set up by former Harvard contract law, bankruptcy and commercial law professor Elizabeth Warren, appointed on 09/17/10 as "Consumer Czar" for President Obama and Special Advisor to the Treasury Secretary.

After it opened on 07/21/11, President Obama nominated Ohio Attorney General Richard Cordray to head the CFPB. Mr. Cordray's confirmation was blocked by at least 44 Republican senators who believed that a single director would have too much unaccountable, unchecked power and authority to set his/her own budget and agenda. The Republican senators preferred that the CFPB be headed by a board or commission.

President Obama went against the will of Congress by appointing Mr. Cordray to head the CFPB on 01/04/12, without Senate confirmation, while the Congress was technically and constitutionally in "pro forma" session. The Senate often holds pro forma sessions specifically to prevent the President from making recess appointments to fill vacancies in federal offices that require the approval of the Senate. The Senate eventually confirmed Mr. Cordray's appointment on 07/16/13 for a five-year term.

Since its inception in CY2011 through end-CY2016, the CFPB was credited with (1) collecting over $11.8B from credit card companies, bank and mortgage companies for abusive practices; (2) creating a user-friendly website for consumer complaints; (3) making information on mortgages, student and auto loans more accessible and understandable; and (4) collecting $589M to be paid in civil penalties as a result of CFPB enforcement work.

On 10/11/16, the Court of Appeals for the District of Columbia ruled that the structure of the CFPB was unconstitutional because its director (Mr. Cordray) was only loosely accountable to President Obama and could only be removed from his position for cause. The court directed an amendment to the Dodd-Frank Wall Street Reform and Consumer Protection Act so that a president could remove the CFPB Director at will. Predictably, the CFPB disagreed with that ruling and elevated the matter to the Supreme Court. As of end-CY2016, the Supreme Court had not heard this case.

This promise was fulfilled.

TY-38	**The Promise:** "...will maintain fiscal responsibility and prevent any increase in the deficit by offsetting cuts and revenue sources in other parts of the government..." **When/Where:** Obama-Biden Plan: "Helping All Americans Serve Their Country" dated 09/11/08. **Source:** http://i2.cdn.turner.com/cnn/2008/images/07/02/national.service.fact.sheet.final.pdf **Status:** Under President Obama, the Office of Management and Budget (OMB) forecasted on 08/22/12 that the U.S. budget deficit would be $1.3B for FY2012, the same as for FY2011, and equal to 7.3% of the nation's Gross Domestic Product (GDP).	0.00

Pessimistic about the ability of Congress and the White House to reduce the nation's federal budget deficit, Standard and Poor's reduced the U.S. credit rating from AAA to AA+ on 08/05/11 -- the first credit rating downgrade in the nation's history.

A bipartisan supercommittee (Joint Committee on Deficit Reduction (aka "Simpson-Bowles Commission") was formed under the Budget Control Act of 2011 signed into law on 08/02/11. Although this Act increased the national debt ceiling to $16.4T, the supercommittee was mandated to identify $1.2T over ten years in federal spending cuts by 11/23/11. If the supercommittee failed to agree on these spending cuts, cuts to national defense in the amount of $600B and another $600B

Chapter 14 - Department of the Treasury

from other agencies would be automatic.

On 11/09/11, Republicans on the supercommittee offered a $1.2T package that included new taxes in the amount of $300B in return for maintaining lower tax rates that originated during the Bush presidency. The supercommittee Democrats rejected this package, claiming that the rich would gain a tax windfall and the middle and poor classes would suffer under the Republican plan.

The supercommittee announced failure to meet the dictates of its mandate on 11/21/11. President Obama promised on the same date to veto any legislation designed to prevent the above automatic cuts, to take effect in CY2013. At the same time, he indicated that he would ignore most of the supercommittee's recommendations.

On 02/13/12, President Obama presented his $3.8T spending plan. Interpretation of this 10-year plan reveals that annual deficits will exceed $6.7T over the next decade despite an estimated $4T in deficit reduction initiatives. At the same time, the national debt held by foreign investors was projected to grow to $18.7T by FY2021, equivalent to 76.5% of the U.S. national economy.

As of 09/03/12, the national debt which was increased by President Obama by $5.4T since he took office in CY2009, breached the $16T level.

The promise to "maintain fiscal responsibility and prevent any increase in the deficit" was not fulfilled. Nor was it apparent to the average American taxpayer that President Obama was committed to reducing/eliminating the deficit other than his repeated insistence that the solution laid primarily in the raising of taxes on the so-called 1% "rich" folks.

This promise was not fulfilled.

TY-39

The Promise: "...will protect workers who fall into bankruptcy as a result of a medical crisis...will create an exemption from the new law's requirement that middle class families extend their debts rather than have them forgiven."
When/Where: Obama-Biden Plan: "Supporting Urban Prosperity," dated 09/11/08.
Source: https://assets.documentcloud.org/documents/550008/barack-obama-2008-supporting-urban-prosperity.pdf
Status: Prior to the Patient Protection and Affordable Care Act (ACA) (Public Law 111-148), signed into law by President Obama on 03/23/10, anywhere from 800K to 1M workers fell into bankruptcy annually due to a combination of loss of job and high medical costs. By some accounts, that number fell to about 643K Americans in CY2013 by their declaring bankruptcy due to medical bills. That reduction was attributed in part to insurance obtained by workers as mandated by the ACA.

Nonetheless, by end-CY2016, no exemption had been created to forgive debts that led to bankruptcy as a result of medical crises.

This promise was not fulfilled.

0.00

TY-40

The Promise: "...believes that we need to ensure that all Americans have access to clear and simplified information about loan fees, payments, and penalties...he'll require lenders to provide this information during the loan application process..."
When/Where: Obama-Biden Plan: "Supporting Urban Prosperity," dated 09/11/08.
Source: https://assets.documentcloud.org/documents/550008/barack-obama-2008-supporting-urban-prosperity.pdf
Status: The Dodd-Frank Wall Street Reform and Consumer Protection Act (H.R. 4173) signed into law by President Obama on 07/21/10 offered expanded mortgage loan terms protection to the home buyer, but did not provide simplified application protections for the types of loans reflected in this promise, which was focused on predatory payday loans.

0.00

Chapter 14 - Department of the Treasury

The Payday Loan Reform Act of 2009 (H.R. 1214) was introduced by Congressman Luis Gutierrez (D-IL) on 02/26/09. This bill would have responded to the basic tenets of this promise but was not enacted and expired with the 111th Congress at the end of CY2010.

While the Consumer Financial Protection Board (CFPB) was known to be working on rules to provide clear and simplified protections for borrowers seeking loans such as payday loans, no rules to that effect were known to have been published by end-CY2016.

This promise was not fulfilled.

TY-41

The Promise: "...will work with his Secretary of Treasury and the Federal Deposit Insurance Corporation to encourage banks, credit unions, and Community Development Financial Institutions to provide affordable short-term and small dollar loans -- and to drive the sharks out of business."
When/Where: Obama-Biden Plan: "Supporting Urban Prosperity," dated 09/11/08.
Source: https://assets.documentcloud.org/documents/550008/barack-obama-2008-supporting-urban-prosperity.pdf
Status: This specific issue (short-term/small dollar loans) was not addressed in the "Dodd-Frank Wall Street Reform and Consumer Protection Act" (H.R. 4173) signed into law by President Obama on 07/21/10. That law addresses only predatory practices related to mortgage loans.

The Consumer Financial Protection Bureau (CFPB) estimates that interest rates charged by payday loan sharks can reach from 300% to as high as 521% for loans made to the underserved. "Underserved" refers to those without checking or savings accounts with an insured depository institution or have such accounts but cannot secure personal loans for whatever reason.

On 03/26/15, President Obama and the CFPB introduced proposed rules intended to require lenders to ensure that borrowers have access to adequate resources to repay their short-term/small dollar loans such as payday loans, vehicle title loans, deposit advances and other loans. By end-CY2016, the proposed CFPB rules had not been published.

This promise was not fulfilled.

Grade: 0.00

SPECIAL FUNDS — GRADE

TY-42

The Promise: "Obama and Biden will create an Advanced Manufacturing Fund to identify and invest in the most compelling advanced manufacturing strategies."
When/Where: Plan for America: "Blueprint for Change," dated 10/09/08
Source: https://www.documentcloud.org/ Obama and Biden's documents/550007-barack-obama-2008-blueprint-for-change.html
Status: On 06/24/11, President Obama announced the creation of an Advanced Manufacturing Partnership between government, industry and academic entities to fund new technology initiatives. This partnership was funded initially at the $500M level.

On 03/09/12, President Obama announced the creation of a new $1B National Network for Manufacturing Innovation, to be started with a $45M federal investment in a pilot institute for "Additive Manufacturing," an initiative that was to receive matching funds from industry and participating states.

The Obama-Biden plan called for the creation of a very specific "Advanced Manufacturing Fund." Despite the nonexistence of such a specific fund as of end-CY2016, points were granted for the new initiatives reflected above.

This promise was fulfilled.

Grade: 1.00

TY-43

The Promise: "...will also direct revenues from offshore oil and gas drilling to increased coastal hurricane protection."
When/Where: Obama-Biden Plan: "Rebuilding the Gulf Coast and Preventing Future Catastrophes",

Grade: 0.00

dated 09/11/08.

Source: https://assets.documentcloud.org/documents/550006/barack-obama-2008-rebuilding-the-gulf-coast-and.pdf

Status: As of CY2012, coastal states were in line to receive direct revenues from offshore oil and gas drilling for hurricane protection -- but not until the CY2016-CY2017 timeframe.

A key factor that drove this promise was the declining ability to reverse coastal erosion in Louisiana's wetlands.

To mitigate the above, Congressman Anh Cao (D-LA) introduced H.R. 5267 on 05/11/10 to amend the Gulf of Mexico Energy Security Act of 2006 to accelerate the increase in the amount of Gulf of Mexico oil and gas lease revenues paid to Gulf states. This bill expired with the 111th Congress at the end of CY2010.

The above bill was replaced in the 112th Congress by the "Strengthening Our Share (S.O.S.) Act" (H.R. 1759) introduced by Congressman Jo Bonner (D-AL) on 05/05/11. No action was taken on this bill beyond initial committee review and it expired with the 112th Congress at the end of CY2012.

The "Offshore energy and Jobs Act of 2015" (S. 1276) was introduced by Senator Bill Cassidy (R-LA) on 05/11/15. This proposed law would have lifted the ban on drilling in the Eastern Gulf and would have increased revenue sharing caps for states along the Gulf Coast. This bill expired with the 114th Congress without being enacted.

Contrary to the basic tenets of this promise, President Obama's FY2016 budget proposal sought to eliminate the allocation of revenues from offshore oil/gas drilling operations to coastal hurricane protection. Instead, he proposed that those revenues be realigned to support national conservation efforts.

This promise was not fulfilled.

TY-44

The Promise: "...will work closely with the state to distribute critical infrastructure dollars...will ensure that no unnecessary red-tape or burdensome regulations are holding up state and local plans, while retaining the need for public accountability."

When/Where: Obama-Biden Plan: "Rebuilding the Gulf Coast and Preventing Future Catastrophes", dated 09/11/08.

Source: https://assets.documentcloud.org/documents/550006/barack-obama-2008-rebuilding-the-gulf-coast-and.pdf

Status: In view of the urgency surrounding the need for more liberal interpretations of Federal Emergency Management Agency (FEMA) rules regarding the disbursement of funds to areas affected by Hurricane Katrina, some red tape was removed as a result of interventions by dispute resolution teams. Key to this effort was the 08/06/09 implementation of an arbitration panel process announced by Homeland Security Secretary Janet Napolitano.

1.00

The arbitration panels were instrumental in resolving disputes and red tape for public assistance projects valued at more than $500K. These projects included road reconstruction and pothole repair, cleaning of drainage catch basins and drain lines, replacement of traffic and street name signs, streetlight repairs, sewer overflow and water supply repairs including drainage millage renewal and hydrant/valve repairs, and power generation system repairs, to name but a few.

By end-CY2016, the cumulative federal share of funding for public works projects for Louisiana was $11.7B, for Mississippi $3.1B, for Alabama $116.8M and for Florida $192.8M.

This promise was fulfilled.

TY-45 | **The Promise:** "...will also strengthen Community Development Financial Institutions (CDFIs), which | 1.00

Chapter 14 - Department of the Treasury

are engaged in innovative methods to provide capital to urban businesses."
When/Where: Obama-Biden Plan: "Supporting Urban Prosperity," dated 09/11/08.
Source: https://assets.documentcloud.org/documents/550008/barack-obama-2008-supporting-urban-prosperity.pdf
Status: Not counting a $100M plus-up under the American Recovery and Reinvestment Act (ARRA) of 2009, the CDFI Fund was appropriated $107M in FY2009, up from $94M in FY2008.

Under President Obama, the CDFI Fund was more than doubled starting in FY2010 as follows:
FY2010....$246.7M
FY2011....$227.0M
FY2012....$221.0M
FY2013....$221.0M (Continuing Resolution)
FY2014....$226.0M
FY2015....$230.5M
FY2016....$233.5M
FY2017....$248.0M

This promise was fulfilled.

TREASURY GPA | 0.36

Chapter 15 - Department of Veterans Affairs

Campaign Promises
Departments -> Veterans Affairs

ITEM	VETERANS AFFAIRS	
	GENERAL	**GRADE**
VA-1	**The Promise:** "...will fully fund the VA so it has all the resources it needs to serve the veterans who need it, when they need it, when they need it." **When/Where:** Plan for America: "Blueprint for Change," dated 10/09/08 **Source:** https://www.documentcloud.org/ Obama and Biden's documents/550007-barack-obama-2008-blueprint-for-change.html **Status:** The final enacted FY2010 appropriation for the Department of Veterans Affairs (VA) was $127.2B, $29.5B above the $97.7B appropriation for FY2009. The FY2010 appropriation included $71.3B for mandatory VA benefits programs, $53.1B for discretionary funding purposes, and $2.8B for the Medical Care Collections Fund (MCCF). For the first time, the VA's FY2010 appropriation included an advance appropriation to ensure uninterrupted funding for medical care for veterans for FY2011. The final FY2011 enacted budget for the VA was $125.5B, a slight decrease from FY2010. VA funding for the remainder of President Obama's two terms in office was as follows: FY2012 - $126.8B FY2013 - $139.1B FY2014 - $168.9B FY2015 - $163.5B FY2016 - $163.5B FY2017 - $182.1B This promise was fulfilled.	1.00
VA-2	**The Promise:** "...will also push to quickly build a new, state-of-the-art Department of Veterans Affairs hospital in New Orleans so that the city's veterans can get top-quality care." **When/Where:** Obama-Biden Plan: "Rebuilding the Gulf Coast and Preventing Future Catastrophes", dated 09/11/08. **Source:** https://assets.documentcloud.org/documents/550006/barack-obama-2008-rebuilding-the-gulf-coast-and.pdf **Status:** Ground was broken on 06/25/10 for a new VA medical complex to be built in New Orleans -- an $800M facility scheduled to open in early-CY2014, 10 years after the Hurricane Katrina severely damaged the VA hospital that existed in the downtown medical district. Construction issues delayed completion of the facility until 11/18/16 and caused cost increases to about $1B. The 31-acre complex contains 1.7 million square feet, 300 outpatient exam rooms, 200 hospital rooms, 20 intervention/surgery rooms, an emergency department, a research facility, rehabilitation services and a mental health division. The hospital employs 2,800 people able to handle 500K outpatient visits annually while serving over 70K veterans in the New Orleans area. This promise was fulfilled.	1.00

Chapter 15 - Department of Veterans Affairs

	HEALTH CARE	GRADE
VA-3	**The Promise:** "Obama will expand "Vet Centers in rural areas so that veterans and their families can get the care they need where they live." **When/Where:** Obama-Biden Plan: "Fulfilling a Sacred Trust With Our Veterans", dated 09/09/08. **Source:** https://s3.amazonaws.com/s3.documentcloud.org/documents/550009/barack-obama-2008-fulfilling-a-sacred-trust-with.pdf **Status:** The Veterans Health Care Budget Reform and Transparency Act signed into law on 10/22/09 included funds for investing in mobile clinics to reach veterans in rural areas. Further, the FY2010 appropriation for the Department of Veterans Affairs (VA) included $250M to continue rural health initiatives and an additional $30M to increase the number of Community Based Outpatient Clinics in rural areas, benefitting approximately 41% of eligible veterans. President Obama's FY2012 budget proposal included an additional $250M to improve access to care in rural and highly isolated areas by veterans and their families. His FY2013 proposal included continuation of the $250M historical funding level to "improve access and quality of care for enrolled veterans residing in rural areas." This promise was fulfilled.	1.00
VA-4	**The Promise:** "...requiring individual, face-to-face post-deployment mental health screenings." **When/Where:** Obama-Biden Plan: "Fulfilling a Sacred Trust With Our Veterans", dated 09/09/08. **Source:** https://s3.amazonaws.com/s3.documentcloud.org/documents/550009/barack-obama-2008-fulfilling-a-sacred-trust-with.pdf **Status:** Face-to-face screenings, designed to help members of the armed forces deal better with stress, also make it easier for them to seek substance abuse treatment, obtain marriage/family counseling, and help prevent suicides. The National Defense Authorization Act for Fiscal Year 2010 (H.R. 2647) signed into law by President Obama on 10/28/09 was successfully amended to provide "person-to-person mental health assessment for each member of the Armed Forces who is deployed in connection with a contingency operation...At a time during the period beginning 90 days after the date of redeployment from the contingency operation and ending 180 days after the date of redeployment..." On 12/19/14, President Obama signed into law the Carl Levin and Howard P. 'Buck' McKeon National Defense Authorization Act for Fiscal Year 2015 (H.R. 3979). This Department of Defense (DoD) bill authorized $30.7B for the defense health program and codified the requirement for annual one-on-one, face-to-face mental health checkups for active duty and Selected Reserve troops, as well as in-person mental health screenings every 180 days during deployment. Under this legislation, the DoD must also provide periodic in-person mental health assessments reports to Congress. This promise was fulfilled.	1.00
VA-5	**The Promise:** "...will establish standards of care for TBI treatment, require pre- and post-deployment screenings and improve case management so that servicemembers get the best possible care." **When/Where:** Obama-Biden Plan: "Fulfilling a Sacred Trust With Our Veterans", dated 09/09/08. **Source:** https://s3.amazonaws.com/s3.documentcloud.org/documents/550009/barack-obama-2008-fulfilling-a-sacred-trust-with.pdf **Status:** According to Pentagon statistics as reported in Congressional Research Service Report RS22452 of 08/07/15, more than 325K troops had been diagnosed with some form of Traumatic Brain Injury during the period CY2000 to mid-CY2015. On 03/08/10, the VA issued Directive 2010-012 that set the standards for the screening and evaluation of possible TBI in Operation Enduring Freedom (OEF) and Operation Iraqi Freedom (OIF) Veterans. This was an initial effort to satisfy the post-deployment screening aspects of this promise.	1.00

Chapter 15 - Department of Veterans Affairs

The Defense Centers for Excellence (DCoE) for Psychological Health and Traumatic Brain Injury has the mission to "develop state of the science clinical standards to maximize recovery and functioning and to provide guidance and support in the implementation of clinical tools for the benefit of all those who sustain traumatic brain injuries in the service of our country." The DCoE operates a 24/7 Outreach Center that provides a source of information to everyone (not only wounded warriors) on psychological health and TBI issues and resources and partners with the VA and a national network of military and civilian agencies, community leaders, advocacy groups, clinical experts, and academic institutions to establish best practices and quality standards for the treatment of TBI. The DCoE's work is carried out across these major areas: clinical care; education and training; prevention; research and patient, family and community outreach.

The Veterans Health Administration has a Polytrauma System of Care to treat and care for Veterans with TBI alone or in combination with other injuries and health conditions.

In its CY2013 report entitled "Returning Home from Iraq and Afghanistan: Preliminary Assessment of Readjustment Needs of Veterans, Service Members, and Their Families", the Committee on the Assessment of the Readjustment Needs of Military Personnel, Veterans, and Their Families of the National Academies of Sciences, Engineering and Medicine continues to stress that its extensive research into TBI treatment is stymied by the apparent non-availability of DoD/VA standards. Through end-CY2016, independent verification of the existence of standards was inhibited by the non-accessibility to DVBIC and DCoE websites by the general public.

The availability of pre- and post-deployment screenings, coupled with improved case management practices indicates that progress was made on the establishment of standards by end-CY2016.

This promise was fulfilled.

VA-6

The Promise: "As the nation's largest integrated health system, the Veterans Health Administration has already been a national leader in reform, particularly with electronic health records and prevention initiatives...will continue this trend to make the VA a leader of national health care reform so that veterans get the best care possible. This includes efforts to improve electronic records interoperability, expand effectiveness research, promote wellness programs, and instill more accountability for performance and quality improvement initiatives."

When/Where: Obama-Biden Plan: "Fulfilling a Sacred Trust With Our Veterans", dated 09/09/08.

Source: https://s3.amazonaws.com/s3.documentcloud.org/documents/550009/barack-obama-2008-fulfilling-a-sacred-trust-with.pdf

Status: On 04/09/09, President Obama announced the creation of a Joint Virtual Lifetime Electronic Record (VLER) to improve care and services to transitioning veterans by facilitating the flow of medical records between the Department of Defense (DoD) and the Department of Veterans Affairs (VA). Once fully developed, VLER will include both administrative and medical information from the day a new recruit enters military service, throughout that servicemember's career, and after that servicemember retires or separates from active or reserve duty.

A proof of concept VLER prototype and production pilot was executed in the San Diego area during CY2009. On 01/30/10, the DoD and VA joined the Nationwide Health Information Network (NHIN). They announced on 03/08/10 that they had progressed to testing capabilities to complete data integration implementation, and were building adaptors to communicate through the NHIN with each other and with private providers.

As of end-CY2016, even private clinics and health facilities, using the Veterans Health Information Exchange (VHIE), had been able to exchange electronic patient records with the VA through the VLER Program, enabling access to patient records of active and retired military personnel who receive care at VA health care facilities.

This promise was fulfilled.

1.00

Chapter 15 - Department of Veterans Affairs

VA-7	**The Promise:** "...increasing the VA budget to recruit and retain more mental health professionals..." **When/Where:** Obama-Biden Plan: "Fulfilling a Sacred Trust With Our Veterans", dated 09/09/08. **Source:** https://s3.amazonaws.com/s3.documentcloud.org/documents/550009/barack-obama-2008-fulfilling-a-sacred-trust-with.pdf **Status:** The Department of Veterans Affairs (VA) FY2010 appropriation included an increase of $300M over the FY2009 appropriation of $4.3B for "programs addressing the wounded, ill and injured, traumatic brain injury, and psychological health." This includes "$1 million to provide education debt relief as a hiring incentive for mental health professionals." The DoD budget for FY2010 included $800M for improving the hiring and retention of psychiatrists and mental health professionals. For FY2011, the President's budget proposal for the Department of Defense included $669M "to provide care for traumatic brain injury and psychological health" and $250M "for continued support of mental health and traumatic brain injury research". Also in the VA FY2011 budget proposal, the President proposed to invest $5.2B in "specialized care" for post-traumatic stress, traumatic brain injury and other mental health conditions. This number went up to $5.8B in FY2012 and $6.2B in FY2013. The VA's budget steadily increased each year of President Obama's two terms in office, with total funding during his second term as follows: FY2014 - $147.9B, FY2015 - $158.6B, FY2016 - $162.6B, FY2017 - $176.9B. These funding increases permitted the increased hiring of mental health professionals. This promise was fulfilled.	1.00
VA-8	**The Promise:** "There will be a longterm need for strengthened specialty care within the VA, including additional polytrauma centers as well as centers of excellence for Traumatic Brain Injury (TBI), PTSD, vision impairment, prosthetics, spinal cord injury, aging, women's health and other specialized rehabilitative care...he will expand the number of these centers of excellence and invest in specialty care." **When/Where:** Obama-Biden Plan: "Fulfilling a Sacred Trust With Our Veterans", dated 09/09/08. **Source:** https://s3.amazonaws.com/s3.documentcloud.org/documents/550009/barack-obama-2008-fulfilling-a-sacred-trust-with.pdf **Status:** When President Obama assumed his office, the VA administered four (4) Polytrauma Rehabilitation Centers (PRC), one each in Richmond, VA; Tampa, FL; Minneapolis, MN; and Palo Alto, CA, supplemented by 21 Polytrauma Network Sites (PNS). These were further supplemented by 80 Polytrauma Support Clinic Teams (PSCT) at the nation's VA hospitals. A fifth PRC was dedicated on 10/25/11 in San Antonio, TX. By the end of President Obama's second term in office, the Polytrauma System of Care (PSC) continued to provide a continuum of integrated care through 5 Polytrauma Transitional Rehabilitation Programs (PTRP) at the five PRCs (up from four), 23 PNS (up from 21), 86 PSCT (up from 80), and 39 Polytrauma Points of Contact (POC), located at VA medical centers across the country. This promise was fulfilled.	1.00
	HOMELESSNESS	**GRADE**
VA-9	**The Promise:** "Launch an innovative supportive services-housing program to prevent at-risk veterans and veteran families from falling into homelessness in the first place." **When/Where:** Obama-Biden Plan: "Fulfilling a Sacred Trust With Our Veterans", dayed 09/09/08. **Source:** https://s3.amazonaws.com/s3.documentcloud.org/documents/550009/barack-obama-2008-fulfilling-a-sacred-trust-with.pdf **Status:** The VA began a $26M pilot program in FY2010 to prevent homelessness and maintain housing stability for veterans' families. Further, the VA began supportive services in FY2010 for low-income veterans living in permanent housing to help prevent the onset of homelessness.	1.00

Supportive Services for Veteran Families (SSVF): This program, authorized by Public Law 110-387 (Veterans' Mental Health and Other Care Improvements Act of 2008), provides supportive services to very low- income Veteran families living in or transitioning to permanent housing. SSVF was designed to rapidly re-house homeless veteran families and prevent homelessness for those at imminent risk of becoming homeless due to a housing crisis. Funds are granted to private nonprofit organizations and consumer cooperatives, which then provide very low-income veteran families with a range of supportive services designed to promote housing stability.

Based on an Annual Homeless Assessment Report from the U.S. Department of Housing and Urban Development (HUD), veteran homelessness during the Obama Administration steadily declined as follows:
CY2009 - 75,600
CY2010 - 74,087
CY2011 - 65,455
CY2012 - 60,579
CY2013 - 55,619
CY2014 - 49,689
CY2015 - 47,725
CY2016 - 39,471

By end-CY2016, three states (Virginia, Connecticut and Delaware) as well as 66 communities had reported to the VA that they no longer had homeless veterans. Also since CY2010, more than 600,000 veterans and their family members have been permanently housed, rapidly re-housed, or prevented from falling into homelessness through HUD's targeted housing vouchers and VA's homelessness programs.

During President Obama's two terms in office, significant progress was made to prevent and end veteran homelessness. The number of veterans experiencing homelessness in the USA declined by nearly half (46%) during the period CY2010-CY2016. The unsheltered homeless population -- those veterans living on the streets, in cars, abandoned buildings or other places not meant for human habitation -- declined by 53% over the same period. The HUD Point-in-Time (PIT) Count estimated that on a single night in January 2017, roughly 39,471 veterans were experiencing homelessness. Of these, 26,404 were sheltered and 13,067 were unsheltered or on the street compared to 45,642 sheltered and 29,958 unsheltered in CY2009.

This promise was fulfilled.

VA-10 **The Promise:** "Expand proven homeless veteran housing vouchers to assist those already on the streets."
When/Where: Obama-Biden Plan: "Fulfilling a Sacred Trust With Our Veterans", dated 09/09/08.
Source: https://s3.amazonaws.com/s3.documentcloud.org/documents/550009/barack-obama-2008-fulfilling-a-sacred-trust-with.pdf
Status: According to a Veterans Administration (VA) and Department of Housing and Urban Development (HUD) report released in 02/11, nearly 76K veterans were homeless on any given night in CY2009, representing about 12% of all homeless adults nationwide that year.

The HUD-VA Supportive Housing (HUD-VASH) program serves hard-to-house, homeless veterans and their families with deep housing subsidies and intensive supportive services. HUD-VASH, a collaboration between HUD and the VA, grew from a small program serving fewer than 2,000 veterans in CY2008 to a major program with the capacity to serve more than 87,000 veterans by end-CY2016. The program contributed substantially to the 47% decline in the number of homeless veterans since CY2010. Thus, there was a measurable increase in the number of housing vouchers made available to homeless veterans during President Obama's tenure.

This promise was fulfilled.

1.00

Chapter 15 - Department of Veterans Affairs

	JOBS	GRADE
VA-11	**The Promise:** "Will put additional resources into enforcement and investigation in order to crack down on employers who are not following the letter and spirit of the law in regards to military reservists." **When/Where:** Obama-Biden Plan: "Fulfilling a Sacred Trust With Our Veterans" dated 09/09/08. **Source:** https://s3.amazonaws.com/s3.documentcloud.org/documents/550009/barack-obama-2008-fulfilling-a-sacred-trust-with.pdf **Status:** The "Uniformed Services Employment and Re-employment Rights Act" (USERRA) has existed since CY1994. This law has re-hiring enforcement mechanisms in place to protect honorably discharged reservists returning from active duty but requires an amendment to ensure that returning reservists are not subjected to discrimination by former employers. In an effort to mitigate this situation, Congressman John Garamendi (D-CA) introduced the "Help Veterans Return to Work Act" (H.R. 3860) on 02/01/12. This bill did not progress beyond referral to the House Committee on Veterans' Affairs. On 07/19/12, President Obama issued a memorandum with the subject "Ensuring the Uniformed Services Employment and Reemployment Rights Act (USERRA) Protections." While this memorandum served to establish a "USERRA Employment Protection Working Group," it did not allocate additional resources to enforce and investigate employer discrimination against reservists returning from active duty. Rather, it simply directed participating agencies to "allocate sufficient resources to effectively implement the requirements of this memorandum, subject to the availability of appropriations." On 09/28/16, Senator Richard Blumenthal (D-CT) introduced the "Uniformed Services Employment and Reemployment Rights Improvement Act of 2016" (S. 3445) to improve the enforcement of employment and reemployment rights of members of the uniformed services. This bill expired with the 114th Congress at the end of CY2016. This promise was not fulfilled.	0.00
VA-12	**The Promise:** "...will create a new 'Green Vet Initiative' that will have two missions: first it will offer counseling and job placement to help veterans gain the skills to enter this rapidly growing field; second, it will work with industry partners to create career pathways and educational programs." **When/Where:** Obama-Biden Plan: "New Energy for America" dated 09/06/08. **Source:** http://energy.gov/sites/prod/files/edg/media/Obama_New_Energy_0804.pdf **Status:** As of 10/11, the jobless rate among Iraq and Afghanistan veterans grew to 12.1% according to Department of Labor statistics, 3% higher than the national average of 9.1% for that month. The 12.1% veteran unemployment rate was up from 10% in 11/10, which was up from 8.4% in 07/10 and up from 7.7% in 07/09. The primary reason for the high veteran unemployment rate was that few of the skills acquired by our warfighters were directly transferable to the civilian sector. Under the Veterans Workforce Investment Program, $7M was allocated to create 3,000 jobs for veterans in the green sector. The Department of Labor had a separate $100M initiative, created under the American Recovery and Reinvestment Act of 2009, that funded green training for veterans. In the private sector, "Green Collar Vets," headquartered in Mansfield, TX, provided "online assistance to veterans in selecting and securing their next career in the rapidly-growing, multi-faceted green industries." On 08/05/11, President Obama announced the creation of a new career readiness training proposal, dubbed a "reverse boot camp," to assist troops returning from Iraq and Afghanistan to better	1.00

transition to the civilian workforce. In his announcement, President Obama also proposed tax credit incentives for companies to hire unemployed and disabled veterans and returning service men and women at a cost of approximately $120M over two years. Legislation supporting these initiatives was signed into law on 08/03/11 as the "Restoring GI Bill Fairness Act of 2011" (H.R. 1383) sponsored by Representative Jeff Miller (R-FL).

The "3% Withholding Repeal and Job Creation Act" (H.R. 674) was introduced by Congressman Walter Herger (R-CA) on 02/11/11. Title II of H.R. 674 is entitled "VOW to Hire Heroes." Subtitle A of Title II, entitled "Retraining Veterans" provided for the retraining of 45K veterans during FY2012 and 54K veterans during the period 10/01/12 through 03/31/14. H.R. 674 was signed into law by President Obama on 11/21/11.

Section 261 of Title II, entitled "Returning Heroes and Wounded Warriors Work Opportunity Tax Credits" granted tax credits of up to $5,600 for employers hiring veterans who have been unemployed for at least six months; granted employers a $2,400 credit for hiring veterans unemployed for more than four weeks; granted tax credits of up to $9,600 for hiring disabled veterans who had been seeking work for more than six months; provided benefits to aging veterans for continued education; provided an additional year of help for job-hunting disabled vets; and allowed warfighters to apply for jobs before being discharged.

While no formal federal level "Green Vet Initiative" was created as promised, the programs initiated and the funds allocated for satisfying the two stated missions constitute promise fulfillment, as does the new tax credit incentives for industry to hire veterans. For example, the Denver-based non-profit organization "Veterans Green Job" has initiated a new "Veterans Green Force" recruitment and placement program that aims to place 300 veterans in "green" jobs.

This promise was fulfilled.

	VETERANS' BENEFITS	GRADE
VA-13	**The Promise:** "To reduce the Veterans Benefits Administration claims backlog, "Obama will hire additional claims workers and convene our nation's leading veterans groups, employees and managers to develop an updated training and management model..." **When/Where:** Obama-Biden Plan: "Fulfilling a Sacred Trust With Our Veterans" dated 09/09/08. **Source:** https://s3.amazonaws.com/s3.documentcloud.org/documents/550009/barack-obama-2008-fulfilling-a-sacred-trust-with.pdf **Status:** As of 06/09, the VA had over 720,000 claims pending. A VA Inspector General report dated 09/23/09 laid the blame for claims processing delays on inadequate VA workload management practices, not on inadequate claims processing personnel resources. The FY2010 Veterans Health Care Budget Reform and Transparency Act signed into law on 10/22/09 by President Obama included resources to continue moving toward his goal of reforming the benefits claims process, increasing funds for that purpose from $1.4B in FY2009 to $1.8B in FY2010. This translated into the VA's ability to hire 1,200 new claims processors in FY2010, bringing that workforce to 14,550 personnel. The number of claims pending action went from 448,000 in 04/10 to 756,000 in 04/11. Claims exceeding 125 days processing time went up from 200,000 in 04/10 to 450,000 in 04/11, with processing time estimated at 180 days. Despite processing over 1M claims in CY2010 and CY2011, the number of claims in progress at end-CY2012 was estimated to be 897,566, 67.6% or 606,754 of which were over 125 days old. The backlog of claims peaked in 03/13 with 611,000 stuck in processing for over 125 days. A year later, that number had gone down to 344,000, an indicator that processing improvements were taking hold.	1.00

The claims processing system became increasingly strained by end-CY2014 as veterans from Afghanistan separated from active service, many of whom had multiple medical conditions. The claims backlog was further exacerbated by the aging of Vietnam-era veterans who were filing for medical benefits and previously unavailable benefits related to Agent Orange exposure. To mitigate that situation, President Obama requested $2.5 billion, an increase of $28 million over FY2014, in his FY2015 budget request for veteran benefits processing.

With the hiring of additional claims processors coupled with mandatory overtime, the veterans claims backlog was significantly reduced. On 06/30/15, the number of initial claims waiting in excess of 125 days for processing was estimated at 194,000. By 12/31/16, that number reportedly went down to about 70,000. Thus, the backlog of VA claims was significantly reduced during President Obama's two terms in office.

This promise was fulfilled.

VA-14

The Promise: "Obama will sign an executive order "ending the unfair ban on healthcare enrollment of certain groups of veterans, including 'Priority 8' veterans who often earn modest incomes."
When/Where: Obama-Biden Plan: "Fulfilling a Sacred Trust With Our Veterans" dated 09/09/08.
Source: https://s3.amazonaws.com/s3.documentcloud.org/documents/550009/barack-obama-2008-fulfilling-a-sacred-trust-with.pdf
Status: Priority 8 veterans are those who either have no service-connected disability or a 0% disability rating, with incomes above specified thresholds based on family size. For the VA's Income Year 2016, income thresholds for eligibility for free VA health care were $32,074 for a veteran with no dependents to $44,104 for a veteran with four dependents (an amount increased by $2,205 for each additional dependent over four).

Under President Bush, Congress authorized the expenditure of $375M to re-enroll some Priority 8 veterans, about 10% of the total number of eligible veterans.

When President Obama signed the Veterans Health Care Budget Reform and Transparency Act on 10/22/09, he acknowledged that "for 500,000 Priority 8 veterans, we're restoring VA health care coverage". According to the VA, the correct number of Priority 8 veterans was closer to 265,000 at the time the law was signed.

This promise was fulfilled.

1.00

VA-15

The Promise: "As president, Obama will meet early in the budgeting process each year with congressional leaders and the nation's leading Veterans Service Organizations (VSOs) to ensure the VA budget is always given must-pass status."
When/Where: Obama-Biden Plan: "Fulfilling a Sacred Trust With Our Veterans" dated 09/09/08.
Source: https://s3.amazonaws.com/s3.documentcloud.org/documents/550009/barack-obama-2008-fulfilling-a-sacred-trust-with.pdf
Status: The House passed H.R. 1016, the Veterans Health Care Budget Reform and Transparency Act of 2009, on 10/08/09 by a vote of 419-1. The measure was then approved by the Senate on 10/13/09. President Obama signed this legislation into law on 10/22/09.

Starting in FY2011, the above Act requires the President to submit a budget request for the VA's medical-care accounts for the fiscal year after the one for which the budget is submitted. The legislation also requires the VA to provide an annual report to Congress by 07/31 of each year, projecting cost estimates in advance of the current year's budget requirements.

Except for one roundtable meeting with VSOs in Phoenix, AZ on 03/12/15, President Obama is not known to have held annual meetings with VSOs to address VA budget issues.

This promise was not fulfilled.

0.00

Chapter 15 - Department of Veterans Affairs

VA-16

The Promise: "Obama will transform the paper benefit claims process to an electronic system that will be interoperable with the VA's health network as well as military records"

When/Where: Obama-Biden Plan: "Fulfilling a Sacred Trust With Our Veterans" date 09/09/08

Source: https://s3.amazonaws.com/s3.documentcloud.org/documents/550009/barack-obama-2008-fulfilling-a-sacred-trust-with.pdf

Status: The VA's 2010 budget included $3.3B to develop electronic health care records, paperless claims systems, and seamless integration of medical and service records with DoD. This level of funding was considered sufficient to get the promised transformation started and implemented.

For FY2011, the actual budget authorization for VA Information Technology (IT) was $2.994B.

Part of the President's FY2012 request for $2.019B for claims processing was for information technology enhancements. Further, of the enacted $3.161B for the VA's FY2012 discretionary funding for information technology, $70M was for the development and implementation of a Virtual Lifetime Electronic Record (VLER) initiative and $148M for a paperless claims processing system.

For FY2013, the President's request for VA IT was $3.327B, $128M of which was specifically for the continued development and implementation of a paperless claims system under the Veterans Benefits Management System.

This promise was fulfilled.

1.00

VA-17

The Promise: "...would also extend the window for new veterans to enroll in the VA from two to five years."

When/Where: Obama-Biden Plan: "Fulfilling a Sacred Trust With Our Veterans", Kansas City, 08/20/07.

Source: https://s3.amazonaws.com/s3.documentcloud.org/documents/550009/barack-obama-2008-fulfilling-a-sacred-trust-with.pdf

Status: Veterans, including "new" veterans, who served in a theater of operations after 11/11/98 are eligible for an extended period of eligibility for health care for five years after their discharge.

H.R. 1460 was introduced by Congressman William Owens (D-NY) on 04/08/11 to provide for automatic enrollment of veterans returning from combat zones into the VA medical system. This bill and others like it such as the "Providing Real Outreach (PRO) for Veterans Act" (S. 1080) introduced during the 112th Congress (CY2011-13) did not get beyond initial committee reviews. These bills would have granted veterans returning from combat tours in Iraq or Afghanistan automatic enrollment in the VA if the terms of their discharge permitted.

However, not all service members got to serve in Iraq or Afghanistan by end-CY2016. Such veterans were assigned to a lower priority group for receipt of VA health care benefits, with those able to afford their own health care placed at the lowest end of the priority scale.

According to a VA representative responding to a telephonic inquiry (1-877-222-VETS), an otherwise qualified "new veteran" can enroll for VA health care benefits at any time and is not limited to two or five years after discharge.

This promise was fulfilled.

1.00

VETERANS AFFAIRS GPA | **0.88**

Chapter 16 - Appointments

Campaign Promises
Other/Miscellaneous -> Appointments

ITEM	APPOINTMENTS	
	AMERICAN INDIAN ADVISOR	**GRADE**
AP-1	**The Promise:** "I'll appoint an American Indian Policy Adviser to my senior White House staff to work with tribes." **When/Where:** Speech at Crow Agency, MT, 05/19/08. **Source:** http://www.youtube.com/watch?v=SU4WR_rcGUA **Status:** On 06/15/09, President Obama announced the appointment of Kimberly TeeHee as his Senior Policy Advisor for Native American Affairs. She served in that position until 04/27/12 when she was replaced by Jodi Gillette. Ms. Gillette served until 05/14/15 and was not replaced. This promise was fulfilled.	1.00
	AUTISM COORDINATOR	**GRADE**
AP-2	**The Promise:** "...will appoint a Federal ASD Coordinator to oversee federal ASD research and federal efforts to improve awareness of ASD and improve the training of medical professionals to identify and treat ASD." **When/Where:** Obama-Biden Plan: "Supporting Americans with Autism Spectrum Disorders" dated 10/30/08. **Source:** https://safeminds.org/wp-content/uploads/Obama-ASD-fact-sheet.pdf **Status:** By end-CY2016, no Federal Autism Spectrum Disorder (ASD) Coordinator had been appointed by President Obama. This promise was not fulfilled.	0.00
	CABINET REPUBLICAN	**GRADE**
AP-3	**The Promise:** "Often stated promise to appoint a Republican to his Cabinet, otherwise stated as "appoint a cabinet of the talents, irrespective of party labels." At one point, Obama stated that he "absolutely" considered it important to have Republicans in the Cabinet." **When/Where:** Throughout campaign. **Source:** http://www.reuters.com/article/politicsNews/idUSTRE49T05X20081030 **Status:** Obama retained Robert Gates as Defense Secretary. On 12/18/08, he added Congressman Ray Lahood (R-IL) as his pick to be Transportation Secretary, a nomination that was confirmed. This promise was fulfilled.	1.00
	CHIEF FINANCIAL OFFICER	**GRADE**
AP-4	**The Promise:** "Will appoint a Chief Financial Officer to oversee the rebuilding following national disasters to minimize waste and abuse." **When/Where:** Obama-Biden Plan: "Rebuilding the Gulf Coast and Preventing Future Catastrophes" dated 09/11/08. **Source:** https://assets.documentcloud.org/documents/550006/barack-obama-2008-rebuilding-the-gulf-coast-and.pdf **Status:** In 09/11, the Obama Administration released its National Disaster Recovery Framework	0.00

(NDRF). The sole, new federal-level position introduced in that plan was that of Federal Disaster Recovery Coordinator (FDRC). The mitigation of fraud, waste, discrimination and abuse is addressed to some extent in the plan, but not the involvement of a federal-level Financial Officer in those efforts.

The following are examples of multi-state disasters that occurred during President Obama's two terms in office:
YEAR/TYPE/LOCATION
2011 - Flood/Mississippi River Valley
2011 - Tornado/Alabama, Tennessee, Georgia, Arkansas, Virginia
2012 - Hurricane Sandy/ Eastern USA
2014 - Tornado/Nebraska, Louisiana, Oklahoma, Illinois, Florida, North Carolina
2015 - Flood/Carolinas
2016 - Hurricane Matthew/Florida, Carolinas, Georgia; Wildfires/West-Southwest

No Chief Financial Officer was appointed in the aftermath of these national disasters.

This promise was not fulfilled.

	CHIEF PERFORMANCE OFFICER	GRADE
AP-5	**The Promise:** "Obama ...will create a focused team within the White House that will work with agency leaders and the White House Office of Management and Budget (OMB) to improve results and outcomes for federal government programs while eliminating waste and inefficiency. This unit...will be ... headed by a new Chief Performance Officer (CPO) who will report directly to the president." **When/Where:** Obama-Biden Plan: "The Change We Need in Washington" dated 09/22/08. **Source:** https://www.politifact.com/truth-o-meter/promises/obameter/promise/405/create-white-house-performance-team-and-chief-perf/ **Status:** Source is cited for confirmation of exact promise wording only, as it existed before original "When/Where" campaign document was deleted from archival websites. On 01/07/09, Obama named Nancy Killefer, a former Assistant Secretary of the Treasury, to this post. Killefer had to withdraw her nomination for failure to pay household help employment taxes. Jeffrey Zients, a board member of several corporations, was nominated to replace Ms. Killefer as the first CPO/Deputy Director of the Office of Management and Budget (OMB) on 04/18/09. On 01/27/12, Mr. Zients was named the Acting Director of the OMB while maintaining his CPO functions until his departure from the OMB to become President Obama's National Economic Council Director on 03/05/14, a position in which he served for the remainder of President Obama's second term in office. Ms. Beth Cobert, formerly a Director and Senior Partner at McKinsey & Company, replaced Mr. Zients until she became Director of the Office of Personnel Management (OPM) on 07/10/15. Mr. Andrew Mayock, a former senior associate for development and international diplomacy at Booz Allen Hamilton and an international trade consultant at Harvard University's Center for Business and Government, was nominated by President Obama to replace Ms. Cobert on 12/14/15. Mr. Mayock was confirmed by the Senate nearly a year later on 12/10/16, but was not sworn in to serve during President Obama's last month in office. This promise was fulfilled.	1.00
	CHIEF TECHNOLOGY OFFICER	GRADE
AP-6	**The Promise:** "Will appoint the nation's first Chief Technology Officer (CTO) to ensure that our government and all its agencies have the right infrastructure, policies and services for the 21st century." **When/Where:** Obama-Biden Plan for Science and Innovation dated 09/25/08 **Source:** https://pubs.acs.org/cen/news/pdf/FactSheetScience.pdf **Status:** Obama's nominee, Aneesh Chopra, formerly the Secretary of Technology for Virginia, required	1.00

Chapter 16 - Appointments

Senate confirmation which was rendered 05/21/09. Mr. Chopra resigned from his position as the first first Chief Technology Officer (CTO) on 02/08/12.

Mr. Chopra was replaced by Mr. Todd Park who served as the second CTO from 03/01/12 to 08/28/14.

The third CTO was Ms. Megan J. Smith, a former Google Vice President, appointed on 09/04/14. She remained as incumbent CTO until the end of the Obama Administration on 01/20/17.

This promise was fulfilled.

DIRECTOR, FEMA	GRADE

AP-7

The Promise: "The FEMA Director will report directly to President Obama, serve a six-year term and will have professional emergency management experience."
When/Where: Obama-Biden Plan: "Rebuilding the Gulf Coast and Preventing Future Catastrophes" dated 09/11/08.
Source: https://assets.documentcloud.org/documents/550006/barack-obama-2008-rebuilding-the-gulf-coast-and.pdf
Status: The Federal Emergency Management Agency (FEMA) exists as a major agency of the Department of Homeland Security (DHS). The Administrator for Federal Emergency Management (aka FEMA Director) reports directly to the Secretary of Homeland Security.

Craig Fugate, former director of the Florida Division of Emergency Management, was confirmed by the U.S. Senate as FEMA Director on 05/12/09.

Mr. Fugate reported directly to the Secretary of Homeland Security throughout his period of service (05/09 to 01/17) in lieu of reporting to the President as promised.

This promise was not fulfilled.

Grade: 0.00

FED REBUILDING COORDINATOR	GRADE

AP-8

The Promise: "...will elevate the federal rebuilding coordinator so that he or she reports directly to the president and so that rebuilding remains a national priority."
When/Where: Obama-Biden Plan: "Rebuilding the Gulf Coast and Preventing Future Catastrophes" dated 09/11/08.
Source: https://assets.documentcloud.org/documents/550006/barack-obama-2008-rebuilding-the-gulf-coast-and.pdf
Status: Janet Woodka was appointed as Gulf Coast Rebuilding Coordinator by the Secretary of Homeland Security on 03/31/09 and reported to Secretary Napolitano, not to President Obama as promised.

Ms. Woodka served as Director of the Office of the Federal Coordinator for Gulf Coast Rebuilding until that office was closed on 03/31/10, at which time she transferred to the Environmental Protection Agency (EPA).

This promise was not fulfilled.

Grade: 0.00

FEDERAL COORDINATING OFFICER	GRADE

AP-9

The Promise: "Immediately following a catastrophe, Barack Obama will appoint a Federal Coordinating Officer to direct reconstruction efforts."
When/Where: Obama-Biden Plan: "Rebuilding the Gulf Coast and Preventing Future Catastrophes" dated 09/11/08.
Source: https://assets.documentcloud.org/documents/550006/barack-obama-2008-rebuilding-the-gulf-coast-and.pdf
Status: The appointment of a Federal Coordinating Officer is mandated under the "Robert T. Stafford Disaster Relief and Emergency Assistance Act," which is an amended version of the "Disaster Relief

Grade: 1.00

Act of 1974."

Reporting to the Director of of the Federal Emergency Management Agency (FEMA), William L. Vogel was appointed as Federal Coordinating Officer on 03/24/10 in the aftermath of flooding in New Jersey.

Gracia B. Szczech was appointed as Federal Coordinating Officer on 05/13/10 in the aftermath of flooding in Tennessee.

By another name (National Incident Commander), the former Commandant of the Coast Guard, Admiral Thad Allen, was designated as the government's point person for the 04/20/10 Deepwater Horizon oil spill in the Gulf of Mexico. He served in that position until 09/10, three months after he retired from the Coast Guard in 06/10.

Federal Coordinating Officers were also appointed in the aftermath of tornado and flooding disasters in Oklahoma, Missouri, Arkansas and other states during the first half of CY2011, after Hurricane Sandy in late CY2012, and other disasters since then.

This promise was fulfilled.

GENERAL	GRADE

AP-10

The Promise: "...in an Obama-Biden administration, every official will have to rise to the standard of proven excellence in the agency's mission."
When/Where: Obama-Biden Plan for America "Blueprint for Change" dated 10/09/08
Source: https://www.documentcloud.org/documents/550007-barack-obama-2008-blueprint-for-change.html
Status: The Internal Revenue Service (IRS) falls under the purview of the Secretary of the Treasury. Upon his nomination for that post, it was learned that Timothy Geithner had evaded paying $26,000 in taxes since the 2001-2002 timeframe, an amount he quickly paid. In this instance, Mr. Geithner had failed to "rise to the standard of proven excellence" in the mission of the department he was nominated and later confirmed to lead.

Another example: Ms. Elizabeth Birnbaum was appointed as Director of the Minerals Management Service (MMS) of the Department of the Interior on 07/15/09. She apparently did not meet the "standard of proven excellence" demanded by her job in the aftermath of the oil spill of 04/20/10 in the Gulf of Mexico. By some accounts she was fired by President Obama on 05/27/10; by other accounts she resigned after criticism over her lax oversight of oil drilling in general and alleged coziness with the industry she was hired to oversee.

To replace Ms. Birnbaum, President Obama selected Mr. Michael Bromwich (a litigation partner at the Fried Frank, Harris, Shriver & Jacobson law firm when selected) to head the MMS, since rebranded as the Bureau of Ocean Energy Management, Regulation and Enforcement. Mr. Bromwich had no experience with oil and gas issues and thus had no "proven excellence" in his appointed mission.

On 06/30/11, General David Petraeus was unanimously confirmed as the Director of the CIA by the Senate. During his relatively short tenure as CIA Director, General Petraeus was discovered to be having an extramarital affair with his biographer, Paula Broadwell. General Patraeus resigned as CIA Director on 11/09/12 and later pleaded guilty to one count of having shared classified CIA information with Ms. Broadwell. The CIA's mission was potentially compromised.

These are but a few examples where this promise was not fulfilled.

0.00

NATIONAL CYBER ADVISOR	GRADE

AP-11

The Promise: "...will establish the position of National Cyber Advisor who will report directly to the President and will be responsible for coordinating federal agency efforts and development of national cyber policy."

0.00

Chapter 16 - Appointments

When/Where: Plan for America: "Blueprint for Change," dated 10/09/08
Source: https://www.documentcloud.org/ Obama and Biden's documents/550007-barack-obama-2008-blueprint-for-change.html
Status: On 12/22/09, President Obama announced the appointment of Howard Schmidt, a former Chief Security Officer for eBay and Microsoft, as National Cyber-Security Coordinator or "Cyber Czar". However, Schmidt reported to the National Security Council through the Deputy National Security Advisor for Homeland Security and Counterterrorism, John O. Brennan, not to the President.

In 05/12, Mr. Schmidt retired and was replaced by Michael Daniel, formerly head of the White House budget office intelligence branch. Like Mr. Schmidt, Mr. Daniel reported to the National Security Advisor and to the head of the National Economic Council.

Under Executive Order 13718 signed on 02/09/16, President Obama established the position of Federal Chief Information Security Officer (CISO). The new CISO does not report directly to the president. Rather, the position is overseen by the Office of the Administrator, Office of E-Government and Information Technology, in the Office of Management and Budget (OMB).

This promise was not fulfilled.

NUCLEAR SECURITY ADVISOR	GRADE

AP-12
The Promise: "Obama will appoint a deputy national security advisor to be in charge of coordinating all U.S. programs aimed at reducing the risk of nuclear terrorism and weapons proliferation."
When/Where: Obama's New Plan to Confront 21st Century Threats, 07/16/08
Source: https://www.presidency.ucsb.edu/documents/press-release-fact-sheet-obamas-new-plan-confront-21st-century-threats
Status: In late 01/09, President Obama appointed Gary Samore, a former Clinton Administration advisor on nonproliferation matters and coordinator of U.S. policy on nuclear, chemical and biological weapons matters, as White House Coordinator for Arms Control and Weapons of Mass Destruction, Proliferation, and Terrorism.

Mr. Samore reported to the National Security Advisor, General (Ret.) James Jones prior to the latter's resignation on 10/08/10. General Jones was replaced by Thomas E. Donilon. Mr. Samore was appointed as Executive Director of Harvard Kennedy School's Belfer Center for Science and International Affairs in 01/13.

Mr. Samore was replaced by Dr. Elizabeth Sherwood-Randall as Coordinator for Defense Policy, Countering Weapons of Mass Destruction, and Arms Control in 04/13, a position she vacated on 09/14 when she was appointed by President Obama to be Deputy Secretary of Energy.

This promise was fulfilled.

Grade: 1.00

PRIVACY/CIVIL LIBERTIES BOARD	GRADE

AP-13
The Promise: "Support efforts to strengthen the Privacy and Civil Liberties Board with subpoena powers and reporting responsibilities."
When/Where: Obama-Biden Plan to Improve Intelligence Capacity and Protect Civil Liberties, 11/16/08
Source: http://webarchive.loc.gov/all/20090429184932/http://change.gov/agenda/homeland_security_agenda/
Status: This promise could have been filed under Homeland Security (HS), but the key tenet pertains to White House level appointments.

As a result of a 9/11 Commission Report recommendation dated 07/22/04 (formally referred to as the "Final Report of the National Commission on Terrorist Attacks Upon the United States"), former President Bush selected three Republicans and one Democrat to serve on the Privacy and Civil Liberties Oversight Board (PCLOB). Only the Chairperson and Vice-Chairperson required Senate confirmation at the time and this was accomplished in 02/06.

Grade: 0.00

Chapter 16 - Appointments

In 01/07, Congress decided that the PCLOB should be reorganized as an independent agency with each member subject to Senate confirmation, serving for overlapping six-year terms with no more than three members being from the same party. By 01/08 the PCLOB, as originally structured, ceased to operate. It would remain nonfunctional for over four years.

In early-08/12, the Senate confirmed four of the PCLOB's five members -- two Republicans and two Democrats -- but failed to confirm its chairman, Democrat David Medine. In 01/13, the White House re-nominated Mr. Medine as chair and the Senate confirmed him on 05/07/13. On 07/09/13, the Board held its first public workshop followed by its first substantive hearing on 11/04/13.

As of end-CY2016, a majority of the PCLOB could submit a written request to the Attorney General (AG) to issue a subpoena on behalf of the board. Within 30 days, the AG must either comply or provide a written explanation for a denial to the board and to the House and Senate Judiciary Committees. Thus after President Obama's eight years in office, the PCLOB itself had no subpoena powers.

This promise was not fulfilled.

SCIENCE/TECHNOLOGY ADVISOR	GRADE

AP-14 **The Promise:** "Will appoint an Assistant to the President for Science and Technology Policy who will report directly to the president, and be deeply involved in establishing research priorities..."
When/Where: Obama-Biden Plan: "Advancing the Frontiers of Space Exploration" dated 08/15/08.
Source: http://www.nasa.gov/pdf/382369main_48%20-%2020090803.2.Space_Fact_Sheet_FINAL.pdf
Status: President Obama's nominee, John P. Holdren, was confirmed by the Senate as Director of the White House Office of Science and Technology Policy (the "Science Czar") on 03/19/09, a position he held throughout President Obama's two terms in office.

1.00

Mr. Holdren also served as Co-Chair of the President's Council of Advisors on Science and Technology (PCAST) during the period 03/09-01/17.

This promise was fulfilled.

SPECIAL ENVOY - AMERICAS	GRADE

AP-15 **The Promise:** "In the past, American presidents have filled the position of special envoy to bring senior-level attention to hemispheric matters...the position was eliminated...in June of 2004. As president Barack Obama will reinstate the position."
When/Where: Obama-Biden Plan: "Renewing U.S. Leadership in the Americas" dated 06/06/08.
Source: https://www.politifact.com/truth-o-meter/promises/obameter/promise/220/reinstate-special-envoy-for-the-americas/
Status: Source is cited for confirmation of exact promise wording only, as it existed before original "When/Where" campaign document was deleted from archival websites.

0.00

Early in President Obama's first term in office, there was some lip service to the effect he and SecState Clinton were considering filling this position, which could easily have gone to a retired or retiring, well-known Senate or House Democrat. This didn't happen.

Former President Clinton was appointed Special Envoy to Haiti -- by the United Nations. That didn't count toward promise fulfillment.

On 02/20/15, President Obama appointed Bernard W. Aronson, a former Assistant Secretary of State for Inter-American Affairs, as a special envoy to facilitate negotiations between the Colombian government and the guerilla warfare Revolutionary Armed Forces of Colombia -- in Spanish: Fuerzas Armadas Revolucionarias de Colombia (FARC). It's interesting that FARC was listed as a terrorist organization by the Department of State at the time.

Chapter 16 - Appointments

By the end of President Obama's second term in office, no Special Envoy for the Americas had been nominated/appointed.

This promise was not fulfilled.

	URBAN POLICY DIRECTOR	GRADE
AP-16	**The Promise:** "Will create a White House Office of Urban Policy...The Director of Urban Policy will report directly to the president and coordinate all federal urban programs." **When/Where:** Obama-Biden Plan: "Supporting Urban Prosperity" dated 09/11/08. **Source:** https://assets.documentcloud.org/documents/550008/barack-obama-2008-supporting-urban-prosperity.pdf **Status:** The White House Office of Urban Affairs was created by President Obama under Executive Order 13503 dated 02/19/09. On that date, President Obama announced the appointment of Adolfo Carrion as White House Director of Urban Affairs, reporting directly to the President and concurrently to Valerie Jarrett (Assistant to the President for Public Engagement and Intergovernmental Affairs) and Melody Barnes (Director of the Domestic Policy Council). Mr. Carrion's White House service ended on 05/03/10 when he was named by President Obama to be Regional Director at the New York and New Jersey Regional Office for the Department of Housing and Urban Development (HUD). On 05/03/10, Mr. Carrion was replaced by Derek R.B. Douglas as Special Assistant to the President for Urban Affairs. Mr. Douglas served until end-CY2011 when he accepted a position as the University of Chicago's Vice President for Civic Engagement. This promise was fulfilled.	1.00

	VIOLENCE AGAINST WOMEN	GRADE
AP-17	**The Promise:** "As president, Barack Obama will appoint a special advisor who will report to him regularly on issues related to violence against women." **When/Where:** Plan for America: "Blueprint for Change," dated 10/09/08 **Source:** https://www.documentcloud.org/ Obama and Biden's documents/550007-barack-obama-2008-blueprint-for-change.html **Status:** The appointment of Lynn Rosenthal as the first White House Advisor on Violence Against Women was announced on 06/26/09. Ms. Rosenthal served until 12/14. She was replaced by Carrie Bettinger-Lopez in 01/15. Ms. Bettinger-Lopez served as White House Advisor on Violence Against Women until the end of the Obama Administration in 01/17. This promise was fulfilled.	1.00

| | | APPOINTMENTS GPA | 0.53 |

Chapter 17 - Transparency & Ethics

Campaign Promises
Other/Miscellaneous -> Ethics/Transparency

ITEM	ETHICS/TRANSPARENCY	
	ETHICS	**GRADE**
TE-1	**The Promise:** "No political appointees in an Obama-Biden administration will be permitted to work on regulations or contracts directly and substantially related to their prior employer for two years. And no political appointee will be able to lobby the executive branch after leaving government service during the remainder of the administration." **When/Where:** Obama-Biden Plan: "Blueprint for Change" dated 10/09/08. **Source:** https://www.documentcloud.org/documents/550007-barack-obama-2008-blueprint-for-change.html **Status:** In one of his first official actions, President Obama signed Executive Order 13490 (Ethics Commitments By Executive Branch Personnel) on 1/21/09. That order addressed all the basic tenets of this promise. But a few loopholes were inevitably found. A few examples where the appointment of approximately 70 former lobbyists to principal government positions early in the Obama Administration was considered problematic, questionable, or borderline unethical: (1) William J. Lynn III was a Raytheon lobbyist for six years, lobbying extensively on a broad range of defense-related issues. He was appointed to be Deputy Secretary of Defense on 02/11/09, with final authority on a number of contract, program and budget decisions. On 1/26/12, Mr. Lynn was selected as Chairman and CEO of DRS Technologies, responsible for Italian multinational company Finmeccanica's efforts in the U.S. in the fields of defense, aerospace and security. (2) Ashton Carter, Defense Acquisition Chief, former consultant to Textron, and later Secretary of Defense. On 5/11/09, the DoD Inspector General ruled that in his judgment, the nature of Carter's previous consulting arrangement with Textron, a major aerospace and defense development and manufacturing firm, should not prevent Carter from objectively making decisions involving the company. (3) Mark Patterson, Chief of Staff to the Secretary of the Treasury, was a lobbyist for Goldman Sachs until 04/11/08. (4) William Corr, Deputy Secretary of Health and Human Services, lobbied as executive director of the "Campaign for Tobacco-Free Kids" until 09/08. President Obama's 01/21/09 Executive Order 13490 banning lobbyists from working in an agency they previously lobbied was either directly violated early in his first term in office, or former lobbyists were given a pass based on very broad interpretations of the executive order. This promise was not fulfilled.	0.00
TE-2	**The Promise:** "...will issue an executive order asking all new hires at the agencies to sign a form	1.00

Chapter 17 - Transparency & Ethics

affirming that no political appointee offered them the job solely on the basis of political affiliation or contribution."
When/Where: Obama-Biden Plan: "Blueprint for Change" dated 10/09/08.
Source: https://www.documentcloud.org/documents/550007-barack-obama-2008-blueprint-for-change.html
Status: On 01/21/09, President Obama signed Executive Order 13490 entitled "Ethics Commitments by Executive Branch Personnel." This order requires that appointees sign forms saying that they were not hired because of political affiliations or contributions.

This promise was fulfilled.

TE-3	**The Promise:** "...will issue an executive order banning registered lobbyists or lobbying firms from giving gifts in any amount or any form to executive branch employees." **When/Where:** Obama-Biden Plan: "Stop Wasteful Spending and Curb Influence of Special Interests so Government Can Tackle our Great Challenges" dated 09/22/08. **Source:** https://www.politifact.com/truth-o-meter/promises/obameter/promise/427/ban-lobbyist-gifts-to-executive-employees/ **Status:** Source is cited for confirmation of exact promise wording only, as it existed before original "When/Where" campaign document was deleted from archival websites. Executive Order 13490 entitled "Executive Order on Ethics Commitments by Executive Branch Personnel" issued by President Obama on 1/21/09, bans registered lobbyists from giving gifts to executive branch personnel. This promise was fulfilled.	1.00
TE-4	**The Promise:** "Obama will use the power of the presidency to fight for an independent watchdog agency to oversee the investigation of congressional ethics violations so that the public can be assured that ethics complaints will be investigated." **When/Where:** Obama-Biden Plan for America entitled: "Blueprint for Change" dated 10/09/08. **Source:** https://www.documentcloud.org/documents/550007-barack-obama-2008-blueprint-for-change.html **Status:** The House is being policed by its Office of Congressional Ethics (OCE) that came into existence in CY2008 before President Obama assumed the Presidency. Over the objections of the Congressional Black Caucus, the 112th Congress majority House Republicans decided to retain the OCE as part of an over-arching House ethics adherence process. In 11/10, as a direct result of the OCE's work, the House Committee on Standards of Official Conduct found Congressman Charles Rangle (D-NY) guilty of 11 ethics violations. The Senate has its own Ethics Committee to investigate its members suspected of ethics violations. In 05/11, Senator John Ensign (R-NV) was investigated for breaking federal laws while trying to cover up an extramarital affair. The Executive Branch of government has no constitutional power/leverage over ethics investigations the House and Senate undertake on their members. Further, the U.S. Constitution contains a "speech or debate" clause which is interpreted as protecting legislative matters from executive branch interference if what a Congressional member did was part of his/her official duties. The invocation of this clause served to kill numerous congressional investigations during the Obama Administration. As of end-CY2016, there was no record that President Obama used the power of his office to influence the creation of an "independent watchdog agency" for Congress. This promise was not fulfilled.	0.00

Chapter 17 - Transparency & Ethics

TE-5	**The Promise:** "...will create a "contracts and influence" database that will disclose how much federal contractors spend on lobbying, and what contracts they are getting and how well they complete them." **When/Where:** Obama-Biden Plan: "Blueprint for Change" dated 10/09/08. **Source:** https://www.documentcloud.org/documents/550007-barack-obama-2008-blueprint-for-change.html **Status:** The government database "data.gov" has a "Lobbying Disclosure Reports" section, but this section does not reflect the promised data. The majority of reports found therein pertain to city and state lobbying data, not federal. An independent website, OpenSecrets.org, does an excellent job of tracking some aspects of this promise, indicating that the data is available if one is dedicated to doing some serious digging. Another excellent resource for data related to this promise is pogo.org. The Project on Government Oversight (POGO) is a nonpartisan independent watchdog that champions good government reforms. POGO's investigations into corruption, misconduct, and conflicts of interest achieve a more effective, accountable, open, and ethical federal government. As of end-CY2016, no specific federal "contracts and influence" database existed, despite the existence of "data.gov" as a potential vehicle for such a database. This promise was not fulfilled.	0.00
TE-6	**The Promise:** "...will create a centralized Internet database of lobbying reports, ethics records, and campaign finance filings." **When/Where:** Obama-Biden Plan: "Blueprint for Change" dated 10/09/08. **Source:** https://www.documentcloud.org/documents/550007-barack-obama-2008-blueprint-for-change.html **Status:** Throughout President Obama's two terms in office, he emphasized that government is more accountable when it is transparent, and that's a principle that he worked to make a reality in his administration. Ethics.gov was created to fulfill this promise. When it existed, anyone could search through the records of seven different datasets: - White House visitor records; - Office of Government Ethics travel reports; - Lobbying Disclosure Act data; - Department of Justice Foreign Agents Registration Act (FARA) data; - Federal Election Commission individual contribution reports; - Federal Election Commission candidate reports; and - Federal Election Commission committee reports When President Obama left office, the ethics.gov website ceased to exist. Nonetheless, the promised database was created during President Obama's tenure in office. This promise was fulfilled.	1.00
	TRANSPARENCY	**GRADE**
TE-7	**The Promise:** "That's what I will do in bringing all parties together, not negotiating behind closed doors, but bringing all parties together, and broadcasting those negotiations on C-SPAN so that the American people can see what the choices are." **When/Where:** Democratic Presidential Debate with Senator Hillary Clinton, Los Angeles, CA, 01/31/08. **Source:** http://www.cnn.com/2008/POLITICS/01/31/dem.debate.transcript/ **Status:** This promise was repeated at least eight times during Candidate Obama's campaign. When	0.00

debates and negotiations on the American Recovery and Reinvestment Act of 2009 and the Affordable Care Act of 2010 took a highest priority position within the Obama Administration and Congress, none of the deliberations were broadcast on C-SPAN. In some cases, Republicans were reportedly denied access to "back room" negotiations.

House Speaker Nancy Pelosi's comment of 03/09/10 on the Affordable Care Act to the effect that "we have to pass the (health care) bill so that you can find out what is in it" did not reflect the transparency expected by the American people. They were insulted.

Subsequent important legislative negotiations such as those leading to the Dodd-Frank Wall Street Reform and Consumer Protection Act 2010, the Continuing Resolution of early CY2011 and those pertaining to raising the federal debt limit and deficit reduction in 07/11 were done behind closed doors, despite President Obama's commitment to have all those talks/deals broadcast on C-SPAN.

It is acknowledged that some congressional discussions on topics such as Troubled Asset Relief Program (TARP) management and financial reform were broadcast on C-SPAN. However, public coverage of other top priority legislation was either inconsistent or nonexistent during the Obama Administration.

This promise was not fulfilled.

TE-8	**The Promise:** "As president, Obama will not sign any non-emergency bill without giving the American public an opportunity to review and comment on the White House website for five days." **When/Where:** Obama-Biden Plan: "Blueprint for Change" dated 10/09/08. **Source:** https://www.documentcloud.org/documents/550007-barack-obama-2008-blueprint-for-change.html **Status:** The Economic Stimulus Bill signed into law by President Obama on 01/29/09, the American Recovery and Reinvestment Act of 2009 signed into law on 02/17/09, and the Patient Protection and Affordable Care Act of 2010 signed into law on 03/30/10 are prime examples of bills passed with no 5-day public review period as promised. When queried about the contents of the proposed Patient Protection and Affordable Care Act of 2010, blatant disrespect for the American taxpayer was voiced by House Speaker Nancy Pelosi on 03/09/10 when she stated "We have to pass the bill so you can find out what's in it..." This promise was not fulfilled.	0.00
TE-9	**The Promise:** "I will not use signing statements to nullify or undermine congressional instructions as enacted into law." **When/Where:** Obama's Responses to The Boston Globe's questions dated 12/20/07. **Source:** http://www.boston.com/news/politics/2008/specials/CandidateQA/ObamaQA/ **Status:** President Bush signed nearly 1,200 nullifying statements during his presidency. Fearing that his prerogatives were being threatened by Congress, President Obama back-peddled on this promise on 03/09/09 by issuing a memorandum that stated: "I will issue signing statements to address constitutional concerns only when it is appropriate to do so as a means of discharging my constitutional responsibilities...". Two days later, on 03/11/09, Obama signed a statement to accompany the "Omnibus Appropriations Act, 2009" circumventing the legislative intent of Congress with regard to contact between federal employees and congressional committee members when it comes to "whistleblowers" reporting fraud, waste and abuse matters. By so doing, President Obama signed a statement he promised he wouldn't sign. This promise was not fulfilled.	0.00

Chapter 17 - Transparency & Ethics

TE-10

The Promise: "...Obama will strengthen whistleblower laws to protect federal workers who expose waste, fraud, and abuse of authority in government."
When/Where: Obama/Biden Plan: "The Change We Need in Washington," dated 09/22/08.
Source: http://webarchive.loc.gov/all/20090429185753/http://change.gov/agenda/
Status: The benefits of protecting whistleblowers are evident. Under the False Claims Act, the federal government successfully prosecuted 417 whistleblower cases in CY2011, up from 231 in CY2008. The CY2011 prosecutions alone recovered approximately $2.3B in taxpayer monies.

On 04/16/11, Senator Daniel Akaka (D-HI) and 14 co-sponsors introduced the Whistleblower Protection Enhancement Act of 2012 (S. 743). It was described as a "bill to amend chapter 23 of title 5, United States Code, to clarify the disclosures of information protected from prohibited personnel practices, require a statement in nondisclosure policies, forms, and agreements that such policies, forms, and agreements conform with certain disclosure protections, provide certain authority for the Special Counsel, and for other purposes."

President Obama signed S.743 into law on 11/27/12.

This promise was fulfilled.

1.00

TE-11

The Promise: "....we need earmark reform. And when I'm president, I will go line by line to make sure that we are not spending money unwisely."
When/Where: Presidential Debate, Oxford, MS, 09/26/08.
Source: http://votesmart.org/public-statement/381008/the-first-presidential-debate-transcript/?search=unwisely
Status: The American Recovery and Reinvestment Act of 2009 was loaded with earmarks, by some accounts up to 9,000. The promised "line-by-line" review was not conducted, reportedly for the sake of expediency. The President did not have "line item veto" powers anyway. All he could have done under the Constitution is either sign the bill when presented to him or return it to Congress with his objections, thereby delaying the process which he sought, at all costs, to avoid.

Another example: A "stopgap" measure extending the spending power of 11 Cabinet-level departments until mid-12/09 was approved by Congress on 10/29/09 (House 247 to 178; Senate 72 to 28) and contained approximately 526 earmarks valued at $341M. No "line by line" review was conducted.

President Obama promised to reduce earmark spending down to the CY1994 level of $7.8B (in nominal dollars). Instead, he signed into law $15.2B of appropriations for 11,124 earmarks during FY2009 and $11.0B of appropriations for 9,192 earmarks in FY2010. The FY2011 $1.1T omnibus spending bill released on 12/14/10 included approximately 6,600 earmarks worth about $8B for specific Senate and House member pet projects and programs.

In the aftermath of the CY2010 mid-term elections, it appeared that both houses of Congress were leaning toward a 2-year moratorium on earmarks. This did not happen as the proposed moratorium was rejected by the Senate on 11/30/10 (39 for, 65 against). However, on 02/01/11, Senator Daniel Inouye (D-HI), who served as Chairman of the Senate Appropriations Committee, announced that the 2-year earmark moratorium would be implemented over Senate Majority Leader Harry Reid's (D-NV) documented objections that President Obama is "absolutely wrong" and "should back off" his opposition to earmarks. The 2-year moratorium expired at the end of CY2012.

An Earmark Elimination Act of 2011 (S. 1930) was introduced in a bipartisan manner by Senators Claire McCaskill (D-MO) and Pat Toomey (R-PA) on 11/29/11. Proponents of this legislation sought to include it as an amendment (S. 1472) to the Stop Trading on Congressional Knowledge (STOCK) Act of 2012. The proposed amendment was defeated (40 for, 59 against) on 02/02/12.

The House had a similar Earmark Elimination Act of 2011 (H.R. 3707) introduced by Congressman

0.00

Jeff Flake (R-AZ) on 12/16/11. No action was taken on this proposed legislation and it expired with the 112th Congress at the end of CY2012.

Earmarks continued into FY2012 but were no longer referred to as "earmarks" but simply as budget "additions" or "policy issues." For example, the FY2012 Defense appropriation alone included 115 committee "additions" valued at $834M.

Although this promise was not intended to eliminate earmarks entirely, just reform them, it did call for "line by line" scrutiny by President Obama of earmarks appended to bills passed by Congress for his signature without public hearings. This didn't happen.

This promise was not fulfilled.

TE-12	**The Promise:** "....will shed light on all earmarks by disclosing the name of the legislator who asked for each earmark, along with a written justification, 72 hours before they can be approved by the full Senate." **When/Where:** Obama-Biden Plan: "Blueprint for Change" dated 10/09/08. **Source:** https://www.documentcloud.org/documents/550007-barack-obama-2008-blueprint-for-change.html **Status:** The 2009 Economic Stimulus Bill was loaded with earmarks, by some accounts up to 9,000. While the House originator of individual earmarks became a matter of public record in this and subsequent bills signed into law by President Obama, the promised written notice 72 hours in advance of Senate approval did not happen. Senator Thomas Coburn (R-OK) introduced the Earmark Transparency Act (S. 3335) on 05/11/10 to require Congress to establish a database that is "unified and searchable on a public website" on which Congressional earmarks are to be posted not later than five days after submission by a requester. This bill was reported by the Senate Committee on Homeland Security and Governmental Affairs on 07/28/10, but no further action was taken by the Senate. This bill expired with the 111th Congress in 01/11. House Rules for the 112th Congress included the proposal that "Earmark information should be posted online in a centralized database. This includes earmarks, earmark requests and related documentation." Following up on this proposed House rule, Congressman Mike Quigly (D-IL) proposed on 01/05/11 that all earmark requests in the 112th Congress be made available for public review. This proposal would have required members of Congress to disclose all requests for funding in their Congressional districts to be posted on their official websites, including official earmark requests as well as soft earmark requests like letters, phone calls, or direct federal agency solicitations. This proposal was rejected by the 112th Congress House leadership. Although a 2-year earmark moratorium was announced by Senator Daniel Inouye (D-HI) on 02/01/11, earmarks reportedly continued through FY2011. But there were positive developments. On 05/17/11, the Chairman of the House Armed Services Committee, "Buck" McKeon (R-CA), published guidelines for submitting amendments to the FY2012 National Defense Authorization Act (NDAA). Such budgetary amendments were not to be considered as "congressional earmarks" and amounts involved could only be for national security purposes. The resultant FY2012 NDAA had 115 such "amendments" valued at $834M. As of end-CY2016, although the "earmark moratorium" was still in effect, sly legislators continued to practice alternative methods to "bring home the bacon" to their constituents. FY2016 earmarks, referred to by some as "congressionally directed spending," were contained in the Consolidated Appropriations Act of 2016 in an amount exceeding $5.1B. In FY2017, the amount went up to $6.8B. The prevailing earmark moratorium rendered moot the basic tenets of this promise. It should be noted, however, that throughout the Obama Administration, Congress did not adopt any process for	0.00

Chapter 17 - Transparency & Ethics

the promised 72-hour written public notification prior to Senate approval of bill "amendments" or "congressionally directed spending" -- whatever the term of choice may have been for earmarks at that time.

This promise was not fulfilled.

TE-13

The Promise: "Obama and Biden will nullify the Bush attempts to make the timely release of presidential records more difficult."
When/Where: Obama-Biden Plan: "Blueprint for Change" dated 10/09/08.
Source: https://www.documentcloud.org/documents/550007-barack-obama-2008-blueprint-for-change.html
Status: During his first full day in office, 01/21/09, President Obama revoked Executive Order 13233 signed by President Bush on 11/01/01 that limited release of former presidents' records. President Obama's Executive Order 13489 superseded Executive Order 13233.

This promise was fulfilled.

1.00

TE-14

The Promise: "...will ensure that federal contracts over $25,000 are competitively bid."
When/Where: Obama-Biden Plan: "Blueprint for Change" dated 10/09/08.
Source: https://www.documentcloud.org/documents/550007-barack-obama-2008-blueprint-for-change.html
Status: On 11/30/09, the GAO published a report revealing that the Small Business Administration issued 68% of its stimulus bill contracts non-competitively, and NASA and HUD issued 37% and 35% of their stimulus contracts this way respectively.

In addition, the GAO cited 5 other agencies for disregarding President Obama's promise by awarding the following percentages of its contracts non-competitively: Transportation (22%), EPA (24%), Homeland Security (25%), Commerce (29%) and Agriculture (30%).

On 01/31/10, Assistant Secretary of State P.J. Crowley informed Fox News that a contract worth more than $24.6 million had been awarded non-competitively by the U.S. Agency for International Development (USAID) to Checchi and Company Consulting, a Washington, D.C.-based firm owned by economist and Democratic Party donor Vincent Checchi. This particular contract was terminated as a result of protests from at least one potential bidder. The point of this example is that no-bid contracts continued to be awarded early in the Obama Administration and were only reversed if discovered and protested.

There are circumstances when contracts exceeding $25K can be awarded on a non-competitive bid basis. Foreign Military Sales (FMS) is an example where a purchaser country can certify to the Department of Defense that it desires to acquire a specific end-item or system from a specific Original Equipment Manufacturer (OEM) on a designated sole source basis. If justified for reasons such as equipment standardization or interoperability purposes, such sole source designation requests are usually honored and contracts are awarded on a no-bid basis.

This promise was not fulfilled.

0.00

TE-15

The Promise: "...is committed to returning earmarks to less than $7.8 billion a year, the level they were at before 1994."
When/Where: Obama/Biden Plan to Slash Earmarks dated 11/10/07.
Source: https://webarchive.loc.gov/all/20090429184437/http://change.gov/agenda/ethics_agenda/
Status: The American Recovery and Reinvestment Act of 2009 alone reportedly contained over 9,000 earmarks valued at over $5B. Altogether, President Obama signed $16.5B of appropriations earmarks (11,124 line items) into law during CY2009.

The total U.S. Government FY2010 budget signed into law by President Obama contained over $15.9B in earmarks (over 9,000 line items).

0.00

Chapter 17 - Transparency & Ethics

The FY2011 $1.1T omnibus spending bill released on 12/14/10 included approximately 6,750 earmarks worth about $8.3B for specific Senate and House member pet projects and programs.

Until the FY2012 earmark moratorium, earmarks were a popular way for congressional members to placate their constituents back home, and President Obama acquiesced to exceeding the promised $7.8B annual limit. Subsequent to FY2012, earmarks continued to exceed $7.8B per year under different names such as "amendments" or "congressionally directed spending."

This promise was not fulfilled.

TE-16

The Promise: "...will ensure that any tax breaks for corporate recipients - or tax earmarks - are also publicly available on the Internet in an easily searchable format."
When/Where: Obama-Biden Plan for America entitled: "Blueprint for Change" dated 10/09/08.
Source: https://www.documentcloud.org/documents/550007-barack-obama-2008-blueprint-for-change.html
Status: On 05/11/10, Senator Thomas Coburn (R-OK) introduced the Earmark Transparency Act (S. 3335) to establish a unified and searchable database on a public website as called for by President Obama during his 2010 State of the Union Address. On the same date, Congressman Bill Cassidy (R-LA) introduced a similar bill (H.R. 5258). No further action was taken on either proposed legislation and they expired with the 111th Congress at the end of CY2010.

During the 112th Congress, the "Transparency in Government Act of 2011" (H.R. 2340) was introduced by Congressman Mike Quigley (D-IL) on 06/23/11. While this bill would have responded 100% to the requirements of this promise, no action was taken on it and it expired with the 112th Congress at the end of CY2012. Congressman Quigley reintroduced this bill on 03/13/14 (H.R. 4245) but it expired with the 114th Congress at the end of CY2016.

Until FY2010, the excellent Office of Management and Budget (OMB) website at "http://earmarks.omb.gov/earmarks-public" (no longer available) reflected earmark data for the period FY2005-FY2010. However, this database did not specifically address tax breaks accorded to corporate recipients of government funds.

This promise was not fulfilled.

0.00

TE-17

The Promise: "...would amend Executive Order 12866 to ensure that communications about regulatory policymaking between persons outside government and all White House staff are disclosed to the public."
When/Where: Obama-Biden Plan for America entitled: "Blueprint for Change" dated 10/09/08.
Source: https://www.documentcloud.org/documents/550007-barack-obama-2008-blueprint-for-change.html
Status: Executive Order 12866 (as amended) was supplemented by President Obama's 01/18/11 signature of Executive Order 13563 entitled "Improving Regulation and Regulatory Review." Executive Order 13563 did not address the issue of disclosure to the public of regulatory policymaking between non-government persons and "all White House staff."

The Senate confirmed Cass Sunstein to lead the White House Office of Information and Regulatory Affairs on 09/10/09 in a 63-35 vote. Just five days later, the White House started to make its visitor list available to the public. A positive step -- but far from the level of disclosure at the heart of this promise.

In 12/09, Mr. Sunstein was directed to initiate a review of the White House's rules on public disclosures and transparency, resulting in the 09/20/11 release of the "Open Government Partnership - National Action Plan for the United States of America."

0.00

Chapter 17 - Transparency & Ethics

On 12/08/09, the Office of Management and Budget (OMB) issued its "Open Government Directive". This directive offered excellent direction to "executive departments and agencies", requiring each such department or agency to develop its "Open Government Plan" and post it on its "Open Government Webpage".

Communications between outsiders and White House staff about regulatory policymaking were not, as of end-CY2016, effectively addressed anywhere. The new "data.gov" website contained information on White House visitors, but did not address in any meaningful detail the influence those visitors may have had on regulatory policymaking.

White House principals and staffers reportedly routinely circumvented procedures. For example, the New York Times reported in 06/11 that hundreds of meetings between liberal political activists, lobbyists, and White House officials went unreported in White House visitor logs because the groups took their business off-site (i.e. to coffee shops near the White House) to discuss President Obama's agenda. In one instance, introductions to the chief executive of a major foreign corporation were reportedly made on a White House side lawn to avoid entering that visitor's name in the official White House visitor registry.

This promise was not fulfilled.

TE-18	**The Promise:** "...will insulate the Director of National Intelligence from political pressure by giving the DNI a fixed term, like the Chairman of the Federal Reserve...will seek consistency and integrity at the top of our intelligence community -- not just a political ally." **When/Where:** Obama-Biden Plan for America entitled: "Blueprint for Change" dated 10/09/08. **Source:** https://www.documentcloud.org/documents/550007-barack-obama-2008-blueprint-for-change.html **Status:** President Obama's nominee as Director of National Intelligence (DNI), Admiral (Ret.) Dennis C. Blair, was sworn in as DNI on 01/29/09. No term limit was attached to his appointment. Blair resigned from this post on 05/20/10. Retired Air Force Lieutenant General James Clapper was confirmed by the Senate as Blair's successor on 08/05/10. There was no term limit attached to this appointment. This promise was not fulfilled.	0.00
TE-19	**The Promise:** "...will require his appointees who lead the executive branch departments and rulemaking agencies to conduct the significant business of the agency in public, so that any citizen can watch these debates in person or on the Internet." **When/Where:** Obama-Biden Plan: "Blueprint for Change" dated 10/09/08. **Source:** https://www.documentcloud.org/documents/550007-barack-obama-2008-blueprint-for-change.html **Status:** As of end-CY2016, neither the heads of executive branch departments nor the heads of rulemaking agencies (with very few and rare exceptions) conducted their "significant" business in public forums. They released the results of that business on a strict "need to know" basis only. This promise was not fulfilled.	0.00
TE-20	**The Promise:** "...will bring democracy and policy directly to the people by requiring his Cabinet officials to have periodic national broadband townhall meetings to discuss issues before their agencies." **When/Where:** Obama-Biden Plan: "Blueprint for Change" dated 10/09/08. **Source:** https://www.documentcloud.org/documents/550007-barack-obama-2008-blueprint-for-change.html **Status:** As of end-CY2016, not all Cabinet officials were known to have conducted "periodic national broadband townhall meetings" to discuss their agencies' affairs.	0.00

Chapter 17 - Transparency & Ethics

Aside from select domestic/local or foreign venues, the Secretaries of Agriculture, Transportation, Treasury, Veterans Affairs, and the Attorney General were not known to have conducted "periodic national broadband townhall meetings" so that the American people could get a sense of what was going on in their organizations. Q&A's fielded by department underlings don't count. President Obama promised Cabinet member interface.

Appearing on Jon Stewart's "The Daily Show" on 10/27/10, President Obama acknowledged that during his first two years in office, "we have done things that some folks don't even know about." The American taxpayer understands that in the interest of national security, some issues simply cannot be discussed in open forums. But President Obama's admission did not contain a national security caveat. Rather, he told the American people that his Administration was not being as forthcoming with them as he promised it would be.

The Secretaries of Defense, Education, State, Interior, Energy, Commerce and several others conducted infrequent town hall meetings. President Obama would have done well to define the word 'periodic.' However, this promise, as interpreted by the 'man/woman on the street,' applied to all Cabinet members and the frequency of broadband-based townhall meetings was meant to be at least once or twice each year.

The White House web site "Open for Questions" did not count as a vehicle for promise fulfillment, as there was no assurance that a taxpayer would receive a response to questions submitted to the White House.

This promise was not fulfilled.

TE-21

The Promise: "...will bring foreign policy decisions directly to the people by requiring his national security officials to have periodic national broadband town hall meetings to discuss foreign policy. They will personally deliver occasional fireside chats via webcast."

When/Where: Obama-Biden Plan: "To Secure America and Restore our Standing," undated.

Source: Source document was available online throughout the Obama Administration. It has since been deleted from all archival websites.

Status: This promise is not to be confused with Promise Number TE-20, which was aimed at town hall meetings to be conducted by members of President Obama's Cabinet.

As of end-CY2016, there had been no such "periodic national broadband town hall meetings" led by his national security officials (i.e. Director of CIA, NSA, National Intelligence, etc.) or, in the case of foreign policy decisions, by the Secretary of State.

This promise was not fulfilled.

0.00

ETHICS/TRANSPARENCY GPA | **0.24**

Chapter 18 - Independent Organizations

Campaign Promises
Other/Miscellaneous -> Independent Organizations

ITEM	INDEPENDENT ORGANIZATIONS	
	CFTC	**GRADE**
IO-1	**The Promise:** "Current loopholes in Commodity Futures Trading Commission regulations have contributed to the skyrocketing price of oil on world markets...will enact simple legislation to close these loopholes and increase transparency on the market to help bring oil prices down and prevent traders from unfairly lining their pockets at the expense of the American people." **When/Where:** Obama-Biden Plan: "New Energy for America" dated 09/06/08. **Source:** http://energy.gov/sites/prod/files/edg/media/Obama_New_Energy_0804.pdf **Status:** In CY2008, oil prices skyrockted to over $147 per barrel. To mitigate the potential repeat of the CY2008 situation, the Commodity Futures Trading Commission (CFTC) released a proposal on 01/14/10 to cap the number of contracts the 10 largest position holders could hold in all markets. Under Section 737 of the Dodd-Frank Wall Street Reform and Consumer Protection Act (aka "Financial Reform Bill") signed into law by President Obama on 07/21/10, the CFTC is bound to "establish limits (including related hedge exemption provisions) on the aggregate number or amount of positions in contracts based upon the same underlying commodity (as defined by the Commission) that may be held by any person, including any group or class of traders..." This initiative to close the oil-related loopholes extended the CFTC's authority to the over-the-counter market for the first time in over 30 years. This promise was fulfilled.	1.00
	CNCS	**GRADE**
IO-2	**The Promise:** "Will build on the foundation of sites like USAFreedomCorps.gov and VolunteerMatch.org and leverage technology to increase awareness of and participation in service opportunities." **When/Where:** Obama-Biden Plan: "Helping All Americans Serve Their Country", 09/11/08. **Source:** http://i2.cdn.turner.com/cnn/2008/images/07/02/national.service.fact.sheet.final.pdf **Status:** Further to the creation of the website "Serve.org" by the Corporation for National and Community Service (CNCS), President Obama signed the Serve America Act (H.R. 1388) into law on 04/21/09. Subtitle G, Section 1704 of the Serve America Act expands on the responsibilities of the CNCS to "...bolster the public awareness of and recruitment efforts for the wide range of service opportunities for citizens of all ages, regardless of socioeconomic status or geographic location, through a variety of methods, including (A) print media; (B) the Internet and related emerging technologies; (C) television; (D) radio; (E) presentations at public or private forums; (F) other innovative methods of communication; and (G) outreach to offices of economic development, State employment security agencies, labor organizations and trade associations, local educational agencies, institutions of higher education, agencies and organizations serving veterans and individuals with disabilities, and other institutions or organizations from which participants for programs receiving assistance from the national service laws can be recruited..." This promise was fulfilled.	1.00

Chapter 18 - Independent Organizations

IO-3 | **The Promise:** "Expand AmeriCorps from 75,000 slots to 250,000..." | 0.00
When/Where: Obama-Biden Plan: "Enable All Americans to Serve to Meet the Nation's Challenges," undated.
Source: https://webarchive.loc.gov/all/20090429185046/http://change.gov/agenda/service_agenda/
Status: The $5.7 billion Edward M. Kennedy Serve America Act, signed into law on 04/21/09, more than tripled the authorized size of the domestic volunteer group AmeriCorps from 75,000 to 250,000 by FY2017. Incremental manpower increases mandated by this law were as follows:
- 88,000 in FY2010
- 115,000 in FY2011
- 140,000 in FY2012
- 170,000 in FY2013
- 200,000 in FY2014
- 210,000 in FY2015
- 235,000 in FY2016
- 250,000 in FY2017

As of end-CY2016, the annual membership for Americorps still averaged about 75,000 annually according to the Corporation for National and Community Service (CNCS). The goal of filling the enacted 250,000 slots by FY2017 was not met.

This promise was not fulfilled.

IO-4 | **The Promise:** "...will engage more interested seniors into public service opportunities by expanding the Senior Corps program..." | 0.00
When/Where: Obama-Biden Plan: "Helping America's Seniors", dated 10/26/07.
Source: https://webarchive.loc.gov/all/20090429185714/http://change.gov/agenda/seniors_and_social_security_agenda/
Status: In the President's 2010 Budget for the Corporation for National and Community Service (CNCS), this promise was covered by the statement: "The President's Budget would expand and improve Senior Corps programs, which connect individuals over the age of 55 to local volunteer opportunities, allowing more retirees to help meet the needs and challenges in their communities."

For FY2009 (pre-Obama), the enacted budget level for the Senior Corps was $213.7M. Expansion of the Senior Corps was not likely possible without a related funding increase. Consequently Senior Corps funding was increased slightly to $220.9M in FY2010, but was funded below the FY2009 level for FY2011, FY2012 and FY2013 ($207M respectively). The funding level for the Senior Corps went down further to the $202.1M level in FY2014, where it remained for the rest of President Obama's second term in office.

This promise was not fulfilled.

IO-5 | **The Promise:** "Will support the creation of an "Artists Corps" of young artists trained to work in low-income schools and their communities." | 0.00
When/Where: Obama-Biden Plan: "Champions for Arts and Culture", dated 09/11/08.
Source: http://muzartworld.org/president-barack-obama-and-joe-biden-champions-for-arts-and-culture/
Status: Section 1302 of the Edward M. Kennedy Serve America Act (H.R. 1388), signed into law by President Obama on 04/21/09 provides, in part, for "skilled musicians and artists to promote greater community unity through the use of music and arts education and engagement through work in low-income communities..." This initiative was to be an offshoot of the "Education Corps" to be established under the above law. However, Congress never established the "Education Corps."

A limited-scope "MusicianCorps" has existed under the umbrella of AmeriCorps to infuse music instruction and service learning into under-resourced elementary and secondary schools in communities with high dropout rates such as in Austin, TX; Denver, CO; and Los Angeles and San Francisco, CA.

The logical organization to assume the responsibility for the creation and management of a national-level "Artist Corps" would have been the Corporation for National and Community Service (CNCS). However, no specific "Artist Corps" had been established under CNCS as of end-CY2016.

This promise was not fulfilled.

Chapter 18 - Independent Organizations

IO-6	**The Promise:** "Will create a Social Investment Fund Network." **When/Where:** Obama-Biden Plan: "Helping All Americans Serve Their Country" dated 09/11/08. **Source:** http://i2.cdn.turner.com/cnn/2008/images/07/02/national.service.fact.sheet.final.pdf **Status:** The creation of a Social Investment Fund occurred under the aegis of the Edward M. Kennedy Serve America Act, signed into law on 04/21/09 by President Obama. Initial funding in the amount of $50M for this fund, now referred to as the "Social Innovation Fund," came to fruition under the Consolidated Appropriations Act of 2010, signed by President Obama on 12/16/09. This promise was fulfilled.	1.00
IO-7	**The Promise:** "...will also create an energy-focused youth jobs program to invest in disconnected and disadvantaged youth." **When/Where:** Obama-Biden Plan: "New Energy for America," dated 09/06/08. **Source:** http://energy.gov/sites/prod/files/edg/media/Obama_New_Energy_0804.pdf **Status:** President Obama created the Clean Energy Service Corps as part of the Edward M. Kennedy Serve America Act he signed into law in 04/09. The Clean Energy Service Corps, part of AmeriCorps, was intended to train people and put them to work installing solar panels, weatherizing low-income homes, conducting home energy audits, and consulting small businesses on their energy use. This promise was fulfilled.	1.00
IO-8	**The Promise:** "Under the current federal work-study program...at least 7 percent of that funding is supposed to go to community service jobs like tutoring...we need to raise the service threshold to 25 percent...will work to help colleges and universities reach the goal of 50 percent in serve-study..." **When/Where:** Obama-Biden Plan: "Helping All Americans Serve Their Country" dated 09/11/08. **Source:** http://i2.cdn.turner.com/cnn/2008/images/07/02/national.service.fact.sheet.final.pdf **Status:** Under Title 34, Chapter VI, Part 675.18 of the Code of Federal Regulations and the Higher Education Act of 1965 (as amended), an institution must use at least 7% of the sum of its initial and supplemental Federal Work-Study (FWS) allocations for an award year to compensate students employed in community service activities. As of end-CY2016, Department of Education rules still indicated that schools must use at least 7% of their FWS allocation to employ students in community service jobs with at least one student employed as a reading tutor or performing family literacy activities. There was no meaningful activity during President Obama's two terms in office to raise the community service threshhold to 25%, let alone 50% for college/university serve-study programs. This promise was not fulfilled.	0.00
IO-9	**The Promise:** "I am also going to create a 5-E Youth Service Corps. The "E's" stand for energy efficiency, environmental education and employment." **When/Where:** Obama Campaign Speech, Hampton, VA, dated 06/05/07. **Source:** https://www.presidency.ucsb.edu/documents/remarks-the-hampton-university-annual-ministers-conference-hampton-virginia **Status:** During the Obama Administration, there existed several programs targeted toward America's youth such as the "America's Great Outdoor Initiative" the "21st Century Conservation Service Corps" and "YouthBuild." As of end-CY2016, there was no sign that a specifically promised "5-E Youth Service Corps" had been established, logically under the Corporation for National and Community Service (CNCS) and the Americorps programs it manages. This promise was not fulfilled.	0.00
IO-10	**The Promise:** "There will be a comprehensive, easily searchable web presence with information about service opportunities, and a full strategy to ensure that people interested in opportunities can find them." **When/Where:** Obama-Biden Plan: "Helping All Americans Serve Their Country" dated 09/11/08.	1.00

Source: http://i2.cdn.turner.com/cnn/2008/images/07/02/national.service.fact.sheet.final.pdf
Status: During the Obama Administration, the Corporation for National and Community Service (CNCS) refined its web site entitled "nationalservice.gov," an interactive program designed to guide individuals to Americorps and Senior Corps volunteer/service programs that may interest them. Nationalservice.gov has a link entitled "Find a Volunteer Opportunity," a site that provides leads to volunteer opportunities in one's specific area as well as permitting entities with volunteering opportunities to register their projects. The search tool is supported by all modern browsers (i.e. Internet Explorer, Google Chrome, Firefox).

This promise was fulfilled.

IO-11 The Promise: "...will tie a plan to give schools a substantial infusion of funds to support teachers and principals and improve student learning to the condition that school districts develop programs to engage students in service opportunities."
When/Where: Obama-Biden Plan: "Helping All Americans Serve Their Country" dated 09/11/08.
Source: http://i2.cdn.turner.com/cnn/2008/images/07/02/national.service.fact.sheet.final.pdf
Status: The perfect vehicle to deliver on this promise was the "Learn and Serve America" (LSA) program. This program offered approximately 1M students from kindergarten through college the opportunity to get involved by integrating community service projects with classroom activities. Funding for the LSA program started to stagnate in FY2009 with funding limited to $37.4M. The LSA budget was hit again in FY2010 (down to $36.5M). Congress killed the LSA program in FY2011.

The promise for a "substantial infusion of funds" was not apparent in President Obama's first budget submission to Congress for FY2010. The rest is history.

This promise was not fulfilled.

0.00

IO-12 The Promise: "...believe that middle and high school students should be expected to engage in community service for 50 hours annually during the school year or summer months. They will develop national guidelines for service-learning and community service programs, and will give schools better tools both to develop successful programs and to document the experience of students at all levels."
When/Where: Obama-Biden Plan: "Helping All Americans Serve Their Country" dated 09/11/08.
Source: http://i2.cdn.turner.com/cnn/2008/images/07/02/national.service.fact.sheet.final.pdf
Status: The Corporation for National and Community Service (CNCS) "Learn and Serve America" program was the perfect vehicle to support promise fulfillment. This program was cancelled by Congress in FY2011.

Other than existing state and district service-learning policies and guidelines, there has been no known development of "national guidelines" or any specific mandate articulated by the Obama Administration to CNCS that ALL middle school and high school students engage in community service.

This promise was not fulfilled.

0.00

IO-13 The Promise: "...will create an agency within the Corporation for National and Community Service dedicated to building the capacity and effectiveness of the nonprofit sector. The agency will be charged with: improving coordination of programs that support nonprofits across the federal government; fostering nonprofit accountability; streamlining processes for obtaining federal grants and contracts, and eliminating unnecessary requirements; and removing barriers for smaller nonprofits to participate in government programs. The agency will make grants to build the infrastructure of the nonprofit sector and capacity of nonprofit organizations, including their ability to ensure accountability, manage volunteers, and improve outcomes."
When/Where: Obama-Biden Plan: "Helping All Americans Serve Their Country" dated 09/11/08.
Source: http://i2.cdn.turner.com/cnn/2008/images/07/02/national.service.fact.sheet.final.pdf
Status: The "Nonprofit Capacity Building Program" (NCBP) was created under the Edward M. Kennedy Serve America Act of 2009 (H.R. 1388/S. 277) (also known simply as the "Serve America Act"). This Act directed the establishment of the NCBP by the CNCS. Its establishment satisfied all of the criteria addressed in this promise, specifically to improve nonprofits' performance in communities facing resource hardships.

Under the Serve America Act, the NCBP was authorized $25M over a period of five years (FY2010-FY2014).

This promise was fulfilled.

1.00

Chapter 18 - Independent Organizations

	EPA	GRADE
IO-14	**The Promise:** "Will establish a goal of making all new buildings carbon neutral, or produce zero emissions, by 2030..." **When/Where:** Obama-Biden Plan: "New Energy for America" dated 09/06/08. **Source:** http://energy.gov/sites/prod/files/edg/media/Obama_New_Energy_0804.pdf **Status:** The proposed "Cap-and-Trade Bill", a two-part regulatory system in which the "cap" is a government-imposed limit on carbon emissions, and the "trade" is a government-created market to buy and sell greenhouse gas credits. This bill (H.R. 2454) was passed by the House on 06/26/09. The above bill did not pass the Senate before the 111th Congress adjourned at the end of CY2010. Had it passed Congress and been signed into law, the above bill would have fallen far short of the "zero emissions" or efficiency goals in "all new buildings" promised by 2030. On 10/05/09, President Obama signed Executive Order 13514 entitled: "Federal Leadership in Environmental, Energy, and Economic Performance." This document mandates that 100% of all new "federal" buildings meet a "zero-net-energy" goal by CY2030. This campaign promise was directed toward "all new buildings," not only toward new federal buildings. As of end-CY2016, the Obama Administration had not established the stated goal on a national scale. This promise was not fulfilled.	0.00
IO-15	**The Promise:** "As President, I will set a hard cap on all carbon emissions at a level that scientists say is necessary to curb global warming - an 80% reduction by 2050...I will also commit to interim targets toward this goal in 2020, 2030, and 2040. These reductions will start immediately..." **When/Where:** Remarks of Senator Barack Obama: Real Leadership for a Clean Energy Future, Portsmouth, NH , 10/08/07. **Source:** https://2008election.procon.org/sourcefiles/Obama20071008.pdf **Status:** Reductions didn't exactly start "immediately" as Candidate Obama promised. The proposed "Cap-and-Trade" initiative was included in President Obama's FY2010 budget proposal of 02/26/09, but warranted no mention in his FY2011 budget proposal. Proposed "Cap-and-Trade" legislation (H.R. 2454) was passed by the Democrat-led House 06/26/09. The Democrat-led Senate did not take any action on this bill before the 111th Congress expired at the end of CY2010. In essence, Senate Democrats abandoned a 7-year effort to pass some version of "Cap and Trade" legislation that would have addressed climate change by regulating and taxing the carbon emissions of power plants and other companies. With Republicans in control of the House since the 11/10 elections, it was unlikely that they would support any new version of the "Cap and Trade" bill prior to the end of President Obama's first term in 01/13. This was supported by the view of many (rightly or wrongly) that the setting of artificial caps on carbon dioxide emissions would not be as effective as the employment of practical solutions such as the pursuit of natural gas by drilling into shale formations (i.e. fracking). Draft legislation entitled the "Energy Tax Prevention Act of 2011" was unveiled on 02/02/11 by Congressman Fred Uption (R-MI). One of the stated purposes of this proposed act was to prevent the EPA from "imposing a backdoor cap-and-trade tax" on industries identified as polluters that would ultimately raise the cost of gasoline, electricity, fertilizer and groceries for the American consumer. Meanwhile, a U.S.-Finnish study revealed in 07/11 that the extent of global warming during the period CY1998-CY2008 was less than publicized by other studies. Despite an increase in carbon dioxide emissions during that period, global temperatures reportedly dropped slightly, a condition attributed to China's increased use of coal-fired power plants that release sun-blocking sulfates. Further, the 7th International Climate Change Conference held in Chicago, IL in 05/12 concluded that global temperatures had cyclically declined since CY2000 and that this decline would continue through at least CY2030.	0.00

Chapter 18 - Independent Organizations

The bottom line, however, was that President Obama promised to address the setting of a "hard cap" on carbon emissions "immediately" (meaning shortly after his 01/09 inauguration). This was not done.

This promise was not fulfilled.

IO-16	**The Promise:** "Will increase fuel economy standards 4 percent per year ..."

When/Where: Obama-Biden Plan for America entitled: "Blueprint for Change" dated 10/09/08.
Source: https://www.documentcloud.org/documents/550007-barack-obama-2008-blueprint-for-change.html
Status: The Corporate Average Fuel Economy (CAFE) standards are U.S. regulations enacted in CY1975 to improve the average fuel economy of cars and light trucks sold in the USA. Resources under the Environmental Protection Agency's (EPA's) Federal Vehicle and Fuels Standards and Certification program are responsible for issuing certificates and ensuring compliance with these CAFE standards, as established by the National Highway Traffic Safety Administration (NHTSA).

From CY1990 to CY2010, CAFE requirements for passenger cars were flat at 27.5 miles per gallon (mpg). Starting with CY2011, CAFE requirements for passenger cars increased as follows:
CY2011....30.4 mpg (a 10.6% increase over preceding year)
CY2012....33.3 mpg (9.5% increase)
CY2013....34.2 mpg (2.7% increase)
CY2014....34.9 mpg (2.1% increase)
CY2015....36.2 mpg (3.7% increase)
CY2016....37.8 mpg (4.4% increase)
Average increase per year: 5.5%

CAFE requirements for light duty trucks for CY2009 and CY2010 were 23.1 and 23.5 mpg respectively. Starting with CY2011, CAFE requirements for light duty trucks increased as follows:
CY2011....24.4 mpg (a 4.0% increase over preceding year)
CY2012....25.4 mpg (4.1% increase)
CY2013....26.0 mpg (2.4% increase)
CY2014....26.6 mpg (2.3% increase)
CY2015....27.5 mpg (3.4% increase)
CY2016....28.8 mpg (4.7% increase)
Average increase per year: 3.5%
Combined passenger car and light duty truck average increase per year: 4.5%

This promise was fulfilled.

1.00

IO-17	**The Promise:** "I am committed to pursuing greater funding for the EPA."

When/Where: Candidate Obama letter to the National President, American Federation of Government Employees, AFL-CIO, dated 10/20/08.
Source: https://litwinbooks.com/obamas-letter-on-the-epa/
Status: The Environmental Protection Agency's (EPA's) FY2009 budget authorization under President George W. Bush was $7.633B. Under President Obama, this was supplemented by the American Recovery and Reinvestment Act (ARRA) of 2009 in the amount of $7.220B for a total FY2009 budget of $14.853B.

Using the pre-ARRA budget authorization for FY2009 ($7.6B) as a marker, the EPA's enacted budget authority during the ensuing years was as follows:
FY2010....$10.3B
FY2011.....$8.7B
FY2012.....$8.5B
FY2013.....$7.9B
FY2014.....$8.2B
FY2015.....$8.1B
FY2016.....$8.1B
FY2017.....$8.3B

This promise was fulfilled.

1.00

Chapter 18 - Independent Organizations

IO-18

The Promise: "...will restore the strength of the Superfund program by requiring polluters to pay for the cleanup of contaminated sites they created."
When/Where: Obama-Biden Plan: "Supporting Urban Prosperity", dated 09/11/08.
Source: https://assets.documentcloud.org/documents/550008/barack-obama-2008-supporting-urban-prosperity.pdf
Status: The "Superfund" moniker came about after the passage into law of the "Comprehensive Environmental Response, Compensation and Liability Act (CERCLA) of 1980." Under this Act, the U.S. Government was able to collect nearly $4B in taxes from the chemical and oil industries. These funds were used by the EPA to clean up some of the approximately 650 orphaned sites (toxic sites for which there is no longer an identifiable Potentially Responsible Party (PRP)). This tax was left to expire in CY1995, at which time the fund had about $6B. This $6B ran out in CY2003 and any EPA cleanups since (one or two dozen per year) have been paid by the U.S. taxpayer through funds appropriated by Congress.

President Obama's FY2010 budget proposal called for the reinstatement of excise taxes to collect $1B to clean up the nation's most toxic sites under the EPA's Superfund program. But, the taxes were deferred "until CY2011, after the economy recovers." The taxes were forgotten after CY2011.

During President Obama's two terms in office, Congress did not act on the prerequisite reinstatement of some form of excise tax on the oil and chemical industries. Bills such as the "Polluter Pays Restoration Act" (S.461) introduced by Senator Frank Lautenberg (D-NJ) on 03/02/11, or the "Superfund Reinvestment Act" (H.R. 1596) introduced by Congressman Earl Blumenauer (D-OR) on 04/15/11, had little-to-no chance of getting beyond preliminary committee reviews.

The "Superfund Polluter Pays Restoration Act of 2014" (S.2679) was introduced by Senator Cory Booker (D-NJ) on 07/29/14 to amend the Internal Revenue Code of 1986 to reinstate the financing for the Hazardous Substance Superfund in the form of excise taxes levied on polluters to pay for the cleanup of contaminated sites. This legislation expired with the 113th Congress at the end of CY2014. Senator Booker reintroduced this Act on 12/14/15 and it expired without enactment at the end of CY2016 with the 114th Congress.

Under CERCLA 106 (42 U.S.C. Section 9606), PRPs can be ordered to clean up their own toxic sites. The EPA is also empowered to fine non-compliant entities up to $25,000 per day for each non-compliant day.

As of end-CY2016, no legislation had been passed/enacted to strengthen the Superfund by reinstating excise taxes to be levied on polluters.

This promise was not fulfilled.

0.00

IO-19

The Promise: "...will reinvigorate the drinking water standards..."
When/Where: Obama-Biden Plan: Promoting a Healthy Environment" dated 10/08/08.
Source: https://www.energy.gov/sites/prod/files/edg/media/Obama_Cap_and_Trade_0512.pdf
Status: The Environmental Protection Agency (EPA) conducts a review of Drinking Water Standards every six years to assess the validity of its National Primary Drinking Water
Regulations (NPDWRs). The CY2010 review indicates that regulations pertaining to 71 contaminants were validated, with 4 subject to revision. A CY2016 report indicates that regulations pertaining to 76 contaminants were validated, with 8 such regulations subject to review.

The Safe Drinking Water Act (SDWA) of 1974 remains the principal legal vehicle under which the EPA sets legal limits of contaminants in drinking water. SDWA allows individual states to set their own drinking water standards, so long as those standards meet the EPA's standards.

Reinvigoration of the nation's drinking water standards under President Obama started with the American Recovery and Reinvestment Act of 2009 which provided a supplementary $6B to the EPA for its Clean Water and Drinking Water State Revolving Funds (SRF).

On 02/02/11, the EPA announced that it would regulate the presence of perchlorate and 16 other cancer-causing chemicals (referred to as "volatile organic compounds") in drinking water, reversing a Bush Administration decision not to regulate perchlorate. As of end-CY2016, the EPA had not yet established a

0.00

maximum contaminant level goal for perchlorate, nor had it published definitive rules or regulations to address the presence of numerous cancer-causing chemicals in drinking water.

There was no significant reinvigoration of the EPA's drinking water standards during President Obama's two terms in office.

This promise was not fulfilled.

IO-20 **The Promise:** "...will continue leadership in protecting national treasures like the Great Lakes from threats such as industrial pollution, water diversion, and invasive species."
When/Where: Obama-Biden Plan: Promoting a Healthy Environment" dated 10/08/08.
Source: https://www.energy.gov/sites/prod/files/edg/media/Obama_Cap_and_Trade_0512.pdf
Status: For the last budget enacted under President George W. Bush, no funds were appropriated specifically for Great Lakes Restoration Initiatives (GLRI).

President Obama's FY2010 budget submission to Congress included $475M for an "interagency Great Lakes restoration initiative, which will target the most significant problems in the region, including invasive aquatic species, non-point source pollution, and contaminated sediment." This was the amount ($475M) enacted by Congress for the GLRI for FY2010. For FY2011, the EPA's budget for GLRI was annualized under Continuing Resolution conditions at $475M.

The promise to "continue leadership" in this area was fulfilled.

1.00

IO-21 **The Promise:** "...will call for full and stringent enforcement of all applicable laws related to Florida's water resources, including the Clean Water Act, the Endangered Species Act, and the Safe Drinking Water Act."
When/Where: Obama-Biden Plan: "Protecting Florida's Waterways" dated 10/16/08.
Source: http://news.caloosahatchee.org/docs/Obama_On_Florida_Waters.pdf
Status: In 01/10, the EPA issued a proposed rule establishing nutrient criteria for Florida's water resources. In doing so, the EPA committed to issue a final rule by 10/15/10 for lakes and flowing waters. The final rule entitled "Water Quality Standards for the State of Florida's Lakes and Flowing Waters" was published in the Federal Register on 12/06/10.

The final rule for Florida's estuaries and coastal waters was published in the Federal Register 12/18/12.

This promise was fulfilled.

1.00

IO-22 **The Promise:** "...will encourage federal partnership with the state of Florida and local municipalities in researching new and innovative ways to insure the health and safety of Florida's waters."
When/Where: Obama-Biden Plan: "Protecting Florida's Waterways" dated 10/16/08.
Source: http://news.caloosahatchee.org/docs/Obama_On_Florida_Waters.pdf
Status: As of end-CY2016, there is no sign of any new, formal "federal partnership" between a U.S. Government entity (i.e. the EPA) and the State of Florida to protect Florida's waters.

This promise was not fulfilled.

0.00

IO-23 **The Promise:** "...will establish policies to help high-growth regions like Northeast Florida with the challenges of managing their water supplies...will restore better federal financing for water and wastewater treatment infrastructure so we can protect the St. John's..."
When/Where: Obama-Biden Plan: "Protecting Florida's Waterways" dated 10/16/08.
Source: http://news.caloosahatchee.org/docs/Obama_On_Florida_Waters.pdf
Status: The St. John's River Water Management District (SJRWMD), operating largely under Florida's Surface Water Improvement and Management (SWIM) Act of 1987, and in partnership with the City of Jacksonville, the Florida Department of Environmental Protection, and other local government partners, implemented a $700M plan on reclaimed water projects. Under a River Accord signed in 07/06, SJRWMD also spent $150M on water reuse cost-share projects over a 10-year period ending in CY2016.

The goals of SJRWMD's efforts were to reduce point source (wastewater and industrial discharges) pollution, reduce nonpoint source (stormwater) pollution, reduce bacteria in the tributaries, restore degraded aquatic habitat, increase water quality compliance and enforcement, and increase public awareness of river issues.

0.00

Chapter 18 - Independent Organizations

More than 20 reclaimed water projects were expected to remove from the St. John's River approximately 1.6M pounds of nitrogen per year and 32M gallons of wastewater per day (or 10B gallons of wastewater per year by CY2025, without direct federal involvement).

As of end-CY2016, there was no sign of any "policies" established by the Obama Administration to help Northeast Florida manage its water supplies.

Federal financing assistance for the SJRWMD was minimal during the Obama Administration. For FY2010, federal funding accounted for only 0.7% of the SJRWMD's budget of $254M. For the FY2011-2012 budget cycle, federal funding accounted for only 0.4% of the reduced SJRWMD budget of $204M. The reduced SJRWMD budget trend continued for the remainder of President Obama's two terms in office, culminating in federal financing of only about 1% of the SJRWMD's $132.9M budget for the FY2016-17 budget cycle.

This promise was not fulfilled.

IO-24

The Promise: "...amending the Clean Water Act to clarify that it protects isolated wetlands."
When/Where: Obama-Biden Plan: "Supporting the Rights and Traditions of Sportsmen" dated 08/06/08.
Source: https://www.kentuckyhunting.net/threads/obama-sportsmen-issues.61174/
Status: The Clean Water Restoration Act of 2009 (S. 787), introduced by Senator Russel Feingold (D-WI) on 04/02/09, was reported on by the Senate Committee on Environment and Public Works on 06/18/09. This proposed bill would have clarified that the Clean Water Act includes protection of the nation's wetlands. This legislation was placed on the Senate Legislative Calendar on 12/10/10 where it sat when the 111th Congress expired at the end of CY2010.

No similar legislation was introduced during the remainder of President Obama's two terms in office.

This promise was not fulfilled.

0.00

IO-25

The Promise: "...will work to provide low-income communities the legal ability to challenge policies and processes that adversely affect the environmental health of low-income and minority communities."
When/Where: Obama-Biden Plan: Promoting a Healthy Environment" dated 10/08/08.
Source: https://www.energy.gov/sites/prod/files/edg/media/Obama_Cap_and_Trade_0512.pdf
Status: Executive Order 12898 signed by President Clinton on 02/11/94 directs federal agencies to develop environmental justice strategies to address environmental effects on minority and low-income populations.

On 03/21/11, the Deloitte Consulting firm issued its report entitled "Evaluation of the EPA Office of Civil Rights" in which it found that the EPA's Office of Civil Rights (OCR) had not adequately adjudicated Title VI complaints (allegations of discrimination against communities affected by the EPA's environmental rules). In some cases, complaints had been queued for adjudication for over eight (8) years.

A 04/05/11 report by the Environment News Service (ENS) further stated that the OCR staff suffered from "the absence of the rudiments of organizational infrastructure - well-documented policies and procedures, standardized processes, and effective systems...staff members are often confused about their job duties."

In 08/11, the heads of 17 government departments and agencies signed a Memorandum of Understanding (MOU) on Environmental Justice and Executive Order 12898. While this MOU ultimately helps low-income communities to more effectively engage with Interagency Working Group on Environmental Justice (EJIWG) members on environmental justice issues, no proof can be found substantiating that any work has been done by the Obama Administration to provide low-income and minority communities the "legal ability" to challenge what they deem to be negative environmental health policies.

This promise was not fulfilled.

0.00

IO-26

The Promise: "...will work to strengthen the EPA Office of Environmental Justice and expand the Environmental Justice Small Grants Program, which provides non-profit organizations across the nation with valuable resources to address local environmental problems."
When/Where: Obama-Biden Plan: Promoting a Healthy Environment" dated 10/08/08.

0.00

Source: https://www.energy.gov/sites/prod/files/edg/media/Obama_Cap_and_Trade_0512.pdf
Status: While the EPA does not publicize its break down of manpower resources for Environmental Justice (EJ) functions, it is clear from online data that the EPA's enacted budget in FY2010 ($10.3B) had fallen to $8.0B by President Obama's last budget year of FY2017. At the same time, the EPA's total personnel strength fell from 17.2K in FY2010 to 15.4K by FY2017. With these cited budget and personnel reductions, it is likely that the EPA's EJ Office was not strengthened in any significant way.

The EPA's Environmental Justice (EJ) Small Grants Program supports and empowers communities working on solutions to local environmental and public health issues. The program is designed to help communities understand and address exposure to multiple environmental harms and risks.

Grants not exceeding $30K each are awarded to support:
a. - Activities designed to educate, empower and enable communities to understand the environmental and public health issues and to identify ways to address these issues at the local level, and
b. - Research activities related to the Comprehensive Environmental Response, Compensation and Liability Act (CERCLA), Section 311(c).

In FY2009 (President George W. Bush's last budget year), the EJ Small Grants Program was funded at the $800K level. During President Obama's two terms in office, funding was provided at the following levels: FY2010 - $1M, FY2011 - $1.2M, FY2012 - $1.5M, FY2013 - $0, FY2014 - $0, FY2015 - $1.2M, FY2016 - $0, FY2017 - $1.2M. Since the EJ Small Grants Program was not funded during all eight budget cycles of President Obama's two terms in office, an average of those eight years reveals that the grants program was funded at an average of $762.5K per year, a decrease when compared to President Bush's last budget year ($800K).

This promise was not fulfilled.

IO-27 The Promise: "...the Environmental Protection Agency will strictly monitor and regulate pollution from large Concentrated Animal Feeding Operations (CAFOs)...with fines for those who violate tough air and water quality standards."
When/Where: Obama-Biden Plan: Promoting a Healthy Environment" dated 10/08/08.
Source: https://www.energy.gov/sites/prod/files/edg/media/Obama_Cap_and_Trade_0512.pdf
Status: Under the Clean Water Act, an Animal Feeding Operation (AFO) is a facility in which livestock or poultry are housed in confinement for a total of 45 days or more in any 12-month period and crops are not grown over the facility for feeding/grazing purposes. A CAFO is an AFO with more than 1,000 animals. A facility with 300-999 animals may be classified as CAFOs if pollutants are discharged from a manmade conveyance or are discharged directly into waters near the animal housing area. Facilities with fewer than 300 animals may also be classified as CAFOs if the EPA or State permitting authority determines that the facility contributes to water pollution.

On 05/28/10, the EPA released its guidance document entitled "Implementation Guidance on CAFO Regulations - CAFOs That Discharge or Are Proposing to Discharge" (EPA-833-R-10-006). While this document is not legally enforceable, it does provide clarification of regulatory requirements.

As part of the EPA's 2008-2010 CAFO enforcement strategy, a CAFO that discharges pollutants under the Clean Water Act must have a State/National Pollution Discharge Elimination System (S/NPDES) Permit. EPA regulations also require permits for CAFOs that "propose" to discharge at some point in the future, whereas CAFOs that have the "potential" to discharge pollutants do not require a permit.

Sanctions for CAFO S/NPDES permit violations include severe civil and criminal penalties for each day of violation. Basic monetary penalties could be up to $32,500 per day. Stiffer criminal penalties of up to $50,000 per day or three years' imprisonment, or both, could be levied for negligent or knowing violations of the Act. A fine of up to $250,000 or 15 years' imprisonment (or both) could be levied if a violation is considered "knowing endangerment" and leads to the imminent danger of death or serious bodily injury of another person.

This promise was fulfilled.

IO-28 The Promise: "...will work with my scientific advisors to develop a strategy to protect marine life and ensure that the mechanisms we choose to implement that strategy are effective. My administration will ensure that

Chapter 18 - Independent Organizations

sound science -- not ideology or profits -- guides federal environmental policy."
When/Where: Candidate Obama response to Greenpeace letter dated 12/03/07.
Source: Source document was available online throughout the Obama Administration. It has since been deleted from all archival websites.
Status: On 06/12/09, President Obama unveiled his "Ocean Protection Plan," dovetailing the standards set by President Bush in CY2006. In doing so, President Obama announced the creation of an Interagency Ocean Policy Task Force to be led by his chief environmental advisor, Ms. Nancy Sutley, to come up with a recommended policy/strategy for protecting and restoring "the health of ocean, coastal and Great Lakes ecosystems and resources."

The Task Force issued its interim report on 09/10/09. This interim report recommends (1) a national policy emphasizing the importance of our oceans, (2) the establishment of an interagency National Ocean Council, and 9 categories for action to manage the largest issues facing our oceans, coasts and the Great Lakes. Among these proposals is coastal and marine "spatial planning" as the answer to protecting marine life.

The final Task Force recommendations report was released by the White House on 07/19/10. With it, President Obama signed Executive Order 13547 entitled "Stewardship of the Ocean, Our Coasts, and the Great Lakes." That Executive Order establishes the policy for the United States to "use the best available science and knowledge to inform decisions affecting the ocean, our coasts, and the Great Lakes, and enhance humanity's capacity to understand, respond, and adapt to a changing global environment."

This promise was fulfilled.

FAA	GRADE

IO-29 **The Promise:** "Will work with Congress to modernize the nation's air traffic control system." — **1.00**
When/Where: Obama-Biden Plan: "Strengthening America's Transportation Infrastructure" dated 10/09/08.
Source: https://transportist.org/2008/02/
Status: President Obama's FY2010 budget outline proposed $800M for a 'Next Generation (NextGen) Air Transportation System', a long-term, 24-satellite constellation to improve the ground-based Air Traffic Control (ATC) system by CY2025. The actual enacted amount for NextGen was $867.7M in FY2010, a 24% increase over FY2009.

Also in CY2009, a Department of Transportation (DOT) Inspector General report stated that the FAA's computer systems remained vulnerable to cyber attacks by criminals, terrorists, or other nations. The FAA's position on this matter was that it had accorded priority to upgrading critical ATC systems, while ignoring the improvements needed in those systems' intrusion detection capabilities. This left vulnerable to attack the operational systems that control communications, surveillance and flight information used to keep flying aircraft at safe distances from one another.

On 10/20/10, the FAA announced it had awarded TASC a 10-year $828M contract to help launch the NextGen network by 2025. Under this initial progress initiative, TASC was tasked to work on advanced systems engineering, investment and business case analysis, planning and forecasting, and business, financial and information management support services.

The President's FY2011 budget proposal included an increase to $1.14B (from the FY2010 enacted amount of $867.7M) for NextGen. The government's NextGen Air Transportation System initiatives excluded funding to equip commercial aircraft with the new onboard systems they will need to interface with the new ground-based air traffic control stations.

On 08/01/10, President Obama signed into law the 15th extension of the last multi-year aviation bill that expired in 09/07. This stopgap measure remained in effect until 09/30/10. By that date, it was anticipated that both houses of Congress would agree on the contents of the $34.5B FAA Reauthorization Bill of 2009 (H.R. 915) so that the $22B needed to upgrade the air traffic control system's WWII-era radars with the NextGen satellite-based system at the nation's busiest airports by CY2014 could be appropriated. This didn't happen and H.R. 915 expired with the 111th Congress at the end of CY2010.

Since then, major airlines reportedly lost confidence in the FAA's ability to field NextGen GPS-based capabilities in the relatively near term. According to a DOT Inspector General report of mid-05/11, the FAA was found deficient in its inability to produce an "integrated master schedule" for NextGen. The report further specified some FAA NextGen design decisions that threatened the entire program's cost (estimated at between $29B and $42B for equipment, software and training by CY2025) and schedule targets.

On 02/03/11, the FAA announced that it would spend $4.2M to equip JetBlue Airways aircraft with advanced onboard systems to prove to other carriers that such investments on their part would accrue significant savings in the long term. As of end-CY2012, the JetBlue initiative has proven that the adaptation of NextGen technologies results in fuel savings, faster approaches, more direct routes, and more system capacity.

After 23 funding extensions, the Senate finally approved the $63B FAA Air Transportation Modernization and Safety Improvement Act (H.R. 658) on 02/06/12. President Obama signed this bill and it became law on 02/14/12. One of the key tenets of this bill is the annual authorization of $3B for the development of the NextGen ATC system.

This promise was fulfilled.

IO-30 **The Promise:** "...will direct the new FAA Administrator to work cooperatively with the frontline air traffic controllers to restore morale and improve working conditions and operations at the agency."
When/Where: Obama-Biden Plan: "Strengthening America's Transportation Infrastructure" dated 10/09/08.
Source: https://transportist.org/2008/02/
Status: The Government Accountability Office (GAO) issued a report on 11/30/09 (GAO-10-89) addressing the continuing morale problem at the FAA. In that report, the FAA was ranked 214 out of 216 best places to work in the federal government based on a study published by the Partnership for Public Service and American University's Institute for the Study of Public Policy Implementation.

According to the GAO report, although the FAA had created "a performance-based culture that could improve employees' workplace satisfaction," only 55% of the FAA's workforce was under performance-based compensation and there was no accountability for the plan's success. Part of the issue was that a contract between the National Air Traffic Controllers Association (NATCA) and the FAA resulted in the removal of NATCA's 16,000 members (45% of the FAA's workforce) from the performance-based pay system -- granting them automatic pay raises.

According to Congressman John Mica (R-FL), the morale problem was partially attributed to the fact that "Congress has failed to reauthorize the FAA for the longest period in decades...With no reauthorization, and a significant lack of fairness in its personnel system, don't expect morale at FAA to improve." President Obama signed the 17th 3-month extension of the FAA on 12/30/10.

Meanwhile, the 111th Congress failed to pass an FAA reauthorization bill, greatly jeopardizing policy, long term acquisition planning, safety projects and Air Traffic Control (ATC) modernization initiatives. During the first half of its term, the 112th Congress didn't do any better. As a consequence, the FAA's funding ran out on 07/23/11 (ATCs were not affected). 4,000 FAA employees and about 24,000 airport construction workers were furloughed and the FAA lost about $160M per week from fuel tax and ticket revenues. Consequently, morale at the FAA continued to decline more than three years into President Obama's first term in office. On 08/05/11, the Senate passed legislation by unanimous consent to approve a 21st extension to the FAA Reauthorization Bill for a period of six weeks, thereby permitting FAA and airport construction workers to return to work. A 22nd and 23rd extension through 02/17/12 followed.

Finally on 02/06/12, the Senate approved the $63B FAA Air Transportation Modernization and Safety Improvement Act (H.R. 658) (introduced by Congressman Mica on 02/11/11). President Obama signed this bill and it became law on 02/14/12. Key features of this legislation bore directly on FAA and specifically on ATC morale and working conditions such as Title II (NextGen Air Transportation System and Air Traffic Control Modernization) as well as Title VI (FAA Employees and Organization). Sections within these titles addressed FAA and ATC training and scheduling as well as addressing facility conditions. Consequently, morale and working conditions slowly began to improve within the FAA in general and within the ATC corps in particular.

This promise was fulfilled.

1.00

Chapter 18 - Independent Organizations

	FCC	GRADE
IO-31	**The Promise:** "...the Federal Communications Commission should provide an accurate map of broadband availability using a true definition of broadband instead of the current 200 kbs standard and an assessment of obstacles to fuller broadband penetration." **When/Where:** Obama-Biden Plan for Small Business, dated 09/11/08. **Source:** https://www.politifact.com/truth-o-meter/promises/obameter/promise/27/change-standards-for-determining-broadband-access/ **Status:** Source is cited for confirmation of exact promise wording only, as it existed before original "When/Where" campaign document was deleted from archival websites. The FCC released the National Broadband Plan on 03/16/10. Some provisions of the plan follow: - make broadband available to all U.S. residents; - connect 100M U.S. households to "affordable" 100 Mbps broadband service by 2020; - connect anchor institutions such as hospitals, schools and government buildings in every U.S. community to 1 Gbps broadband service in the next decade; - restructure the FCC's Universal Service Fund and redirect $15.5B from traditional telephone subsidies to broadband deployment over the next decade. This promise was fulfilled.	1.00
IO-32	**The Promise:** "...true broadband to every community in America..." **When/Where:** Obama-Biden Plan for Science and Innovation dated 09/25/08 **Source:** https://www.faseb.org/portals/2/pdfs/opa/2008/obamafactsheetscience.pdf **Status:** The American Recovery and Reinvestment Act of 2009, signed into law 02/17/09, has $7.2 billion earmarked for improving the U.S. broadband infrastructure, particularly in rural/remote areas, under management of the FCC. Of this amount, $4.7B went to the Department of Commerce's National Telecommunications and Information Administration for broadband deployment, adoption and data collection. The FY2010 budget submitted by President Obama included an additional $1.3B under the U.S. Department of Agriculture's (USDA's) budget plan to increase broadband capacity in rural areas. Further, the President's FY2011 budget proposal includes "$418M in USDA loans and grants to move rural communities into the modern information economy." The FY2011 budget proposal also includes $24M to initiate what may become known as the "Broadband Technology Opportunities Program Administration." There is a significant issue that may hinder promise fulfillment in the near future. A planned nationwide broadband wireless network may interfere with spectrum reserved for satellite communications services reserved for Global Positioning Systems (GPS). Such interference could impact commercial, private and military aviation, 911 responders (police, ambulance, fire), and consumer navigation devices. A 06/30/11 report from the U.S. GPS Industry Council to the FCC revealed that a start-up firm called "Lightsquared" has been developing a wireless-by-satellite network that could potentially knock out 500M GPS receivers used by first responders, commercial and military aviation, and others. "Lightsquared" maintained that the use of filters on its devices and on the potentially affected GPS receivers could allow its services and GPS technologies to operate on the same band of satellite spectrum. This potential anomaly was resolved in 02/12 by the FCC disallowing the fielding of Lightsquared's solution. As of 11/01/11, Congress was considering legislation to authorize the FCC to conduct incentive auctions for about 120 MHz of spectrum from broadcast TV to be allocated to wireless uses. Instead, the FCC made 95 MHz of government-controlled wireless spectrum available for commercial use on 03/26/12. According to a Congressional Research Service report dated 12/28/16, there remain two ongoing federal funding vehicles to fund broadband infrastructure: the broadband and telecommunications programs at the Rural Utilities Service (RUS) of the U.S. Department of Agriculture and the Universal Service Fund (USF) programs under the Federal Communications Commission. As of end-CY2016, only about half of rural residents enjoy a download speed faster than 25MB per second.	0.00

34M Americans do not, 23.4M of them residing in rural areas. To mitigate this situation would, by some accounts, cost about $80B more than the amounts appropriated as of end-CY2016.

This promise was not fulfilled.

IO-33 **The Promise:** "...will reform the Telephone Universal Service Program, direct the FCC to better manage the nation's airwaves, and encourage public-private partnership to get more low-income communities connected."
When/Where: Obama-Biden Plan: "Supporting Urban Prosperity" dated 09/11/08.
Source: https://assets.documentcloud.org/documents/550008/barack-obama-2008-supporting-urban-prosperity.pdf
Status: The Universal Service Reform Act of 2010 (H.R. 5828) was introduced on 07/22/10 by Congressman Frederick Boucher (D-VA) and Lee Terry (R-NE). This bill was intended to improve and modernize the Universal Service Fund (USF) by reining in the size of the fund and promoting broadband deployment, going beyond the "telephone" aspect of this promise. This bill was referred to the House Committee on Energy and Commerce and expired with no further action at the end of CY2010 with the 111th Congress.

Nonetheless, by the end of President Obama's two terms in office, the USF had four distinct components, each of which supported the goal of reform:
--1. On 10/27/11, the FCC approved a 6-year program to transfer funds from the USF to a new $4.5B per year "Connect America Fund." This program subsidizes telecommunications services in rural and remote areas. Its "Mobility Fund" pays wireless carriers that expand services to under-served areas in a public-private arrangement.
--2. Low Income (Lifeline): On 03/31/16, the FCC instituted reforms to the Lifeline program by extending broadband services to low income households in addition to existing Lifeline benefits such as helping low income citizens acquire phone services (both landlines and cellphones).
--3. Rural Health Care: The first of three components, Telecommunications Program, provides subsidies to healthcare providers for telehealth and telemedicine services. The second, initiated under President Obama, is the Healthcare Connect Fund that provides support for high-capacity broadband connectivity to eligible health care providers (HCPs) and encourages the formation of state and regional broadband HCP networks. The third is a Pilot Program that provides funding for up to 85% of costs of constructing/implementing broadband networks at the state or regional level.
--4. E-Rate Program for Schools and Libraries: Provides subsidies for Internet access to schools and libraries. Since CY2011, this program was expanded to include schools on tribal lands, schools that serve children with physical, cognitive and behavioral disabilities as well as schools serving children with medical needs, some juvenile justice schools, and those with 35% or more students eligible for the National School Lunch Program.

In CY2013, President Obama sent a memorandum to the FCC and other federal agencies directing them to report more complete data about the use of spectrum, with the possibility of sharing/selling additional airwaves in the competitive wireless market. The memo was part of his efforts to provide high-speed Internet to the most remote reaches of the country while also providing faster smartphone service within a few years.

As a consequence of the above, the Telephone Universal Service Program has been reformed to the point of extinction on President Obama's watch.

This promise was fulfilled.

IO-34 **The Promise:** "...will support the transition of existing public broadcasting entities and help renew their founding vision in the digital world."
When/Where: Obama-Biden Plan: "Connecting and Empowering All Americans Through Technology and Innovation" dated 11/13/07.
Source: https://www.wired.com/images_blogs/threatlevel/2009/04/obamatechplan.pdf
Status: For FY2010, Corporation for Public Broadcasting (CPB) funding by the federal government was set at $420M under regular appropriations, plus $36M for digital conversion and $25M for radio interconnection. These amounts were supplemented by $25M under the Consolidated Appropriations Act of 2010 for "fiscal stabilization grants to public radio and television stations, which have experienced a downturn in revenues due to the recession."

President Obama's budget proposal sought a 50% increase in funding to $59.5M for digital conversion in

FY2011, but Congress appropriated $36M for the CPB's transition to digital broadcasting.

This campaign promise was to "support the transition" of public broadcasting from analog to digital media, a goal that was achieved by the CPB prior to the end of President Obama's two terms in office.

This promise was fulfilled.

IO-35 **The Promise:** "...strongly supports the principle of network neutrality to preserve the benefits of open competition on the Internet....will protect the Internet's traditional openness to innovation and creativity and ensure that it remains a platform for free speech and innovation that will benefit consumers and our democracy."
When/Where: Obama-Biden Plan: "Connecting and Empowering All Americans Through Technology and Innovation" dated 11/13/07.
Source: https://www.wired.com/images_blogs/threatlevel/2009/04/obamatechplan.pdf
Status: Net neutrality is the principle that all Internet content, sites, platforms, applications, devices, services and networks are to be treated equally. Some FCC oversight of the Internet is arguably warranted to ensure that Internet providers do not exercise favoritism or block access to Internet sites that offer competing products or services.

In 04/10 under the Obama Administration, the FCC received a court decision that the FCC has no regulatory authority over Internet service providers. Google and Verizon responded by offering a commitment to net neutrality if accompanied by limited enforcement authority for the FCC where violations were detected. To many, this formulation of "neutrality" left many loopholes.

On 12/21/10, the FCC passed net neutrality rules that appeared to provide equal access to the Internet. In reality, the new rules gave the U.S. Government a say in how the Internet would be operated and managed, and how broadband services and networks would be respectively priced and financed.

The new rules do not apply to wireless access the same way they apply to broadband access. Under these new rules, Internet providers would technically be able to slow down wireless access to sites on a selective basis. Further, mobile network providers would have the legal right to stop access to Internet content or applications -- again on a selective basis.

1.00

While President Obama's support of the principles of net neutrality were not in question, unless the FCC revised its 12/21/10 rules and issued new, more comprehensive rules to include wireless applicability, the promise to protect the Internet's "traditional openess" was not being fulfilled. Because of this, the House deleted funding for FCC enforcement of net neutrality from the draft FY2012 Financial Services Appropriations bill in mid-CY2011.

On 11/10/11, the Senate voted 52-46 to reject the House bid to repeal the FCC's net-neutrality rules that would prevent Internet service providers from speeding up or slowing down website access. Meanwhile, the service provider Verizon filed a lawsuit in federal court, claiming that the FCC's net neutrality rules violated the right to free speech. The Verizon case was assigned to the D.C. Circuit Court of Appeals. The court overturned the FCC's net neutrality rule on 01/14/14. After this ruling, the FCC introduced a proposal that would allow companies providing Internet access to charge content providers such as Google extra for faster, more reliable service. This proposal generated protests as it came up for an FCC vote and a lengthy public comment period in 05/14.

On 03/12/15, the FCC released the details of its new net neutrality rules which were published on 04/13/15. Several internet providers filed suit with the D.C. Circuit Court of Appeals, which heard the case in 12/15. The court issued its ruling in 06/16 in favor of the FCC, stating that the Internet should be treated as a utility, not as a luxury. With this ruling, President Obama's promise to "support" net neutrality became reality.

This promise was fulfilled.

IO-36 **The Promise:** "...will encourage industry not to show inappropriate adult-oriented commercial advertising during children's programming."
When/Where: Obama-Biden Plan: "Connecting and Empowering All Americans Through Technology and Innovation" dated 11/13/07.

0.00

Chapter 18 - Independent Organizations

Source: https://www.wired.com/images_blogs/threatlevel/2009/04/obamatechplan.pdf
Status: In 1974, the National Advertising Review Council (NARC) established the Children's Advertising Review Unit (CARU), administered by the Council of Better Business Bureaus (CBBB). As a self-regulatory program to promote responsible children's advertising, CARU monitors and reviews advertising directed to children, initiates and receives complaints about advertising practices, and determines whether such practices violate children's programs standards.

In addition to CARU's efforts, the Children's Television Act of 1990 is enforced by the FCC to serve children's information and educational needs. Under this Act, the FCC can also impose fines on broadcast companies that violate the limits on the use of advertising during children's programming.

In 07/09, FCC Chairman Julius Genachowski recommended to the Senate Commerce Committee that parents be empowered with the tools to determine appropriate TV content for their children in lieu of more government regulation of TV content.

On 05/28/10, the FCC fined seven TV stations a total of $250K for violating children's programming rules. These rules limit commercial advertising time during children's shows to 10.5 minutes per hour on weekdays and 12 minutes per hour on weekends. But adult-oriented advertising is not specifically addressed in the Act cited above.

In 06/12, FCC Commissioner Robert McDowell estimated that the FCC had a backlog of approximately 1.48M indecency complaints on file tied to 9,700 broadcasts (the number of backlogged complaints when President Obama was sworn in for his first term was 1.6M). During the period 09/12 to 02/13, the number of backlogged indecency complaints was reduced by 70% from 1.48M complaints to 465K. This rapid reduction was attributed, by the FCC, to cases exceeding the statute of limitations, cases that had insufficient information, and cases that were foreclosed by settled precedent.

On 04/01/13, the FCC sought public comment on whether to change its "current broadcast indecency policies or maintain them as they are." As of end-CY2016, the FCC had failed to propose any new indecency policy.

This promise was not fulfilled.

IO-37 **The Promise:** "...will encourage improvements to the existing voluntary rating system, exploiting new technologies like tagging and filtering, so that parents can better understand what content their children will see, and have the tools to respond."
When/Where: Obama-Biden Plan: "Connecting and Empowering All Americans Through Technology and Innovation" dated 11/13/07.
Source: https://www.wired.com/images_blogs/threatlevel/2009/04/obamatechplan.pdf
Status: The FCC announced in 02/11 that it was looking at an improved "V-Chip" to replace the V-Chip mandated to be installed on all TV sets with screens over 13 inches manufactured since CY2000. Nonetheless, the FCC guidelines for applying ratings had no legal force and did not apply to news and sports broadcasts.

A study published by the Geisel School of Medicine at Dartmouth, NH in late CY2016 revealed that TV-Y7 rated shows, intended for children age 7 and older, had similar levels of violence as TV-MA shows, intended for mature audiences, despite having lower levels of sex, alcohol and tobacco on TV-Y7 shows compared to shows for older audiences.

There is no record anywhere that President Obama aggressively pursued improvements to the TV industry's voluntary rating system during his two terms in office.

This promise was not fulfilled.   0.00

IO-38 **The Promise:** "...will work to give parents the tools to prevent reception of programming that they find offensive on television and on digital media."
When/Where: Obama-Biden Plan: "Connecting and Empowering All Americans Through Technology and Innovation" dated 11/13/07.
Source: https://www.wired.com/images_blogs/threatlevel/2009/04/obamatechplan.pdf
Status: The primary tool to prevent reception of offensive TV programming is the "V-Chip," which blocks   0.00

Chapter 18 - Independent Organizations

programs on the basis of their ratings category (Y, Y-7, FY-FV, G, PG, 14, and MA). The V-Chip was mandated in the Telecommunications Act of 1996 to be built into all television sets manufactured starting in CY2000. The V-Chip guidelines have no legal force and do not apply to news, sports programming and regular commercial break advertising.

The basic tools for restricting the reception of offensive programming on TV existed long before President Obama arrived on the national scene. Those tools could be improved, but the basic "V-Chip" has existed on all TVs with a screen larger than 13 inches since CY2000.

Tools to prevent similar reception via the Internet also exist. See Promise Number IO-45 for a listing.

This promise was not fulfilled.

IO-39 **The Promise:** "...will encourage the creation of Public Media 2.0., the next generation of public media that will create the Sesame Street of the Digital Age and other video and interactive programming that educates and informs."
When/Where: Obama-Biden Plan: "Connecting and Empowering All Americans Through Technology and Innovation" dated 11/13/07.
Source: https://www.wired.com/images_blogs/threatlevel/2009/04/obamatechplan.pdf
Status: For reference purposes, "Public Media 1.0" consisted of 20th Century public broadcasting, cable access, nonprofit satellite set-asides, and focused national and international journalism. These media occasionally hosted political debates, aired major Congressional hearings, reported news, and broadcast cultural events. "Public Media 1.0" was also limited in generating public conversations by the "one-to-many" structure of mass media.

"Public Media 2.0" was intended to become media both for and by the public. The plan was for "Public Media 2.0" to be multiplatform, participatory, and digital. It would be held together by a combination of four features: (1) a trusted national network to coordinate communication and media practices, (2) funding for content creation, curation and archiving, (3) partnerships among outlets, makers, and allies, and (4) the standards and measurements that providers of public media uphold.

Since 1967, the Corporation for Public Broadcasting (CPB) has relied heavily on federal funding for its Public Broadcasting System (PBS) and National Public Radio (NPR) services. During President Obama's two terms in office, federal funding for CPB's operations was $420M in FY2010, rising to $445M by FY2017. To ensure its survival, "Public Media 2.0" would have required increased funding from taxpayers as well as the corporate world and partnering foundations.

While several successful experiments with the evolution of "Public Media 2.0" were conducted during the first years of President Obama's terms in office (i.e. $36M was projected for digital conversion, $25M was projected for the Public Radio Interconnection System (PRSS) and $27.3M was projected for its "Ready to Learn (RTL) programs in FY2010), progression from the "Public Media 2.0" concept to its acceptance by the general public did not occur.

None of President Obama's eight budget proposals addressed "Public Media 2.0" as one of his priorities, nor is he known to have come out publicly to "encourage" its creation since assuming the Office of the Presidency. In fact, his own National Commission on Fiscal Responsibility and Reform recommended on 11/10/10 that the American taxpayer stop funding the CPB by FY2015.

"Public Media 2.0" remained at the conceptual stage as of the end of President Obama's first term in office and essentially disappeared from public attention during his second.

This promise was not fulfilled.

0.00

IO-40 **The Promise:** "...will promote greater coverage of local issues and better responsiveness by broadcasters to the communities they serve."
When/Where: Obama-Biden Plan: "Connecting and Empowering All Americans Through Technology and Innovation" dated 11/13/07.
Source: https://www.wired.com/images_blogs/threatlevel/2009/04/obamatechplan.pdf

0.00

Status: Localism is an old FCC regulatory requirement that radio and TV stations must meet to receive and maintain their broadcast licenses going back to Title III of the 1934 Communications Act. On 01/14/10, FCC Commissioner Robert McDowell stated that "all of us should be asking why the Commission needs to devote scarce time and resources to reviving any old localism rules at all...Broadcasters must adapt to meet the needs and desires of their communities if they want to stay alive."

The perceived intent of this promise was interpreted by many as a new effort for the FCC to enforce the 1949 Fairness Doctrine. On 08/08/11, FCC Commissioner McDowell acknowledged that the FCC could find a 'back door' way to impose localism rules without congressional concurrence and in doing so, would find a way to implement the principles of the Fairness Doctrine which was formally revoked a few days later on 08/22/11.

Despite Commissioner McDowell's comments above, promoting "localism" was not an Obama Administration priority up to end-CY2016. Nonetheless, the FCC's core policy goals since the Communications Act of 1934 remained unchanged throughout President Obama's tenure: localism, diversity and competition.

This promise was not fulfilled.

IO-41 The Promise: "...will encourage diversity in the ownership of broadcast media, promote the development of new media outlets for expression of diverse viewpoints, and clarify the public interest obligations of broadcasters who occupy the nation's spectrum."
When/Where: Obama-Biden Plan: "Connecting and Empowering All Americans Through Technology and Innovation" dated 11/13/07.
Source: https://www.wired.com/images_blogs/threatlevel/2009/04/obamatechplan.pdf
Status: On 05/25/10, the FCC launched its Quadrennial Regulatory Review 2010 of broadcast media ownership, as mandated by Congress, to determine whether rules preventing any broadcast company from controlling too many media properties in the same market still served the public interest.

Five rules were the focus of the FCC's studies: (1) local TV ownership, (2) local radio ownership, (3) newspaper/broadcast cross-ownership, (4) radio/TV cross-ownership, and (5) dual network rule. It's important to note that these rules were initiated and probably more relevant/effective in the days when there were only three TV networks and local newspapers were plentiful. Some of these rules have since been loosened/deregulated by the FCC.

On 07/21/10, the FCC filed a brief with the 3rd U.S. Appeals Court defending its CY2007 decision to weaken the Newspaper/Broadcast Cross-Ownership (NBCO) rule, a rule that was designed to protect local communities from media monopolies and increase diversity in the broadcast media marketplace. Congress didn't agree.

The Quadrennial Regulatory Review 2014 was conducted with much of the same results.

In 08/16, the FCC adopted by a 3-2 vote the Second Report and Order, which left the rules largely unchanged. The item also reinstated the television Joint Sales Agreement (JSA) attribution rule and the revenue-based eligible entity standard for ownership diversity purposes, and required the disclosure of shared services agreements (SSAs) for commercial television stations. By 12/16, several parties were seeking reconsideration of various aspects of the Second Report and Order and challenges to the item were pending in the U.S. Court of Appeals for the Third Circuit.

As of end-CY2016, the FCC had not taken the actions necessary to permit fulfillment of President Obama's campaign promise to encourage diversity in the ownership of broadcast media.

This promise was not fulfilled.

0.00

IO-42 The Promise: "...supports efforts to provide greater technical assistance to local and state first responders and dramatically increase funding for reliable, interoperable communications systems...supports a more rapid turnover of broadcast spectrum to first responders."
When/Where: Obama-Biden Plan: "Supporting Urban Prosperity," dated 09/11/08.
Source: https://assets.documentcloud.org/documents/550008/barack-obama-2008-supporting-urban-prosperity.pdf
Status: According to a Congressional Research Service (CRS) report entitled: "Funding Emergency

1.00

Communications: Technology and Policy Considerations" dated 01/05/12, the U.S. "has yet to find a solution that assures seamless communications among first responders and emergency personnel..."

Part of the solution to acquire a more reliable, interoperable communications system was the pursuit of the "Next Generation 9-1-1 (NG9-1-1) system. To expedite the transition to NG9-1-1, President Obama signed into law the "Middle Class Tax Relief and Job Creation Act of 2012" (H.R. 3630) on 02/22/12. This law defined NG9-1-1 as an Internet Protocol-based system that "supports data or video communications needs for coordinated incident response and management" and "provides broadband service to public safety answering points or other first responder entities."

To make this all happen, President Obama's FY2013 budget proposal sought over $10B derived from the sale and reallocation of spectrum. Specifically, the President's request proposed to reallocate D Block spectrum valued at over $3.1B, and provided $7B to support the deployment of this network, including up to $300M to fund R&D and support for standards and technologies to ensure the network capabilities met the mission requirements of public safety.

This promise was fulfilled.

FTC	GRADE

IO-43 **The Promise:** "I'll institute a five-star rating system to inform consumers about the level of risk involved in every credit card."
When/Where: Obama Campaign Speech, Raleigh, NC dated 06/09/08.
Source: http://www.nytimes.com/2008/06/09/us/politics/09transcript-obama.html?pagewanted=1&_r=1
Status: On 04/30/09, the House voted in favor of the Credit Card Accountability Responsibility and Disclosure Act of 2009. Also known as the Credit Card Act of 2009, the Senate passed it on 05/19/09. President Obama signed it into law on 05/22/09. The major reforms introduced by this new law: bans unfair rate increases, prevents unfair fee traps, plain sight/plain language disclosures, accountability, and protections for students and young people. While the foregoing were all positive steps with regard to consumer credit card protections, there was no "five-star rating system" established by this legislation.

The Credit Card Safety Star Act of 2009 (S.900) introduced by Senator Ron Wyden (D-OR) on 04/27/09, as an example, would have responded to this promise but failed to garner congressional interest and expired with the 111th Congress at the end of CY2010.

This promise was not fulfilled.

Grade: 0.00

IO-44 **The Promise:** "will create a Credit Card Bill of Rights to protect consumers."
When/Where: Obama-Biden Plan to Revitalize the Economy, 2008
Source: https://webarchive.loc.gov/all/20090429185145/http://change.gov/agenda/economy_agenda/
Status: After an initial 04/23/09 meeting with credit card company leaders and passage of legislation for the promised Bill of Rights for credit card holders, Obama signed the Credit Card Accountability, Responsibility and Disclosure (CARD) Act - also known as the Credit Card Bill of Rights - on 05/22/09.

On 08/22/10, the final reform provisions of the CARD Act took effect. Since that date, consumers have been protected against unreasonable fees and penalties for late payments, as well as unfair practices involving gift cards. This law also made the terms of credit cards more understandable and put a stop to hidden over-the-limit fees and other practices designed to trap consumers. It restricted rate increases that applied retroactively to old balances. And the CARD Act prevented companies from increasing rates within the first year an account is opened.

This promise was fulfilled.

Grade: 1.00

IO-45 **The Promise:** "...will require that parents have the option of receiving parental controls software that not only blocks objectionable Internet content but also prevents children from revealing personal information through their home computer."
When/Where: Obama-Biden Plan: "Connecting and Empowering All Americans Through Technology and Innovation" dated 11/13/07.
Source: https://www.wired.com/images_blogs/threatlevel/2009/04/obamatechplan.pdf

Grade: 0.00

Chapter 18 - Independent Organizations

Status: Enforced by the Federal Trade Commission (FTC), the Children's Online Privacy Protection Act (COPPA) that became effective on 04/21/00 gave parents control over what information websites could collect from their children. Any website for children under 13, or any general site that collects personal information from children it knows are under 13, is required to comply with COPPA.

Under COPPA, sites have to get a parent's permission if they want to collect or share a child's personal information such as full name, address, email address, or cell phone number.

Quite a few software packages are available to help parents control a child's Internet experience and protect the child in the process. These range from the free "K9 Web Protection" by BlueCoat, to paid applications such as Internet Child Protection, NetNanny, CyberSitter, SafeEyes, Puresight PC, CyberPatrol, McAfee Family Protection, FilterPak, imView, and others.

As of end-CY2016, there was no record that President Obama had taken steps to "require" that parents have the option of receiving parental control software.

This promise was not fulfilled.

NARA	GRADE

IO-46 **The Promise:** "...will institute a national declassification center to make declassification secure but routine, efficient and cost-effective."
When/Where: Obama-Biden Plan "Blueprint for Change" dated 10/09/08.
Source: https://www.documentcloud.org/documents/550007-barack-obama-2008-blueprint-for-change.html
Status: A 05/27/09 presidential memo directed the National Security Advisor to come up with recommendations toward promise fulfillment within 90 days. The White House Office of Science and Technology Policy took up this mission with the institution of its "Declassification Policy Forum".

Over the period 07/01/09-07/05/09, no less than 15 well-founded recommendations were received via this forum that, if/when implemented, would directly support the creation of a National Declassification Center (NDC).

On 07/08/09, a document entitled "A Concept of Operations for a National Declassification Center" was released by the National Archives and Records Administration (NARA), an organization subordinate to the Archivist of the United States. This document proposed the creation of the NDC at a NARA facility in College Park, MD.

On 12/29/09, President Obama signed Executive Order 13526 creating the NDC.

This promise was fulfilled.

Grade: 1.00

NASA	GRADE

IO-47 **The Promise:** "...supports congressional efforts to add at least one additional Space Shuttle flight to fly a valuable mission..."
When/Where: Obama-Biden Plan: "Advancing the Frontiers of Space Exploration" dated 08/15/08.
Source: http://www.nasa.gov/pdf/382369main_48%20-%2020090803.2.Space_Fact_Sheet_FINAL.pdf
Status: Although the additional mission was signed into law under the Bush Administration, credit is given to the Obama Administration for funding it in NASA's FY2010 budget of $18.7B on top of the $1B provided for NASA under the American Recovery and Reinvestment Act of 2009.

Among the budget highlights: "an additional flight may be conducted if it can safely and affordably be flown by the end of 2010". Space Shuttle "Discovery" was rolled out on 09/20/10 for its 39th and final flight to the International Space Station (ISS). It lifted off on 02/24/11.

A second additional flight (STS-134) by the shuttle "Endeavour" lifted off on 05/16/11 for a 16-day mission to the ISS, carrying a $2B Alpha Magnetic Spectrometer particle detector and spare parts. "Endeavour's" last mission successfully ended on 06/01/11.

Grade: 1.00

Chapter 18 - Independent Organizations

On 10/21/10, NASA announced that a third additional shuttle flight (STS-135) was necessary to stock the ISS with food, water and other supplies needed to sustain a crew of six for one year. STS-135, flown by the shuttle "Atlantis," lifted off for a final 14-day shuttle mission to the ISS on 07/08/11. When "Atlantis" came back to planet Earth on 07/21/11, it was retired and shuttle missions to the ISS ended.

This promise was fulfilled.

IO-48	**The Promise:** "Will enlist other federal agencies, industry and academia to develop innovative scientific and technological research projects on the International Space Station." **When/Where:** Obama-Biden Plan: "Advancing the Frontiers of Space Exploration" dated 08/15/08. **Source:** http://www.nasa.gov/pdf/382369main_48%20-%2020090803.2.Space_Fact_Sheet_FINAL.pdf **Status:** During the President Obama's two terms in office, Department of Defense (DoD) investment in space systems dropped from about $10B FY2009 to just over $6B by FY2016. The greatest reductions during this timeframe were in space research and development contracts, reduced from $6B to about $3B. Federal organizations were funded (albeit at a reduced level) in research involving the International Space Station (ISS). Academic - By end-FY2016, the following were among the top new (since CY2009) academic entities participating in scientific and technological research projects involving the ISS: State Universities of Michigan, Alabama, Florida, Hawaii, Alaska, and Washington; Baylor College of Medicine; Cornell University; and Columbia University. Industry - By end-FY2016, approximately 30 new companies (since CY2009) were ranked among the top 100 non-federal organizations involved in scientific and technological research projects with the ISS. This promise was fulfilled.	1.00
IO-49	**The Promise:** "Will stimulate efforts within the private sector to develop and demonstrate spaceflight capabilities." **When/Where:** Obama-Biden Plan: "Advancing the Frontiers of Space Exploration" dated 08/15/08. **Source:** http://www.nasa.gov/pdf/382369main_48%20-%2020090803.2.Space_Fact_Sheet_FINAL.pdf **Status:** NASA's Commercial Crew and Cargo Program was launched on 08/04/09 by the issuance of solicitation JSC-CCDev-1. As of mid-CY2010, at least five contracts had been awarded against the above solicitation "to stimulate effort within the private sector to develop and demonstrate human spaceflight capabilities. This effort is intended to foster entrepreneurial activity leading to job growth in engineering, analysis, design, and research, and to economic growth as capabilities for new markets are created." The Space Exploration Technologies Corporation (SpaceX) received Federal Aviation Administration (FAA) approval for the 12/08/10 launch to low-earth orbit and recovery of a reusable "Dragon" capsule powered by an 18-story "Falcon 9" rocket. The ultimate objective of that extremely successful debut test flight was to someday transport cargo and astronauts to the International Space Station (ISS) and beyond. That goal came to fruition on 05/22/12 when SpaceX launched it first trial mission carrying 1,000 lbs of equipment and supplies to the ISS. Under a $1.6B contract with NASA, SpaceX then launched the first of 12 regularly scheduled supply missions to the ISS on 10/07/12. The second successful "Dragon" mission splashed down in the Pacific Ocean on 03/26/12. Meanwhile, operating under a $1.9 billion contract for eight resupply flights to the ISS, Orbital Sciences Corp. of Dulles, VA launched its first Antares rocket test flight in 04/13 from NASA's Wallops, VA facility. Orbital then launched its first cargo delivery "Orb-1" Cygnus spacecraft to the ISS on 01/09/14. Given SpaceX's and Orbital Sciences Corporation's steady progress toward filling the void left by the cessation of shuttle flights to the ISS, private sector efforts have evidently been stimulated. This promise was fulfilled.	1.00

Chapter 18 - Independent Organizations

IO-50 — **The Promise:** "...will use the ISS for fundamental biological and physical research to understand the effects of long-term space travel on human health and to test emerging technologies to enable such travel."
When/Where: Obama-Biden Plan: "Advancing the Frontiers of Space Exploration" dated 08/15/08.
Source: http://www.nasa.gov/pdf/382369main_48%20-%2020090803.2.Space_Fact_Sheet_FINAL.pdf
Status: In 05/09, President Obama established the "Review of U.S. Human Space Flight Plans Committee" to assess planned human spaceflight activities so that the nation can achieve "its boldest aspirations in space."

A Government Accountability Office (GAO) report dated 11/09 states that full research utilization of the International Space Station (ISS) will be impeded by (1) the Administration's plans to halt Space Shuttle activities in the CY2010/11 timeframe, (2) high cost for launches and developing research hardware and the absence of a reliable funding stream for research on the ISS, and (3) limited crew time available for research due to fixed crew size (only 6) and the need to conduct other maintenance and safety activities. The limited payload of alternate international shuttle capabilities also exacerbates this dilemma.

To ensure the best return on the American taxpayer's investment of $49B for ISS design, development and assembly over a 25-year period, the President's Human Space Flight Plans Committee advised him that it would be unwise to de-orbit the ISS in CY2015 after only 5 years of full operations after its final assembly. In response, President Obama announced on 04/15/10 that he would seek extended funding for the ISS through CY2020. For FY2011, he obtained $2.7B for ISS operations, an amount increased to $2.8B in FY2012 and to $3.0B for FY2013. The annual budget for ISS operations was close to $4B by end-CY2016, and was expected to remain at that level through CY2024.

On 03/27/15, Astronaut Scott Kelly flew to the ISS on board Russian Soyuz Mission TMA-16M. He remained on board the ISS for nearly one year, during which time biological and physical research was conducted to determine the effects of long-term travel in a space environment.

This promise was fulfilled.

1.00

IO-51 — **The Promise:** "Will consider options to extend International Space Station (ISS) operations beyond 2016."
When/Where: Obama-Biden Plan: "Advancing the Frontiers of Space Exploration" dated 08/15/08.
Source: http://www.nasa.gov/pdf/382369main_48%20-%2020090803.2.Space_Fact_Sheet_FINAL.pdf
Status: Original plans were for NASA to deorbit the ISS in the first quarter of 2016. The Summary Report of the Review of U.S. Human Space Flight Plans Committee dated 09/08/09 and issued by the Augustine Committee recommended "that the return on investment of ISS to both the United States and the international partners would be significantly enhanced by an extension of ISS life to 2020..."

President Obama apparently listened to this advice, as his FY2011 budget proposal states in part: "...provides funds to extend operations of the Space Station past its previously planned retirement date of 2016." As of end-CY2016, the ISS was expected to remain operational through CY2024.

This promise was fulfilled.

1.00

IO-52 — **The Promise:** "Will endorse the goal of sending human missions to the Moon by 2020, as a precursor in an orderly progression to missions to more distant destinations, including Mars."
When/Where: Obama-Biden Plan: "Advancing the Frontiers of Space Exploration" dated 08/15/08.
Source: http://www.nasa.gov/pdf/382369main_48%20-%2020090803.2.Space_Fact_Sheet_FINAL.pdf
Status: On 02/01/10, President Obama announced his decision to cancel the Constellation Program (CxP) effective with the FY2011 NASA budget. Although NASA had already spent about $10B on this project, he stated his preference to dedicate research and development dollars toward new technologies for an eventual mission to Mars and beyond.

On 07/15/10, while considering the National Aeronautics and Space Administration Authorization Act of 2010, the Senate Committee on Commerce, Science and Transportation unanimously agreed to cancel the $150B return-to-the-moon program by cancelling the Ares I rocket in favor of a larger heavy-lift rocket to be developed starting in CY2011 for more distant missions after CY2015.

This promise was not fulfilled.

0.00

Chapter 18 - Independent Organizations

IO-53	**The Promise:** "Will enlist international partners to provide International Space Station (ISS) cargo re-supply and eventually alternate means for sending crews to the ISS." **When/Where:** Obama-Biden Plan: "Advancing the Frontiers of Space Exploration" dated 08/15/08. **Source:** http://www.nasa.gov/pdf/382369main_48%20-%2020090803.2.Space_Fact_Sheet_FINAL.pdf **Status:** The introductory portion of President Obama's FY2011 budget proposal ("Laying a New Foundation for Economic Growth") talks about reinvigorating space science and exploration by forging "international partnerships." However, the President's budget proposal for NASA itself in that same budget proposal appears to contradict the stated goal. President Obama's FY2011 budget proposal for NASA includes the statement: "The Budget funds NASA to contract with industry to provide astronaut transportation to the International Space Station as soon as possible, reducing the risk of relying solely on foreign crew transports for years to come." As of end-CY2016, NASA still relied solely on Russia for its transport of human cargo to the ISS. The fact that no less than five (5) of Russia's launched, space-destined missions crashed in CY2011 alone was not a confidence builder in this sole source of transport to/from the ISS. Enlisting new "international partners" since the original Space Station Intergovernmental Agreement (IGA) was signed on 01/28/98 with Russia, Japan, Canada and the member states of the European Space Agency has not happened. Brazil once partnered with NASA to provide ISS hardware, but cancelled that contract due to cost issues. Chinese participation is opposed by U.S. lawmakers. This promise was not fulfilled.	0.00
IO-54	**The Promise:** "...will support a robust research and technology development program that addresses the long-term needs for future human and robotic missions. He supports a funding goal that maintains at least 10 percent of the total exploration systems budget for research and development." **When/Where:** Obama-Biden Plan: "Advancing the Frontiers of Space Exploration" dated 08/15/08. **Source:** http://www.nasa.gov/pdf/382369main_48%20-%2020090803.2.Space_Fact_Sheet_FINAL.pdf **Status:** Since assuming the presidency, President Obama's budget requests have been supportive of NASA's exploration objectives but have fallen short of the 10% goal he and NASA established for "Exploration Research and Development (R&D)" as detailed below: Year --- Total Exploration Systems Budget --- Exploration R&D Budget --- Percentage FY2010 --- $3,625.8B --- $299.2M --- 8.25% FY2011 --- $3,821.2B --- $232.3M --- 6.08% FY2012 --- $3,707.3B --- $303.0M --- 8.17% FY2013 --- $3,705.5B --- $296.7M --- 8.01% FY2014 --- $4,113.2B --- $302.0M --- 7.34% FY2015 --- $3,542.7B --- $331.2M --- 9.35% FY2016 --- $3,996.2B --- $355.4M --- 8.89% FY2017 --- $4,184.0B --- $157.2M --- 3.76% This promise was not fulfilled.	0.00
IO-55	**The Promise:** "Will support increased investment in research, data analysis, and technology development across the full suite of exploration missions including the Mars Sample Return mission and future missions to the Moon, asteroids, Lagrange points, the outer Solar System and other destinations" **When/Where:** Obama-Biden Plan: "Advancing the Frontiers of Space Exploration" dated 08/15/08. **Source:** http://www.nasa.gov/pdf/382369main_48%20-%2020090803.2.Space_Fact_Sheet_FINAL.pdf **Status:** This promise is not to be confused with space exploration by humans and does not contradict the President's cancellation of the Constellation program for a return to the Moon by humans (Promise IO-52 refers). Rather, the President's FY2011 budget proposal clearly stated that he supported and wanted to provide $1B annually through FY2015 for "space science research grants and dozens of operating missions and telescopes currently studying the planets and stars as well as many more in development - including a telescope to succeed the Hubble Space Telescope, missions to study the Moon, and two Mars exploration missions."	1.00

Chapter 18 - Independent Organizations

Supportive of this goal, President Obama in 04/10 reversed an earlier decision to cancel the Orion Crew Exploration Vehicle in which the U.S. Taxpayer had invested $4.8B. In response, NASA's Human Exploration Framework Team (HEFT) recommended that NASA begin immediately to develop a heavy lift rocket, derived from the space shuttle, and capable of transporting 100 metric tons into orbit.

On 09/30/10, Congress passed the 2010 NASA Authorization Act, clearing the way for the $6.9B development of a heavy-lift space launch system (SLS) capable of carrying 70-100 metric tons (and later 130 metric tons) into low Earth orbit, as well as a $3.92B Multi-Purpose Crew Vehicle (MPCV). Congress also set a 12/31/16 deadline for NASA to reach an "operational capability" for these new systems. A separate Senate appropriations report proposed that funding for the SLS be capped at $11.5B through FY2017, and the MPCV be capped at $5.5B. NASA publicly acknowledged that these funding limits were insufficient to reach the mandated operational targets.

On the plus side, NASA successfully launched its "Juno" mission to Jupiter on 08/05/11. The objective of this mission was to investigate Jupiter's magnetic field, learn how the planet was formed and evolved, whether it has a solid core, and whether it has or had water.

On the minus side, insufficiency of funding was evident in NASA's acknowledgement on 01/02/11 that it would need an additional $82M in CY2011 to complete testing of the $2.5B "Curiosity" NextGen Mars rover. Funds were found and "Curiosity" was lauched on its 8.5 month, 354M-mile mission to Mars on 11/26/11. The rover safely landed on Mars on 08/05/12.

Because of reduced funding for planetary exploration from $1.5B in FY2012 to $1.2B in FY2013, NASA cancelled the start of its Mars Sample Return program, and delayed the launching of probes to distant planets and the launching of Discovery-class explorer missions.

The James Webb Space Telescope (JWST) to be launched in 10/18 to replace the Hubble Telescope was also in jeopardy. In 11/11, Congress decided not to cancel the JWST but limited funding to complete the project to $8B.

Despite perturbations in funding authorizations addressed above, the Orion project was successfully launched on its initial test flight on 12/5/14, landing in the Pacific Ocean 4.5 hours after its launch. Among several long-term goals, Orion could put a human on the surface of Mars after CY2030.

This promise was fulfilled.

IO-56	**The Promise:** "Will stimulate the commercial use of space and private sector utilization of the International Space Station. He will establish new processes and procurement goals to promote the use of government facilities." **When/Where:** Obama-Biden Plan: "Advancing the Frontiers of Space Exploration" dated 08/15/08. **Source:** http://www.nasa.gov/pdf/382369main_48%20-%2020090803.2.Space_Fact_Sheet_FINAL.pdf **Status:** In President Obama's FY2011 budget proposal for NASA, a section entitled "Supports Promising Commercial Space Transportation" specifies that "A strengthened U.S. commercial space launch industry will bring needed competition, act as a catalyst for the development of other new businesses capitalizing on affordable access to space, help create thousands of jobs, and help reduce the cost of human access to space." The key factor of this promise was to "stimulate" commercial participation in the space program. This promise was fulfilled.	1.00
IO-57	**The Promise:** "...will work to launch "without further delay" the Global Precipitation Measurement mission, an international effort to improve climate, weather, and hydrological predictions through more accurate and more frequent precipitation measurements." **When/Where:** Obama-Biden Plan: "Advancing the Frontiers of Space Exploration" dated 08/15/08. **Source:** http://www.nasa.gov/pdf/382369main_48%20-%2020090803.2.Space_Fact_Sheet_FINAL.pdf **Status:** On 12/02/09, NASA approved the Global Precipitation Measurement (GPM) mission to proceed to its implementation phase with its primary collaborator, the Japanese Aerospace Exploration Agency (JAXA). The	1.00

Chapter 18 - Independent Organizations

mission: study global rain, snow and ice to better understand our climate, weather, and hydrometeorological processes.

On 05/10/10, NASA awarded a $48.5M contract to Bell Aerospace and Technology Corporation for the GPM Microwave Imager Instrument Flight Unit 2 which was to be identical to the Flight Unit 1.

The GPM Core Observatory (Flight Unit 1) was launched on 02/27/14 from JAXA's Tanegashima launch site. Funding for Flight Unit 2, referred to as a "Low Inclination Orbiter," was cancelled by Congress under the FY2012 budget.

The basic premise of this promise was fulfilled.

IO-58

The Promise: "...will expand the use of prizes for revolutionary technical achievements that can benefit society, and funds for joint industry/government rapid-to-the-consumer technology advances."
When/Where: Obama-Biden Plan: "Advancing the Frontiers of Space Exploration" dated 08/15/08.
Source: http://www.nasa.gov/pdf/382369main_48%20-%2020090803.2.Space_Fact_Sheet_FINAL.pdf
Status: Since CY2005, NASA has awarded $4.5M to 13 different teams responding to 19 competitions for creative solutions to problems that NASA seeks to resolve. Its "Centennial Challenges" program has produced solutions from students, "citizen inventors", and entrepreneurial firms for technologies ranging from lunar landers, space elevators, fuel-efficient aircraft to astronaut gloves.

In CY2009 alone, five competition events were held with winners declared in four of them, winning $3.65M in prizes.

To further solidify President Obama's commitment to fulfilling this promise, his Administration's policy to "increase the use of prizes and challenges as tools for promoting open government, innovation, and other national priorities" was released by the Office of Management of Management and Budget (OMB) on 03/08/10.

This promise was fulfilled.

Grade: 1.00

NASC — GRADE

IO-59

The Promise: "Between 1958 and 1973, the National Aeronautics and Space Council oversaw the entire space arena for four presidents; the Council was briefly revived from 1989 to 1992. Barack Obama will re-establish this Council reporting to the president. It will oversee and coordinate civilian, military, commercial and national security space activities. It will solicit public participation, engage the international community, and work toward a 21st century vision of space that constantly pushes the envelope on new technologies as it pursues a balanced national portfolio that expands our reach into the heavens and improves life here on Earth."
When/Where: Obama-Biden Plan: "Advancing the Frontiers of Space Exploration" dated 08/15/08.
Source: http://www.nasa.gov/pdf/382369main_48%20-%2020090803.2.Space_Fact_Sheet_FINAL.pdf
Status: The National Aeronautics and Space Council (NASC) was established during the Eisenhower Administration under the National Aeronautics and Space Act of 1958. It was disbanded in 1973, later to be reformed as the National Space Council by President George H.W. Bush in 1989.

This council was again disbanded when in 1993 its functions were assumed by the National Science and Technology Council.

In order to bridge a gap between the civil and military space agencies, President Obama promised to re-establish the NASC. There was no known activity during his two terms in office that led to the NASC's resurrection.

This promise was not fulfilled.

Grade: 0.00

NATIONAL INFRASTRUCTURE BANK — GRADE

IO-60

The Promise: "... creating a National Infrastructure Reinvestment Bank to expand and enhance ... existing federal transportation investments... The Bank will receive ... $60 billion over 10 years, to provide financing to transportation infrastructure projects across the nation."
When/Where: Stated in Obama-Biden Plan: "Strengthening America's Transportation Infrastructure" dated 10/09/08.

Grade: 0.00

Chapter 18 - Independent Organizations

Source: https://webarchive.loc.gov/all/20090429184932/http://change.gov/agenda/homeland_security_agenda/
Status: The National Infrastructure Bank Act of 2007, during the Bush Administration, was the first step toward creating the promised bank. Under this bill, an independent entity of the government led by a five-member board of directors would be tasked with evaluating and financing regional and national infrastructure projects. The bank would develop a financing package for a selected project with credit from the government. The financing package could include direct subsidies, direct loan guarantees, long-term tax-credit general purpose bonds, and long-term tax-credit infrastructure project specific bonds. The Infrastructure Bank, however, would not replace existing formula grants or earmarks for infrastructure. This initiative expired with the 110th Congress.

A new bill, entitled the National Infrastructure Development Bank Act of 2009 was introduced by Representative Rosa DeLauro (D-CT) on 05/20/09, did not get further than the House Financial Services Committee, and expired with the 111th Congress at the end of CY2010.

Meanwhile, President Obama's FY2010 budget outline of 02/26/09 included $5 billion for the creation of a National Infrastructure Bank and showed projected outlays of $25 billion for infrastructure improvement projects over the FY10-FY14 timeframe....short of the promised $60 billion goal. This bank was not created under the FY2010 budget.

But, this National Infrastructure Reinvestment Bank, as promised or by any other name, was forgotten in President Obama's FY2011 budget submission which, instead, proposed the creation of a National Infrastructure Innovation and Finance Fund to be funded at the $4B level under the purview of the Department of Transportation (DOT). This sounded a lot like the intent of the original promise, but the projected funding profile was inconsistent with the promise of "$60B over 10 years." This proposal did not go anywhere and under Title XII, Section 2202 of the Department of Defense and Full-Year Continuing Appropriations Act (H.R. 1473), DOT National Infrastructure Investment funds were limited to $528M for FY2011.

With the arrival of the 112th Congress in 01/11, Congresswoman DeLauro introduced a new National Infrastructure Development Bank Act (H.R. 402) on 01/24/11. This government-owned bank would be capitalized at a level of $5B per year for five years. This bill got no further than the House Financial Services Committee and expired with the 112th Congress at the end of CY2012.

On the Senate side, Senator John Kerry (D-MA) introduced a bill entitled "American Infrastructure Financing Authority" (AIFA) (S. 652) on 03/17/11. This government entity would be authorized to make loans not exceeding $10B during each of its first two years of operation, then not exceeding $20B during each of the following seven years, and not exceeding $50B during any fiscal year thereafter. This bill sat with the Senate Committee on Finance until it too died at the end of the 112th Congress.

On 12/13/11, Congressman Raul Grijalva (D-AZ) introduced the "Act of the 99%" (H.R. 3638) which included the establishment of a "National Infrastructure Development Bank" to be capitalized at the $5B level for five years starting in FY2012. This bill did not progress beyond initial House committee reviews and also expired with the 112th Congress.

Lastly, President Obama included the creation of a National Infrastructure Bank in his FY2012 and FY2013 budget proposals. However on 07/20/12, the Congressional Budget Office (CBO) reported that the creation of such a bank would significantly duplicate current programs such as the Department of Transportation's "Transportation Infrastructure Finance and Innovation Act" (TIFIA) program.

This promise was not fulfilled.

NEA	GRADE
IO-61 **The Promise:** "Will "support increased funding for the National Endowment for the Arts."" **When/Where:** Obama-Biden Plan: "Champions for Arts and Culture" dated 09/11/08. **Source:** http://muzartworld.org/president-barack-obama-and-joe-biden-champions-for-arts-and-culture/ **Status:** When President Obama assumed the presidency in 01/09, the National Endowment for the Arts was funded at $155M, the amount subject to be increased.	0.00

Chapter 18 - Independent Organizations

The $787 billion American Recovery and Reinvestment Act of 2009 economic stimulus bill signed into law 02/17/09 by President Obama included $50M in supplementary funding for the NEA.

President Obama then proposed to raise the FY2009 allocation of $155M to $161.3M. The House and Senate passed the final version of the bill for FY2010, increasing President Obama's proposed amount to $167.5M.

In the face of budget cutbacks, NEA funding was reduced to $154.6M for FY2011 against the President's request for $161.3M. NEA's budget was further reduced to $146.2M for FY2012, consistent with the President's request. For subsequent years during President Obama's two terms in office, the NEA was funded as follows: FY2013....$146M, FY2014....$146M, FY2015....$146M, FY2016....$147M, and FY2017....$149M.

Despite a promising start for increased funding of the NEA in FY2010, that funding started to fall below the last Bush Administration budget level in FY2011. What would have been reflected as a positive grade up until FY2011 was reversed in FY2012 when President Obama's budget request for the NEA fell below the FY2009 enacted level and stayed below that level for the remainder of his two terms in office. This indicates that his "support" for increased NEA funding was short-lived.

This promise was not fulfilled.

OMB	GRADE

IO-62 **The Promise:** "...will reform federal contracting and reduce the number of contractors, saving $40 billion a year."
When/Where: Obama and Biden's Plan for America: "Blueprint for Change," dated 10/09/08
Source: https://www.documentcloud.org/documents/550007-barack-obama-2008-blueprint-for-change.html
Status: Implementation of the reform called for in this promise would likely be an action for OMB's Office of Federal Procurement Policy (OFPP).

On 03/04/09, President Obama ordered a government-wide review of federal contracting practices with a view to increasing competition and accountability. He repeated his 09/08 promise that federal contracting reform would save $40B per year. His memorandum was published in the Federal Register in the same timeframe.

Understanding that government contracting reform must also come from within, President Obama instituted the "Securing American Value and Efficiency" (SAVE) Award program in CY2009, which over the ensuing three years produced over 75,000 cost-cutting ideas from federal workers among which dozens were included in the President's subsequent annual budget proposals. Contracting reform, however, required supporting legislation.

On 05/06/10, Senator Russ Feingold introduced the "Federal Contracting Oversight and Reform Act of 2010" (S. 3323) that sought to bring more transparency to the government contracting process.

On 07/13/10, Congressman Mike Quigley (D-IL) introduced H.R. 5726, also entitled the "Federal Contracting Oversight and Reform Act of 2010."

Neither of the above bills were acted upon beyond preliminary committee review by the time the 111th Congress expired at the end of CY2010. No exact or near-exact replica of the above bills was introduced during the 112th Congress, except for purpose-specific contracting reform bills (i.e. "Comprehensive Contingency Contracting Reform Act" (S. 3286) or "Overseas Contractor Reform Act" (H.R. 3588), etc.). Both of these bills expired with the 112th Congress at the end of CY2012 anyway.

With the 03/09 issuance of a Presidential Memorandum to the heads of relevant agencies and departments, President Obama took initial steps toward promise fulfillment. This promise would have been considered as fulfilled if appropriate legislation had been signed into law. While federal contracting during his two terms decreased somewhat, his stated $40B per year goal was not met.

This promise was not fulfilled.

Grade: 0.00

OPIC	GRADE

IO-63 **The Promise:** "...will provide initial capital for an SME [Small and Medium Enterprises] Fund...through the

Grade: 0.00

Chapter 18 - Independent Organizations

Overseas Private Investment Corporation [OPIC]...The SME Fund will be designed to provide seed capital and technical assistance to catalyze the establishment of job-creating small and medium enterprises, and to build the capacity of entrepreneurs to translate their ideas into viable businesses..."
When/Where: Obama-Biden Plan: "Strengthening Our Common Security by Investing in Our Common Humanity", dated 09/11/08.
Source: https://www.cgdev.org/sites/default/files/archive/doc/blog/obama_strengthen_security.pdf
Status: The Small and Medium Enterprise (SME) existed as an OPIC program long before President Obama ran for office. In short, the SME Finance Program has two forms of eligibility:
- SME Direct Loan Eligibility for U.S. corporations with less than $250M in revenues and U.S. individuals or investment entities with less than $67M in equity.
- SME Loan Eligibility (Expedited Approval Process) for U.S. corporations with less than $35M in revenues and individuals or investment entities with less than $27M in equity.

One of the most effective U.S. SME support programs is the Small Business Innovative Research (SBIR) program, in existence since CY1982 and funded at over $2B annually. But this promise focused on OPIC's international SME support programs.

OPIC itself has committed hundreds of millions of dollars to the SME sector in collaboration with financial giants such as Citi and GE Capital. In Central America alone, SME's were financed in the Pre-Obama era (pre-CY2009) as follows: Costa Rica $60M, El Salvador $47.5M, Guatemala $35M, Honduras $37.5M, Nicaragua $12.5M and Panama $7.5M.

When this promise was made, OPIC was in the process of investing $150M in private SMEs in Jordan.

OPIC also committed $100M to Garanti Bank of Turkey in 12/09 to finance its medium-to-long term loans to SME clients. The same bank received another $400M in financing from OPIC in CY2012.

So the promise to provide "initial capital" to OPIC's SME support program was without foundation.

This promise was not fulfilled..

IO-64 **The Promise:** "...will provide initial capital for...creation of regional 'SME Universities' supported by America's business schools."
When/Where: Obama-Biden Plan: "Strengthening Our Common Security by Investing in Our Common Humanity", dated 09/11/08.
Source: https://www.cgdev.org/sites/default/files/archive/doc/blog/obama_strengthen_security.pdf
Status: As of end-CY2016, there was no sign that any specific regional Small and Medium Enterprises (SME) "Universities," not to be confused with Society of Manufacturing Engineers (SME) student chapters, had been created during President Obama's two terms in office.

This promise was not fulfilled.

Grade: 0.00

OPM | GRADE

IO-65 **The Promise:** "...will thin the ranks of Washington middle managers, freeing up resources both for deficit reduction and for increasing the number of frontline workers."
When/Where: Obama and Biden's Plan for America: "Blueprint for Change," dated 10/09/08
Source: https://www.documentcloud.org/documents/550007-barack-obama-2008-blueprint-for-change.html
Status: While the national budget deficit caused individual government organizations and agencies to cut spending by up to 10%, and such spending cuts meant job cuts, there was no direction from President Obama's White House that specifically ordered the thinning of middle manager ranks as promised.

One could argue that cuts in one area would simply shift the Washington-area middle managers from their current organizations to new organizations to fill positions mandated by health care reform, financial reform, and other spending projects that President Obama championed while he was in office.

Neither the Office of Personnel Management (OPM) nor the Office of Management and Budget (OMB) are known to have a database specifically designed to report middle manager personnel strengths and fluctuations.

Grade: 0.00

Chapter 18 - Independent Organizations

We have seen no specific proof that the ratio of middle managers to frontline workers in the Washington D.C. area was reduced during President Obama's two terms in office.

This promise was not fulfilled.

SBA	GRADE
IO-66 **The Promise:** "will work to help more entrepreneurs secure both traditional and alternative means of financing, expand the network of lenders, make interest rates for SBA loans more competitive with the private sector, and simplify the loan approval process." **When/Where:** Barack Obama and Joe Biden: Small Business Emergency Rescue Plan, undated. **Source:** https://www.washingtonpost.com/wp-srv/politics/documents/obamasmallbusinessrescueplan.pdf **Status:** On 03/16/09, Obama announced plans to facilitate credit applications by small businesses by increasing the percentage of loans backed by the U.S. Government (via the SBA) from 75% (over $150,000) or 85% (under $150,000) to 90% across the board, as well as waiving certain fees for SBA-backed loans. This was codified in the Small Business Jobs Act of 2010 (H.R. 5297) signed into law by President Obama on 09/27/10. Under Section 1206(e) of this law, the network of lenders was expanded by the entry "Any lender that is participating in the Delegated Authority Lender Program of the Export-Import (Ex-Im) Bank of the United States...shall be eligible to participate in the Preferred Lenders Program." This act also simplified, to some extent, the loan approval process. In 06/15, Congress decided not to renew the the 70-year old charter of the Ex-Im Bank to continue extending new loans. The bank will continue, however, to service the $110 billion in loans already extended. This promise was fulfilled.	1.00
IO-67 **The Promise:** "Strengthen Small Business Administration programs that provide capital to minority-owned businesses, support outreach programs that help minority business owners apply for loans, and work to encourage the growth and capacity of minority firms" **When/Where:** Obama-Biden Plan for Small Businesses, dated 09/11/08. **Source:** https://www.politifact.com/truth-o-meter/promises/obameter/promise/16/increase-minority-access-to-capital/ **Status:** Source is cited for confirmation of exact promise wording only, as it existed before original "When/Where" campaign document was deleted from archival websites. The American Recovery and Reinvestment Act (ARRA) of 2009 provided $730M to the Small Business Administration (SBA) to supplement the FY2009 appropriation of $615M for a total of $1.345B. The ARRA also enhanced the SBA's lending and investment programs so that they can reach more small businesses, including minority-owned businesses. Another example of how President Obama succeeded in strengthening the SBA occurred in FY2011 when Congress awarded a supplemental appropriation to the SBA, increasing its regular appropriation of $837M by $963M for a total of $1.800B. The foregoing are two examples where President Obama managed to strengthen the SBA. In Section 4103 of the Small Business Jobs Act of 2010 (H.R. 5297) signed into law by President Obama on 09/27/10, a subparagraph entitled "Outreach to Minorities, Women, and Veterans" calls for institutions receiving capital investments under the program to provide "linguistically and culturally appropriate outreach and advertising in the applicant pool describing the availability and application process for receiving loans." This promise was fulfilled.	1.00
IO-68 **The Promise:** "Will support entrepreneurship and spur job growth by establishing a small business and micro-enterprise initiative for rural America." **When/Where:** Obama and Biden's Plan for America: "Blueprint for Change," dated 10/09/08 **Source:** https://www.documentcloud.org/documents/550007-barack-obama-2008-blueprint-for-change.html	1.00

Status: The American Recovery and Reinvestment Act (ARRA) signed into law on 02/28/09 recognized and improved support to the nation's small businesses. Included in the ARRA was $6.9B in discretionary appropriations for "rural development activities such as...rural business programs..."

President Obama's FY2010 budget submission of 02/21/09 proposed $20B in loans and grants "to support and expand rural development activities, including small businesses...". Of this amount, $61M was proposed for "microentrepreneur" assistance programs, $250M for rural America's development of renewable energy, and $70M for rural revitalization, education and land grant programs, to name a few.

The President's FY2011 budget proposal for the Department of Agriculture goes further by supporting the USDA's Rural Innovative Initiative under a $2.6B line item for rural development.

This promise was fulfilled.

IO-69

The Promise: "...would direct the Small Business Administration to amend regulations under the Small Business Act that provide preferences in federal contracting to small businesses owned by members of socially and economically disadvantaged groups to include individuals with disabilities."
When/Where: Obama-Biden Plan: "Empower Americans with Disabilities," dated 09/06/08.
Source: http://www.thearc.org/document.doc?id=3073
Status: Numerous references to this preferential treatment promise were made by President Obama during 2009, but no specific actions, either in his annual budget proposals nor the American Recovery and Reinvestment Act of 2009 point directly to the fulfillment of this promise.

Several small business "set-asides" such as the '8(b)' program for minority and/or women-owned business already exist. While policy set forth in Section 1313 of the Small Business Jobs Act of 2010 (H.R. 5297) calls for all federal agencies to provide "small business concerns with appropriate opportunities to participate as prime contractors and subcontractors in the procurements of the Federal agency," no specific preference for the disabled (other than disabled veterans) was addressed by the Small Business Administration in the form of amended regulations during President Obama's two terms in office.

This promise was not fulfilled.

0.00

IO-70

The Promise: "Expand the Small Business Administration's loan and micro-loan programs which provide start-up and long-term financing that small firms cannot receive through normal channels."
When/Where: Obama-Biden Plan for Small Businesses, dated 09/11/08.
Source: https://www.politifact.com/truth-o-meter/promises/obameter/promise/36/expand-loan-programs-for-small-businesses/
Status: Source is cited for confirmation of exact promise wording only, as it existed before original "When/Where" campaign document was deleted from archival websites.

7(a) loans are the SBA's primary program for providing financial assistance to small businesses. 504 loans provide long-term, fixed rate financing for major fixed assets that promote business growth and job creation.

The president's FY2011 budget request asked Congress to increase the maximum size of 7(a) loans from $2 million to $5 million, and increase the size limits on 504 loans from $2 million to $5 million on regular projects and from $4 million to $5.5 million for manufacturing projects. This request was approved in subsequent appropriations.

This promise was fulfilled.

1.00

IO-71

The Promise: "...will implement the Women Owned Business contracting program that was signed into law by President Bill Clinton, but has yet to be implemented by the Bush Administration."
When/Where: Barack Obama and Joe Biden: Small Business Emergency Rescue Plan, undated.
Source: https://www.washingtonpost.com/wp-srv/politics/documents/obamasmallbusinessrescueplan.pdf
Status: On 03/02/10, the Small Business Administration (SBA) announced a proposed rule that would expand federal contracting opportunities for Women-Owned Small Businesses (WOSB), making it available for 60 days to the public for comment.

1.00

The studies found that WOSB's were under-represented in the federal contracting marketplace in 83 industries. President Obama opted to create one comprehensive rule embodying the results of all previous studies. The new proposed rule included the following major provision: "To be eligible, a firm must be 51 percent owned and controlled by one or more women, and primarily managed by one or more women. The women must be U.S. citizens. The firm must be "small" in its primary industry in accordance with SBA's size standards for that industry.

In order for a WOSB to be deemed "economically disadvantaged," its owners must demonstrate economic disadvantage in accordance with the requirements set forth in the proposed rule."

Implementation of the WOSB program, sometimes referred to as the "8(m)" program, took effect on 02/04/11 for manufacturing contracts valued at less than $5M and less than $3M for other contracts as announced in the 10/07/10 edition of the Federal Register.

On 12/19/14, President Obama signed into law the National Defense Authorization Act (NDAA) for FY2015. Section 825 of the NDAA authorized federal agencies to award sole-source contracts to women-owned small businesses eligible for the WOSB Federal Contract Program, giving women the same level of access to the federal contracting marketplace as other disadvantaged groups.

This promise was fulfilled.

	SSA	GRADE
IO-72	**The Promise:** "The SSA's [Social Security Administration's] disability claims backlog has reached a record high of 755,000, up from 311,000 in 2000. The average wait time for an appeals hearing averages 505 days and...can exceed three years...Barack Obama and Joe Biden are committed to streamlining the current application and appeals procedures to reduce the confusion that surrounds these important programs." **When/Where:** Obama-Biden Plan: "Empower Americans with Disabilities" dated 09/06/08. **Source:** http://www.thearc.org/document.doc?id=3073	0.00

Status: In FY2009, the number of claims received by the Social Security Administration (SSA) was about 2.8M. At the end of FY2009, there were 779K claims for disability benefits awaiting hearing before Administrative Law Judges. These judges hear appeals from claimants who were initially denied benefits.

In FY2010, the number of initial disability claims rose to 3.1M. The SSA saw a $1B increase in its budget for FY2010, up to $11.4B. This increase should have permitted information technology improvements that could have improved the claims processing turn-around time. This didn't happen. The SSA was also to open eight new hearing offices. This also didn't happen.

It was estimated that with the 5,800 additional personnel the SSA was to hire in FY2010 and increased overtime to handle an escalating workload, the SSA should have been on track to eliminate its claims processing backlog by FY2013. Federal budget cuts put the brakes on this potential momentum -- the SSA was under a hiring freeze and had no funds for overtime for its current staff.

There were over 759K disability claims pending at the end of FY2011, down from 842K in FY2010. This number went down slightly to about 750K at the end of FY2012.

The number of backlogged disability claims caused some disability applicants to wait nearly four years (over 1,400 days) before their disability benefits could begin. While 270 days is the SSA's goal for settling claims, a goal that the President's FY2013 budget proposal claims would be met for disability appeal hearings by 09/13, 316 days was the actual average the SSA was experiencing as of end-CY2012.

In FY2016, the SSA's budget was $12.6B, largely unchanged since FY2010 ($11.4B), while serving 6M more people than in FY2010.

By end-CY2016, the backlog had swelled to nearly 1 million applications, about a 30% increase over CY2012. The average wait for a hearing had swelled to 602 days. Also by end-CY2016, there were reportedly 7,400 people on waitlists who had died while awaiting claim resolution, according to a report issued by the SSA's Inspector General.

By the end of President Obama's two terms in office, the SSA had reportedly hired 500 new administrative law judges, bringing the total of such judges to about 1,600. More than 600 support staff were also hired to assist with the backlog.

This promise was not fulfilled.

IO-73 **The Promise:** "...will also ensure that the SSA [Social Security Administration] has the funding it needs to hire judges and staff and to invest in technology to expedite final decisions. Obama supported the $150 million increase in the SSA's budget that was vetoed by President Bush this year. As president, he will continue to work to ensure that the SSA has the resources it needs for hiring and to more effectively process its caseloads."
When/Where: Obama-Biden Plan: "Empower Americans with Disabilities" dated 09/06/08.
Source: http://www.thearc.org/document.doc?id=3073
Status: Based largely upon the President's request, the FY2010 budget for the Social Security Administration (SSA) was $11.4B, a 10% increase over the FY2009 enacted level. This increase was intended to permit the SSA to hire about 5,800 replacement and 1,300 new personnel largely intended to replace the SSA's information technology infrastructure.

In FY2011, reality set in. The SSA was supposed to receive $12.4B but operated on its FY2010 budget of $11.4B. The SSA also lost $200M in funds intended for addressing its claims backlog. Those funds were taken by Congress as part of the stopgap measure to prevent a government shutdown in 03/11.

SSA's plans to open eight new SSA hearing offices were postponed. There was also a hiring freeze in effect for FY2011 at the SSA and no funds were available for overtime to pay the current staff to accelerate elimination of benefits payments caseload backlogs. FY2012 hiring was limited to positions classified as critical to the SSA.

As of early-CY2013, the SSA did not have the resources it needed for hiring additional personnel and to more effectively process its caseloads. In fact, the SSA acknowledged a loss of 4,000 personnel in FY2011, another 3,000 in FY2012 and lost an additional 2,000 in FY2013 due to budget cuts.

The completion of efforts to develop a Disability Case Processing System (DCPS) and Health Information Technology (Health IT) systems to replace up to 54 COBOL-based systems currently used will be a huge step in mitigating caseload backlogs. As of end-CY2016 the DCPS had not been rolled out/activated.

Nonetheless, the funding increase promised to SSA to hire judges and invest in technology improvements was delivered during President Obama's first term in office.

This promise was fulfilled.

1.00

TRADE REPRESENTATIVE	GRADE

IO-74 **The Promise:** "...will use trade agreements to spread good labor and environmental standards around the world."
When/Where: Obama-Biden Plan to Revitalize the Economy, 2008
Source: https://webarchive.loc.gov/all/20090429185145/http://change.gov/agenda/economy_agenda/
Status: At the start of the Obama Administration, the USA had Free Trade Agreements (FTA) with 17 countries (Canada, Mexico, Israel, Jordan, Singapore, Chile, Australia, Morocco, Bahrain, Oman, Peru, Dominican Republic, Costa Rica, El Salvador, Guatemala, Honduras and Nicaragua). By end-CY2016, three countries had been added (South Korea, Colombia and Panama) as FTA partners. Each of these agreements contained labor and environmental standards.

In addition to the above, 10 countries entered into Trade and Investment Framework Agreements (TIFA) with the USA during President Obama's two terms in office (Angola, Argentina, Armenia, Bangladesh, Myanmar, Iceland, Laos, Libya, Maldives, South Africa). These were supplemented by three regional TIFAs: Caribbean Community (CARICOM), Economic Community of West African States (ECOWAS), and Gulf Cooperation Council (GCC) Framework Agreement. Labor and environmental considerations are reflected in each of these agreements.

1.00

Chapter 18 - Independent Organizations

On 02/12/13, President Barack Obama called for a Transatlantic Trade and Investment Partnership (TTIP) between the European Union (EU) and the USA. Opposition to the TTIP within the EU led to years of unsuccessful negotiations by the time President Obama left office in 01/17 due largely to labor and environmental concerns from the EU citizenry, among many.

The Trans-Pacific Partnership (TPP), also called the Trans-Pacific Partnership Agreement, is a trade agreement between Australia, Brunei, Canada, Chile, Japan, Malaysia, Mexico, New Zealand, Peru, Singapore and Vietnam. China refused TPP participation largely due to the environmental and labor requirements imposed therein by the USA. President Obama signed the TPP on 02/04/16, but the Senate had not ratified that agreement by the end of his tenure in the Oval Office.

This promise was fulfilled.

INDEPENDENT ORGANIZATIONS GPA	0.50

Campaign Promises

Other/Miscellaneous -> Miscellaneous Promises

ITEM	MISCELLANEOUS PROMISES	
	AL GORE	**GRADE**
MP-1	**The Promise:** "I will make a commitment that Al Gore will be at the table and play a central part in us figuring out how we solve this problem. He's somebody I talk to on a regular basis. I'm already consulting with him in terms of these issues, but climate change is real." **When/Where:** Obama Statement at a Town Hall Meeting, Wallingford, PA, 04/02/08. **Source:** https://www.cbsnews.com/news/obama-gore-will-be-at-the-table/ **Status:** It's unclear what Candidate Obama meant by "at the table," a term he used frequently during his first presidential campaign. But this comment should not be interpreted as Obama offering former Vice President Gore a cabinet position. Ultimately, any meaningful interface between President Obama and Nobel Prize Laureate Gore on climate change issues were invisible to the public during President Obama's two terms in office. On 11/13/08, Gore's office advised President-Elect Obama's White House transition team that Gore did not want to be considered to fill the position of "Climate Czar" under President Obama. The two met to discuss climate issues prior to the CY2009 international negotiations held in Copenhagen, Denmark -- a conference that produced no substantive, enforceable targets for global warming pollution, only a "rhetorical agreement," according to Gore. On 06/22/11, the magazine "Rolling Stone" published a 7K-word essay written by former Vice President Gore that accused President Obama of having failed to lead the U.S. and international communities on the issue of global warming. This promise was not fulfilled.	0.00
	BIPARTISANSHIP	**GRADE**
MP-2	**The Promise:** "...and I believe that there are a lot of Republicans who hunger for that kind of bipartisan approach -- that's what I will offer as President of the United States." **When/Where:** Democratic Presidential Debate, Las Vegas, NV, dated 11/15/07. **Source:** http://www.youtube.com/watch?v=kIjQCzIli9Q **Status:** While this specific promise was made within the context of national security and foreign policy, the prevailing theme was bipartisanship on all fronts. President Obama addressed the House Republican Retreat in Baltimore on 01/29/10. He stated during that address: "Bipartisanship, not for its own sake but to solve problems, that's what our constituents, the American people, need from us right now. All of us then have a choice to make. We have to choose whether we're going to be politicians first or partners for progress; whether we're going to put success at the polls ahead of the lasting success we can achieve together for America." With few exceptions, bipartisanship did not prevail during President Obama's two terms in office. Nonetheless, he did try to communicate his willingness to work with the Republican sides of the	1.00

Chapter 19 - Miscellaneous Promises

House and Senate early in his first term as evidenced by his address to the House Republican Retreat depicted above.

This promise was fulfilled.

MP-3

The Promise: "I will call for a standing, bipartisan consultative group of congressional leaders on national security. I will meet with this consultative group every month and consult with them before taking major military action."
When/Where: Campaign Speech entitled "A New Beginning," Chicago, IL, dated 10/02/07.
Source: http://www.presidency.ucsb.edu/ws/index.php?pid=77015
Status: A consultative group was not formed during President Obama's two terms in office, despite a bipartisan study and recommendation to do so.

Further, President Obama did not meet monthly with a bipartisan representation of legislative leaders on military/national security matters.

This promise was not fulfilled.

0.00

MP-4

The Promise: "...put an end to the petty partisanship that passes for politics in Washington..."
When/Where: Obama Campaign Speech entitled "League of United Latin American Citizens," Washington, D.C., 07/08/08.
Source: http://www.presidency.ucsb.edu/ws/index.php?pid=77598
Status: The American Recovery and Reinvestment Act of 2009 was passed with only three (3) Republicans in the Senate (none in the House) voting for it.

The Patient Protection and Affordable Care Act (H.R. 3590) was even worse, with all Republicans in the House and Senate voting either against it or not at all (as in the case of Senator Isakson, R-GA).

The Dodd-Frank Wall Street Reform and Consumer Protection Act (H.R. 4173) passed the Democrat-controlled House on 12/11/09 without one single Republican vote and passed the Democrat-controlled Senate with support from only three Republican and two Independent Senators.

On these big bills, there was absolutely no significant bipartisanship.

After the Republicans won control of the House in the 11/10 elections and to prevent "petty partisanship" from continuing, a first meeting took place on 11/30/10 between President Obama and top Congressional leaders from both parties. In an address to the media following this meeting, President Obama focused on the "hyperpartisan climate" in which "both sides come to the table. They read their talking points. Then they head out to the microphones, trying to win the news cycle instead of solving problems." This statement is one of many that set the stage for continued animosity between Congress and the White House.

To be fair, bipartisan compromises were reached to extend Bush-era tax cuts (H.R. 4853), repeal "Don't Ask, Don't Tell (H.R. 2965)," and ratify the "New START" treaty with Russia (signed into law on 02/02/11). These are but a few significant examples.

Nonetheless, it was evident that "petty partisanship" would continue, making progress on such dicey issues as a new Development, Relief, and Education for Alien Minors (DREAM) Act, immigration reform, etc. virtually impossible.

Meanwhile, President Obama missed no opportunities to insult Congressional Republicans. On 10/17/11, he mocked their intelligence by stating that Republicans were "not smart enough" to understand his $447B jobs bill and he therefore had to present it to Congress in smaller pieces so that Republicans could understand them.

0.00

Chapter 19 - Miscellaneous Promises

As of end-CY2016, with Republicans controlling both houses of Congress, the page on "petty partisanship" had not been turned.

This promise was not fulfilled.

CAMPAIGN FINANCING	GRADE

MP-5

The Promise: "If I am the Democratic nominee, I will aggressively pursue an agreement with the Republican nominee to preserve a publicly financed general election."
When/Where: Midwest Democracy Network Presidential Candidate Questionnaire, dated 11/27/07.
Source: https://www.wisdc.org/images/files/pdf_imported/MDN-Presidential-Questionnaire-responses.pdf
Status: The amount of public financing for a candidate's campaign after nomination is established and limited by the Federal Election Commission (FEC) based on funds made available by the Department of the Treasury from contributions made by individuals on their tax return ($3 per person on CY2008 and CY2012 IRS Form 1040).

After winning his party's nomination on 08/27/08 for the 2008 general election, it became clear that Candidate Obama was doing extremely well with private funding from small donors, principally through the Internet. He reportedly received about $745M for the CY2008 campaign and $782M for the CY2012 campaign from private sources.

Based on his success in raising money through social media, Candidate Obama retreated/flip-flopped from pursuing public financing, did not "aggressively" engage with his opponent at the time on this issue, and shunned public campaign financing altogether. That funding would reportedly have been limited by the FEC to about $85M for each nominee.

This promise was not fulfilled.

Grade: 0.00

COLLEGE FOOTBALL	GRADE

MP-6

The Promise: "....we should be creating a playoff system. Eight teams. That would be three rounds to determine a national champion....I'm going to throw my weight around a little bit..."
When/Where: Interview on CBS New Program "60 Minutes" dated 11/17/08.
Source: http://www.youtube.com/watch?v=3WDuQe89kJM
Status: Among the principal complaints against the college football Bowl Championship Series (BCS) when Candidate Obama promised to "influence" change were that the methodology employed to select championship game participants consisted of subjective voting assessments coupled with the ability for an undefeated team to finish a season without being afforded the opportunity to play in that year's national championship game. Further, a team could lose its own conference championship but still be selected to play in the BCS championship game.

President Obama's desire for a college football playoff system was repeated several times during his first term in office, most notably on 04/23/09 when he received the Florida Gators champions at the White House. During his remarks to that winning football team, he stated "You guys are the national champions. I'm not backing off the fact we need a playoff system." This remark became reality on 06/26/12 when university presidents approved a National Collegiate Athletic Association (NCAA) plan to institute a four-team playoff system. The structure: four teams, two semifinals played in bowl games during the New Year holiday, followed by a national championship game played about a week later. The four-team playoff system was activated with the CY2014-CY2015 college football season.

President Obama didn't get the eight teams he wanted in the new college football playoff system. However, he most likely influenced the creation of the new four-team playoff system.

This promise was fulfilled.

Grade: 1.00

MISCELLANEOUS PROMISES GPA	0.33

Campaign Promises

Other/Miscellaneous -> United Nations

ITEM	UNITED NATIONS	
	CONVENTION PARTICIPATION	**GRADE**
UN-1	**The Promise:** "Will re-engage with the U.N. Framework Convention on Climate Change (UNFCC) - the main international forum dedicated to addressing the climate problem." **When/Where:** Obama-Biden Plan for America entitled: "Blueprint for Change" dated 10/09/08. **Source:** https://www.documentcloud.org/documents/550007-barack-obama-2008-blueprint-for-change.html **Status:** President Obama addressed the UNFCC at the Copenhagen Climate Change Conference of the Parties (COP15) on 12/18/09. According to a document entitled the "Copenhagen Accord," a 2010 deadline for reaching a legally binding climate treaty between UNFCC participating nations was dropped and no global target for cutting greenhouse gases was set. President Obama elected not to attend COP16 (Cancun), COP17 (Durban), COP18 (Doha), COP19 (Warsaw), and COP20 (Lima) during which the finer points of a binding agreement were ironed out. He finally attended COP21 in Paris during which participating nations concluded what is now known as the "Paris Climate Change Agreement." This promise was for President Obama to "re-engage" with the UNFCC, and he did. This promise was fulfilled.	1.00
UN-2	**The Promise:** "...will renew America's leadership by making the United States a signatory to the UN Convention on the Rights of Persons with Disabilities..." **When/Where:** Obama-Biden Plan: "Empower Americans with Disabilities," dated 09/06/08. **Source:** http://www.thearc.org/document.doc?id=3073 **Status:** The USA became the 141st signatory of the United Nations Convention on the Rights of Persons with Disabilities (CRPD) on 07/30/09. Ratification of the CRPD by the Senate is a different matter altogether. This promise was for the USA to become a signatory to the CRPD and this happened. Then-Candidate Obama did not promise that he would get it ratified by the Senate. This promise was fulfilled.	1.00
UN-3	**The Promise:** "...will also create a Global Energy Forum of the world's largest emitters to focus exclusively on global energy and environmental issues." **When/Where:** Obama-Biden Plan for America entitled: "Blueprint for Change" dated 10/09/08. **Source:** https://www.documentcloud.org/documents/550007-barack-obama-2008-blueprint-for-change.html **Status:** In 03/28/09, President Obama initiated the Global Energy Forum under a different name: the "Major Economies Forum on Energy and Climate (MEF)." There are 17 participating countries that together account for about 80% of the world's greenhouse gas emissions: Australia, Brazil, Canada, China, the European Union (EU), France, Germany, India, Indonesia, Italy, Japan, South Korea,	1.00

Mexico, Russia, South Africa, the United Kingdom, and the United States. Note that while France, Germany, Italy and the United Kingdom were members of the EU at the time, theirs was an individual membership.

This promise was fulfilled.

UN-4	**The Promise:** "...will ensure that the U.S. provides leadership in enforcing international wildlife protection agreements, including strengthening the international moratorium on commercial whaling. Allowing Japan to continue commercial whaling is unacceptable." **When/Where:** Candidate Obama response to a Greenpeace letter dated 03/16/08. **Source:** https://www.distantocean.com/2010/03/theres-an-ahab-in-the-white-house.html?cid=6a00d834200af253ef0133ec3bafd2970b#comment-6a00d834200af253ef0133ec3bafd2970b **Status:** The International Convention for the Regulation of Whaling (ICRW) was originally signed by the USA and 14 other nations, including Japan, on 12/02/46. Under the ICRW, the International Whaling Commission (IWC) was created. The IWC adopted a moratorium on commercial whaling in CY1982 and created a Southern Ocean Whale Sanctuary in CY1994. Japan was the sole member of the IWC to oppose this santuary and continued its commercial whaling practices. The 61st annual meeting of the IWC in Madeira, Portugal on 06/22-24/09 under USA chairmanship and with 71 of the 85 "contracting governments" participating. Nothing came out of this meeting that strengthened the moratorium on commercial whaling. The meeting's report indicated that Japan caught 1,000 whales during the 2008/2009 whaling season under a "special permit." The 62nd annual meeting of the IWC took place in Agadir, Morocco on 06/21-25/10. The "Future of the IWC" was a prominent agenda item, because the future existence if the IWC was uncertain. During this meeting, talks aimed at reducing whaling by Japan, Norway and Iceland collapsed. Even a compromise plan proposed by the USA and other anti-whaling nations that would have allowed these three countries to resume commercial whaling but at significantly lower levels and under tight monitoring failed. On 07/20/11, Commerce Secretary Gary Locke recommended that sanctions be levied against Iceland based on his belief that Iceland was in violation of the Pelly Amendment to the "Fishermen's Protective Act of 1967." His letter to President Obama stated that Iceland was "conducting fishing operations which diminish the effectiveness of an international fishery conservation program." President Obama waived the requested sanctions on 09/15/11. Without the promised Obama Administration leadership, Japan continued its whaling activities in the North Pacific and Antarctic regions as a compromise move to permit continued approval of catches by the Alaskan Inuit tribe under a clause allowing Aboriginal subsistence whaling. On 03/31/14, the International Court of Justice (ICJ) in The Hague, Netherlands ordered a temporary cessation of Japan's Antarctic whaling activities in the southern Pacific Ocean, stating that Japan's harvesting of 850 whales annually was excessive to its stated "scientific research" requirements. As of end-CY2016, after a brief hiatus in the CY2014-15 timeframe, Japan resumed its commercial harvesting of primarily minke whales under the guise of "scientific research." This promise was not fulfilled.	0.00
UN-5	**The Promise:** "will...make the Millennium Development Goals, which aim to cut extreme poverty in half by 2015, America's goals." **When/Where:** Obama-Biden Plan: "To Secure America and Restore our Standing," undated. **Source:** https://s3.amazonaws.com/s3.documentcloud.org/documents/550007/barack-obama-2008-	1.00

Chapter 20 - United Nations

blueprint-for-change.pdf

Status: At the Millennium Summit of CY2000, eight major goals were set by the United Nations, principal among which was to halve the number of people living on less than $1.25 per day -- a goal to be reached by CY2015. These became known as the Millenium Development Goals (MDGs).

In an address to the United Nations MDG Review Summit on 09/22/10, President Obama confirmed the adoption of the UN's MDG as America's goals by stating: "...this can be our plan, not simply for meeting our Millennium Development Goals, but for exceeding them, and then sustaining them for generations to come."

The United Nations "Millenium Development Goals Report of 2015" indicated that the proportion of people living on less than $1.25 a day fell from 47% in CY1990 to 14% in CY2015, a reduction from over 1.9B people to less than 840M -- less than half the CY1990 rate.

This promise was fulfilled.

	NUCLEAR NON-PROLIFERATION	GRADE
UN-6	**The Promise:** "...will work with our allies and other countries to achieve a successful outcome in 2010 that strengthens the Non-Proliferation Treaty (NPT)." **When/Where:** Fact Sheet: "Confronting 21st Century Threats" dated 07/16/08. **Source:** https://www.presidency.ucsb.edu/documents/press-release-fact-sheet-obamas-new-plan-confront-21st-century-threats **Status:** President Obama presided over a historic summit meeting on 09/24/09 at the UN during which 13 other Heads of State and Government and the UN Security Council pledged support to mitigate "long-stalled efforts to staunch the proliferation of nuclear weapons and ensure reductions in existing weapons stockpiles, as well as control of fissile materials." This resulted in the unanimous adoption of UN Resolution 1887 which called for the setting of realistic goals for the 2010 Nuclear Posture Review (NPR). The month-long conference that ended on 05/28/10 in New York served as a recovery from the failed NPR of 2005. The 2010 NPR also served to reaffirm the commitment of 189 countries toward the NPT. Further, President Obama succeeded in securing strong language on safeguards, NPT compliance, support for the International Atomic Energy Agency (IAEA), and his detailed plan for nuclear disarmament. This was reflected in a final document that included an action plan for disarmament, nonproliferation, peaceful uses of nuclear energy, and eventually attaining a nuclear weapons-free zone in the Middle East. This was a small step towards strengthening the NPT. This promise was fulfilled.	1.00
UN-7	**The Promise:** "...will convene a summit in 2009 (and regularly thereafter) of leaders of Permanent Members of the UN Security Council and other key countries to agree on implementing many of these measures on a global basis." **When/Where:** Fact Sheet: "Confronting 21st Century Threats" dated 07/16/08. **Source:** https://www.presidency.ucsb.edu/documents/press-release-fact-sheet-obamas-new-plan-confront-21st-century-threats **Status:** This promise relates to the prevention of nuclear terrorism. The first Nuclear Security Summit was held in Washington, D.C. on 04/12-13/10 (not CY2009 as stated in this promise), with a focus on nuclear terrorism. Its result was a non-binding, non-enforceable, non-treaty communique that reflected a dubious international commitment to secure all nuclear materials by CY2015. Three other Nuclear Security Summits were held: The second summit was held in South Korea in CY2012, the third summit was held in The Netherlands in CY2014, and the fourth (and last) summit was held in Washington, D.C. in CY2016 This promise to "convene a summit" was fulfilled.	1.00

Chapter 20 - United Nations

UN-8	**The Promise:** "...will work with the Senate to secure the ratification of the CTBT at the earliest practical date and will then launch a diplomatic effort to bring on board other states whose ratifications are required for the treaty to enter into force." **When/Where:** Fact Sheet: "Confronting 21st Century Threats" dated 07/16/08. **Source:** https://www.presidency.ucsb.edu/documents/press-release-fact-sheet-obamas-new-plan-confront-21st-century-threats **Status:** On 10/13/99, the Senate rejected ratification of the Comprehensive Nuclear Test Ban Treaty (CTBT), signed by the USA on 09/24/96. Ratification by signatory countries is considered crucial to keeping the wider-scoped Nuclear Nonproliferation Treaty viable. As of end-CY2016, 166 of 183 countries had ratified the CTBT. The USA was one of the 5 nuclear-capable countries that had signed the CTBT but had not yet ratified it. Before the CTBT can take effect, ratification by signatories China, Egypt, Iran and Israel is also required. So too is signature and ratification by India, North Korea and Pakistan. Support from two-thirds of the Senate is required for ratification of the CTBT by the USA to take place. This promise was not fulfilled.	0.00
UN-9	**The Promise:** "...will crack down on nuclear proliferation by strengthening the Nuclear Non-Proliferation Treaty so that countries like North Korea and Iran that break the rules will automatically face strong international sanctions." **When/Where:** Obama-Biden Plan for America entitled: "Blueprint for Change" dated 10/09/08. **Source:** https://www.documentcloud.org/documents/550007-barack-obama-2008-blueprint-for-change.html **Status:** During President Obama's two terms in office, North Korea and Iran adopted an "in your face" attitude and continued to develop nuclear capabilities with impunity. A nuclear security summit involving 38 heads of state and 9 senior national representatives was convened in Washington, D.C. in mid-04/10, the first of four similar summits. President Obama then met with international partners at the United Nations in 05/10 to review global efforts on nuclear non-proliferation. While these events led to stronger international sanctions against Iran, nothing of substance came about against North Korea to supplement the sanctions imposed against that country after two nuclear tests in CY2006 and CY2009. Since then, North Korea succeeded in building a uranium enrichment plant and completed work on a new long-range ballistic missile launch site at Donchang-ri. It tested such a missile in 02/13, on President Obama's watch. Shipping/transportation loopholes in the sanctions against North Korea facilitated its illegal exportation of ballistic missiles, components and technology to the Middle East (notably Iran). North Korea is also suspected of having helped Myanmar build a nuclear reactor and plutonium extraction plant that would have permitted Myanmar to build nuclear weaponry as early as CY2014. However, the new government of President Thein Sein promised Senator John McCain (R-AZ) in 06/11 that it was abandoning its pursuit of any nuclear capabilities. During the 21-nation Asia-Pacific Economic Cooperation (APEC) conference held in Hawaii on 11/12-13/11, President Obama failed to convince the leaders of Russia and China to join him in pushing for more severe sanctions against Iran in the aftermath of a UN International Atomic Energy Agency (IAEA) 11/11 report that Iran was rapidly developing nuclear weapons. The promised 'automatic' implementation of sanctions against any country that breaks the rules (such as Iran and North Korea) did not happened. In fact, on 01/12/16 President Obama signed an	0.00

Chapter 20 - United Nations

Executive Order revoking a 20-year system of sanctions against Iran for pursuing a nuclear weapons program.

This promise was not fulfilled.

UN-10

The Promise: "...will...work with other nuclear powers to reduce global stockpiles dramatically by the end of an Obama presidency."
When/Where: Fact Sheet: "Confronting 21st Century Threats" dated 07/16/08.
Source: https://www.presidency.ucsb.edu/documents/press-release-fact-sheet-obamas-new-plan-confront-21st-century-threats
Status: The only nuclear power with which the USA has aggressively worked with the objective of nuclear stockpile reductions is Russia. A "New START" treaty was signed on 04/08/10 in Prague by Presidents Obama and Medvedev. It was ratified by the U.S. Senate in a 71-26 vote on 12/22/10, and by the Russian Government on 01/28/11.

The "other nuclear powers" addressed in this promise (i.e. France, United Kingdon, China, Pakistan, India, etc.) have not been engaged meaningfully to reduce their nuclear stockpiles. We won't even address North Korea and Iran.

This promise was not fulfilled.

0.00

UN-11

The Promise: "...will institutionalize the Proliferation Security Initiative (PSI), a global initiative aimed at stopping shipments of weapons of mass destruction, their delivery systems, and related materials worldwide...will expand the responsibilities of its members, not only in stopping illicit nuclear shipments, but also in eradicating nuclear black market networks."
When/Where: Fact Sheet: "Confronting 21st Century Threats" dated 07/16/08.
Source: https://www.presidency.ucsb.edu/documents/press-release-fact-sheet-obamas-new-plan-confront-21st-century-threats
Status: The Proliferation Security Initiative (PSI) was initiated by President Bush on 05/31/03 to interdict shipments of weapons of mass destruction (WMD) and related materials (chemical, biological, nuclear) to terrorists and countries believed to harbor desires to develop and/or produce WMD.

105 countries have recognized the PSI, including Russia, based on participation and not membership. China, concerned about the legality of interdictions, has declined to participate in PSI, as have, notably, North Korea, Indonesia, Iran, Myanmar, Syria and Pakistan.

As of end-CY2016, the PSI's effectiveness was hindered by scarce financial resources, lack of global coverage, unresolved issues regarding inspection of vessels in international waters, the absence of any permanent institutional structure and the absence of any requirement for participants to accept any binding legal commitments to carry out the intended interdictions.

This promise was not fulfilled.

0.00

UN-12

The Promise: "...will lead a global effort to secure all nuclear weapons materials at vulnerable sites within four years - the most effective way to prevent terrorists from acquiring a nuclear bomb."
When/Where: Obama Campaign Document "A 21st Century Military for America" dated 11/26/07.
Source: https://www.scribd.com/document/6245756/Barack-Obama-on-Defense-Issues-A-21st-Century-Military-for-America
Status: President Obama provided leadership and guidance during the 04/12-13/10 Nuclear Security Summit held in Washington, D.C.

During this summit, 47 nations succeeded in establishing concrete actions and decisions ranging from securing all of the world's vulnerable nuclear materials within 4 years to reducing the availability of highly enriched uranium and plutonium.

0.00

However, the Director General of the International Atomic Energy Agency (IAEA) acknowledged on 02/14/11 that the IAEA remained concerned about reports that Iran and North Korea continued to build new nuclear facilities and continued research on nuclear weaponization. Further, the IAEA issued a restricted report to its board and to the UN Security Council in early 11/11 that described Iran's nuclear work as "specific to nuclear weapons."

As of end-CY2016, nuclear weapons materials were believed to be available to bad actors Iran and North Korea, a status unchanged from the pre-Obama era. Consequently, the risks related to their potential acquisition by terrorist organizations remained extremely high throughout President Obama's two terms in office.

This promise was not fulfilled.

UN-13	**The Promise:** "...will stop the development of new nuclear weapons..." **When/Where:** Obama-Biden Plan "Blueprint for Change" dated 10/09/08. **Source:** https://www.documentcloud.org/documents/550007-barack-obama-2008-blueprint-for-change.html **Status:** IRAN: On 06/09/10, the UN Security Council voted 12 to 2 in favor of U.S. sponsored sanctions against Iran over its suspected nuclear program, believed by the UN International Atomic Energy Agency (IAEA) to be for the development of new nuclear weapons. These sanctions were not effective and Iran continued to develop new nuclear capabilities. As a result of an 11/11 IAEA report, President Obama tried to convince the leaders of Russia and China to join him in pushing for more severe sanctions against Iran during the 21-nation Asia-Pacific Economic Cooperation (APEC) conference held in Hawaii on 11/12-13/11. Neither nation supported President Obama's initiative and the matter was not brought up for a UN Security Council vote. NORTH KOREA: UN Security Council sanctions against North Korea have been imposed repeatedly since North Korea first conducted nuclear tests in CY2006. These sanctions did not deter North Korea. Its development of long-range nuclear weapons continued throughout President Obama's second term in office. MYANMAR: Throughout President Obama's first term in office, North Korea (with Russian assistance) was suspected of transferring nuclear technology and resources to Myanmar for that country to develop nuclear capabilities by CY2014. By end-CY2012, however, the State Department reported that these suspicions were without basis. Myanmar, however, is known to continue its nuclear research initiatives with Russian assistance. SYRIA: In cooperation with North Korea and Iran, Syria is known to have a nuclear research facility. A Syrian nuclear reactor at Kibar near the city of Deir al-Zor on the banks of the Euphrates River was destroyed by Israel in 09/07. Since then, Syria has been uncooperative with the IAEA in the UN's efforts to determine the extent of Syria's nuclear weapons development efforts. Based on IAEA reports, Syria is believed to possess up to 50 tons of natural uranium, enough material for three to five bombs once the enrichment procedure is completed. To that end, an enrichment capability is believed to have been built by end-CY2016 at a nuclear facility near Qusayr north of Damascus, or at another nuclear facility just outside Damascus near the border with Lebanon. PAKISTAN & INDIA: Both countries do not participate in the Treaty on the Non-Proliferation of Nuclear Weapons (NPT) nor the Comprehensive Nuclear Test Ban Treaty (CTBT). These two countries remained in competition with one another in the development of new nuclear weapons throughout President Obama's two terms in office. ISRAEL: Israel is not a party to the Treaty on the Non-Proliferation of Nuclear Weapons (NPT). In response to a perceived nuclear threat from Iran, Israel is believed, according to open source materials, to possess weapons-grade plutonium sufficient to produce about 200 nuclear weapons. The development of new/updated nuclear capabilities continued unabated during President Obama's	0.00

Chapter 20 - United Nations

two terms in office at Israel's Shimon Peres Negev Nuclear Research Center near Dimona.

This promise was not fulfilled.

UN-14

The Promise: "...will lead a global effort to negotiate a verifiable treaty ending the production of fissile materials for weapons purposes."

When/Where: "Arms Control Today" 2008 Presidential Q&A: President-elect Barack Obama (pp. 31-36)

Source: https://www.jstor.org/stable/23628543?refreqid=excelsior%3A67406c6547d537aca1cd7ae0819e7229

Status: Candidate Obama promised to "lead" the world in negotiating a Fissile Material Cutoff Treaty (FMCT), cutting off future production of fissile material for nuclear weapons. Before him, so did President Bill Clinton who tried in 1993, and President George W. Bush who tried in 2006.

On 04/05/09 in Prague, President Obama proposed to negotiate "a new treaty that verifiably ends the production of fissile materials intended for use in state nuclear weapons," on the premise that verification of an FMCT was both desirable and do-able.

After eight years, by end-CY2016, the Obama Administration had accomplished little else than to formulate a proposal at the 03/16 CD to establish a working group to negotiate an FMCT, reminiscent of a similar proposal made at the CD on 08/11/98.

This promise was not fulfilled.

0.00

UN-15

The Promise: "...will propose a new multilateral initiative to control existing fissile materials, under which nations will provide regular declarations of their fissile material holdings, secure their materials to the highest international standards of physical protection, declare increasing amounts of material as excess to defense needs and transform such excess materials to forms no longer useable in nuclear weapons as soon as practicable."

When/Where: "Arms Control Today" 2008 Presidential Q&A: President-elect Barack Obama (pp. 31-36)

Source: https://www.jstor.org/stable/23628543?refreqid=excelsior%3A67406c6547d537aca1cd7ae0819e7229

Status: This promise is not to be confused with Promise UN-14, which pertains to the production of fissile materials. This promise addresses the control of existing fissile materials.

The 2010 Nuclear Security Summit held in Washington, D.C. on 04/12-13/10 and attended by 47 nations/ international entities, focused on how to better safeguard existing fissile materials, specifically weapons grade plutonium and uranium. The Review Conference Action Plan included language on the importance of transparency and verification regarding fissile material (Actions 19 & 21). However, the Summit ended with a non-binding communique that did not specifically address the actions that need to be taken to control existing fissile materials. Rather, broad statements were included in the communique such as "endeavor to fully implement all existing nuclear security commitments" and "support the implementation of strong nuclear security practices."

Similarly, the communique issued at the end of the 03/26-27/12 Nuclear Security Summit in Soeul, Korea was not specific about any real progress made by the participating nations other than "to make every possible effort to schieve further progress" in defined areas. The word "fissile" does not even appear in that communique.

As late as 03/16, senators from President Obama's own party begged him in writing to pursue goals such as "ensuring the security of fissile, radiological, and other nuclear materials..."

By end-CY2016, there were approximately 2,000 metric tons of highly enriched uranium (HEU) and Plutonium 239 (Pu) in the world. There remained two primary impediments to effective verification,

0.00

control and disposal of these fissile materials:
- questionable accuracy of knowledge about holdings of fissile materials and past production, given reportedly lost or incomplete records, and
- limited access to fissile materials in active military use due to the classified nature of individual nation military environments.

Thus, the international control of existing fissile materials was no better after President Obama's eight years in office than it was prior to CY2009.

This promise was not fulfilled.

UNITED NATIONS GPA	**0.40**

Appendix A
First Term

President Obama's Approval Rate
(Average Among Major Polling Organizations)

2009	%	Trend
Inauguration Day - 20 January 2009	63.3	
January 31, 2009	61.8	↓
February 28, 2009	64.2	↑
March 31, 2009	61.5	↓
April 30, 2009	61.6	↑
May 31, 2009	60.8	↓
June 30, 2009	59.5	↓
July 31, 2009	53.7	↓
August 31, 2009	51.2	↓
September 30, 2009	52.5	↑
October 31, 2009	51.7	↓
November 30, 2009	50.3	↓
December 31, 2009	49.8	↓
Average Approval Rating for 2009:	**56.6**	↓

Source: http://www.realclearpolitics.com/epolls/other/president_obama_job_approval-1044.html

President Obama's Approval Rate
(Average Among Major Polling Organizations)

2010	%	Trend
January 31, 2010	49.3	↓
February 28, 2010	47.8	↓
March 31, 2010	48.6	↑
April 30, 2010	47.9	↓
May 31, 2010	47.4	↓
June 30, 2010	46.6	↓
July 31, 2010	45.3	↓
August 31, 2010	46.5	↑
September 30, 2010	45.0	↓
October 31, 2010	46.0	↑
November 30, 2010	45.9	↓
December 31, 2010	45.4	↓
Average Approval Rating for 2010:	**46.8**	↓

Source: http://www.realclearpolitics.com/epolls/other/president_obama_job_approval-1044.html

President Obama's Approval Rate
(Average Among Major Polling Organizations)

2011	%	Trend
January 31, 2011	50.7	↑
February 28, 2011	49.3	↓
March 31, 2011	47.4	↓
April 30, 2011	45.9	↓
May 31, 2011	51.2	↑
June 30, 2011	47.2	↓
July 31, 2011	44.6	↓
August 31, 2011	43.0	↓
September 30, 2011	42.5	↓
October 31, 2011	44.3	↑
November 30, 2011	43.2	↓
December 31, 2011	46.8	↑
Average Approval Rating for 2011:	**46.3**	↓

Source: http://www.realclearpolitics.com/epolls/other/president_obama_job_approval-1044.html

President Obama's Approval Rate
(Average Among Major Polling Organizations)

2012	%	Trend
January 31, 2012	47.0	↑
February 29, 2012	48.6	↑
March 31, 2012	47.3	↓
April 30, 2012	47.6	↑
May 31, 2012	48.0	↑
June 30, 2012	47.9	↓
July 31, 2012	47.4	↓
August 31, 2012	47.7	↑
September 30, 2012	49.8	↑
October 31, 2012	49.7	↓
November 30, 2012	51.0	↑
December 31, 2012	53.4	↑
Average Approval Rating for 2012:	**48.8**	↑

Source: http://www.realclearpolitics.com/epolls/other/president_obama_job_approval-1044.html

Appendix A
Second Term

President Obama's Approval Rate (Average Among Major Polling Organizations)		
2013	**%**	**Trend**
Inauguration Day - 21 January 2013	52.1	
January 31, 2013	52.3	↑
February 28, 2013	50.9	↓
March 31, 2013	47.6	↓
April 30, 2013	48.3	↑
May 31, 2013	47.7	↓
June 30, 2013	46.0	↓
July 31, 2013	45.4	↓
August 31, 2013	44.2	↓
September 30, 2013	44.1	↓
October 31, 2013	43.9	↓
November 30, 2013	40.1	↓
December 31, 2013	42.6	↑
Average Approval Rating for 2013:	**46.1**	↓

Source: http://www.realclearpolitics.com/epolls/other/president_obama_job_approval-1044.html

President Obama's Approval Rate (Average Among Major Polling Organizations)		
2014	**%**	**Trend**
January 31, 2014	43.4	↑
February 28, 2014	43.0	↓
March 31, 2014	43.1	↑
April 30, 2014	43.8	↑
May 31, 2014	43.6	↓
June 30, 2014	41.9	↓
July 31, 2014	41.7	↓
August 31, 2014	42.0	↑
September 30, 2014	41.7	↓
October 31, 2014	42.1	↑
November 30, 2014	42.0	↓
December 31, 2014	43.2	↑
Average Approval Rating for 2014:	**42.6**	↓

Source: http://www.realclearpolitics.com/epolls/other/president_obama_job_approval-1044.html

President Obama's Approval Rate (Average Among Major Polling Organizations)		
2015	**%**	**Trend**
January 31, 2015	46.0	↑
February 28, 2015	44.1	↓
March 31, 2015	46.0	↑
April 30, 2015	45.7	↓
May 31, 2015	45.3	↓
June 30, 2015	46.4	↑
July 31, 2015	46.1	↓
August 31, 2015	44.9	↓
September 30, 2015	45.3	↑
October 31, 2015	45.8	↑
November 30, 2015	44.2	↓
December 31, 2015	43.6	↓
Average Approval Rating for 2015:	**45.3**	↑

Source: http://www.realclearpolitics.com/epolls/other/president_obama_job_approval-1044.html

President Obama's Approval Rate (Average Among Major Polling Organizations)		
2016	**%**	**Trend**
January 31, 2016	46.9	↑
February 29, 2016	46.4	↓
March 31, 2016	49.0	↑
April 30, 2016	48.3	↓
May 31, 2016	48.8	↑
June 30, 2016	50.1	↑
July 31, 2016	49.8	↓
August 31, 2016	51.4	↑
September 30, 2016	50.3	↓
October 31, 2016	52.5	↑
November 30, 2016	54.0	↑
December 31, 2016	53.6	↓
Average Approval Rating for 2016:	**50.1**	↑

Source: http://www.realclearpolitics.com/epolls/other/president_obama_job_approval-1044.html

Appendix B
First Term

Dow Jones Industrial Average (As of End of Month)

2009	Index	Trend
Inauguration Day - 20 January 2009	8,228.1	
January 31, 2009	8,000.8	↓
February 28, 2009	7,062.9	↓
March 31, 2009	7,608.9	↑
April 30, 2009	8,168.1	↑
May 31, 2009	8,500.3	↑
June 30, 2009	8,447.0	↓
July 31, 2009	9,286.7	↑
August 31, 2009	9,496.2	↑
September 30, 2009	9,712.2	↑
October 31, 2009	9,712.7	↑
November 30, 2009	10,344.8	↑
December 31, 2009	10,428.0	↑
Average Index for 2009:	**8,897.4**	↑

Source: http://www.google.com/finance?client=ob&q=INDEXDJX:DJI

Dow Jones Industrial Average (As of End of Month)

2010	Index	Trend
January 31, 2010	10,067.3	↓
February 28, 2010	10,325.3	↑
March 31, 2010	10,856.6	↑
April 30, 2010	11,008.6	↑
May 31, 2010	10,136.6	↓
June 30, 2010	9,774.0	↓
July 31, 2010	10,469.8	↑
August 31, 2010	10,014.7	↓
September 30, 2010	10,788.0	↑
October 31, 2010	11,118.4	↑
November 30, 2010	11,006.0	↓
December 31, 2010	11,577.5	↑
Average Index for 2010:	**10,595.2**	↑

Source: http://www.google.com/finance?client=ob&q=INDEXDJX:DJI

Dow Jones Industrial Average (As of End of Month)

2011	Index	Trend
January 31, 2011	11,891.9	↑
February 28, 2011	12,226.3	↑
March 31, 2011	12,319.7	↑
April 30, 2011	12,810.5	↑
May 31, 2011	12,569.7	↓
June 30, 2011	12,414.3	↓
July 31, 2011	12,143.2	↓
August 31, 2011	11,613.5	↓
September 30, 2011	10,913.3	↓
October 31, 2011	11,955.0	↑
November 30, 2011	12,045.6	↑
December 31, 2011	12,217.5	↑
Average Index for 2011:	**12,093.4**	↑

Source: http://www.google.com/finance?client=ob&q=INDEXDJX:DJI

Dow Jones Industrial Average (As of End of Month)

2012	Index	Trend
January 31, 2012	12,632.9	↑
February 29, 2012	12,952.0	↑
March 31, 2012	13,212.0	↑
April 30, 2012	13,213.6	↑
May 31, 2012	12,393.5	↓
June 30, 2012	12,880.0	↑
July 31, 2012	13,008.6	↑
August 31, 2012	13,090.8	↑
September 30, 2012	13,437.1	↑
October 31, 2012	13,096.5	↓
November 30, 2012	13,025.6	↓
December 31, 2012	13,104.1	↑
Average Index for 2012:	**13,003.9**	↑

Source: http://www.google.com/finance?client=ob&q=INDEXDJX:DJI

Appendix B
Second Term

Dow Jones Industrial Average (As of End of Month) — 2013

2013	Index	Trend
Inauguration Day - 21 January 2013	13,649.7	
January 31, 2013	13,860.6	↑
February 28, 2013	14,054.5	↑
March 31, 2013	14,578.5	↑
April 30, 2013	14,839.8	↑
May 31, 2013	15,115.6	↑
June 30, 2013	14,909.6	↓
July 31, 2013	15,499.5	↑
August 31, 2013	14,810.3	↓
September 30, 2013	15,129.7	↑
October 31, 2013	15,545.7	↑
November 30, 2013	16,086.4	↑
December 31, 2013	16,576.7	↑
Average Index for 2013:	**15,083.9**	↑

Source: http://www.google.com/finance?client=ob&q=INDEXDJX:DJI

Dow Jones Industrial Average (As of End of Month) — 2014

2014	Index	Trend
January 31, 2014	15,698.9	↓
February 28, 2014	16,321.7	↑
March 31, 2014	16,457.7	↑
April 30, 2014	16,580.8	↑
May 31, 2014	16,717.2	↑
June 30, 2014	16,826.6	↑
July 31, 2014	16,563.3	↓
August 31, 2014	17,098.5	↑
September 30, 2014	17,042.9	↓
October 31, 2014	17,390.5	↑
November 30, 2014	17,828.2	↑
December 31, 2014	17,823.1	↓
Average Index for 2014:	**16,862.4**	↑

Source: http://www.google.com/finance?client=ob&q=INDEXDJX:DJI

Dow Jones Industrial Average (As of End of Month) — 2015

2015	Index	Trend
January 31, 2015	17,164.9	↓
February 28, 2015	18,132.7	↑
March 31, 2015	17,776.1	↓
April 30, 2015	17,840.5	↑
May 31, 2015	18,010.7	↑
June 30, 2015	17,619.5	↓
July 31, 2015	17,689.9	↑
August 31, 2015	16,528.0	↓
September 30, 2015	16,284.7	↓
October 31, 2015	17,663.5	↑
November 30, 2015	17,719.9	↑
December 31, 2015	17,425.0	↓
Average Index for 2015:	**17,488.0**	↑

Source: http://www.google.com/finance?client=ob&q=INDEXDJX:DJI

Dow Jones Industrial Average (As of End of Month) — 2016

2016	Index	Trend
January 31, 2016	16,466.3	↓
February 29, 2016	16,516.5	↑
March 31, 2016	17,685.1	↑
April 30, 2016	17,773.6	↑
May 31, 2016	17,787.1	↑
June 30, 2016	17,930.0	↑
July 31, 2016	18,432.2	↑
August 31, 2016	18,400.9	↓
September 30, 2016	18,306.1	↓
October 31, 2016	18,143.6	↓
November 30, 2016	19,123.6	↑
December 31, 2016	19,762.6	↑
Average Index for 2016:	**18,027.3**	↑

Source: http://www.google.com/finance?client=ob&q=INDEXDJX:DJI

Appendix C
First Term

U.S. National Unemployment Rate
(As of End of Month)

2009	%	Trend
Inauguration Day - 20 January 2009	7.2	
January 31, 2009	7.8	↑
February 28, 2009	8.3	↑
March 31, 2009	8.7	↑
April 30, 2009	9.0	↑
May 31, 2009	9.4	↑
June 30, 2009	9.5	↑
July 31, 2009	9.5	→
August 31, 2009	9.6	↑
September 30, 2009	9.8	↑
October 31, 2009	10.0	↑
November 30, 2009	9.9	↓
December 31, 2009	9.9	←→
Average Unemployment for 2009:	**9.28**	↑

Source: Dept of Labor - Bureau of Labor Statistics

U.S. National Unemployment Rate
(As of End of Month)

2010	%	Trend
January 31, 2010	9.8	↓
February 28, 2010	9.8	←→
March 31, 2010	9.9	↑
April 30, 2010	9.9	←→
May 31, 2010	9.6	↓
June 30, 2010	9.4	↓
July 31, 2010	9.4	←→
August 31, 2010	9.5	↑
September 30, 2010	9.5	←→
October 31, 2010	9.4	↓
November 30, 2010	9.8	↑
December 31, 2010	9.3	↓
Average Unemployment for 2010:	**9.61**	↑

Source: Dept of Labor - Bureau of Labor Statistics

U.S. National Unemployment Rate
(As of End of Month)

2011	%	Trend
January 31, 2011	9.2	↓
February 28, 2011	9.0	↓
March 31, 2011	9.0	←→
April 30, 2011	9.1	↑
May 31, 2011	9.0	↓
June 30, 2011	9.1	↑
July 31, 2011	9.0	↓
August 31, 2011	9.0	←→
September 30, 2011	9.0	←→
October 31, 2011	8.8	↓
November 30, 2011	8.6	↓
December 31, 2011	8.5	↓
Average Unemployment for 2011:	**8.94**	↓

Source: Dept of Labor - Bureau of Labor Statistics

U.S. National Unemployment Rate
(As of End of Month)

2012	%	Trend
January 31, 2012	8.3	↓
February 29, 2012	8.3	←→
March 31, 2012	8.2	↓
April 30, 2012	8.2	←→
May 31, 2012	8.2	←→
June 30, 2012	8.2	←→
July 31, 2012	8.2	←→
August 31, 2012	8.0	↓
September 30, 2012	7.8	↓
October 31, 2012	7.8	←→
November 30, 2012	7.7	↓
December 31, 2012	7.9	↑
Average Unemployment for 2012:	**8.07**	↓

Source: Dept of Labor - Bureau of Labor Statistics

Appendix C
Second Term

U.S. National Unemployment Rate
(As of End of Month)

2013	%	Trend
Inauguration Day – 21 January 2013	7.8	
January 31, 2013	8.0	↑
February 28, 2013	7.7	↓
March 31, 2013	7.5	↓
April 30, 2013	7.6	↑
May 31, 2013	7.5	↓
June 30, 2013	7.5	→
July 31, 2013	7.3	↓
August 31, 2013	7.2	↓
September 30, 2013	7.2	→
October 31, 2013	7.2	→
November 30, 2013	7.0	↓
December 31, 2013	6.7	↓
Average Unemployment for 2013:	**7.37**	↓

Source: Dept of Labor - Bureau of Labor Statistics

U.S. National Unemployment Rate
(As of End of Month)

2014	%	Trend
January 31, 2014	6.6	↓
February 28, 2014	6.7	↑
March 31, 2014	6.6	↓
April 30, 2014	6.2	↓
May 31, 2014	6.3	↑
June 30, 2014	6.1	↓
July 31, 2014	6.2	↑
August 31, 2014	6.1	↓
September 30, 2014	5.9	↓
October 31, 2014	5.7	↓
November 30, 2014	5.8	↑
December 31, 2014	5.6	↓
Average Unemployment for 2014:	**6.15**	↓

Source: Dept of Labor - Bureau of Labor Statistics

U.S. National Unemployment Rate
(As of End of Month)

2015	%	Trend
January 31, 2015	5.7	↑
February 28, 2015	5.5	↓
March 31, 2015	5.5	→
April 30, 2015	5.4	↓
May 31, 2015	5.5	↑
June 30, 2015	5.3	↓
July 31, 2015	5.3	→
August 31, 2015	5.1	↓
September 30, 2015	5.1	→
October 31, 2015	5.0	↓
November 30, 2015	5.0	→
December 31, 2015	5.0	→
Average Unemployment for 2015:	**5.28**	↓

Source: Dept of Labor - Bureau of Labor Statistics

U.S. National Unemployment Rate
(As of End of Month)

2016	%	Trend
January 31, 2016	4.9	↓
February 29, 2016	4.9	→
March 31, 2016	5.0	↑
April 30, 2016	5.0	→
May 31, 2016	4.7	↓
June 30, 2016	4.9	↑
July 31, 2016	4.9	→
August 31, 2016	4.9	→
September 30, 2016	5.0	↑
October 31, 2016	4.9	↓
November 30, 2016	4.6	↓
December 31, 2016	4.7	↑
Average Unemployment for 2016:	**4.87**	↓

Source: Dept of Labor - Bureau of Labor Statistics

Index

A

Abortion, 81, 151
Add Value to Agriculture, 184
Adult-Oriented Commercial Advertising, 291-292
Advanced Manufacturing Fund, 245
Advanced Technology Vehicles Manufacturing, 75
Advanced Technology, 28
Affordable Care Act, 81-102, 151, 229-244, 270, 3124
Affordable Child Care, 84
Affordable Housing Trust Fund, 135, 136
Afghanistan, 19-36, 158, 191, 199, 212, 251, 256
African Growth and Opportunity Act, 185
After-School Programs, 45
Age Discrimination in Employment Act, 176
Agribusiness, 3
Aid to the Americas, 209
Air Traffic Control System, 287
Air Traffic Controller Morale, 288
Air Transportation Modernization/Safety Act, 288
Al Gore, 311
Al Qaeda, 24, 35, 114, 129, 132, 133
Alaska Natural Gas Pipeline, 77
All-Electric Vehicles, 63, 65
Alternative Minimum Tax, 237
Alternative Sources of Energy, 168
America Houses, 203
America's Voice Corps, 203
American Clean Energy and Security Act, 72, 78, 143
American Indian Advisor, 259
American Opportunity Tax Credit, 41
American Taxpayer Relief Act, 3, 41, 229, 232, 233, 235, 237
American-Israel Public Affairs Committee, 213
Americorps, 278
AMTRAK Funding, 225
AnonCoin Anonymous Cryptocurrency, 109
Anti-Counterfeiting Trade Agreement, 122
Anti-Monopoly Laws, 5
Anti-Satellite Capability, 203
Anti-Trust Enforcement, 152
Anti-Trust Laws, 151
Armenian Genocide Resolution, 210
Arms Export Control Act, 194
Army Force Generation Model, 37
Army National Guard, 25, 37
Army Reserve, 25, 37
Army Strength, 22
Artist-Museum Partnership Act, 239
Artists Corps, 278
Arts Education Grants, 53
Arts Education, 44
Assistance to Israel, 213
Autism Coordinator, 259
Autism Spectrum Disorder, 81
Autism Treatment Insurance Coverage, 82
Auto Plant Loan Guarantees, 75
Auto Plant Retooling Tax Credits, 75

B

Bankruptcy from Medical Crisis, 244
Bankruptcy Law, 139, 140
Best Practices to Accommodate Disabled Workers, 174, 123, 123, 123
Bicycle and Pedestrian Usage of Roads/Sidewalks, 222
Bioforensics Program, 130
Bipartisan Consultative Group, 312
Bipartisanship, 311
BitcoinDark Anonymous Teleported Currency, 110
Border Security, 103-104, 205-206
Broadband – National Plan, 289
Broadband Infrastructure, 289
Broadcasting Negotiations on C-SPAN, 269
Bush-Era Tax Cuts, 233, 312
Business Incubators, 13
Byrne Justice Assistance Grant Program, 156

C

Cabinet Republican, 259
Campaign Financing, 269, 313
Cancer Clinical Trials, 84
Cancer Patient Navigation & Follow-Up, 83
Cancer/Cancer Research, 82-83
Cap-And-Trade, 72, 143, 281
Capital Gains Taxes, 227, 235
Carbon Capture, Utilization and Storage Projects, 75-77
Carbon Neutral Buildings, 281
Career Pathways Innovation Fund, 176
Caribbean Basin Security Initiative, 209
Carried Interest, 236
Cellulosic Ethanol, 69, 74
Centennial Challenges Program, 301
CEO Pay Tax Deductibility, 238
Charter School Expansion, 47-49, 112
Cheaper Drug Prices, 98
Chemical Facility Anti-Terrorism Standards, 129
Chemical Plants Security Standards, 120
Chemical Security Assessment Tool, 130
Chief Financial Officer, 259
Chief of the National Guard Bureau, 36
Chief Performance Officer, 260
Chief Technology Officer, 260
Child and Dependent Care Tax Credit, 236
Child Screening for Disabilities, 85

INDEX

Children's First Agenda, 47
China Currency Value Manipulation, 186
China Respect for Human Rights, 187
China Support - Sudan, Burma, Iran and Zimbabwe, 188
Citizen Corps Program, 106, 117
Civil Rights Abuses, 154
Civilian Assistance Corps, 200
Civilian Extraterritorial Jurisdiction Act, 158
Civilian Response Corps, 201
Clean Alternative Fuels, 68
Clean Coal Power Initiative, 77
Clean Coal-Fired Plant, 77
Clean Energy Projects, 77
Clean Energy Service Corps, 279
Clean Technologies Deployment, 75
Clean Technologies Venture Capital, 74
Clean Water Act, 148, 284
Climate Change, 11, 143, 187-202, 209, 281, 311, 315
Climate Records, 11
Cloakcoin Anonymous Currency Network, 109
Coast Guard, 104
Code of Conduct for Outer Space Activities, 203
Collective Bargaining Rights, 181, 182
College Access Challenge Grants, 43
College Education, 41
College Football, 313
Combatant Commanders, 201
Combating Autism Act, 81
Combating Autism Reauthorization Act, 82
Commerce Control List, 194
Commodity Futures Trading Commission, 277
Common Sense Regulations, 242
Community College Partnership, 43
Community College, 43
Community Development Block Grants, 136, 138-140
Community Development Financial Institutions, 245
Community Development, 138
Community Oriented Policing Services for Katrina, 162
Community Oriented Policing Services, 155
Community Service Jobs, 279
Community-Based Interventions, 87
Comparative Effectiveness Research, 102
Competitive Energy Efficiency Grants, 64
Comprehensive Everglades Restoration Plan, 145
Comprehensive Immigration Reform Act, 126
Comprehensive National Cybersecurity Initiative, 106
Comprehensive Nuclear Test Ban Treaty, 318
Comprehensive Peace Agreement, 183
Concentrated Animal Feeding Operations, 286
Conservation Easement Tax Incentive, 145
Conservation Reserve, 6, 145, 149
Conservation Security, 6
Consular Affairs, 190-191
Consumer Financial Protection Bureau, 137, 243
Consumer Product Safety Commission, 186
Contracts and Influence Database, 269

Controlled Burns, 7
Copyright System, 15, 122
Corporate Average Fuel Economy, 67, 282
Corporate Bankruptcy, 167
Corporate Taxes, 227
Corporation for National and Community Service, 277
Corporation for Public Broadcasting, 290, 293
Corps of Engineers, 27, 42, 146
Council for Higher Education Accreditation, 46
Counterterrorism Data Layer, 121
Credit Card 5-Star Rating System, 295
Credit Card Bill of Rights, 295
Critical Infrastructure and Key Resources, 116
Critical Infrastructure Dollar Distribution, 246
Critical Infrastructure Protection Plan, 116
Crop Insurance, 3-4
Cross-Leveling, 36
Cuban Americans Unrestricted Rights, 207
Cyber Crime, 106
Cyber Security Standards, 110
Cyber Security Strategy, 105
Cyber Threat Intelligence Integration Center, 121
Cybersecurity Act, 105, 107, 110
Cyberspace Policy Review, 105
Cyprus Political Settlement, 192

D

Darfur Genocide, 183
DASH Bitcoin-Based Electronic Currency, 109
Data Security, 13-14, 107
DEA Efforts Against Drug Gangs, 162
Debt Cancellation, Heavily Indebted Poor Countries, 240
Defend Trade Secrets Act, 108
Defense Acquisition Reform, 17
Defense Acquisitions System, 20
Defense Advanced Research Projects Agency, 28
Defense Contract Officer Corps, 19
Defense Contracting, 18-19
Defense Contractor Performance, 19
Defense Logistics Agency, 29
Defense of Marriage Act, 164
Defense Spending, 27
Deferred Action for Childhood Arrivals, 124
Deferred Action for Parents of Americans, 124
Dependence on Foreign Oil, 67-68, 72
Detention Facility Closure, 113, 114
Development, Relief & Education for Alien Minors, 124
DHS Budget Authority, 103
Dickey-Wicker Amendment, 101
Digital Electricity Grid, 69
Diplomatic Relations with Cuba, 208
Direct Diplomacy with All Nations, 197
Direct Talks with Iran, 214
Direct-Deposit IRA Account, 179
Director, FEMA, 261

INDEX

Disabled Access Tax Credit, 174
Disease Management Programs, 89
Diversity in Broadcast Media Ownership, 294
DoD Quadrennial Defense Review, 17, 201
DoD Science & Technology, 28
Dodd-Frank Wall Street Reform Act, 135, 137, 141, 244-245, 270, 277, 312
Domestic Violence, 162
Don't Ask/Don't Tell, 22, 312
Doughnut Hole Medicare Part D, 96-98
DOW Jones Industrial Average, Appendix B, 325
Drinking Water Standards, 283
Driving, Ridesharing & Public Transit Benefits, 223
Drug Courts, 159
Drug Rehabilitation Programs, 160
Dry-Cask Storage, 79

E

Early Assessment Program, 42
Early Head Start, 86
Early Learning Council, 46
Earmark Moratorium, 271
Earmark Reform, 270
Earned Income Tax Credit, 171, 232, 235
Economic Substance Doctrine, 234
Economic Support Fund for Mexico, 125
Educating Young Hunters and Anglers, 143
Education Aid to Pakistan, 212
Educational and Cultural Exchange Program, 196
Electrical Grid, 62
Electricity Demand Reduction, 61
Embryonic Stem Cell Research, 101
Emergency Management Performance Grants, 119
Employee Free Choice Act, 180
Employer Health Plan Reimbursement, 90
Employment Cost Index, 29
Employment Non-Discrimination Act, 168
End Racial Profiling Act, 153
Energy and Climate Partnership of the Americas, 202, 208
Energy Conservation, 61
Energy Consumption, 63
Energy Efficiency & Conservation Block Grant, 61, 64
Energy Efficiency, 10, 14, 61-62, 64, 66, 69-70, 71, 75, 168-170, 208, 279
Energy Infrastructure Protection, 119
Energy Policy Act of 2005, 70, 76
Energy-Efficient Appliances, 76
Environmental Health Issues, 91
Environmental Response, Compensation & Liability, 283
EPA Office of Civil Rights, 285
EPA Office of Environmental Justice, 286
Equal Employment Opportunity Commission, 169
Equal Remedies Act, 152
Estate Tax Law, 232
European Union Sanctions on Iran, 188, 213

European Union, 100, 122, 188, 192, 203, 210, 212-214, 309, 315
Everglades Restoration, 145
Every Student Succeeds Act, 49
Evidence-Based Interventions, 87
Executive Bonuses During Bankruptcy, 167
Export Control Reform Initiative, 194
Extreme Rendition, 164

F

Fair Sentencing Act, 157, 172-173, 175
Family and Medical Leave, 175
Farm Bill, 3-10
Farming Practices, 8
Federal Building Energy Retrofits, 71
Federal Charter School Program, 47
Federal Contracting Compliance Program, 170
Federal Contracting Reform, 303
Federal Coordinating Officer, 261
Federal Emergency Management Agency, 54, 91, 111-112, 246
Federal Employee Health Benefits Plan, 89
Federal Employees with Disabilities, 171
Federal Energy Consumption Reduction, 71
Federal Energy Regulatory Commission, 120
Federal Green Products Investment Program, 170
Federal Rebuilding Coordinator, 261
Federal Research and Development Funding, 177
Federal Workforce Training & Green Technologies, 169
First Responder Communications, 294
Fish and Wildlife Service, 143
Fissile Materials Control, 317
Fissile Materials Production, 321
Five-E (5-E) Youth Service Corps, 279
Fixed Term for Director of National Intelligence, 275
Fixing America's Surface Transportation Act, 62, 221
Flexible-Fuel Vehicles, 70-71
Foreclosure Moratorium, 139
Foreclosure Prevention Fund, 140
Foreign Aid Spending, 198
Foreign Area Officers, 26
Foreign Intelligence Surveillance Act, 127
Foreign Service Personnel Strength, 196
Forest Service, 7
Four Singles ("4 Singles") Initiative, 195
Fraud Enforcement and Recovery Act, 155
Free Application for Federal Student Aid, 56
Free Community College Tuition, 43
Freedom of Choice Act, 151
Freight Rail Security Grant Program, 119
Fuel Economy Standards, 66, 282
FUTURE Act, 77
Future Years Defense Program, 31

INDEX

G

General Education, 44
General Election Public Financing, 313
Generic Drugs, 97, 99
Geneva Conventions, 114, 115
Global Education Fund, 199
Global Energy and Environment Initiative, 185
Global Energy Corps, 205
Global Health Initiative, 219
Global Nuclear Stockpile Reduction, 319
Global Precipitation Measurement, 300
Government Flexible-Fuel Vehicles, 70
Great Lakes Collaboration Implementation Act, 149
Great Lakes Restoration Initiative, 149, 284
Great Plains and Eastern Forests Protection, 148
Green Building Market, 70
Green Jobs Creation, 168
Grid Modernization Commission, 62
Ground-Launched Cruise Missiles, 39
Group of Eight (G-8), 197, 205
Guantanamo Bay, 113-115
Gulf Area Schools Infrastructure, 54
Gulf Coast Medical Infrastructure, 95
Gulf Opportunity Zone Act, 230

H

Habeas Corpus, 114
Habitat Restoration, 145
Hair-Trigger Alert, 38
Handling of Detainees, 114
Haqqani Network, 35-36
Hate Crimes, 154
Head Start, 46, 85-86
Health Care System Overhaul, 87
Health Equity & Accountability Act, 90
Health Info Tech for Economic & Clinical Health, 87
Health Information Systems, 87
Health Information Technology, 87-88, 98, 117, 308
Health Infrastructure 2020, 205
Health Insurance Exchange, 87, 92
Healthful Environments for Children, 85
High Assurance Platform, 109
High School Dropout Intervention, 48
High School Graduation Rates, 48-49, 52
High Speed Rail Networks, 224
Hiring Incentives to Restore Employment Act, 228
HIV/AIDS Global Fight, 200
Home Affordable Refinance Program, 140
Homeland Security Budget, 115
Homeland Security Grant Program, 117
Homeowner Obligation Made Explicit, 137
Hospital/Medical Provider Reporting, 89
Housing Crisis, 141

Human/Robotic Space Mission Research, 299
Hurricane Katrina, 27, 54-55, 95-96, 111-112, 136-137, 162, 177, 224, 230, 246, 249

I

Immigration & Customs Enforcement Agency, 103,122-123, 189
Immigration and Nationality Act, 123
Immigration Bill, 125, 127
Immigration, 123
Improving Regulation and Regulatory Review, 274
Improvised Explosive Device, 23, 30, 35
Incandescent Light Bulbs, 64
Independent Watchdog Agency, 268
Individual Taxes, 229, 231
Individuals with Disabilities Education Act, 47
Infrastructure Information Collection Program, 116
Innovation Clusters, 14
Insurer Payment of Premium Share, 94
Integrated Gasification Combined Cycle, 77
Intellectual Property, 15, 108, 122, 190
Intelligence Community Databases, 121
Intercity Bus Security Grant Program, 119
Intercity Passenger Rail, 119
Intermediate-Range Nuclear Forces, 39
International Aerospace Markets, 195
International Atomic Energy Agency, 204, 215, 318, 320
International Court of Justice, 316
International Fund for Ireland, 193
International Space Station, 296-300
International Tax Havens, 240
International Traffic in Arms Regulations, 194
International Whaling Commission, 316
International Wildlife Protection Agreements, 316
Internet Crimes Against Children Task Force, 161
Internet Parental Control, 295
Internet Use to Exploit Children, 161
Iraq, 19-33, 191, 200, 207, 210-213, 250-251, 254, 257,
Iraqi Refugees, 199-200, 212
Islamic State of Iraq and Syria, 34, 129
Israeli Missile Defense Systems, 217
Israeli-Palestinian Peace Process, 215

J

James Webb Space Telescope, 300
Jobs Access and Reverse Commute, 223
Joint Comprehensive Plan of Action – Iran, 215
Joint Military Programs, 23

K

Katrina Recovery Employment and Training, 177

INDEX

Kurdistan Workers Party, 211

L

Land and Water Conservation Fund, 145, 147-148
Land Use, 9
Land-Grant Colleges, 10
Landowner Incentive Program, 146
Landsat Data Continuity Mission, 149
Latin America/Caribbean Crime Mitigation, 158
Latin America/Caribbean, 207
Law Enforcement Cyber Center, 106
Learn and Serve America Program, 280
LEOCoin Peer-to-Peer Payment System, 109
Lilly Ledbetter Fair Pay Act, 152
Loan Application Process Improvement, 244
Lobbying Reports, Ethics Records, Finance Filings, 269
Local Emergency Planning, 117
Low Carbon Fuel Standard, 67-68
Low Emissions Coal Plants, 69
Lugar-Obama Initiative, 131

M

Madrasas, 199, 212
Make College a Reality Initiative, 41
Making Work Pay Tax Credit, 235-236
Mandatory Minimum Sentences, 157, 160-161
Manufacturing Extension Partnership, 11
Manufacturing, 11
Marine Corps Strength, 22
Marine Life Protection, 286
Marriage Penalty, 232
Matthew Shepard Act, 154, 164
Medicaid and SCHIP Expansion, 94
Medicaid, 95
Medical Infrastructure, 96
Medicare Homebound Rule, 98
Medicare, 96
Methane Digesters, 9
Metropolitan Medical Response System, 106, 117
Micro-Enterprise Initiative for Rural America, 305
Middle East Partnership Initiative, 218, 219
Middle East, 132, 188, 192-193, 199, 204, 207, 210-211, 215, 218-219, 317-318
Migration and Refugee Assistance, 199
Military Advisors Corps, 25
Military Aid to Pakistan, 35
Military Commissions Act, 114
Military Contractor Standards, 18
Military Deployment Policies, 24-25
Military Families Advisory Board, 25
Military Humanitarian Missions, 31, 33
Military Reserves, 36
Military Reservists – Rehiring Rights, 254

Military Skillsets, 24
Millennium Challenge Corporation, 218
Millennium Development Goals, 316
Mine Resistant Ambush Protected Vehicle, 30
Minimum Wage, 171
Modernizing Public Health Labs, 87
Monero Open-Source Untraceable Currency, 109
Mortgage Professionals Fraud, 155
Moving Ahead for Progress in the 21st Century Act, 62, 68, 223

N

NASA Programs for K-12, 45
National Aeronautics and Space Council, 301
National Air Traffic Controller Association, 288
National Asset Database, 116
National Bio- and Agro-Defense Facility, 131
National Biodefense Analysis & Countermeasures, 130
National Bioforensic Analysis Center, 130
National Biological Threat Characterization Center, 130
National Board for Professional Teaching Standards, 57
National Broadband Townhall Meetings, 275, 276
National Catastrophe Insurance Reserve, 118
National Commission on People with Disabilities, 171
National Counterterrorism Center, 121
National Cyber Advisor, 262
National Declassification Center, 296
National Domestic Threat Assessment, 129
National Endowment for Democracy, 202
National Endowment for the Arts, 54, 83, 302
National Forests Protection and Restoration, 146
National Health Service Corps, 91
National Housing Trust Fund, 135
National Infrastructure Policy, 221
National Infrastructure Protection Plan 2009, 116
National Infrastructure Protection Plan 2013, 110, 116-117
National Infrastructure Reinvestment Bank, 301
National Institute on Disability & Rehab Research, 55
National Institutes of Health Budget, 102
National Land Imaging Program, 149
National Nuclear Security Administration, 131
National Oceanic and Atmospheric Administration, 11, 42, 145
National Organic Certification Cost Share Program, 4
National Park Service, 147
National Preparedness System, 113
National Rifle Association, 158
National Space Policy, 203
National Special Security Event, 119
National Strategy, Trusted Identities in Cyberspace, 13, 15, 107
National Utility Grid, 62
Nationalservice.gov Web Site, 280
Natural Fire, 7
Navy Modernization, 32

INDEX

Navy Phased Modernization Program, 32
Navy Research & Development, 30
Navy/Coast Guard Interoperability, 104
Network Neutrality, 291
New Drugs, Vaccines and Diagnostics, 91
New Hire Political Affiliation Influence, 267
New Market Tax Credit, 230
New Nuclear Weapons Development, 320
New Orleans Medical Complex, 96, 249
New Orleans Protection, 27
New Orleans Regional Transit Partnerships, 224
New Orleans Rental Property, 136
New Strategic Arms Reduction Treaty, 37-39, 312, 319
Next Generation Technology Education, 53
NextGen Air Transportation System, 287
NextGen Secure Computers, 108
No Child Left Behind Act, 50-51
No Tax Increases, 235
Nonprofit Capacity Building Program, 280
Nonprofit Security Grant Program, 119
North American Wetlands Conservation Act, 143
Northern Ireland, 193
Nuclear Forces, 38
Nuclear Non-Proliferation Treaty, 317-318
Nuclear Security Advisor, 263
Nuclear Security Summit, 79, 317-321
Nuclear Warheads, 38
Nuclear Waste, 79
Nuclear Weapons Materials Security, 131, 319-320
Nuclear Weapons Reduction, 39, 317, 319
Nurse-Family Partnership, 85-86

O

Odious Debt, 204
Office of Special Education & Rehabilitative Services, 55
Office on Violence Against Women, 163
Offshore Oil and Gas Drilling Revenues, 245
Oil and Gas Drilling Leases, 78
Oil Company Windfall Profits, 79
Oil Consumption Reduction, 67
Oil Price Reduction, 277
Open Fields Incentives, 9
Opening of Consulates, 191
Operation Enduring Freedom, 21, 30, 36, 250
Operation Stonegarden, 117
Osama bin Laden, 131-132, 212
Overseas Buildings Operations, 191

P

Paid Leave, 172
Paid Sick Days, 173
Pakistan Counterinsurgency Capability Fund, 35
Pakistan, 35-36, 40, 131-133, 199, 210, 212, 318-320

Participation in Service Opportunities, 277
Passenger Rail Investment and Improvement Act, 225
Patent & Trademark Office, 15
Patent Laws, 16
Patent System, 15
Patient-Centered Medical Home, 89
PATRIOT Act, 127, 128-129
Pay Discrimination, 152
Pay-As-You-Go (PAYGO) Budgeting Rules, 242
Peace Corps Strength, 198
Pell Grants, 28, 56
Pension Fund Disclosures, 179
Pension Protection During Bankruptcy, 167
Permit Purchase of Foreign Drugs, 100
Personal Data Security, 106
Personal Data Victim Disclosure, 107
Personal Exemptions and Itemized Deductions, 233-234
Petty Partisanship, 312
Physical/Cyber Security Standards, 110
Pipeline and Hazardous Materials Safety Admin, 120
Plug-In Hybrid Vehicles, 63, 65-75, 240
Political Appointee Ethical Limitations, 267
Port Security Grant Program, 119
Pre-Existing Conditions, 82, 92
Pre-Filled Tax Forms, 238
Pregnancy, 81, 100
Premium Percentage for Patient Care, 94
President Obama Approval Rate, Appendix A, 323
President's Emergency Plan for AIDS, 200, 218
Presidential Policy Directive 8, 113
Presidential Policy Directive 21, 110, 116-117, 120
Presidential Study Directive on Global Development, 218
Prison-to-Work Incentive Program, 160
Privacy/Civil Liberties Board, 263
Private Lender Education Subsidies, 56
Private Sector Spaceflight Development, 297
Production Tax Credit, 228
Proliferation Security Initiative, 319
Promise Neighborhoods, 52
Protect Roadless Areas, 8
Protecting Americans from Tax Hikes Act, 231
Protection of Florida's Water Resources, 284
Public Conduct of Government Business, 275
Public Housing Operating Fund, 137
Public Mass Transportation Projects, 222
Public Media 2.0, 293
Public Review and Comments of Bills, 270
Public/Commuter Transportation, 223
Public/Private Arts Partnerships, 54
Publicly Traded Partnerships, 229

R

Race to the Top Program, 48, 57-58, 86
Racial Profiling, 126, 153
Radio and Television Localism Requirements, 294

INDEX

Rebuilding the Gulf Coast, 27, 54, 95-96, 111, 118, 136, 162, 177, 224, 230, 245-246, 249, 259, 261
Refundable Mortgage Interest Tax Credit, 238
Rehabilitation Act, 175
Release of Jailed Scholars and Activists, 206
Release of Presidential Records, 273
Renewable Energy Production Tax Credit, 228
Renewable Energy, 9, 10, 68-69, 72, 75, 78, 168-169, 208, 228
Renewable Portfolio Standard, 72, 78
Research Grants, 55, 298
Reserve Deployment Policies, 36
Responsible Fatherhood and Healthy Families Act, 163
Restoring Fiscal Discipline, 242
Retirement Account Withdrawals, 237
Retirement Savings Tax Credit, 178
Risk Management Agency, 4
Road Home Applications, 136
Rural Area Doctors, 91
Rural Revitalization, 5, 306
Russia, 21-23, 37-40, 131, 193, 197-198, 203, 205-206, 214, 298-299, 312, 316, 319-320

S

Safeguarding U.S. Leadership and Security Act, 194
Safety of Foreign Imports, 186
Saint John's River Water Management District, 284
School Accreditation, 46
Science Assessments, 52
Science, Technology, Engineering and Math, 51, 57
Science/Technology Advisor, 264
Secure Our Borders, 103
Securing American Value and Efficiency Award, 303
Security Vulnerability Assessment, 130
Senator George Mitchell, 210, 216
Senior Corps Program, 278, 280
Sentencing Disparities, 157
Serbian Community and Religious Sites Protection, 191
Serve America Act, 277-280
Serve-Study Programs, 279
Shadowcash Decentralized Cryptocurrency, 109
Shared Security Partnership Program, 205
Short Range Ballistic Missile Defense, 217
Short-Term/Small Dollar Loans, 245
Signing Nullifying Statements, 270
Simpson-Bowles Commission, 243
Sliding Scale Tax Credits, 239
Small and Medium Enterprises Fund, 303
Small and Medium Enterprises Universities, 304
Small Business Health Tax Credit, 229
Small Business Innovative Research, 304
Small Business Investment Expensing, 228
Small Business Jobs Act, 231, 305-306
Small Business Jobs and Credit Act, 227
Small Business Loan/Micro-Loan Programs, 306

Small Business Refundable Tax Credit, 229
Small Business Set-Asides, 306
Small Community Air Service, 221
Small Owner-Operator Business Tax Credit, 231
Smart Grid Investment Matching Grant, 62
Smart Growth Considerations for Transportation, 222
Social Innovation Fund, 279
Social Investment Fund Network, 279
Social Security Disability Claims Backlog, 307-308
Social Security Increased Funding for Staff, 307
Social Security Payroll Tax Cap, 238
Soldier-Wearable Acoustic Targeting System, 29
Southwest Border, 103-104
Space Shuttle, 296, 298, 300
SpaceX, 297
Special Advisor – Violence Against Women, 265
Special Envoy – Americas. 264
Special Inspector General for Afghan Reconstruction, 33
Special Tax Breaks for Oil and Gas Companies, 80, 227
Speech at a Major Islamic Forum, 202
Stability of Iraq and Region, 210
Standard of Proven Excellence, 262
State Department QDDR, 201, 218
State Energy Program, 66
State Homeland Security Program, 106, 117
State of Our Energy Future, 73
State of the World Address, 117
State, Local, Tribal and Private Sector, 121
State/National Pollution Discharge Elimination, 286
Stop-Loss Program, 25
Strategic Arms Reduction Treaty, 37
Strategic Offensive Reduction Treaty, 38
Strategic Petroleum Reserve, 73
Strengthen Small Business Administration, 305
Strengthen Whistleblower Laws, 271
Striking Workers, 172
Student Aid, 43, 56
Students With Disabilities, 47, 55
Subsidies to Medicare Advantage Plans, 94, 96-97
Sudan People's Liberation Movement, 183
Summit of the Americas, 159, 202, 208
Superfund Program, 283
Supplemental Budgets, 27
Support for Building Blocks of Democracies, 207
Sustainable Communities Planning Grants, 138
Swamp Buster, 6

T

Taliban, 20-21, 35-36
Tax Credit for Plug-In Hybrid Purchase, 240
Tax Earmarks, 274
Tax Incentives for Relocation to Gulf Coast, 230
Taxation of Seniors, 231
Teacher Mentoring Programs, 58
Teacher Pay Increases, 59

INDEX

Teacher Performance Assessment, 57-58
Teacher Recruiting, 57
Teacher Residency Programs, 59
Teacher Service Scholarships, 57
Teaching, 57
Telephone Universal Service Program, 290
Teleport, 110
Television V-Chip, 292
Temporary Assistance for Needy Families, 176
Terrorism, 117, 129
Texas Clean Energy Project, 77
Tiahrt Amendment, 157-158
Torture Without Exception, 165
Trade Laws/Agreements Enforcement, 189
Trade Secrets Protection, 108
Transit Security Grant Program, 119
Transportation Improvement Program, 62
Tribal Homeland Security Grant Program, 119
Troubled Assets Relief Program, 135, 140-141, 228, 270
Turkish and Iraqi Kurdish Relations, 211
Turkish Membership in European Union, 211

U

U.N. Convention – Regulation of Whaling, 316
U.N. Convention – Rights of Persons w/Disabilities, 315
U.N. Framework Convention – Climate Change, 315
U.N. Major Economies Forum on Energy & Climate, 315
U.N. Nuclear Posture Review, 317
U.N. Security Council, 317
U.S. Army Special Operations Command, 26
U.S. Geological Survey, 149
U.S. Munitions List, 194
U.S. National Unemployment Rate, 327
U.S.-Caribbean Security Dialogue, 209
U.S.-China Human Rights Dialogue, 187, 188
U.S.-Israel Relationship, 215
Undocumented Immigrants, 122-125
Unemployment Insurance, 180
Uniform Code of Military Justice, 115
United Nations High Commission on Refugees, 199
Universal Service Fund, 289
University Partnership Programs, 42
Unmanned Aerial Systems, 103
Unmanned Aerial Vehicle, 28
Untraceable Internet Payments, 109
Urban Area Security Initiative, 115, 117
Urban Policy Director, 265
USA FREEDOM Act, 127-128
USAID Complex Crisis Fund, 217

V

VA Centers for Rural Areas, 250
VA Electronic Health Records, 251
VA Hospital for New Orleans, 249
VA Polytrauma Rehabilitation Center, 252
Veteran – Ban on Priority 8 Healthcare Enrollment, 256
Veteran – Benefits Administration Claims Backlog, 255
Veteran – Electronic Benefit Claims Processing, 257
Veteran – Employment/Re-Employment Rights, 254
Veteran – Extend Enrollment Window, 257
Veteran – Green Vet Initiative, 254
Veteran – Homeless Housing Vouchers, 253
Veteran – Homelessness, , 252
Veteran – Job Creation Act, 255
Veteran – Mental Health Screenings, 250
Veteran – Supportive Services for Families, 253
Veteran – Traumatic Brain Injury, 250
Veteran – Virtual Lifetime Electronic Record, 257
Veterans Affairs Funding, 249, 252, 256
Veterans Health Information Exchange, 251
Videotaping of Interrogations, 153
Violations of Personal Privacy, 106, 111
Violence Against Women Reauthorization Act, 163, 175
Visa Process for Artists/Art Students, 190
Voter Fraud, 155

W

Washington Middle Managers Reduction, 304
Waste Isolation Pilot Plant, 79
Water Conservation Initiative Challenge Grants, 147
Weapons of Mass Destruction, 131, 206, 263, 319
Weatherization Assistance Program, 65
Wetland Reserve Program, 149
White House Fleet Plug-In Conversion, 66
Wildfires, 7
Wildland Fire Management, 150
Wildlife Habitat Incentive Program, 149
Women-Owned Business Contracting Program, 306
Women-Owned Small Businesses, 306
Work Opportunity Tax Credit, 174
Workforce Investment Act, 175
Working Lands for Wildlife Program, 149
Workplace Pension Plan, 178
World Trade Organization, 189, 214-215

Y

Young People Insurance Coverage, 93
Youth Jobs Program, 279
YouthBuild, 177
Yucca Mountain, 79

Z

Zero-Emissions Buildings, 70
Zero-to-Five Plan, 86

About the Author

Originally from the northern Maine town of Madawaska, John E. Beaulieu completed his initial studies in Quebec City and Montreal, Canada. Following nearly three years in Qui Nhon, South Vietnam in the early 1970's, he pursued a military career at NATO's military headquarters in Belgium followed by tours of duty in the Defense Attaché System in Zaire, Algeria, Niger and Haiti. He retired from the Army in 1989 as a Chief Warrant Officer and recipient of three Defense Superior Service Medals (DSSMs), Bronze Star, Purple Heart and numerous other decorations and honorifics such as Officer and Knight in the National Order of the Republic of Niger. Mr. Beaulieu then pursued a second career as a Department of the Navy civilian specialized in Foreign Military Sales of the Navy's E-2C and E-2D Airborne Early Warning aircraft to existing and potential operators on a worldwide basis. He retired from the Civil Service in 2012. Mr. Beaulieu holds a Bachelor's and a Master's of Science degree in Business Management. He resides in Annandale, Virginia with his wife of 48 years, Wanda, who was instrumental in the final review and editing of this book. Her unwavering support and attention to detail made it possible for its publication to come to fruition.